T5-CQD-235

TRINITY COLLEGE, WASHINGTON, D. C.

COLLEGIUM DEO UNI TRINOQUE SACRUM

Trinity College
WASHINGTON, D.C.

The First Eighty Years
1897–1977

Sister Columba Mullaly
S.N.D. deN., Ph.D.

Christian Classics, Inc.
POST OFFICE BOX 30, WESTMINSTER, MARYLAND
1987

First published, 1987

© 1987 by TRINITY COLLEGE, WASHINGTON, D.C.

ISBN 0-87061-139-9 Paperback Edition
0-87061-140-2 Cloth Edition

Library of Congress Card Number: 87-071310

PRINTED IN THE UNITED STATES OF AMERICA

DEDICATION

". . . The real Trinity has little to do with bricks and mortar; it dwells the country over in lives and hopes. The real Trinity is unchangeable." Letter of Mary R. Walsh '12 to the editor of the Trinilogue, 1925.

To the Trinity women in all parts of the country and in many other countries who by quiet, unassuming, perhaps unknown service, or by widely acclaimed, eminent achievement in the home, in public office, in the professions in all spheres of endeavor, are influencing those around them by their lives—to the real *Trinity—this book is dedicated.*

Introduction

This history has been long in the making (more than eighty years) and long in the writing (almost fifteen years). It was preceded by a brief typed history in 1906, by a mimeographed history in 1909, and by the published *Historical Sketch of Trinity College* by Sister Mary Patricia Butler for the twenty-fifth anniversary of the opening of the college, and by entries in the Catholic Encyclopedia first and second editions. It leaves the college flourishing in the late 1970's, facing staunchly toward the twenty-first century. Some of the sources of information for this history form outline histories themselves: The Trinity College *Record* from 1907 to the late 1920's when its college chronicle and alumnae notes were replaced by the *Alumnae Journal* of *Trinity College* which still continues as a source of firsthand data, a history in itself.

The long debated subject of "the first" has been treated in the early chapters. Suffice it to say here that the founders were convinced that they were breaking new ground, founding a college for women under Catholic auspices with curriculum of university grade, a national clientele, and not growing out of an already established secondary school. Later years revealed that several academies had been developing into colleges and had conferred degrees before 1897, the nearest being Notre Dame of Maryland in Baltimore. Yet even Cardinal Gibbons, a great friend of Notre Dame of Maryland, did not equate the two colleges. He wrote to Sister Julia that he did not envision any other college of the type of Trinity "in the next twenty-five years." Those years did, however, see the development of a number of Catholic women's colleges in various parts of the country. Trinity does stand as the first of the type intended by the founders.

This history has been organized in such a way as to be four histories of the college from four points of view. The period until the first graduating class in 1904 is treated chronologically. Chapter 4 develops the history of the faculty and administration; Chapter 5 the Academic Program through the years; Chapter 6 Student Life; Chapter 7 the non-academic influences that helped make a Trinity education. The final chapter, The Alumnae, is a brief summary of "the product" of the college. The author recommends to the Alumnae Association a full-fledged history. The Trinity College Alumnae deserve a book of their own.

Several other topics that could have been treated have been omitted: The whole subject of the education of Notre Dame Sisters, the Religious Educators' Foundation, and Education for Parish Service. The author also suggests that "Trinity and Women's Higher Education" would make a good graduate dissertation topic.

The author specially thanks Sister Margaret Claydon who first urged the writing of this history; and, with her successors in office, and the Sisters of Notre Dame of the Trinity College community, encouraged and supported it through the years; Sister Mary Frances McCarthy who gave valuable assistance in preparing the typescript for publication; and Mrs. Marsha Mattarrese and Mrs. Julie Garrett who typed the manuscript.

SISTER COLUMBA MULLALY, S.N.D., PH.D.

Trinity College History

General Plan

Glossary of Trinity Terms

Necessary for younger readers to understand parts of this history.

Aventine: One of the hills on the original campus, site of the present library building.

Blue Bird Hill: Wooded hill at north end of the campus, separated from college buildings by a deep ravine. It was cleared of trees and hill and ravine leveled in the 1980's.

Cafeteria: The lower level of Alumnae Hall. This is the "cafeteria" mentioned as the center of student activities from 1929 for forty years. The Dining Halls were converted to cafeteria style to accommodate the large student body of the late 1960's. The lower level cafeteria was the site of the first "smoker" on campus. The faculty dining room and the Education for Parish Services room now occupy this area.

Class Days: Days chosen by each class (freshmen to senior) for all-college celebration in their honor. They are not holidays from class. They were student inaugurated and have changed through the years. These should be distinguished from the formal day in Commencement Week called Class Day.

Colors: Each class since the beginning has had a "class color," used in banner, decorations, emblems of all kinds. The class of 1904 chose red; 1905 blue; 1906 green; 1907 gold (or yellow). These four colors have been perpetuated by the formal bequest by each graduating class of its color to the incoming freshmen. Thus a continuous relationship of color has linked every fourth class to its predecessors. It is not uncommon to hear an alumna say to another (much older or younger) "Oh! You were a blue, too."—or a red, green or gold.

Court: The "quadrangles" between South Hall and O'Connor Hall, and between O'Connor Hall and North Hall of the Main Building. These were formerly called South and

North Courts. Now they are Seymour Court (south), and (north) the direct route to and from Alumnae Hall and the elevator in Main.

Fountain: For about sixty years a picturesque fountain with a curbed basin adorned the south slope of "the Aventine" (q.v.). It was near what is now the Franklin Street gate in what is now a faculty parking lot.

Quads: Not quadrangles, but rooms housing four students during the crowded years before Cuvilly Hall was built.

Red Rose Inn: A roadhouse or tavern operated, when the college opened, by the Rose family. It was on old Lincoln Road across from the then back gate of the college. In 1913 the college bought the Rose estate including the Inn, thus extending the campus to Fourth Street. The building has had various uses (see text). It was razed in the late 1950's to clear the site for new Cuvilly Hall. The first student rathskeller on the ground floor of that hall was called the Red Rose Inn.

Well: The "Well," center for many student celebrations through more than eighty years, is a light well which rises from the Marble Corridor to the Dome with railings on all floors. It was called by the early faculty "The Atrium," but the students called it the Well and the Well it has remained.

CARDINAL'S RESIDENCE,
408 North Charles Street

Baltimore, *June 21, 1897.*

Sister Julia,

Provincial of the Sisters of Notre Dame of Namur,

Dear Mother:—I heartily congratulate you on the good news you send me,—that you are about to erect a college for the higher education of Catholic young women, in our National Capital, and near by the grounds of the Catholic University of America.

I hereby give my endorsement, approval and blessing to your noble work and I pray that it may succeed beyond your most sanguine expectations.

Such an institution under your able and experienced direction and in the shadow of our great University, will, I am convinced, offer educational advantages to our young women which can not be found elsewhere in our country. It will relieve the University authorities from the embarrassment of refusing women admission, many of whom have already applied for the privilege of following our courses, and will be a light and a protection in faith and morals to that class of students while pursuing the highest branches of knowledge. Your work, with that of the University, will complete and crown our whole system of Catholic education; will be a blessing to our country and a glory to our Church.

Praying God's blessing most abundantly on you and all your works, I am, dear Mother,

Faithfully yours in Christ,

James Cardinal Gibbons

Printed in the *Catalogue* 1900–1901, 1901–1902

Abbreviations

Advisory Board Minutes 1900–1926	Ad. Bd. Min.
Annals of Notre Dame, Mt. Pleasant, Liverpool, England	MPA
Archives of Trinity College	TCA
Baltimore Archdiocesan Archives	BA
Board of Trustees Minutes 1897–1978	B. T. Min.
Dictionary of American Biography	DAB
Foundations of Trinity College *ms* (by Sister Mary Euphrasia Taylor)	Fd. S. E.
Journal of Sister Mary Euphrasia	*Jour.* I, II
Minutes of the Auxiliary Board of Regents of Trinity College 1898–1978 ("Ladies' Board")	ABR

THE COAT OF ARMS

The coat of arms of Trinity College consists of a main field of red (gules) charged with a gold triangle, the conventional heraldic emblem of the Blessed Trinity. Upon the triangle is placed an open book, gold-edged and bound in gold, bearing the motto of the College: *Scientia Ancilla Fidei* (Knowledge the Handmaid of Faith). The chief (or upper compartment of the shield) is of blue (azure) charged with three mullets (stars, here of five points) in silver (argent).

The red and blue chosen for the fields are the component colors of purple. Thus the College colors of Trinity—properly "livery" colors—which are purple and gold, are represented by the constituents of purple and by the gold of the triangle and of the edges, binding, and clasps of the book.

The name of the College, Trinity, is recorded heraldically by the triangle, the three clasps of the book, the three words of the motto, and the three stars in chief.

The purpose of the College is shown by the open book, the heraldic symbol used for institutions of learning.

Thus, according to the intention of M. Pierre de Chaignon de la Rose, the shield "identifies its owner—Trinity College—as clearly as the conventions of heraldry permit."

The chief is designed, first of all, to indicate Notre Dame; and for this reason Our Lady's heraldic colors, azure and argent, have been used, as well as the star, significant in heraldry of one of her titles, Stella Maris. In this way the relation of the institute of Notre Dame to the College finds expression.

Finally it is to be noted that the three stars in the chief appear in exactly the position which they occupy in the arms of the Washington family. This reminiscence serves to recall the location of Trinity College in Washington.

Contents

PART I *Foundations*

PART II *The Solid Core*

5. The Academic Program

6. Student Life

PART I

Foundations

CHAPTER ONE

Women and the Moment

". . . for the creation of a master-work . . . two powers must concur, the power of the man and the power of the moment, and the man is not enough without the moment . . ." Matthew Arnold[1]

THE CLIMATE for literary masterpieces required by Arnold may foster other creative activities. Trinity College in Washington, D.C. sprang in 1897 from just such a combination of "man and moment" as Arnold supposes, but in this case "woman" would be more appropriate. The nineteenth century, a period of advance in science, in literature, in philosophical and theological controversy, and, in the U.S. especially, of expansionism, and of passionate interest in the spread of education for all, was drawing to a somewhat tumultuous close. Its last decade has been given many facile titles. None is more appropriate than the "moulting nineties" implying a shedding of the old to develop and emerge into new and greater times—"emergence from old ways, the dropping of old standards, old ideas, old political allegories, old concepts of human relations, old disciplines of religion and family life . . . suggests youthful hospitality to the new which came crowding in every field."[2]

Throughout the century the education of girls and later their higher education was a subject of vital interest. The greatest thrust of the century in this field was for secondary schools, "academies," "seminaries," high schools, leading the way to women's higher education and in some instances developing into full degree granting colleges. Thomas Woody's *History of Women's Education in the United States,*[3] Jessie Bernard's *Academic Women,* U. of Pa. 1964, and Mabel Newcomer's *A Century of Higher Education for American Women,* N.Y. 1959, offer excellent documented surveys of the development of higher education for women in the U.S., its struggles, its achievements, the strong opposition it faced throughout the century. By the 1890's the idea that

1. *Essays in Criticism,* London-N.Y., 1900, p. 5. It is interesting to note that Matthew Arnold's "bread-and-butter job" was in education. He was one of Her Majesty's Inspectors of Schools and more than once his signature appears in the records of Notre Dame Training College, Liverpool, praising work there, after an official visit. MPA.
2. W. L. Whittlesey of Princeton quoted in *Our Times,* Vol. I, p. 185.
3. 2 Volumes, Science Press, 1929. Note especially Chapters VIII and IX of Vol. I.

young women had the intellectual ability for higher studies was being gradually accepted,[4] though there was still strong opposition in some quarters to their making use of that ability. Charles F. Thring, for example, wrote in 1894 "the old and tiresome question . . . of intellectual ability is closed,"[5] and the U.S. Commissioner of Education's Report for 1897 strengthens this opinion. Yet the subject continued as a vital topic of discussion.[6]

Opposition to the higher education for women persisted through the '90's and beyond. The popular novelist Ouida (Louise de la Ramée) writing of the "New Woman," also in 1894, "objected to the belief held by so many 'that there is no good education without a college curriculum.' Such an idea, she thought, was both 'as injurious as erroneous.' Though college education 'may have excellencies for men . . . for women it can only be hardening and deforming.' "[7] She thought that the "publicity of a college must be odious to a young woman of refined and delicate feeling."

Others declared that college gave too great freedom from woman's[8] limited sphere, that it would be injurious to health and would destroy her "womanly nature." Most terrible of all would be the decline in the marriage rate of college women and the decline in the birth rate. Nevertheless, young women continued to seek "higher studies" in normal schools, in post graduate years of the academies or seminaries and in degree-granting colleges and universities. In 1890, there were 56,000 women in regular sessions of institutions of "higher learning" including all the types of schools listed above. This was 2.2% of 18–21 year-old women and 35.9% of all students enrolled. By 1900, this had increased slightly to 2.8% or 85,000, 36.8% of all students enrolled.[9] American Catholic young women were among the 2.8%, but more were eager for university grade study in a college that was Catholic.

Therefore, an important aspect of the climate into which Trinity College was born may be found in the state of the Catholic church in the United States in the late 1890's. McAvoy's *The Great Crisis in American Catholic History,* 1895–1900[10] gives a well-documented, easily readable account of the development of "the Catholic minority" up to the "Americanism" crisis of the last years of the century, as well as an analysis of that crisis and its results. The nucleus of the Catholic church

4. Woody, *op. cit.* Vol. II, p. 157.
5. Quoted in Woody, Vol. II, p. 158.
6. Cf. Newcomer, pp. 1–3, also Chapter 2, pp. 5–32, p. 255.
7. *North American Review* (1894) CLV III, 614–15. Quoted in Woody, Vol. II, p. 152.
8. Woody, Vol. II, p. 204.
9. *91st Annual Edition of Statistical Abstract of the U.S.*, 1970, direction of Wm. Lerner, U.S. Department of Commerce. G.P.O.
10. McAvoy, Thomas T., C.S.C., Chicago (Regnery Co.) 1957.

in the United States, chiefly English colonists with a few Irish and French Canadians and the Catholic Indians converted by early missionaries, was augmented in the nineteenth century by French-Spanish Catholics of the Louisiana Territory, the Spanish of California and the Southwest, but especially by very large Irish and German immigrations from the 1840's on, with other smaller groups of European origin. The American principle of freedom of religion from domination by the state as well as the "melting pot" mentality helped these varied elements to join their fellow citizens in social, economic, political life while remaining staunchly Catholic in faith.[11]

By the 1890's friction between the German bishops and the main body of the rest of the bishops whom they called "Irish" and the "Americanism" crisis, to which it was related, were attracting the attention of both the Catholic and the secular press. "Americanism" in this context had as its central problem "the extent of the adaptation of Catholic practices to the American milieu. Those favoring adaptation were the Americanists—the Americanizing prelates whether they were of American, Irish, French or German birth. Those opposed felt that these adaptations were heretical."[12] The pseudo-heresy, named in Europe "Americanism," was little known by Catholics in America except among the bishops and theologians, but was hotly debated in Europe, especially in France. This debate was sparked by the translation into French, ten years after its peaceful publication in the United States, of Elliot's *Life of Isaac Hecker*, the founder of the Paulist Fathers. The principles of freedom of religion embodied in the American Constitution applied in Hecker's life came as joyous good news to Catholics in France, but as dangerous heresy to some French theologians and prelates who attempted unsuccessfully to have both the *Life* and "Americanism" as they interpreted it condemned. The Pope in a letter addressed to Cardinal Gibbons on the subject, January 27, 1899, ended controversy, but did not condemn. He expressed confidence in the American bishops' ability to judge conditions in their own country.

These aspects of the climate in the last decade of the century are relevant to Trinity College because of the far-seeing, liberal views of those who encouraged its foundation as well as an explanation for the violent opposition in some quarters to the establishment of the college and even of the fears and doubts expressed by the Superior General of Notre Dame at Namur, Belgium.

11. This is a brief simplification with no pretense of covering all facets or details. For these the reader should refer to other sources, such as McAvoy, *op. cit.*, with its excellent bibliography and *Immigration and American History*, edit. Henry Steele Commanger, U. of Minn. Press, 1961, especially the chapter "Immigration in American Life: A Reappraisal," by Oscar Handlin.
12. McAvoy, *op. cit.*, p. x.

The American hierarchy was still struggling to help the large body of immigrants who were Catholics to prepare for full participation in the privileges of free American citizenship.[13] Their three major concerns were Americanization of newcomers, education, and cooperation with other agencies in political, social, and industrial reform.

In the 1890's the bulk of Irish Americans were still concentrated on the industrial eastern seaboard, though there were strong Irish groups in other parts of the country. Considerable numbers had settled in Chicago, in Cincinnati, on the farmlands of Minnesota or had gone west with the railroads. German American concentration, on the other hand, was largely Middle-western with Milwaukee, Cincinnati, and St. Louis as centers.

> To the Irish themselves, they were Americans though Catholic. Their cultural differences with this "Yankee" neighbor they attributed to religious prejudice, not without cause, and to them their differences with the German and Pole and Canadian French were caused by the lack of Americanism on the part of these "foreigners."

> The German Catholic immigrants were never as poor economically and culturally as the persecuted Irishmen. Most of them could have remained in their old world homes, and they knew and loved their folk songs and folk lore in their native languages.[14]

Their life tended to center around their parish and school where German language and culture were preserved. "They established a German language press and many social and cultural societies."

Protest against what they considered the "inferior" status of German parishes in large cities, concern over the consequences of a Wisconsin state law requiring English in schools and that children attend school in their own school district [the reverse of the present bussing problem] and finally Cahenslyism[15] formed the substance of friction.

The intervention of individual members of the faculty and Board of Trustees of the Catholic University made this whole, apparently unrelated, problem into an important element in the environment and climate surrounding Trinity's beginning. The name of Schroeder especially appears in news releases in the Washington, Baltimore and New York daily papers as well as in the German and English Catholic press, in 1897, in violent opposition to the founding of the college.[16]

The Sisters of Notre Dame de Namur took a steady, vigorous part in the nineteenth century movement for maintaining and improving the

13. McAvoy, *op. cit.*, p. 59.
14. *Ibid.*, p. 62.
15. *Ibid.*, pp. 64–66, 72 ff.
16. *McAvoy, op. cit.*, pp. 172 ff. Cf. Ellis, John Treacy, *The Formative Years of the Catholic University* (*passim*), C.U.A. Press, 1946 and Hogan, Peter, S.S.J. *Catholic University, 1896–1903*, C.U.A. Press, 1949, pp. 95–100.

education of girls in Ohio, New England, Philadelphia, Washington, D.C. and in California.[17] The high esteem in which they were held in 1897 was backed by fifty-seven years of experience in the United States, as well as by the excellent reputation of the Notre Dame Schools and teacher-training colleges in Belgium and England. Dr. Thomas J. Conaty, Rector of the Catholic University, said on the first visit of Sister Mary Euphrasia and Sister Georgiana to discuss the college project:

> Although Notre Dame is of all other orders the one I would desire to have undertake such work yet I never would have dared to ask you. I have spoken to several religious orders, and particularly to the Holy Cross. I have also been stirring up the Sisters of Mercy at Pittsburgh asking them "Why not start Higher Education, *send some of your subjects to Europe, let them take degrees*?" [sic] If I had only known that Notre Dame would undertake it, I would ask no others.[18]

The congregation was founded in Amiens, France, in 1804 by Julie Billiart—now St. Julie—and Françoise Blin de Bourdon to meet the most pressing educational need of the times, the elementary education of the poor for whom no schools were provided. These two dedicated women have been associated since 1794 in shared prayer and work to alleviate the sufferings caused by the Revolution and the Reign of Terror. The goal they set for the little group who formed the first Sisters of Notre Dame was not only to educate the poor children of one place, but to go wherever they were needed. Julie's vision was worldwide for the education of girls. It resulted first in the removal of the group to Namur when the bishop of Amiens tried to hem them into his diocese. Though Julie died in 1816 and Françoise in 1838, the vision brought eight Sisters of Notre Dame on a six week Atlantic crossing to New York and thence to Cincinnati in 1840 while six others sailed with Father de Smet on an eventful seven month trip around Cape Horn to Oregon in 1844.[19]

From Cincinnati the Notre Dame schools in the mid-West and on the eastern seaboard were launched. The Gold Rush drew the Sisters from Oregon to meet the needs of the exploding population of California. Notre Dame is closely connected with the history of California and of Catholic education on the Pacific Coast.[20]

17. *Sister Louise,* Sister Helen Louise [Nugent]. New York (Benziger), 1931. This book gives throughout a good picture of the growth, spirit and influence of the religious congregation in the U.S. The Introduction is a concise, accurate account of the history of the Sisters of Notre Dame de Namur.
18. Ms *Foundations*, p. 56.
19. *Willamette Interlude.* Sister Mary Dominica McNamee, S.N.D. de N., Palo Alto, California, 1959, XIII, p. 302.
20. *Light in the Valley,* Mary Dominica McNamee, S.N.D. de N., Berkeley, California, 1967.

The "moment" imbued as we have seen with the ferment of change, of expansionism, of intellectual, economic and sociological progress foreshadowed many of the problems that have developed in the twentieth century. The power of this moment concurred with the power of the "man" embodied particularly in two experienced women educators, and in the group of scholarly men of faith who gathered to encourage, advise, defend them in their pioneering work. These were: Sister Julia (Susan McGroarty), Superior of the Sisters of Notre Dame de Namur in the United States; Sister Mary Euphrasia (Ella Taylor), Superior of the Convent at North Capitol and K Streets, Washington, D.C.; James Cardinal Gibbons, Archbishop of Baltimore and Chancellor of the Catholic University of America; the Rector and Vice-Rector of that university, Doctors Thomas Conaty and Philip Garrigan; and two brilliant young scholars of the university faculty, Doctors Edward A. Pace and Thomas J. Shahan.

From the perspective of eighty years one can observe a source of the enduring characteristics of the college in the varied preparation of these men and women, in the necessary tensions and resolution of tension involved in their working together. The geographical spread of their origins and experience, their varied competences were reflected in Trinity College.

Sister Julia (Susan McGroarty),[21] wise, gentle, but firm in decision, brought to the work of foundation fifty years of experience in education, as teacher and administrator, as friend and counselor of youth, as builder of solid educational programs as well as of solid buildings. Irish by birth, she had come with her family to Cincinnati, Ohio, in 1831 at the age of four, and had grown up in that German-Irish middlewestern city. Educated by the Sisters of Notre Dame from their first days in Cincinnati, she became a member of the congregation in 1846. Under the guidance of Dutch-born Belgian Sister Louise Van der Schriek and in close cooperation with other Belgians she developed into an understanding, successful teacher. Teaching experience in the academy in Cincinnati and in Roxbury, Massachusetts, as well as some years as "mistress of boarders" in the latter school led to her appointment to be superior of the six-year-old Notre Dame school in downtown Philadelphia. For twenty-five years Sister Julie presided over the growth and development of Notre Dame's educational work while she exercised in that city a widening influence. The many friends she made in Philadelphia were life-long friends. Her experience in those years prepared her for a wider sphere of work. She planned and directed the building of the large dignified academy on South 19th Street, known as West Rittenhouse Square. She supervised the development of the edu-

21. DAB Vol. X, pp. 244–5; *Sr. Julia,* by Sr. Helen Louise, esp. Intro. pp. VII-X and Chapter I and Chapter XII.

Sister Julia McGroarty, Foundress.

cational program there, while continuing work in the parish schools and establishing classes for the negro children which later developed into St. Peter Claver's school.

In 1886 Sister Julia succeeded Sister Louise as superior of the Sisters of Notre Dame in the Middle West and on the Eastern seaboard. From

1892 until her death her jurisdiction included also the California convents. Keeping abreast of the best in education she encouraged what we would call today a "cooperative study of curriculum and methods" on all levels of Notre Dame education in the United States. The product of this study was the *Course of Study*, first printed in 1888, revised, enlarged and reprinted in 1895, to be used in all Notre Dame schools.[22]

Sister Mary Euphrasia, a "southern lady" of English descent, was born in Richmond, Virginia and grew up in North Carolina.[23] In the spring of 1897, she was forty-five years old. From her correspondence with Sister Julia,[24] she emerges as a woman of unlimited energy, impulsive though with tenacity of purpose when once launched on a project, deeply spiritual though using a multiplicity of "devotions," somewhat socially snobbish, impressed by position and family, popular in her time, a prolific letter writer without benefit of secretary or typewriter. Her letters are very open, chatty, eager for action. To that very eagerness backed by practical common sense the college owes much. Because of it Sister Mary Euphrasia, during the hectic months from March to August 1897, urged, entreated, prodded, explained and acted as executive agent on the spot for college planning, especially for the choice and purchase of land to begin. She had interests and "connections" with what Barbara Tuchman calls "the small world that was Washington's elite" in the 1890's.[25] From this "small world" she gathered the ladies who helped her in promoting the college. Her "connections" were both family and Washington: "Mr. Beale, my sister's uncle-in-law," Mr. and Mrs. Talty, Secretary Sherman, Miss Seward, Senator Carter's wife; many important people in civic and political life whose names will appear later. The affectionate, admiring support of alumnae of Notre Dame Academy throughout the Washington area gave added strength to her efforts. She was interested in what would be called in 1971 "development": promotion, public relations, fund-raising. The scholarly affairs she knew were important, but she left them to others whose greater potential she discerned clearly. Her part was to urge to action, to organize the material provided and to utilize all resources available for a sound beginning for the college.

James Cardinal Gibbons, sixty-three in 1897, had been born in Baltimore, Maryland, spent his childhood in Ireland, and his adolescent years in New Orleans where he helped support his widowed mother

22. "Plan of Studies," 1894. Printed 1895. A copy is in the Trinity College Archives (T.C.A.).
23. Keenan, Sister Angela Elizabeth, *Three Against the Wind*, Westminster, Md. (Christian Classics), 1973.
24. Ms *Foundation* of T.C. and elsewhere in TCA.
25. *Proud Tower*, London, 1966, p. 123.

James Cardinal Gibbons.

by clerking in a grocery store and continued his interest in classical literature. After college at St. Charles in his native state of Maryland, he entered St. Mary's Seminary, Baltimore, and was ordained to the priesthood June 30, 1861. Interesting accounts exist of Civil War incidents in his first parish in rural Maryland.[26] Three post-war years as secretary to Bishop Spalding of Baltimore served as immediate preparation for his long career as a bishop. He was consecrated in 1868, the youngest bishop in the U.S., served in North Carolina, in Richmond, Virginia, and finally (1877) in Baltimore where he was Archbishop for forty-three years.

> In North Carolina, the future Cardinal received some of the strongest of the impressions which helped to shape his career. . . . His work brought him into much contact with non-Catholics, who were attracted by his winning personality, broad tolerance and rare intellectual force. . . . Where there was no Catholic church he preached in court-houses, Masonic lodge rooms, and even in Protestant churches the use of which was offered him. He studied the non-Catholic viewpoint in order that he might make his appeal with hopefulness. While he was serving this vicariate, the Ecumenical Council of the Vatican was called, of which he was the youngest member. . . . During this trip abroad he was impressed with the difficulties of the relations between Church and State in Europe as compared with the American system. A diary of the Council which he kept, published in *The Catholic World* (February to September, 1870), attracted much attention.[27]

> In the press his appointment [as Cardinal 1886] was hailed on the ground that he thoroughly identified with American life and institutions and that he interpreted the spirit of his country.[28]

He defended labor's right and saved the Knights of Labor and Henry George's *Progress and Poverty* from ecclesiastical condemnation in the U.S. His view was that discussion of labor and economic questions ought not to be stifled. He had met President Andrew Johnson when that President attended the closing exercises of the Second Plenary Council of Baltimore, and he came in personal contact with every subsequent President down to Harding. Some of them, especially Cleveland, Roosevelt and Taft, were warm personal friends.

> The celebration in 1889 of the centennial of the Catholic Hierarchy in America was marked by a week of imposing observances in Baltimore, organized by Gibbons, in which the Church's complete identification with American institutions was emphasized. A Congress of Laymen was held in connection with this celebration.[29]

In that same year the Catholic University of America was founded in Washington, D.C. with Gibbons as chairman of its board of trustees. Cardinal Gibbons, therefore, in 1897 was in an excellent position to

26. DAB, Vol. VII, 239–241.
27. DAB, p. 239.
28. *Ibid.*, p. 240.
29. *Ibid.*, p. 241. Cf. *Ellis, Gibbons*, Vol. I, p. 424 and its footnote, Baltimore 95-S-9 Gibbons to Satolli, Sept. 5, 1897.

support and encourage the Sisters of Notre Dame in the foundation of a college. Professor John Treacy Ellis, in his scholarly biography of Cardinal Gibbons, reinforces this statement.

> The Cardinal was likewise able to calm the fears of Cardinal Satolli, Prefect of the Congregation of Studies, when the Roman prelate grew apprehensive over locating a women's college within a few blocks of the university. Gibbons explained that Trinity College would not be part of the university proper and that its courses would be taught almost entirely by the Sisters of Notre Dame de Namur. He made known to Satolli that the rumors reaching Rome about the relationship of the two institutions were, as he expressed it, "utterly false or grossly exaggerated, and are the offspring of ignorance or malice."[30]

The other four men listed here among the founders of Trinity College were all from the very new Catholic University of America, its Rector and Vice-Rector, Drs. Conaty and Garrigan, and two enthusiastic young faculty members Doctors Pace and Shahan. Each had his own specific contribution to making the college what it became.

Thomas James Conaty, a forty-nine year old priest from New England, had just entered his duties as second rector of the university when the first steps toward planning for Trinity College were taken in March, 1897. Born in Ireland, he had been three years old when his family settled in Taunton, Massachusetts, where he attended the public schools. After secondary education in Montreal, he entered Holy Cross College, Worcester, graduating in 1869. Seminary training, again in Montreal, prepared him for ordination in 1872 for the diocese of Springfield. From 1887 to 1897 he was pastor of Sacred Heart Church in Worcester.

> During this period he displayed an active interest in civic as well as ecclesiastical life. His gifts as an orator attracted wide attention. He became a leader in his community and exerted far-reaching influence in movements that dealt with educational, moral and social problems. . . . He served on the Board of Education of Worcester for fourteen years and on its Library Board for six. He was one of the founders and president, 1893–1897, of the Catholic Summer School of America established originally at New Haven, Connecticut, and later permanently located at Cliff Haven, New York. He was active in founding the association of Catholic colleges later known as the National Catholic Education Association, and was its president, 1899–1903.[31]

Not only his position as Rector of the Catholic University, but especially his connection with and work for the Catholic Summer School

30. Ellis, *Gibbons*, Vol. I, p. 424. Cf. previous footnote reference to this letter in Baltimore Archdiocesan Archives.
31. DAB, Vol. IV, p. 337.

gave an opportunity for spreading the news of the new college to a widely dispersed, interested clientele. After his appointment in 1901 as bishop of Monterey-Los Angeles, he continued his interest in making Trinity known in the far West.

Philip Joseph Garrigan came at the age of four with his family from Ireland to Lowell, Massachusetts. Educated in the public schools of that city, he worked for a few years, earned his bachelor's degree from St. Charles College, Ellicott City, Maryland and studied theology at the seminary in Troy, New York. After ordination he served for two years in Worcester, Massachusetts until he was called back to Troy as director of the seminary. From 1875 to 1889 he was rector of St. Bernard's Church, Fitchburg, Massachusetts. "Here he displayed unusual administrative ability and keen interest in parochial education and won local distinction as a preacher."[32] In 1889, he "accepted the invitation of Rector J. J. Keane to serve as vice-rector of the newly established Catholic University of America. Chosen as a Northerner who might popularize the University in Catholic circles of New England, Garrigan proved an able executive who calmly went his way during the era when the new institution was subject to bitter criticism and stood loyally by Keane in the controversy which led to the latter's 'deposition.' He also aided materially in the foundation of Trinity College, a neighboring school for the higher education of women." That aid and friendship continued not only during the founding years, but after his installation as first Bishop of Sioux City, Iowa in 1902 until his death in 1919.[33]

Thomas Joseph Shahan (September 11, 1857–March 9, 1932) of the "founders" shared with Dr. Pace connections of longest duration with Trinity College. From the 1897–1900 period, when he was untiring in scholarly, practical advice on curriculum, courses of study, preparation of faculty, through his years of teaching in the college until his appointment to the Rectorship of the University in 1909, and up to his retirement in 1928, his interest in and affection for the faculty, students and alumnae of Trinity never lessened. Yet no mention of this involvement appears among his many assignments in the Dictionary of American Biography entry.[34]

He was born in Manchester, New Hampshire, of Irish parents, "immigrants of some culture, who acquired a small competence in the mill towns of New England without acquiring a slavish obsequiousness to their 'Yankee betters.'" After study in Sulpician College in Montreal,

32. DAB, Vol. VII, p. 167.
33. He was especially interested in studies. Largest donor in original equipment of chemistry laboratory. Later gifts to laboratory noted in annual reports of President.
34. DAB, Vol. XVII, 16; cf. "Bishop Shahan and Trinity," by Sister Wilfred (Elsie Pasons '04) *Trinity College Record*, April, 1932, pp. 131–135.

and the American College and Propaganda in Rome, where he was considered a "brilliant student of prodigious memory and great versatility," he received the S.T.D. in 1882. For six years he served in the diocese of Hartford, Connecticut as pastor of St. John's, as chancellor of the diocese and secretary to the Bishop of Hartford.

> When in 1888 he was invited by Monsignor John J. Keane to lecture at the pontifical Catholic University at Washington in church history, Roman law and patrology, he continued his studies at the Sorbonne and the Catholic Institute in Paris, at the Roman Seminary, and at the University of Berlin, where he specialized in history and learned German. In 1891 he began his lectures.[35]

He was a voluminous writer with a "somewhat redundant" style, an enthusiastic teacher who emphasized the German seminar method, and a life-long advocate of and worker for higher education.

Dr. Edward Aloysius Pace[36] was a Southerner. He was born in Starke, Florida, July 3, 1861, the first Catholic child to be born in that little town and destined to become its most famous citizen. His father, George Edward, was a plantation owner, later a merchant in Jacksonville, who was descended from 17th century English settlers in Virginia, and his mother was Margaret Kelly from Nova Scotia. He was educated at the Starke Institute, the Duval County High School, old St. Charles College, Ellicott City, Maryland, and the North American College in Rome. He received the doctorate in Theology in 1886 "after a brilliant course that brought him to the attention of Pope Leo XIII." Although requested for service at North American College, he was recalled to be chancellor of his native diocese of St. Augustine. "In 1888 Pace was chosen for the faculty of the projected Catholic University of America in Washington, D.C. He spent a year of study in Louvain and Paris and two years under the psychologist Wilhelm Wundt in Leipzig, receiving his Ph.D. in psychology *magna cum laude* in 1891. The remainder of his career was spent at the Catholic University of America as professor of psychology 1891–1894 and of philosophy 1894–1935 and in various official positions."[37] He taught at Trinity College 1900–1924.

In 1891, Pace established at the Catholic University one of the first psychological laboratories in America; in 1904 he was chairman of the

35. *Ibid.*
36. DAB, Vol. XXII (supplement 2, publ. 1958), pp. 506–7, *Priest, Administrator, Counsellor, Educator,* Memorial booklet, privately printed in 1963, the 25th anniversary of his death. A plaque in his honor erected in Starke, Florida, St. Edward's Church. Career highlights, pp. 26–28 are Appendix VII; *The Catholic University Bulletin*; Vol. 6, No. 3, May, 1935 Memorial Issue; *New Scholasticism*, XXXV, 2, April, 1961, pp. 141–151; Program of "Exercises in Honor of the Centenary of the Birth of the Rt. Rev. Edward A. Pace, S.T.D., Ph.D." Nov. 21, 1961, C.U.A. School of Philosophy.
37. DAB *ibid.*

experimental psychology section of the International Congress of Arts and Sciences held in St. Louis; in 1926 he became the first editor of C.U.'s *Studies in Psychology and Psychiatry*. He was an editor of *Catholic Encyclopedia* 1907–1914. With Thomas E. Shields he founded and was first editor of the *Catholic Educational Review* (1911). He wrote the post World War I Pastoral Letter for American Bishops (1919) discussing among other subjects, capital and labor, marriage and family, education and problems of international relations. He was a founder of the American Catholic Philosophical Society and editor with J. H. Ryan of *New Scholasticism* (1925–1936). He was Chairman of the American Council on Education, 1925–1926.

> Solidly grounded in Philosophy and Theology, possessed of a wide culture, and equipped with a thorough knowledge of his subjects, Pace had great powers of lucid explanation as a teacher and a writer. He was a pioneer both in scientific psychology and in modern scholastic philosophy in America. The bibliography of his writings numbers almost 300 titles.
>
> In education, in addition to these general aims, his interests included improved methods of teaching religion, the liturgical revival, courses of study for students for the priesthood, and the development of graduate studies, particularly in philosophy and psychology. . . . Because of its solid and original character, his work has had a deep and lasting influence on American Catholic educational theory and practice.[38]

Dr. Pace, the youngest of the group intimately associated with the foundation of the college, continued his interest until his death in 1938. His name will reappear frequently in the following pages, as closely involved in the formulation of curriculum and entrance requirements, in the continuing process of accreditation, and in the college's participation in professional educational associations. He was in today's language a resource person who could be consulted in many fields from student attitudes to appropriate Scripture quotations for the inscriptions for Notre Dame Chapel. He taught at least one course at Trinity College from the opening until 1924.[39]

38. DAB Vol. XXII, Supplement II, 1958, p. 507.
39. Cf. References throughout this history, especially the philosophy, psychology, and education departments. Also "Souvenir of an Uncle," Marguerite Pace Corcoran, 1911, in *Alumnae Journal*, Summer, 1967, pp. 240–243; Msgr. Edward A. Pace *obit.* by Sister Julia Stokes, S.N.D. (Helen Stokes) '13, *Alumnae Journal*, May, 1938, p. 34.

CHAPTER TWO

Strong Foundations 1897–1900

IN THE ATMOSPHERE described in the preceding chapter, the actual history of Trinity College, Washington, D.C. began in March, 1897. Five months of enthusiastic activity, frustration, anxiety, deliberation, premature publicity, violent opposition and momentous decision led to the act of incorporation of Trinity College on August 20, 1897. The record of those months alone forms a microcosm that typifies not only the spirit of the closing years of the century, but the history of the college through its more than eighty years of service. Three years of foundation laying, preparing curriculum and faculty, setting requirements, recruiting students, seeking funds and constructing a building, reached fruition with the opening of the college in the fall of 1900.[1]

On Sunday afternoon, March 7, 1897, three days after the inauguration of President McKinley,[2] Sister Julia McGroarty, Superior of the Sisters of Notre Dame in the United States, and Sister Mary Euphrasia Taylor, Superior of the Convent at North Capitol and K Streets in Washington, "drove[3] to Eckington and Brookland, suburban villages of great beauty in the neighborhood of the Catholic University." They were looking for a suitable site outside the city, for a "second foundation at Washington," an academy for girls. That Sister Julia, an educator of long experience, fully aware of the contemporary thrusts toward better advanced education for girls, "secretly longed for a college" was known to few. She delegated to Sister Mary Euphrasia, her "man on the spot," the business of seeking approval from Cardinal Gibbons for

1. A valuable addition to the material of this chapter is "The Foundation of Trinity College and the Design of a Program of Higher Education for Women," by Mary Hayes, S.N.D., a paper delivered at the American Catholic Historical Society, December 30, 1982.
2. For McKinley's second inauguration in 1901 all the students of the college were present at the ceremonies. *First Annual Report of Trinity College, 1900–1901.*
3. This is the first reference to the many drives in Mrs. Talty's carriage on business for Trinity. Cf. Appendix I.

a new academy as well as of consulting Dr. Garrigan, Vice-Rector of the Catholic University of America, about the feasibility of the project. She, herself, left for Massachusetts to continue her schedule of visiting her sisters in that state, intending to return when needed.[4]

Sister Mary Euphrasia lost no time arranging appointments with Dr. Garrigan and with Cardinal Gibbons. On March 11, Dr. Garrigan "gave . . . an hour and a half of his valuable time," discussing the plans for a second Notre Dame school. The list of topics for consideration included suggestions of friends "that we open a house for select pupils in the northwest (fashionable quarter); the propriety of being represented *just as we are* in this city of educational institutions,"[5] the need for more outdoor space and finally, reflecting the fears of the time, the establishment of a "Protestant College" [Eckington College?] near the university to which Catholic children had begun to go.[6]

Dr. Garrigan replied with cordial approval, but amplified considerably on the idea of a new academy. The Ladies of the Sacred Heart and the Sisters of the Holy Cross, he said, had "in turn desired to come and establish an annexe" to the Catholic University. The Board of Trustees had approved but not Cardinal Satolli, Apostolic Delegate to the United States until 1896. The plan was also "discountenanced by the heads of both orders."

He went on to outline what might be called the first plan for the college, which he felt sure the Cardinal would approve. "We must have the new foundation," he said, "a college for Higher Education. It must be a boarding school; one that will receive pupils from all over the United States who after finishing in parochial day, and boarding schools (ours particularly)[7] will come here to continue their studies in our college, lectures being given by the University professors in some branches, the Sisters supplying the others; all the pupils attending the *public* lectures of the University, and possibly some private ones under chaperonage of a lady employed by us for that purpose. Our proposed schedule would be compared with that of the University. . . ."

Here we find mention for the first time of those now well-known *twenty applicants* who had been refused admission to Catholic University because they were women and who had "entered other annexes, *all Protestant or infidel,* where they are in danger of losing their faith."

4. Throughout the material cited from the *Ms Foundations,* the italics are Sister Mary Euphrasia's.
5. The fact that the academy on N. Capitol Street was registered in Washington as a Parochial School, even though the full academic course had always been followed, irked Sister Mary Euphrasia.
6. The material for this chapter is drawn chiefly from Sister Mary Euphrasia's manuscript *Foundations of Trinity College* (abbreviated *Fd.* S.E.).
7. It is well to note that when the college opened students came from both public and private academies and high schools and not just "ours particularly." A study of registration records appears later in this work in Chapter 5.

Sister Mary Euphrasia's letter of March 13 reporting to Sister Julia is full of "what Dr. Garrigan said," his argument for a college. It shows her own complete acceptance of the idea.

> I fear you think me very eager, very enthusiastic, but it is because such an opportunity comes but once in a life time, and but in one place in the world! *Where elsewhere have we a Catholic University under the direct supervision of our Holy Father offering to work hand in hand with a religious institute for the benefit of our pupils and of American society at large? Will such an offer ever come to us again?*

She, too, like Arnold believed in the "power of the moment."

The plans of other Sisters were rejected, Dr. Garrigan said, because they entailed co-education. The city, he said, has cultural advantages "under proper chaperonage." [Of course!] In summing up his arguments for a college he strikes a vital point: "*It is the need of the times, the especial need of the place. Not so much for the inhabitants, perhaps, as for those of the country at large.* It is what the present system of boarding schools is tending towards. . . ."

The Cardinal came Saturday afternoon March 13 when he was "in the city, [for] next Sunday," and Sister Mary Euphrasia was careful to keep to the original request. "Our beloved Cardinal came promptly at five o'clock and went at once to business. I spoke to him just as to Dr. Garrigan; *making no mention* of the latter's idea." He desired time for reflection and to consult Doctors Conaty and Garrigan. As good pastor of all, he was concerned for the effect on other Catholic schools in Washington. One bit of his very practical advice was based on hard experience: they should buy land quickly. Land that Catholic University had bought for $500 an acre would now be $5000 an acre, he warned.

The fact that the telephone, though in use, was not yet in 1897 the ordinary method of communication between those even in the same city is helpful in following the activity of Sister Mary Euphrasia and Dr. Garrigan during the next few weeks. Letters sent by messenger between the Convent on North Capital Street and Catholic University leave a written record of developments. These, added to letters to Sister Julia reporting progress, formal letters to the Cardinal [T.C. Archives and Baltimore Archdiocesan Archives] and the manuscript *Foundation of Trinity College* and *Journal of Trinity College 1897–1900,* make it possible to share the feverish activity, the sustained devotion to accomplishing a necessary work, the frustrations and fears, and especially the deep trust in God of the founding months—and the years—until the actual opening of the college.

Early on Sunday, March 14, Sister Mary Euphrasia sent a note to Dr. Garrigan which elicited a reply the same day saying that he did not hope to see the Cardinal that day, but, he wrote:

> . . . I have mentioned your good work to Very Rev. Rector [Dr. Conaty] to get his endorsement of all I had said to you for I was a little fearful that I might have taken a great responsibility on myself in advising you as strongly as I did. But I was pleased to find that he was even stronger than I dared to be. He says that your community is the one to accomplish this work.[8] He had already begun to stir up the Srs. of the H. Cross on the project, as I had, but he agrees with me that you are the community for this work. So you see your case is in most friendly hands.
>
> In the meantime, dear Sister, because the work is of great importance to your family, to religion and to the university also, I know that you will all pray fervently that no wrong step may be taken as we will also do. [Original in T.C.A., copy in Fd.S.E., pp. 21–22]

The next day, March 15, Dr. Garrigan visited the convent to say that he had met the Cardinal after all and told him of the college project. He had been requested "to call and say that in a few days he [the Cardinal] would assemble his council to deliberate with them concerning the matter." That day Sister Mary Euphrasia wrote to the Cardinal asking time to gather necessary data before presenting the plan. [Balt. Archives–1st about college 95K8]

Two letters of March 16 show prompt action. Sister Mary Euphrasia requests "a brief outline of the work expected in the proposed college." She will leave in the morning for Massachusetts to consult Sr. Julia. Dr. Garrigan answers: "It is going very fast to think of courses of studies at this distance from the realization of the material part of your project. I should think it enough to decide on the general character of your school, its aim and scope." He advises her to send for catalogues of other colleges and includes with his letter the Vassar, Wellesley, and Catholic University catalogues. The "aim and scope" given in his "humble opinion" fills the rest of the letter. As it forms the broad outline of the plan and expresses the attitude of the founders, the rest of this letter is cited as a whole. [Original letter also in T.C.A.]

> . . . It should, in my humble opinion, aim at work that would rest on the full Courses and diploma of our Catholic female Academies and public high schools. In that sense it would be post-graduate, or as we say more correctly graduate work. This should give the name and character to your new institution. It would not interfere with existing institutions, as it would not do work they are already doing, and in some instances at least doing well. These institutions would not then antagonize you; you should make them your friends, in order to make them feeders to your school. Therefore you should aim at work that is not done by any, even of our best academies today, and take our young Catholic women to a higher plane than has been so far reached by our Catholic schools; in a word do for them what Vassar

8. Cf. Fd. S.E. Fr. Purbrick S.J.'s opinion of S.N.D.'s, pp. 38–39; also Dr. Conaty's p. 58. [Edward Ignatius Purbrick, English Jesuit Provincial]

and Wellesley and Bryn Mawr are doing for American women. For this attainment you must not imitate these institutions in their entire curricula. I think they offer too much and accomplish less. Take the studies that suit womanhood, whether for use or adornment, such as will fit a young woman for positions that become her sex (and you know that the range of such positions has of late been much extended) and ground your student in the knowledge of these studies, so that she will know the branch, can think in it, write of it, enjoy it no matter in what form it comes before her through life; may correct erroneous notions about, no matter when, or by whom presented, and in fine by teaching, can from proper material produce others such as she is herself, aglow with true knowledge, and anxious to communicate the flame to others. You must teach history Sacred and profane, *philosophy* and *ethics*. Letters, especially English. And perhaps *Journalism*, Chemistry, and some other natural sciences *Physiology, Pedagogy, Painting, Music, Political* and *Social* economy as well as others that will be suggested might enter into your courses. Send for the Catalogues or Year Books of the leading Female Colleges, and examine their studies. I send you that of Vassar and our own Year Book the latter you may retain but Vassar return to me if you please, as it does not belong to me.

If I can say anything or do anything else useful to you, command me.

Yours in Christ Phil. J. Garrigan

Armed with this material and eager to report in person "considering the slowness and unsatisfactory character of written transactions," Sister Mary Euphrasia set out on March 17 for Worcester, Massachusetts to consult Sister Julia. There she met also Sister Georgiana who was asked to add her experienced judgement to the planning. Back in Washington Sister Mary Euphrasia wrote a formal letter to the Cardinal, March 22, [Balt. Archives 95L4] giving progress to date and requesting an appointment to "submit to your Eminence a few points of the general plan which Sister Julia is preparing for presentation to your council." Attached to this letter in the Baltimore Archives is a handwritten copy of these "few points" labelled "Notre Dame Sisters about founding a post-graduate institution near Catholic University." This is the first official statement of the projected plan. [Also copy in Fd. pp. 39–40] Therefore, it follows here in its entirety. Five months and many discussions later, the act of incorporation omits the word Catholic in the statement of purpose.

Location	Vicinity of Catholic University
Aim	Higher Education of Catholic Y. Women
Conditions of Admission to our College	Graduation from Academy of good standing or from Public High School

Intentions	Purchase ground at once Announce opening for 1900 Advertise throughout U.S.
Means of Support	Tuition of students with any bequests that the public may wish to offer.

At the interview on March 29 with Cardinal Gibbons this plan was discussed point by point in a friendly, encouraging manner. The fact that this would be a "post-graduate"[9] course would, the Cardinal thought, "obviate objections" such as the fears of other religious orders in Washington. In regard to taxes on land which might be acquired, but not yet built upon or used for college purposes while plans were being perfected, he suggested consulting Mr. Waggaman, the business manager of the University.

During the whole interview, the Cardinal showed encouragement for the project. His interest extended to each detail of the outline. In about ten days, he said, he would meet his council, with Doctors Conaty and Garrigan present for consultation, having delayed the meeting to give the Sisters "a little time" for consideration, consultation and planning.

That evening Sister Georgiana arrived "at 9:45 p.m." after the long trip by train from Boston.

> . . . the next morning Sister Mary Euphrasia and she went to visit several estates in the neighborhood of the University. Good Mrs. Talty's carriage was at their disposal and this dear friend who drove herself was as much interested as the Sisters were.[10]

The letters of both these explorers of the vicinity of the University (Sister Euphrasia's enthusiastically exuberant, Sister Georgiana's agreeing in substance, but giving more practical details such as prices) show that they considered at that time three estates: the Chase-Sprague, the Stewart, and the Robinson. No mention is yet made of what actually became the Trinity campus known later as "the Glenwood Cemetary or Michigan Avenue site." To understand better the problem of land selection facing the planners, it is necessary to realize that the whole area was in 1897 far outside the city, Florida Avenue, then named "Boundary Street" being the city limit. North Capitol Street extended only to the end of the lettered streets. Michigan Ave-

9. "Post-graduate" as used in these early discussions of the college meant after fulfilling the requirements for graduation from an academy or high school, post-secondary school graduation. The more usual meanings of graduate and undergraduate work in higher education appear under "Classification of Students" in the earliest catalogues of Trinity College. Cf. 1901–1902, pp. 12–13.
10. Mrs. Talty's account of the acquisition of land for Trinity, written some years later, appears as Appendix I.

nue followed the south boundary of the Soldiers Home property and stopped abruptly about where Franklin Street now (1972) joins it. Fourth Street was the main direct road to the University from downtown. The Chase land, "on the main road to the University" was favored by Dr. Garrigan because he thought the house big enough for a beginning. Sister Mary Euphrasia found it "not nearly as large as I had anticipated" and "very dilapidated." "The land however is beautifully graded, and the view charming, commanding a full sight of the University buildings [sic] and Eckington." Sister Georgiana writes merely that it was "the remains of what was formerly a fine place. . . . If the price is $100,000, it would take another hundred thousand to put the grounds in any kind of repair."

Both Sisters agreed that the adjoining Stewart place was not suitable. The Vineyard, owned by the Robinsons was eminently suitable—even the down-to-earth Sister Georgiana called it "the ideal spot"—but it was not for sale! Bounded on two sides by Soldiers Home property and on the other two by [what is still] Harewood Road, "it stands above Soldiers Home and the University, and between them." "There is not an eye-sore in sight." "The little path through the pines to the stile-way . . . would admit a seven minutes walk, I think, to the University building [only one, this time]." A new spur of the electric or horse car could come directly "to our gate."

Their hearts were set on this place though it was not for sale, and Mr. Waggaman was asked to make inquiries through a lawyer, Mr. Williamson. That negotiations continued for nearly two months is evidenced by a letter of Mr. Conway Robinson[11] to Mr. Williamson, May 24, 1897. The owner's description of the property is even more glowing than that of the Sisters. No agreement on price or conditions of sale could be reached.

Meanwhile, Dr. Garrigan came to say that the Cardinal's Council would meet on Monday (April 5). The two Sisters, therefore, spent two more days in land exploration, discussion and preparation for a formal interview with Dr. Conaty. On Saturday, April 3, they "went to the University and sent in their cards." The account of what followed shows not only turn-of-the-century etiquette, but the light-hearted informality with which it was brushed aside to reveal the sincere cooperation and close involvement of the heads of the Catholic University in the proposed college. Only direct quotation from Sister Mary Euphrasia's manuscript account can give the true picture. "Very reverend Dr. Conaty," it says

> . . . gave them a most gracious and cordial welcome and recognizing Sister Georgiana with the quick friendly impulse of a boy said "Hello" but

11. T.C.A. Robinson Land.

immediately *added* [sic] with his gentlemanly courteousness apologized by saying "Sister please pardon the expression but I was so glad to see you." He commenced by congratulating us on accepting the work, and on the broad-minded progressive spirit exhibited. "Although Notre Dame is of all other orders," he said, "the one I would desire to have undertake such a work, yet I never would have dared to ask you. I have spoken to several religious orders, and particularly to the Holy Cross. I have also been stirring up the Sisters of Mercy at Pittsburg asking them Why not start Higher Education, send some of your subjects to Europe, let them take degrees? If I had only known that Notre Dame would undertake it, I would ask no others." On being asked when he would advise to begin; he answered emphatically "Strike while the iron is hot." Dr. Conaty then added: "In June I commence my lecture tour and everywhere I can advertise your work, as soon as you are ready let us know. We shall publish it far and wide. Get the land bought." Dr. Garrigan who at that moment was passing through the corridor was called in and the question, when to begin was proposed to him. He advised not to set a time, but in the near future say we shall open. Let students send in their applications, suggest courses of studies in preparation. Not wise to set a time before the material part is more advanced; get an option on certain desirable places, a written agreement so that within a certain time, the place cannot be sold to another. Consult Mr. Waggaman, our businessman. On one of the Superiors expressing some doubt, as to the ultimate success of the undertaking. Rev. Dr. Conaty said success was certain he had never known Notre Dame to undertake anything in which it did not succeed. We should train subjects, select proper minds to put to study, perhaps send them abroad. Not so much in the study itself as in the scientific manner of imparting it. . . . Then as regards the council we are going in your interests, and to represent you. It will be to our credit, for it is something we have been asked to do, but could not do. You are going to provide a home near the University. . . . As to requisites for admission Dr. Conaty said: The applicants must know French and German, these are the languages in which the sciences are written and they should have at least a readable knowledge such as high schools and academies give generally. Your college is for post-graduates.[12]

That day also (April 3) a letter from Sister Julia addressed to both Sister Mary Euphrasia and Sister Georgiana arrived. She was ill and "hors de combat" for an indefinite time with plenty of time to think. She wrote her thoughts which she wanted communicated to Dr. Garrigan because "in this as well as in all other matters we must be true to N.D., be fair and square. . . ."

Had I known the probable outcome of it I would never have taken the step, as it is I would not hesitate to take it up, if I can see our way to make it a success. I have seventy years' experience, have erected through the able assistance of my able Sisters three large institutions, so why should we fear

12. *Fd.* S.E. p. 65. Cf. note p. 22.

> to fail, simply because one element of success is wanting (the money). We are considered by the outside world immensely wealthy, because we manage our own affairs, have no man of business, have never asked anything of anyone, gone on by degrees. This must like Minerva spring forth fully armed Cap à Pie. I think of all the apparatus, and everything else. For the sake of the work we must not fail or it will put it back twenty years or kill it. With what we are doing in Belgium and Scotland, there is no reason to fear but want of money, so let us count the cost before we beg. I would not disappoint the Cardinal and other friends for anything. I write this on the flat of my back, and will send it at once. There is much I would like to say. I have been studying Vassar and Wellesley both asking for unlimited means.

This letter was followed by a telegram that Sister Julia's illness was serious.

On Monday, April 5,[13] as planned, Cardinal Gibbons' Council, his "consultors" as he called them, met and "warmly approved" the proposed "post-graduate institution for women in the vicinity of the Catholic University." In his letter reporting this news, the Cardinal added:

> As for myself, I am persuaded that such an institution, working in union with though entirely independent of the Catholic University, will do incalculable good in the cause of higher education, and I am happy to give the project my hearty approval.

This letter was received in Washington on April 7, one month from that first carriage drive to the pretty little suburban villages. Meanwhile a cablegram, dated April 1, 1897, and still preserved in the Trinity archives, came from Namur, Belgium. "Approve, hoping you can find means and subjects. Aimee." Since "Aimee" was the Superior General of the Sisters of Notre Dame, approval seemed complete and the work of planning could begin in earnest.

Letters and telegrams between Washington and Holyoke, Massachusetts kept Sister Julia in almost daily touch with developments, describing properties, giving cost estimates and receiving wise advice in return. Her two closest advisors, Sister Georgiana from New England and Sister Mary Borgia from Ohio conducted business and correspondence for Sister Julia, keeping her informed while she was forced to take the long overdue complete rest prescribed by doctors.

Early in April, after the official approval, Sister Mary Euphrasia asked Mr. Waggaman, the "man of business" for Catholic University, to get options on various properties until a decision could be made. Dr. Garrigan came to visit on the tenth. He said that Mr. Waggaman was slow. "I thought," wrote Sister Mary Euphrasia, "in one way that was

13. On this day Theodore Roosevelt was named Assistant Secretary of the Navy. Before the first degrees were granted, he was President of the United States.

not bad just now! Dr. Garrigan is so very anxious that the land be bought, because then one can work!" In spite of negotiations and many more visits to properties, no option was actually taken until June 9. Then, it was for thirty days on the "Michigan Avenue" land and in the name of Mr. Maurice Talty. The actual purchase was not until July. This fact is anticipated here, because in mid-April some one (possibly a dissident member of the Catholic University faculty) wrote to Cardinal Satolli[14] in Rome that: "the Sisters of Notre Dame had bought a place near the Catholic University, and were going to build a University for Women . . . that the Professors [of] the Catholic University would be the teachers, and that the students of both places would attend the classes of the professors . . . that there would be an 'amalgamation of sexes'—co-education." This private erroneous report was unknown to those most concerned with the foundation until August—when violent opposition became public. Yet the seeds of misrepresentation had been sown before even an option on land had been secured or any announcement of plans had been made.[15] The approval was not as complete as it seemed to the founders.

April was spent in considering ways and means of support while continuing the land hunt. Letters to "the Floods," a wealthy Catholic family in California who were friends of Notre Dame, and plans to call on Mr. and Miss Flood when they came east date from early in the month. Sister Julia, though somewhat better, could not come to Washington, but approved of seeking funds. "Without money we cannot involve ourselves and ruin the work!" she writes. "Sister Georgiana will write for me as I can write only essentials." From Washington came details of progress, affectionate sadness that Sister Julia could not come herself, and a strong plea that she send her two advisors to add their opinions, because no written descriptions of the land would suffice. On advice from Sister Julia, Sister Mary Euphrasia wrote, on April 14, and called on Archbishop Martinelli, the Apostolic Delegate, on April 25, to inform him of all that had been done and was planned for the future. Monsignor Martinelli showed interest, and did not tell her then that he had received a letter from the Holy Father inquiring about the rumors he had heard. He simply wrote back, as he told her four months later, "that there was not to be co-education. I wrote to him as

14. Former Apostolic Delegate at Washington, and an opponent of the Catholic University.
15. Early in April as we know, after the Cardinal's Council approved (April 5) the plan for a college, Sister Mary Euphrasia asked Mr. Waggaman, the "man of business" for Catholic University, to get *options* on various properties. *This* may be the "buying of land" reported to Rome. The sites under consideration then *were* closer to the University than final purchase of the Glenwood Cemetery land. Also, Sister Mary Euphrasia was still on April 26 thinking joyfully of the Robinson place as "ours." Her enthusiasm may have leaked!

soon as you left me and I thought that that was the end of it." He was mistaken.

Many pages of the manuscript account are devoted to such lively descriptions of properties that one is tempted to reproduce them. They give an insight into the nature of the area at the time as well as a basis for tracing growth and change of this section of Washing during eighty years. The "Commissioners Map" of the city, referred to, is still preserved at Trinity College. It makes intelligible the 1897 descriptions of places and streets. North Capitol Street extended only to the end of the alphabet streets,[16] though First Street, N.W. did extend as far as the South Gate of the Soldiers Home grounds. Michigan Avenue bordered the south boundary of those grounds with a projected extension along the eastern boundary to join the road in front of the University. "The Main Road from the city" to the University on which the "electric car" line ran was Fourth Street, N.E.

By the end of April, interest had narrowed down to the "Michigan Avenue property,"[17] the northern end of land owned by Glenwood Cemetery. Dr. Garrigan turned from other estates to focus on it. Mr. Beale advised it. Mr. and Mrs. Talty had always favored it. Enthusiastic letters from Sister Euphrasia elicited a telegraphic reply: "I will not go so fast. I must see my way through. Sr. Julia." Sister Mary Euphrasia put her trust in God, redoubled her prayers and wrote back:

> But now I must write $ and ¢ [dollars and cents] again. I am sure I frightened you, dearest Sister Superior, when I wrote about the 24 and 48 hours. You see those gentlemen, with Secretary Sherman at the head are 'Land Speculators.' This land we have in view belongs to the Glenwood Cemetery. Sec. Sherman has eye on it for a good speculation. (If he knew we needed it how quickly he would secure it!) Mr. Beale was invited to go in with them. Now if Mr. Beale could buy it for us, ahead of this speculation, that would and will be our only chance to get it. This accounts for the hurry. He said to me that if we would certainly take it, he would be willing to pay cash down $4,000 or $5,000 on 30 or 60 da. time and this is what I had not time to say in detail the other day, as the carriage was waiting. This would really be either an option, or a sale at small payments, to bind the bargain, and get the deed. You could then announce your purchase and intention of opening the school.
>
> I did not like to put the question if there would be any interest charged, because for two months it would be only $50. 6% being the legal rate here. The other payment would be probably a third down in cash etc. as usual in those sales. Now, dearest Sister Superior, I am certain you will not let the

16. An X Street is projected on that map, though it seems never to have materialized, nor have Y or Z. The names of streets beyond the alphabet have since been changed to the orderly two-syllable and three-syllable alphabet as the city grew.
17. This property, now part of the campus of the college, is described at length in the manuscript *Foundations*, pp. 88–89, 105–110.

> opportunity slip for want of confidence when you recollect all that the good God has done for you in the past! and see the example of the Catholic University! How they regret this want of confidence. 'See how Dr. Garrigan says: I could so easily have had it endowed.' He thinks this is no risk whatever for us. People will not endow nothing. Once the land is secured, you can ask them to endow Halls, libraries, observatories. This will mean to endow the land on which it stands also.
>
> June will soon be here, and if we are not ready for the announcement of the Rector, what an opportunity lost! Of course they will not wait for us; they will say we have failed them and get somebody else, and after the benefit of their own experience, and all that the good God has given us through Mr. Beale's enlightening us regarding these speculators, would we not blame ourselves?

This brought results. May 6, Sister Julia's two advisors, Sister Mary Borgia and Sister Georgiana arrived "very hopeful and thoroughly interested in the project." They visited and discussed the various proposed sites, visited buildings and conferred with administrators at Catholic University and at "the Columbian University" [now George Washington University], consulted Mr. Beale, Mr. Waggaman, and Mr. Talty. They shuttled by train back and forth to Philadelphia where Sister Julia was now continuing her convalescence, "studying out plans for the buildings and for the studies," and worrying about money. Some one who died recently, Sister Mary Euphrasia wrote, had "left some hundreds of dollars to the Sisters . . . small compared to the hundreds of thousands needed. Perhaps our college is to be built by small contributions by many people." In the perspective of the years that stands out as a prophetic statement!

A letter from Namur, in mid-May, to Sister Julia showed Mère Aimée's appreciation of the importance of the project and of the difficulties it entailed. "The Bishop of Namur and our chaplain," the letter continues

> went to Rome in April. When His Lordship presented the Canon to the Holy Father and told him he was our chaplain His Holiness exclaimed: 'The Sisters of Notre Dame do so much good. I send a special blessing to the Rev. Mother and to all the Sisters throughout the Institute.'

There is still no indication of the mid-summer storm against the college that had been brewing since April.

Sister Mary Euphrasia wrote eloquently on May 25 of her ideas on the value of higher education, of the advantages of Washington, D.C., of the need to act quickly with trust in God.

> Now since every one here—and where could they understand the subject so well as at the heart and centre of the movement?—who has been approached concerning endowments, says *that the land must be bought, and*

the announcement publicly made before any successful step can be taken, will you not see in all, the wonderful workings of God to bring this matter around, His own hand, and be encouraged to bravely venture? I feel confident, dear Sister Superior that when once you will have said "*Duc in Altum,*" and have abandoned the foundation to the providence of God to do *all* that will be needed for its beginning and continuance, that He will Himself take up the work and carry it through. It seems to me dearest Sister Superior, that if to you there appeared in this undertaking as much pure undivided glory to God as *I* feel there would be, that your faith would be so great, that you would have courage to go straight ahead, in spite of every misgiving and obstacle that could arise on the part of others. Would that I could impart to you some of the ardor with which my own heart is filled! I must confess that from the very outset I felt a great affection for the project. . . .

. . . I have thought in reference to the subject of higher education itself, that though in the beginning God chose for the work of converting the world, twelve simple and ignorant fishermen, yet when the time came for them to begin their labors, by a miracle He transformed them into brilliant intellectual orators ready to give to every one "a reason for the faith that was in them," and to the Gentiles He deputed St. Paul a rhetorician and a man of culture thus reaching human nature through human means. How necessary it is, then, that our influential Catholic women should be trained to give to society, not only the force of their example, valuable though that must ever be!—but the benefit of a more enlightened knowledge than the cleverest girl in her teens can acquire, and that from a Catholic source!

Now our dear Institute is considering the undertaking of a work that will meet the need of the Church to-day! . . . The Church's glory is God's glory. St. Catherine of Sienna in the fourteenth, St. Teresa in the sixteenth century was each in turn the glory of the age in which she lived. But little later Helen Lucretia Cornaro, Piscopia, a *Benedictine Nun* filled, with glory to Padua, the chair of Philosophy, in that university and other women held chairs with honor in the same seat of learning. All this even women who are non-Catholics are proud to advance, and it is no slight refutation of the error of those who declare that the Church is an enemy of 'progress' to remind them that, nearly three hundred years before Harvard, Yale, or Cornell had opened their doors to women, the Catholic Church through her universities, had forestalled their 'progress.'

Now *the Church approves that we take up the work of Padua!* Shall not God's honor be advanced, if not equally, yet in the same line?

After this fervent *apologia* she turns to the practical side and puts forth a "development plan" worthy of professional acceptance in the 1970's.

To come now to the practical point of my letter, dear Sister Superior which is to suggest a means to carry out this great plan, may I say that if we are to succeed in the material part, we must *seek every assistance that the influence of those high in station* can afford us! We must not content ourselves with *writing*: we must *send* and even *go* to those who could help us. The

> undertaking being *unusual*, we must take the *unusual means*, in an *unusual manner*, and so we shall *perfectly observe propriety*! The project is so grand, the incentives so great, that we must be free and confident in asking. I do not presume to advise you, dearest Sister Superior—I think you know me too well to so misjudge,—but may I urge that, these written requests of the kind too often find their way to the waste basket. And that there can without extraordinary difficulty, certainly be found some one who will do this service for the Institute! You know it is not for ourselves we would ask. Whilst it is for the Church, it is also for our country; so we must start out with the very highest approval of both Church and state. If our Methodist President is chary of his name, we shall be content with that of his Catholic attorney!!! Seriously dear Sister Superior we must go to all our friends amongst senators, congressmen, ministers, Catholics and Protestants alike, and if this one will not give an impetus to the work, that one will, and so *through failures*, perhaps, *we shall succeed*. Now Washington offers many advantages just now from its cosmopolitan character, and every day of May and June are invaluable to you. Later, Congress will have disbanded, the University dispersed, and there will continue this weary wait.

The evening of May 27 saw Sister Julia in Washington. Though still not able to "see their way," she gave Sister Mary Euphrasia "freedom for three months to act and to take an option for that time on one of the properties." Having made her decision Sister Julia acted with dispatch; conferred with all the "on the spot" advocates of the college; agreed on the "Michigan Avenue property" and secured the option (June 9) for a month; called together her "experts": Sister Mary Nepomucene, experienced in building planning and construction; Sister Anne de Marie, the artist who later taught in the college; and Mr. Edwin F. Durang, the Philadelphia architect whose work she valued.

On June 14, Sister Julia wrote a letter to be presented by hand to Cardinal Gibbons that they had "secured a site . . . of twenty acres on Michigan and Lincoln Avenues for $40,000." Because of its "proximity to the Catholic University and the Soldiers Home," she wrote, "Its surroundings can never degenerate."

"We are preparing its public announcement and outlining the plans for the buildings which will be useful and plain, yet not unworthy of so great an undertaking." She thinks that while these preparations are going on, it will be possible to assess the probable reaction of the "general Catholic public"—"Everything will depend on the first impression." As part of the first publicity she hopes to have a formal letter of approval from Cardinal Gibbons as well as his support for full cooperation by the "Reverend Gentlemen of the Catholic University," and that there be "but this one Catholic college for the city of Washington during the years of the near future?"

June 15, before the letter had been presented, the first news leak occurred.

> . . . owing, perhaps to a *misunderstanding* on the part of Reverend Gentlemen, to whom the cherished secret of the College had been imparted in confidence, the whole affair was made public through the New York and Washington papers [and] . . . extensively copied. The papers, as frequently happens, exaggerated the account, and stated that one year from the following September the College would be opened. This caused great consternation to dear Sister Superior [Sr. Julia], and chagrin to our kind friends at the University, who advised as the only remedy for misstatements to publish an authoritative account as widely as possible as soon as the purchase of land would be completed.[18]

Four days later, Sister Mary Euphrasia went to Baltimore to keep the appointment with Cardinal Gibbons. She presented Sister Julia's letter and the draft of a letter of approval which had been composed by Dr. Garrigan and which they hoped the Cardinal would sign for publication. She was received "most graciously." ". . . His Eminence said that it was a duty and to his interest, to give to the foundation of the new College all the encouragement and support in his power; that in order to draw to ourselves the support of those who would be the best friends of the institution, the Religious Orders, we should both write to and visit them, obtaining thus their cooperation and support."[19]

After careful consideration, a few dictated revisions and deletions, he agreed to the formal letter of approval. He would make no restrictions on the establishment of other colleges, but ". . . anticipated no rival College, of the same plane, coming into existence; in the distant future, in Chicago, perhaps, there might arise a College similar, but without the existing inducements, but that could, there and then, do us no harm." In this forecast he was wrong, as the history of Catholic higher education for women has shown.[20]

"At graduation, next year, and the remainder of this, we should engage Dr. Conaty to speak in favor of higher education and the New

18. A July 9 letter from Sr. Mary Euphrasia to Sister Julia adds to this: I understand now the way the subject first got into print and think it only just to exculpate the Downings who spent $10 in telegrams, the night of June 14th trying to get the piece away from the N. York Journal fruitlessly. *Our good Father Gillespie* sent the word to the Times Sunday night (daily paper here) and though Maggie and Mr. Downing succeeded in keeping the Times quiet that day, the piece had already gone to N.Y. on *Father Gillespie's assurance that it was all right to publish it*. I think Dr. Conaty was rather hard on the Downings, and it is quite sure that he sent for the Associate Press to arrange for a publication on Wednesday. I do not expect a reply to this. I only thought that charity demanded that the Downings should have fair play especially after their $10.00!!!
19. He particularly recommended the School Sisters of Notre Dame, and especially their Normal School at Govanstown, Maryland, whose pupils he would gladly see in our classes.
20. In late 1897, Dr. Pace gave to Sister Euphrasia two books on college life: *The American College Girl*, by Rose McCook and *College Training for Women*, by Kate Holladay Claghorn (L.C. 1507C5). *Fd.* S.E. II, p. 28, January, 1898.

College." The suggestions for raising "a convenient sum" by asking "a good many rich persons to contribute $100 for a building fund" seemed feasible to him. "Make your appeal," he commented, "by *private* letter. *Write all you choose.* You can easily find out the rich people, and they will suggest others: in this way, you will give a dignified impression, which would be lost if you exposed publicly your need *in the very beginning*. People know that such works cannot be carried on without public support, and they will respond to private demands."[21]

"After Sister Mary Euphrasia returned from Baltimore with the letter and its approbation," Sister Julia went back to Philadelphia until the deeds could be signed and the formal press release sent out. A title search on the land was begun on June 23. "It seems," wrote Sister Mary Euphrasia, "that this must be done here in all sale of real estate now, and I suppose elsewhere the same. Mr. Riggs told me that where an ordinary lawyer formerly sufficed, they now pass it over altogether to a Real Estate Title Insurance Co." Preparation continued for an official announcement to be released simultaneously in all parts of the country as soon as the deed was delivered. The two Sisters, Dr. Garrigan and Dr. Conaty corresponded or conferred for the next three weeks on content, method, detail in order to insure an effective announcement. A summary of the plan of action appears in a letter of July 6 [Sr. Mary Euphrasia to Sister Julia]:

> . . . The nine hundred of the Associated Press are reached by themselves, by telegraph, hence the short notice they give, and the reason that they desire us to send the full acct. by mail so as to have it reach the office of each paper the afternoon their telegram reaches. I have therefore sent copies enough for each Daily of good repute to a confidential person at each of the following cities, the others to be reached by the brief notice of the Associated Press, those receiving the whole acct. from us, receiving also the brief notice through the Associated Press if belonging to it—Boston, Springfield, Worcester, N. York, Providence, Baltimore, Washington, St. Louis, Chicago, Milwaukee, San Francisco, San Jose, Galveston, New Orleans, Richmond, Asheville, N. Carolina, Summer Resorts, Cleveland, Ohio, Cinti. Montreal, Savannah, Atlanta, Charlestown. To the Catholic papers, being weeklies we shall mail so as to reach them on the same day the Asso. Press sends the telegram. Now I thought dear Sister Superior that Sr. M. Flora could send them out for you in *Philada.* by one of the servants or a friend the afternoon you would receive any telegram or letter saying what day to distribute them. We have already prepared to send envelopes for all the persons to whom we have sent copies addressed thus (an envelope enclosed) the date to be yet supplied. To California and Galveston I will tel-

21. The letter was a statement to be circulated concerning the college. A handwritten copy is No. 95 G 6 in the Baltimore Archdiocesan Archives. Printed copies are in the Trinity College Archives and in early catalogues of the college. One is attached to Balt. 95G6.

> egraph the date, if not belonging to Asso. Press whose list I am expecting today. I will see to the Catholic papers in Philadelphia as I think it may save that much trouble. There must be about a dozen good dailies in Philada. Baltimore has seven—Dear Sister Superior I have just rec'd your telegram and will attend to the matter of printing the Cardinal's letter, and have written to hurry the surveying, and the closing up of the business. . . . How much you have accomplished in Phil. all those letters to the bishops!

As late as July 6 four surveyors were still "out at our place" with Mr. Talty correcting the platting, but the transfer of deeds was expected on July 8 and the press announcement set for "next Wednesday week." Dr. Garrigan on July 7 wrote from Massachusetts: ". . . let me congratulate you on the passing of the deed! Thank God, now the die is cast! . . . The good work[22] is planned, and it will and it must grow." Sister Julia returned on the eighth expecting the deeds, "however some weary days intervened before they came"—not until July 17, in fact, and by that time she had been called by urgent business to Cincinnati and they had to be sent for her critical examination. In the meantime, "Mr. Fitzgerald, member of Congress from Massachusetts, and many other prominent gentlemen of Washington were written to," and

> Thinking that the Deeds that were promised for July 8th were certain to come before the 15th, simultaneous advertisement appeared in all the papers of the U.S.—The Associated Press as well as other Press Associations, and independent papers, showed extreme generosity and courtesy. Letters were sent to the President and to all the distinguished members of the U.S. Government. Mr. Lentz, a member of the House of Representatives from Ohio kindly delivered them, and a few days after, a cordial acknowledgment for the greater number was joyfully received.[23]

By the end of July Sister Julia was again under the doctor's care. It was "over-exertion" he said and she must do "no mind-work whatever, not one line of writing, in a word, no application of any kind." If she had rested six months as advised by the Holyoke doctor she would now be able to work. She was deeply concerned about the validity of the deed, about taxes, insurance, about water, sewage and gas—and about the well-meaning helpfulness that had brought about the premature announcements of June. On August 1 she "penned a note." After that, except for a note here and there, Sister Mary Borgia again took

22. It is in this letter that he tells Sr. Mary Euphrasia that Sister Julia "says that you are the founder of Trinity College whoever may get the credit. I perfectly agree with her in all that, and I am glad that Washington City can claim the initiative in so great and important a work."
23. Clippings of articles published in more than forty newspapers, both the daily press and Catholic weeklies in cities widely distributed throughout the country are preserved in *Clipping Book I* and Auxiliary Board Notes, both in the Trinity College Archives.

over as much of her responsibility as she could, acting as scribe and general assistant.

"The reaction of all I went through since I arrived in Philadelphia," Sister Julia wrote,

> came near putting me "hors du combat," for good and all. I intend writing to Dr. Garrigan to tell him the exact state of affairs. For six months I must have rest. You know I never in my fifty years took a week, now I must or go under the daisies and butter-cups. Now to all to whom you have any right to say anything, answer we have bought the ground, we are getting our plans, etc., that an immense educational institute as a college will take time to mature, etc.—that we shall certainly not open next October. I think it may be well to write to the Cardinal, tell him by the order of our two doctors, I must have six months rest. In the meantime I will be drawing up our *moral* plan, while Mr. Durang is attending to the outside. Sr. M. Bor. wrote him yesterday. Now for something just as serious. I am not satisfied with the *title*, in which not one reference is made to the *Chief Justices' three decisions*. I thought it was to have been written on the face of it. *All this notwithstanding the Chief Justices' decision to the contrary;* I have a feeling we will have trouble from this, and I here record my warning note! Thanks to good Doctors Garrigan and Conaty and all friends. Get all the information you can on any and all subjects and let me have it. I am sorry I cannot tell you my conversation with Abp. [Archbishop] Ryan, who did not think we would have all smooth sailing with the Archbishops. No more strength for today. I am glad the dear Sisters enjoyed Trinity site, they may go again on an outing. God bless you.

On August 11, she wrote: "All right for the Incorporation which I return. I am sorry to leave out the word Catholic since that is really our 'raison d'etre.' We must be careful or we will fail. I am having a pattern of a seal drawn—will send it for you to see. *Faith* in Latin will be the base. . . . Write me everything. I enclose you two or three notices of Trin. [sic] College which you may not have seen. I am glad of a little adverse criticism! It will help." This was the first indication of the storm of adverse criticism that was to appear in many parts of the country in mid-August, threatening continuation of the work. The sketches of the seal were mailed two days later with a letter expressing her satisfaction that "Mr. Durang has been on and is so pleased with the site! If we only had the money!" That last cry has been rising steadily from the Trinity College campus through the years since then and bids fair to continue for many more.

"The deed," she continues, "seems all right, but before we begin to build we shall have the approval of Congress." Then a bit of practical advice: "Before the meeting of the Bishops, indeed at once, I would like you to have a post or two, painted white, put up at the future entrance, that everyone may see that we are not at the *gate* of the University. That will set people right." More than white painted posts was needed before the furor of the next weeks could be quieted.

There is a short break in the manuscript *Foundations*. Then the report continues.

> In the meantime disadvantageous reports were circulating. August 21st, a telegram from the Cardinal wishing the immediate presence of our Superior Mary Euphrasia at his residence in Baltimore occasioned a series of journeys during the next few weeks. . . . In obedience to the desire of His Eminence, [she] left immediately for the episcopal residence Baltimore.
>
> The kind prelate as was his wont received [her] graciously. The conversation however was of so confidential a nature that [she] was forbidden to repeat it; but he said that trouble was menacing Trinity, that Sister Superior Julia should be informed that further work had to be stopped until he gave notice to proceed, that he entertained grave fears of the result of machinations against it which were most serious on account of their hiddenness.
>
> In reply to respectful questions, he admitted that the trouble came from the German element in the West and principally through a Mgr. Shroeder, Prof. of Dogmatic Theology at the Catholic University, who, on account of animosity to the noble institution, stirred up a host of contradictory statements against the work, and this fomented the jealousy of other religious orders of women. At the conclusion of the interview, the Cardinal told Sr. Mary Euphrasia that he would send for her in a few days when he hoped to be able to speak less mysteriously. In the meantime he desired her to keep very strictly the confidence he had given her, but insisted that she must mention to Mother Julia that all work must be stopped. As Sister Superior was just recovering from her recent prostration, Sr. Mary Euphrasia, fearing the consequence of a sudden alarm, begged His Eminence that she withhold the information until something more definite was told her. To this he agreed, on condition that the work was momentarily suspended. . . . Sr. Mary Euphrasia, however, was not at all daunted, and told His Eminence that for her part, she was not alarmed, as she had every confidence that God would himself carry through a work in which His Hand had been visible from the beginning; that nothing could discourage her.

Writing later to Sister Julia, she told of this:

> Well, dearest Sister Superior, isn't this "a wheel within a wheel!" It reminds me of our own Mere Julie's times! But how grateful we ought to be to have a great prelate *on* our side, when, but for God's goodness, we might have had one against us! I think you would have had a hearty laugh at my expense had you heard me giving what must have sounded like a lecture on confidence in God to the Cardinal Abp. of Baltimore.

During this visit the Cardinal read to Sister Mary Euphrasia the answer he was sending to the Apostolic Delegate "hasten[ing] to correct the mistaken reports." He wrote:

> Trinity College as the prospectus states is simply intended to be a school of higher studies or for post-graduate curriculum (Cf. note p. 22) and, of course, lays no claim to the dignity of a university. . . . When in my letter of approval I referred to it as aiming to accomplish for women what the Catholic University was doing for men, and relieving [sic] the University Authorities from the embarrassment of refusing admission to women, I simply meant it would provide a higher course of studies for young ladies. . . . Trinity College will have no official organic connection whatever with the Catholic University. The faculty will be supplied by the community of Notre Dame [who] might invite Professors from the University or from Georgetown College to give lectures. . . . On inquiry I now find that the College is one third of a mile from the Catholic University. . . .
>
> As for the Sisters of Notre Dame of Namur, . . . they enjoy the merited confidence of the Holy Father who knew them and esteemed them when he was Nuncio at Namur [Brussels]. They are also esteemed by the Belgian and American Bishops for their piety, learning, and spirit of discipline and devotion to the cause of Catholic truth. . . .
>
> [The proposed college] has met with the warm approval of a large number of the Hierarchy of the United States, of the Very Rev. Father Purbrick, provincial of the Jesuits of the English Province, and even of the President of the U.S. and Members of the Cabinet, who have written us cordial letters of congratulation. . . . I shall direct the Mother Superior to call on Your Excellency . . . with all the other information you may require.

On her return to Washington Sister Mary Euphrasia went immediately to the Apostolic Delegation only to learn that Archbishop Martinelli was escaping the Washington heat by visiting the Augustinians in Atlantic City. Dr. Rooker, one of his aides, sowed seeds of more anxiety by asking: "Is your Mother in Europe in sympathy with this work? The Belgians are very conservative." To the answer that she had already approved and was "very progressive, even more so than we are," he asked: "Are you sure? . . . write everything [to your Mother] and explain all to her. Send her copies of your letters to Rome."

Meanwhile, the convent on North Capitol Street "had been besieged by newspaper reporters who said that it was generally asserted that Mgr. Schroeder had prevailed on the Holy Father to put a stop to the project. Several articles treating of the matter had already appeared in the newspapers throughout the country. . . ." Hoping to stem the tide of criticism and to give these reporters "something to satisfy their editors," Sister Mary Euphrasia repeated the main points of the plan which had been published in the synchronized press releases of July 15, being careful to mention "no time for the starting of the building or the opening of the College." As a result articles vindicating the college plan, and incidentally publicizing the project, appeared August 27 and 29 in the *Boston Herald*, August 28 in the *Washington Star* and August 29 in *Washington Post, Baltimore Sun, Washington Herald.*[24] These were copied or repeated in the press of other cities, but no attempt at a complete compilation has been made here. One statement in the *Boston Herald* article [Aug. 27] is especially interesting in the light of later developments in the fight for women's rights. "A great deal of indignation," it states, "is being expressed in Catholic circles over this news [opposition] concerning the women's college. Mgr. Schroeder is credited with sending the information to Rome, since he is the only professor [at Catholic University] who did not heartily approve the founding. . . . Should the Pope condemn this movement, there is talk of a memorial *addressed to him by the Catholic women of the United States protesting.*" [Italics added]

The morning after her impromptu press conference, August 26, Sister Mary Euphrasia and a companion, properly wearing the heavy Notre Dame outdoor hooded cloak, started off by the ten o'clock train to call on Archbishop Martinelli in Atlantic City. They arrived at 3:30, conducted their business and caught the 4:45 "fast" train which reached Philadelphia at 7:00, used the time of waiting for the Washington *express* to send telegrams, and arrived home at 10:45 p.m. Apart from the very important conference with the Apostolic Delegate, that August journey itself appears, in the late twentieth century, a heroic endeavor. No wonder Archbishop Martinelli showed concern. To the Sisters' amusement, "the apparent weight of our cloaks appeared to excite in him a great compassion" [and] "regret that the two sisters would not remain overnight at Atlantic City, enjoying the sea breezes and the proffered hospitality of the Ladies of the S.H. [sic]."

Her main object, however, was clarification and defense of the plans and work that had reached the stage, just six days before, of incorporation of the College. Therefore, Sister Mary Euphrasia brushed aside all consideration of physical discomfort to use every precious minute in frank discussion of present problems. It was now that she learned of the unfounded mid-April criticisms which Msgr. Martinelli had thought definitively answered at that time, and of a recent letter from the Holy Father himself seeking information. [Cf. pp. 26–29] She repeated in detail the steps so far completed toward founding Trinity College, summarized the previous day's interview with Cardinal Gibbons, and answered questions to the satisfaction of her host. She, too, asked penetrating questions about jurisdiction and authority. Letters to Rome from all concerned, the Sisters of Notre Dame, the Cardinal of Baltimore, and the Apostolic Delegate are reflected in the discussion and copied into the manuscript *Foundations*. The temptation to reproduce in full this informal original account is strong. Only the fact that

24. Clippings are in T.C.A.

all relevant material appears elsewhere in this narrative prevents its inclusion as too repetitive.

August 29 and September 7 Sister Mary Euphrasia continued the "series of journeys" to Baltimore for consultation with Cardinal Gibbons. For the first of these she was able to take with her Sister Mary Olympia who was *en route* to Cincinnati "thinking it a good opportunity to inform [Sister Julia] of all that was going on in a less disturbing way than by letter." A full discussion of the visit to Archbishop Martinelli, of the contents of letters to be sent to Rome and Namur, and of the sources of opposition led to the decision that the Sisters of Notre Dame should address their letters to Cardinal Ferrata, the Cardinal Protector of the Congregation, for presentation to Cardinal Rampolla, Secretary of State rather than to Satolli.[25] "His Eminence told Sr. Mary Euphrasia that he had received a letter from Cardinal Satolli about "the rumors rife in Rome" which he read to her.

> I should acquaint Your Eminence with the fact that rumors have reached us here that the Srs. of Notre Dame are about to erect a University for Women, and in the vicinity of the Catholic University. Every week I receive papers from the U.S. containing accounts of the University, and these are mostly unfavorable, being an amalgamation of facts. There are three points that are dwelt upon. (1) That the University is to be in the vicinity of the Catholic University. (2) That the teachers are to be the same for both schools. (3) That there is to be a mixture of the students in the classes (co-education). I am sure, however, that notwithstanding these facts Your Eminence's prudence will provide against the occurrence of improprieties.

The afternoon of August 29 on her return from Baltimore, Sister Mary Euphrasia received a visit from "the first good and loyal friend of Trinity," Dr. Garrigan, who had just returned to the university from his vacation. He had kept informed of developments during his absence, and had written to encourage her to "be a brave little Sister and work hard."

During this visit she learned much that unravelled the mysteries of the past few days. It was the first time she learned that Cardinal Satolli was unfavorable to the University: that he was hand in glove with the German element in the West, so inimical to the University; that it was he (Cardinal Satolli) who had transmitted to the Holy Father the misstatements received from Msgr. Schroeder, about the "new kind of University."

September brought more hope. The *Catholic World* in its issue for that month published an "authoritative statement" about the proposed

25. He had been the first Apostolic Delegate in Washington until 1896. Considered up to this time by S.N.D.'s as their friend and an advocate of Catholic University.

Trinity College, (Cf. Appendix II) thus inaugurating a history of friendship and cooperation between the Paulist Fathers and the college that continues to the present. Letters from Cincinnati reflect support and encouragement. Sister M. Olympia wrote that she had given all the messages and that Sister Julia was interested and "enjoyed many things that you feared might worry her. Let me tell you for your consolation that our dear Superior's whole trust is in God, and all these little details do not disturb her in the least. It is consoling also for you to know that [she] feels that you have the confidence of the reverend gentlemen, and that she will let you act."

Sister Julia herself wrote: "I am quite amused at the noise the quiet old S.N.D.'s are making for the first time in this country. . . . 'If God be for us, who shall be against us?' I am not in the least troubled . . . and provided we get $$ I do not fear! I would much rather have the storm before we begin than a breeze later which might insure a feeling of distrust and thus injure the work."

Before the end of the month she was back in Washington where she stayed until November, able again to take an active part in Trinity business.

To the September 7 meeting with Cardinal Gibbons, Sister Mary Euphrasia had taken draft-letters over which she had been laboring, and some very strong advice from Dr. Rooker of the Apostolic Delegation to write fully and truthfully to the Reverend Mother in Namur, to Cardinal Ferrata, and to the Holy Father. "Remember," he said, "it is *business* not charity you have to write . . . don't *write a sentimental letter*. Put the facts and *put them strong*. Other people have written all manner of lies about you to the Holy Father—*Why shouldn't he hear the truth now?*" The account of this meeting with Cardinal Gibbons in the manuscript *Foundations* shows not only the mutual respect and down-to-earth cooperation of the conferees, but the frank and friendly informality of their working relationship. They agreed, after careful consideration of each statement, on the texts of letters to Cardinal Ferrata, and to Cardinal Rampolla for presentation to the Holy Father. The same facts would be sent to the Superior General of Notre Dame in Namur. To insure promptness of dispatch, Sister Mary Euphrasia was given the privacy of the episcopal library to make the final copies immediately. (The full text of these letters follows p. 250 in *Fd. S.E.*)

Though the hoped for approval did not reach Washington until November, this meeting and the "authoritative statement" seem to mark a turning point. Public opposition subsided. The Board of Trustees was organized and met twice in special sessions. Planning went quietly forward. Sister Mary Euphrasia's letter to Sister Julia,[26]

26. T.C.A. Drawer II.

dated November 30, 1897, refers to an excerpt about Trinity from a November 13 letter of Cardinal Rampolla to Archbishop Martinelli, Apostolic Delegate at Washington. It was, she wrote, "Dictated to me by Cardinal Gibbons and translated from the original Italian." The momentous statement is simple: "His Holiness after having considered the matter well, thinks that there should be nothing more said concerning the difficulties in the way of the project of the erection of an Institute for females in the vicinity of the Catholic University." This statement settled the chief opposition to the college. The founders could turn to financial and academic problems. Sister Mary Euphrasia, however, would have liked to have a formal, public approval by the Apostolic Delegate, but Dr. Rooker would not let her present the request. His explanation of diplomatic intricacies is enlightening. "Now," he said, "*this thing stands this way*:

> *Rome has stuck its finger in the pie! It is not going to say aloud that it has pulled it out again,* but it *has* pulled it out, just the same, *and it means you to go ahead! When you will be successful,* you can get *any amt. of blessings and approbations direct from the Holy Father himself*, but until you are Rome is not going to meddle again. So now, you see, Monsignor Martinelli is *obliged* (I am trying to quote his [own] words!) to act *from a diplomatic standpoint. He can't speak when Rome does not*. He *wants* you to *succeed,* and he will be glad to see *this kind of thing* to go up, but *he can't* say *so, because he represents Rome*. If you asked him to endorse you *and you had to say that he refused, it would do you harm. Consequently, it is better for you not to ask him.*

He (Dr. R.) wanted something *strong* in favor of Trinity in the papers."[27]

The years have proved his wisdom. The Trinity College of the late twentieth century is stronger because of its American roots free of undue interference from overseas.

The American emphasis appears repeatedly in documents of this early period, in the decision that the fund raising group should consist of American ladies, the rejection of the project for a prestige seeking campaign among foreign friends in high places, the rejection of the "Album" of donors to be presented publicly to Prince Albert of Belgium.

The indefatigable Sister Mary Euphrasia turned her attention immediately to the practical business of seeking financial support and public approbation from influential people as her correspondence and her

27. Dr. Rooker was right. After the college had opened, the *Annals I* Jan. 13, 1901, record that letters came from Rome "wishing success to the college, convey[ing] the blessing of His Holiness on Sister Julia and expressing congratulations on the success of Trinity College."

hastily jotted *Journal* begun in December 1897 show.[28] These journal entries give the first indication that she was aware of the national feeling that would develop by the summer of 1898 into the "Splendid Little War"[29] with Spain about Cuba. She writes that she went

> To call upon the heads of the Cath[olic] Legations and Sir Julian Pouncefort. The former were much interested, and gave cordial letters, except the Minister from Spain, Mr. Depuy de Lome, the Spanish Government being a little bitter towards the U.S. on account of its presumed friendliness for Cuba.[30]

In spite of her enthusiasm, the December *Journal* notes the frustrations, as well as the successes, of the visiting campaign. "I also called upon many distinguished and wealthy persons in the city," she wrote. "They generally seemed interested, and promised assistance, though in many cases, likewise, the iron 'Not at home' rendered them *inaccessible*.! One lady sent me down 50¢ by the servant, refusing to see me! It is wonderful with how little scruple they refuse to see Religious! They allege 'so many calls'! How many are listened to?!!" These experiences must have crystalized in her mind the need of some organized assistance in fund-raising.

The January *Journal* concentrates on "the pamphlet,"[31] its printing and distribution, but by the thirty-first "Dr. Gerrigan called to say that I should go to see the Chairman of the House, and of the Senate, District Appropriations, to ensure an appropriation for Mich.[igan] Ave.[nue]." An alumna of the academy, Mrs. Purcell, made the appointment and on February second

> Sr. Hermance and I went to see Mr. Grount, M. C. from Vermont, Chairman of House Com. on Appropriations. He was very courteous, and said that the House had passed over Mich. Ave. in making appropriations, and advised us to see Mr. Allison, Chairman of the Com. on Appropriations for the Senate. He kindly furnished the address (1124 Vermont Ave.). We went, and found the Senator preparing for a dinner. He saw us for a moment, and promised to attend to the matter for us. We were to *write* to him at once.[32]

28. Cf. letter of May 25 and development plan, pp. 29–30. Cf. also Fd. Bk. II, p. 19 about plan—Dec. 1897 for contributions from Notre Dame pupils and alumnae.
29. Frank Freidel, *The Splendid Little War*. New York, 1958, p. 9, quotation from John Hay, U.S. Ambassador to England: "It has been a splendid little war; begun with the highest motives, carried on with magnificent intelligence and spirit, favored by that fortune which loves the brave." Not all would agree with Hay as the book goes on to show.
30. *Journal* No. I, p. 1.
31. A copy is in the scrapbook "Early Hist. of Trinity College." Cf. Eliza E. Starr "St. Jerome's School" and Sara Carr Upton "House-on-Aventine."
32. *Journal I*, p. 10, Feb. 2, 1898.

This business of appropriation for extending and grading Michigan Avenue dragged on through the months of 1898.[33] As late as December 23 the *Journal* notes:

> I sent Srs. Therese of S. H. and Gertrude of B. S. to see Sen. Allison about Mich. Ave., Mr. Talty having told me that the bills were being rushed through Congress for the District. Mr. A. [llison] was as usual most kind and fatherly, and said that there was not a moment to lose. 'Have patience, but be active,' he said, and let Capt. Beach, Head Com[missioner] of Engineering, recommend it, and make an estimate, and write me a letter asking to have it passed as an amendment.[34]

On Christmas Day she extracted a reluctant promise from Dr. Garrigan to call on the Engineer Commissioner, reluctant because he was more concerned with the building than pushing the road through. On December 29 she herself went to "see dear Sen. Allison about Mich. Ave."

The concern with "the pamphlet" and negotiations for the extension of Michigan Avenue, even the "war craze" did not interfere with Sister Mary Euphrasia's fund-raising efforts. On February 9, she had "received a letter from Sr. Supr. Julia, saying that our dear Mother [in Belgium] forbad building until she would have seen her in August,[35] and until the money was provided." "The latter comes in slowly," she added. She "went to call upon several Senators or their wives, in the interest of the Avenue and Trinity." She "found Mrs. Sen. Carter[36] of Montana, very kind, also, Mrs. Lodge of Mass. and the Countess de L.[ichtervelde] I saw at her hotel, who gave me the names of several persons to see." On February 28, she went "to see many rich persons, but notably the Vicomtess de Santo Thyrso, who will endeavor to get us letters of introduction to millionaires in New York. She is a charming young Portuguese lady; very bright, very *wise*."

Through February and March 1898, while the papers were full of the investigation of the Maine disaster, of worsening conditions in Cuba, of the Alaska Homestead Act, Sister Mary Euphrasia continued undaunted her work for the college. In early March she added Mr. Fitzgerald, Congressman from Massachusetts, to those "on the Hill" who worked for the Michigan Avenue appropriation. On March 4 he assured her that he was "carefully watching proceedings." The Count-

33. Cf. Correspondence Mich. Ave., Dr. II and *Jour. I* passim.
34. *Jour. I*, pp. 34–5.
35. The adverse criticism of 1897 had reached the Superior General and made her uneasy about what her American Sisters were undertaking.
36. This is the first mention of Mrs. Thomas H. Carter, who from that time until her death in 1932 was an untiring friend and worker for Trinity. *Obit. Alumnae Journal*, Feb. 1933, p. 20.

ess de Lichtervelde[37] sent a message that she "had made arrangements with Mrs. Senator Hanna for me to go to New York" but "Mrs. H. had not understood the good little Countess" and that trip did not materialize. "Moreover," she writes, "the times do not seem propitious, at the moment, as the 'war craze' is still aflame and people's pockets closed." She mentions also "Mrs. Henderson, Florida Avenue and 16th Street," the recognized leader of Washington society. "She is a Unitarian, but promises to do something amongst her Cath.[olic] acquaintances for the college." In all the replies the "doing something" was still very vague. By the middle of March she realized the necessity of organized help from others besides the Sisters. Even her persisting interest in foreign prestige was beginning to fade in the face of outspoken advice especially from Dr. Garrigan against the project of an album of contributors to be presented to the young Prince Albert of Belgium during his visit to America. It was *not American*. I "will speak with some representative American women," she wrote, "before doing anything public." That consultation resulted before the end of the month in the Ladies Auxiliary Board of Regents of Trinity College.

As late as March 19 she mentions "the album." Mme. Romero, she writes, had agreed to "lead the album," but "I went to see Mrs. Leiter, and though kindly received, was most cordially refused any assistance! She was feeling indignant over having been called a 'heretic' by a priest!" No wonder Sr. Mary Euphrasia was glad to have suggestions of names from Professor Maurice Francis Egan. He sent her to call on Mrs. William Winthrop "a delightful woman" who helped plan whom to invite to work with her. On the twenty-first the Journal reads: "Met Miss Olive Risley Seward [niece and adopted daughter of the former Secretary of State] who had been wanting to meet some one from Trinity College.[38] She has a fine physique and is a magnetic woman." That magnetism and Mrs. Winthrop's kindly interest were effective, for on March 27 four ladies, Miss Marie Patterson, Miss Olive Risley Seward, Mrs. William Winthrop (Alice Worthington W.), and Mrs. Maurice Francis Egan came to the convent to plan a meeting of "prominent ladies interested in Trinity." They discussed methods of "collecting moneys," the selection of ladies, the plan that members be resident in Washington, D.C., one from each state called "Regent." Mrs. Win-

37. March 12. The Journal notes: "dear little Countess de Lichtervelde [wife of the Belgian Minister] . . . sent by the young Prince Albert, heir apparent of Belgium, now visiting Washington. . . . He would see us tomorrow A.M. after the 9 o'clock Mass at *old* St. Matthews, Penna. Ave. . . . We must meet him tomorrow, with a letter for him to sign, in favor of Trinity College. His Mother, the Countess of Flanders, told him to be *sure to see the Belgian Srs., his compatriots*. The Countess and the young prince seemed unaware that there were in 1898 very few, if any, of his compatriots among the American Sisters of Notre Dame.

38. Note that the college was already spoken of as an entity.

throp refused the presidency of the proposed board because of health, though she chaired the first meeting, on March 31, of the "Auxiliary Board of Regents of Trinity College."

That historic first "meeting of the Auxiliary Board of Regents at Trinity College was held at the Convent [on North Capitol Street] March 31, 1898.[39] Present were Sister Euphrasia, Mrs. Winthrop, Mrs. Bland, Miss Daingerfield, Miss Dorsey, Mrs. M. F. Egan, Miss Emily Mason, Miss Patterson, Mrs. Reid, Mrs. Robinson, Miss Seawell and Mrs. Vance." Mrs. Thomas H. Carter, wife of the Senator from Montana, who was to be for more than thirty years a loyal and enthusiastically active member of the Board is not listed until the second meeting, April 13. Miss Olive Risley Seward, too, seems to have been absent from this meeting, though she had been at the preliminary group on March 27, and was elected president of the board at the April 13 meeting.

The organization of the "Auxiliary Board of Regents" initiated a new phase in the work for the college, the close involvement of lay women with the Sisters of Notre Dame and their counsellor-colleagues from the Catholic University. The first meeting adopted broad lines of policy which were in accord with the future thrust of the college. The ladies rejected a plan for seeking the support and prestige of distinguished foreign ladies. They voted firmly for an *American* plan of "forming local committees in the different states to collect funds for Trinity College." The original members set themselves the task of involving Catholic women actively for the higher education of women. "The method of collecting money was decided as follows—one lady for each state to be appointed and called *Regent for the State she represents,* with the power to appoint *Vice-Regents* in her individual state."

Dr. Philip Garrigan, Vice Rector of the Catholic University, in his address offered "to help all he could in this magnificent work which had for its object the higher education of Catholic girls who desire to take a higher course than could be obtained at any of the many excellent schools and academies. At Trinity young women would receive a moral and religious training as well as advanced instruction. . . . Mrs. Sherman[40] and the other ladies associated with her sowed the small seed some twenty five years ago from which Trinity came and the ladies present should be impressed with the result of well organized

39. Minutes ABR, orig. p. 2 T.C.A., used throughout this section. Cf. Chapter 7 for an account of the eighty-year history of the Auxiliary Board.

40. Mrs. William Tecumseh Sherman, wife of the Civil War General, and daughter of the long time Senator from Ohio, Thomas Ewing, helped to bring the Sisters of Notre Dame to Washington, where they opened an academy as well as a night school for working girls at N. Capitol and K Streets in 1873.

work: there were only eleven present, but the Lord converted the world with twelve poor men and what could not be accomplished if all worked with energy and good will. In working for Trinity we were also specially honoring our Blessed Lady since she is the Patron of the United States. . . . it was necessary to work and work hard, not to be content to wait and see what the result will be, but take part and push the work along vigorously; write fifty letters a day if necessary and see that the work was made a success. Dr. Garrigan particularly recommended frequent meetings as a means of keeping up interest in the work, and he ended by again assuring the ladies of the interest he felt in the success of Trinity College and his willingness to help in any way he could."

Even in that exciting spring and summer of 1898 when the papers were full of news of investigation of the *Maine* explosion, of war with Spain, and of the Klondike gold rush, the ladies followed Dr. Garrigan's advice to meet frequently, recruit members and work hard. Officers, except the president, were elected at the first meeting: Vice-President, Miss [Marie] Patterson; Recording Secretary, Miss [Sara Carr] Upton; Corresponding Secretary, Mrs. Egan, wife of Professor Maurice Francis Egan, one of the first lay professors of Catholic University. Sister Mary Euphrasia, Miss Patterson and Miss Olive Risley Seward were elected to be the executive committee.

An article, "Catholic Life in Washington," by Mary T. Waggaman in the March 1898 *Catholic World*[41] included two paragraphs on the proposed Trinity College. This supplied one more impulse to the interest of the members of the new Auxiliary Board in work for the higher education of women. In the June issue[42] of the same magazine appeared "The House on the Aventine," by Sara Carr Upton, Recording Secretary of the Board, about the "Roman Palace of Marcella, a beautiful widow, allied to the imperial family," where in the late fourth century a group "of thoughtful patrician women had gradually drawn together, satiated with wealth and luxury, and now restless and eager in their reaction toward something to satisfy their mental and moral craving." Here the great reformer and Scripture scholar Jerome met and trained his co-worker Paula. This house is cited not only as an early convent, but as an early center for women scholars. As such it was used in the publicity material for the new college.

At the second meeting, April 13, the Auxiliary Board elected Miss Risley-Seward president and adopted a constitution. "Miss Patterson in the chair after calling the meeting to order said a few words about

41. Vol. LXVI, pp. 821–838.
42. Vol. LXVII, pp. 633–643.

Trinity College itself, that though it would enjoy many privileges from its proximity to the University, it was to be in no sense an annex like Harvard but an independent college like Vassar or Bryn Mawr."

Both the manuscript copy of the constitution and copies of the first little printed pamphlet (3½ × 5½ inches, 6 pp.) are extant. Article I stated: "The Board is organized as the Auxiliary Board of Regents of Trinity College and consists of ladies who have associated themselves together for the purpose of assisting and equipping Trinity College, Washington, D.C." That purpose has continued through the years, though the word "equipping" was dropped in the mid-1930's. The college catalogue 1936–1937 drops the word Regents and lists the "Trinity College Auxiliary Board" as associated for the purpose of assisting Trinity College. Article III states that "the Sister in Charge" shall be Treasurer. Other officers were to be elected annually.

One tangible result of the April 13 meeting was a letter, typed, duplicated and circulated to prospective members. Signed by the officers and listing "Regents" for sixteen states it is the earliest public expression of the serious purpose and wide scope of the work envisioned by these ladies of 1898. It is given here in its entirety:

Washington, D.C., April 18, 1898

Dear Madam:

You have been suggested as one who would naturally be interested in a project for the higher education of women. The Sisters of Notre Dame, in their zeal for Christian truth and the good of modern society, have undertaken to establish a college for women, the standard of which shall be in no way below that of Smith, Vassar, Wellesley, or Bryn Mawr. They have bought a beautiful site for the buildings in an exceptionally desirable locality of the National Capital, which is fast becoming the educational as it is the political centre of the nation, and where proximity to great libraries, universities and the scientific departments of the government lend peculiar advantages. We, the undersigned, feel that we owe it to our sex as well as to religion, to give our active co-operation in the work of erecting and equipping the first hall or building of a group to be known to future generations as Trinity College. The Sisters have proved themselves eminently fitted for educational work by their past success, but are debarred by their habit from going about in public to solicit patronage and assistance, and we women in the National Capital concerned, as many of us are, in the interests of far-away States and sections, have formed a plan of work in which we hope to enlist your practical interest, and we feel sure that much can be accomplished by good organization and Christian unity.

We enclose your copy of a pamphlet stating the plan and purpose of the College, and also a copy of Articles IV and V of our Constitution.

Should you be willing to join us in this work, which will be a monument for all time for those who take part in its inception, we shall be heartily glad to welcome you as one of us and communicate with you more in detail.

OLIVE RISLEY SEWARD, President

Marie Patterson, *Vice President*	Sister Mary Euphrasia, *Treasurer*
Sara Carr Upton, *Recording Sec'y*	Katharinee Egan, *Cor. Sec'y.*

REGENTS

Mrs. R. P. Bland, Missouri	Miss Roach, North Dakota
Mrs. Thom. H. Carter, Montanta	Mrs. Geo. Crogan Reid, D.C.
Mrs. Thos. H. Carter, Utah	Mrs. W. C. Robinson, Connecticut
Miss Daingerfield, Virginia	Miss Mollie Eliot Seawell, Va.
Mrs. Maurice Francis Egan, Pa.	Miss Olive Risley Seward, N.Y.
Miss Ella Lorraine Dorsey, Md.	Miss Sara Carr Upton, Maine
Miss Emily Mason, Virginia	Mrs. Zebulon B. Vance
Miss Marie Patterson, Missouri	Miss Elizabeth Sherman, Ohio

Miss Charlotte Lincoln (pro-tem.), Ohio

Note: Pamphlets and other printed matter concerning the College, may be had on application to Sister Mary Euphrasia, Convent of Notre Dame, North Capitol and K Streets, Washington, D.C.

Sister Euphrasia wrote in the Journal that Miss Seward was elected president and that "Mrs. Carter and Mrs. General Vincent joined us." On April 16 she left for Cincinnati to confer with Sister Julia because Cardinal Gibbons "approves highly, but is displeased because we do not begin building, as he thinks we are hampered by Europe." Others, too, were concerned. "Mrs. Winthrop," she wrote later in the month, is "very anxious that we begin to build. So are all the friends of the college if we did nothing more than 'put up stakes' as Dr. Conaty says. They all fear harm to college by delay."

Before a week after the second meeting had passed, the *New York Times* (April 22), and papers throughout the country, headlined: "War has come," followed the next day by "Marines Off to War." The Auxiliary Board, however, met May 2 and June 6, to plan their campaign and set a policy to be followed in organizing the work in their home areas during the summer. Though the *Journal* recorded: "The war prevents much being accomplished just at present," the minutes give no evidence of waning interest. Mrs. Carter expected to initiate work immediately in Montana, Mrs. Bland in Missouri, Miss Roach in Minnesota, and Miss Seawell in Virginia even though "the War with Spain is so absorbing an interest in the West." At the May meeting, after discussion about the duties of Vice-Regents,

> Mrs. Carter proposed that the Executive Committee draw up a set of instructions for Vice-Regents. It seemed to be the sense of the Board that its policy should be thoroughly understood by the Regents with certain broad lines, 1st that though the Regents will not receive a less [sic] subscription than twenty-five dollars, no limit is placed on amounts to be received or

collected by Vice-Regents, 2nd that no money shall be raised for Trinity by lotteries and 3rd that as the Board has taken pains to procure all authority requisite, and as subscriptions for Trinity are in no sense parochial collections, no special permission is further needed from the clergy; and that beyond this general policy, the instructions are to be governed by the different circumstances of the localities.

Sister Julia made the acquaintance of the ladies after this meeting and seems to have won their respect and admiration which lasted until her death in 1901. At the June 6 meeting, the last before the summer, Sister Euphrasia stated "that *Sister Loyola of the Georgetown Visitation has made application for two pupils* and that the answer has been that *the college hopes to be ready by the year 1900.*" On this hopeful note the Board "adjourned until the 1st Monday of October." That date proved too optimistic, since only Mrs. Carter was back in Washington by then, and the reconvening was delayed until November.

Meanwhile, the war fought itself out by mid-August [Aug. 13], the Klondike gold rush continued in earnest, and Sister Julia with others traveled to Namur for the Golden Jubilee celebration for Sister Aimée, the Superior General, where "she felt the coolness" because of Trinity College plans. En route she visited the Notre Dame Training College in Liverpool, England.[43] The annals of that institution record on August 6 the arrival of "five Superiors of America." Though Sister Julia observed and consulted about the higher education work being done in conjunction with the University of Liverpool, the annals record only an important convent event. For Sunday, August 7th, they record in beautifully curlicued handwriting: "We kept Sr. Superior's Feast, viz. the grand repasts today." In the evening, "our singers gave us a Musical Performance, both in honour of Sr. Superior, and of Sr. Julia, whose Golden Jubilee of Profession occurred whilst they were at Sea. Our American Sisters were highly delighted with the Sisters' Band, choruses and comical recitations." This interlude of enjoyment was especially beneficial to Sister Julia who faced unexpected misunderstanding at Namur because the criticisms of 1897 seem to have tardily reached the Superior General at Namur, the "Aimee," who had cabled approval the year before. The visit to the Training College at "Mt. Pleasant," Liverpool bore fruit for Trinity College by bringing the foundress into renewed direct contact with Notre Dame educators in England. A year later she sent Sister Josephine Ignatius and Sister Mary, both destined for the faculty of Trinity, for an extended stay (Oct. 26, 1899 to June 26, 1900) in England,[44] Scotland and Belgium studying methods and student life. Their base of operations was Mount Pleas-

43. M.P.A, Aug. 6, 1898ff.
44. M.P.A., Oct. 26, 1898 and ff.

ant. In 1900, when Trinity College opened, Sister Mary Josephine of the Liverpool college was one of the faculty, lecturing in English literature.

In Washington during that hot summer, "affairs relating to the college were at a stand-still. The vacation passed by quite uneventfully. The community of N. Capitol and K now and then enjoyed a trip out to the new grounds to breathe the pure air." It was "excessively warm, 95° to 100° average. . . ." September 14, the Sisters in Washington celebrated "on the Trinity grounds" in union with the Golden Jubilee event at Namur. "The autumn [sic] weather was delightful—the grass green yet and perfectly dry, while the warm sunshine so tempered the soft air as to make it as balmy and pleasant as a summer's day. . . . A surprise in the form of hot coffee, ice-cream and confections were [sic] [was] sent out from the city by our kind friend, Mr. Talty, who also lent conveyances to take the Sisters out." Pleasant it was and refreshing—but still no sign of building.

In late September, Dr. Stafford, the popular, scholarly assistant pastor at St. Patrick's church, recommended a Miss Davis, an "expert mathematician" for the faculty "in case Trinity succeeded. Dear me!"

Sister Julia returned directly to Cincinnati without stopping in Washington. The *Journal* notes: "Something unfavorable must have occurred, as nothing encouraging for Trinity has been written me." The circular about the trip contained "not a word about the great project except that the building would commence when resources would warrant no risks, and as the money was not forthcoming no idea of commencing could be entertained at present." Her delegate in Washington, however, "never faltered in her confidence." She redoubled her prayers and her efforts through Senator Alison of Iowa, Chairman of the Senate Appropriations Committee, to have money appropriated for improving and extending Michigan Avenue.

October 26, 1898, the Board of Trustees held its *First Annual* meeting without the presence of Sister Julia. Those in 1897 were called "special meetings." The chief business recorded was the election of members and officers. Sister Mary Euphrasia, as Secretary-Treasurer of the Board and Treasurer of the new Auxiliary Board was the liaison between the two. By the end of October she could record that Sister Julia "sent some hundreds of dollars" and that Miss Seward had reappeared after the summer's dispersal making possible an enthusiastic meeting of the "Executive Board." Between this and the much less "enthusiastic" meeting of the full Auxiliary Board several disheartening events occurred.

After "consulting Our Lord in prayer," Sister Mary Euphrasia wrote to "Miss Caldwell (Mme. la Marquise de Merinville) about our College. . . . She came with Mrs. Donnelly, her aunt, and being foundress of the Catholic University [sic] I allowed the Sisters to meet her. She is a most charming woman; very bright, out-spoken and strong in her ideas. Has a bitter prejudice against *the Jesuits,* (!!) and was afraid that Trinity was going to do them [Catholic University] harm, but Mgr. Conaty assured her of the contrary. She said she would *like* to help us, but was afraid that we would bring in Jesuits!"

The Rector of Catholic University, Dr. Conaty, visited later that day, feeling "extremely bad that we will not begin to build. . . . He *says* that his intention is to remove the obstacles to beginning." He must have come after meeting with two ladies of the Auxiliary Board because the minutes of their November 7 meeting state: "Miss Seward and Mrs. Carter reported results of an interview held the day before with Monsignor Conaty in which he expressed his deep sympathy with the plan and idea of the Sisters of Notre Dame, but saying also in very decided terms that he and other officers of the University were losing interest because the work was not being pushed and that matters should be started at least and something begun: that other Sisters stood ready to come forward and begin the work at once."[45]

At that same November 7 meeting the Board indicated plans for a benefit lecture on higher education of women to be given either in early December (1–15) or early January. Mrs. Egan was delegated to invite the Bishop of Peoria, John Lancaster Spalding, an outstanding scholar and advocate of higher education. The Vice-President, Miss Patterson, and the Recording Secretary, Miss Sara Carr Upton, were authorized "with all respect to Sister Euphrasia" to write directly to Sister Julia to tell her of their conference with Dr. Conaty and to ascertain the status of work for the college to date. After Miss Seward's declaration that the Board should be enlarged, the names of twelve ladies were proposed as possible members. Sister Euphrasia again proposed that an "album be started for 1000 persons to subscribe 100 dollars each for building the 1st Hall, to be called the Hall of the Auxiliary Board," but again did not receive support for the idea.

Of this meeting Sister Mary Euphrasia commented in the *Journal*: "to my astonishment, the Ladies all declared that unless we began our College at once, and the work was pushed forward, they would dissolve themselves as a Board! However, they pledged themselves to work heart and soul to accomplish something, and considered that they had had a very enthusiastic meeting! I fear it is more talk than work with them." She was feeling disappointment about the "album"

45. I have not found corroboration for this statement about "other Sisters." Cf. earlier pages of this chapter. Dr. Conaty's later correspondence and more than one lecture given by him in the spring of 1899 show continued interest and support. He was perhaps using "shock treatment" to get results.

and not a little rebuffed by the direct contact with both Dr. Conaty and Sister Julia, though she went ahead undaunted, as subsequent correspondence, the *Journal* and the *Foundations* show.

The ladies of the Board, too, threw themselves whole-heartedly into work for "the lecture." Though Miss Seward was ill, the regular December meeting was held at the Convent. After preliminaries the

> rest of the meeting was devoted to the discussion of the arrangements for *Bishop Spalding's lecture*. Through the disinterested good will of the Catholic University the Bishop will give one of the 2 lectures [sic] which he agreed to give for the University, for the purposes of Trinity College on the 16th of Jan. 1899, at 4:15 p.m. The secretary reported from Miss Seward who was too ill to be present, that according to instructions she had seen Dr. Harris, the Commissioner of Education, relative to making an introductory address, or presenting Bishop Spalding with a few words, and that he had agreed to do so. It was decided that the Executive Committee should appoint the various committees on invitations, etc. etc. and Sister Euphrasia is to procure the invitation lists of the Catholic University and Georgetown College which have been offered.

A second meeting was held that month, December 16, at Miss Seward's home, 2109 Pennsylvania Avenue, with eight members present. Sister Mary Euphrasia was not there though the day before she had visited the ailing Board President "to explain to her my views about the meeting to be held at her house. . . ." The answer to the Board's letter to Sister Julia had come and the meeting had been called to learn its contents. The letter was read and the minutes record that Sister Julia said

> that although the Sisters do not intend to wait until the whole sum is raised, that she and her Council are determined not to begin hampered by debt, and cannot promise to begin work at once, though one substantial endowment would make the work easy. That at present they feel they are 'making traditions,' drawing up plans and looking around for help, and that the work must not be begun in a hurry. The sentiment of the Board . . . was that it was a very decided and reasonable statement of the policy of the Sisters and that while the efforts of the Board must not be relaxed yet it relieves the Board from the necessity of looking for immediate results in the way of raising money which seem impossible to realize, and that they must work quietly and slowly without discouragement that the interest does not progress in ratio with theirs.

The immediate focus of work must be Bishop Spalding's lecture for which they had great hopes and the organization of Associate Boards in other cities.

"The question of a hall was then discussed and it was agreed that the lecture room of the Columbian University [later George Washington

University] should be applied for. . . . In default of that the Shoreham or the Washington Club and a more limited number of invitations." Mrs. Maurice Francis Egan was to apply for the hall and "to attend to the matter of having suitable notices by the press in due time before the lecture and to ask several of the students of the Cath. Univ. [sic] to act as ushers on the occasion."

This lecture, the first major undertaking of the Auxiliary Board, though not nearly the hoped-for financial success, was so influential in publicity and public relations for the college that it will be treated here at some length. The lecturer, John Lancaster Spalding,[46] Bishop of Peoria, Illinois, was a Kentuckian. A descendent of Thomas Spalding who settled in the Maryland colony in 1650 and a nephew of Martin John Spalding, the 7th Bishop of Baltimore; he was an outstanding liberal leader and advocate of higher education in the American church in the last two decades of the century, a strong supporter of and "moving force" in the establishment of the Catholic University of America.

The hall of Columbian University [G.W.] was successfully reserved. The invitation committee worked zealously. Sister Euphrasia wrote

> Invitations in large numbers were sent out accompanied by our dear Sister Superior Julia's card. Among those which were most courteously responded to we may mention the President and Mrs. McKinley's who regretted that pressing business prevented them from accepting the pleasure of hearing Bishop Spalding's lecture. We were particularly gratified by the response of the Worcester Class of '99 [N.D. Academy] who sent a check to the Auxiliary Board to help defray expenses. This and the little offering of the community were most acceptable.

In addition to those sent out from "lists" each lady who desired had twenty invitations to send to her own friends with her personal note or card.

While preparations continued, Sister Mary Euphrasia kept up her efforts for Michigan Avenue, badgering a reluctant Dr. Garrigan (who was more interested in starting to build) to go to see the Engineer Commissioner and herself going to Senator Allison during the last week of 1898. The January 3 meeting of the Auxiliary Board dealt chiefly with lecture arrangements, but the Convent on North Capitol Street at K was the center of activity. That Sisters of the community worked eagerly for the project and that important visitors called on them both before and after the lecture, is clear from the delightfully detailed pages of the Ms *Foundation* account.

46. *DAB*.

On Thursday, January 12, '99, Sister Superior received a letter from Bishop Spalding stating that he would be in Washington on Friday a.m. 13th. The University lecture was to take place that very evening. The weather was most unpromising, a perfect mist of sleet thickened the atmosphere and glazed the already frozen ground, so that walking was difficult and dangerous. The Bishop was not able to get to the University as he stated he would be there to give our messenger the synopsis of his discourse which was asked. Not knowing this, John made his way to the University with great difficulty and had to retrace his steps as the Bishop was at the Shoreham Hotel. His Lordship sent word that he would be at the convent himself with the manuscript at one o'clock. . . . Only a few Sisters [were ready] when the side door-bell rang. The rain was pouring down, and the garden walks all glassy as the Bishop stood with his hand on the knob and came in saying: "Is Mother Euphrasia here? I am Bishop Spalding, am in a great hurry going to the University" and in he walked to the Holy Family [community room], sat down while pulling out his Ms. lecture and asked to have it type-written and sent back to him. Then with his benevolent smile he said promptly: "If you wish you can have it printed in pamphlet form, send the proofs to me, and I shall add if necessary to make it more effective; it may help on the great work." He left promising to return on Monday to see the Community. The twenty-five pages which the lecture covered were mimeographed with all possible speed, and the copy the Bishop asked for, type-written. Twenty-five copies were taken off—the illegibility of the Bishop's writing as well as the 500 sheets which the copies covered, and which had to be taken off singly was a great labor as was also the folding and directing to the different newspaper offices that expressed great eagerness to have them—an explanatory circular also was mimeographed and sent with each. Our dear Sister Superior Julia received the first copy, and must have had it even before the lecture was delivered.

The promised Sunday visit was also described in detail ending in an emphatic statement by Bishop Spalding: "Remember no progress in things divine or human is made except through effort. Mother Julia must begin at once."

On the day of the lecture several priests among others, called at the convent for cards, and during the morning our venerated Cardinal who came to preside at the lecture stopped in on his way from the depot to Gonzaga where he was invited to stay while in Washington. He was accompanied from Baltimore by the Superior of the Sulpicians, and was met at the depot by our kind rector Fr. Galligan, S.J. While the three gentlemen were in the parlor, Bishop Spalding and Father Lee came to the door to ask to see Sister Superior on business and being in haste to meet an appointment they did not wish to come in. Superior however prevailed on the Bishop to step in for a few moments, he met the Cardinal, the Jesuit and the Suplician with a cordial greeting and friendly shake-hands, conversed a few moments, then kissed His Eminence's ring and left. Father Lee remained outside in the carriage. Sister Superior knowing that it gave the Cardinal pleasure to say Mass for us or rather that he always gave us that privilege of saying his Mass in our chapel, asked him to come next morning to which he kindly assented.

Early in the afternoon four Sisters of Mercy from Mt. St. Agnes College, Baltimore, came also to attend the lecture which was to begin at 4:15 o'clock, and asked hospitality for the night. The request was granted as it began to rain and there was no possibility of returning to Baltimore that night. . . . They were the first to tell us of the grand success of the lecture in regard to the immense audience and the enthusiasm it enkindled. The streets were lined and hundreds of persons could not gain admittance the hall was so completely thronged aisles and all.

The first to arrive after the lecture was an old friend of Notre Dame from Massachusetts who traveled to Washington for the "great event."

Rev. Father O'Reilly from Lawrence was announced just as our community bell called us to six o'clock and as the Sisters of Mercy were in the hall at the moment, Sister Superior could not with propriety avoid inviting them in. The conversation became general, our Sister guests were quite at ease and being genial and evidently well-bred ladies, they made it extremely pleasant. Rev. Father O'Reilly expressed all his kind interest in Trinity, was so charmed with the lecture that on being asked to tell us of it, he said that if he attempted to describe it, he would spoil it. The *eloquence* of the *inspired orator was* inimitable. The reverend father declared that he felt proud of being one of Sister Superior Julia's first advisers on the grand project and that he was preparing a fair for its benefit in which he hoped to be imitated by many of his colleagues. "Sister Superior must begin to build" he exclaimed! "Is it not better to fail than not to attempt a worthy work which might be ours?" He left us impressed with his earnest goodness and we thanked God for his friendliness to Notre Dame.

Notwithstanding the unfavorable weather, the University lecture was numerously attended, the highly cultured of the city and surroundings thronged the hall and felt well repaid for the inconvenience attending their coming.

As the discourse has been printed in pamphlet form, I shall add here a few remarks of our Sister guests. The Bishop used no notes, and the lengthy discourse, made longer by the addition of more effective words thrown in by the grand orator and incomparable educator, was all too short; every word was listened to with avidity, and when Notre Dame as the favored order to whose zeal and efficiency the grand undertaking was entrusted, was mentioned a burst of applause filled the crowded hall so that the Bishop had to wait several moments till the enthusiasm subsided, and when he uttered emphatically: "Trinity College will be built! Trinity College must be built! Trinity College shall be built! and we are men, and where is our chivalry if we do not favor the grand work!" the applause was louder and more prolonged. A lady, seated near Rev. Fr. O'Brien Pardow, ex-provincial of the Jesuits, asked what he thought of it. He answered, "I would build it today if in my power." Dr. Harris, U.S. Commissioner of Education, called the audience to order and when silence prevailed said that those who wished to be introduced to His Eminence, to the Apostolic Delegate, Mgr. Martinelli and to the Rt. Rev. Bishop would be received in the library and lecture rooms. These were courteously thrown open for them by the Columbian Professors who all attended the lecture. Receptions in Washington are social ceremonies that are seldom dispensed with in the upper circles. The entire Faculty of the Catholic University also attended. Srs. of Charity of the Academy of St. Vincent, Srs. of Holy Cross, the German School Sisters of Notre Dame, and the heads of educational houses were present. Surely God will inspire persons to aid in time, but as, "The combat and not the victory proclaim the hero," if the financial success had been greater, Notre Dame's glory had been less.

A letter[47] to Sister Mary Euphrasia written two days later by the Rector of the Catholic University sums up temperately the results of the lecture.

I must congratulate you upon the magnificent success which crowned your efforts for the lecture of Bishop Spalding. The audience was very representative, most influential and the results for Trinity must be far reaching. The lecture was a scholarly presentation of the claims of woman for the higher education and all who heard must realize that Trinity is a duty before us. The Cardinal, the Papal Delegate, the heads of all our Educational institutions, clergy and laity, are now pledged to Trinity's success. I hope that new courage will come to you to urge the beginning of the work. In my judgment it is fatal to delay. The Bishops of the country have been appealed to and have splendidly responded. Our hopes have all been aroused, many young women in view of the promises are preparing for it. They will turn to Protestant schools and the work of the past year and a half must be done over. The Sisters must trust in divine Providence and with what they have go ahead and redeem the promises. Failure now means almost death to the higher Education of women and delay is as bad as failure. Our clergy and lay people are aroused now and if lethargy comes, it will be hard to arouse them again. Notre Dame is the talisman and trusting in Our Lady and [what] your order has always done, why can the work not begin. I have never had any doubt of its success if once begun but I fear the good name of Notre Dame and the future of the College, if something be not done soon to make good the promises so publicly made.

I cannot help writing you this as I feel it all intensely after Bishop Spalding's splendid appeal.

Trusting that your superiors may realize how we are all bound up in Trinity and how we suffer by delay and commending my work to your earnest prayers.

I am yours sincerely in S.C.J.
Thomas J. Conaty

47. T.C.A.

The consistent refrain from friends and well-wishers during these weeks as well as in the preceding months was "Build!" This friendly pressure plus the success and widespread press coverage of the *Woman and the Higher Education* lecture seems to have brought about the momentous decision. On January 29 the Journal notes the arrival of a letter[48] from Sister Julia that she has decided to begin the building—at last!

With $43,084 including a $10,000 loan on the Convent of Notre Dame on North Capitol Street and "gifts and donations" to date, the South Wing was begun.[49] Before the opening in 1900 nearly $200,000 more had been borrowed with the Notre Dame houses in Washington and Philadelphia as surety. Notre Dame convents in New England, Ohio, and California had contributed $23,000 toward the work. Ground was broken at a private, informal ceremony on June 21, 1899. The cornerstone was laid December 8, 1899. Both these events are reported in the *Washington Post* and other papers, notably "Miss Conway's *Pilot* of Boston. The first students arrived November 3, 1900, and classes began on the seventh.

The months between were seething with preparation both academic and material. Sister Julia, more frequently in Washington herself, gathered there her "experts," Sister Anne de Marie, the artist, and Sister Mary Nepomucene, "the builder," who worked with Mr. Durang of Philadelphia, the architect of the building. Mr. Maurice Talty, a staunch friend throughout the early years, not only cooperated with the construction firm of McShane, but donated men, labor and equipment for the early stages of the building, while he succeeded in having the "electric cars" routed to Brookland past the college on the new Michigan Avenue extension.

Sisters destined for the faculty were studying intensively. Sister Josephine Ignatius and Sister Mary spent from October 1899 to June 1900 in England.[50] The others gathered at Waltham, Massachusetts for courses with professors from Harvard and M.I.T.

In April 1899, Sister Julia spent two weeks in Washington. The manuscript *Foundations* records that

> . . . while in the city [she] met and talked at length with the ladies of the Board and many others, made friends for the College by the devotedness

48. The date of this letter January 27, 1899, is the same as the date on the Pope's letter to Cardinal Gibbons, *Testem Benevolentiae*, ending the "Americanism" controversy, a coincidence noted years later.
49. Treasurer's Report 1897–1901, T.C.A. and Bd. of Trustees Minutes.
50. The annals of the Notre Dame Training College, Liverpool for 1899 record their arrival: "Sister Josephine Ignatius of Roxburgh, Pens. [sic] and Sister Mary of Cincinnati arrived here, to obtain chiefly in Saint Mary's Hall, practical information for their future work in Washington." St. Mary's Hall was established in cooperation with the University of Liverpool.

> and zeal of Sr. Superior's chief support in this work, Sr. Mary Euphrasia. All who met Sister Superior were charmed with her simplicity and geniality and gave [her] every encouragement to begin building the College, now so greatly needed. Several of the University Clerical and Lay Professors called to pay their courtesy to Sr. Superior, and to offer a friendly word for Trinity, notably Doctors Garrigan, Shahan, Kerby, and the lay professors, Drs. Neill, Shea, Bolling. Acting on Dr. Kerby's suggestion Sister Superior and Sr. Mary Euphrasia called at the University to see the Very Rev. Dr. Bouquillon, whom [she] asked to draw up a plan of study for Trinity. He impressed Sister Superior very favorably and he gave her some wise ideas regarding College life and training, which he had gained from his experience of colleges and students at home and abroad.

Doctors Pace and Egan as well as the Rector, Dr. Conaty, had been so long associated with the planning that the manuscript account takes them for granted without need of listing.

When Sister Julia left for visits to Philadelphia and several cities in Massachusetts, Sister Mary Euphrasia accompanied her so that she could learn more about higher education by visits to colleges for women. In mid-April

> Sister Mary Euphrasia accompanied by Sr. Anne de Marie visited Bryn Mawr College, not far distant from Philadelphia to take notes and glean any information that might prove useful in our own College. Trinity was not unknown to either faculty or students, as its fame, ideal though it still is, reached them through the eloquence of the great and learned Bishop of Peoria. On the occasion of his lecture as recorded herein, Jan. 16, President Thomas assembled the students in the College chapel, introduced our new and noble venture to them, and desired that they should take a deep personal and educational interest in Trinity College. This the Sisters learned from Miss Milos, Sec'y of the Institution, who, in the absence of the President, chaperoned the visiting party through its many beautiful and useful parts, and finally gave them into the hands of Miss Clarke, a teacher of English in a school preparatory to the College. This lady was more than kind, and left nothing undone to promote the Sisters' comfort and pleasure. She had a nice luncheon prepared, and the Catholic servants, very neatly dressed, were so happy to have this occasion to serve the Sisters, whom they "so rarely see." In their round of the College the Sisters made the acquaintance of five students, who were Catholics—a further proof that Trinity will fill a want in our system of education!
>
> Before leaving Philadelphia, Sister Mary Euphrasia very willingly yielded to Sister Superior's suggestion that she be her companion to New England, and [sic] after a few days of preparation at home, was again en route for Philadelphia, there to meet Sister Superior, in whose genial and happy company she was privileged to spend more or less of the next two weeks. Arriving at Springfield on the 27th, the next day Sister Superior and Sr. Mary Euphrasia went to Holyoke, and at noon, in answer to Sr. Superior's summons, Sr. Josephine Ignatius arrived, destined to join them in their

round of inspection. In the early afternoon, Sister Mary Euphrasia and Sr. Josephine Ignatius, accompanied by one of the graduates of our Sisters, visited Mt. Holyoke College. Providence placed them in the car with a teacher of this institution who offered her time and kindness to show the Sisters about. This was gratefully accepted and there was little, if anything, which the Sisters did not see, learning even the details of purchase from this faculty of courteous teachers. The hilly beauty of the surroundings of this college makes its hundred acres of land a dream for the mind to feast upon.

The Sisters met with an equally cordial reception accompanied by generous sharing of experience at Smith, Wellesley, and Radcliffe. For the last two visits they were joined by Sister Georgiana, who had been concerned in Trinity planning from 1897. One excerpt from the descriptions of these visits does not duplicate what has already been quoted and forms a link with the Auxiliary Board efforts, for Miss Seward and Miss Dorsey were actively organizing in Boston, Providence and New York especially.

> Through the kindness of Miss Seward, Sr. Mary Euphrasia had a letter of introduction to Miss Irwin, Dean of Radcliffe College and this probably prepared the way for the very cordial reception which she gave the Sisters. At this institution the Sisters had the gratification of assisting at the lesson of Prof. Robinson on "Milton's Paradise Lost" in lieu of the requested Philosophy class which did not assemble that day.

Miss Emma F. Carey, sister of the foundress of Radcliffe, had already become an earnest worker for Trinity College and president of the newly formed Boston Associate Board, or "Vice-Regent for Boston."

The Boston Associate Board was organized as the result of interest awakened at a "Concert and Lecture for Trinity College" under the auspices of the Notre Dame Alumnae of Boston and Vicinity, April 30, 1899, in the Boston College Hall. The lecturer, the Rev. Dr. Conaty, Rector of the Catholic University, spoke on "The Work of Catholic Women in Education." Among other activities, the Boston Board sponsored later in the year, Nov. 14, a lecture "Women and the Higher Intellectual Life"[51] by Thomas I. Gasson, S.J. This was copyrighted by Emma Carey and printed as a pamphlet by the University Press, Cambridge.

While still in New England, Sister Mary Euphrasia represented Sister Julia in a "personal interview with Bishop Harkins [of Providence, R.I. to] give a more satisfactory account of the college and its progress than had been gleaned from newspaper articles. . . . [The bishop] showed great regard for all that was said about the College. Moreover, he promised his support to the work and his presence at the inauguration of a Board of Regents for the college, should Miss Seward pass

51. T.C.A. Drawer II.

that way to establish it . . . since this interview he has placed the college before his warm personal friend, Bp. Healy of Portland, for the purpose of obtaining likewise his support and interest." Associate Boards in Providence, Woonsocket, Pawtucket and other Rhode Island cities actively supported the nascent college. The results of their interest extend to the present in the form of scholarships and a loyal, active, alumnae chapter.

New York, too, was "on the move." "About the middle of April the Misses Seward and Patterson went to Baltimore" to call on Cardinal Gibbons. They sought an introduction to the Archbishop of New York in preparation for a visit to New York to make Trinity College well known there and to reach some of the city's wealthy Catholics.

> His Eminence was very willing to do anything in his power for Trinity, and was pleased at their suggestion to call upon the most Rev. Archbp. Corrigan but advised them to avoid the subject of funds. Miss Seward accordingly left for New York, April 19th, and in company with her friend, Mrs. Thos. Wren Ward, a prominent Catholic lady of New York City, called upon Achbp. Corrigan. The magnetic interest of Miss Seward drew forth the same from the Archbishop who expressed himself a friend of the College, but like His Eminence desired that the subject of funds be waived. However, later in the conversation he himself opened the way for the generally unwelcome topic of ways and means. He said he could readily understand how far-reaching such an institution would be in its power for good to the country at large, having, as it did, a national character, and thereby it was logical to conclude, the whole body, not a few individuals should support it. Happy in having obtained the Archbishop's friendly interest, without which she could do nothing, Miss Seward lost no time in making arrangements for a meeting of ladies prominent in social and educational circles to be held at the home of Mrs. Ward . . . at which Achbp. Corrigan had agreed to preside. The date was set for April 27th, and the Archbishop faithfully responded, being in fact, the first to arrive and next after him his co-adjutor, Mgr. Farley. The former stood at the door, welcoming each guest that appeared. Both these dignitaries made addresses apropos of the subject that caused the gathering, and to their eloquent words were added those not less so from the Hon. Judge Daly of New York who, as President[52] of the Catholic Club promised some financial good from their society the coming winter. About two hundred were in the audience and the seed of Miss Seward's almost inspired words, who was the last in order to make a plea for Trinity, fell on fruitful soil, as the sequel will show.

That sequel was threefold. A New York Associate Board was organized with Mrs. Thomas Wren Ward as Vice-Regent. Judge Daly's promise was fulfilled in a reception held December 12, 1899, four days after the cornerstone of the college was laid, at the Catholic Club, 120 Central Park South for the members of the Auxiliary Board of Trinity

52. The Judge was chairman of the Committee on Catholic Interests and past president.

College and the New York Associate Board whose names and addresses are listed in the invitational leaflet. "The object of the present reception," says the leaflet,

> is to enable the ladies . . . to lay before the Catholic families of New York the importance of the work, and to enlist their sympathy with the movement. While colleges for the higher education of women are springing up all over the United States, there is no such institution for Catholic women. If a young lady, after graduating from the Sacred Heart, Mount St. Vincent or any of our Academic institutions, desires to take a Post Graduate course, she cannot do so without going to Bryn Mawr, Radcliffe, Barnard, Wellesley, Smith or some other well-known women's college not conducted under Catholic auspices.

The third and more immediate sequel was Miss Annie Leary's change of heart. That lady had declared that she had "no interest in the College or the higher education of women," that she would stop into the meeting for a moment, but not stay. "Entrapped by the interesting program and infused by the enthusiasm of all," she stayed two hours and left asking for more detailed information. After further visits with Miss Seward she gave an initial hundred dollars, "considering it an honor to be among the founders of the College" and was "inspired" to give the chapel to Trinity College, in memory of her family. On a visit to Washington she signed on May 27 a contract prepared by the Sisters' lawyer, Mr. Colbert, for the Arthur Leary Memorial Chapel to cost $55,000. Though a check for $15,000 was duly delivered by "young Mr. Stafford" sent from New York by Miss Leary, the chapel was never built. The lady felt "aggrieved that the *place of the crypt* is not under the altar." That and other grievances cooled Miss Leary's ardor so that future generations were saved a pseudo-Gothic church attached to the end of South Hall.[53] Work on the chapel was suspended Nov. 21, 1899. The initial payment had been used for the Gothic windowed addition to South Hall that now houses the faculty lounge and some offices. The second floor was, from 1902–1941, the "chemical laboratories." The first floor was for years the Music Department, and student publication offices, and, 1941–1963, the Alumnae Office. Thus Miss Leary's generosity has benefited Trinity through the years, though her pious "inspiration" for a chapel where her family would be buried did not materialize. She never completely severed connections with the college and was elected Regent for New York in 1903.

During the summer of 1899, while the building was gradually rising, academic planning, student recruitment, and faculty preparation con-

53. The early catalogues carry an architect's drawing of the college which includes the proposed Gothic chapel.

tinued. In spite of a disturbing letter from the Superior General in Belgium expressing grave doubts that the conditions of her approval had been fulfilled, Sister Julia went steadily forward. Since she was convinced it was too late to abandon the project approved by both civil and ecclesiastic authorities, she confided her worries to few, and courageously took responsibility for the college without what the Cardinal had called "undue interference from abroad."[54] She arrived in Washington June 1 with Sister Georgiana, met the "Ladies of the Board," heard of the progress of the New York and Boston Associate Boards, and conferred about building plans. On the eighth she and Sister Mary Euphrasia went to the Catholic University to discuss Trinity College plans with the Vice Rector. "He advocates," says the *Journal*, "a large-hearted, generous minded policy towards the future students, having as few rules as possible, and as little restraint. The government to be largely moral!" The seeds were being sown for the policy that made Trinity, even in its small beginning, a "college for women, not a glorified school for girls" as successive Deans have emphasized. In August, 7.4 more acres were purchased from the Glenwood Cemetery corporation "and 6 acres of Michigan Avenue, which, though belonging to the government, will probably be the source of some remuneration later, on the part of the Government always so kind." (That last phrase so characteristic of Sr. Mary Euphrasia, who referred to the chairman of the Senate Appropriations Committee as "*dear* Senator Alison," is another clue to her success in public relations.)

In October of that year (1899) the first prospective student arrived and was disappointed to find the college not open. She went to "one of the Visitation Convents" to study in preparation for opening in 1900. She may have met at least one other future Trinity student there because Bishop Farley of New York called at the convent with Dr. Garrigan in mid-October to say that his niece at Visitation hoped to come to Trinity next year. "He says," recounts the *Journal*, "our Admissions Examinations are considered severe. I said they were adapted to our own pupils." There were also four graduates of Notre Dame Academies in Ohio, Massachusetts, and Pennsylvania gathered for a post-graduate year (1899–1900) conducted entirely in French at the Philadelphia Academy while awaiting the opening of the college.

The Auxiliary Board held two meetings in November, on the sixth and twenty-eighth. Letters from Miss Cary in Boston, Mrs. Ward in New York, and Miss Lindsay in St. Louis gave encouraging reports of the work for the college. Miss Seward, the president, had been in Eng-

54. On her way to Washington, Sr. Julia consulted Father Purbrick, Provincial of the Jesuits, who had formerly been the Provincial in England and knew the Sisters' work there. He was "strongly in favor of the college." He offered to write a letter which could be shown to the Superior General.

land that summer combining an information gathering tour of inspection of higher education with her vacation. Her "letter from London was read explaining her absence . . . telling of her visit to the Training School at Liverpool, in which she expressed herself very much delighted with all she saw. . . . [She was] even more sure, though she never doubted the fact, that the Sisters of Notre Dame were capable of doing all they promised." At the November 28 meeting, at which she presided, "Miss Seward sketched in broad outline the Conference at Stockport, England, August 28–30, mentioning and quoting certain of the English Bishops and Cardinal Vaughan. They said the Catholic College was 'a great movement' and they watched with deep interest the Church in America."

The minutes of this meeting record the discussion of questions most frequently asked about the college. These were not only listed with the answers "authoritatively returned by the Superior of the Order through the Auxiliary Board," but were reproduced by mimeograph for distribution, and incorporated in Miss Dorsey's pamphlet to be used on her student recruitment journeys. This list (cf. Appendix IV) concludes with the statement: "Every question laid before the Sisters is discussed with great care, which accounts for the slow formulation of the three several questions that most vitally interest the public—discipline, curriculum, finance."

Before returning to Washington, Miss Seward had been present at the Boston meeting and Father Gasson's lecture "Women and the Higher Intellectual Life," and had visited New York for conferences about Trinity, especially a last attempt to persuade Miss Leary to continue with her gift. She urged the members to attend the reception in their honor to be given by the N.Y. Catholic Club,[55] December 12. Some of the ladies had been demurring because they had not received individual invitations as would have been according to proper etiquette! Interest in the college prevailed. The ladies, after attending the simple cornerstone-laying ceremony on December 8, journeyed to New York for the reception on the twelfth. (cf. p. 59).

As the building rose and the actual time of opening drew closer, the months of 1900 took on for those directing operations on the scene in Washington, for the Sisters chosen for the faculty, and for the Auxiliary Board and other friends of the college, an air of immediate preparation. It was then that Ella Lorraine Dorsey, an original Board member, emerged as an effective, enthusiastic, tireless worker for Trinity College. Descendant of an old southern Maryland family, she grew up quietly in Georgetown, the admiring daughter of a well-known au-

55. N.Y. Catholic Club founded 1883 by "Catholic gentlemen who are governed by a spirit of devotion to the Church," an early example of Catholic lay organization. Cf. "Catholic Church of New York," *Catholic Encyclopedia*, Vol. III, 1st edition, 1908.

thor.[56] She herself was a "liberated woman," earning her living as a full-time government employee at the United States Patent Office. In January, 1900, her concise, practical article about the college was printed in booklet form and released to the press. It was published in many cities across the country and served as a recruiting and promotional tool in the following months. The booklet included the answers to ten "questions most frequently asked," (cf. Appendix V) as well as ways to raise money for the college even if one is not wealthy. Elected Recording Secretary of the Auxiliary Board, February 5, 1900, in March she was appointed by that board to travel forming Associate Boards, and by Sister Mary Euphrasia to represent the college as what we would call today an "admissions recruiter and public relations representative." Her meticulous expense account shows that in 1900 she was at least two months on the road using her annual leave and an "excess leave" of thirty-five and a half days. The trips were financed chiefly by the proceeds of a Harp Recital held May 2 at the Columbia theatre, by $118.26 from the Sisters to replace salary lost through "excess leave," and by a pass on the Western Pacific Railway from Chicago to Butte, Montana, furnished by Mrs. Thomas H. Carter.

May 7, 1900, Miss Dorsey addressed the Catholic Author's Guild of New York City about Trinity College. In late June she was in Cleveland to speak to the Associate Board and interested friends. This meeting "in the auditorium of the Ursuline College" is enthusiastically reported in the June 29 *Catholic Universe* as part of a "six weeks' tour of the principal cities of the East and West . . . to spread the knowledge of the aims, the aspirations and practical equipment of the new college for the higher education of Catholic women." "One hundred and fifty candidates presented themselves for the first examinations," the article states. "The next will take place in August. The standards of the college are exceptionally high." Having stirred the ladies of Cleveland to work to establish a scholarship, "Miss Dorsey left on an evening train for Chicago. There the movement has been espoused by Eliza Allen Starr, the well-known Catholic writer and art critic." Thence she expected to go as far as Montana and perhaps to San Francisco. This western journey lasted, according to her expense account (Appendix IV), from June fifteenth to August first and included Cleveland, Cincinnati, Chicago, Milwaukee, St. Paul, Butte and other cities in Montana, and a week in Yellowstone Park. This last, we can hope, a

56. . . . "my first and only claim on the public is that I am the daughter of my beloved Mother, Anna Hansen Dorsey, the pioneer of light literature in America, one of the most remarkable women of her generation and a Laetare Medalist, the medal in her case being given for distinguished services rendered Religion, Literature *and* Education. When I add that the medal is conferred for services rendered Religion *or* Literature *or* Education, you will perceive the compliment in her case. T.C.A. Drawer II pencilled notes about her family.

vacation, though it is carefully itemized in a separate expense account. She did not go as far as San Francisco.

In mid-August, Miss Dorsey was in New York again, talking about the college to the students of the National Catholic Summer School at Cliffhaven at a reception in her honor. In October she was again on the road revisiting Chicago and Cleveland. The trip (Oct. 11–16) according to the expense account cost $36.56 and used an extra five and a half days of excess leave. By that time members of the faculty were beginning to gather in Washington at the Convent on North Capitol Street. The *Dean's Notebook* begins with a series of fourteen answers to questions submitted by Miss Dorsey on the eve of her departure. The work begun in 1897 and intensified that summer of 1900 continued unflaggingly until the death of Ella Lorraine Dorsey more than thirty years later.

The college, destined to open in early October, was delayed because the "imposing granite building" was not yet habitable. The New York *Daily Tribune* published a full column article, datelined "Washington, September 22 (Special)," with details about the college and a 4 × 6" cut of the architect's drawing of the building captioned "*Trinity College for Women*. It is to be opened in Washington, November 1." "The courses of study," the article states, "are planned according to the best standard of American educational systems. . . . As announced in newspaper articles heretofore, only freshman and special students will be received during the year 1900–01. When the college is developed, there will be the usual classification of students that is found in all higher colleges. . . ." One paragraph captioned *Mistress of Mechanics* describes the work of Sister Mary Nepomucene, "the builder" mentioned on an earlier page. It deserves citation here, providing a fitting close to the chapter and a prologue to the arrival of students and faculty.

> The plans for the college were made by Sister Mary of Notre Dame, who kept in close touch with the architect, E. Durang, of Philadelphia, when he was making the contracts and specifications. Sister Mary visits the college daily and directs the workmen and contractors what to do, watching all the time to see that nothing is neglected. One of the stonecutters said the other day: "You can't do Sister Mary, for last Saturday, when she thought some skeleton work was being done on the fourth floor, she went right up the ladders to see about it, and, sure enough, made the boss carpenter go back up there and fix something." Sister Mary is a "mistress of mechanics," and, notwithstanding she is nearly sixty years of age, when it is necessary to climb ladders to the fourth story of a building she has no hesitancy about doing so. She is much pleased with the progress which has been made on the building, for when the cornerstone was laid last December there was some doubt as to whether it could be completed by the beginning of the next school year.

CHAPTER THREE

Pioneer Years, 1900–1904

The First Academic Year: 1900–1901

TRINITY COLLEGE had now been an entity for nearly three years, recorded in documents, embodied in acres of land, in the stone of a slowly rising building, in entrance requirements and curriculum plans, in the aspirations, doubts and determination of the founders and those who staunchly supported them. In the fall of 1900 the college came alive. Students and faculty met and academic work began.

Sisters for faculty and staff gathered at Notre Dame Convent on North Capitol Street during October. The Dean began, on October 10, her notebook: "Events of College Life Each Year." On October 25 Sisters of the Trinity community moved into a partially finished South Hall, an event recorded in community annals as well as Dean's Notebook. A brief note from the latter is sufficient:

> "The Trinitarians left the hospitable shelter of our Convent at K and N. Capitol Streets in three parties and reached Trinity at 11:00 a.m. . . . Dr. Garrigan brought the Blessed Sacrament at 2:30 p.m. to the newly arranged temporary chapel (in 1974 the east end of the Language Laboratory). . . . That night the Talty family sent a caterer's supper, ample enough to satisfy a Community three times more numerous than we are."

The next morning Dr. Garrigan celebrated the first mass on campus after which all sang the *Te Deum*.

Sunday, October 27 saw the first faculty meeting. Several others followed in quick succession to prepare for the official beginning of college work.

The first four students arrived November third and by the seventh there were nineteen students, the freshman class of 1904, at the opening academic assembly in "St. Paula," the present Room 250. A student eye-witness description of the opening days, written by one of the first arrivals for the *Trinity Record* (to celebrate the college's tenth anniversary) still retains a validity not attainable elsewhere.[1]

Who of us, I wonder, who witnessed the opening of Trinity just ten years ago would have dared to prophesy the future which is now her present and her past? A building hopelessly unfinished, a handful of brave religious, a little group of earnest students, a vast deal of that enthusiasm without which nothing great is ever accomplished, much kindly encouragement from friends, enough discouragement to ensure the stability of the undertaking and mark it with the indispensable seal of the Cross—those were the conditions under which it all happened.

And this is how Trinity first opened its doors to its students. It was Saturday noon, November 3, 1900, when amidst a depressing downpour of rain four students and one Sister wended their muddy way from the car track to the front door. When I said that Trinity opened its doors, I should have been more explicit—Trinity opened its *door*, for it had only one in a state resembling anything like completion. But where, oh, where was that door to be found? Our little party of pioneers steered their course to the front door (near Dean of Students' Office—for many years the "S.G. Door") only to find it partly boarded over and, wanted to go to College, but how could we if there was no door by which we could enter? We tried to remember that "in the bright lexicon of youth there's no such word as *fail*," and by calling to mind a few other classic quotations equally suited to the occasion, we at last found that "other door," whose perpetually recurring refrain was beginning to haunt us.

It happened to be the door which is now sacred to the postman, for that end of the building alone was finished.[2] [End of South Hall near back staircase.] Once safely inside, our welcome was as warm as its three predecessors had been cold and we began, under its beneficent influence, to feel our zeal for learning and our responsibility as pioneers grow and increase within us. The first subject of our course was dinner and we had it in the room now used as the studio, which had to serve as refectory for both Sisters and students (separately, of course) until Christmas. After it followed in due order a visit to the Chapel—in St. Jerome's—to our own rooms—all on the 3d and 4th floors, south wing, front, and to as much of the rest of the house as was finished. No, not finished, for no part of the building could claim that distinction and many were the prophets of woe who asked how any one could possibly carry on classes in *that* place? What made it

1. *Trinity College Record*, Vol. IV, pp. 247–253. Signed E.M.P. '04, it was written by Sister Wilfred du Sacre Coeur, Elsie Parsons, the first alumna to become a Sister of Notre Dame, to return to the faculty, to hold an administrative office (Dean 1924–32). The article has been reprinted in college publications for the twenty-fifth and fiftieth anniversaries, and now enters the history to stay. Cf. *Annals* Vol. I, Nov. 3, 1900. "At 12:30 pm Sister Blandina of S.H. arrived from Philadelphia with four students—Miss McGorrisk of Des Moines, Iowa, Miss Jessie Johnston of Milwaukee, Wisc., Miss Scallon of Handcock, Mich. and Miss Elsie Parsons of Philadelphia. These were the first students to enter Trinity. They came in a heavy downpour of rain and had quite a little search to find the entrance door."
2. The present window door in faculty office 176.

South Hall, 1900.

possible was the brave spirit of Sister Superior Julia, then provincial Superior of the Sisters of Notre Dame and preeminently foundress of the College, and the courage and generosity of that first community who faced positive hardship in order to make Trinity possible.

As for us students, the whole experience was one delightful picnic and it was a matter of much merriment to us that there was no gas in the house those first days, so that we had to perform all our evening evolutions by candle-light, that we had to wade through inches of sawdust and shavings and climb up temporary and delightfully precarious stairways. And if the absence of glass in the doors of our rooms necessitated the hanging of draperies—artistic and otherwise—it also singularly facilitated intercommunication and produced a comfortable feeling of interest in your neighbor's doings. Even real drawbacks had their ludicrous side—thus, the ubiquity of the workmen had something sociable about it and their prompt arrival at 7 A.M., perhaps in *your* room, meant that you were decidedly expeditious in getting down to breakfast. And if they persistently hammered outside the room where we were trying to follow a lecture, they also favored us with numerous musical selections, ranging in repertoire all the way from "Two Little Girls in Blue" to "Die Wacht am Rhein," and "Cavalleria Rusticana." Sometimes these interludes strained our risibilities to the breaking point, as when one day a carpenter working at the baseboards outside the present French room, (Room 248) then used for English, yielding to the seductions of a piano which, in default of other room, was ornamenting the corridor, started to pick out on it, with his *thumb*, as far as we could make out, "The wearing of the green." An English lesson of exceeding seriousness was going on at the same time, and the teacher, seeing the worried expression of our quivering faces, gravely requested one of the students to ask that man to stop. Which being done, the tension increased, but the lesson proceeded.

By November 6th there were nineteen students in the house, and the next morning, that all might be well begun, we had the Mass of the Holy Ghost in the dainty little Chapel arranged in St. Jerome's. (Room 259) The Mass was said by the Very Rev. Dr. Garrigan, then Vice-Rector of the Catholic University and Chaplain to the students of Trinity College, now Right Rev. Bishop Garrigan of Sioux City, Iowa.

At 10 A.M. the same day there was an assembling of Faculty and students in solemn conclave in St. Paula. St. Paula, interested reader, was the one-time name of the present museum (Room 250) and former Chapel, and the room opposite, wherein flourished the higher mathematics until the new building was opened and wherein are now to be found those fountain-heads of learning,—pens, ink, and paper of French-exercise fame,—in those days rejoiced in the euphonious appellation of St. Eustochium. (Room 251) It fulfilled the functions of the present Social Hall, but do not believe for an instant that we ever attempted to pronounce its name—all our efforts in that line were limited to looking intelligent when the Dean pronounced it. In St. Paula then, behold us gathered. At the desk Sister Superior Julia, who first addressed us on the *reasons* for undertaking the College; at her right Sister Superior Lidwine, President of the College, who spoke to us next in order, on our opportunities and the great things expected of us; at her left Sister Josephine Ignatius, Dean of the Faculty, who outlined a college day as it was to be. The Faculty were also present and were introduced in due order, after which there was an adjournment of the meeting, and the first lesson at Trinity took place at 11.30 that morning—it was an English lesson and was given by Sister Mary Josephine, who had come to us all the way from England. Other lessons followed—and by the next morning we were ready for regular work. Here is the program of studies of that first day:

8.30—Assembly.
Mathematics.
9.30—Church History.
10.30—Intermission.
10.45—Greek.
11.45—English.
12.45—Intermission.
2.30—French.
3.15—German.
4.00—Intermission.
4.30—Help given by teachers in class-rooms.
5.30—Free.
6.00—Social Ethics.
6.30—Supper.

7.00 – Social Hour.
8.00 – Study in rooms.
9.30 – Lights out.

It will be seen at a glance how little time there was for anything but hard work with Social Ethics at 6 P.M., Social Hour – which was a sort of general recreation with a different member of the Faculty presiding each evening, from 7 to 8, and lights out at 9.30. But we *did* work hard, one and all of us, and no one seemed to think it at all strange that we should; on the contrary, the usual advice of our many distinguished visitors could be summed up in these two words "hard work"!

The first lecture was given by Very Rev. Monsignor Shahan at 9.30 on that 8th of November, and Very Reverend Dr. Pace began his course in Philosophy on the 12th, holding his first lessons in the Ancient Languages Room (Room 246) now known to fame as the Dean's office. The course in Religion was given on Friday afternoons by our reverend Chaplain and the lectures usually took place in the corridor outside the German room, all other available space large enough for community and students being occupied by the workmen.

That first academic year with the three that followed, until degrees were conferred, established lasting patterns of college life, though some practices were found unsuitable before the year was out. The "social ethics" was gone by Christmas and the supervised social hour quickly followed; but the basic framework for future growth and development emerged clearly in the months of 1900–1901. Chapters on faculty, curriculum, student body, alumnae, development and public relations, as well as on the physical plant with its builders and maintainers will attempt to trace that growth through three quarters of the twentieth century to the vastly different – yet somehow similar – college of today. Because the college is an organic entity[3] it is difficult to separate these subjects from one another. Necessarily, some overlapping will occur, yet for continuity of individual topic and to avoid the sometimes deadly dull effect of strict chronology, this will be the format.

The rigorous schedule of studies was put immediately into operation so that by November 18 the Faculty Minutes record the first student protest to the Dean. "Some students were fretful under so many hours of labor" (Faculty Minutes, p. 5). They claimed they had 29 hours of class, while the Dean patiently demonstrated that their class load was only 21 hours. A study of the freshman records for 1900–1901, of the Dean's report of the year to the Advisory Board in May 1901, and of the courses of study in the catalogue, makes possible a clearer picture

3. After writing this, the author was happy to find in Sister Julitta Larkin's article on the college at its fiftieth anniversary *Trinity College Record*, 1948–49, pp. 68–72, 195–200. "What keeps a college going once it is started? Growth and Development – the characteristics of an organism" (p. 195).

of the student program than the stark time schedule for one day presented on page 68. That gives the spartan timetable for a typical day the actual classes of November 8, 1900. All the students, however, did not take all subjects every day. Required for all were:

English Rhetoric and Composition	2 hours
English Literature	2 hours
Church History	2 hours
Introduction to Philosophy	1 hour
German—differentiated according to preparation	3 hours
French—grammar, lectures on history and literature, or prose composition, conversation, critical study of authors, lectures on 19th century literature	3 hours
History—Roman or Europe since 1815	1 hour

Greek, Latin, Mathematics for qualified students as well as extra work to remove entrance "conditions" for those who needed it, filled the heavy schedule of study.

Even "special students" had to have the entrance requirements and take at least fifteen hours a week of regular class work. Piano lessons for those who had achieved a high degree of proficiency before entrance might be taken in addition to the academic schedule since several young ladies wished to "keep up their music." Art lectures began in February 1901 and studio work in September 1902. The more advanced mathematics classes were "for students intending to specialize in science." The botany, chemistry and physics laboratories were not equipped until September of 1902. All candidates for the A.B. degree were required to take at least one science before senior year. After the pioneer years a science was required of all sophomores until the 1930s when the requirement was transferred to the freshman program.

Faculty interest in the individual student dates from the earliest months. December 3, 1900, the Dean began her series of monthly visits to each student in her room "to give report of classwork and comment on studies and courses." December 12 saw the first "examination in review of the month's college work" the beginning of monthly tests in vogue at Trinity for half a century. At one of the earliest faculty meetings, the teachers were strongly recommended to be available to students in classrooms during the late afternoon, thus establishing from the beginning the "office hour-problem hour" concept that has been integrated into the Trinity program through all its changes.

Meanwhile, the "Ladies' Board" and the Sisters of the College administration were deep in preparation for the ceremony of Dedication, a long-anticipated great event. The Board, still under the direction of Sister Mary Euphrasia, met November 5, 9 and 20 at the North Capitol Street Convent. All other business was postponed until December to allow time for detailed arrangements for the day of dedication set for November 22. The Sisters at the college were to concentrate on the morning activities, blessing of the building, Solemn Pontifical Mass and catered breakfast for guests, while the ladies of the board would take responsibility for the grand reception in the afternoon. The result was a day of ceremony impressive even after seventy-five years. A near full-page spread in the *Washington Post* and articles in *The Star* and in newspapers in all parts of the country list the dignitaries of church, state and *academia* who were present among the hundreds of guests. A more intimate and lively view of the coordination of effort, the practical attention to detail that went into preparation, come from the annals of the community of Sisters of Notre Dame at the college, the minutes of the Ladies Auxiliary Board and from students' reminiscences.

When one realizes that the students' dining and reception room, the large room which in the 1970s houses Alumnae, Development and Admissions offices, had to be transformed overnight into a chapel for the Pontifical High Mass; and, while guests were enjoying their catered breakfast in class rooms and corridor of the second floor, cleared, re-arranged and decorated as the "imposing reception hall" for the afternoon—when one realizes all this one has some idea of the gigantic undertaking that Dedication Day was for the small group of workers. Two thousand invitations for the morning, and one thousand for the afternoon were addressed by Sisters at Trinity and at North Capitol Street, helped by ladies of the board. Bids for refreshments were sought from the two best caterers, Raucher's and Demonet's. "Miss Dorsey spoke earnestly on the subject of having the refreshments adequate." Miss Sherman was appointed to try to get Marine Band members for the music at the reception. "Miss Dorsey undertook to get the flags needed for decoration from the War and Navy Departments."

The Ladies of the Auxiliary Board
of
Trinity College
request the honor of your presence
Thursday afternoon, November twenty-second
Nineteen Hundred
from three to five o'clock
to meet
The Reverend Mother Provincial
of the
Sisters of Notre Dame de Namur
and the
Faculty of Trinity College

There were formal invitations from the College to the dedication mass and breakfast, but the author has not succeeded in finding an extant copy. A copy of the above invitation is pasted into the minute book of the Ladies Auxiliary Board.

Four days later, Nov. 9, Mrs. Egan reported that "Rauscher finds he can give the Board: bouillon, coffee, cream and sugar, sandwiches, chocolate and whipped cream with small cakes for the number named (300–400) for $45.00–$6.00 additional being charged for three waiters." This was accepted since the Sisters had accepted Rauscher's for the breakfast and "as he has all his men on the ground, it will be a simpler matter for him to serve the refreshments for the afternoon." Besides, this bid was $20.00 less than Demonet's! That could be used toward paying the musicians from the Marine Band who "explained that as members of the musicians' union they could not volunteer, as it would make their fellow-members feel they were cutting the ground from under their feet, but, he [the leader] added, they would willingly volunteer should their commanding officer express a wish. The cost per man is $4.00 with $8.00 for the leader." About transportation for the musicians ". . . the Board decided if they volunteered a Herdic should be chartered to take and bring them. If they were regularly engaged at union prices, they could furnish their own transportation. This could be easy and inexpensive as the North Capitol Street car goes nearly to the barracks and quite close to the college." Though Miss Sherman was to communicate with the commandant again through Mrs. Reid, the union prevailed. "Five men and a leader (were) engaged at $28.50. The instruments were chosen to avoid the expense of a piano since the college did not yet have one."

Mrs. Egan was appointed to see Major Sylvester, Chief of Police, to have "policemen for duty at Trinity on the 22nd in view of the large number of vehicles and visitors on foot that will be coming and going all day. . . ." Sister Euphrasia "made arrangements with the Brookland Road" so that on the day "cars would be run every seven minutes, instead of every fifteen minutes, between the hours 9:30 to 11:30 a.m., and 2:30 to 5:30 p.m."

The question of protocol concerned some of the ladies. "The Sisters being the hostesses and the board the medium of introduction, the question arose as to how and by whom the introductions should be made." Sister Euphrasia announced a procedure agreeable to all: "The President, Mrs. Carter, will introduce to the Mother Superior, the Honorary President, Miss Seward, will introduce to the Cardinal and Monsignor Martinelli."

On November 20 the final program was announced. As the ceremonies began at 9:45 the ladies were to assemble at the college by 9:30.

The minutes end with what must have been a momentous statement for those ladies who had been working for three years in support of the college. "The meeting was adjourned with the announcement that the next time we met it would be at Trinity" for the Dedication Day.

At Trinity, Sister Mary Euphrasia was in and out making final arrangements, directing, coordinating the efforts of the college community and of the Ladies Board. By the nineteenth she had written out some items regarding the order of exercises "a document for the information of all." There were no classes so that teachers and students were free to help. "Chairs stored away in the attic, eighty in number were brought down . . . to the first floor by elevator." Students helped in this process, no mean labor if one remembers that the "elevator" was the hand-operated, rope-pull dumb waiter that serviced South Hall for thirty years! Convent rooms were occupied by carpenters putting together temporary extra tables to accommodate visiting religious of other orders. Visiting Sisters of Notre Dame were put to work. "Father Burke (John J.) the Paulist, who was to have charge of the sanctuary, stayed until eight tacking carpet etc. Sister Georgiana assisted in dusting the chairs in the body of the chapel. Sisters Anne de Marie and Agnita stayed up after the community retired. Sister M. Rosalia from North Capitol and K stayed overnight."[4]

On the Thursday, November 22, the community annals record that after their earlier-than-usual breakfast Sister Julia gave the Sisters a general review of assignments for the day:

> "Sisters Georgiana, J. Ignatius and Raphael will attend to the visitors from the East; Sister Mary will look after those from Ohio. Sister Agnes Mary and Anne Madeleine those from Philadelphia. Sr. Blandina will be in the little room across from the chapel which will serve as a bureau of information for reporters and others seeking news. Sister Odilia will take charge of the visiting religious, while Sister M. Borgia and I will stay in the parlor to receive the Cardinal and Papal Delegate and Sister Lidwine will look after such people as Commissioner Harris and the president of Bryn Mawr.
>
> At nine o'clock the flag was raised over the college and at 9:30 guests began to come in. The Sisters' refrectory was given up for a hat room for the clergy. Rooms had been fitted up for the Cardinal, the Delegate and each of the Bishops. At twenty minutes before ten, Dr. Garrigan brought the Cardinal over from the University.[5]

The description that follows of this day is taken from Sister Mary Patricia Butler's, *Historical Sketch of Trinity College,* 1897–1925, pp. 33, 35.

4. Annals, Vol. 1.
5. Annals, Vol. I, November 22. Cf. *Washington Post,* Nov. 23, 1900.

The dedication took place on November 22, feast of St. Cecilia (1900). His Eminence Cardinal Gibbons was the officiating prelate at the blessing of the building and Monsignor Martinelli, the Papal Delegate, was the celebrant of the Mass. The Cardinal, preceded by a cross-bearer and two acolytes carrying torches and accompanied by Very Reverend William Byrne, Vicar General of Boston, and Very Reverend Doctor Dumont, S.S., of the Catholic University, went through all the corridors sprinkling walls and floors with holy water and reciting from the Ritual the prayers for the Blessing of a House and Convent and the Blessing of a College. The choir took up the *Laudate Dominum* as the procession moved back to the altar steps. Here a solemn blessing was given by the Cardinal, who then retired to his throne at the Gospel side of the sanctuary. The officers of the Pontifical Mass were: celebrant, Monsignor Martinelli, Papal Delegate; assistant priest, the Reverend James T. O'Reilly, O.S.A., of Lawrence, Mass.; deacon, the Reverend Timothy Brosnahan, of Waltham, Mass.; subdeacon, the Reverend Doctor Rooker, secretary of the Papal Legation; deacons of honor to His Eminence the Cardinal, the Very Reverend F. L. M. Dumont, S.S., of the Catholic University, and the Reverend Owen A. Clark, of Providence. R.I.; deacons of honor of the Mass, the Very Reverend William Byrne, D.D., Vicar General of Boston, and the Very Reverend Doctor O'Hara, president of Mount St. Mary's College, Emmitsburg, Md. There were also present the Right Reverend C. A. McDonnell, Bishop of Brooklyn; the Right Reverend Monsignor Van de Vyver, Bishop of Richmond; the Right Reverend John M. Farley, then Auxiliary Bishop of New York, later Cardinal Archbishop; the Right Reverend P. J. Donahue, Bishop of Wheeling; and the Right Reverend Monsignor Nugent of Liverpool, England. The master of ceremonies was the Reverend John J. Burke, C.S.P., at that time editor of *The Catholic World*, and the music was by a choir of seventeen Paulist students, under the direction of Messrs. Finn, C.S.P., and Casserly, C.S.P., now Father Finn, of the world-famous boys' choir of the Paulist Church, New York, and Father Casserly, missionary, New York. Dumont's sixth tone Gregorian Mass was sung.

The sermon was by the Right Reverend Monsignor T. J. Conaty, D.D., rector of the Catholic University, who chose for his text the fifth and sixth verses of the forty-fourth Psalm: "With thy comeliness and thy beauty set out, proceed prosperously, and reign, because of truth and meekness and justice, and thy right hand shall conduct thee wonderfully." It was so fine a discourse that the United States Commissioner of Education, who was present, embodied it that year in his Report.

There were present some fifty priests, including Jesuits, Sulpicians, Marists, Augustinians, Benedictines, Paulists, and Franciscans. Representatives of all the religious orders of women in and around Washington were also in attendance at the Mass. The congregation was composed of men and women prominent in public and social life, many of them non-Catholics. The diplomatic corps was well represented by ambassadors and their wives; the government by senators, congressmen, and others; there were members of all the learned professions and of the faculties of other colleges.

Though the chapel was improvised for the ceremony, it presented a scene of great beauty. The superb room, with lofty ceiling moulded in pure Greek designs and upheld by Corinthian columns, was all pure white, with a white and gold altar, decorated with chrysanthemums and candles in tall golden candelabra. The only spots of color were three great paintings on the walls; the thrones for the prelates, heavily draped in scarlet; and the magnificent cloth-of-gold vestments worn by the officers of the Mass.

More intimate details from those present supplement the formal account. Sister Blandina from "the little room (called for today, 'the Bureau of Information')" writes that she

"can see dear Sister Superior Julia. She sits reading her prayer book,—no doubt, following the ceremony according to the Ritual. . . . How I wish I could photograph the scene I am delighting in! . . . During the sermon I can hear Monsignor Conaty's voice . . . but a group of reporters are comparing notes near me, and so I can give you no extracts, but I am sure a verbatim report will be secured. . . . There are about five hundred persons seated in the body of the chapel on small chairs borrowed from a hall in the city. . . .

Some belated priests are in the corridor; six reporters are taking notes; the ushers (fine gentlemen) are standing at the chapel door—thus far there has been not the slightest hitch or slip. The sisters of North Capitol Street are in a side sacristy; Sisters M. Borgia, Georgiana, Agnes Mary and Mary Euphrasia are with Superior Julia. Sister Lidwine, S.H., and the Trinity Community are behind them."

Upstairs the caterers are busy. They have laid thirty tables in the lecture hall, and down the long corridor there are covers for two hundred and ten guests. I went up to look at them so as to tell you just what it is like. . . .

General Vincent is placing cards at the plates. He is usher for the President at the White House and his staff of assistants include such men as the Head of the District of Columbia and Maurice F. Egan. . . .[6]

Other points of view can be gained from letters and later actions of those present. The U.S. Commissioner of Education included Monsignor Conaty's sermon in his annual official report and President M. Carey Thomas gathered her Bryn Mawr students in assembly to tell of the new college and urge them to do anything they could to encourage it.

"Monsignor Martinelli, like all people of importance" writes Sister Mary Borgia, "is very simple. He speaks English with difficulty. I met Father Teeling escorting the Secretary of State through the building. In reply to a remark of mine the reverend gentleman said "We have Trinity College now

6. *Reapers*, December 1900, pp. 127–130.

and we must make the best of it." . . . Secretary Hay seemed very much amused."

"At the afternoon reception, a lady appeared in a black bonnet close to her face with fine white muslin fluting inside. She looked very cute. . . . Later she was introduced as a lay sister from Georgetown, accompanying the Senior Class, about twelve in number."

"Father Clark of Providence, seemed very much interested. At least, four times I met him showing persons the house."

The next day the students had a holiday and the Sisters slept late—until *6:00 a.m.*! By Monday, college life was in its regular full swing.

From the perspective of more than seven decades, the first year, after the extraordinary event of the Dedication, developed for the college at least four enduring characteristics. First, deep-seated concern on the part of faculty, administration and staff Sisters not on the faculty, for the academic and physical welfare of the individual student, for providing suitable living facilities, for setting standards, curriculum and teaching methods of a level comparable to the best in contemporary collegiate education. Second, the motivation of the students that kept them conscientiously at study through long hours, though not always without protest, but without need of the frequent advice of eminent visitors to "work hard."[7] Third, the constant stream, through that year especially, but continuing in succeeding years, of eminent visitors: statesmen who had heard of the college, friends from "home" of the Ladies of the Auxiliary Board, Bishops from all parts of the United States and from abroad, pastors or friends from all the cities where Sisters of Notre Dame taught, parents or older sisters with possible applicants for the next year, any important academic or ecclesiastic visitor to the Catholic University accompanied by Dr. Conaty, Dr. Garrigan, Dr. Pace, Dr. Shahan or Dr. Kerby, Sisters of many religious orders, and faculty members from Catholic University and Georgetown College. Fourth, an appreciation of the educational and cultural advantages of the location in Washington, D.C.

On December 3, all the students went to the Capitol where they "attended the opening of Congress at 12:00 noon. They left the college at 10:30 a.m., returned at 2:30 p.m. Classes 3 to 6 p.m." (Dean's Notebook.) On December 8, the anniversary of the laying of the cornerstone of the Main Building, the chapel was moved from the small room in South Hall to the large hall on the second floor at the southwest corner of "the college building." (Room 250) The *Annals* note a "Civic holiday"

7. The chapter on Student Life will treat in more detail the activities, social and academic, of the early students.

On campus, c. 1904.

on the twelfth for the centenary of Washington City. Study continued earnestly all during that last month of the nineteenth century as students and faculty worked to make up for the late opening date. No Christmas vacation had been planned so that when a week's respite from class was announced, all but four students stayed to participate fully with the Sisters in the Christmas and New Year celebrations in the permanent (until 1910) "new chapel." Enthusiastic reminiscences of students who stayed described that vacation as "best ever."

One of the Sisters writes more specifically:

> "December 21, Friday. Dr. Shahan's Church History lecture on History of the feast of Christmas. . . . Vacation began at noon. . . . All but four students stayed at the college. . . . Miss Johnston of Milwaukee and Miss Linehan of Connecticut started for home on the 20th. . . . E. Parsons and N. Mahoney left in the afternoon for Philadelphia." (Annals I).

"Dr. Garrigan had presented each student a nicely printed booklet "Lead Kindly Light" as a souvenir of the first Christmas at Trinity." (Dean's Notebook.)

There was a solemn high midnight mass celebrated by Dr. William Kerby, the Sisters' Chaplain, assisted as acolyte by his friend Dr. Shea, Professor of Physics at Catholic University. Dr. Garrigan, the students' Chaplain and Vice-Rector of the University came in the early morning for three Christmas masses. At all of these both Sisters and students joyfully assisted. The rest of the week was given over to more mundane rejoicing as well as to preparation for the New Year which would usher in the Twentieth Century.

On New Year's Eve:

> "At 3 p.m. the students offered their New Year greeting to Sister Superior Julia and the community. Miss Bugg played an overture, Miss Blanche Gavin delivered a salutatory; Miss Alice Gray read a little poem, an offering of good wishes that had been written for the occasion by Alice Wasserbach and Miss Dooley read an original address. They sang two choruses—the Holy City and Lead Kindly Light and Miss Rotterman played a piano solo. Sister Superior Julia made a pleasant little address and it was all over by four o'clock." (Annals I).

Dr. Garrigan celebrated the midnight mass to welcome the new century and "preached an enthusiastic sermon in which he pictured the future of Trinity." During the day, while the faculty were receiving the many distinguished visitors "to pay New Year Calls" the students had "all gone down (to the White House) to see the diplomats as they offered formal greetings to the President."

On January 3, 1901, classes were resumed "with full attendance." The Dean's Notebook proclaims as heading for its January entries: "*20th Century*." Probably the best extant summary of the first academic year is the Dean's Report "spread upon the minutes" of the Auxiliary Board at its first meeting at the college in April, and repeated in somewhat more polished form to the Advisory Board at its first meeting in May. It is quoted here from the minutes of Auxiliary Board of Regents of Trinity College.

"What has the College done?

1. Kept its promise to open on November 7, 1900.
   Formed and opened its classes on November 8, 1900.
   The Course of Lectures on Church History was opened by Rev. T. J. Shahan D.D. on November 8.
   The course in Philosophy was opened by Rev. E. Pace D.D. on November 12.
   The course in Religion was opened by V. Rev. Doctor Garrigan on January 10, 1901.

Extra Lectures

2a The students attended the Course of Advent Sermons given in St. Aloysuis Church by Rev. F. Pardow.

b Attended the Catholic University Extension Course during the Fall and Winter Terms.

c Had two lectures on Ancient and Modern Greece at the College given by Professor Laotsakos.

d Had two illustrated lectures by the V. Rev. Dr. Griffin on the Isle of Man and Venice.

e Had Course of 4 lectures on Art, and 4 on Hygiene given by two members of the faculty.

f Attended a French lecture on Modern French Literature through the kindness of Mr. Boeufre, Chancellor of the French Legation.

Social Life

Attended matinees and saw Sarah Bernhardt and Maude Adams in the French and English versions of l'Aiglon.

Have attended University Celebrations of Patronal Feasts on December 8 and March 7. Teas at homes of ladies of Auxiliary Board. The President of the Class met the Literary Society and heard a lecture from Mr. George Kennan at the home of the Recording Secretary.

Have receptions every Friday P.M.

Have receptions and serve tea on Sundays from 3 to 5 p.m.

Have visited with chaperone:

The Government buildings, Corcoran Art Gallery, Inauguration Ceremonies, Mount Vernon on Easter Monday.

The regularity and morality of the students is of the most satisfactory character, indeed it is exemplary.

"They are happy, united and industrious" says V. Rev. Dr. Garrigan the Chaplain and Confessor of the College.

Some Rules formulated as need showed itself:

1. No invitations for evening entertainments may be accepted by the students as a body.
2. No invitations for all the students are accepted, unless presented through the President or Dean.
3. Gentlemen who are strangers must present letters or credentials of character to the President or Dean.
4. Saturday is the college holiday unless another holiday occurs during the week.

"They enjoy the fullest liberty consistent with Order and Duty" (Dr. Garrigan).

What are the Needs of the College

I. Endowments for Lecture Courses
Physical Laboratory
Chemical Laboratory
Botany and Biology

II. Furniture for new students rooms, as tables, chairs, bureaus, bookcases
III. Geological and mineral specimens, maps and charts.
IV. Very pressing needs are:
a telephone and fire alarm.

(signed) Sr. Josephine Ignatius
Dean of the Faculty

The new catalogue for 1901–1902, called by the Dean "Our New Year Book," went to the printer April 29.[8] The Advisory Board met May 9. Year-end examinations in all courses were scheduled May 20–May 31. Items from the *Dean's Notebook* conclude our record of the first academic year.

"June 2. Trinity Sunday. High Mass. Students attended University to hear the Baccalareate Sermon.

June 3. Trinity Monday. Pic-Nic on the grounds for the students.

June 5. Students attended the Commencement at University.

June 6. Closing exercises. Apostolic Delegate presided. Address by Dr. Garrigan. Student speeches and musical selections.

This finished the year's academic work. D. G. for all His help."

In the next three years the college reached full stature with four year courses of study; Sophomore, Junior and Senior classes added to the original Freshmen until the Conferring of Degrees on the class of 1904 (always the "top" class) June, in the new O'Connor auditorium. Several of the enduring student "societies" date from this period, notably the Glee Club, Dramatics, a Literary Society with Greek letter title and the Sodality. A student advisory council, a first small step toward student government, conferred earnestly and sometimes explosively with the administration about regulations. "The Corps of Professors and Teachers," as the faculty was still called as late as 1910, increased to meet the needs of the expanding curriculum.

The O'Connor[9] gift of their large art collection and the building to house it was formally accepted by the Board of Trustees, October 20, 1903. Work of this center part of the Main Building, O'Connor Hall, progressed rapidly so that the gallery could be solemnly dedicated with an address on Art History by Dr. Thomas Shahan during the first Commencement Week, and degrees conferred in the auditorium. The front door and foyer with the adjoining parlors and the rooms above comprised a second O'Connor gift and were not completed until 1905

8. For greater detail see chapters on faculty and curriculum.
9. O'Connor gift will be included in more detail in a later chapter.

Walking a requirement. One hour a day, out of doors.

Baseball, 1905. On the Aventine.

Student Room, c. 1905.

Picnic to Rock Creek Park.

Dramatics, 1904. Antigone *on the site of the present Fine Arts Wing.*

when the first students who were not "pioneers" had entered college. It serves, therefore, as a fitting symbol of the beginning of a new era. Let it stand with its inscription "Collegium Deo Uni Trinoque Sacrum" as the gateway from the Pioneer years to the present.

Sister Mary Patricia Butler's *Historical Sketch of Trinity College 1897–1925* covers accurately and well the first quarter century of that time. This history will not duplicate her work but will begin at once the chapters with differentiated subject matter proposed earlier.

PART II

The Core

CHAPTER FOUR

Administration and Faculty

THE ORIGINAL faculty of Trinity College, called at least until 1910 "The Corps of Professors and Teachers," numbered thirteen including the President and the Dean of the College. Three of these, "The Professors," were from the Catholic University: Dr. Philip J. Garrigan, Vice-Rector of the University, who taught religion and acted as the students' chaplain until he was appointed Bishop of Sioux City, Iowa in 1902; and the two brilliant young scholars, Dr. Thomas Shahan who introduced the German Seminar Method and taught Church History until he was appointed Rector of the University in 1909; and Dr. Edward A. Pace who introduced the scientific, experimental approach to psychology from the beginning and taught philosophy at Trinity until 1924. These three had been among the co-founders of the college and continued their interest in and work for it all their lives. Close cooperation and sharing of faculty between the two institutions Trinity and Catholic University continued until the late 1930's when accrediting agencies objected to "over-lapping" faculties.[1]

The other original faculty members were Sisters of Notre Dame, well educated women, experienced teachers of "advanced students" in the academies, each competent in her field. Only one had a degree when the college opened, though they had been gathered at Waltham, Massachusetts for courses with Professors from Harvard and M.I.T., and continued "in service" study with Catholic University professors, soon earning the official parchments that still seem to signify to accrediting agencies that faculty members are competent.

Because the catalogue did not include a list of faculty until 1911 and did not name the Sisters individually until 1922, it has been necessary to search out these early members in faculty minutes and other college documents, in Notre Dame community records, in the recollections of their students, and in their own writings (according to custom never signed except as S.N.D. or "by a Sister of Notre Dame"). There were,

1. It is interesting to note that thirty years later, in the 1960's the sharing of faculty was one of the *new* ideas suggested for alleviating the problem of faculty shortage in higher education.

the first year, twenty-two Sisters of Notre Dame in the Trinity community of whom ten were faculty members. The devoted, indispensable work and unique influence of the others in the making of the college will be described in Part III of this book.

The ten Sisters of Notre Dame on the original faculty were:

Sister Lidwine (Mary Lee) of the Sacred Heart, President and Superior of the Community (1900–1902)
Sister Josephine Ignatius (Alice Tierney),[2] Dean of the College (1900–1903)
Sister Anne de Marie (Ann Elizabeth Roche), Secretary of the College, Art (1900–1902)
Sister Mary Josephine (Anna Short), English Language and Literature (1900–1903)
Sister Raphael of the Sacred Heart, M.D., (Lucy Pike), Greek[3] (1929–1940)
Sister Mary (Margaret Henretty), Latin—Dean (1903–1921)
Sister Odilia (Mary E. Funke), German (1900–1937)
Sister Blandina of the Sacred Heart (Abigail Shea),[4] Mathematics, later Physics (1900–1904)
Sister Anne Madeleine (Julie Rose Guerin), French (1900–1919)
Sister Mary Hilda (E. McDonald) Music (1900–1901)

Of these Sisters Raphael, Mary, Odilia and Anne Madeleine remained at Trinity College for many years. The President, Sister Lidwine, was succeeded in 1902 by Sister Georgiana who had been associated with the college planning since 1897.[5] In 1903, Sister Josephine Ignatius, because of ill health, passed on the office of Dean to Sister Mary who had accompanied her in the months of study and observation of colleges in England in 1899 and who continued as Dean until 1921, known to nearly a quarter century of students as "Sister Mary Dean". The "Sister from England", Sister Mary Josephine from Notre Dame College, Liverpool, remained on loan at Trinity sharing her knowledge of Old, Middle, and Modern English language and literature until 1903. Sister Anne de Marie, an artist who had been a consultant all through the planning for the original building, established the first art studio and gave lectures on art history while acting as Secretary of the college until February 1902. She was replaced in both these positions by Sister Florence Louise (Catherine Delany) whose imposing presence was known to Trinity students for the next twenty-five years.

2. *Obit. Record*, June 1922, p. 173.
3. Cf. p. 89, pp. 108–111.
4. *Obit. Record*, April 1914, p. 108 (insert).
5. Cf. Chapter II: *passim*.

Early faculty. Student Album, May Day, 1908.

Sister Blandina,[6] described by contemporaries as a brilliant teacher, guided the advanced mathematics students through to graduation, established the physics laboratory and with the help of professors from the Catholic University, prepared her successor, Sister Marie Cecilia (Josephine Mangold) in mathematics before leaving the college in 1904.

Sister Raphael of the Sacred Heart, the teacher of Greek, was a practicing physician, one of the few women M.D.'s from Boston University before she became a Sister of Notre Dame in 1890. Besides her Greek classes in those early years, she gave lectures on hygiene and acted as health consultant for both students and faculty. With Dr. Thomas Verner Moore she began the biology department in 1912 and taught that subject until her appointment to the presidency of the college in 1920. Her biography is one of the *Three Against the Wind* in Sister

6. *Obit. Record*, April 1914, p. 108 (insert).

Angela Elizabeth Keenan's 1973 book, in which many affectionate reminiscences of Sister Raphael by her students show the influence of her knowledge and her personality on the college through its first quarter century and beyond.

Parisian born and educated, Sister Anne-Madeleine brought to the college faculty many years of teaching experience, especially that of directing the post-graduate "Year Entirely in French" at the Academy of Notre Dame, Philadelphia. She established high standards of achievement for credit in the French Department which she ruled firmly, but gently, until her death in 1920.[7]

Sister Odilia, Boston born daughter of German parents, an enthusiastic, conscientious German scholar, established high standards for the language and literature courses of the German Department which she directed—with one break—until her retirement in 1937. Throughout the early years of the college, Sister Odilia continued her scholarly work. She earned her doctorate in German from the Catholic University in 1916, just before the United States entered World War I and German studies were, shortsightedly but effectively, wiped out of American education. Sister Odilia became, during the years of the German black-out, the Registrar of the college, taking over the records from the Dean's office and organizing a separate office according to then current practice. She also taught some religion classes at that time, but as soon as possible after the war she set herself to re-build her life's work. Though German never reached its former eminence in the college, the department was again firmly established. She died on the eve of World War II before she could know of the adoption of a more enlightened policy of encouraging rather than obliterating the "enemy's language."

The original faculty members were joined in the succeeding years by others until in June 1906 when the student enrollment was 104, the President could report to the Advisory Board that the faculty numbered 26, seven "Professors" from Catholic University and nineteen Sisters of Notre Dame. There were lay men and women teaching single courses as early as 1903 but the first two full-time lay faculty members, Miss Elsie Kernan and Senora Rita Lesca de Ruiz, joined the faculty after its first decade. They are listed in the catalogue of 1912–13, though Miss Kernan, at least, began teaching in the fall of 1910.

Most of the Sisters of Notre Dame on the faculty during the twenty years before the catalogue listed their names, will be mentioned in connection with their departments in the chapter on curriculum. A few, however, who as young religious joined the faculty in 1901, 1902 and

7. Cf. "Historical Sketch," *Trinity College Record*, Vol. 20, 1926, p. 84. Retirement 1919, President's Report, May 31, 1919. *Obit. Record*, December 1919, p. 248.

1903, who attained tenure before that word was in vogue, and who so strongly influenced the educational program that they acquired legendary status, in spite of the era of anonymity, deserve special mention. Of these, Sister Julie de la Sainte Famille (just try to remember *do-la-sol-fa-me,* she used to say), *the* Sister Julie of English 15 fame, came at the beginning of the year 1901–1902.

Still in her twenties, with a keen analytical mind, dry wit, boundless energy, enthusiasm for English literature and exact expression of thought, she taught with, while she learned from, Sisters Mary Josephine and Mary Patricia. Decades before the "New Criticism" Sister Julie was emphasizing the need of studying the work itself to understand it, not just learn about it. She guided the students who established a literary magazine, *The Trinity College Record,* in 1907, and the *Trinilogue* in 1911. For more than twenty years she dominated the English Department, before leaving Trinity in 1922 for Emmanuel College in Boston. She returned in 1929 to teach a new generation of Trinity students until elected in 1938 to represent the American Sisters of Notre Dame on the General Council in Namur, Belgium. With the same indomitable spirit that animated her teaching she remained at her post during the whole of World War II, having refused to be evacuated with other Americans when war broke out.[8] Her old age was spent in her native Massachusetts working meticulously on her scholarly history of the Rule and Constitutions of the Sisters of Notre Dame de Namur. For hundreds of alumnae Sister Julie symbolizes the best of English teaching at Trinity College.[9]

That year, too, Sister Marie Cecilia came to assist in teaching German while continuing her study of more advanced courses in mathematics with Sister Blandina.[10] From 1904 to her death in 1934 her gentle, kindly personality as well as her store of mathematical knowledge were at the service of generations of mathematics and science students who found in her not only a scholarly, demanding teacher, but an interested friendly adviser through college years and long after.

In September 1901, Sister Gertrude of the Blessed Sacrament (Margaret Dempsey) was appointed Treasurer of the College, a position she held until 1935, though from 1932 failing health made her assume a more and more consultative job. Sister Gertrude had been one of the original incorporators of Trinity College in 1897 and, through close association with Sister Mary Euphrasia Taylor, had continued her interest in and work for its foundation and lasting welfare. She had a

8. Her description of the bombing of the Notre Dame Motherhouse in Namur, May 1940, is printed in the *Alumnae Journal,* Nov. 1940, pp. 5–11. Namur was bombed a second time in 1944.
9. Obituary by Elizabeth Hanlon '40, *Alumnae Journal,* Spring, 1958, p. 129.
10. *Annals I,* Jan. 1902, Ms. T.C.A.

close association with the Auxiliary Board of Regents from its beginning which continued until her death.[11] For years she was the chief link between that Board and the President of the college.

The Science Courses were initiated in September 1902. In preparation for this step Sister Louise of St. Stanislaus Delamare had come in May 1901 to spend a year developing Botany courses and equipping the "Botanical Laboratory" in what is now Room 244. She continued to teach the Botany courses after the department became Biology with the addition of zoology in 1912, until the year before her death in 1918. Sister Mary Isabelle Mahoney arrived in April 1902, full of youthful enthusiasm, to establish the Chemistry department. The courses and "Chemical Laboratory"[12] flourished under her direction until 1921 when she entered on a short term as Dean of Students before going to Emmanuel College in 1924. To her deep interest in photography the historian owes many contemporary pictures of students and college activities for the first twenty years.

Another of the "greats" who joined the college ranks in 1902 was Sister Mary Patricia Butler who came for English and to take charge of the growing library. That she was a popular, effective teacher may be seen from the statement of Marie Madden '08 written many years later.

> As professor of English Literature and particularly of Poetry, she opened wide horizons on the realities of life with her pungent criticisms and her sense of poetic values, focussing a shaft of light from a classical past where the eighteenth century seemed as fresh as the twentieth and the Bible as vivid as today." (*Alumnae Journal*, Vol. 14, May, 1941, No. 3)

Increasing deafness forced Sister Mary Patricia to give up teaching to make the library her full-time occupation. The excellence of her work may be judged by *A History of the Trinity College Library* by Sister Dorothy Beach, third college librarian.[13] Not only did she build up a solid curriculum-oriented collection and the nucleus of a rare book collection, but found time to write. To her we owe the *Historical Sketch of Trinity College, 1897–1925* as well as short articles in the *Catholic Historical Review* and a thick volume, *Notre Dame Foundations in the United States to 1925.*

11. Sister Gertrude's mother, aunts, and sisters were members of the Board and listed in the Association of Founders. Five of her nieces and three grandnieces are Trinity alumnae. Cf. a brief biography of Sister Gertrude by her niece Mrs. Charles Fahy '19, T.C.A.
12. This laboratory, initially equipped in large part by Bishops Harkins of Providence and Garrigan of Sioux City and materially supported by them for many years, occupied the east end of South Hall until the opening of the Science Building in 1941.
13. Catholic University of America, 1951. Unpublished M.A. dissertation.

Before 1904 graduated Dr. John Creagh had replaced Dr. Garrigan[14] as teacher of Christian Doctrine, delivering his "scholarly series of Sunday Morning Lectures." Dr. Charles P. Grannan, the Scripture scholar who had given "valuable aid in preparing a systematic course in Biblical Science" was teaching Scripture courses. Dr. William Kerby had begun Sociology. Dr. Mitchell Carroll, Dean of Classical Languages at Columbian University (now George Washington) and Miss Dorothy Sipe, a Bryn Mawr alumna and a Ph.D. candidate at Columbian taught Senior Greek and Latin respectively. The number of Notre Dame members had grown to sixteen. Dr. Thomas Shields had begun teacher education with "Principles and Methods of Pedagogy." Dr. Shahan and Dr. Pace aided him by giving "Ancient and Medieval Education" and "History of Modern Education," while Church History and philosophy courses remained under their direction. Of the last two, the President reported in 1904 that their "lectures throughout the four years have been most potent and most successful in laying the foundation of thorough scholarship, many-sided culture and true Catholic spirit."

One other young Sister of Notre Dame who came to Trinity in the pioneer period was Sister Marie Louis Hummel. Beginning in 1903 she was a student of Dr. Grannan and Dr. Shields. She became their assistant later and succeeded both on the faculty. For more than twenty years she taught Scripture to all Freshmen and Sophomores. From the midteens to 1927 she taught education courses, and after the death of Dr. Shields in 1920, directed the department. Through conscientious in-service study she earned the Ph.D. in education from Catholic University in 1924. She was Dean of Studies 1932 to 1941 when she retired from the faculty to become, for six years, Superior of the community of Sisters of Notre Dame at Trinity. In her old age Sister Marie Louis returned to live at Trinity until her death in 1968.[15]

The Trinity College faculty has consistently through the years controlled curriculum development and greatly influenced book selection for the library. The results of this perennial interest in what is best for "today's student" may be seen in the chapter on curriculum. The composition, growth, and organization of the faculty itself is the concern of this chapter. Extant documents from the Dean's office or excerpts from President's Reports make it possible to compare these aspects at intervals from 1900–1974. In the earliest years the structure was simple. The President held ultimate responsibility for the college as a whole but delegated its practical day-to-day operation to the Dean, making her in

14. A tribute to Dr. Garrigan appears in the description of the farewell to him in the ms. *The Woman*, second issue, May 25, 1902. T.C.A.
15. *Obit. Trinity College Newsletter*, Feb., 1968, p. 7; *Alumnae Journal*, Winter, 1968, p. 79.

effect the chief executive officer. The "teachers and professors" taught, the latter usually with an assistant to take roll and mark papers.

From October 1900, regular faculty meetings were held and minutes kept. For the first few years the Sisters, "the resident faculty," met weekly on Sunday morning with the Dean or President presiding. They were joined by the "Professors" at times during the year when especially important matters, such as curriculum or course changes, or degree requirements were on the agenda (Cf. for example, Faculty Minutes, February 16, March 23, 1901). By 1920 meetings were scheduled less frequently, monthly as a rule, and continued so until 1940. The "Professors" were consulted, but were usually not present. The growing number of laywomen, with a few men, on the faculty met with department groups or learned faculty decisions through their department heads. Full faculty meetings, with all expected to be present, began in 1941. They were held quarterly until 1965, and monthly, during the academic year, since then. Increasingly, the faculty works through committees of interdepartmental membership which report to the full faculty.

Through all these years the size and composition of the faculty has changed gradually, but radically. Until the 1940's no differentiation of full, part-time or "shared" members can be discerned in faculty listings. In the 1911–1912 catalogue a faculty list appears for the first time. The next year, 1912–1913, the list included the six "Professors", two lay women, and the departments in which Sisters of Notre Dame taught, but no names of individual Sisters. This format continued until the 1922–1923 catalogue lists the complete faculty in the order of appointment, but without ranking. Not until 1941 were the conventional academic ranks used for the Trinity Faculty. In the era of the 1940's, too, the title "lecturer" was given to part-time teachers who held full-time positions in other institutions, including Catholic University, and who presented written approval of their "home" administration to teach at Trinity.

The faculty of Trinity, as will be seen from Table I, has always been predominantly women, as befits a college for women. Except in the early 1930's, the percentage of women has never fallen below 70% of the total faculty. Even at its lowest ebb it was more than half, 57%. The number of Sisters of Notre Dame increased for the years cited in the table, except the last; but not in proportion to the growth of the faculty. In 1969–70 they comprised only 32% of the total faculty. The percentage has been even lower since then. In the decade of the 1950's the analysis of the composition of the faculty became more complex so that yearly statements of faculty statistics were issued, grouping the total faculty according to various principles of division. Three of these statements are reproduced here to give a more comprehensive view of the

TABLE I. *Aspects of Composition of the Faculty, 1900–1974*

Year	Sisters	Lay Women	C. U. Prof.	Other Clergy	Lay Men	Total	Percentage Women	Percentage S.N.D.
1900–1901	10		3			13	76	76
1903–1904	16	1 (G. W.)	6		1 (G. W.)	24	71	67
1912–1913	20	2	6			28	79	71
1922–1923	23	11	11		1 (C. U.)	46	78	50
1932–1933	21	11	17	1	4	56	57	38
1949–1950	24	25	3	3	2	57	85	42
1959–1960	30	32		6 priests	6	74	84	41
1969–1970	37	50		3 clergy	28	118	73	32
1973–1974	31	44		3	29	107	70	29

Note: Administration and part-time members included without differentiation in all totals in this table.

composition of the faculty in the last twenty years (see Tables II, III, and IV).

Organization and Administration

Robert L. Williams writes[16]: "The administration of academic affairs in a college or university is the means of ensuring order and economy in that institution's educational activities. The task does not stop there, however. Orderly and economical operations are admirable only so long as they further the main purpose—education." One continuing benchmark of the Trinity College administration and faculty, which shows through all study of growth and change, is adherence to that "*main purpose—education.*" There has been a deep-seated reluctance to making a distinction between faculty and administration as such. Administrative officers and professional librarians have cherished their faculty membership resisting consistently any division that might separate them from the mainstream of educational endeavor.

> The college's management, affairs and business concerns (1975) are vested in a Board of Trustees numbering not fewer than nine or more than fifteen members. At least one third of the Board's membership is drawn from the Congregation of the Sisters of Notre Dame. The faculty and the student body each elect two non-voting representatives to the Board. Responsibility for the development of academic policies and programs rests primarily with the faculty, which relies heavily on the work of standing committees, most of them including representatives of the administration, the faculty and the student body.[17]

16. Preface to *The Administration of Academic Affairs in Higher Education*, University of Michigan Press, 1965, p. V.
17. Trinity College Catalogue, 1975–76, p. 7.

TABLE II. *Faculty Statistics (1959–1960)*

	N	Full Time	Part Time	Administration (not otherwise counted)
Priests	6	4	2	
Sisters	30	23	5	2
Laymen	6		6	
Lay Women	32	18	11	3
Total:	74	45	24	5

Note: This does not include the two Sisters on leave of absence for study in Europe.

Ranks		Administration with Faculty Status (not ranked)
Professors	13	President
Associate Professors	11	Librarian
Assistant Professors	7	Assistant to Librarian
Instructors	18	Reference Librarian
Lecturers	11	Registrar
Assistants	3	Assistant Registrar
	63	Director of Reading Clinic
		Asst. Dean of Students
		Business Officer
		Doctor
		Placement Director
		11
Total: 74		

The development of administrative organization in the college reflects, with local adaptations, such development in American higher education in general. It is in turn reflected in the changes indicated by the data of Tables I to IV.

The office of the Dean, until 1918 the only administrative office, was divided as need or changing academic usage required. New administrative offices were established to carry on the increasingly complex business of running a college until the faculty statistics of 1969–70 listed seventeen administrative officers, six of whom were lay people. (Table III) The Dean, during the greater part of the first two decades (1903–1921), Sister Mary Henretty, had been, as we have seen, an original faculty member. As the college grew, her office extended. Her experience as an educator, her understanding of the "modern" college girl with a growing need for self determination, her capacity for directing without seeming autocratic or domineering made it possible for her to grow with the office. One function that appears not to have been under the Dean's Office was admissions. The secretary of the college, Sister Anne de Marie followed by Sister Florence Louise, was "admis-

TABLE III. *Trinity College Office of the Dean*

Faculty Statistics – 1969–1970 October, 1969

I. Teaching Faculty by Rank[a]

Rank	Ph.D.	M.A.	B.A.	Totals
Professor	12	2	0	14
Associate Professor	7	8	0	15
Assistant Professor	19	12	1	32
Instructor	0	19	4	23
Lecturer	7	5	2	14
Total Teaching Faculty	45	46	7	98 (incl. 9 on leave)

II. Lay and Religious Faculty: Full-Time and Part-Time

		Full-Time		Part-Time[b]	Totals
Clergymen		1		2	3
Sisters		16 (Teaching) 11 (Administrative) 8 (On leave)		1 (Teaching) 1 (Appointed)	37
Laymen		17 (Teaching) 1 (Administrative)		9 (Teaching) 1 (Appointed)	28
Laywomen		34 (Teaching) 5 (Administrative) 1 (On leave)		9 (Teaching) 1 (Appointed)	50
Totals:	94	68 (Teaching) 9 (On leave) 17 (Administrative)	24	21 (Teaching) 3 (Appointed)	118

TOTALS: Total Faculty: (Teachers and Administrative Officers)

Religious	40
Lay	78
	118

[a]The 45 Ph.D.'s are from 25 universities. Eleven from the Catholic University of America, 3 from Johns Hopkins University, 3 from Georgetown University, 3 from St. Louis University, 2 from George Washington University, 2 from Penn State University, 2 from Columbia University, 2 from Fordham University. The remaining 17 are from the University of Chicago, University of Cincinnati, Duke University, Harvard University, University of Illinois, University of Maryland, The New School for Social Research, Rutgers, the State University, Stanford.

[b]Twenty-one part-time teachers = 7 full-time equivalent. Based on the full-time equivalent, the total teaching faculty numbers 75 (68 full-time, 21 part-time).

sions officer." The latter also assigned students' rooms with the attendant business of signing contracts. The matter of paying bills, of course, came under the authority of the Treasurer. All else concerning students was in the Dean's domain.

TABLE IV. *Trinity College Office of the Dean*

Faculty Statistics–1976–1977 October, 1976

I. Teaching Faculty by Rank

Rank	Ph.D.	M.A./M.S.	B.A./B.S.	Other	Totals
Professor	12	2	0	0	14
Associate Professor	8	4	0	0	12
Assistant Professor	9	3	1	0	13
Instructor	0	8	0	0	8
Lecturer (part-time)	15	25	8	1	49
Total Teaching Faculty	44	42	9	1	96 (includes 2 on leave)

The 44 doctorates held by the teaching faculty are from 24 universities. Ten are from Catholic University, 3 from George Washington University, 2 from Johns Hopkins University, 2 from New York University, 2 from St. Louis University, 2 from Columbia University, 2 from the University of California, 2 from the University of Maryland, 2 from the University of Kentucky, 2 from Georgetown University, and 2 from American University. The remaining thirteen are from the University of Rome, University of Louvain, University of London, New School for Social Research, Ukranian Free University, Yale University, University of Illinois, Fordham University, University of Indiana, University of Pennsylvania, Rutgers University, University of Virginia, and Duke University.

Totals:		Teaching Faculty		Enrollment	
Administrative Officers and Appointed Members	32	Full-time	44	Full-time	
Teaching Faculty	96	Part-time: FTE (52 total)	17	Undergraduates	394
	128	Total (FTE)	61	MAT	19
				PMP	16
					429
				Part-time	160
		Faculty-Student Ratio: 1:9.7		Total (FTE)	589

II. Lay and Religious Faculty: Full-Time and Part-Time

	Full-Time	Part-Time	Totals
Clergymen	1 (Teaching) 1 (Administrative) 0 (On leave)	3 (Teaching) 0 (Administrative) 0 (On leave)	5
Sisters	14 (Teaching) 14 (Administrative) 1 (On leave)	2 (Teaching) 3 (Administrative) 1 (On leave)	35
Laymen	5 (Teaching) 3 (Administrative) 0 (On leave)	21 (Teaching) 0 (Administrative) 0 (On leave)	29
Laywomen	23 (Teaching) 10 (Administrative) 0 (On leave)	25 (Teaching) 1 (Administrative) 0 (On leave)	59

(continued)

TABLE IV. *(continued)*

	Full-Time	Part-Time	Totals
	43 (Teaching)	51 (Teaching)	
	28 (Administrative)	4 (Administrative)	
	1 (On leave)	1 (On leave)	
Totals:	72	56	128

TOTALS:	Total Faculty: (Teachers and Administrative)	
	Religious	40
	Lay	88
		128

Comparative Faculty Statistics

	1978–79	1979–80	1980–81	1981–82	1982–83	1983–84
Teaching Faculty Size Total	82	79	82	83	87	86
Full-time Equivalent	54	55	55	57	60	60
Administration and Support Personnel	25	24	23	22	21	20
% F-T faculty with doctorate	57%	55%	65%	71%	71%	73%
% all faculty with doctorates	45%	43%	52%	59%	60%	60%
% tenured faculty	52%	45%	46%	46%	44%	40%
Faculty-Student Ratio	1:10.8	1:11.7	1:11.9	1:11.7	1:10.6	1:9.4

Sister Odilia's taking over of the records in 1918 when she took the first steps toward establishing a separate Registrar's Office began the division of the Dean's duties. In 1921, when Sister Mary left Trinity, the Dean's work was reorganized. The supervision of studies (curriculum, faculty, student programs of study) became a separate office. All other aspects of student life remained under the Dean. It is regrettable that in the process of modernization the first title assigned to the new office was Assistant Dean, because the idea of subordination of function entered then and was long prevalent. Though the title soon became Dean of Studies, and the offices were co-ordinate for years, working together for the good of the students, the title of Dean remained in the non-academic office until 1943 when the catalogue lists a Dean of Students and a Dean of Studies. In 1965 the Academic Dean became "Dean of the College" for the first time since the division of 1921.

In spite of later recognized anomalies in the organizational chart for those years, the Deans devoted themselves to the good of Trinity College students. Their achievements as well as the difficulties of their offices will be reflected in the chapters on Student Affairs and on Curriculum. The product of their educational endeavors will appear in the

Sister Catherine Marie Lee and Jane O'Boyle.

chapter on Alumnae as well as in the description of the administrations of the presidents with whom they served. Their names and the dates of their tenure of office given on p. 101 provide a source for reference.

The records of students' marks and academic status were kept in the Dean's Office until 1918. At that time Sister Odilia (Funke), prevented from teaching German by World War I regulations, organized a separate Registrar's Office and became the first Registrar. Admissions activities continued to be carried on by the Secretary of the College, Sister Florence Louise, until she retired and left Trinity in the late 1920's.[18] Sister Margaret of the Trinity (Sweeney) succeeded as Registrar with the admissions work transferred to the Registrar's Office. After her

18. For Lowell, Mass., where she lived in retirement until her death in 1932.

sudden death, Sister Mary Mercedes (Robb) became Registrar and served from 1935 to 1954. In the latter part of that time Sister Catherine Marie Lee was her assistant. Sister Sheila Doherty, with Miss Jane O'Boyle as assistant, replaced Sister Mary Mercedes in 1955. Sister Mary Lawlor was Director of Admissions from 1952–1957. In 1961, Sister Sheila again divided the work of the Registrar's Office, setting up a separate Admissions office with herself as Director until 1969 when she was replaced by Sister Patricia Langan. Miss Jane O'Boyle became Registrar. In 1968 Sister Catherine Marie Lee became Registrar and Miss O'Boyle became Associate Dean. Sister Catherine Marie was the Registrar until the late 1970's.

Deans of Trinity College
1900–1981

Sister Josephine Ignatius (Anna Short)	1900–1903
Sister Mary (Margaret Henretty)	1903–1921

Deans of Students

Sister Mary Isabelle, M.A. (Mary Mahony)	1921–1924
Sister Wilfred du S.C., Ph.D. (Elsie Parsons)	1924–1932
Sister Angela Elizabeth, Ph.D. (Angela Keenan)	1932–1942
Sister Ann Francis, Ph.D. (Catherine Hoey)	1942–1961
Sister Marie Joan, M.A. (Joan Kentz)	1961–1963
Sister Janice Marie, M.A. (Janice Moran)	1963–1965
Sister Ann Gormly, Ph.D. (was Sister Francis)	1965–1971
Miss Winifred Coleman, M.A.	1971–1980

Dean of Studies

Sister Berchmans Julia, M.A. (Julia Shumacher)	1921–1932
Sister Marie Louis, Ph.D. (Alma Hummel)	1932–1941
Sister Columba, Ph.D. (Catherine Mullaly)	1942–1953
Vice President for Academic Affairs	1953–1965

Academic Dean

Sister Elizabeth Woods, Ph.D.	1965–1970
Sister Margaret Finnegan, Ph.D.	1970–1974
Sister Mary Ann Cook, D. Phil.	1974–1978
Jean Willke, Ph.D.	1978–1981
Karen Weis Kershenstein, Ph.D.	1981–1985

In its first eighty years Trinity College has had eleven presidents, eight of whom were also Superiors of the Notre Dame community resident at the college. They have all been, as even the 1968 revision of the by-laws of the Board of Trustees requires, Sisters of Notre Dame de Namur. The complete list follows.

Presidents of Trinity College, 1900–1982

Sister Lidwine of Sacred Heart (and Superior)		1900–1902	Mary Lee
Sister Georgiana (and Superior)		1902–1907	Bridget Flannelly
Sister Julia of the Passion (and Superior)		1907–1911	Anna M. Overend
Sister Catherine Aloysius (and Superior)		1911–1920	Anna Crotty
Sister Raphael of the Sacred Heart (and Superior)		1920–1929	Lucy Pike
Sister Julia of the Trinity (and Superior)		1929–1932	Edith McDonald
Sister Berchmans Julia (and Superior)		1932–1940	Julia Shumacher
Sister Catherine Dorothea		1940–1953	Mary Fox
Sister Berchmans Julia (Superior)	1940–1941		
Sister Marie Louis (Superior)	1941–1947		
Sister Marie Claire (Superior)	1947–1948		
Sister Evelyn Marie (Superior)	1948–1953		
Sister Mary Patrick (Superior)		1953–1959	Mary Furdon
Sister Margaret		1959–1975	Margaret Claydon
Sister Berchmans Julia (Superior)	1959–1962		
Sister Ann Francis (Superior)	1962–1968		
Sister Joan Bland (Superior)	1968–1969		
Community Goverment	1969–		
Sister Rose Ann Fleming		1975–1981	
Sister Donna Jurick		1982–	

Note: Sister Dorothy McCormick was acting president 1981–1982

The first President, Sister Lidwine, though one of the youngest when she took office[19] remained at Trinity only a year and three months. The achievement of her administration was the actual opening of the college and guiding it through the first academic year into the second. She had the difficult job of being the pioneer leader in a work in the planning of which she had not been so closely involved as most of her associates. During the first academic year she had the benefit of the experience of the foundresses. Sister Julia spent most of her time at Trinity providing a source of strength as well as of wise counsel. Sister Mary Euphrasia was still at the convent on North Capitol Street, directing the Ladies Auxiliary Board, and treasurer of the Board of Trustees, a mixed blessing for the new president. A competent administrator, Sister Lidwine must have felt herself hampered that first year by the control of the Board of Trustees, by the earlier experience of Sister Euphrasia and the more dominant members of the Auxiliary Board.

Soon after the death of Sister Julia in November, 1901, trouble surfaced over the management of the finances and especially over the relationship with the Ladies Auxiliary Board of Regents. In January and February, 1902, led by the indomitable Miss Olive Risley-Seward, thirteen members of the Ladies Auxiliary Board of Regents resigned. The

19. She was 40 years old in 1900. Sister Margaret Claydon was 36 when she became president. Sister Raphael was 62 and the others in their 40's or 50's.

Board of Trustees held a special historic session February 17, 1902. The minutes might be called, "The case of Sister Lidwine vs. Ladies Board." Each trustee's opinion about the relation of the Auxiliary Board to the Board of Trustees was recorded. Discord within the Auxiliary Board, its division into parties, the "apparent impossibility of securing a peaceful election of a new President" led to the decision to suspend its meetings indefinitely. Sister Lidwine resigned as President of the College. Sister Mary Euphrasia resigned as a member of the Board of Trustees and as its Treasurer for five years.[20] The foundation years were over.

Neither of these resignations was an abrupt move. Sister Euphrasia had returned in January from a five month stay in Europe with the announcement on February 8 that she would be going to a new assignment as Superior of the Notre Dame Academy on Court Street in Cincinnati. She left Washington after the Board meeting on February 17, 1902, having come to Trinity to say goodbye the day before. During her years in Cincinnati and later in California she never lost interest in the college.

College life had continued smoothly through the first semester of 1901–1902.[21] On January 22 the students and faculty enjoyed an illustrated lecture on Scotland by Dr. Griffin. Sister Lidwine had made herself an expert in the operation of the college's up-to-date projector, the Magic Lantern, and was, we suppose, the lecturer's chief assistant on this occasion. Examinations and the students' retreat followed. On February 6, she told the Sisters that she was expecting a new assignment. February 21 she "took formal leave of the students in St. Jerome's Hall with the faculty present." Miss McGorrisk gave a "farewell address" and roses were presented.[22] Then on February 24 Sister Lidwine of the Sacred Heart, first president of the college, left Washington for Chicopee, Massachusetts. The annals of the community record a touching departure ceremony.

The next day Sister Georgiana, the new president, arrived from Waltham, Massachusetts, "accompanied by two Sisters, a novice (to study)—and nine trunks!" Sister Georgiana had been closely associated with the early plans for Trinity College from the spring of 1897,[23] had been active in work for the college in the Boston area, and had never lost her interest in its welfare. Most of the "nine trunks" that amazed the annalist contained useful articles as gifts for the college from the

20. Her account of Trinity College funds from June, 1897 to January, 1901 appears as Appendix III. An appreciation of her work as co-foundress appears throughout the first three chapters of this history.
21. President's report to the Advisory Board, May 14, 1902.
22. A student description of this ceremony appears as a "special" on pp. 68–69 of the manuscript magazine *The Woman*, March 25, 1902.
23. Cf. Chapter II, *passim*.

Sisters in Massachusetts. She "met the students that afternoon and gave them an ice-cream supper that evening." The annals continue, "Prince Henry of Germany was in Washington and most of the students went down to the Capitol to catch a glimpse of His Royal Highness. The weather was stormy."

In spite of the "stormy weather" that greeted her arrival, Sister Georgiana began her administration immediately with calm common sense and practical energy. She was named treasurer of the corporation and went down to the bank to have her signature recorded "according to the laws of the District of Columbia."[24] She persuaded the Board of Trustees to revoke its decision against the Auxiliary Board of Regents and set about healing the rift in that organization.[25] Though Miss Risley-Seward and her close followers never returned to that Board, they retained their interest in the college as well as cordial relations with its new president. Miss Seward herself continued to serve on the Advisory Board of Trinity College. The work of the Associate Boards in many parts of the country continued without interruption, apparently unaware of any problem in Washington.

Sister Georgiana guided the college through its first accreditation and four commencements. Before she left in August, 1907, the central part of the Main Building had been finished and plans for the "North Wing" were in progress.

A tribute of appreciation of Sister Georgiana introduced her successor's report to the Advisory Board, June 8, 1908.

> "An adequate recognition of all that Sister Georgiana has done for the College", she said, "would necessarily begin with the earliest page of its history, for she was from the first intimately associated with the work of Trinity's revered foundress, our late Sister Superior Julia. It was, however, in February, 1902, a few months after Sister Superior Julia's death that Sister Georgiana was appointed to guide the further development of the College, then in its second year of its actual work. There were at that time but two classes, the freshmen and the sophomores, with a total enrollment of fifty-one students. The official records show that under Sister Georgiana's able leadership there was steady progress along all lines. The student body and faculty increased from year to year; the college walls were twice extended; the educational facilities were enriched by very creditable laboratory equipment, by large additions to the library, and by the acquisition of a magnificent art collection; the number of available scholarships was raised from six to twelve; the curriculum was annually developed and strength-

24. *Annals III*, March 7, 1902. "Sister Superior was obliged to go to the bank to leave her signature, according to the laws of the District of Columbia. Sister Gertrude was her companion and both were so impeded with mud that they were about to leave their rubber overshoes in the car. The conductor offered to take charge of them, have them cleaned, and returned to the College, which he accordingly did."
25. Auxiliary Board of Regents Minutes, January–June, 1902.

ened; the requirements for degrees, as well as for admission, were carefully adjusted to the highest national standards, and Trinity was placed upon a secure, officially recognized footing with colleges of the first class.[26] In the name of the College, therefore, I am happy to express the gratitude so justly due to Sister Georgiana."

The *Annals*, February 8, 1910, record a ten day visit which she made to Trinity College to see the completed Main Building with the North Wing in use. The President's Report, 1921, announced her death in the preceding year and again praised her contribution to the college.

During the administration as third President of the college, 1907–1911, of Sister Julia of the Passion (Anna Overend) the growth, both physical and academic, of the college continued. An up-to-date "Circular of Information" in 1907 aimed to

1. make the college more widely known
2. answer questions on admissions requirements and the high school preparation of candidates
3. "to ensure uniformity and thoroughness in preparatory studies . . ."
4. "to establish beyond further question the right of Trinity's entrance standards to full credit given those of other colleges of the first class."

The president's annual report in May, 1908 includes a good analysis of college admissions in the United States at the time. The report for 1910–11 again deals with admissions and transfer standards. The B.S. degree requirements were definitely settled in 1909. Other curricular developments belong rather in the chapter on that subject.

Sister Julia of the Passion built North Hall, thus completing in 1909 the Main Building begun in 1899. She had an outdoor basketball court built, and the tennis courts repaired. She encouraged further development of the Alumnae Association which had been formed on the first Degree Day in 1904. The Association was separately incorporated in 1909, applied for admission in the Association of Collegiate Alumnae, elected a member to the Advisory Board of the college; and by 1911 had, in addition to its national entity with $700 in the bank, three local chapters: Boston, New York, Worcester.[27] She received the Amanda Holohan bequest of art, the Catherine Baker Holohan Scholarship, and established the Harriet Arnold Annuity. With her support, Mrs. Thomas Carter, President of the Auxiliary Board of Regents, carried on a successful program of increasing its membership and completing its

26. By the U.S. Commissioner of Education, as well as the Regents of the State of New York and the educational authority of the State of Pennsylvania.
27. Dean's Report, 1911.

first Anna Hanson Dorsey Memorial Scholarship. She left Trinity College August 16, 1911 after five years with a record of achievement worthy of the praise which she had given her predecessor in her first report to the Board.

The nine years of Sister Catherine Aloysius Crotty's administration, 1911–1920, spanned the decade of transition from the pre-war years of the century through World War I to the first post-war year. By 1912 the first two lay women had joined the faculty as full-time members. About sixty alumnae were teaching in high schools or academies in various parts of the country. Honoria Shine '09 had earned her M.D. and Bertha Strootman her LL.B. It had become necessary for the students "to have room-mates," thus doubling the capacity of the Main Building. Seniors, juniors, and sophomores could attend dances at Georgetown College and Catholic University. The long protested "chaperone rule" was abolished except for dances. Student government, "on trial" in 1912–13 reached full-fledged status with the senior class of 1914. Land between Michigan Avenue and Girard Street,[28] and the "Rose Estate on Lincoln Avenue" were purchased with "money received from the houses of Notre Dame." The former Red Rose Inn on the Lincoln Avenue land was temporarily fitted up for scientific purposes. The history of this building (Old Cuvilly) through its use as an infirmary, as Graduate Hall, as student dormitory, as psychology experimental laboratory, and as fine arts building will appear in later chapters which will also give accounts of the students' activity for women's suffrage, their war effort, and the "great flu epidemic." (cf. Dean's Report, 1919)

In the academic field, the scholastic year was established at "the standard requirement of thirty-six weeks," emphasis was placed on building up the graduate department. Dr. Claxton, the United States Commissioner of Education, paid an official visit to the college. His letter re-affirming approval of the college was printed in 1914, widely distributed and appeared in the yearly catalogue until 1930. In 1912, Trinity was one of the first colleges accepted for affiliation with the Catholic University, and in 1915 joined that University's 25th Anniversary celebration.[29] For five years, 1914–1919, the college experimented with accepting candidates from accredited schools by certificate without further examination. Sister Catherine Aloysius' report for 1919 announced the end of the "certificate privilege for entrance." College

28. Sold in 1930's for development when Franklin Street was cut through and Lincoln Road closed at Trinity's campus. Board of Trustees Minutes, Special Meetings, February and October, 1912; Annual Meeting, October 30, 1912.
29. The 1912 President's Report (*Adv. Bd. Min.*) details the good effects of affiliation to Catholic University and the 1915 Report eulogizes C.U.'s help through the years. It also mentions the many dignitaries who visited Trinity while celebrating the university's silver jubilee.

Elizabeth, Queen of the Belgians with the Class of 1920.

Board, Trinity College, Catholic University affiliation or New York Regents' examinations were required of all applicants. The custom of granting degrees with distinction was introduced, but used sparingly; the Alumnae Association was admitted to membership in the Association of Collegiate Alumnae[30] and even hosted its national meeting April 12, 1917 with President M. Carey Thomas of Bryn Mawr chairing a session; the college was placed on the first Association of American Universities list (1917) of colleges whose graduates were competent for work at European Universities; in 1919 the first honorary degree was conferred on Elizabeth, Queen of the Belgians; and two post-war scholarships for French students were established.

Other accomplishments of Sister Catherine Aloysius' administration should not be overlooked: her interest in the higher education of the Sisters of Notre Dame and her long-range planning for the future physical development of the college. The first of a long line of summer sessions for S.N.D.'s was held at the college in 1912 with eighty present. The summer session of 1916 was a workshop for music teachers conducted by Mme. Von Unschuld. Watching the steady growth of the college (348 students in September, 1919) she added to her encouragement of the already growing chapel and gymnasium funds a strong recommendation that a "Drive for Funds" for a new dormitory be ini-

30. Later, American Association of University Women.

tiated. The implementation of this recommendation fell to her successor to whom she passed on her office at the end of the summer of 1920.[31]

That successor, Sister Raphael Pike, undertook competently the work of up-dating and carrying the college forward into the ebullient post-war decade of the 1920's. A fascinating personality in her own right, a veteran of twenty years on the faculty, having been one of the original group, she faced the office of president with unprecedented experience. Her biography has been written by Sister Angela Elizabeth Keenan.[32] Her presidency (1920–1929) began in a year of remarkable change, not only at Trinity College and in higher education in general, but in the "post-war world." The Report of the President at the end of her first year makes it clear that a new era had begun. She pays tribute to six early friends of the college: Sisters Georgiana and Mary Borgia who died in 1920 and Cardinal Gibbons who died on March 21, 1921 had all participated in the foundation of the college in 1897 and had retained a continuous active interest in Trinity. Dr. Thomas Shields, founder of the education department both at Catholic University and Trinity College; Bishop Harkins of Providence, a benefactor during the years; and Mrs. Maurice Francis Egan, a member of the Auxiliary Board from 1898 completed the lists in the 1921 report.

Thus the new era began not only with a new president at Trinity College, but a new Archbishop of Baltimore; a new vice-rector at Catholic University, Dr. Edward A. Pace, "now in his twenty-first year of lecturing at Trinity . . . revered and beloved by hundreds of our students all over the country"; a new Provincial Superior of the Sisters of Notre Dame, Sister Francis of the Sacred Heart "who knows Trinity College work thoroughly"; and a Superior General who "is very broad-minded, able to recognize and willing to meet the needs of the times." With her own experience, in the spirit of the times, with the support of enlightened advisers, Sister Raphael began her administration. In nine years she modernized administrative structure, financial methods, and academic program, pushed forward the building program, had the campus landscaped for the first time, and encouraged the alumnae in their projects for the college and in participation in national organizations.

March 19, 1921 ground was broken for Notre Dame Chapel which was dedicated in May 1924.[33] Independent audits of college finances date from the early 1920's.[34] A fund-raising firm, John Price Jones Co., was engaged in 1923 to organize the "campaign" for financing a new

31. Board of Trustees Minutes; November 26, 1919; May 11, 1920.
32. In *Three Against the Wind,* Westminster Press (Md.), 1973.
33. More detail of buildings will appear in Part III.
34. *Board of Trustees Minutes,* October 31, 1923; October 30, 1924.

Dedication of Notre Dame Chapel, 1924.

dormitory-dining hall building. Miss Loretta Lawler, class of 1915, became also in 1923 the first chairman of alumnae fund raising and full-time alumnae Secretary to administer the Fund Drive. Alumnae Hall, built in the later years of the decade, was occupied in September 1928.

Meanwhile, the administrative re-organization described earlier in the chapter, the modernization of the curriculum and catalogue, an increase in the number of lay members of the faculty,[35] the initiation of "Study Abroad" and exchange students from France and Spain programs came under Sister Raphael's intelligent keen-eyed approval. On April 15, 1921 the college was inspected "by Mr. Charles W. Hunt of Columbia University, an expert on higher education and representative of Professor Jones . . . rating colleges in the Middle and Atlantic States [*sic*]." His visit was reported at "a meeting of college presidents at Swarthmore in October and the committee again put Trinity in the first rank"—and on the list of members of the Middle States Association. In April 1922 Trinity became an institutional member of the American Council on Education. Four delegates of the Trinity College Alumnae attended the First Annual Convention of the American Association of University Women. During the years of her administration, Sister Ra-

35. The earliest extant "contract" or letter of agreement is addressed to Miss Elsie Kernan, 1921. T.C. Archives.

Sister Berchmans Julia (Julia Schumacher).

phael was ably assisted not only in academic affairs, but in detailed supervision of building projects by the Dean of Studies, Sister Berchmans Julia Schumacher, who continued that assistance to her successor until she herself was appointed President in 1932.

The last paragraphs of a tribute to Sister Raphael by Loretta Lawler in the *Alumnae Journal*[36] in summing up the achievements of her administration show the affectionate appreciation of those who know her well.

> In that difficult decade, just closing, many trying adjustments have been found necessary by all classes of people, but perhaps none more difficult and trying than those in regard to the relations between the College and the students. It is again characteristic that these adjustments were accomplished with dignity and with real understanding of the changing currents in the life around her, the essential outgrowth of the knowledge and wisdom gathered during her life of devoted service to youth. In her relations with the Alumnae, it is not possible to give an adequate estimate of her deep interest and active cooperation which included not only practical good-will but the making of numerous adjustments to facilitate the work. Everything that she touched, the administration of the College, contacts with the students and Alumnae, from the splendor that is the Chapel to the modern efficiency of the kitchens in Alumnae Hall, from the landscaping of the grounds to the furnishings of the rooms, all received the personal impress of her unbounding energy and amazing versatility.
>
> And yet the enlarged College, the numerous improvements, the buildings, beautiful and complete as they are, are not all she has left to Trinity. Her tolerance, her interest in the new, her ability to orientate herself and the College in these changing times, her essentially broad attitude of mind, in short, have permeated the whole structure of college life, and have become part and parcel of that intangible something, which is the spirit of her culture, classical and yet all Christian, the spirit of Trinity. Her light, like the glowing, vital colors of her beloved Chapel, will continue to illumine and to touch with beauty the life and spirit of the place. So that though Trinity relinquishes her to fruitful, happy years elsewhere, it can never entirely lose her.

Trinity never did "entirely lose her." She returned in 1935 to spend her last years in retirement among her Sisters of the Trinity Community until her death in 1940. Appropriately her funeral mass was in Notre Dame Chapel, built by her, a lasting memorial of her service to Trinity College.

Sister Julia of the Trinity (Edith McDonald, 1911), the sixth president, entered upon her office in the summer of 1929 in an atmosphere of enthusiasm and hope. The college had reached its highest enrollment, the physical plant was up-to-date and adequate for future growth, and the academic program was in competent hands. The Alumnae were delighted that one of their own had been appointed and welcomed her officially at Reunion 1930. Patricia Flinn wrote in the *Alumnae Journal*:

36. Vol. 3, No. 1, June 1930.

> Sister Superior Julia of the Trinity was born in Minneapolis, Minnesota, and brought to her class no little of that characteristic Western spirit of energy, enthusiasm and zeal which marked the activities of 1911 from the very start. This class made important traditions, initiating the *Trinilogue* and general daily Communion among the student body, for it was at their request that the Student's Mass was changed so as to precede breakfast instead of to follow it as heretofore. Sister Superior's literary talents found congenial work in the Literary Society and on the editorial Boards of the *Record* and the *Trinilogue*. For two years she taught in St. Martin's Sunday School, Washington, thus foreshadowing the teaching life she was later to follow. The year following her graduation was devoted in great part to travel and then shortly afterwards she entered the Mother House of the Sisters of Notre Dame at Namur, Belgium.
>
> The last year of her novitiate saw the bombardment of Namur in the early days of the War. She shared the difficult experiences of the German occupation when the Convent was turned into a Hospital for the wounded, but in the Spring of 1915 her return to the United States was arranged. The trip took seven weeks instead of the customary ten days. Sister Superior related some of the experiences of these days for the *Record* at the time of the tenth re-union of her Class. In September of 1915, she took up teaching at Trinity, becoming a member of the Faculty of English, of which she became the Head on the transfer of Sister Julie to Emmanuel College in Boston. Her student interests in the Literary Society, the *Record* and the *Trinilogue* were revived with enthusiasm and as Faculty Advisor of these undertakings, the girls always found her ready with valuable suggestions, wise advice and hearty support. Her active interest in the problems of student life found a new field in cooperation with the Student Government Board. So that when Sister Superior Julia of the Trinity received the appointment as President of Trinity College last August, she brought to her new task intimate acquaintance with the problems of College administration, not only from the point of view of a member of the Faculty but also from close observation and daily contact with the conditions of student life today.[37]

The optimism of her welcome, backed by the loyalty to the college and the quiet practical determination of the new president were urgently needed. Before the hopes expressed above were in print, the stock market crash of October 1929 had signaled the end of the great post-war prosperity and the beginning of the then still unrecognized great depression of the 1930's.[38] In retrospect, the great achievement of her administration would seem to be keeping the college in existence during the first years of depression, yet a study of those years shows a calm unflurried atmosphere and steady attention to the main goal,

37. Vol. 3, No. 1, Summer, 1930.
38. Mitchell, Broadus, *Depression Decade*, Vol. IX Economic History of the United States, New York, 1947, Chap. 1, pp. 25–54.

the higher education of the rapidly waning number of students.[39] The yearly audited financial statements were pronounced "satisfactory" by the Board of Trustees though the custom of borrowing on short term loans from various banks "on the credit of the college . . . for necessary operating expenses" during the summer months became necessary. This type of loan was authorized first by the Board August 7, 1929. Special consideration was given to seniors whose sudden financial plight made their staying in college a serious problem. The Alumnae took the first steps toward student aid in specific cases of known need. Student publications in the *Record* and the Alumnae Association activities reported in the *Journal* reflect a college getting on with the job in spite of unsettling conditions. The first daughter of an alumna registered in 1929, the first "Trinity Granddaughter." Gertrude Cloonan, 1933, was the daughter of Eleanor Griffin Cloonan, 1904. The reorganization of the curriculum was completed in these years so that each student's program included one major subject with at least one related minor to form her major field. This new arrangement appeared first in the catalogue of 1932–1933. The revision of the by-laws of the Board of Trustees and "amendment of the charter in accord with the revised statutes of the District of Columbia" was proposed and discussed in the meetings of October 29, 1930 and February 20, 1931. The work was completed in the following administration, in 1935.

With admission of women to the newly organized Graduate School of Arts and Sciences at the Catholic University, Trinity College concentrated on the undergraduate program for young women, leaving women's graduate study to the university. The catalogue for 1932–1933 reflects, in its new statement on "Graduate Work," the change which had been taking place.

> Special arrangements for Graduate Work have been made with the Catholic University of America. Living accommodations for a limited number of students are available at Graduate Hall[40] on the campus of Trinity College. Inquiries for particular information in reference to Graduate Work should be addressed to the Dean of the Graduate School, Catholic University, Washington, D.C.

Sister Julia of the Trinity left Washington in the summer of 1932 for further study at Oxford, England, in preparation for the return to English teaching at Emmanuel College in Boston. After World War II she was elected assistant to the Superior General of the Sisters of Notre Dame de Namur. In 1961 at the fiftieth reunion of the Class of

39. A student body approaching the 500 mark in 1929 dwindled to a low of 287 in 1933. Registrar's Records.
40. Old Cuvilly on Lincoln Road.

1911, she received an honorary Doctor of Letters from Trinity College. She is living now (1974) in Connecticut, in active, fruitful retirement, still intensely interested in the progress of the college.

The seventh president, Sister Berchmans Julia (Julia Shumacher), at forty-eight years of age, had already served Trinity for twenty years as a faculty member and administrator. The *Alumnae Journal*[41] writes of her as

> known to us from our earliest day at Trinity when we first looked upon that amazing miracle that is the Schedule Board and learned to know the Dean of Studies who understood and was responsible for all its intricacies. She has known Trinity for many years and is well acquainted with its problems. She brings to her office a splendid capacity for administrative work and sympathetic interest in the various phases of life and activity that are part of Trinity.

When Sister Berchmans Julia assumed the responsibility for the college in 1932, the Depression had reached its lowest point. It was the time of greatest unemployment nation-wide, of the "bonus army's" march on Congress, of the "Shame of Anacostia Flats," of disillusionment with policies of back-to-the-land and local relief, and especially of the height of bank failures or suspensions, and of the currency crisis.[42] The enrollment of the college was the lowest since 1918. The new president, in the face of national disaster, reflected in the college, needed the experience, "splendid capacity for administrative work and sympathetic interest in the various phases of life" at Trinity and more needed, in fact, the courage, the decisiveness, the long-range vision of the truly great in time of stress. These she demonstrated in the eight years, 1932–1940. It is possible to identify three special areas of strength in her administration: (1) her enduring interest in the academic program,[43] in students and alumnae; (2) her ability for re-organization shown chiefly in carrying through the revision of the charter and bylaws of the Board of Trustees and of the scholarship fund, and culminating in the proposal to separate the office of President of the college from Superior of the religious community; and, finally, (3) her ability in the planning and direction of building and of physical plant improvement.

The financial difficulties of the time (not mentioned by the new president) are reflected only in the low enrollment and in the minutes of the Board of Trustees which record the authorizations to borrow on

41. November 1932, p. 5. The writer's experience did not take her back beyond the Dean's office to the philosophy classes or the physics laboratory.
42. Mitchell, Broadus, *Depression Decade*, p. 102–110. Cf. *New York Times* and Federal Reserve Reports of the period.
43. Cf. Chapter 5 Curriculum, the academic program.

"note or notes of Trinity College" more frequent and larger sums "for the uses and purposes of the college." At the annual meeting of the Board, October 26, 1932, the audited financial report was studied in detail. The financial status of the college was pronounced "entirely satisfactory"—though not "excellent" as in the 1920's. The next year, however, the report was "accepted and filed." The drama implied in these succinct statements remains hidden while significant developments in the college continued through the decade under the calm direction of Sister Berchmans Julia and her faculty.

Extensive remodeling and modernization of the "old building" brought more baths, showers and improved lighting to students' living space, refurbished classrooms and redecorated parlors and offices as the enrollment slowly climbed. The Alumnae Association collaborated not only in recruiting students, but in helping those at the college. The Alumnae Vocational Guidance Committee organized, in cooperation with Sister Angela Elizabeth, a Vocational Guidance Bureau for students and young alumnae, which served through the decade.[44] When the student publications' funds were wiped out in the national financial crash the Alumnae came to their aid. The president of the class of 1933 wrote

> This year, as never before have we witnessed here at Trinity some of the best examples of generosity ever known to us in our lives—the generosity of the Alumnae to the Class of 1933. Not only did they aid us in our Commencement activities, but they made possible the publication of our *Trinilogue* and *Record*. And so it is to the Alumnae of Boston, New York, Rhode Island, Philadelphia, and Washington that we wish to express our deep appreciation for the loyalty and interest which they have shown and the work they have done for us.[45]

The first Alumnae Council with representatives of all Chapters and Classes was held November 28–29, 1936 in Washington, D.C. Alumnae activities of the late 1930's concentrated on fund-raising for scholarships and the Jubilee Fund for a new science building, though recruiting continued. The first daughter of an alumna (Trinity Granddaughter) Gertrude Cloonan, daughter of Eleanor Griffin Cloonan, 1904, graduated in 1933. By 1936 there were eighteen "grand-daughters" on campus.[46] These were years of earnest activity in social service, "Catholic Action," the Catholic Evidence Guild, both at college and in Alumnae groups. Some idea of the relationship of the president of the

44. *Alumnae Journal;* November 1932, p. 12; June 1933, pp. 72–73. This developed into the guidance and counselling service of the Dean's Office under Sister Ann Francis, and finally the Counselling Center of the late 1960's and the 1970's.
45. *Alumnae Journal,* May 1933, p. 39. Aileen Crimmings.
46. *Alumnae Journal,* June 1933, p. 79; November 1936, p. 17.

college to the Alumnae emerges from messages or reports of National Alumnae Presidents to the association. Typical of these is that of Florence T. Judge in 1937.[47]

> Whatever measure of success the present administration (of the Alumnae Association) may have had is due in great part to the friendly interest and guidance of Sister Superior Berchmans Julia. Without her wholehearted cooperation many of the accomplishments of the Association would have been impossible.

The revision of the bylaws of the Board of Trustees of the college continued. At the Annual Meeting, October 30, 1934, Mr. Daniel O'Donoghue, legal counsel, explained the new statute and the proposed Act of Congress needed to implement it. This "new charter" (H.B. 3477 of the 74th Congress) confirming the incorporation of 1897 and restating it to fit existing laws of the District of Columbia was passed by Congress April 8, 1935.[48] Acceptance of the "new charter" and bylaws was signed by all nine members of the board at a special meeting, May 23, 1935 and the heraldic form of the seal designed by Pierre Chagnon de la Rose was adopted to replace the 1897 allegorical version. Both these actions were confirmed at the annual meeting, October 25, 1935. At that same meeting the Advisory Board and the Associate Boards in various cities outside Washington "which have not functioned for several years" were discontinued. Meetings of the Ladies Auxiliary Board, scheduled monthly since 1898, were changed to three or four a year. The effective work done by the Associate Boards during the first quarter century of the college[49] had been gradually assumed in their areas by Alumnae Chapters, a fact which in itself attests to the success of the student recruiting, public relations, and fund-raising of those early friends of Trinity College.

The college took advantage, in the later years of the decade, of government programs established under the Federal Emergency Appropriation Act of 1935, especially the National Youth Administration and the Works Progress Administration. Students benefited from NYA jobs into the 1940's. With the help of qualified WPA personnel, Sister Julia Stokes was able to prepare a new scholarly catalogue of the O'Connor Art Collection.

The deaths of Bishop Thomas Shahan, Sister Florence Louise, and Mrs. Thomas H. Carter in 1932; of Miss Ella Lorraine Dorsey in 1935; and of Sister Mary (Dean 1903–1921), Dr. William J. Kerby and Bishop William Turner in 1936—all pillars of strength from the past—emphasized the transition that had been re-focusing the sights of the college community toward its second-half century. This is vividly exemplified

47. *Alumnae Journal*, June 1937, p. 67.
48. Copy in the Board of Trustees Minutes, May 23, 1935.
49. Minutes of the Ladies Auxiliary Board of Regents 1898–1930 *passim*.

in the Jubilee Fund for a long overdue science building, in the negotiations for closing Lincoln Road, the cutting through of Franklin Street, and the sale of the property across the new Franklin Street between Girard Street and Michigan Avenue.[50]

In 1936 the Board of Trustees accepted from Mrs. Minna Schmidt of Chicago a collection of four hundred authentically costumed figurines of outstanding women of the world. This valuable collection which had been created for the Century of Progress Exhibition in 1933 was on exhibit in O'Connor Art Gallery and later in the rare book room of the library for nearly forty years until deterioration of many figurines forced the decision to put them in storage where they remain in 1975.

One of the privileges most cherished by Trinity College alumnae has been membership first in the Association of Collegiate Alumnae (from 1915) and in its successor the American Association of University Women, which from 1917 to 1947 required inclusion of the college on the approved list of the Association of American Universities.[51] Trinity's place on that list, though confirmed by an A.A.U. visiting committee in 1932, was threatened later by the need of larger and up-to-date facilities for the science departments. Though a new science building had for years been given priority among the needs of the college in the catalogue, it remained an unfulfilled need, and in 1939 Trinity was suspended from "the List." The college was formally re-instated on "The List" in 1941.

Writing to the Alumnae, March 7, 1940, Sister Berchmans Julia announced the decision to begin the science building, "Trinity's greatest need, not considering the means required for realizing it." Making the only public reference to financial difficulty of her whole administration, she continued:

> In 1932–1933 the architects worked on the plans for the new science building. Before these were completed the depression was upon us. This obliged us to give up the idea as we could not run any financial risks during such uncertain times. Now the student enrollment is getting back to normal and we feel encouraged to begin again, so we have taken out the blueprints once more. Our science teachers are absorbed in the plans for their new quarters and are enjoying in imagination their new laboratories equipped with modern laboratory devices.[52]

The Alumnae President, Catherine Crimmings, immediately issued a call. "Trinity seldom calls on us for help," she wrote, "but she will need assistance now—and to whom can she turn if not to her own graduates?" Fifteen years and a great depression had intervened since the silver jubilee drive for Alumnae Hall. Now "erection of the Science

50. Board of Trustees Minutes: November 20, 1937; June 11 and Oct. 5, 1938.
51. Cf. Chapter 5, section on accreditation for a more detailed account of A.A.U. and the A.A.U.W.
52. *Alumnae Journal*, March 1940, p. 26.

Building should lend zest to our efforts, and . . . the entire building—or a good portion thereof—might well be our tribute to Trinity on her fiftieth birthday."

Long before that "fiftieth birthday," in November 1941 (just in time to avoid the building priorities of World War II), the science departments moved into the new building. Sister Berchmans Julia had succeeded in the administrative re-organization that brought about the appointment of a new "academic president" separate from the superior of the religious community and devoted herself with all her experience in technical construction to supervision of the work on the Science Building, the crowning event of her administration. She remained at Trinity as Vice-President until 1942. After many years of successful apostolate, directing schools of Notre Dame in North Carolina and in Pennsylvania she returned in her retirement to live with the Sisters at Trinity College. Active and interested in all college affairs, using now her baptismal name, as Sister Julia Schumacher (but still B.J. to her friends) she is "at home" to visiting alumnae, ninety-one years old in 1975.

Sister Catherine Dorothea (Mary Fox), Trinity's eighth president, began her thirteen year administration in August, 1940. A graduate of Radcliffe College, with a doctorate from Boston College, she had taught in the Boston public schools before entering the Sisters of Notre Dame de Namur. After experience as a successful member of the English Department of Emmanuel College in Boston[53] where she was a colleague of Sister Julie (cf. p. 91), she had established in 1934 Trinity Preparatory School, Ilchester, Maryland, and led it to full accreditation by the Middle States Association of Colleges and Secondary Schools. With this background and with vigorous enthusiasm she assumed her responsibilities as "academic president" of the college, the first who was not also superior of the religious community, and the first since 1920 from "outside the college."

Engraved announcements of her appointment were sent out by the Board of Trustees. The alumnae welcomed her perhaps a little cautiously as she came to face the "new problems, the inevitable problems attendant on growth and development." "We bring every possible support and confidence to our new president, Sister Catherine Dorothea, who has come to share our life at Trinity and to lead us to new strength and greater power," wrote the editor of the *Alumnae Journal* that fall.[54]

53. Cf. Tribute by Anne M. McNamara *Alumnae Journal* Autumn, 1954, pp. 10–11.
54. Autumn, 1940, p. 5. The Alumnae Association President, 1939–1943, Catherine Crimmings '32, did much to ease the transition to the new administration. She worked closely with Sister Berchmans Julia, organized the "Jubilee Fund" drive for the science building and, loyally supporting Sister Catherine Dorothea's efforts during the first three years of her administration, made the new president known to alumnae in all parts of the country.

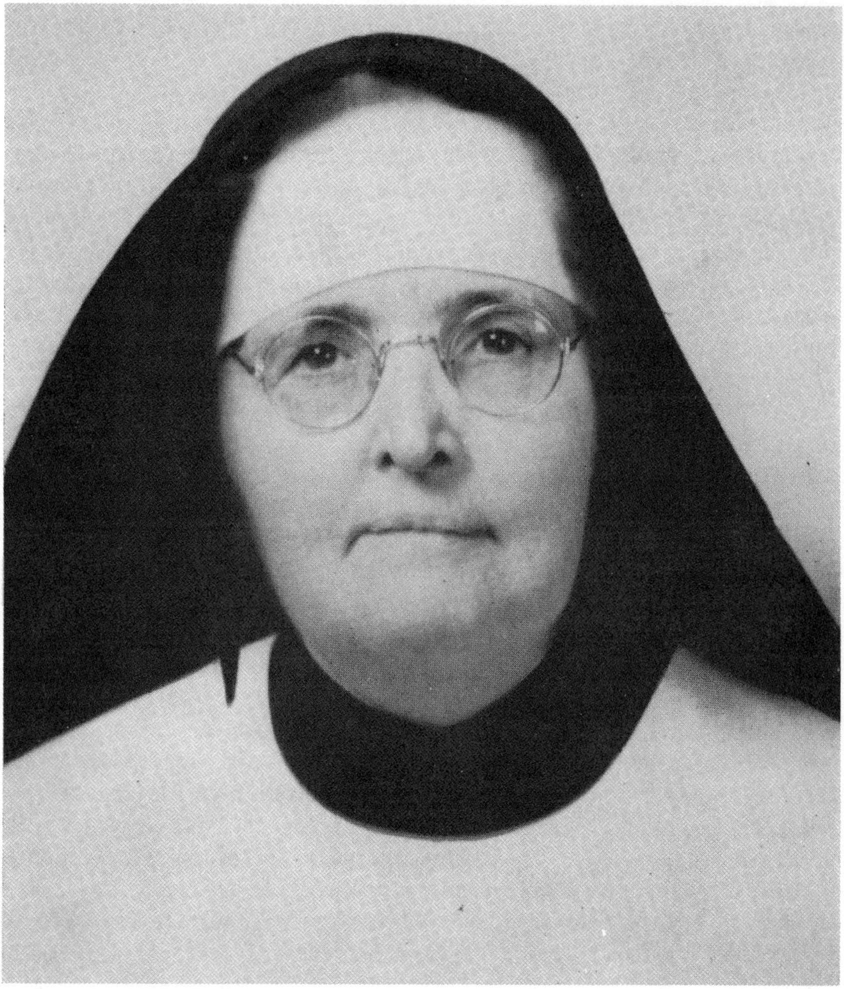

Sister Catherine Dorothea Fox, Ph.D.

The tentative attitude of the alumnae was soon dissipated, so that Sister Catherine Dorothea could write in 1953 when illness forced her retirement:

> In reviewing the past thirteen years, I realize that one of the most satisfying of my activities at Trinity was, my dear Alumnae, my contact with you. I cannot thank you enough—individually, as Chapters, as an Association—for your never failing interest in the College, for your cooperation in all our plans, for your enthusiasm and appreciation of student accomplishments, and for other countless proofs of your loyalty.[55]

55. *Alumnae Journal*, Autumn, 1953, p. 5.

The first year, besides "getting to know" the alumnae, faculty and students, Sister Catherine Dorothea spent much time in preparation for the visit of a committee of the Association of American Universities which was expected in the fall of 1941. While Sister Berchmans Julia supervised the construction of the Science Building, the new president focused on the academic program, faculty organization, and on student recruitment, continuing and building-up the nationwide geographic distribution of the student body. She sent questionnaires to the classes of 1932–1939 to provide up-to-date information about recent alumnae, applied the faculty ranking system, by then customary in American higher education. In November 1941 she was able to write to the alumnae: "You have already received the good news that with the completion of the Science Building, the College has been confirmed in its former status with the Association of American Universities."[56]

A month after this happy announcement, the United States was precipitated into World War II, and the college faced the added problems of a nation at war. Four of the first five years of Sister Catherine Dorothea's administration and to a much lesser extent the last three, 1950–1953, were war years, a fact that necessarily affected the life of the college and decisions made, as will be evident in the following pages.

As the "academic president" without the duties of religious superior, Sister Catherine Dorothea was able to give her whole time to the academic program, to faculty and students; to active participation in professional associations and meetings dealing with higher education; to writing articles and speeches, and to encouraging wider student participation in worthwhile activities off-campus. She studied and wrote an article on the history of the 1897 foundation and the achievements of Trinity College since its opening in 1900.[57] Her coming to Trinity coincided with the centenary of the arrival of the first Sisters of Notre Dame de Namur in America so that one of the first events of her administration was announced at the Alumnae Council in Pittsburgh, November 3, 1940: ". . . in commemoration of the 100th anniversary of the Sisters of Notre Dame in this country we had a Mass sung for our Sisters in Notre Dame Chapel on November 1 and Dr. Moore delivered a beautiful sermon, in which he paid high tribute to the Sisters for the fine work they are doing."[58]

The advent of 1942 brought the necessity of decisions about "accelerating the curriculum" or changing its emphasis, about defense activities and other student activities in a nation at war. Early in the year

56. *Alumnae Journal*, Autumn, 1941, p. 3.
57. Extant in T.C. are typescripts of this historical sketch of Trinity College, with research notes attached in the handwriting of Sister Julia (Stokes) '13, long a member of the Trinity faculty. It was printed in the catalogue of 1942–43.
58. *Alumnae Journal*, November 1940, p. 2. Cf. Ellen Ganey *editorial*, pp. 3–5.

Sister Catherine Dorothea, with "the presidents of about twenty-five privately controlled liberal arts colleges, including Radcliffe, Wellesley, Smith, Mount Holyoke, Wheaton, Vassar, Bryn Mawr, Sweet Briar, Skidmore, Wilson, St. Elizabeth's, Manhattanville, New Rochelle and other colleges located on the eastern seaboard," met in informal conference at Barnard College to discuss these problems. There was "a unanimous agreement that the acquisition of true culture cannot be accelerated, and that women's colleges should do their utmost to preserve the normal four-year program, while contributing as much as possible to national needs."[59] Basic principles evolved at that meeting and accepted at Trinity were in summary:

1. At present there is no compulsion for acceleration for college women comparable to that required for men by the Selective Service Act. Acceleration for men, however, together with the inevitable educational sacrifices demanded by war, accentuates the necessity of educating women as broadly and as soundly as possible.
2. There is a reasonable distinction between expediency and long-range planning. While recognizing the prime necessity of winning the war and while holding ourselves ready to do what is expedient to that end, we must not lose sight of the long range values of education.
3. Both "education" and "training" are necessary at the present time. Education in the true sense cannot be hastened unduly. Training of a practical nature is obviously a necessity.
4. Although acceleration may hasten the date of graduation, no such arbitrary resolution can hasten maturity, and the need of mature judgment and mature personality will be greater in the future than in the past.[60]

These principles continued to be guidelines throughout the war and post-war years, in planning and in faculty efforts toward curriculum development at Trinity.

The war years 1941–1945 were a time of intense activity in all areas of college life. Though many students did not return in September 1942 because of widespread fear that Washington would be an early bomb target, the enrollment soon began, paradoxically, a steady upswing. This was due partly to the fact that families with college-age sons at war were financially able to send their daughters to college instead, as well as to the first principle, expressed above, that "the inevitable educational sacrifices demanded by war, accentuate the necessity of educating women as broadly and as soundly as possible." It was a time of defense work by students and alumnae, of "Trinity in Uniform," of

59. "Trinity and Defense," *Alumnae Journal*, Winter, 1942, pp. 47–49.
60. *Ibid.*, p. 47. Note: the idea of acceleration germinated and came to fruition much later in an era of peace in the late '50's with early admission to Trinity College of competent high school juniors, and with the individually planned programs of the 1970's.

streamlined Commencements, and travel restrictions, of blackouts and Red Cross courses—and of intensified work for peace.[61]

The first war Commencement Week, 1942, not yet affected by wartime transportation restrictions, included the solemn dedication of the new Science Building with an Academic Convocation of representatives from many colleges and an address by Dr. Hugh Stott Taylor, Dean of the Graduate School of Princeton University.

One of the wartime Commencements, 1944, was the most tragic of all commencements. Msgr. George Johnson, eminent university professor, beloved Trinity teacher of an earlier decade, acknowledged leader of Catholic education, founder of the Campus School of the Catholic University, was the speaker. "The extraordinary character of the address caught and held the listeners immediately. There was a profound and attentive quiet upon that Commencement audience—of all audiences perennially nervous."[62] In the midst of that speech Dr. Johnson collapsed and died. He said: "We have still much to learn about educating for Christ in a world that knows not Christ—." "He had not faltered for a single syllable but suddenly he stopped—lifted his hand as if a light had blinded him—and fell swiftly as a tree struck down by lightning in a forest. His brother priests on the platform raised their hands in absolution. Dr. Moore made a hasty examination. The Archbishop rose, blessed the graduates, and dismissed the audience. The quiet was unbroken as our Seniors filed out—in the same order they had come in."[63] All, as of one mind, went directly upstairs to Notre Dame Chapel.

September 1942 brought Sister Ann Francis (Catherine Hoey '24) to Trinity as Dean of Students,[64] and in December of that year Sister Columba (Catherine Mullaly '25), already a member of the English Department, was appointed Dean of Studies.[65] These two, working together and with the president throughout her administration and into those of two succeeding presidents, were directly concerned with the students for two decades. In 1942, also, Trinity College joined the College Entrance Examination Board.[66] Though the college and the Board had been founded in the same year and the board examinations had been used to a greater or lesser extent through the years, this was the beginning of full membership.

61. Cf. *Alumnae Journal*, Spring '43, pp. 86–88.
62. *Alumnae Journal*, '44, pp. 70–73.
63. *Alumnae Journal*, Summer '44, p. 103, obituary by Ellen A. Ganey, which deserves full reading, pp. 100–103.
64. *Alumnae Journal*, Autumn '42, p. 12.
65. *Alumnae Journal*, Spring '43, p. 93.
66. The first Catholic college to become a member.

At the invitation of Mrs. Jouett Shouse, President of the Institute of Women's Professional Relations, Sister Catherine Dorothea attended the Conference on War and Post-War Demands for Trained Personnel, in Washington, April 9–10, 1943.[67] A note on the program indicates that information was available and recruiting agents present for WAAC, WAVES, SPARS, Marines, Red Cross, Army Nurses, and the National Register of Scientific and Specialized Personnel. Undergraduates were urged to remain in college, but alumnae were eagerly sought.

The usual problems of college administration continued to occupy the president, problems of faculty organization, of faculty salaries, of adjusting to changing times, of growing enrollment taxing available space and of a precarious financial outlook, of preparation for the Middle States Evaluation at the end of the decade. In the summer of 1946, Sister Catherine Dorothea participated in the Workshop on College Organization and Administration at the Catholic University, presenting a paper "The College Faculty and Its Development."[68] At the end of the decade, writing for the Alumnae, she stated clearly in "Trinity Looks to the Future" financial needs of the college at mid-century.[69] Because "some alumnae have wondered why Trinity was silent amidst the far-sounding appeals of other colleges," she wrote:

> . . . . The academic world today is overshadowed by alarming implications against privately controlled colleges that have appeared in the *Report of the President's Commission on Higher Education*. All independent colleges and universities are threatened, and especially the small Catholic liberal arts college. In these post-war days Catholic colleges are literally struggling for existence; we are courageously and with faith bending every effort to maintain high academic standards and to preserve our Christian ideals of education, while we labor to balance our budget.

After describing the fund-raising efforts to well-known, highly-endowed institutions, the large gifts they received the year before and a comparison of the basic fees of eastern women's colleges (all higher than those at Trinity) she continued quite bluntly:

> And what of Trinity? Let us not interrupt this presentation of facts and figures to evaluate the contrasting outcomes of our educational endeavors,[70] but let us keep in mind that we live in a material world and that we

67. Program, TCA, Drawer VI.
68. Printed in *Catholic University Bulletin*, Vol. 14, No. 3, November 1946, pp. 7–10 and as a chapter of the *Proceedings* of the workshop.
69. *Alumnae Journal*, Winter, 1949, pp. 44–45.
70. She emphasized this in speeches and *Alumnae Journal* articles throughout her administration.

must face the peculiar material difficulties of our times. Trinity in common with all colleges is suffering from the current financial crisis, but unlike secular colleges, we have no real endowment and no surplus on which to draw. We could not operate without what has been truly called our "living endowment," that imaginary capital, the income of which would be necessary if the Sisters were paid for their services to the College.[71] Vassar, on the other hand, has an actual endowment of $16,000,000, and, during the last year, 1947–1948, received many gifts, of which the following are two: for scholarships and general educational purposes, $98,527; for the library, gifts of more than seven hundred individuals and groups, including one gift of $10,000 and one other of 9,200 books. In contrast, we might state here that last year the Trinity College library received as gifts $125.45 and 240 books. And last year Trinity College received not one capital gift for scholarship aid—a regrettable fact, since we had scholarship applications from a large number of excellent students who were financially unable to matriculate here. Our gift of $2,500 from the Alumnae Fund, for which we were deeply grateful, was used immediately to install a new lighting system in the main reading room and reference rooms of the library.

. . . . It is a well-known fact that a college receives in student fees, at the most, well below 60 per cent of what she gives her students. At the present time operating expenses have increased 50 per cent. Last year, of the $450 each Trinity student paid for board, we spent $429.28 on food and wages. What was left for plumbers, painters, electricians, for furniture, dishes, and utensils? Similar facts might be told of each department, scholastic and domestic, and we have no reserve fund; only a debt as of June 30, 1948 of $419,131 on the Science Building.

This array of facts may have come as a surprise to some alumnae. The information served to raise their sights with a practical outcome in the announcement in June 1949 of a Fiftieth Anniversary Fund drive led by Edith Callaghan '31, to raise $50,000 for the college in its golden jubilee year. The golden jubilee of the opening of the college was celebrated throughout the fiftieth academic year, 1949–1950. It began in November with an impressive three day program,[72] a fitting successor to the dedication ceremony of November, 1900 and reaching a climax in the Alumnae Reunion at Commencement 1950. Honorary Degrees were conferred at the Academic Convocation, November 5, on three distinguished women: Helen C. White, novelist and Professor of En-

71. This concept of "living endowment" first put forward by Dr. Edward Pace circa 1915 has become in the accounting systems of the intervening years the "contributed services" of the present financial statements. The fact remains that, as from 1900, the Sisters of Notre Dame still receive living expenses only amounting approximately to one third of their pooled salaries and contribute the rest to the college. Now as in 1949 "we could not operate" without it.

72. Program of events, *Alumnae Journal*, Autumn, 1949, p. 19. At the convocation of that weekend, the Sisters of Notre Dame joined the other members of the faculty in the academic procession for the first time.

glish at the University of Wisconsin, Mother Mary Joseph, foundress of the Maryknoll Sisters, and Jane M. Hoey (1914), internationally known social worker with an impressive record of public service in the New York State and Federal Governments.

The editorial in the Alumnae Journal, Winter 1950,[73] describes in Ellen Ganey's inimitable way that event.

> At the Solemn Dedication of Trinity College in November 1900, Monsignor Conaty, Rector of Catholic University, preached the sermon containing the memorable words, "Vivat, Floreat, Crescat." That stirring prayer has been quoted many times in the fifty years that have seen its fulfillment. It came to mind most poignantly during the Jubilee Weekend this past November, with which the College formally opened the Fiftieth Anniversary Year.
>
> Our Archbishop came to Trinity on Thursday preceding that weekend to offer Mass for a student body numbering just under five hundred, and a faculty of close to sixty—a far cry from the handful of pioneer students and the few Sisters and "Reverend Doctors" who made up the personnel of the College fifty years before. It was fitting that the sermon should be preached by a professor from Catholic University,[74] for from the earliest beginnings of Trinity College, her faculty has been distinguished by gifted scholars and teachers from "the institution around the bend," to use Sister Mary's vivid phrase.
>
> At the Solemn Requiem Mass on Saturday, Monsignor Conaty himself was remembered with all the other devoted friends of Trinity who, with faith in her high purpose, saw her through those first difficult years. Father Ignatius Smith preached, and his warm and moving words awakened vivid memories and prayerful gratitude.
>
> The Academic Convocation on Saturday afternoon was brilliant and colorful. Father Louis Ryan, O.P., of our Department of Theology was Marshal for the long procession of student representatives, alumnae delegates, our own faculty of Sisters, priests, lay men and women, and official delegates of over a hundred universities and colleges, come to do Trinity honor on her fiftieth birthday. Dr. James Van der Velt, O.F.M., whom many of our young alumnae know as their distinguished professor of psychology, led the line of delegates as the representative of Louvain. It was a long line, splendid with ermine and velvet, with the crimson and blue and gold of academic costume.
>
> Georgetown's President Hunter Guthrie, handsome and impressive in his robes as doctor of the University of Paris, gave a brilliant address. The conferring of the honorary degrees by Archbishop O'Boyle was a thrilling experience. The citations of the three remarkable women who received them are published in this issue of the *Journal*. They explain, better than could any words of ours, the unique contribution made by each of the three to American Catholic life in our time. Trinity is proud to number all three as

73. pp. 56–59.
74. Rev. Edmond Benard, S.T.D. Theology Department, Catholic University.

her "alumnae," but she must be forgiven for the special pride she feels in the one who has worn her gold and purple these many years,[75] who has never failed to recognize the "royal right to serve" that it bespeaks.

The Tea and Reception which followed the convocation were held in Social Hall and surely a more distinguished company has never graced a Trinity parlor.

The climax of the great weekend of commemoration came with the Pontifical Mass of Thanksgiving, the Mass of the Most Blessed Trinity, celebrated on Sunday morning by the Apostolic delegate. Dr. Jordan was the Assistant Priest, Dr. Ziegler, the Deacon, and Dr. Weber, one of the Deacons of Honor. Father Burke's magnificent sermon, we are privileged to be able to publish in its entirety in this issue of the *Journal*. The students from St. Paul's College sang the Mass, as Paulist seminarians have sung Masses on every important Trinity occasion since the first Mass of dedication in November, 1900.[76]

The prayer of Monsignor Conaty uttered on that day has indeed been answered. It was a brave prayer to speak aloud and publicly. There was so little that *seemed* auspicious. Higher education for women was yet young and there were many good friends in the Church who felt this venture by the Sisters of Notre Dame, into a wholly untried field, imprudent, to say the least. But the few Sisters who started Trinity had firm faith and undaunted hope; the little handful who made up our first red class—of 1904—had courage and enthusiasm and determination; the Rector of the University who voiced the prayer, with his brother professors had vision and confidence and fraternal devotion to the new little sister college. Because of these priests, Trinity students from the very beginning have enjoyed the distinction of being taught by men. Trinity College has indeed lived—come to beautiful flower—and already borne abundant fruit—developed and grown, not only in years and numbers, but in grace and strength. She is forever young but no longer youthful with the pains and struggles of the young, nor with the carefree ways that the young know because they are sheltered and protected as they grow. Trinity turns now to the years of her maturity, in humble gratitude for the place of eminence to which God has raised her, wise with the ancient wisdom of a true daughter of the Church, who has known from her earliest years that knowledge is but the handmaid of Faith.[77]

During the fiftieth academic year, "Trinity College was visited on March 5-7, 1950, by a Committee representing the Commission on Institutions of Higher Education of the Middle States Association of Colleges and Secondary Schools for the purpose of conducting an evaluation.[78] Since the United States Commissioner of Education no

75. Jane M. Hoey '14.
76. Two of the Paulist seminarians of 1900 attended this Mass representing the Paulist Fathers: Rev. Richard Cartwright, C.S.P. and Rev. Thomas S. O'Neil, C.S.P.
77. *Alumnae Journal*, Winter, 1950, pp. 56–57.
78. Opening sentence of the report of that committee.

longer rated colleges as in the early years of the college and since the Association of American Universities wishing to "get out of the business of accreditation" had discontinued in 1947 its prestigious "List"; approval by the regional associations had become increasingly significant.[79] The report of this team was favorable and the college was re-affirmed in its accreditation. "Trinity College," the report states, "evidences an unusual unity of spirit and cooperation among its administrative personnel" whose members "are well prepared and very conscientious in the performance of their duties." In the faculty they found "a realistic, dedicated and interested attitude. The faculty represent a good academic cross section of American and foreign colleges and universities since they hold degrees from some forty-seven institutions."[80] It was noted, however, that the "next years will be critical ones for the establishment of a certain teaching morale which will derive from continuity of service."

"This will compensate for the great change of teaching personnel which has occurred within the last years as an outcome of the retirement of some faculty members who had given long service and the resignation of others." As a result nearly half the faculty in 1950 had less than three years of service and "not yet fully integrated to the Trinity teaching traditions." The report recommended more faculty committees to help "accelerate this important process of integration." The selection of students for entrance and the "sensible and valid process of weeding out of students who did not perform well in college," the curriculum, the "simple and thorough system of academic counseling" with both Deans working together, the testing program, the good record of alumnae in graduate schools, the library, the "plant and equipment" were all praised, though needed improvements were suggested. The library especially needed a new building. The areas of organization and of finances drew the strongest criticism and recommendations for revision and up-dating. The anomalous position of the studies office[81] and the fact that "the Superior of the religious community . . . is the chief executive in all matters of community including finance and business management" were noted. Therefore, the committee recommended a revision of the by-laws of the Board of Trustees, the establishment of a lay advisory board,[82] the re-organization of the accounting system of Trinity College "to conform to the accepted standards of educational accounting," and an "annual audit made by a certified public accountant[82] who is thoroughly acquainted with the best

79. Cf. "Accreditation" in Chapter V.
80. Middle States Report, 1950, pp. 5, 11.
81. Mentioned earlier in this chapter, p. 99.
82. Both these measures constituted revivals of earlier practices discontinued since the mid-1930's depression crisis.

procedures in college finance and who has no direct relation to the institution."

In the next three years Sister Catherine Dorothea threw herself into the affairs of the college, attempting to implement the recommendations of the evaluation committee as well as to maintain the high quality of the areas they praised; and into work for women's education in a wider sphere beyond the college. She was a member of the executive committee, to plan a national conference on "Women in a Defense Decade" to be held September 27–28, 1951 in New York which would "discuss what women's attitudes, philosophy, and activities should be in the next ten years."[83] Later, in an article for the alumnae, she described the scope of this conference and some of its outcomes.[84] She took the first steps toward revision of the by-laws of the Board of Trustees and the establishment of a lay advisory board, though the completion of this work fell to her successors. In collaboration with Sister Evelyn Marie Crowley, the Superior of the Trinity community, she also worked toward improvement of the business and financial methods in use in the college.

In 1952 the college again conducted a modernization of finances, the first since the mid-1930's. Sister Alice Clement (Monica Davis '34) was appointed business officer and treasurer of the college. Fortified by courses in accounting for higher education, by membership in the Association of College and University Business Officers, and by the advice of Mr. Wittler of Haskins and Sells she introduced the budget process and revived annual professional auditing of the college finances. Haskins and Sells have been the auditors since that time. Sister Alice Clement, who returned to her family name as Sister Monica Davis in the late 1960's, continued to supervise the financial affairs of the college until 1975. Sister Dorothy McCormick replaced her, again up-dating the financial program.

Meanwhile, though her activity appeared to continue unabated, Sister Catherine Dorothea's health was deteriorating rapidly. Only those closest to her had any idea of her suffering, so that when it became necessary for her, in the summer of 1953, to resign the active life of the presidency of the college, the announcement came as a shock to her many friends. She retired to the Provincial House at Ilchester, Maryland, where she bravely thought that with extra rest she might continue work as Director of Education for the Sisters, but very shortly after her arrival there the Infirmary claimed her. The months until August 4, 1954 when death brought her release were spent in great suffering patiently borne. Her letter to the alumnae in the *Alumnae*

83. President's Report, 1951.
84. *Alumnae Journal*, Spring 1953, pp. 93–95.

Journal, Autumn, 1953 has been quoted at the beginning of this account of her administration.[85]

In that same *Journal*, Ellen A. Ganey paid tribute to Trinity's eighth president. "In October, 1940," she wrote, "we noted the arrival of a new administrator in these words:

> We bring every possible support and confidence to our new president, Sister Catherine Dorothea, who has come to share our life at Trinity and to lead us to new strength and greater power! We had, of course, no idea of *how* new the strength and how great the power. The growth of Trinity in the past thirteen years is due very largely to her—its growth in distinction and achievement, its growth in the intangible ways of deepened wisdom and spiritual intensity. Trinity has been blessed by a very great president, one who gave herself without reservation to the interests of the College, one who showed profound personal concern for each individual student. She has shared our lives to an extent we could never have dreamed possible and whatever position she holds in the Province, she will continue to lead us. Sister Catherine Dorothea has our grateful prayers for her rapid return to health and the lasting affection of all who love Trinity.[86]

The *Journal* of one year later published her *In Memoriam* with tributes of high praise, by her successor Sister Mary Patrick; Bishop John M. McNamara; Mother Eleanor O'Byrne, R.S.C.J.; Mrs. Henry Gratton Doyle, a Radcliffe College classmate; Miss Anne Marie McNamara of the English faculty of Catholic University, a former student at Emmanuel College; and for the whole Trinity household both alumnae, faculty, and students by Ellen A. Ganey, Executive Secretary of the Alumnae Association.

> Even those who knew her well were amazed that she suffered so selflessly, so completely, without complaint or fear, with unfailing gratitude to those who ministered to her, and with more than a hint that she was embracing her agony as the royal privilege befitting a spouse of a suffering King.
>
> And so we knew her—a delightful and brilliant personality, a strong and wise educator, a great and beautiful soul.[87]

Her funeral mass was celebrated in Notre Dame Chapel at Trinity College, filled with her colleagues, her Sisters, her family, her former students and her many friends.

Sister Mary Patrick (Mary Furdon), former Provincial of the Maryland Province of the Sisters of Notre Dame, was Trinity's ninth president. She began her administration in the summer of 1953 as the

85. p. 119.
86. *Alumnae Journal*, Autumn, 1953, p. 7.
87. *Ibid*.

alumnae were preparing for their fiftieth anniversary celebration. She devoted herself with characteristic enthusiasm to her new position, learning to know the alumnae, faculty and students, facing the problems of finance and college development, trying to fill the gap left by the loss of Sister Catherine Dorothea.

The report of the Middle States evaluation committee in 1950 had called attention[88] to a flaw in the administrative organization that made the "academic president" subordinate in matters of budget and finance to the superior of the Notre Dame Community though they worked together and the president exercised considerable influence. The "division of authority" of 1940 had not been complete. Now an attempt was made to meet this criticism by still another arrangement. The new president was appointed both president and superior, but of the president's functions she kept for herself only finances, development, and public relations activities; and delegated to a vice-president for academic affairs the administration of the academic aspects of the college and representation of the college at meetings of professional, educational organizations, while the Dean of Students continued the supervision of student life. During the six years of her administration Sister Mary Patrick kept in close touch with all aspects of the college by a daily informal meeting with the Vice-President and the Dean of Students. Not until the appointment of Sister Margaret Claydon in 1959 did the "division of authority" become complete and the president of the college, who was not also superior of the community, assume complete responsibility for the administration of the college. The over-all authority of the Board of Trustees, of course, continues as it has since 1897.[89]

The changes that summer of 1953, difficult as they were for many, were put into perspective for the alumnae by Ellen A. Ganey as only she could do, while she linked them to the alumnae's fiftieth birthday.

> The autumn of 1903 was marked at Trinity by interesting events in the sphere of college administration. Sister Georgiana was in her third year as Superior and President. The Provincial Superior, Sister Agnes Mary, made her first visit, remaining a month to study the curriculum which had, as of that year, developed into a full college course. And from the Latin Department came one Sister Mary to begin her first year as Dean. Curiously enough, the fall of '53 had also brought about certain administrative changes. Our Superior, Sister Evelyn Marie (Helena Crowley, '25) did not finish her term at Trinity but was appointed Provincial with her headquarters at Ilchester. The Provincial's visits are now happily frequent and easily accom-

88. Cf. p. 127 earlier in this chapter.
89. Cf. Sister Margaret Claydon's article on the Board of Trustees, *Alumnae Journal*, Winter, 1969, pp. 60–61.

Sister Mary Patrick Furden (seated) with Deans: Sister Ann Francis Hoey, Sister Columba Mullaly.

plished, and the college curriculum, needless to say, is well-known to Superior Evelyn Marie. She has been succeeded in office by Sister Superior Mary Patrick, lately Provincial Superior of the Baltimore Province, who also bears the title of President of the College. Sister Catherine Dorothea's letter (page 5) explains this necessary change. Sister Ann Francis (Catherine Hoey, '24), we are happy to report, begins her twelfth year as Dean (she will equal Sister Mary's record yet!),[90] and Sister Columba (Catherine Mullaly, '25) has come down from the second floor to the Marble Corridor to occupy, as Vice President of the College, the office previously used by Sister Catherine Dorothea.

These changes always require adjustment—adjustment made with ready generosity and quiet simplicity by the Sisters as is the way of Notre Dame. The adjustment is not always accomplished with so much grace by those under their care. It is conceivable that the students of 1903–04 lamented with undue regret the end of Sister Josephine Ignatius' term as Dean, however much they may have liked the lady who left the Latin Room to succeed her! Experience has taught us that Providence orders all for the best interests of Trinity, and in the present instance we welcome a Superior and President of wide and long experience in administration, who knows Trinity

90. She outdid it, continuing as Dean of Students for nineteen years.

Sister Alice Clement (Monica Davis '34).

and its problems well. Sister Superior Mary Patrick is blessed with warmth and sincerity; she inspires immediate confidence and the assurance that Trinity's future is safe in her hands.[91]

Cooperating with and approving Sister Alice Clement's[92] competent financial reorganization, Sister Mary Patrick focused during the first two years of her administration on repairing, redecorating and generally "brightening up" the existing student facilities and planning needed expansion to meet growing enrollment. Backed by the Board of Trustees, she and Sister Alice Clement negotiated Trinity's first government loan for construction of a new student residence hall, the first new building on campus since the Science Building was finished in 1941. Ground was broken September 23, 1956, Cap and Gown Sunday, for "new" Cuvilly Hall, so called since it rose on the site of "old"

91. *Alumnae Journal*, Autumn '53, p. 7.
92. Third treasurer of Trinity College, known since the late 1960's as Sister Monica Davis.

Cuvilly of historic memory.[93] It was dedicated with ceremony on Cap and Gown Sunday 1958.

Meanwhile, in June 1954, the Alumnae Association celebrated its golden jubilee and Trinity welcomed her first "Golden Girls," the class of 1904, for their fiftieth reunion. Later that summer the college community was saddened by the death on August 4 of Sister Catherine Dorothea at Ilchester. Her funeral mass was celebrated as was fitting in Notre Dame Chapel at Trinity. Sister Mary Patrick wrote for the *Alumnae Journal*[94] a description of her last days and of the funeral. Much of that issue of the *Journal* was a memorial to Trinity's eighth president.

The thirteenth Alumnae Council[95] met at Trinity October 2–4, 1954, with the general topic "Catholic Alumnae in Volunteer Services." Aspects of volunteer work in education, among the aged and in civic life were presented by Mary Leonard '23, Eleanor Skahan Hickey '23, and Catherine Cray Eichenlaub '21, all experienced workers in those fields. This was Sister Mary Patrick's first Alumnae Council. Her report of the college and her "vision of Trinity's future, the needs of the college, and the means by which she hopes to attain their fulfillment" were received with interest by the alumnae present.

These "means" grew in the remaining years of Sister Mary Patrick's presidency to include, besides alumnae cooperation, the founding of the Father's Club (1956), the establishment of a Development Office with a full-time Director, and the Trinity College *Newsletter*, (1956), the founding of the Lay Board of Trustees in 1956 (an advisory board for the governing board of the college),[96] the campaign for funds for a new library, and the Washington Citizen's Advisory Committee (1959). In 1957 the business office moved to larger, modernized quarters.[97]

A convocation of the whole college, with representatives of the various boards, commemorated in October 1957 the sixtieth anniversary of the foundation of Trinity College. Dr. John Meng, dean and later president of Hunter College, a Trinity husband and father, member of the Lay Board was the speaker.[98] In 1958 the Father's Club sponsored the expansion and updating of the language laboratory which had first been established by the Pittsburgh Chapter ten years earlier.

January 29, 1959 at a special ceremony Mrs. Clara W. Berwick of Norwood, Massachusetts, presented to the college a collection of hand-

93. See Part III of this history for greater detail. Also *Trinity Newsletter* March 1957 and December 1958.
94. Autumn, 1954, pp. 13–14.
95. *Alumnae Journal*, Autumn 1954, pp. 15–19.
96. All of these organizations will be treated at greater length in Part III, Chapter 7, of this history. Cf. also *Newsletter*, March, 1957 (for Lay Board).
97. By 1973 these "quarters" had again been expanded to include both the "old" and the "new" offices at the north end of the Marble Corridor.
98. *Newsletter*, March 1958—picture.

carved ivories valued at $46,000.[99] This was housed at first in the Library Rare Book Room, but later moved to specially lighted cases in the O'Connor Art Gallery.

During Sister Mary Patrick's whole administration she cooperated with Sister Columba and Sister Ann Francis showing a great interest, without interference, in the academic life of the college, in the growing number of student and faculty fellowships, in the annual faculty forums on such topics as Excellence in Higher Education, Curriculum Revision, Independent Student Work. She watched with pride the achievement of students in their own government, in national student organizations such as the National Federation of Catholic College Students, and the National Student Association. When her six-year term as President and Superior ended in 1959, Sister Mary Patrick was convinced by her experience of the need of a president whose authority covered all facets of college administration. She succeeded in convincing the Board of Trustees as well as the Sisters of Notre Dame to take the final step in the "division of authority" and appoint such a president. She left Trinity College in the summer of 1959, sure of the competence of her young successor, turning with characteristic enthusiasm to other works in the Maryland Province of the Sisters of Notre Dame. She died at Villa Julie Infirmary on June 6, 1969, honored by the whole province and is buried in the Sisters' cemetery in Ilchester, Maryland.

Trinity's tenth president, Sister Margaret Claydon was, at thirty-six, the youngest to be appointed to that office and one of the youngest college presidents in the country in 1959. She was educated in the public schools of New Rochelle, New York, graduated in 1945 from Trinity College and the next year entered the Sisters of Notre Dame de Namur at Ilchester, Maryland. She earned her M.A. and Ph.D. from the Catholic University of America and had the experience of six years on the Trinity faculty as well as of a summer seminar at Oxford University and a year as an exchange professor at Notre Dame College of Education in Glasgow, Scotland where she was when appointed to the presidency.

In the summer of 1959 Sister Margaret began her new work with whole-hearted commitment, symbolized through the years by the signing of all her letters: "Devotedly in the Trinity." Her long administration spanned years of expansion, of significant change in the city, in the country, in the church, in higher education, and problem years of worldwide unrest reflected in college life by student unrest, of constant financial needs, of radically changing trends in enrollment and in curricular development, and in administrative and faculty organization.

99. *Newsletter*, April 1959.

Sister Margaret Claydon, Ph.D., 1960.

As an alumna and a member of the faculty Sister Margaret was cordially welcomed back from her exchange-year in Scotland. Ellen A. Ganey wrote in the *Alumnae Journal* that autumn in 1959[100]:

> The new president is well prepared to direct Trinity women, for besides her student years—the early forties when war made sacrifices (many small ones and a few very large ones) the order of the day for our girls, Sister Margaret was for six years a member of the ever-distinguished English faculty. Her outlook is that of a true scholar who looks beyond the immediate, and her values take form and color from richest traditions of Notre Dame and Trinity. We look to her with expectancy, certain of strong and sensitive leadership, trusting that she in turn will rely on her sister alumnae for any

100. p. 4f.

support, material or moral, perceptible or prayerful, which her plans for Trinity's future may require.

Sister Margaret herself stated the theme that would characterize her administration. "My whole care," she wrote, "is to maintain the tradition of excellence in Trinity's academic program." In an article "Trinity—Old and New"[101] she developed this idea.

> In the few meetings of higher education that I have already attended, in the educational journals, memos, bulletins, letters to presidents that I have been reading I have met repeatedly the exhortation for "education of excellence" and "education of the whole individual" . . .
>
> At Trinity today the spiritual, the intellectual, the social frameworks are fundamentally the same [as through the years]. . . . yet, because Trinity is a living organism, it is a growing one. It is rooted firmly in the past, but that past is the foundation on which the structure of the present is built, and the emerging structure of the present must be one capable of development for the future.
>
> Trinity exists not for imparting knowledge for knowledge's sake, but for the formation of educated Catholic women who have been trained under the standard of "*Scientia ancilla fidei,*" women who have mastered a certain amount of knowledge, yes, but who have realized its ancillary function in the progress from time to eternity. Trinity women should be those of strong, vibrant faith whose knowledge has helped in the setting of goals, the forming of attitudes; women who are critical in the true sense of the word; women of discernment; women who are leaders because their faith has pointed out the goals, and whose knowledge has indicated the means by which these goals are reached. . . .

A survey of the sixteen years of Sister Margaret's administration reveals six chief areas in which she was actively and whole-heartedly involved: the faculty and academic programs of the college, carrying through the goals stated above; student life and welfare even through the unrest of the late 1960's; fund-raising, development and building to meet growing needs; woman's higher education in general and Catholic higher education in particular; the works and welfare of her religious congregation, the Sisters of Notre Dame de Namur; and, finally, the wider sphere of national and international educational organizations in which she achieved a prestigious position. Through all of these activities the interest, affection, support, cooperation, and financial contribution of the alumnae, both individually and as an Association, were a source of strength to her.[102]

101. *Alumnae Journal*, Autumn, 1959, pp. 6–7.
102. Early in her administration, *Look* magazine in its Washington issue, April 26, 1960, included a feature article on Sister Margaret, "She Teaches Girls to Think," pp. 63–65. Illustrated.

Each of these areas will be treated in more detail in later chapters. As in the account of preceding administrations this will be a summary. It will complete the survey of the first seventy-five years of the college as shown in the administrations of ten presidents.

In close collaboration with the vice-president for academic affairs and three succeeding academic deans (cf. list p. 101), Sister Margaret affirmed and encouraged full faculty participation in the academic program of the college. Semi-annual Honors Convocations with academic procession, an eminent speaker, student awards and from 1961 the presentation to an alumna of the Julie Billart Medal were held for the ten years from 1959–1969. Faculty Forums, Symposia, "Think Sessions" (day-long workshops[103] on such subjects as "Education for the Dialogue" 1960, "Focus on the Individual," "Excellence in Teaching" and "Where We Stand") which were organized by the deans through the years gained from her enthusiastic support. Early in her administration she worked with the faculty academic policy committee to study reorganization of the curriculum which initiated in 1961 a more concentrated rearrangement of subject matter to help students avoid too great diffusion of attention or fragmentation of study at any one time. This "four course system," a local adaptation of the "three-three plan" popular in the 1960's, formed the pattern of study for Trinity students for most of the decade.

The year long self study in preparation for the Middle States Association Evaluation of March 1961 involved not only administration and staff, but practically every full-time faculty member so that all could feel a sense of accomplishment when the evaluating team approved with the statement: "Trinity College fulfills its stated goals and objectives very well. . . . It is a good college with exciting intellectual activity and unusual morale." More specifically the report affirms:

> Proof that Trinity's curriculum and course of study develop the students' potentialities and stimulate their scholarly interests is evidenced by (1) the relatively high percentage of entering students who graduate; (2) the number of competitive fellowships won by Trinity graduates, such as Woodrow Wilson and Fulbright Fellowships; (3) the substantial number of graduates undertaking advanced study immediately after graduation or in later years; (4) the type of positions graduates hold; and (5) the contribution made by Trinity alumnae to worthwhile community, national, and church activities.

While praising the library, the report strongly emphasized the need of an adequate, new building to house the collection and facilitate services. Through the work of Sister Martha Julie, Vice-President for De-

103. *Alumnae Journal*, Winter '60, p. 72, *et al.*

velopment, in close cooperation with the Lay Board especially Mr. Francis Friel of Philadelphia and Mr. Thomas Locroft, the Washington architect, with the Father's Club, with the librarians and with the alumnae the new library was built. It was dedicated in May, 1963 with Louis Wright, the librarian of the Folger Shakespearean Library, as principal speaker in the presence of many eminent guests of the library world, of *academia* in general, and friends of the college from business and civic life. Under the direction of Sister Helen Sheehan and her staff the books had been moved in one day in early spring to the new building.[104] In her Report 1959–1966 Sister Margaret Claydon wrote:

> The year 1962 saw the Library Building emerging from the former site of the Aventine Hill. Faculty and students themselves moved the entire collection of books into new quarters, a move which prompted a male faculty member to hang a sign in his office: "Never underestimate the power of a woman nor the college that educates her." Since that day the library has been an important center not only for study, but for meetings and "study-dates.". . . The old quarters of the library were converted into a faculty lounge and faculty offices, office space for Alumnae, Development, Public Information, and Admissions Offices.

As her attention was drawn more insistently to the manifold areas of college administration, to travel in support of Trinity, and as her participation in wider circles of higher education outside the college grew, Sister Margaret's interest in the academic welfare of the college never diminished. She encouraged Dr. Irena Roberts of the Chemistry Department in her research on education for the mature woman (1964) and an institute on the subject at Trinity in 1965 with Dr. Mary Bunting, Atomic Energy Commissioner as principal speaker. Though Dr. Roberts work was cut short by her untimely death in 1966, it came to fruition later in Trinity's "Degree Completion Program" initiated and fostered by Dr. Joan Kinnaird of the History Department. She worked with the Dean, Sister Elizabeth Woods, and her steering committee in preparation for the 1968 Middle States Association "Case Study" which again resulted in high commendation for the college.

In her printed report of the first seven years of her administration Sister Margaret wrote of the faculty:

> A college is only as good as its faculty. I rejoice in the competence of the 62 laymen (36 women, 26 men) and 31 Sisters of Notre Dame which distinguishes Trinity's teaching corps. Their advanced degrees are from more than 75 universities, among them Harvard, Johns Hopkins, Yale, Oxford,

104. *Washington Star* headline "Never Underestimate the Power of a Woman" and picture. Cf. *Alumnae Journal,* Spring '63, "The Big Move" (four pages of pictures immortalize the event).

Cambridge, Louvain and the Sorbonne. More than fifty percent have travelled and studied abroad, with more than forty fellowships to their credit in the last five years. These have been used to further their research and heighten their teaching competence.

Tremendous effort and energy and support have helped to increase faculty salaries over the past seven years. These have been increased 30.2 percent in the last five years. Committee Z of the Association of American University Professors cites Trinity among the top five percent of colleges working for faculty salary improvement.

IN 1959 THE FACULTY SALARY BUDGET WAS $255,500.

IN 1965–66 THE FACULTY SALARY BUDGET WAS $402,775.[105]

In addition to providing Teachers' Insurance and Annuity Association retirement benefits, the College has granted full tuition to daughters of full-time faculty members; has arranged for group life and group hospitalization plans as well as Blue Cross and Blue Shield benefits.

In addition to providing these fringe benefits and salary increases, the College has reduced full-time teaching responsibilities to twelve hours, and to eight hours for department chairmen.

In 1965 and 1966 the College honored those members of the faculty who had given twenty-five or more years of service to the College with the *Pro Ecclesia et Pontifice* medal. These were presented at the faculty dinner after Commencement by Archbishop Patrick A. O'Boyle to:

1965: Sister Ann Julia, Professor of Philosophy
Miss Ellen A. Ganey, Executive Secretary of the Alumnae Association
Sister Helen, Librarian
Sister Mary Robert, Associate Professor of Physics
Dr. Eva J. Ross, Professor of Sociology
Sister St. John Nepomucene, Professor of Chemistry
Sister Therese of the Blessed Sacrament, Professor of English
Mrs. Hubert J. Treacy, Associate Professor of Physics
Dr. Mary C. Varnhorn, Professor of Mathematics

1966: Sister Columba, Vice President

1967: Sister Ann Francis Hoey, Dean of Students, 1942–1961; Professor of Education

Miss Marian Louise Pierce, who had succeeded Señora de Ruiz in the Spanish department, had been honored for twenty-five years of service at a reception on her retirement in 1957 and Miss Elsie Kernan in 1936.

In the years from 1967 to 1975, the president honored others in appreciation of twenty-five years of service on the faculty:

105. In 1975–1976 the budget for faculty salaries was $736,678.85.

1968	Dr. Ilona Ellinger, Professor of Art
1970	Mrs. Margaret Giovannini, Professor of English
1971	Miss Jane O'Boyle, Associate Dean
1973	Miss Margaret Durbin, Associate Professor of Physical Education; Dr. Edna Fluegel, Professor of Political Science; Sister Marie Dimond, Professor of Biology
1972	Sister Monica Davis (Alice Clement), Treasurer Sister Catherine Marie Lee, Registrar, Sister Marion Timothy Walsh, Science Librarian
1975	Sister Dorothy Beach (Francis Mary), Librarian

Table V, "Growth of Trinity College," 1959–1966 taken from Sister Margaret's report, shows graphically the trend of those years, the years of implementing the recommendations of the Conference on Education Beyond the High School,[106] of taking seriously the Tichton Report,[107] resulting in Trinity's Ten-Year Projection 1963–1973. Sister Margaret, however, states clearly (almost prophetically as the future proved):

> Even as I look back over the past seven years, I look ahead to Trinity's future, to her place in the whole educational scene of these United States. Invited to join the College Research Center along with Briarcliff, Connecticut College, Hollins, Mount Holyoke, Randolph-Macon Woman's College, Smith, Sweet Briar, Vassar, and Wheaton, a new and most important phase of Trinity's apostolate began. It is important that among the best women's colleges in the country Trinity be in their number. Trinity cannot stop growing, cannot stop planning, cannot relax into a comfortable *status quo*. Her faculty, committed to the education of women, is dedicated and selfless. Her students are earnest and capable and restless—seeking the best possible education for their roles in contemporary world.

A Pilot Program initiated in 1968 to experiment with methods of allowing students more individual responsibility for their own education spear-headed the curriculum revision of 1970. Of this the Dean, Sister Margaret Finnegan, wrote in the *Alumnae Journal*[108]:

> In March, 1969, a Task Force was established, composed of faculty members of the Committee on Curriculum and Academic Policy and of students, which was mandated to examine, in the light of the contemporary scene, all aspects of the then-current curriculum, and more especially the system of required courses set up to guarantee the breadth requisite for a liberal arts degree. The faculty devoted two days to discussing and refining the reports of this Task Force, and on February 17, 1970, voted to endorse a curriculum

106. Constituent Member Meeting, American Council on Education, "Education Beyond the High School," March 19–20, 1956. Sister Columba had attended as a delegate of the Association of American Colleges.
107. Cf. footnote, p. 142.
108. "The New Curriculum," *Alumnae Journal*, Summer, 1970, pp. 195–198. Cf. Chapter 5, "Curriculum," for more detail.

TABLE V. *Growth of Trinity College Between 1959–1960 and 1965–1966*

	1959–1960	1965–1966	Percentage of Increase
Student Enrollment	646	916	42%
Faculty	73	93	27%
Religious	37	31	(−16%)
Lay Men	7	26	271%
Lay Women	29	36	24%
Library Holdings	75,600	96,618	28%
Cost of College Operation	$1,304,770	$ 2,352,919	80%
General Fee	$ 1,850	$ 2,450	32%
Student Aid (Scholarship)	$ 80,337	$ 128,422	60%
Endowment	$ 729,378	$ 1,249,198	71%
Contributed Services	$ 115,078	$ 142,087	26%
Gift Support	$ 167,221	$ 338,601	102%
Campus Size	34 acres	58 acres	71%
Plant Value	$5,167,865	$10,384,361	101%
Number of Buildings	5	8	

based on "responsible choice with (responsible) guidance." A faculty committee with student representation was set up to work out the implementation of the changes, and several faculty meetings were held to consider the work of this committee. By the pre-registration week in May, procedures had been worked out to allow students who wished to take advantage of the curricular revisions for 1970–1971 to do so. (Students who preferred to remain under the traditional curriculum were given that option.) All members of the Class of 1974 will follow the New Curriculum, which does not represent a radical break with the past, but rather that logical development and reallocation of academic resources which seem to be called for by the "changing times."

The choice in 1968 of Trinity College by the Middle States Association for a Case Study, instead of an evaluation, which was followed by a commendatory report served to indicate continuing recognition of the academic excellence of the college, as did the establishment in 1970 of a Phi Beta Kappa chapter on campus. A Master of Arts in Teaching Program for Urban Schools began in 1966.[109] Limited at first to English in secondary schools, it later included history, sciences, foreign languages on both elementary and secondary levels as well as courses in teaching

109. A Master of Arts in Teaching program for Sisters of Notre Dame teaching in elementary schools had been initiated in the 1950's and successfully administered by Sister Ann Julia Kinnirey, then Director of Education for the Maryland Province.

the mentally retarded and an award-winning Bi-lingual Bi-cultural program. The graduate program in Pastoral Ministry began in 1973 to fill a growing need in the Post Vatican II Church in America.[110]

Throughout the years of her administration Sister Margaret manifested her lively interest in the students and their activities which had begun in her own student days and matured during her teaching experience. She rejoiced not only in their individual academic awards, their student research projects in chemistry, biology, economics, English and others; but she was an enthusiastic supporter of their sports, dramatics, Glee Club and volunteer civic, religious, and educational activities. In cooperation with five successive Deans of Students (cf. list p. 101) she encouraged the work of the Student Government, acclaiming the NSA Welling awards, the 50th Anniversary celebration of Student Government, and suffering with the students through the difficulties of reorganization to a new form of Student Association, the modernizing of time-honored traditions, and the unrest, protests, and boycott of the end of the decade and into the seventies. In spite of firm action in 1970 by both President and Board of Trustees, the students realized Sister Margaret's interest in their welfare, a fact which helped to heal bruises and lead into calmer times.[111]

Sister Margaret came to office as the wave of drastically increased enrollment, observed and planned for by educators through the decade of the fifties, was reaching higher education. In the face of very rapidly increasing enrollment (the popularly called "Battle of the Bulge in education") she set to work to provide living space and academic facilities for more students. Cuvilly Hall had just been finished with the aid of a government loan, under the Housing Act of 1950, and occupied in 1958. With the help of alumnae, of three successive Development Directors, and of the Lay Board, the Fine Arts addition to O'Connor Hall (1960), the Library (1963) and Kerby Residence Hall (1965) were built. She and Sister Monica Davis, Treasurer, with the active participation of the other executive officers, prepared a Ten-Year projection (1963–1973) following the guidelines of the Tichton Report.[112] This projection exactly foretold the needs of the expanding college for five years until the unprecedented events of 1968 invalidated all projections in higher education as in many other fields: civic, economic and social. With Sister Martha Julie Keehan, Vice-President for Development 1959–1963, who emphasized the personal approach to alumnae giving; Directors of Development Sister Ann Paul Shuman (1963–65) and Roger Schifferli (1965–1975) who initiated the "New Resources for Trinity"

110. Cf. Chapter on Curriculum for greater detail.
111. Cf. Chapter 6 for details of student activities.
112. Tichton, Sidney G., *Ten Year Budget*, Fund for the Advancement of Education, 1951 (Revised 1961).

Hugh P. McFadden, Esq. First Lay Chairman of the Board of Trustees.

program, the "Concerned Action" program with its Lewis Foundation Challenge grant, and the 75th Anniversary Fund, with the $75,000 O'Neill challenge grant, Sister Margaret saw annual giving for Trinity grow from $205,097 in 1958–1959 to $669,438 in 1974–1975.[113]

113. Cf. Chapter 7 for more detail.

Trinity College, as has been seen in an earlier chapter of this history,[114] has had an independent Board of Trustees since August, 1897. Until 1969 the members of this governing board were all Sisters of Notre Dame de Namur with the one exception of Archbishop of Baltimore (or of Washington after the division of the archdiocese). The Sisters, however, were advised and aided by the eminently competent lay men and women of the Ladies Auxiliary Board (since 1898), the Advisory Board (1900–1935), the Fathers' Club (1956–1965), the Lay Board of Trustees (1957–1971) and the President's Council (1972 to the present), and other friends with expertise in finance and in higher education. By 1968, the Board of Trustees, convinced that the times required changes, revised its By-laws to include lay members. Sister Margaret wrote in the *Alumnae Journal*[115]:

> . . . . Recognition of their (lay men and women) contribution coupled with the impact of the Vatican II documents impelled the fifteen S.N.D. trustees to consider the removal of restriction for membership on the Corporate Board. A new Act of Congress was sought to remove such restrictions. . . .
>
> Finally, in September, 1968, after much discussion, many suggestions and revisions, the Board of Trustees voted approval of the by-laws as prepared by the College counsel. . . . The restructuring calls for at least one third of the membership to be Sisters of Notre Dame, for a liaison trustee from the advisory Board of Lay Trustees elected by that board, and for an alumnae trustee elected by the Alumnae Association. . . . The step that the College takes at this moment is one of confidence in God. It is not a revolutionary step, but rather a logical development of the revolution we inherited from those valiant women of the 1890's who provided for a separate, independent Board of Trustees.

It is difficult to separate into clear-cut categories Sister Margaret's other three areas of interest,[116] and those of the college during her administration, for the strengthening of women's higher education, especially Catholic women's colleges, for the renewal of Catholicism in the light of Vatican Council II, for ecumenism, for the international mission of the Sisters of Notre Dame de Namur in education. A partial list of workshops and Lecture Series initiated and organized by Trinity College faculty members during the decade of the 1960's reflects activity on campus in these areas.[117]

114. Chapter 2, "Strong Foundations." Cf. Sister Margaret Claydon's article, *Alumnae Journal,* Winter, 1969, pp. 60–61.
115. Winter, 1969, pp. 60–61.
116. Cf. p. 136.
117. Programs, copies of speeches, participants. T.C. Archives. Cf. also *Trinity Newsletter* and the *Alumnae Journal* for descriptions.

B'nai B'rith—Trinity College Conference, February 22, 1962. "Pluralism in America"

Seventh Workshop in Instructional Programs in Spirituality. August 17–26, 1964.

Six Lectures on the Constitution on the Liturgy. October 18–November 22, 1964. In preparation for the introduction of the New Liturgy, Advent, 1964.

Pluralism, Politics, Persons, Their Impact on the Catholic Woman's College Today, July 5–24, 1965.

B'nai B'rith—Trinity College Conference: Dialogue, February 22, 1966.

Education for Ecumenism: Workshop for Teachers, June 13–30, 1966.

Colloquium: Trinity in Post-Vatican II. August, 1966.

Catholic Women's College Conference, April, 1969, organized by student officers. Keynote address by John J. Meng, Ph.D., Executive Vice President of Fordham University.[118]

Women's Place Conferences, series of four, day-long conferences, February and March, 1973, on Women in Science, in Business, Government and Law, in Communications and the Media, and in Community Development.[119]

In 1967 Sister Margaret emerged as the champion of Catholic women's colleges when her answers to Jacqueline Grennan's announcement of the "secularization" of Webster College were widely publicized in the press.[120]

Sister Margaret's deep interest in her religious congregation spanned the sixteen years of her administration. As a Sister of Notre Dame de Namur she kept up her close ties with and interest in the activities of the community at Trinity College, and of the Maryland Province. For several years, until obliged to resign because of the needs of her office as college president, she served on the Provincial Council. She organized the Notre Dame Education Association of Sisters from all American provinces which met annually during the 1960's. She was one of the Maryland Province Delegates to the Special Renewal General Chapter of the Sisters of Notre Dame 1967–1969. She actively cooperated with Sister Ann Julia Kinnirey, Director of Education, and the Notre Dame Education Center, for the education of young Sisters of Notre Dame, and later with the Religious Educators Foundation for educating young teachers not only of Notre Dame, but of other orders who wished to join. In 1970 she initiated and carried through with the cooperation of the Notre Dame community at Trinity College an international meeting of Sisters of Notre Dame at the College. *Notre Dame*

118. *Alumnae Journal,* Spring, 1969, pp. 120–124; *Newsletter,* June, 1969.
119. *Trinity News,* March, 1974, p. 2.
120. T.C. Archives. Sister Margaret Claydon's Papers. Cf. "Academic Freedom and the Catholic Woman's College," *Alumnae Journal,* Summer 1967, p. 294.

1970 was not an official chapter or assembly, but an invitational meeting to which Sisters from Belgium, England, South Africa, Swaziland, Rhodesia, Brazil, and all parts of the United States responded. The editor of the *Alumnae Journal* introducing her report wrote[121]:

> Recognizing the intense need for personal and communal reflection, Sisters from far-reaching parts of the world came together at Trinity for two weeks of the summer to "stand there," to discuss . . . to reflect . . . and to change.
>
> Their object was to listen to two voices—the Voices of the Seventies and the Voices of Notre Dame, and to ask themselves the question, "Are we really speaking the same language?" It was for all a time of political and social as well as religious awakening. The issues which were aired at the conference are not the exclusive concerns of the Sisters of Notre Dame—in fact, such topics as the Third World Movement, the secular university, and the problems of the ghetto, sound more like the programs of a student-staffed free university than the concerns of a religious conference.

That statement, from a young editor who a short time before was a part of student life herself, is high praise. Her whole article[122] is a perceptive analysis of the meeting and worth reading.

From the press conference arranged for her in the early weeks of her administration by Mary Tinley Daly, '24, publicity director, Sister Margaret began to move out into the "wider sphere of national and international educational"[123] life. That news conference which emphasized her youth, her educational philosophy and her goals for the future, generated articles not only in the Washington papers, but in the secular and religious press throughout the country reminiscent of the nationwide publicity about the founding of the college in 1897.[124] A paragraph in *Time* magazine, and a picture interview in *Look* magazine's Washington issue of April 26, 1960, "She Trains Girls to Think,"[125] introduced her to a wide audience as well as to delighted alumnae throughout the country.

Sister Margaret actively participated in the work of national associations for higher education, was a member of commissions of the American Council on Education, the Association of American Colleges, and on the Board of Trustees of the Middle States Association of Colleges and Secondary Schools, the Board of Trustees of Emmanuel College, Boston, and of the Board of Directors of the National Council of Independent Colleges and Universities. She was a member of the *Pacem in Terram Conference* in New York 1965 and spoke on higher edu-

121. Autumn, 1970, p. 4.
122. "Notre Dame International," *Alumnae Journal*, Autumn, 1970, p. 407.
123. Cf. p. 136.
124. Cf. p. 33.
125. This article was cited with an Award of Merit by the APRA.

cation in various cities.[126] She gave the closing general address, "Inheriting a Revolution," at the convention of the National Catholic Educational Association in New York, April 22, 1965. She was on the executive committee of that organization and the president of its Department of Higher Education, 1968 to 1970. In 1971 she was one of nine American delegates to the Second International Congress of Delegates from Catholic Universities sponsored by the Sacred Congregation for Catholic Education.

> As the only woman to participate in the conference and as an American representing a freestanding college, Sister Margaret's role was unique. This is the first year that free-standing colleges, as opposed to universities, have been recognized by the International Federation of Catholic Universities—with the stipulation that they offer at least one graduate program leading to a masters degree. Sister Margaret and Monsignor Terrence Murphy, President of the College of St. Thomas in St. Paul, Minnesota, proposed that all four year degree granting institutions of higher learning be admitted to the Federation. This proposal, which was accepted, will primarily affect Catholic colleges in the United States, where these four year liberal arts institutions are prevalent.
>
> During the discussion of the role of theologians in Catholic higher education, Sister Margaret made another interesting point. She was successful in having the delegates acknowledge that competent theologians might be women as well as men.[127]

In 1974, Sister Margaret Claydon "announced that she would leave office at the end of the 1974–75 academic year, taking a sabbatical at that time before returning to teaching and research."[128] She was rounding out sixteen years of service as president, the longest administration in Trinity history. "I have been honored," she stated,

> to serve Trinity in these years of exciting challenge. I believe that there are many opportunities ahead for institutions of higher learning for women. Another woman with new ideas and perspectives should be given the opportunity I have had to shape the future. When I leave during Trinity's Seventhy-fifth Anniversary Year, I will leave with great faith in women's colleges and in Trinity's continuing role in the education of women. I shall leave a college which is looking to the next seventy-five years with enthusiasm and vigor.

The Board of Trustees, whose bylaws require that the president be a Sister of Notre Dame de Namur, appointed a search committee with representatives of the trustees, the administration, faculty, alumnae, and students to find the eleventh president of Trinity College.

126. T.C. Archives—Sister Margaret Claydon's papers.
127. *Trinity News*, Winter, 1972, p. 2.
128. *Trinity News*, July 1974.

Sister Margaret Claydon, c. 1970.

In a letter to the alumnae,[129] Sister Margaret Claydon not only explained her reasons for resigning, to leave Trinity's needs to "a new president for a new season"; but she stated firmly:

> I do not intend, however, that my last year (the sixteenth) be a "lame duck" year, but one of continued effort in Trinity's interest. The primary concern in 1974–1975 will be to raise endowment funds for increasing the

129. *Alumnae Journal*, Spring 1974.

> endowment of the College. If we could begin to work towards attaining six million dollars in endowment, we could insure Trinity's continuance into the next century. My goal for next year will be $750,000.
>
> For my part, despite other opportunities available to me, I have one desire and that is to return to teaching Trinity women. I would like to spend the year 1975–76 in study and research and then return to teaching in 1976–77.

That last year was, indeed, a busy and fruitful one. In November 1974 new concentrations were added to the curriculum: Business Administration in the Economics Department, Bilingual Bicultural Elementary Education, Early Childhood and Special Education in the Education Department. Sister Margaret continued crusading for the advancement of education for and about women. She mourned the death of the Honorable Paul Aikin, Chairman of the Board of Trustees, but turned confidently to the newly elected Board President, Pierce Flanigan. In 1975 the faculty held an all-college dinner to honor her. She was the commencement speaker at the Catholic University and received a second doctorate from that institution, honorary this time. On the same day she presided for the last time at Trinity's Commencement, advising the seniors to go forth to serve others and so make full use of their Trinity education.

At the Reunion, the Alumnae expressed their appreciation at the banquet with speeches, cheers, and gifts for one of their own who was celebrating her own thirtieth reunion. Having introduced her successor, Sister Rose Ann Fleming, at the Board of Trustees meeting earlier in the year, Sister Margaret drove off from Trinity in late June in the Ford Maverick given her by the alumnae to spend a "refresher" year as a Visiting Fellow at Timothy Dwight College in Yale University. In September 1976, she rejoined the faculty as Professor of English.

Sister Rose Ann Fleming began her administration as eleventh president of Trinity College on July 1, 1975. She continued the celebration of the college's seventy-fifth anniversary year. That gala year culminated on December 8, 1975 with the solemn inauguration ceremony for Sister Rose Ann, the first of its kind at Trinity, and a formal reception for friends, held at the Belgian Embassy. Seventy-seven institutions and associations of higher education sent delegates to the inauguration ceremony and honorary degrees were granted to Representative Corinne C. Boggs of Louisiana, Margaret F. Grace, and Patricia Sullivan Lindh '50, an eminent worker in politics and Special Assistant for Women to President Ford. The Trinity Award was presented to Claire Boothe Luce and Abigail Quigley McCarthy.

The first two years of Sister Rose Ann's administration, which fall within the scope of this history are best summarized by excerpts from her own report to the Board of Trustees: "Recent Growth 1975–1978."

Sister Rose Ann Fleming, Ph.D. with Anne Hooley '15 and Barbara Kennelly '58.

At a time when many small, private, women's colleges have allowed their struggle for fiscal solvency and increased student enrollment to distract them from their primary obligation of providing, maintaining, expanding, and constantly evaluating an academic curriculum of quality and depth, Trinity, over the past three years, has had an encouraging record of success in all these areas.

THE "NEW CURRICULUM"

Trinity's financial stability depends, in great measure, on its enrollment. It is significant, therefore, that a large percentage of Trinity's students claim to have been drawn to the college by its academic reputation. But an academic reputation is not acquired overnight. From the beginning, Trinity's vigilant concern for the quality of its academic program has prevented complacency and ensured constant evaluation and periodic revision of its curriculum. As a result, its programs and courses have always combined perspectives that are both historical (in the best tradition of the liberal arts) and contemporary. The recent development of the "new curriculum" bears witness to the continuance of this vigilance even to the present day.

One year before Harvard University introduced its widely-publicized core curriculum for undergraduate students, Trinity College introduced its "new curriculum"—more properly known as the General Program of 1977. Designed to control the breadth and depth of the student's search for knowledge by requiring courses in the humanities, the social sciences, the physical and natural sciences, and mathematics, the General Program of 1977 fosters a community of scholarship at Trinity by ensuring a common body of knowledge to which subsequent studies can be related, particularly in a student's major field.

To facilitate the student's personal growth and development and to assist her in exploiting to the full the relationship between her liberal arts program and her career goals, the Counseling and Career Development Center, reorganized in 1977, offers individual counseling services as well as workshops and seminars on such key issues as job interviewing skills, résumé writing, and job campaigning strategies.

In addition, many academic departments now offer internships or practica that enable the student to gain on-site experience in her chosen field even before graduation. Two examples, out of the many that might be cited, will give some indication of the relevance and scope of such experiential learning. Serving as research assistant to the Director of Music at the National Shrine of the Immaculate Conception, music major Joellen Brassfield, '80, organizes files, searches out full scores or complete editions of musical compositions, marks the bowing of orchestral parts, and performs a number of other tasks related to her chosen field. In a very different atmosphere, psychology major Kim Strange, '80, gains both clinical and experimental experience under Dr. Lourdes Ortega of St. Elizabeth's Hospital by working directly with alcoholics, studying their files, and presenting papers on her findings.

ADMISSIONS

As in the past, tuition income is still Trinity's largest source of revenue. But tuition income is no longer able to sustain Trinity's operational costs.

Like most women's colleges, Trinity also knew a time—in the 50's and mid-60's—when the greatest problem of an Admissions Officer was not how to attract more students to the college, but how to reject, without alienating, a large proportion of those who applied for admission. Today, all that is changed. Admissions has become a game of skill, and the successful Admissions Officer is the one who knows the rules of the game. Fortunately for us, Trinity's Admissions Officer is one of the successful ones. She knows that recruitment in the late 1970's must be active, not passive; that the tried-and-true sources of freshman applications must be supplemented with new sources; that she must use new methods of recruitment if she is to compete successfully for students in today's nationally shrunken pool of applicants; that Trinity has much to offer and much to learn from the nontraditional (usually adult) student. As a result of her efforts, the number of freshmen rose steadily from September 1975, when only 83 freshmen matriculated, to September 1978, when 142 matriculated—a striking 71% increase.

By reason of this welcome increase in the number of freshmen enrolled each year, Trinity is able to move steadily toward its optimal enrollment of 800 undergraduate students. When this goal has been reached, the funds currently being used to supply the deficit between tuition income and operational expenses can be used for other important purposes (e.g., deferred maintenance, debt retirement, faculty salary increase).

Academically, both recent graduates and present students continue the Trinity tradition of significant scholarly achievement.

FISCAL STABILITY

One of Trinity's primary goals over the last few years has been the reestablishment of fiscal stability. As many educational institutions have learned to their grief, this is not an easy goal to reach. But Trinity *has* reached it. Within the span of four short years, as the following statistics will show, Trinity has succeeded in turning an operating deficit of nearly half a million dollars into an operating surplus of nearly a quarter of a million dollars.

The transformation was accomplished by a variety of means and through the generosity of a multiplicity of friends. Some of the major steps are listed below.

1. In 1977, Mr. James P. Farrell, husband of Kathryn Fisher Farrell, '25, established a $50,000 Challenge Gift Fund to match on a dollar-for-dollar basis all gifts to the college received after May 9 and before June 30 of that year. Thanks to the generosity of Mr. Farrell and of Trinity's Alumnae, who met the challenge, Trinity was able, with the $100,000 thus generated, to make the last payment of the 25-acre West Campus and hence to decrease our indebtedness by a substantial amount.
2. Subsequently, with funds realized from the sale of this undeveloped tract of land across Michigan Avenue from the main campus, Trinity began to rebuild its depleted unrestricted endowment fund. The investment income from these unrestricted funds is available for a number of purposes, including debt retirement as well as annual operating expenses, "seed money" for new academic ventures, and increased faculty salaries.
3. In 1977–1978, Trinity was successful in meeting the terms of a one-for-three Challenge Grant of $75,000 from the National Endowment for the Humanities with $225,000 in "new money" contributed by our Alumnae.
4. Under the leadership of Mrs. John Fitzer (Isabel Seymour, '53) and the inspiration of the NEH Challenge Grant, moreover, Trinity's Alumnae and friends responded so generously to the Annual Fund Drive for 1977–1978 that contributions soared over the $800,000 mark, placing Trinity tenth in the list of women's colleges receiving the most generous support from their constituents. The addition of these unrestricted funds to Trinity's annual income was a substantial boon to the college.
5. During the same period, Trinity restructured its debt service from short to more manageable intermediate terms, thus improving the cash flow and helping to bring the current deficit under control.

a) Since 1975, by a series of special arrangements with HUD, Trinity has been able to defer payment on the dormitory bonds for Cuvilly and Kerby Halls. As a result, the college has not had to make a cash outlay for principal or interest over the past three years.

b) The college also requested and received a moratorium from July 1976 to March 1979 on principal payments on a loan from the Electrical Workers Benefit Association (EWBA).

But these moratoria will not last forever. In 1979, the college must renew its debt retirement payments to both HUD and EWBA. When this occurs, Trinity's gradually increasing income from unrestricted endowment will acquire a new significance as a means of ensuring that the college will never again be compelled to operate at a deficit in order to make such payments.

6. Through a series of "leadership" dinners, at which she has described specific Trinity needs to prospective benefactors of the college, and through subsequent individual appeals to those who had been invited, Trinity's president has been extremely effective in broadening the base of our fund-raising activities and in securing large gifts for the college. As presently planned, these "leadership" dinners will continue to be held in various parts of the United States.

RESTORATION, RENOVATION, MODERNIZATION, BEAUTIFICATION

Because of the necessary deferral of routine maintenance and major repairs during the decade of financial exigency from which the college has just emerged, Trinity's buildings are presently in a regrettable state of disrepair.

It is a pleasure to report, therefore, that the college Physical Plant Committee is aware of the situation and has already drawn up a Five-Year Plan (1978–1983) for restoring the college buildings to their former dignity and elegance.

First impressions are important. Because Main is the building most frequently visited by prospective students and other guests of the college, it is there that the work of restoration, renovation, judicious modernization, and beautification will begin. During December and early January, detailed projections and cost estimates are being prepared by the firm of Metric Management and Engineering in Philadelphia, Pa. They will be presented to the president in final form toward the end of January and work on Main will commence shortly thereafter.

INCREASED ENDOWMENT

Trinity has now weathered the worst of the financial storm that so recently threatened it. Revenues have been increased by improved tuition income as well as by grants and gifts and challenge funds to a point where

Pope John Paul II, presiding at Ecumenical Prayer Service, Notre Dame Chapel.

a balanced budget is again a reality; expenditures are under control; the debt retirement service has assumed manageable proportions; and the college once again has an endowment fund.

Even more importantly, the college also has a viable short-term and long-term *program,* not just for ensuring the continuance of this financial stability into the future, but also for increasing endowment funds to a level

The Pope Blessing the Sick, Kerby Hall lawn.

that can be expected to forestall a repetition of the recent financial crisis in the future.

Trinity's new development plan for 1978–1979—the introduction of a program of Deferred Giving and Pooled Incomes—is directed precisely toward this latter goal of increasing our endowment fund to a level that will obviate future crises. Although it is still in its initial stages, it gives promise of being a most effective instrument for achieving this purpose.

Secretaries

This chapter should not end without a mention of the secretaries who have assisted in the administration. Four whose able and long service span the years since the 1940's have been chosen to represent the many. Miss Mary Julie Casey (T.C. '45) was the executive secretary to Sister Catherine Dorothea during the second half of her administration. Mrs. Marsha Matarrese, began in the 1950's as secretary to the Vice President, helping also the Dean of students and members of the faculty. Early in Sister Margaret's administration she was promoted to Administrative Assistant to the President. She served with unusual competence in that capacity until the 1970's when she became for a short time Associate to the Director of Development, before leaving Trinity for other fields of service.

Miss Fredericka Hodder organized and efficiently ran the first separate Office of Faculty Secretary in the 1960's and early 1970's. She was succeeded by Mrs. Julie Garrett as Director of Faculty Support Services, who still presides in that office.

CHAPTER FIVE

The Academic Program

The visible change in higher education in America since 1900, quickening yearly since the end of World War II, has been so swift that one is likely to underestimate the deeper continuity that persists. Yet that continuity is frequently a more important fact than the changes. WILIAM C. DE VANE[1]

FROM THE perspective of more than three-quarters of a century, it is possible to identify the values that Trinity has aimed to develop, and to encourage in young women for nearly eight decades. This list includes academic competence to the best of individual potential; maturity, including critical thinking and decision-making guided by principle and based on a consideration of more than one aspect of a problem; a sense of responsibility; active service for others in social, economic and political life and finally a convinced personal Christian commitment. We must remember that these values do not "sprout up" by magic. They are not attained to the same extent by all. They represent a slow growth through the years of college and need not only instruction, but the interaction of faculty and students, of life together in and out of class, in student government, in the myriad activities that college life provides.

The college has offered since the turn of the century an educational program that has changed to meet the demands of changing times, a solid program that echoes the educational ideals of St. Julie Billiart who believed in getting to essentials.

A survey of the aims and objectives of the College will give meaning to the academic history attempted in this Chapter. The nearly 8,000 alumnae show how well these aims were achieved. In 1897, reflecting on the need for the college she was to help found, Sister Mary Euphrasia wrote: "How necessary it is, then, that our influential Catholic women should be trained to give to society, not only the force of example, valuable though that must ever be: —but the benefit of a more enlightened knowledge than the cleverest girl in her teens can acquire, and that from a Catholic source! . . . The cry of the age is knowledge."[2]

1. *Higher Education in Twentieth Century America,* Cambridge, Mass., 1965, p. v.
2. Ms. *Foundations,* pp. 33–4. Cf. 1898 pamphlet (catalogue), p. 23.

Incorporated August 20, 1897 as an institution for the higher education of women, the college opened in November, 1900. The first catalogue announces the advantages of Washington: "Close by is the Catholic University; the Capitol, the National Library, the museums and art collections which are important aids to study, may be easily reached from the college."

In 1905, the Dean, Sister Mary, concluded her report of the academic year with a statement of her belief in the lasting values of a Trinity education: ". . . I would add that every effort has been made on the part of the Reverend Professors and of the Faculty, to instill into the hearts of the Trinity Students principles of honor and virtue and to mold their characters as well as to develop their intelligence. Immediate results may not always be visible, but we must assuredly believe that the years passed at Trinity are a well-spent, if arduous, sowing-time which cannot fail to produce a rich and abundant harvest in after-life."

An essay written by a senior of 1910, Agnes Brady, on the adaptability of a college course illustrates that the Trinity student nearly seventy years ago was indeed "modern." She wrote:

> The days of the backboard and rigidity in education are gone, never to return. Instead of trying to gain the desired erect carriage by being fastened to a board, the college girl, exponent of the strenuous life, goes in for athletics, and illustrates enthusiastically her belief in the "sound mind in a sound body" theory. And the change finds its parallel in the development of the mental energies. The old methods aimed to produce what were considered desirable types, and the process must have been painful. Small wonder one bright little girl wished mournfully that she had lived in the time of Charles II, "for then education was very much neglected." But the increased attention given to the developing of individuality, together with the universal change from static to dynamic methods, has been followed by a recognition of the need of plasticity. Knowledge no longer, but power is the watchword. A real education should not aim at permanent adjustment, but should rather give to each individual the power to adjust himself to shifting phases of his environment, so as to react upon it beneficially. [Today's student would not have used the masculine pronoun.]
>
> . . . From the very beginning of her course the college girl is taught that she is a social being, that she must render social service, and help to carry out the social purpose. This does not mean that she is commanded to devote herself to settlement work or other charities, although many college graduates have become actively interested in such enterprises. She simply learns that she must give generously since she has received much, that she is expected to react for good upon her environment. A college education, if it means anything, means a broadening of sympathies. The wider outlook attained by a mental development carefully guided, and, as well, the absolute, matter-of-course democracy of college life, both aided and abetted by

> that dearest gift of the gods, a sense of humor, surely ought to give the broad sympathy which has been pronounced the touchstone of true culture.

The President of the college reported in 1914:

> In these days when Suffrage, Social Service, professional and industrial activities appeal so strongly to the intellect and the sympathies of women, it is difficult for her (sic) to keep to a *via media* and not be carried away to one extreme or another.

The Dean's Report of 1922 notes that "one cannot fail to realize that the problems confronting the young people of the present day are more complicated than those of the past generation. . . . We need women carefully trained in secular sciences . . . with those spiritual principles that alone can carry them safely through life."

The following statement of "ideals" or "aims" appeared in the catalogues from 1911 to 1949 with the deletion of the somewhat dated material in brackets.

> IDEALS.—Not only in the instruction given in the various college courses, but throughout the careful ordering of the whole college life with its religious influences and its uplifting associations, its liberties and its restraints, a twofold idea is kept in view; the *true scholar*, with knowledge many-sided as well as thorough, with a firm grasp of first principles, a just judgment, a well-trained power of reasoning, a cultured appreciation of all that is true, and good, and beautiful; the *true woman*, with a clear reverent sense of her duty to God, herself, and her fellow-creatures, with every womanly gift and virtue well developed, with a strong, self-reliant character, and with resourceful ability for highest womanly service, whatever be her destined sphere of life or her chosen field of labor.
>
> These qualities of mind and heart are what Trinity's degrees are meant to stand for. These are the ideals which brought Trinity College into existence, [built its walls, established its curriculum] encouraged its work, and ensured its growth. These are the aims which are constantly held before the student [from the day of her entrance upon college life until the final hour when the seal of approval is placed upon her finished course.] (Catalogue 1911–1912)

Between 1955 and 1960, the faculty studied in detail and reaffirmed the aims and objectives of the college, and approved the new statements published in catalogue and faculty handbook: These statements reflect sixty years of value oriented education. I shall quote these slightly overlapping, but complementary statements:

> Trinity College by the circumstances of its foundation is committed to Catholic principles and to a level of education equal to the best in the United States. . . . Her efforts are directed toward the training of the intellect and will, the development of principles and the discipline of mind imparted by

Faculty Meeting, 1960's.

the mastery of bodies of knowledge. Her objective is then the formation of persons prepared and willing to make decisions, and to serve in effecting them; *the formation of the truly educated Catholic woman able to take her full place in spiritual, intellectual, and civic life*. A study of the changes appearing in the catalogue through the years shows that there has been a continuing process of development from decade to decade and even from year to year in conformity with the needs of the times. Such a study reveals also an awareness on the part of administrators and faculty of the impact of world affairs on American education with a consequent emphasis on the personal responsibility of each student to become a loyal American citizen. Student life, regulated since 1912 by Student Government, has fostered the spirit of democracy and the best qualities of leadership. (Catalogue of 1960–1961, p. 11).

. . . The Trinity woman, the goal of this objective, is a mature, self-disciplined person able to consider the problems that confront her in contemporary society both national and international and to direct her actions by principle. She is, in the context of undergraduate work, truly educated intellectually, the possessor not only of a body of knowledge against which to judge present events, but of a competent scholarly foundation in at least one subject matter field that she can continue on the graduate level, if she so chooses. Finally, she is a Catholic woman, living according to her faith, without ostentation in whatever sphere her activity lies. She is keenly conscious of, and guides her actions by the true doctrines of the Church not only in her personal life, but in social, economic, and civic affairs as well. (1960–1961 Faculty Handbook, p. 3.)

Since 1960, more than fifteen years of the future have become past. The exciting teen-age population explosion, with its consequent expansion in college enrollments; the years of student unrest; economic, political crises national and international have happened. Vatican II has happened. The Trinity College student of the mid-seventies appears to be different from her predecessors but in essence she is the same, a young woman of her own time. The college can, therefore, still state in its current catalogue (1975–1976):

> In face of multiple challenge, Trinity College reaffirms, in this its seventy-fifth year, its commitment to service as a liberal arts college, a Catholic college, a college for women in the nation's capital.
>
> *A liberal arts college:* Trinity is a liberal arts college and more. In the belief that a liberal education constitutes the best foundation for a fully human, productive life, Trinity's faculty stands committed to pursuit of the liberal disciplines. By way of helping students analyze and interpret relationships between their liberal studies and the world of work, the college seeks to provide courses exploring the interconnections. For example, languages and the social sciences are set into the context of bilingual/multicultural interaction; economics, psychology, sociology and political science are brought to bear in examining the practical worlds of business and social organization; aesthetic values, the ability to speak and write effectively, knowledge of photography and design are explored for their bearing on visual and verbal communication; theology and philosophy, the natural and physical sciences, for their relationships to pressing societal questions. The college also seeks to join its curriculum with effective academic advising and personal and career counseling so that, drawing on a whole range of resources, students can lay a broad, flexible foundation for a variety of careers; define their own personal and career goals; test these goals and gain confidence through practical experience; and utilize their knowledge responsibly for society.
>
> *A Catholic college:* Trinity welcomes students of all faiths, and invites them to be serious about their values and beliefs. The college seeks to create a climate supportive of free exploration and intelligent, principled choice—especially through its honor system, demanding continual effort to live with integrity, to accept responsibility for personal action, to consider the social implications of individual decisions; and through its curriculum, requiring students to translate their personal values, priorities and goals into a liberal arts program of their own making. Courses are offered in theology, scripture and religious thought. Daily liturgy, special programs sponsored by Campus Ministry, and informal dialogue on questions of value and belief are also available. By such means, Trinity provides students an opportunity to grow in understanding of their own and others' religious traditions, and to explore the bearing of these traditions on contemporary experience.
>
> *A college for women:* Trinity stands in its seventy-fifth year as a college dedicated to meeting the educational needs of women. These needs have changed since 1897. Today, the college enrolls women of various ages and life-styles, women with and without family responsibilities, with and with-

out careers, with part-time as well as full-time status. Much of Trinity's richness as a woman's college resides in this diversity.

In the nation's capital: A liberal arts college in Washington, Trinity encourages its students to utilize fully, by formal and informal means, the educational potential of its location. In particular, field work, practica and internships are viewed as valuable means of applying and testing, deepening and broadening knowledge gained through lectures, discussion and reading. Such experiences are arranged at the departmental level, rather than through a central office, with a view to ensuring the best possible placement and supervision.

And more: Trinity has combined a deepening of its original commitment with responsiveness to new needs. Three coeducational programs oriented toward community service have created a rich diversity in the college's learning population and expanded undergraduates' options for study in the fields of sociology, education (including bilingual/multicultural education) and theology. In 1973, recognizing the critical need for improving the court system, Trinity established the first and only undergraduate Court Management Program; currently, a high percentage of the students enrolled are court employees, men and women who bring to their classes a wealth of practical experience. There are also two graduate programs oriented to community service: the Master of Arts in Teaching Degree Program, established seven years ago; and, more recently, the Pastoral Ministry Program, leading either to a certificate or a Master of Arts degree.

Trinity stands today, in its seventy-fifth year, a liberal arts college, a Catholic college, a college for women in the nation's capital—and more.

Admissions

The selection of satisfactorily prepared students who could profit by and develop through the course of study "planned according to the best standards of our American system" has been important since the beginning. Entrance examinations were required of all. Descriptions of subject matter to be tested rather than number of years of high school study were issued. These descriptions as published in the announcements of 1898 and 1899 were criticized as making the examinations very severe (cf. Chapter 2, p. 61, for an example). They were, however, in accord with the strong movement for improvement in college admissions at the turn of the century. A study of these first entrance requirements as well as of those that followed shows that the founders and early faculty were familiar with and approved the work of the committee on secondary school studies (Committee of Ten) of the National Educational Association under President Charles W. Eliot of Harvard.[3] "Its effect was to supersede, in many secondary schools, a program of

3. "Report of the Committee of Ten," *Educational Review*, Vol. 7, The U.S. Commissioner of Education was a member and later showed great interest in the new Trinity College.

short and miscellaneous courses by a program of relatively few subjects carried for four or five hours per week, and for at least half a year."[4] The successor of this committee was that on College Entrance Requirements (Committee of Twelve) whose report, after four years of study, was published in 1899 and led to official announcement, November 17, 1900, of the College Entrance Examination Board, the month that Trinity College opened to students. Though "Board Examinations" were first administered in 1901, most colleges, even board members, continued to administer their own examinations. The founders of Trinity College benefited by what Claude Fuess[5] called the "gradual clarification of thought which took place during the last quarter of the nineteenth century in an effort to make education a sound process of evolution."

Admission to the college in the first twenty-five years was under the supervision of the "Secretary of the College," who during most of that time was Sister Florence Louise Delaney, assisted by a Board of Admissions. From 1926 to 1955 the Registrar's Office was also the Admissions Office. In 1952 Sister Mary Lawlor was appointed chairman of the Admissions Committee and acted as Director of Admissions until 1955 when Sister Sheila Doherty, the new Registrar, again combined admissions with her other duties. In 1961, an Admissions Office separate from the Registrar's Office was established: Directors of Admission since that time have been Sister Sheila Doherty (1961–1968), Sister Patricia Langan (1968–1972), Hawthorne Farr of Johnson Associates (1972–1974), Mrs. Judith Boerner (1974–1976), Miss Margaret McNally (1976-). All these people and the admissions committees that assisted them have been confronted through the years with problems of selection and changing requirements that have seldom been realized by others not involved with their work. A faculty board or committee on admissions has functioned in the admissions process throughout the seventy-five years. References are made to it in early president's and dean's reports and some minutes of meetings are extant. Alumnae through the whole period from 1904 have been active in varying degrees in recruiting students and aiding the admissions office.

An over-all view, from 1899 to the present, of Trinity College admission requirements shows clearly defined periods: 1899–1908, 1909–1919, 1920–1932, 1933–1945, 1946–1954, 1955–1966, 1967–1975. These approximately ten-year periods reflect a knowledge of and steady determination to adhere to "the best standards of our American system" of higher education, changing with the times while aiming for continuity of excellence. The college catalogue for 1900–1901 states:

4. Monroe's *Cyclopedia of Education*, Vol. II, p. 58, col. 2, N.Y. 1915.
5. Claude M. Fuess, *The College Board*, the First Fifty Years, Columbia U. Press, 1950, p. 26.

It is highly desirable that in the academies of the country there should be uniformity as to the courses of study and requirements for graduation. In view of the differences that actually exist, and in order that the ability of each applicant may be fairly tested at the beginning of her college course, all candidates for admission must take the entrance examination.

Certificates will be given to those students also who pass the entrance examinations simply as a test.

In 1901, the examinations will be held June 3, 4, 5, 6, at Trinity College; also in Boston, New York, Philadelphia, Baltimore, New Orleans, St. Louis, Cincinnati, Columbus, Pittsburgh, Chicago, Dubuque, San Jose, San Francisco, and Montreal. There is a fee of five dollars for examinations taken at places other than Trinity College.

Blank forms of application may be obtained at any time from the Secretary of the College. These applications, accompanied by a deposit of ten dollars, must be filled out and returned before April 15 of each year. (p. 13)

A *Notice for Examinations* is interpolated before the time schedule for entrance examinations of 1901. It states:

Students who desire to work for a degree, must present at entrance Latin, English, French or German, History and Mathematics. Greek is not obligatory at entrance, but must be studied in the College during Freshman and Sophomore Years.

The modern language not presented at entrance must be studied in the College, as both French and German are required for degrees.

Special Students are exempted at entrance from examinations in Greek, Latin and Mathematics, but not from English, one modern language and History.

By the next year the introductory statement about admissions had been set. The following statement appears in the catalogues from 1901–1902 to 1907–1908 without change except in dates:

1. All students, hearers excepted, must have passed the entrance examination.

2. The certificates of academies, or college preparatory schools, or high schools are not accepted in place of the entrance examination. Students who have completed the Freshman Course in a college of good standing may be admitted to the Sophomore Class without examination in the studies specifically covered by their certificates. Such students must present statements as to the courses previously pursued and the grade attained in each subject.

3. At least one month before the entrance examination a candidate for admission must file an application properly filled in and signed. It should be accompanied by a deposit of ten dollars. Application blanks may be obtained from the Secretary of the College.

ENTRANCE EXAMINATION

4. In 1901 the entrance examinations at Trinity College will begin on June 3 and September 16; in 1902, on June 2 and September 15.

By special arrangement, the June examination may be taken at one of the centres. There is a fee of five dollars for examinations taken at places other than Trinity College.

This statement is followed by a list of centers and the description of subject matter for testing. The 1901–1902 list covers nineteen centers in cities across the country from Boston, New York and Philadelphia to San Francisco and San Jose, only six of which were Notre Dame Academies. The 1907–1908 catalogue lists forty centers, distributed through eighteen states and Montreal, Canada. Since only ten of these centers were directed by Sisters of Notre Dame de Namur, the list bears witness to the interest in and cooperation with the new college in Washington of other congregations of religious as well as of public schools in all sections of the country not only in the Northeast, but in the South, Southwest, Mid-west and West.

By 1903 the entrance requirements were specifically listed: Latin and two other languages; English; United States and Greek, Roman, or English history; algebra and plane geometry. In place of the third language the candidate might offer Advanced Mathematics, Physics, Chemistry, or Botany, but the language would have to be taken in college. These are all described as subjects for examination. It is interesting that as early as 1899 statements appeared that indicate concerns of the faculty which have continued for nearly eight decades. The catalogue for 1902–03 is quoted here. Its English statement concludes: "All writing must give evidence of knowledge of diction, sentences, and paragraphs. No candidate will be accepted whose work is notably defective in spelling, grammar, idiom, punctuation, or division into paragraphs." The College Board Writing Sample required in the 1960's gives evidence of the continuing struggle, as do the faculty concerns of the mid-1970's. After the 1902–03 Mathematics requirement appears a warning: "This part of the examination presupposes a thorough knowledge of *Arithmetic*." Even Sputnik and the "new math" have not eliminated the need for such warnings for contemporary applicants.

The first mention of the carefully defined "unit" of high school work occurs in the 1908–09 catalogue (pp. 17–19) in the revised statement on admission to the freshman class.[6] Here, too, appears a table of equivalent examinations of the College Entrance Examination Board which could be taken instead of Trinity College examinations. Since this

6. The first Bulletin of Information for applicants was prepared by Sr. Georgiana and published in 1907. Cf. President's Report to Advisory Board, 1908.

admissions statement, a definite improvement over earlier versions remained with slight changes in the catalogues until 1919, it is reproduced in full here. Among the changes during those ten years were the addition of music and religion as electives, the modification of the mathematics requirement from 3 to $2\frac{1}{2}$ years through the same content was required and the inclusion from 1914 to 1919 of admission by certificate from "schools accredited by Trinity College or affiliated to the Catholic University, Washington, D.C."

ADMISSION TO THE FRESHMAN CLASS

Students are admitted to the Freshman Class of Trinity College after the successful completion of a high-school or academy course of four years. There is no high-school or academy attached to the College.

As evidence of the thoroughness of their preparation for admission to College, candidates must pass examinations in subjects amounting to sixteen (16) unit courses of high-school work. The accepted definition of a unit course is, *a course of study covering a school year of not less than thirty-five weeks, with five class periods of at least forty-five minutes each per week.*

The studies to be presented in satisfaction of this requirement are named in the following list. The amount of preparation required in each subject is indicated by the number of units assigned to that subject.*

The subjects prescribed for all candidates for admission are:

English	3 units
History	1 unit
Mathematics	3 units
Latin	4 units
The Major Requirement in Greek, or French or German	3 units

In addition to the above fourteen (14) units, each candidate must present two (2) units from the following subjects:

The Minor Requirement in one of the languages not offered for major standing	2 units
History (in addition to the amount prescribed above)	1 unit
Physics	1 unit
Chemistry	1 unit
Botany	1 unit

*Although no formal entrance examination is held in Religion, it is expected, needless to say, that the program of every Catholic high-school and academy will give to this all-important subject at least four (4) points, i.e., the equivalent of one period each day throughout the entire course of four years. The teaching should be thorough and systematic so that the student will be well prepared to profit by the courses in Religion and Sacred Scripture which constitute a regular and important part of the system of prescribed studies throughout the College course.

Where "conditions" in the entrance requirements do not exceed two (2) units a candidate may be admitted to the Freshman Class on probation.

"Conditions" must be removed during the academic year at the time appointed for special examinations. [A fee of $1.00 was charged after 1911 for these examinations.]

The standard to be attained in all subjects accepted in satisfaction of the requirement for admission is the standard set by the College Entrance Examination Board of the National Educational Association. The following table of equivalent examinations indicates the subjects that must be offered by Candidates who wish to take the examinations of the College Entrance Examination Board instead of those set by Trinity College:

TABLE OF EQUIVALENT EXAMINATIONS

COLLEGE ENTRANCE EXAMINATION BOARD EXAMINATION		TRINITY COLEGE EXAMINATION	
Subjects		*Subjects*	*Units*
English, *a* and *b*	=	English	3
History, *a* and *b*, or *c* and *d**	=	History	1
Mathematics, *a* (*i* and *ii*) and *c*	=	Mathematics	3
Latin, *a* (*i* and *ii*), *b*, *c*, *d*, *l*, and *m*	=	Latin	4
One of the following: Greek, *a* (*i* and *ii*), *b*, *c*, *f*, and *g* French, *a* and *b* German, *a* and *b*	=	*Major Requirement in one of the following:* Greek, or French, or German	3
One subject from Group I or two subjects from Group II: *Group I:* Greek, *a* (*i* and *ii*), *b*, *f*, and *g* French, *a* German, *a* *Group II:* History, *a*, or *b*, or *c*, or *d* (nor offered above) Physics Chemistry Botany	=	*Two units to be chosen from the following:* The Minor Requirement in one of the languages not offered for major standing (Greek, or French, or German)	2
		History (in addition to the amount prescribed above)	1
		Physics	1
		Chemistry	1
		Botany	1

*Any other combination of the divisions of History will be accepted.

The Regents' Academic Diploma (State of New York) will be accepted in lieu of entrance examinations in those subjects in which the candidate has pursued the course outlined in the admission requirements of Trinity College or of the College Entrance Examination Board. No Diploma granted more than two years before the applicant presents herself for admission to College will entitle the holder to exemption from examination. No form of Regents' certificates other than the Academic Diploma will be accepted in lieu of the examination in any subject.

ADMISSION TO ADVANCED STANDING

Upon the presentation of satisfactory evidence of proficiency in advanced studies, a candidate may be admitted to the sophomore, junior, or senior class. Application for advanced standing must be accompanied by (1) official statements of the candidate's record in her various college studies, (2) letters or other evidence showing the opinions of her instructors in regard to her scholarship and character, (3) a letter of honorable dismissal from the college which she is leaving, and (4) a catalogue or announcement of the college that she leaves in which are plainly marked every requirement for admission and course of instruction for which she has received credit.

The requirements for admission to advanced standing are, in brief, the following:

1. The requirements for admission to the freshman class.
2. All the prescribed studies already pursued by the class to which the candidate seeks admission.
3. As many elective studies as the candidate would have pursued if she had entered the class at the beginning of the freshman year.

A candidate may be admitted in spite of deficiencies in some of these studies but no candidate so admitted will be recommended for a degree until she shall have made good all such deficiencies.

The pattern of wide geographical distribution and varied secondary school backgrounds of the students, noted in the first classes, was well established by 1905–06, when the enrollment reached a hundred. The hundred students were from 24 states, from 82 schools of which 42 were Catholic Academies or parochial high schools under the direction of sixteen different religious congregations, and 36 were public high schools and four private schools with lay faculty.[7] Though this varied background of the Trinity student body has fluctuated at times during the seventy years since this analysis was made, it has, on the whole, been maintained as a study of the "Register of Students" published in the catalogues from 1901 to 1974 will show.

For five years from 1914 to 1919 the college admitted students from schools on its approved list by certificate showing that they had completed the requisite preparation. These students were "regarded as upon probation during the first half year, and those deficient in preparation [were] dropped whenever the deficiency [had] been clearly demonstrated." The catalogue announced that the certificate privilege would be withdrawn from schools whose students were deficient "during a term of years." A different type of admission by certificate, in accord with then current trends, was later introduced and described in the catalogues from 1932 to 1945 as an alternate to the entrance by

7. President's Report to the Advisory Board, 1905–1906. Cf. also Report of 1908–1909.

examination. In those years a student might be admitted by certificate if she ranked in the highest fifth of her class and all other requirements were fulfilled, and if the Regents or Catholic University examinations were not available to her. This, however, was subject to the approval of the Admissions Board. In 1936 the upper fifth rank was changed to "college certificate grades," but all else remained in effect until 1945.

The "new Plan" of admissions, to be effective September 1919, was announced in the catalogue of the previous year. It would supersede admission by certificates. This plan is substantially the College Entrance Examination Board's "radical idea" of comprehensive examinations which by 1915 had become "plain common sense." The new plan was, said the catalogue, "Similar to that adopted by Harvard, Princeton and Yale in prescribing a test of the quality of the applicants' scholarship and intellectual power." There was no change in subject matter requirements and the old plan was not completely abandoned. That Trinity College, in 1919, was in step with good practice in the women's colleges as well as in those mentioned above appears in Fuess'[8] statement that in 1919 "four women's colleges—Mount Holyoke, Smith, Vassar and Wellesley—all of them thitherto supporters of the so-called certificate system of admission, adopted in its place the Board's examinations, and soon expressed their preference for the New Plan." The catalogue statement that remained substantially unchanged from 1919 to 1932 follows:

METHODS OF ADMISSION (1919–1932)

There are two methods of admission to Trinity College.

I. OLD PLAN.—Under this plan a candidate must present at entrance $15\frac{1}{2}$ units in prescribed subjects obtained in one of the following ways: [16 units from 1922]

1. From examinations taken at Trinity College. [Dropped in 1923]
2. From examinations conducted by the College Entrance Examination Board.
3. From Catholic University Examinations given to affiliated schools.
4. From Regents' Examinations of the State of New York.

II. NEW PLAN.—The examinations required in this plan are of the type known as comprehensive examinations offered by the College Entrance Board.

The new method depends on two kinds of evidence:

1. Evidence submitted by the school, consisting of
   a. A school report covering the entire record of subjects and grades for four years.

8. Fuess, Claude M. *The College Board, Its First Fifty Years,* New York, Columbia U. Press, 1950, p. 84.

b. A statement from the school principal including an estimate of the applicant's scholarly interests, special ability, and character.

2. Evidence submitted by the candidate, consisting of

Four comprehensive examinations, selected from each of the following groups:

(1) English or History, selected by the applicant.
(2) A foreign language, selected by the applicant.
(3) Mathematics, or Chemistry, or Physics, selected by the applicant.
(4) A fourth subject, designated by the applicant from the subjects which may be offered for admission. This choice must be approved by the Committee on Admission of the respective colleges.

These four examinations must be taken at one time.

At least two examinations must cover more than two admission units* each.

In each subject chosen the comprehensive examination covering all the units offered by her for admission must be taken by the applicant.

It is desirable that applicants furnish school records and state the subjects selected for examination before February fifteenth of the year in which the examinations are to be taken. Candidates may apply for admission, however, at any time prior to the September examinations.

The Committee on Admission of the individual college must give its permission, based upon the evidence submitted by the school, before the applicant may take the examinations.

Under the new plan the candidate, if admitted to college, will be admitted free from all conditions. Failure to meet completely the standard in both kinds of evidence required will not necessarily involve rejection of the applicant; the Committee may accept unusual excellence in one part of the credentials submitted as offsetting unsatisfactory evidence or even failure in another part. If the candidate fails of admission in June she will not be debarred from taking examinations under the old system in September, but she may not take the comprehensive examinations for admission under the new plan before June of the following year.

It is believed that this new type of admission combines the best elements of the present certificate system and of the examination system in that it requires the school record and estimate of character, and also demands examinations designed to test the candidate's intellectual power, not alone her memory of prescribed facts. Furthermore, the method offers the applicant the fullest opportunity to show her ability in subjects in which she believes herself best qualified.

This plan substitutes a uniform method of admission in place of the various certificate forms now used by many colleges and gives the school entire freedom in the sequence of its work, making no requirement of certain subjects in the last years.

Comprehensive examinations according to the new plan will supersede admission by certificate after September, 1919.

---

*Note—A unit as defined by the College Entrance Examination Board represents a year's study in any subject in a secondary school, constituting approximately a quarter of a year's work.

ENTRANCE REQUIREMENTS
FOR THE DEGREES OF
BACHELOR OF ARTS (A.B.)

Prescribed		*Electives*	
English	3 units	Two units must be chosen from the following subjects:	
Latin	4 units	Minor Language	2 units
Major Language (Greek, French, German or Spanish)	3 units	(Not offered for Major Language)	
History	1 unit	History	2 units
Mathematics	2½ units	Solid Geometry	½ unit
		Trigonometry	½ unit
		Physics	1 unit
		Chemistry	1 unit
		Botany	1 unit
		Zoology	1 unit
		Music	1 unit
		Total	15½ units

BACHELOR OF LETTERS (B. Litt.)

Prescribed		*Electives*	
English	3 units	6½ units must be chosen from the following subjects:	
History	1 unit	Major Language	3 units
Major Language (Latin, Greek, French, German or Spanish)	3 units	Minor Language	2 units
Minor Language	2 units	History	3 units
Latin must be either the Major or Minor Language.		Algebra	1½ units
		Plane Geometry	1 unit
		Physics	1 unit
		Chemistry	1 unit
		Botany	1 unit
		Zoology	1 unit
		Music	1 unit
		Total	15½ units

BACHELOR OF SCIENCE (B.S.)

Prescribed		*Electives*	
English	3 units	One unit must be chosen from the following subjects:	
Latin	2 units	Trigonometry	½ unit
French	3 units	Physics	1 unit
German	3 units	Chemistry	1 unit
History	1 unit	General Biology	1 unit
Algebra—2d year	1 unit	Botony	1 unit
Plane Geometry	1 unit	Zoology	1 unit
Solid Geometry	½ unit	Total	15½ units

Although Trinity College's own entrance examinations were dropped from the list under the "old plan" in 1923, a schedule of examinations at the college in September of each year was in the catalogues until 1932. After that until 1939 there was a statement that a limited number of "old plan" examinations would be given at the college in September for the removal of "conditions" resulting from failure in other examinations or from incomplete high school courses. All this, however, presupposed the "permission of the Board of Admissions."

The curricular re-organization of 1932 explained to the alumnae in the *Journals* of May, 1932 and February, 1933, did not involve fundamental changes in entrance requirements. Since only one degree was to be awarded (the A.B.), the list of subjects required was the same for all candidates for admission with a note about pre-medical candidates. Entrance was by examination: College Entrance Board, Catholic University, New York State Regents; or by certificate for candidates ranking in the highest fifth of their class at the end of senior year in accredited high schools. Science remained an elective. For the first time the language, reduced to six units, was adjustable: 4 or 3 units of Latin and 2 or 3 of a modern foreign language. The evolution of the Trinity language requirement and an indication of the anxieties of both candidates and admissions officers is reflected in Table VI of language requirements 1900–1975. The pattern set up in 1932 endured with very little change until 1945. That year the College Entrance Examination Board Scholastic Aptitude Tests were first required of all candidates. Scholarship applicants had to take also three achievement tests. Two years later (1947) all candidates were required to take three achievements: English Composition, a language, a science or social studies. Four years of high school with sixteen academic units remained basic. Trinity College had joined the College Entrance Examination Board in 1942 and as a member was making full use of the examinations.[9]

Though from 1900 to 1945 sciences were *electives*, except for admission to the B.S. program, or the pre-medical course, the 1946–47 catalogue first listed one unit of chemistry, biology or physics as an entrance *requirement* for all candidates.

The pressure of numbers of applicants, eased by the building of Alumnae Hall (and drastically by the Depression), again made itself felt in the mid-1940's as is evidenced by a statement that appeared in the 1945–46 catalogue:

> Candidates are urged to apply for admission as early in their senior year as possible since rooms are assigned according to date of application. Selection of candidates for admission, however, is not regulated by date of application.

This form of the statement appeared one year only. Misunderstanding brought on by overlooking the second sentence caused the admissions committee some difficulty. Later catalogues carry differently worded, expanded statements about time of application with no men-

9. Margaret Thorne '49 was later Director of the College Board Testing Program. Cf. Her article "The Place of Testing in College Admissions," *Alumnae Journal*, Autumn, 1963, pp. 9–10, 75.

TABLE VI. *Foreign Language—Entrance Requirements*

Dates	No. of Units	Composition*
1900–1906	9	4 Latin, 3 Mod. or Greek, 2 another
1906–1932	7	4 Latin, 3 French or German 3rd lang. elective
1932–1942	6	4 or 3 Latin; 3 or 2 modern
1943–1945	5	3 Latin; 2 modern
1946–1967	5	Latin deficiency could be made up in college if 3 modern, 2 Latin
1967–1974	4	4 one language or 2 of two languages (no mention of Latin)
1974–1975	Basic Statement—no tabulation of subjects	

*Note: In the early catalogues the languages were given not in units but as "Latin, a major language and a minor language" which was equivalent to what is recorded in the table.

tion of rooms, or the order of the dates of application, beginning, from 1946 to 1958, with the phrase "since the size of the freshman class is limited."

The format of the catalogue was changed in 1945, 1949, 1959, 1967, 1971 and 1975 and the admissions statement was re-written several times during that period, but the actual content of requirements continued in the pattern that had been detailed in the preceding pages. Various aids for inquiring applicants were added periodically. An application blank was inserted before the admissions statement from 1955 to 1970. The section on scholarships was expanded in 1959 to "Financial Aid." Pictures were printed throughout the text of the catalogue from 1959–1975 and maps of the campus and of access to the college from 1971 to 1975. All these were used as aids for the Admissions Office. The major struggle of admissions officers during these thirty years was with the language requirement (Table VI) and with the traditional "sixteen units and high school graduation" in the face of sweeping changes on the secondary school level and in the Trinity College curriculum. Advanced placement by C.E.E.B. Advanced Examinations first appeared in the catalogue statement in 1958, though the entrance examinations had already been used for a decade to place students in advanced classes in language, mathematics, and science. In 1958, also, the early decision plan was announced whereby a student could be assured in the fall of her senior year in high school of admission to Trinity, contingent on the successful completion of that year. This plan was changed in 1970 to that of "rolling admissions."

In 1961 the first five candidates for early admission enrolled at Trinity College after their junior year in high school.[10] They scored

10. *Washington Post*, May, 1965. Cf. Trinity College *Newsletter*, Dec. 1969, p. 2. In the 1970's this program became the "High School Articulation Program." Cf. Catalogue, 1974–75, p. 26.

very high in the College Board Examinations, had completed the requisite sixteen units, and were judged by their secondary school advisors sufficiently mature to enter college. The success of these pioneer "early admission" students encouraged the college to continue the policy. At the end of their freshman year several of them returned to their high schools to take part in graduation ceremonies with their classes. Then all continued college courses to receive degrees as high ranking members of the class of 1965. In 1967–1968 when there were 20 such students on campus an evaluation study of the program[11] reported favorably on its value and it continues to the present (cf. current catalogue).

The admissions statement of 1967–1968[12] is the first to omit the mention of Latin and to include the following paragraph, although the tabulation of required and elective subjects was still published until 1974.

> In adhering to the above policy, it is the intention of the College to remain flexible enough to allow for admission of students of diverse preparation and stable enough to maintain the high standards upheld by Trinity College. This flexibility and stability assure those enrolled of a solid education among individuals capable of interaction on all levels.[13]

This survey of the process of selection of a student body capable of profiting by a "course of study planned according to the best standards of our American system" can end fittingly by citing in part the current admissions statement, designed for the students and the individualized curriculum of the mid-1970's. No tabulation of required subjects has been included since 1974.

> The selection of candidates for admission to Trinity College is made by a committee composed of members of the administration and faculty. The Admissions Committee admits students of good character who qualify academically and who have demonstrated interest in procuring the kind of education outlined in the college catalog.
>
> Trinity seeks students who give evidence of academic potential, have a record of scholastic achievement, and manifest breadth of interest. The college regards these characteristics to be important if students are to take full advantage of the opportunities it affords for their intellectual and personal growth. The Admissions Committee gives consideration to applicants whose academic preparation is deficient in a particular area if they have compensating strengths in other areas.

11. Conducted by Sr. Ann Francis Hoey, Ph.D., former Dean of Students, and then Professor of Education and a member of the Admissions Committee.
12. p. 29 of catalogue.
13. Catalogue 1975–1976, p. 31.

Both in its undergraduate programs for women and in its coeducational graduate programs, Trinity College welcomes a diverse student mix and in no way discriminates on the basis of race, color, religion or nationality. Trinity is committed to affirmative action.

Secondary School

Academic growth at Trinity College will depend in part on the student's preparation in secondary school. A strong secondary school program will ensure greater freedom and flexibility at the college level and will enable the student to take full advantage of the opportunities Trinity offers.

Candidates for admission should complete a secondary school course of study, including sixteen units from among the basic academic disciplines: English, history, foreign language, mathematics (algebra, geometry, or trigonometry), laboratory science (biology, chemistry, or physics), social science. Beyond meeting the minimal requirements for high school graduation, each student should pursue in greater depth those academic areas of special interest and importance to her. For example, while some mathematics is required of all students, a heavier concentration is recommended for premedical students and for the following majors: mathematics, psychology, economics, physics, chemistry and biology.

Curriculum, Degree Requirements, Academic Standards

The curriculum of Trinity College, that "whole body of courses offered by an educational institution or by a department thereof,"[14] has developed gradually, according to the goals stated earlier in this chapter, from the simple statement in the first catalogue to the latest revision of 1976. The 1900–1901 outline provided the base on which faculties have built through nearly eight decades. It states on page 16:

> The system of instruction that has been adopted at Trinity College is partly the once universal college method and partly the elective method. The courses leading to the degree of Bachelor of Arts, and to the degree of Bachelor of Science will be the following, required or elective: Religion—Doctrine, Bible, Liturgy; Philosophy; History of the Church; Greek, Latin; English, German, French, Spanish; Mathematics; Physics, Chemistry, Biology, Geology; History, Political Science; History of Art and Architecture; Pedagogy; also courses auxiliary to the study of the modern languages: Anglo-Saxon, Old French and Middle High German.
>
> Of these subjects, Religion, Philosophy and History of the Church are prescribed studies extending through a course of four years. English is prescribed until Senior year; History until Junior Year. Students in Arts will be required to take an elective course in Science for one year.
>
> The entire course open to the Freshman Class consists of prescribed studies. (Cf. Chapter 3 for details)

14. The author has chosen to accept "the usual sense" of *Webster's Unabridged Dictionary* rather than the far-reaching, complicated definition found in educational texts.

Studies for the Bachelor of Arts and Bachelor of Letters degrees were organized into general requirements and specialized "groups." Eight groups were listed with details of content: Greek and Latin (whose great prestige lasted through thirty years), Latin and German, Latin and French, Latin and English, German and French, English and German, English and French, and History and Political Science. Included in this last group were sociology and economics, showing that social science made an early start, though its blossoming came later. Teacher education (pedagogy) began in 1903 as an elective. The same eight groups were listed in the catalogue until 1921, with the following addendum beginning in 1902: "Other groups which students may desire to elect are subject to the approval of the Faculty"; and in 1905 the first student graduated with a Bachelor of Science in Chemistry and Mathematics. The students "desired to elect" so many different groups that by 1921 the pattern had to change.

Significant stages in curriculum development appear as one studies the academic program in retrospect.[15] For the first twenty years, 1900–1921, under the direction of the first two deans: Sister Josephine Ignatius, and Sister Mary, the original curriculum as described in the preceding paragraphs was in effect. Though the prevailing custom in higher education required 120 credit hours for the bachelor's degree, Trinity College required 132 to allow the extra hours for scripture, religion, and church history without "weakening" the value of the degree in the opinion of professional educators and others who might not agree with the college plan. The 1921 revision, effected by Sister Berchmans Julia[16] changed only the system of "groups." Instead each student elected at the beginning of sophomore year two major subjects, not necessarily related, to be pursued during the remainder of the course. A minimum of eighteen semester hours beyond freshman prerequisites was required in each major subject in addition to the prescribed studies and free electives that would complete the 132 semester hours for the degree.[17] (Table of Degree Requirements in Appendix VIII) The 132 hour requirements persisted until 1960 when not only the changes in attitude of secular universities, but the framework of the "four-course system" brought about the modification to 128 semester hours—still above the customary 120 hours.

An editorial, "The Educational Reformation and Trinity,"[18] by Julia O'Neill, gives the background of the curricular changes of 1932 and describes the success of Trinity students in the national testing programs of that time. The catalogue for 1932–1933 and the *Alumnae*

15. The dates 1921, 1932, 1935, 1941, 1956, 1960, 1970 and 1976 mark these stages.
16. Cf. pp. 99–102.
17. Cf. class load as described in Dean's Report, June 1, 1904—Sr. Mary's first report.
18. *Alumnae Journal*, May 1932, pp. 64–65.

Journal[19] give the specifics of curricular change. The student elected, at the end of freshman year, one major subject and one or two subjects related to the major to be pursued during the rest of her course. For the degree a minimum of 48 semester hours in this major concentration beyond freshman requisites (divided 30-18) had to be completed. General requirements and electives made up the 132 semester hours needed. Only one degree, Bachelor of Arts, was to be granted. Science majors and pre-medical students arranged their programs to accommodate the general requirements as well as the dictates of their specific field. (Table of Requirements from 1932–1933 Catalogue in Appendix.) The aspects of the new curriculum that interested the alumnae[20] in addition to those given above were that prescribed science was given in freshman year instead of being a traditional sophomore hurdle; that the Latin entrance requirement was slightly reduced and "Freshman Latin" was now an elective; that American Constitutional history, long a senior requirement, was also an elective; and that all education courses could count toward the degree instead of a maximum of twelve semester hours. This reorganization, the fruit of eleven years experience as Dean of Studies, was effected by Sister Berchmans Julia (Julia Schumacher) just before she became president of the college in 1932.

In the next twenty-five years shifts in organization of subject matter, greater diversification of course offerings, and changes in methods of presentation kept pace with developments in higher education to continue the improvement of the Trinity College educational program without sacrificing the essential values of the traditional curriculum. The reorganization in 1932, which introduced the single major field with a related minor, was a first step in a long-range development culminating, in the 1950's, in the integrated Christian culture program of the freshman and sophomore year[21] and the increased emphasis on individual student activity and seminar work in the major departments. An important milestone in that development was the introduction, in 1935, of the comprehensive examination in the major subject required of all students in the spring of their senior year. This has done much to promote a competent scholarly attitude in each succeeding generation of students. Though there has been some questioning of format and efficacy of comprehensive examinations in the 1970's, the faculty still affirms their use.[22]

The institution in 1939 of a testing program for freshman evaluation and placement according to need and ability, and the follow-up of each

19. February 1933, p. 18f.
20. *Alumnae Journal,* February 1933, p. 18.
21. Cf. "Trinity's 'Christian Culture' Program," Sr. Ann Julia Kinnirey, *Alumnae Journal,* Autumn, 1951, pp. 17–20.
22. Cf. Faculty Minutes.

student to supervise achievement in upperclass work, added to the strength of the academic program of the college.[23]

College Board Examinations had always been used in conjunction with the college's own entrance examinations and for selection of scholarship winners. In 1942 Trinity College joined the College Entrance Examination Board, *thus becoming the first Catholic college for women to be a member of the Board.* In 1945 College Entrance Board Examinations were required of all applicants. The scores have been used, during much of the time since, not only for selection of candidates for entrance, but also for many of the placement and guidance functions mentioned above.

The increased interest in social sciences led in 1940 to the establishment of separate major work in economics and to the strengthening and modernizing of the sociology major, and greater stress on international relations in the political science major. Major work in art (restricted to history of art, 1945–1971) and in music was also introduced at this time. Courses in all these subjects had been offered over the years.

The opening of the new Science Building in 1941 gave increased facility to the well established science programs. Interest in the sciences and in mathematics was marked in the next fifteen years and science majors found excellent positions in industry, in government, in the professions, and in research. They were well prepared in their special fields, but were not confined entirely to science in their undergraduate work, since all students, no matter what their major, took the core of required languages, history, literature, philosophy and theology. Graduates of the pre-medical course made a fine record in medical school in the tradition of their predecessors since the first Trinity alumna M.D., Dr. Honoria Shine, 1909.[24]

The serious scrutiny of college programs during the war years 1941–1945 focussed attention on the value of liberal education in any age of technological advance. That was the period of the "Harvard Report," *General Education in a Free Society,* and of many other such studies. The extensive literature published in the 1940's made clear that the college had been wise in its strong consistent policy of avoiding the trivial and the merely technical in its offerings. As Frank Aydelotte wrote in *Breaking the Academic Lockstep*:

> . . . The very foundation of our democracy is our conception of liberal education and the freedom of the mind which that implies. Upon the broad

23. This was initiated and directed by Sr. Ann Julia Kinnirey working with the deans.
24. Cf. "Bound by the Oath of Hippocrates," Sister St. John Nepomucene Fennessey, S.N.D. '15 Chairman, Chemistry Department, *Alumnae Journal,* Winter, 1965, pp. 76–77 for Trinity's M.D.s to 1965.

> liberal training of youth in our high schools and colleges our future will depend. This fact is widely realized and it is not surprising that men everywhere are discussing anxiously in these days the future of liberal studies.

The college took steps to continue its curriculum development on lines that would insure a liberal education suited to the mid-twentieth century. Careful experimenting in the teaching of philosophy to make it more vital and applicable to the life situations of the students resulted in great interest in that field which had always been a requirement, but in the 1950's became more popular as an elective and, by student request, was opened for major work. In 1947 a course in theology based on the *Summa Theologica* of St. Thomas was introduced to replace the religion courses. This course, correlated with the philosophy and with history, formed a central core of the curriculum around which the student formed her program. In 1950 Sister Catherine Dorothea described the Trinity participation in the Inquiry into postwar conditions in American Colleges 1945–1948.[25]

Another feature of that decade of development was the establishment in 1949 of the modern language laboratory, one of the first fully equipped college laboratories of this kind. The laboratory facilitated the work of oral-aural practice in foreign languages, and has proven its worth in the years of its existence.[26] It was one of the methods used to bring modern technology to the aid of the age-old disciplines. The literature of both the classical and modern foreign languages have formed an important part of the curriculum from the beginning. Even in the face of almost total neglect of languages in many schools, the language entrance requirements were maintained and continued work in college required of all students. The major work in these language fields continues to be chiefly literary, but in keeping with contemporary interest in linguistics, some time was devoted to language study also. The latest addition to the languages offered was Chinese. This language was taken by only a few students, but was found helpful to students of far-eastern history who looked forward to State Department or other government work.

Those years also saw a healthy growth and expansion of the History Department. The introduction of special interest seminars, the opening of area studies to students of marked ability, and increased awareness of the role of international relations, of economics, as well as of government, led to the formulation of excellent individual programs of study.

25. *Alumnae Journal*, Spring, 1950, pp. 109ff.
26. The first language laboratory was financed by the Pittsburgh Chapter of the Alumnae Association. Later, expansions, reorganizations and modernizations were made possible by grants from the Raskob Foundation and the President's Council as well as from the college budget. For greater detail, see pp. 200–202 later in this chapter.

In cooperation with the Political Science Department, an interdepartmental major in history and government was established in 1951. The chief changes in the English Department, by tradition one of the largest and strongest major departments, were the requirement of a course in literary criticism for all major students, and of a senior coordinating seminar.

The launching of Sputnik I, October 4, 1957, reverberated on American campuses with disturbing intensity. Trinity College was affected as was the rest of higher education in the United States. Reflecting on these repercussions evident in the January, 1958, meeting of the Association of American Colleges and their implications for Trinity, Sister Columba, then Vice President for Academic Affairs, wrote[27]:

> All the great media of mass communication are devoting much time these days to the subject of higher education or to what the President's Committee calls "education beyond the high school," accepting the fact that the same education for all is not feasible. Causes for this concentration of attention may be found first, in the very large number of young people in the age groups which will provide the potential college students of the 1960's and 1970's, the "Tidal Wave" which educators have been trying to plan for during the 1950's; secondly in the Advertising Council's fine campaign to keep the value of higher education before the American people and to help them appreciate their obligation to support it; but finally, and most explosively, in the excitement caused by Russia's technological advantage over us as symbolized by the Sputnik episode.
>
> The first two of these causes have brought about movements that have been quietly and efficiently progressing for several years. College administrators, The President's Committee on Education Beyond the High School, many regional and state meetings, individual speakers and writers—all have been facing the problems of education and working toward their solution through practical, definite action. The third focusing cause, however, has brought about something near panic. Crisis—challenge—Sputnik—Oh! Science—Science—Science. . . . Whatever shall we do?

After quoting briefly from Rev. Thurston Davis'[28] speech, from the report of the AAC's Commission on Liberal Education, and from an article by Yale's President Alfred Whitney Griswold, she states Trinity College policy in the face of this new crisis.

> There should be emphasis on mathematics and the physical sciences, but not *dominant* emphasis. The dominant emphasis must be on the education of the individual as a whole. We at Trinity College are proud of our science achievement. The Science Building, its equipment, the faculty of the science and mathematics departments are worth our pride. Yet we are not compla-

27. "Where do we Stand?" Sister Columba Mullaly, Vice President, *Alumnae Journal*, Winter 1958, pp. 61-63.
28. Editor of *America*.

Faculty Forum: Small Discussion Group: l.-r. Nancy Brown, Sister Frances Butler, Sister Mary Lawlor, Sister Sheila Doherty.

cent. We, like all our educational neighbors, are alert to the need for careful self-criticism, for evaluation and revision of curricular content, for constant striving for improvement.

Science has an honored place at Trinity. The science or mathematics student has the opportunity for excellent training in her major field, but she is not dominated by science to the exclusion of all else. Like students in all fields she has a strong balance in the basic requirements of history, literature, philosophy, and theology.

We need science, yes, but we need social science, too. We need the humanities, the languages. Most of all, we need the philosophical principles and theological truths that will enable us to use all the rest of knowledge effectively in a world aghast at the thought of outer space.

To face the world crisis with serenity requires more than knowledge, more than technical excellence. The Trinity of today, like the Trinity of the past, is confronted with the task of educating women to meet the needs of their times.

It is our responsibility to build women, mature, competent to face problems, to explore possibilities of solutions—women strong in faith, self-reliant, practical—not dreamers. Adherence to the liberal arts does not imply an unrealistic attitude. The culture of the past is needed to give meaning to the near chaos of the present. Nuclear fission does not require atomistic, fragmentary education. As atomic energy can be used for building as well as for destruction, so we hope with the help of the Most Holy Trinity who made both man and atom to build the Trinity woman for the space age.

The academic year 1957–58 revealed that Trinity's science departments were prepared for the spotlight focused on them. Not only were the elementary and major courses thorough and up-to-date, but senior research seminars were keeping abreast of current developments in their fields. The physics department, for example, had introduced (before Sputnik) solid state physics, the first undergraduate women's college course in that subject. In March 1958 students took upon themselves the project of "educating scientifically" the whole college. Chemistry, Biology, Physics and Mathematics Clubs "inspired by the recent advances and resulting upsurge of interest in science this year . . . joined forces in an effort to present a practical and attractive picture of science to the non-science major"[29] for Science Day, March 13, 1958.

The visiting professors that year reflected the scientific emphasis. Spanish Circle and the American Association of Teachers of Spanish sponsored the visit of Dr. Robert Picard of the Universities Madrid and Bordeaux, and Miss Margaret Leddy of Pius X School of Liturgical Music interested students in the fine arts and humanities by her lectures and seminars in medieval and renaissance music as part of the Arts Program of the Association of American Colleges. Yet science visitors seemed very important in the year of Sputnik.

Dr. Louis R. Maxwell, specialist in solid state physics at the U.S. Naval Ordinance Laboratory, came in January, under the auspices of the American Institute of Physics and the American Association of Physics Teachers, as a part of a broad, nationwide program to stimulate interest in physics. Earlier in the term Trinity was one of the sponsors and hosts for a series of seven lectures on mathematical topics given by *Dr. Richard D. Shaefer,* head of the department of mathematics at the University of Connecticut. The series was under the auspices of the Mathematical Association of America and the National Science Foundation. The chemists also profited by a National Science Foundation grant, which helped provide the American Chemical Society's Division of Chemical Education with a visiting lecture program. Under this program *Dr. Harold Gomez Cassidy* of Yale shared with the chemistry students his knowledge of chromatography, and lectured to the student body on Science and the Humanities. Chemistry majors from nearby colleges came to Trinity for Dr. Cassidy's classes and discussions.[30]

29. Helen L. Murphy, '58, a chemistry senior, in a descriptive article in the *Alumnae Journal,* Spring, 1958, pp. 130–131.
30. *Alumnae Journal,* Winter, 1958, p. 71.

The "Alumnae College," a day of classes for returning alumnae at the May reunion was science-oriented that year.[31] The conjunction of the International Geophysical Year (IGY) and the interest generated by the Sputniks determined the theme. Each of the two main papers dealt with subject matter of lasting importance as well as current interest. Sister St. John Nepomucene, Professor of Chemistry, brought to her "History of the Geophysical Year" competence in organization and presentation as well as research experience in the history of science. Father Francis J. Heyden, S.J., Director of the Georgetown Astronomical Observatory not only introduced his space-age audience to some of the mysteries of outer space, but succeeded in making understandable to the lay mind some of the major steps in the historical development of today's preoccupation with the subject. "Recent Developments in Cancer Chemotherapy" by Dr. Howard W. Bond of the National Institutes of Health; "Nuclear Physics Today and Tomorrow" by Dr. James G. Brennan of Catholic University; "Whither Genetics" by Sister Marie Therese Dimond, Associate Professor of Biology at Trinity; and "Solid State Physics" by William J. Whelan, Lecturer in Physics at Trinity completed the panel under the capable chairmanship of Mrs. Eileen Treacy, Associate Professor of Physics at Trinity.

The change to the "Four Course Plan" was not a content change in curriculum or degree requirements. It was rather a reorganization of both subject matter and time schedule to meet a "felt need" (to use a bit of educational jargon). During the scholastic year 1959–1960, departmental reports to the President as well as frequently reiterated faculty and student opinion emphasized dissipation of effort and the fragmentation of much of the students' knowledge because students took too many subjects at the same time. Schedules were too heavy, it was said, and too many courses were two or three hours a week—occasionally, even one hour a week. Out of this situation grew the idea of the four-course plan.

The Committee on Curriculum and Academic Affairs[32] worked on the problem through many hours of meetings. They reached the decision to shift emphasis from semester hours to courses, and developed a plan which was embodied in the statement on degree requirements in the catalogue.

In preparation for the plan, the departments were asked to reorganize subject matter so that students would take only four courses at a time in order to encourage greater concentration and deeper understanding. Each course was to constitute one-fourth of the student's

31. "Alumnae College-Science Day," May 30, 1958, *Alumnae Journal*, Educational Supplement, Autumn, 1958.
32. For membership of the Curriculum Committee see *T.C. Catalogue* 1959–60, p. 13.

time and was considered to be roughly equivalent to four hours of class and the study time needed in preparation for those classes. It was hoped that the new plan would give the students opportunity to deepen their knowledge by

(1) focusing attention on fewer subjects at a time;
(2) concentrating class time and allowing longer uninterrupted periods of study, allowing most students a day free of classes for library or laboratory work (this last never really worked out for all, but a valiant attempt was made);
(3) providing opportunity for more independent study, seminar work, and participation in research.

The departments were asked to reorganize subject matter. It sounds quite simple. Faculty members are competent scholars who not only know their fields but also know how to teach them. Our system of liberal learning, of academic freedom, of academic excellence presupposes this—but faculty members by their very permanency, by their dedication to their own disciplines tend to resist change in the framework of their lives. The change was effected by a great amount of good will, long departmental discussions, some trial and error—and continuing self-criticism—continuing until it brought about the 1970 changes.

The program as it evolved is described in the catalogue:

> The requirement for graduation is determined by the quantity and quality of the work completed. The quantity of work is measured by course units. A course represents one-fourth of a student's academic work for one semester. For graduation thirty-two courses are required, with twelve in a concentrated area, of which at least seven should be within one department. The additional requirements are: theology—four courses; philosophy—two; literature—three; social science or history—three; art or music—one course; language—two courses; science—two courses. A two-year non-credit sequence in physical education is prescribed. The quality of work is indicated by the quality ratio, according to which the student must maintain an average of C, and cumulatively for the degree.

There was flexibility within the framework for more individual choice than is apparent at first glance. The freshman requirement was modified so that the student might choose social science immediately and delay science or language to sophomore year, if she did not intend to do advanced work in those fields.

As the decade of the sixties progressed, faculty and students became more restive in the framework of the "four-course plan." In December 1967 the President of the College appointed a Carte Blanche Committee of faculty and students funded by a grant from Esso to study the problem and make suggestions. Their report to the president and the faculty,

Sister Thérèse's Seminar in English A.

dated April 1, 1968,[33] stated: "The explosive growth of knowledge is almost all traditional disciplines and the emergence of many new, essentially interdisciplinary, areas of study make the traditional liberal arts curriculum an inadequate instructional tool today." They suggested and gained approval for an individualized approach spelled out in some detail to be tested by a pilot group from the class of 1972 who would be entering as freshmen in September 1968. The work of the Carte Blanche Committee, the Pilot Program and the faculty-student Task Force that succeeded them eventuated in the innovative curriculum of the seventies.

In early 1970 the faculty approved the new curriculum, described in the academic dean's article in the *Alumnae Journal*[34]:

> In March, 1969, a Task Force was established, composed of faculty members of the Committee on Curriculum and Academic Policy and of students, which was mandated to examine, in the light of the contemporary scene, all aspects of the then-current curriculum, and more especially the system of

33. This report with the report of the evaluation of the Pilot Program is in the Trinity College Archives.
34. "The New Curriculum, a Union of Stability and Dynamism," Sister Margaret Finnegan, *Alumnae Journal*, Summer, 1970, pp. 195–198.

required courses set up to guarantee the breadth requisite for a liberal arts degree. The faculty devoted two days to discussing and refining the reports of this Task Force, and on February 17, 1970, voted to endorse a curriculum based on "responsible choice with (responsible) guidance." A faculty committee with student representation was set up to work out the implementation of the changes, and several faculty meetings were held to consider the work of this committee. By the pre-registration week in May, procedures had been worked out to allow students who wished to take advantage of the curricular revisions for 1970–1971 to do so. (Students who preferred to remain under the traditional curriculum were given that option.) All members of the class of 1974 will follow the guidelines of the New Curriculum, which does not represent a radical break with the past, but rather that logical development and reallocation of academic resources which seem to be called for by the "changing times." . . .

The Trinity curriculum which aspires to continue to provide for these "changing educational needs of women as these develop with the changing times" must continue to provide a "union of stability and dynamism" which is to say it must balance tensions—among others, the perennial tension of unity and diversity. For there is on the one hand a very real need for shared traditions, shared experiences, shared problems and values, and on the other very real differences of competence and interest. Almost every ground of curricular argument speaks for commonality. A complex culture cannot function without a substantial core of shared values, for even the store of practical means on which we draw to solve problems arises from a shared lore, tradition, idiom, from the wealth of allusion, simile, metaphor, even the very sentence rhythms by which we communicate layer on layer of meaning.

But it is equally true that a complex culture requires diverse cultivation of diverse talents. The academic community would fall apart from boredom if everyone were the mirror image of every one else—as would any other community. It is the exchange of different experiences and different points of view which nourishes both the learning process, and the person, the liberally educated, the liberated person. Such exchanges exist to serve the diversities of interest which constitute the world of scholarship in the broadest sense, and require the widest possible variety of alternatives, since from consideration of these arises the varied habits of the mind which support and nourish the freedoms of the liberated.

It appears to be the considered judgment of the faculty, as manifested by their overwhelming vote of approval, that the New Curriculum, based on responsible choice with responsible guidance, will best serve these freedoms at this time. Under the New Curriculum each student will be free to draw up her individual program of study, subject of course to the requirements of her major department, but free in the sense that she is correlatively accountable for searching out and formulating a statement outlining the curricular coherence underlying her responsible choices, which will replace the traditional program of general requirements. In a very real sense her program will be authentic and will represent her appropriate voice in a matter which affects her so intimately. The proximate goal of the pattern or choices for any one semester must always be justified in the context of her ultimate goal of becoming a truly liberated person.

The role of her faculty adviser will be to encourage and counsel her in every step of the process, insuring that she understands the importance of incorporating breadth into her education by taking courses in the varied areas of humanities, languages and fine arts, social sciences, natural sciences, and mathematics. Although the New Curriculum permits a good deal of latitude in these choices, each student's program, after being approved by the adviser, will be evaluated by the Guidance Committee, and programs which give cumulative evidence of premature specialization will be returned to the student for re-formulation and re-submission.

Departmental chairmen, who have in the past borne the responsibility of guiding majors, will continue to supervise major programs in their disciplines, but the guidance of students will be distributed among the faculty at large in order that each student may receive maximum opportunity for individual guidance. This pooling of diversities of experience and insight in a joint intellectual effort is something that most students see as an indispensable aspect of their education. The enterprise of learning, far from being formless and undisciplined will acquire, it is hoped, a new quickening from this consolidation process, from the meeting of minds in a cooperative venture that is meaningful to the student and to her adviser, with each discovering that both are necessary for successful participation in the reflexive critical scrutiny due a program and a statement of purpose of such importance to the individual student.

The faculty does not, however, indulge in a mindless certainty that it has hit upon the final solution for all curricular needs. Built into the implementation of the Task Force recommendations there is provision for a very careful series of evaluations by faculty and students separately and together, each in the fashion appropriate to its competence.

In the early 1970's the increasing development of the practicum course became evident. The practica offered academic credit for work experience closely related to the student's field of study or career goals. Such work was under the joint supervision of the student's major department and a competent advisor in the government, business, labor or educational organization where she worked. In 1972, practica were offered in the departments of Economics, Education, Music, Political Science, Sociology, and Psychology while others were considering them. In that year the faculty decided to devote itself to careful planning of programs of this sort after accepting the concept of practica for college-wide application. An article[35] describing in some detail the practica of the Sociology Department ended with a paragraph that sums up well this whole trend in modernized curriculum.

35. "Education in an Ivory Tower . . . or a College Without Walls," *Alumnae Journal, Winter, 1972, pp. 7–11. Cf. Academic News (students Education Committee), Autumn, 1978, for other modern developments in the use of media in course work. Cf. also "New Opportunities,"* *Trinity News*, April, 1972, pp. 1–3.

> Last year's Commission on Future Directions for Trinity, appointed by Sister Margaret Claydon to investigate all aspects of the life of the college, strongly recommended that faculty and administration "emphasize the potential of Trinity as an urban college, and as a college in Washington, D.C." To accomplish this end, the Commission specifically recommended that "the college make an unambiguous commitment to the development of practicum courses, and that this commitment be reinforced by departments involved in such courses. The development of such courses should take into consideration the concerns and the welfare of the individual student, and should constitute, in addition, a real contribution to the work of the agency, the institution, or the community group for whom the student will be working."

The "careful series of evaluations" in tune with reactions on many campuses in the mid-1970s led to the faculty approved "back to basics curriculum" of 1977 which is getting off the ground as this chapter ends. A *Trinity Times*[36] interview with Sister Mary Ann Cook, Academic Dean, and Betsy Hoffmann, of the Student Education Committee, and a *Washington Post*[37] front page article provide its essence. There will again be a general program, a "common pool of knowledge" required of all students as well as depth in one or more subjects of their choice. A good description of both the 1970 and 1977 curricula may be found in the catalogue 1979–1980 (pp. 40–46).

Through all these eighty years a thread of continuity in the Trinity curriculum can be traced. Expansion, modernization, reorganization, change of emphases over the years leave the program a liberal arts curriculum adapted to the needs of the times and keeping abreast of current developments in the various scholarly disciplines. How successful it has been in different eras of Trinity College history may be judged by the lives and achievements of the alumnae.[38]

A closer look at the history of the subject matter fields and of those responsible for them; some mention of supplementary enriching developments such as international exchange, study abroad, internships and practica; of graduate work; of the library as a strong bulwark of the curriculum—all these are necessary to complete a survey of Trinity's academic program and lead to a summary history of accreditation.

Languages and Literature

Though courses in philosophy, fine arts, science, mathematics, history, "pedagogy" and other social sciences were required or available

36. February 9, 1977.
37. February 21, 1977.
38. Chapter 8 of this history.

to the pioneer students, the original academic program was heavily weighted toward languages and literature. The classics, both Latin and Greek; and the modern languages, English, German, and French, were the strongest elements of the curriculum in the first decade. Spanish was introduced in 1911. Of the sixteen members of the class of 1904, five specialized in Greek and Latin, one in Greek and German, the rest in combinations of two languages. Until 1930 there were one, two or three Greek and Latin majors heading the degree lists in nearly all classes.[39] Combinations with Latin dominated the "groups" up to 1920 when those with English took over for the next two decades, at least. It must be remembered, however, that the Bachelor of Science degree was awarded until 1933 to those specializing in sciences and mathematics and that combinations of history, sciences, mathematics and the social sciences with one of the languages became more numerous after 1910.[40] By 1918 the Dean was saying in her annual report that history, English, political science, and French were the most popular electives and that small percentages elected Latin, Greek, and mathematics. For this last group we can judge that the students either specialized or did not take them beyond the general requirement.

Italian courses began in 1920 and developed into a major field from 1939 until 1948 under Dr. Alba Zizzamia. In the years 1949–1952, the Italian courses were taught by Dr. Alessandra Liuini del Russo and Mme von Mayer who combined French and Italian in their schedules. Though no Italian majors were graduated after 1951, the major requirements remained in the catalogue until 1960. Since 1952, a sequence of two or three courses a year has been offered, taught by Miss Antoinette Melignant. Courses in other languages have been offered at various periods as the times or demand warranted. Gaelic in the 1920's and early 1930's; the "critical languages" (Portuguese, Russian, Chinese[41]) after World War II and Korea; elementary Japanese in the 1970's. Of these, Russian alone became a major concentration under Sister Mary Frances McCarthy, Ph.D., with the help of a series of Russian born assistants. The others were used chiefly to supplement area studies and were dropped when demand decreased. Dr. Natalie Kalikin worked with her from 1962 and has directed the Russian majors since 1967. The few majors have been drawn from both Trinity and Catholic University through an agreement and continues under it.

A tabulation of major fields of graduates from 1944 to 1964 showed that, though numbers fluctuated in individual languages, a little more than 8% of all graduates in that period specialized in foreign lan-

39. Classes with none were 1906, 1909, 1916, 1918, 1922, 1926, 1928.
40. Booklet: "Degrees Conferred, 1904–1925," Trinity College, Washington, D.C. Several copies in T.C. Archives. Cf. also Trinity Catalogues.
41. Cf. T.C. Newsletter Oct. 1959, July and October, 1960.

TABLE VII

	1944–1959		1960–1964	
	N	%	N	%
Sciences and Mathematics	338	21	160	22
Humanities and Fine Arts (includes foreign languages)	766	47	338	46
Social Sciences	525	32	233	32

Data for the decade since were not available at the time of writing.

guages. The same analysis,[42] made at a time when sciences appeared to be dominating the curriculum, shows a surprising balance in percentages of graduates in three areas during the twenty year period. The figures are almost exactly the same for the fifteen year period 1944–1959 and that for 1960–1964. They are given in Table VII. Data for the decade since were not available at the time of writing.

Of the strong departments of the first decade (Latin and Greek, English, French, German), English and French have best survived the many changes of the years. The decline of the classics followed the widespread trend in American colleges, though they maintained their influence at Trinity through the 1930's into the 1940's, declining more slowly than in many comparable colleges. The separate departments of Latin and Greek were combined in 1946 into "Classical Languages and Literatures." The struggle to keep Latin as an entrance requirement reflects the widespread change in secondary school curricula (Cf. Table VI) as well as the decline in the number of entering students prepared to undertake advanced study in classical languages. The findings of the *Classical* Investigation of 1924 were studied and analyzed by faculty and by students of the course "Teaching Latin in Secondary School" who enthusiastically carried the results into teaching experience. High school Latin, however, was dying and college classics were soon to follow, though not to the extent of complete extinction.

Alumnae of all generations remember with affectionate admiration the succession of great teachers of classical languages: Sister Raphael of the Sacred Heart, M.D., A.M.,[43] of the original faculty, Sister Mary Albania (Burns), Ph.D., Sister Mary (Henretty) who taught Latin for the first three years until her appointment as Dean in 1903, Sister Mary Josephine, Sister Wilfred du Sacre Coeur, Ph.D. (Elsie Parsons, 1904),

42. T.C. Archives: Sister Columba Mullaly's notebook for the period. Data used in self-studies for Middle States Evaluations.
43. Lucy Pike, M.D., A.B., A.M., later (1912) founder of the Biology Department and President of the College, 1920–1929. Her biography is in D.A.B. and *Three Against the Wind*. Cf. typed draft, pp. 89, 108–111.

Sister Julia, A.M., L.H.M., B. Litt, (Oxon) (Helen Stokes, 1913), Sister Ann Julia, Ph.D. (Helen Kinnirey, 1925), Sister Margaret Mary (Fox), Ph.D.

Though all these classics teachers have been written up in some part of this history, the following excerpt from the 1946 *Trinilogue* must be inserted here because it sums up well the attitude of generations of students toward one whose career in the department was cut short by illness in mid-life.

> Those who had the good fortune to take classes in the Latin Department will not soon forget the magic of Sister Julia. . . . (We) not only became familiar with Horace, Cicero and Virgil, but also absorbed from Sister Julia's great store of knowledge a world of ideas and experience outside the realm of the classics. (p. 23)

Others assisted in classics for a longer or shorter time, but these are the names remembered through the years.

For those Greek and Latin majors of the class of 1904,[44] Dr. Mitchell Carroll, Dean of Classics at the Columbian University (now George Washington University) taught senior Greek students, reading with them Aristotle's *Poetics* and selected odes of Pindar. Miss Dorothy Sipes, a Ph.D. candidate at the same university, taught senior Latin when Sister Mary became Dean. A generation later, in 1924, when Sister Wilfred became Dean, her junior and senior Latin classes were taken for several years by a young instructor from Catholic University, Dr. Roy J. Deferrari, who was later the first Dean of the Graduate School and finally for many years General Secretary of that university. Thus classics provided early examples of inter-institutional sharing in addition to the invaluable contributions of the "professors" described in earlier chapters of this history.[45]

Classical Languages and Literatures is still a department in the Trinity curriculum, though it is often necessary to teach aspiring students the elements of the languages before they can undertake advanced work. The statement from the 1975–1976 catalogue sums up the present classics program:

> The Classics curriculum offers courses for the major and non-major. It affords the student opportunity to experience the breadth of classical learning through study of its language and literature. Related courses in ancient history, archaeology, linguistics, philosophy and theology broaden and enrich the department's offerings.

44. Cf. p. 93.
45. A complete list of Catholic University professors who taught at Trinity College in various departments up to 1939, the year of the university's Golden Jubilee, is extant in the Trinity College Archives. Cf. Chap. 7.

MAJOR REQUIREMENT: Eight courses, including at least three in Greek beyond 101, and three in Latin beyond 123. Related subjects strongly suggested: Art 432, History 511, 512 (CU), Linguistics. (p. 45)

The flourishing German Department of the early years with its courses in drama, poetry and narrative of various periods, its Old and Middle High German, its lectures conducted in the language became a casualty of World War I.[46] In the 1920's, its founder Sister Odilia Funke, Ph.D., re-introduced German and laboured to rebuild the department. It, however, never again reached its lost position. Sister Odilia was assisted in the 1920's by Sister Mary Kostka Kemper in the 1930's by a former student, Sister Mary Ellen Goerner, Ph.D. (Marguerite Goerner 1927), who replaced her after her retirement and continued to direct German studies until the early 1950's when she went to Villa Julie College as vice-president. Mrs. Clara Rathjens, M.A., taught German from 1951 to 1962, the first year with Sister Mary Ellen, 1952–1960 alone in the department, and finally 1960–1962 with Sister Mary Frances McCarthy, another of Sister Odilia's majors who had gone on to a doctorate in German. In the decade of the 1960's and early 1970's, Sister Mary Frances aided by two young German professors Dr. Schulz and Dr. Schacher from Catholic University worked innovatively for the German and with Dr. Kalikin for the Russian Departments. She established the German Study-Travel summer programs and the year abroad in Germany[47] as well as interdepartmental courses in German and Russian literature in English. Though the students of German continued to receive a thorough course in language and literature, the number of majors remained few. Work in that department is, since Sister Mary Frances became the president of Emmanual College, Boston, under the supervision of Dr. Kalikin, using the facilities of the Washington Consortium of Universities.

Sister Ann Madeline,[48] Paris born Julie Rose Guerin, already in 1900 an experienced and very capable teacher, established the French Department firmly on a level favorably comparable to French in colleges of the time. Strong emphasis on the spoken language and on French literature and culture characterized the teaching from the beginning. Study with Sister Ann Madeline presupposed competence acquired in high school and proved by examination. Remedial work ("make up courses") was available, but not for college credit. Courses in elementary French for college credit did not come into being at Trinity until the 1940's, during World War II. The earliest catalogues show that even freshmen who did not offer French as one of their subjects for entrance

46. Cf. Chapter 4, p. 89.
47. "Trinity in the Black Forest" by Sr. Mary Frances McCarthy, *Alumnae Journal*, Winter '70, pp. 67–72. Cf. "Study Abroad Programs" later in this chapter.
48. Her religious name seems to have been anglicized as was S.N.D. custom at the time.

Sister Mary Frances McCarthy, Ph.D. German and Russian.

were expected to have studied it. The French course required for freshmen in this category reads like an "intermediate French" course of later years, including dictation, prose composition, readings, and "Introduction to the History and Literature of France to prepare for detailed work in the different epochs." All other freshman students took French including prose composition, committing to memory of entire selections, and critical study of selections and the reading of five or six whole works. Sophomores, juniors and seniors in more advanced courses continued "critical readings" and prose composition as well as lecture series in French covering in the sophomore and junior years "the movements," poetry, drama, novel, oratory, criticism of seventeenth and nineteenth centuries up to "l'heure présente." Not much emphasis seems to have been given to the eighteenth century in these series, though there is a course (Course C) which includes an "Outline of the

French Literature of the Eighteenth Century" and a "general view of the social and political institutions of the period." Seniors took "Grammaire Historique, Phonetique, Morphologie (Darmesteter). Study of Old French. *Chanson de Roland, Aucassin et Nicolette.* Poesie Provencale (Mistral). French Journalism."

Until 1918 Sister Ann Madeline continued direction of French studies. She was joined in 1912 by Sister Marie Eugenie (Eugénie L. Lescesne) as her "assistant." The Dean's Report in 1918 mentioned that French continued to be one of the most popular subjects. Later that year, as World War I ended, the college joined in the Association of American Colleges plan to offer scholarships to students from allied countries. Trinity offered board "residence," tuition and living expenses to two French students: one, "Miss de Percin,"[49] was an advanced undergraduate student and the other a graduate student, Germaine Augier. Both later received Trinity degrees and Miss Augier taught for a time in the French department of the college. These two began the long line of "foreign exchange" students who have studied at Trinity from not only France, but Spain, Germany, Belgium and Italy.

The pioneer of the French department, however, was no longer able to direct operations. The president's report of May 31, 1919, announces:

> Giving in to ill health, Sister Anne [sic] Madeline, who has been head of the French department since the opening of Trinity, was obliged to resign her position after twenty years of untiring and incalculable service to the college and 55 years in the class-room. Her place has been in some measure filled by a Sister who has worked closely with her as assistant in the department, and two extra instructors have been employed to help in the constant increasing classes in French."

Though with the reticence characteristic of the time in referring to the S.N.D.'s on the faculty, Sister Catherine Aloysius mentioned no names, we know that the new head of the French department was Sister Marie Eugenie Lescesne who continued to teach French at Trinity until her retirement in 1949. The names of the "two extra instructors" do not appear in any catalogue or extant list. For a few months in 1920 (January to May) a Soeur Ignace came from Belgium. Miss Germaine Augier taught in the department until 1923. Sister Marie Lioba Bieler, Swiss-born linguist and gentle, cultured lady, "helped out" 1920–21 and returned in 1925 to share Sister Marie Eugenie's labors until her retirement in 1943. In the 1930's, Sr. Emmanual Doherty also taught with them. During the years from 1920 until the mid-1940's, French "foreign exchange" students conducted classes in conversation and

49. Marie Renée de Percin, La Rochelle, France. In 1980 Mme. Marie de Percin Lauzeral visited Trinity and spoke to the French Club.

what was called "French civilization" while themselves studying in various departments of the college.

As early as 1909, the French department offered a "Teachers' Course: A study of the aims and methods in teaching French. A review of the essentials of Grammar, Pronunciation, reading, composition. Practice in teaching." It was open to all students one hour a week with the permission of the instructor. By the 1920's, only seniors could take it with the same permission, of course. In the 1930's as a result of the "Modern Language Association Study" of 1929, it was a two hour course on aims and methods of teaching French in Junior and Senior High schools. In the 1950's it developed into a three hour course offered in alternate years and by 1960 had become "Language Methodology." It moved, in 1966, out of the French department to be "interdepartmental." By 1975, language methodology had become Linguistics, an area separate from the language departments, listed in the catalogue under social sciences.

A study of the yearly catalogues for the last twenty-five years will show the faculty changes and curriculum re-organization that has

Mme. Eda Levitine and Sister Maura Prendergast.

developed the present French department. It aims to achieve for the late twentieth century student what Sister Ann Madeline aimed to do as the century opened. During those years, Sister Margaret Therese Evans, Sr. Helen Denise Cronin, Mme. Von Mayer, Dr. Alexandra Liuni del Russo, Dr. Rosario Adriazola, Dr. Sylvia Washington and others for brief intervals carried on the department. A 1975 statement for prospective students describes the current department.

> The study of French at Trinity can concentrate on literature or on the cultural-lingual approach. In either case, the proficiency that the student of French achieves benefits her not only in her course work but at the many French lectures, films, and art collections in Washington. The French student participates in the works of Voltaire and Balzac, the films of Truffant (without the stilted English subtitles) and the novels of Camus. She opens

Mme. Sylvia Washington Bâ.

her mind to a new experience, to a part of the world's population that was once obscured by a language barrier. The reign of Louis XIV and the Battle of Waterloo become as meaningful as the presidency of Thomas Jefferson and the Civil War.

Two programs which originated in the French department, Study Abroad and the Language Laboratory, have grown to include all the modern language departments. They will therefore be treated at the end of this section rather than with the French Department.

Spanish

Spanish was a "late-comer" to Trinity, having been added to the curriculum in 1911. Dating, however, from the beginning of the second decade, the department has a venerable tradition of nearly seventy years of contribution to the academic life of the college. The president's report, May 30, 1912, announced:

> The growing interest in Spanish in all American colleges, influenced us to begin its study last September, and many students entered upon its courses with delight and enthusiasm. The work in this department has been carried on by Señora Lezca de Ruiz and has been efficient and satisfactory in every detail.

The "many students" who studied Spanish "with delight and enthusiasm" seem to have considered it supplementary to their main program because Spanish does not appear as a declared major subject in the degree lists until 1919—when one student offered French and Spanish.[50] During the period of two major subjects, 1922–1932, there were several Spanish majors in each class. The largest number offering Spanish as one major were in the classes of 1926 (9) and 1927 (10). During the twenty years of her devotion to Trinity students, Señora Rita Lesca de Ruiz had the usual nameless assistants from time to time, but she taught the bulk of the classes herself.[51] Her health began to fail in the early 1930's, and she retired in 1932. It was her successor, Miss Marion Louise Pierce, who participated in the curricular re-organization and established the requirements for Spanish major work in the new program which graduated its first three majors in 1935.

Señora died in 1937. One of her former students wrote of her then[52] as a loved "modest, affectionate little lady," "our motherly confidant

50. There had been a graduate student who offered French and Spanish for the M.A. in 1915.
51. One of these was Mercedes Hayden, a *magna cum laude* student of languages of the class of 1920 who taught with Señora in the early 1920's. Her name appears in the complete faculty list published in the catalogue of 1922–23.
52. Edith Duncan, '25 in the *Alumnae Journal*, Nov. 1937, p. 13.

and capable instructor." "Those of us," she wrote "who sat in her small classroom at Trinity can recall vividly the personal interest she had in each of us and the un-Latin patience with which she guided us through faltering Spanish ways."

The 1932–1933 catalogue which announced the new curricular organization of one major with related minors also carried for the first time the name of Miss Marion Louise Pierce, M.A., and the newly stated requirement language for the Spanish major. Miss Pierce continued to direct the Spanish department until her retirement in 1956. She was assisted in the early 1940's by Professor René Samson, from 1948–1951 by Señorita Blanca Gutierrez del Rio and from 1951 by Sister Francis (Ann Gormly, '45), a modern language major whose Ph.D. was in Spanish, French and Italian and who replaced Miss Pierce in 1956. Sister Francis directed the department, even after her appointment as Dean of Students in 1965, until 1971. The present chair of the department, Sister Joan Mary Hill, Ph.D., joined the Spanish department in 1970. Through the 1950's and 1960's, into the 1970's, the catalogue shows the names and qualifications of those who taught for short periods. A few only will be mentioned: Señorita Maria Montero who, as "native speaker" taught conversation courses from 1952 to 1961; Señorita Marguerita Mendoza-Cubillo who taught literature 1964–1968; two from other departments where they later settled permanently: Dr. Rosario Adriazola from French and Dr. Liliana Gramberg from art; and Mrs. Anna Modigliani de Lynch who is still with Sister Joan Mary Hill in the department.

The Spanish major has always been a language and literature combination with emphasis on spoken word and a knowledge of the literature of Spain and of Latin America. From 1961–1973 Portuguese was also offered as an aid to Latin American Area Studies. The table referred to earlier in this chapter[53] shows that there were 56 Spanish majors in the period from 1944–1964, a steady stream of small numbers with the largest group of six in 1951. Spanish continues in this trend into the late 1970's. A contemporary description written about 1975 will serve to sum up this section.

> The Spanish Department at Trinity gives students a strong program in Spanish literature and, with the help of the language laboratory, a proficiency in the spoken word. . . . For students interested in preserving diversity in the United States, proficiency in Spanish enables them to teach Bicultural-Bilingual courses; for students interested in Social Sciences, this proficiency helps them understand the unique problems and needs of many Latin-Americans.

53. p. 190.

Louise Pierce.

Sister Francis (Ann Gormly), Ph.D.

THE LANGUAGE LABORATORY

The establishment in 1949 of the modern language laboratory, one of the first fully equipped college laboratories of this kind, was an outgrowth of the French Department's pioneering, funded in part by a gift of the Pittsburgh Alumnae Chapter. It was intended, however, for use by all modern language classes. The laboratory had its roots in a

Sister Joan Mary Hill, Ph.D.

powerful short-wave radio and an early model SoundScriber in Sister Marie Eugenie's French classroom. There students of the 1940's listened to French broadcasts from Radio Brassaville when Paris was unavailable during the war years and recorded their voices for criticism of pronunciation and inflection on scratchy little green disks.

The first language laboratory was equipped in what is now Room 262.[54] It was called at first the Modern Language Studio and described

54. A plaque still on the door of that room expresses the gratitude of the college to the Pittsburgh Chapter.

by Sister Catherine Dorothea Fox, president of the college, in an illustrated article for the alumnae in 1949.[55] After summarizing the trend away from foreign language study in American colleges and the self-evaluation of the Trinity foreign language departments, she writes of the new project to assist in carrying out the objectives expressed by the language departments.

> Trinity has converted the former German Room[56] (second floor south) into a language studio, equipped with various mechanical devices to assist the students in acquiring thorough language training and skill. Physically, the room is provided with acouti-celotex ceiling, carpeted floor and draped windows for sound purposes. The Radio Corporation of America sent an engineer to confer with us and to carry out our plans. As a result we have a very attractive studio with enough variety in electronic equipment to attract and assist students on all levels of language accomplishment, and yet so arranged that, as the classes increase in number and proficiency, more equipment can be added.

Not only increased use of the "studio," but rapid development in the field of electronic equipment soon made expansion and newer type equipment necessary. In 1958, with the help of funds from the Raskob Foundation and the Class of 1942, under the meticulous supervision of Sister Margaret Therese Evans, the laboratory was enlarged and re-equipped. Three rooms on the opposite side of the South Hall corridor were combined to make the present laboratory (Room 259) where the "latest electronic equipment was installed." Since then, periodic up-dating, supervision, and repair have kept the now elderly laboratory at the service of language students. The names of three people to whom the language laboratory owes its continuing service and effectiveness will be remembered by many alumnae are those of Sister Margaret Therese Evans, Mrs. Katalina Quander Masembwa, and Mrs. Anna Modigliani de Lynch.

Foreign Study

Study abroad for Trinity undergraduate credit began in 1928. Before that students had traveled and alumnae had earned degrees in England and in Europe, but "junior year in French" with Erin Samson's Paris Study Groups for College Women, under Catholic auspices,[57] was the undergraduate debut in this field. The first description in the

55. "The New Modern Language Studio," *Alumnae Journal*, Autumn, 1949, pp. 4–6. Cf. *Newsletter*, July, 1963.
56. Now Room 262.
57. Two illustrated brochures from the early and mid-1930's for the program are extant in the Trinity Archives. Catalogue 1932–1933, p. 68 and following years to 1942.

catalogue appears at the beginning of the French Department offerings in 1932.

THE JUNIOR YEAR IN FRANCE

Students who have chosen French as their major subject may be allowed to spend Junior year in France as a member of "The Paris Study Group for Catholic Colleges." Undergraduates are thus enabled to spend nine months in France, follow courses at the Sorbonne and the Catholic University in Paris, visit other countries during the holidays, and return to College the following September where they will be accepted as Seniors.

The group is supervised by a former member of the Trinity College faculty at present attached to the Catholic University in Paris. The students live with the best type of French families where they speak the language and gain some knowledge of French life and customs.

Only those students will be recommended who have a high average in their work and who seem well qualified to represent the College. For further information, apply to the Dean or to one of the French Professors.

Catalogue 1932–33, p. 68

The 1943–44 catalogue announced that the junior year in France arrangement would be resumed when "foreign travel is possible." In the late 1940's, a few students benefited from Miss Samson's experienced supervision, but the Paris Study Group never returned to its former status.

In the last three decades, various study abroad programs, both for summer and for the full scholastic year have been developed not only by the modern language departments, but also by the history, English and, on an individual basis, by classics and social sciences. Examples of these programs included the German one cited earlier,[58] the Sophomore Year in England (1965–present) in which a small group of English, History or Political Science majors spend a year in Oxford,[59] Junior Year in Spain in cooperation with the New York University group, and more recent French study-travel programs for both summer and the year at Aix-en-Provence. By the late 1960's, this aspect of the curriculum had developed to such an extent that a college-wide policy was formulated. The catalogues[60] from 1967 to 1975 have carried a full statement of policy and procedure for undergraduate study abroad.

58. p. 192.
59. Cf. catalogue 1970–71, p. 54, p. 60. Also: *Alumnae Journal*, Winter 1966, pp.104–107 and *Newsletter*, July 1965, August 1967.
60. Cf. catalogue 1967–1968, p. 23. Also: "Traveling with Trinity," *Alumnae Journal*, Autumn 1963, pp. 11–19; "Trinity in England," *Alumnae Journal*, Winter, 1969, pp. 74–78.

ENGLISH

From 1900 English has been an important part of a Trinity education. The English department is one of the original academic departments that has weathered the years well. The mini-profiles of two of the early English faculty, in Chapter 3, give the flavor of teaching in the first two decades.[61] The statement in the catalogue of 1901–1902 sets the pattern for succeeding years. "The courses in English," it says,

> are arranged in three sections: Rhetoric and composition; English Literature; and the elements of philology. During the Freshman and Sophomore years one course in each section is required from all students. English is prescribed for the Junior Year but the courses are elective. The courses for the Senior Year are open only to the students who have elected the English groups.[62]

Until the curriculum re-organization of 1932, all students continued to take three years of English whatever their major subjects, though only English majors were required to take old and middle English language and readings. Anglo-Saxon (Old English) and Middle English with readings in the language continued as a major requirement until 1961.

As the courses were lettered rather than numbered in the catalogue until 1914, the famous English 15, "English Poetry from the publication of the Lyrical Ballads to the present day," can be traced by number back only to 1914, but its fame long outlasted its metamorphasis in 1932 to English 151.

Sister Mary Josephine, the "Sister from England" as she was called, founded the English department and taught literature and "philology" until 1903 when she returned to Notre Dame Training College, Mount Pleasant, Liverpool, whence she had come as a loan to the new college. She was joined in 1901 by the young Sister Julie[63] whose name became identified with English at Trinity in the first two decades, and in 1902 by Sister Mary Patricia.[64] Professor Maurice Francis Egan, first chairman of the Catholic University English department, lectured at Trinity in 1903–1904 and even earlier had come for Literary Society meetings. Twenty years later the president's report mentions the "pleasant rebinding of old ties" when Dr. Maurice F. Egan gave a series of four lectures on Modern Drama to "appreciative young auditors." Sister Helen Louise (Mary F. Nugent) taught in the department from 1908 to 1915. The President's Report of 1920 mentions Miss Rebecca Shanley's course

61. pp. 68–70.
62. Catalogue 1901–1902, p. 40.
63. Cf. Chapter 4, p. 91.
64. Cf. Chapter 4, p. 92; Obituary by Marie Madden, 1908 in *Alumnae Journal*, May 19, 1941, pp. 57-58; also cf. library section of this history.

A class in English C (238).

in Business English. Sister Julia of the Trinity[65] (Edith McDonald, '11) joined the English department in 1915, teaching with Sister Julie and replacing her as head of the department until 1929. With her in the 1920's, and continuing after her, were Sister Loretta du Sacre Coeur (McGarry) (1921–1948), Sister Mary Mercedes (Robb) (1922–1935) and Sister Therese (Sullivan) who taught courses while studying for her

65. Sixth president of the college, cf. pp. 111–114.

doctorate 1927–1930 and returned in 1933 to devote herself to "*her* English majors" until her retirement in 1967.[66] Students from 1932 to 1938 remember with appreciation the classes of Dr. Arthur Deering who taught literature during those years.

Writing in 1950, when greats of the third quarter of the century—Mrs. Margaret Giovannini, Mr. William Force Stead, Sister Therese Sullivan—were already putting their prestigious stamp on English, Sister Columba Mullaly wrote of the fifty year old department[67]:

> Facing the task of writing about the English Department for alumnae readers takes real courage. Telling you "how we do it now" when to hundreds of you English at Trinity means Sister Julie de la Sainte Famille, Sister Julia of the Trinity, Sister Angela Elizabeth or others—perhaps even Sister Mary Josephine or Sister Mary Patricia—would seem rash indeed, but for two things. First, in spite of your habit of cherishing memories of "our day," you would not be satisfied to have college or curriculum remain static. Secondly, though there have been developments with the changing times, and there will need to be further changes in the future in accord with tendencies in college English, we of "the Now" hope that the core, the solid meat, of the English offerings has remained essentially unchanged. All students still must take two years of English, but the sophomore survey has replaced "English 15" as the formidable hurdle, and courses after sophomore year are optional. English majors still must take Old English and Chaucer, and still must haunt the library to the attempt to keep up with long reading assignments for all courses. A statement of the objectives of the department and of some of the means used in working toward those objectives will allow you to judge for yourselves both the changes and the underlying continuity which links the English student of 1950 with her predecessors.
>
> The objectives of the English Department may be divided into two groups: those which apply to all students of the college, and those which apply specifically to English majors. Through the required courses of the freshman and sophomore years, the department aims to develop in all students those reading and writing skills which will be necessary for their advanced college courses, and, as far as time will permit, an appreciation of literature which may form a basis for leisure-time enjoyment. In addition, the department aims
>
> 1. to give the major student a knowledge and appreciation of the development of the English language and of the literature in English;
> 2. to develop in her an increasing ability to evaluate critically works of poetry and prose;

66. Cf. Chapter 4, faculty profiles. Tribute by Ila Ware Klein, '50, in *Alumnae Journal*, Spring, 1978 and by Marie Noonan Sabin, '53, at Reunion Banquet, May, 1978.
67. "In the Wake of English 15," *Alumnae Journal*, Autumn, 1950, pp. 4–5.

3. to improve her skill in expressing ideas effectively in writing;
4. to encourage special effort in creative writing by those who have talent.

The differentiated program,[68] which was introduced in 1939 into the freshman year, is the chief means used to attain the general objective. In order to meet the needs, or to encourage the special abilities, of all, the materials of the traditional reading and composition course have been varied. Entering students are grouped on the basis of scores on tests of verbal aptitude, reading comprehension, and mechanics of English. Particular attention is given in the freshman course to improvement of reading and prose expression, and to remedial work. Those students showing proficiency in these typical freshman requirements are exempt from the usual course and introduced to selected works of world literature, while their training in written expression is continued. All freshmen are trained in the use of the library and in the preparation of the documented paper. The "term paper" has the grave importance of the brief and forensic of the days of freshman argumentation courses. Functions formerly belonging to freshman argumentation have been absorbed by the logic course which, through practical applications in deductive and inductive reasoning, and close correlation with the work of the English courses, helps to develop the clear thinking and exact study habits necessary for advanced work.

In the sophomore year, the survey is modified for the major group, who study more intensively periods which will not be covered by later courses, touch but lightly the work of Shakespeare and end with the late eighteenth century. In this course the new major student makes her first attempts at critical evaluation and lays the foundation for later literary study. The non-major survey is more inclusive and less intensive. Seeking to meet the needs of those who may be finishing with this course their formal instruction in English, it covers the chief works of English literature from the beginning through the Victorian Period.

The English major work requires at least thirty semester hours beyond the work already described. This must include Old English and Chaucer, Shakespeare, the Romantic and Victorian poets, nineteenth-century critical writers, one prose writing course, at least one semester of versification, and American literature. Adding a list of electives to this lengthy enumeration would be tantamount to reproducing the catalogue. The most popular elective for seniors is twentieth-century literature which is crowded each year by majors and non-majors alike. The advanced writing courses, short story and advanced composition, open to select groups, aim especially at the attainment of the last of the departmental objectives. The upperclass majors have a one hour course directed toward coordinating the work in their major field. This consists in guided background readings and class discussions emphasizing, for the juniors, the seventeenth and eighteenth centu-

68. Planned and put into operation by Sister Ann Julia Kinnirey working with the Dean of Studies. Cf. Catalogue 1943–44, p. 69 and *Alumnae Journal*, Autumn, 1951, pp. 17–20.

> ries, and, for the seniors, a general view of English literature and a "taking stock" of weaknesses or gaps that should be filled by individual study.
>
> Changes in requirements must come gradually as they have in the past. Probably the greatest need at present is a lessening, or a shifting, of the emphasis still placed on the nineteenth century, now that the twentieth century "hath his halfe cours y-ronne" and our perspective is clearer. Another change should grow from the ardent desire cherished for years by various members of the department for smaller senior groups and more individualized work, at least for the outstanding major students.

Since that mid-century statement, another twenty-five years of the future have become past. Teachers who strongly influenced students and shaped the character of the department in those years include Mrs. Margaret Giovannini, Mr. William Force Stead,[69] Sister Therese of the Blessed Sacrament (Katherine Sullivan, '17)—full professors all even then—Mrs. Nancy Brown who joined the department in 1959 and who chairs it in the 1970's,[70] Sister Margaret Claydon from 1952 to 1959 and enthusiastically back at teaching in the late 1970's after her long fruitful term as president of the college. In the 1940's and 1950's, Sister Columba Mullaly combined some teaching with her work as Dean, shuttling between English and Education and chairing English from 1948 to 1963. Others have taught in the department for shorter times, contributing to the attainment of its objectives.[71] Their names are memorable to their students and are listed in the catalogues, but they form too long a roll to be included here.

The chief trend of these years has been that suggested above, "a lessening, or a shifting, of the emphasis still placed on the nineteenth century, now that the twentieth century 'hath his halfe cours y-ronne'" and greater attention to the individual, to honors work, or to small seminar work. The swing became, perhaps, over the years a bit too far toward a program heavily weighted with the contemporary. In the mid-1970's the department was working toward a balance of earlier periods, nineteenth and twentieth centuries, and American literature. All these elements of development are expressed in the catalogue statement of 1975–76 given here in full to summarize the change and continuity apparent in the English department.

> The department provides all students with the opportunity to become familiar with English as an effective tool in speaking and writing; to discover the roots of the language with regard to its history and structure; to

69. Cf. *Alumnae Journal,* Winter, '65, pp. 59–66: Spring, '67, p. 190 (*obit.*).
70. "Harbison Award for Distinguished Teaching," *Alumnae Journal,* Autumn, '66, p. 63.
71. The eminent Sister Angela Elizabeth Keenan is remembered at Trinity as Dean of Students 1932–1942, as well as English teacher. She will be included in Chapter 6, rather than here.

explore the range of English and American literature from the earliest periods to the present; and to develop special gifts for original writing in various genres. It is hoped that each student will become a thoroughly articulate person, aware of the resources of English and American literary culture. Students are also offered the opportunity of trying out career preferences in several pre-vocational courses, and in practica enabling them to experience career situations off campus.

English majors, who undertake more intensive study in the field, are invited to apply to join the group selected to spend the sophomore year in Oxford, where the college program is conducted in accordance with the traditional tutorial system of the University (see section 4 and below).

Small seminar groups and tutorial sessions also find a place in many other English courses. Each instructor has the freedom to plan courses in the manner that seems most suitable for the material under study; often a combination of lecture sessions, discussion groups, and individual direction proves most workable, and gives impetus to the growth of mature and independent critical judgment.

The American Studies Program provides an interdisciplinary study of American literature, history and culture (see section 10). Students also have the option of pursuing a modified American Studies Program by fulfilling the requirements of an English major with an emphasis on American literature.

Interdepartmental or interdisciplinary courses directed by the department are designated by the letter I following the number.

MAJOR REQUIREMENT: Thirty-two hours above introductory level from courses listed below (excluding pre-vocational and practicum courses). The senior English major is required to take the colloquium (498), and strongly recommended to take a seminar (499). Individual students shape their programs in consultation with their advisors to develop their particular interests within the discipline.

M.A.T. COURSES: All courses in the department are open to M.A.T. students, and special arrangements will be made, if necessary, for their advanced program of study. Such courses will be designated as 500-level courses, and planned for three graduate credits.[72]

Student publications which began under English department auspices and flourished for many years under its supervision are the *Trinity College Record,* a literary magazine begun in 1907, the *Trinilogue,* published yearly by the senior class since 1911, the *Trinity Times,* the newspaper which dates from 1925. The Literary Society (Upsilon Tau) began in 1902 and flourished through more than fifty years as one of the student "co-curricular" clubs. Sister Mary Patricia wrote in the 1920's that in 1903 "The Upsilon Tau, the present Literary Society, gave an evening's readings from modern authors under study in the Soci-

72. Catalogue 1975–76, pp. 46–47.

Mr. William Force Stead with Literary Society officers.

ety, the first mention made of it in College history.[73] These activities will be treated more fully in the chapter on student activities.

Closely related to English, but not actually part of the English department was the work in speech and drama. From 1921 to 1961, the catalogues list courses, called at first Elocution and including Voice, Public Speaking, Dramatic Speech, it developed under Miss Elsie Kernan who from 1921 to 1941 gave full time to courses which finally became Speech and Drama and to the coaching of the Dramatic Society's productions. Elocution courses in the 1920's included psysiology of the voice, phonetics, pronounciation, techniques of vocal expression and interpretation as well as dramatic training. Membership in the Dramatic Society required passing courses in elocution. From 1941 to 1951, a one hour course in speech was required of all freshmen. During these years a series of well prepared young teachers spent from one to five years in the department teaching speech courses and considerably modernizing play production continuing use of the stage in Notre Dame Auditorium. They were Miss Margaret Roberts,[74] Miss Maxine Schlingman, Miss Mary Finnerty,[74] Miss Dorothy Chernuck, and Miss Catherine Hanifin.

73. Historical Sketch of Trinity College, p. 43. Source Dean's Notebooks for 1902–1903. T.C.A.
74. Spent one year only on faculty.

Professors Jean Willke and Margaret Giovannini.

The second name that stands out, after Miss Kernan, in the more than fifty-year history of the department is that of Miss Charlotte Brannen (1951–1962). In 1949, Speech and Drama was removed from its place as addendum to the English department and listed as a department in its alphabetical order. Miss Brannen competently directed its activities for more than a decade, emphasizing remedial speech, public speaking and acting. She produced in cooperation with the Dramatic Society excellent plays, experimenting with then very new techniques such as "theater-in-the-round" and finally succeeding in the decades-old struggle to have young men play the male parts in Trinity plays. After 1962 no speech and drama department appears in the Trinity College curriculum. Dramatic Society plays continue sporadically, but with no resident coach or producer.[75]

History and the Social Sciences

"In the totality of the spectrum of human knowledge . . . the social sciences may serve as a common ground . . . in which man may resolve the disparate elements of science and humanistic learning, and perhaps even discover them to be . . . not latently opposed, but mutually complementary. . . . The social sciences by virtue of ties in both camps, can serve as a bridge, as an intermediate zone of reconcilia-

75. Cf. Dramatic Society in Chapter 6, Student Activities.

tion."[76] If this is true, then history might be considered the bridge between the other humanistic studies and the social sciences. In spite of very definitely stated opinions of members of the present history faculty who insist on the place of their scholarly field among "the humanities," history is closely linked in Trinity curricular development with several of the studies which later were called social sciences. It is, therefore, grouped here to show that relationship, without in any way detracting from the prestige of either history or the social sciences which have become important especially in the decades since World War I.

History

The History Department is one of those that spans the years since 1900.[77] In the catalogue of 1901–1902 the title is "History and Political Science" and included not only ancient, mediaeval [sic] and modern European; American colonial, modern (1876–1900); and constitutional history, a history of U.S. Foreign Relations, and bibliography, but the elements of economics and economic history. The introductory note quoted here shows that the methods of the department of the 1970's have roots in the earliest years. "The object of the prescribed courses in history," it states, "is threefold: to give all students a broad survey of the history of the world; to stimulate individual research and to awaken a critical sense of the philosophy of history. The course is further developed and strengthened by its co-relation with the course in church history.

"The instruction is carried on by means of lectures, recitations, private reading and seminars. The course is outlined to guide private reading and preparation."

Before the first class graduated, the departmental offerings had expanded to include four political science, three economics and two sociology courses. Church history, history of science, history of art, and history of education were listed separately in their appropriate departments. The title became in 1903 "History and the Political Sciences," thus embracing economics and sociology. In 1914, the catalogue carried the title "History and the Social Sciences." The next year the title continued, political science courses were grouped with history while economics and sociology had separate sections under the inclusive title.

76. Sr. Margaret Finnegen at Summer 1963 Faculty Summer Conference reported in Trinity College Newsletter Feb., 1964.
77. "Before the publication of the first Year Book [catalogue], Dr. William J. Kerby and Dr. Charles P. Neill kindly undertook to outline a systematic course in History and Political Science 'which can hereafter be elected as Major Studies by candidates for degrees.'" President's Report to Advisory Board, June 1, 1904.

Three years later, 1918–1919, history at last stood alone separated even from political science. During the first thirty years of the century, though never required of all students,[78] history courses were well populated. A study of the major subjects of those earning B.A. degrees shows that in the classes 1910 to 1932 from 15% to 25% offered history as one of their majors. After the re-organization of 1932 requiring one major subject with a related minor, the percentage of history majors dropped to 6% or 7% but by 1939 was again up to 18% of the class. History was elected as a related minor during all these years to 1948 by from 25% to 35% of each class. From 1942 to 1946, European and American history became separate majors but then united to one basic history major with individual choice of emphasis. From 1932 the specialized histories, except history of education, were encompassed by the department. World War II awakened interest in eastern Europe and in the Far East. From 1944 the history department offered the History of Eurasia and Eastern Europe, popularly called "Russian History." This, with history of the Far East which first appeared in the catalogue in 1954, had developed by the mid 1960's into the Asian Studies Program.

Through the years but especially since the 1950's, the history department has been strongly oriented toward intellectual history. The foreward to an *Alumnae Journal* supplement "History—Focus on Ideas"[79] sums this up well: "Trinity's history courses, like others, are concerned with the past. But the past is manifold, and it is inevitable that historians should emphasize some aspects of it more than others. In Trinity's department the focus is quite frankly on ideas. We are interested above all in what men have thought and believed, and only secondarily in the wars they have fought and the bridges they have constructed in consequence of what they believed." The wording of course descriptions in the last two decades bears this out. During these years, interest and course offerings in American history have continued to increase. History of the American Negro, introduced in 1968 and later developing into courses and seminars in the Black Experience, became part of the American Studies major which was first announced in the catalogue of 1972–1973.

The history department was the first to make a reciprocal agreement with the history department of the Catholic University. The announcement of courses available under this arrangement appeared in 1962.[80] It has participated in the Sophomore Year in England Program since its

78. Except that Constitutional History was required of seniors in B.A. program from 1916–1932. It was taught by Sister Wilfred du Sacre Coeur even after she became Dean.
79. Winter, 1960.
80. Winter 1960.

Sister Joan, Ph.D. (Mary Kate Bland '38).

inception in 1965 and has conducted periodically summer study tours of historical sites in Europe and in England.

Echoes of the 1901 statement quoted earlier can be perceived in the current description of the history major which reflects the years of development, use of up-to-date scholarly techniques while showing basic continuity.

> Students elect history to obtain a rich, full liberal arts background. It is the channel for transmitting the experience of the ages, the inherited cultural tradition, the value system of civilized life. It offers unlimited opportunities for expanding horizons of the mind. Through investigation of human situations not otherwise experienced, history leads to understanding and tolerance for ideas, institutions and ways of life different from our own.
>
> As a major discipline, history is particularly flexible. The student may select an orientation suiting her own individual interests, along with allied courses in art, literature, politics and religion. Courses in non-Western history are available through the Consortium.

Trinity's location in Washington allows a learning experience unavailable elsewhere. The enormous resources of the Library of Congress are accessible for routine class assignments. Museums, galleries, government offices and national monuments serve to enhance historical scholarship. Intensive use of Washington's resources is available through internships.

Training in history offers a foundation for many different careers. Broad reading, the development of critical perspective, the discipline of research, organizational ability, logical presentation of evidence and conclusions, intuitive insight, understanding of human nature—all these prepare the student for a wide variety of different pursuits.

Major Requirement. A minimum of eight courses above the 100 level, according to the following distribution: one course for the periods before 1600; two courses in European history since 1600; two courses in United States history; one seminar, colloquium, or independent research; one contemporary course.[81]

Because of the catalogue anonymity of faculty in the early years, it has not been possible to reconstruct the original history department. A few names surface. Dr. Shahan, of course, shared historical scholarship and German university methods with Trinity students until his appointment as rector of Catholic University. Sister Antoinette Marie (Pratt), who also founded the physics department,[82] taught history from the early years until 1915. She was the first of a long line of Sisters of Notre Dame to earn a doctorate from the Catholic University. It was in history. The records of the Trinity College community reveal that the following taught history: Sister Jeanne of the Nativity (Mary Murphy), 1910–1912; Sister Clare of the Passion (Johanna Lawler), 1912–1921; Sister Marie Virginia (Gertrude Smith, '14), 1919–1926. Others are "lost in the mists of time." Dr. Patrick Browne of Catholic University taught history at Trinity until his death in 1930. Julia O'Neill and Sister Margaret Angela (Frances Haven) taught history in the early 1930's. Then for nearly two decades (1933–1948) history was under the direction of Sister Raphael of the Trinity (Anna Coleman, '04), a former highly successful teacher in the public high schools of Westchester, N.Y. and Sister Marie Lidwine (Katherine Quinn) who came to Trinity from long experience in Notre Dame Academies in various cities. Sister Margaret Mary Fox, Professor of Greek, taught the ancient history from 1940 to 1959. Students of the last thirty years, in addition to instructors who taught a year or two or even a course or two, will remember Sister Carmelita (Mary Fennell), 1944–1954; Sister Joan (Mary K. Bland, '38); Sister Mary Lawlor, 1951–1978; Dr. Harold Hinton,

81. Catalogue 1976–1977.
82. The early faculty, though anonymous to the public, were indeed scholarly "renaissance women" competent in more than one field through arduous self education.

Professor Joan Kinnaird.

Sister Mary Hayes, Ph.D.

Rev. Dr. John A. Ryan. Student snapshot from 1917.

1960–1964 and Dr. Allan Wood III in Far Eastern Area Studies, 1964–1973; Dr. Jean Willke, 1959 to her appointment as Academic Dean in 1978; Dr. John J. Whealen, 1967–1970; Dr. Joan Kinnaird, 1968 to the present; and Sister Mary Hayes ('57) 1967 to the present, who inaugurated the American Studies major.

Political Science

As appears in the section on the history department, political science formed an integral part of that department until 1918. After that, several courses in political science were offered each year allowing for a major "as arranged" in combination with other social sciences and history: Dr. John A. Ryan, the internationally known advocate of social justice, author of *The Living Wage*, founder and long head of the Social Action Department of the National Catholic Welfare Conference, had come to Trinity for economics in 1916. His name with that of Dr. Donald McLean, also a Catholic University professor, appears in the catalogue faculty list for political science throughout the decades of the 1920's and 1930's. In 1941, the young enthusiastic Dr. Mildred Otenasek re-organized and modernized both the economics and political science majors. Dr. John A. Ryan continued to lecture on "Religious and Moral Problems of the State" or "Special Political Problems" until his death in 1945.

With Sister Carmelita (Fennell) teaching the principles course and Dr. Leo Stock the History of the United States Constitution and of American Diplomacy, Dr. Otenasek continued with major work in both economic and political science until 1948. Dr. Edna Fluegel, who developed and influenced the political science department for more than two decades, was appointed to the faculty in 1949. She was a graduate of Marywood College in Scranton, Pa. with a doctorate and Phi Beta Kappa membership from Duke University. She had State Department experience and worked both in London and in San Francisco preparing for the establishment of the United Nations Organization. She was staff worker at the meeting that adopted the U.N. Charter in 1945 and taught at St. Catherine's College in Minnesota before coming to Trinity. During her years at Trinity,[83] Dr. Fluegel also served as a Foreign Affairs Consultant for the U.S. Senate. A senior fellow of the Brookings Institution, Dr. Fluegel was listed in *Who's Who of American Women, Who's Who in the South* and the *American Political Science Directory.*

Throughout the 1950's, Dr. Fluegel strengthened and broadened the political science major emphasizing American political institutions, international relations, and comparative government. By 1960, the course in American Political Institutions included not only readings, but off-campus field work and experience in group research under her personal direction.

The following article by Dr. Fluegel gives an idea of the enthusiastic activity of the Political Science Department of the 1950's and 1960's on which the present is built.

> It's listed in the Catalogue as "Pol. Sci. 122" and is described as "Intensive study of Congress, the Court, the President and the Executive Establishment, Political Parties and Pressure Groups. Readings, off-campus field work, experience in group research. Four hrs., second semester." For Soph-

83. 1949–1972. Emeritus because of ill health 1973. Cf. *Trinity News*, July 1973, p. 4.

omores. Nothing there to indicate a combination of the latest research techniques with the old-fashioned method of learning to swim by being thrown in the water—and nothing that suggests the beaming, "do it yourself" satisfaction that is one of the end products.

What is Pol. Sci. 122? For the professor teaching it, it is a joy to plan and launch, a source of intermediate doubt and anxiety, and, so far, a terminal satisfaction. For the student, it is designed to provide the widest possible use of learning techniques; to link the academic and the actual world of government; to give to the political scientist, whose major is both a science and an art, some of the "feel" the physical scientist gets in the laboratory and some of the creative outlet the artist gets in the studio. For Trinity, it constitutes a utilization of one of its unique advantages—location in Washington. For government officials and employees contacted, the time expended on the students appears to be well compensated. Two of the many quotes this year are revealing. From a Senator: "I envy these students. They are experiencing things I had to wait to get elected to encounter. It is good for us to know that college students are concerned about our problems. Some of their questions stimulated my own interest and had me arguing and discussing with my colleagues." From a government employee: "It was a pleasure to help them. I gained a new insight. My own work suddenly became part of a larger operation and more important."

For the students themselves, the course provides a vivid introduction to their major and a sharp break from the purely academic approach, coming as it does after a year and a half of core subjects. It seems to be a welcome reminder that learning can be and should be "fun," that college is a sort of apprenticeship, that people as well as books are sources of information. Sometimes the scholarly student is "rattled" a little and forced to stretch mentally to master the new techniques where personality and imagination open up new dimensions in the acquisition of knowledge. On the other hand, sometimes the not-so-good student comes into her own—and becomes a better student when she perceives the link between "town and gown" and returns to view "dull" books as the crystallization of the knowledge and experience of live people.

This year Trinity multiplied Allen Drury by 36 and scrutinized seven fields in addition to the one he spotlighted in *Advise and Consent*. All the students started together, then went off for field work in "teams," and then returned to share the results and to take a fresh look at the problems of government. Before they finished, they had worked hard—harder than they expected to work! They had certain advantages this year since it is the second year for the experimental course and some of the initial "bugs" had been eliminated. Senior majors, for example, were enlisted to facilitate initial contacts and to provide perspective, reassurance, and interest. Valuable contacts had also been established in some areas as the result of volunteer work on the Hill and with the political parties by members of the Political Club. A canvass of the students produced some useful leads which were supplemented by suggestions and contacts from last year's experimenters. The change of regime was another factor that was favorable since it added to the drama of government and emphasized the role of men and of institutions. With world attention focused on the Washington scene, no professional briefing was needed to spell out the unique advantages Trinity majors enjoyed in being "on stage"—not for a day's tour or for a week or two of arranged interviews, but for a full semester.

The first class was held on January 30, the Monday after "Inaugural Weekend." This year, unlike the first year the course was given, a basic textbook was used, and roughly three-fourths of it was covered before the students went off on field work. The keeping of a journal, with daily notations of reading and observations, was again scheduled. Students were also required to read *Advise and Consent* and one of the many current books on each of the following official and nonofficial institutions: Presidency, Congress, Political Parties, Pressure Groups, the Court. This preparatory work was accompanied by regular class lectures designed to isolate problems and to stimulate inquiry. Thus the students had a fairly solid core of knowledge before embarking on field work. The first week of field work was common to all—this was the period when Senior majors were used to take small groups of Sophomores around the Hill. This saved considerable time since the Seniors shared with them contacts, tips, and know-how they had acquired more laboriously. Then the students returned to class for further discussion and for completion of group organization.

Eight "teams" sallied forth, charged with the preparation of group reports combining "live" as well as library research on the following institutions: Senate, House, Congressional Committees, Executive Establishment, Supreme Court, Democratic Party, Republican Party, Pressure Groups. Each group had an elected chairman and a secretary. The time allotted was March 22–April 19, during which no classes were scheduled, although the professor was available for consultation during the regular periods and, in addition, met with each group one evening for a combination discussion and social session. Each group prepared both an oral and a written report. Presentation of the former varied, though all the tested TV group presentation methods were utilized. The written reports, well documented, were filed in the library—nowhere in printed form could the groups have obtained the short-cut to collected materials supplied by these reports. The last two weeks of the course were devoted to lectures on the impact on American institutions of the American role in foreign affairs.

This course has now been tested for two years. The results, both in terms of factual knowledge, skill, and professionalization are highly gratifying.[84]

In the 1960's the growing department, while continuing to build on its established foundation and emphasizing methodology and field work, added courses in legislative history and procedures; and enlarged

84. "Course in American Political Institutions Uses Washington as a Laboratory—Trinity's 'Allen Drury' Reporters," Edna R. Fluegel, Professor of Political Science, *Alumnae Journal*, Spring, 1961, pp. 139–140. Cf. "Political Affairs Club," Mary Powers '60, *Alumnae Journal*, Spring, 1960, p. 140.

Dr. Edna Fluegel, a visiting lecturer, Jeane Kirkpatrick and her husband. (l.-r.)

comparative government courses to include more detailed study of non-democratic governments and the strategy and tactics of World Communism. Ably assisted by Mrs. Jeane J. Kirkpatrick (1962–1967),[85] Mrs. Emilia Govan (1964–1970), Mr. D. B. Hardeman (1965–1974) and others, Dr. Fluegel led the department into the 1970's. Dr. Elizabeth James joined the department in 1970 and Dr. William H. Jackson in 1971. After Dr. Fluegel's retirement, Dr. Jackson succeeded her as chairman for two years. Dr. Elizabeth James and Dr. Katherine McGinnis are continuing to keep the department up-to-date in the late 1970's.

Economics

Courses in elements of economics and in economic history appear in the catalogue from 1901 as part of the "History and Political Science" offerings. The Dean's Report of May, 1910, mentions enthusiastically a new course. She wrote: "The new course in Economics opened to the Seniors last Fall proved intensely interesting. Many phases of commercial life, which had never before risen above their mental horizon, were

85. Cf. *Trinity College Newsletter,* February 1964 about her book: *Strategy of Deception.*

thoroughly treated and much information obtained on practical issues, which will undoubtedly be of great value to these young ladies in the future." The new course is listed in the 1909–1910 catalogue as "Modern Economic Problems, A study of the chief economic problems that confront modern society, and an analysis of the movements for social reform that represent attempts to solve the problems."

Until 1916, Dr. William J. Kerby taught economics as well as sociology. That year Dr. John A. Ryan[86] came for economics which he taught until 1920. During the 1920's and 1930's only three courses in economics were offered in the catalogue. They were taught at various times by Dr. Donald McLean, Sister Margaret of the Trinity (Sweeney)[87] who became the registrar, Dr. Wm. Deviny, Sister Mary Agnes of the Infant Jesus (Edith Stowell) who became the second treasurer of the college. In 1940 Dr. Eva J. Ross took over the economics as well a sociology and the next year she collaborated with Dr. Mildred Otenasek in the inauguration of a complete economics major which has developed and been kept up-to-date in the last four decades.

The major of 1941 included (in addition to the traditional basics: principles of economics, economic history and labor economics) economic geography, statistics, money and banking, organization of occupational groups, economic theory and the history of economic thought. In 1943 international economics and public personnel administration were added, and in 1950 economic analysis.

Two names stand out in the more than three decades since 1941 as eminent professors who have left a lasting mark on the economics department: Dr. Mildred Otenasek and Sister Martha Julie Keehan.

Dr. Otenasek chaired the department and taught advanced courses until 1954 when she resigned to be more active in politics in her native Baltimore. During this time in the 1940's and early 1950's, she was assisted at various times by Miss Jean Hewitt, Miss Margaret Conway, Miss Phyllis Burkart and others for specialized courses like statistics.

Sister Martha Julie Keehan directed the department from 1953 to 1963 and again from 1969 to the present. Her competence as a teacher as well as her infectious enthusiasm for the department and for the development of her students are known to generations of economics majors. Through contacts in the United States government, especially the Labor and Commerce Departments, in banking, business and labor organizations she organized student workshops, symposia, and internships making full use of Washington's resources for economics majors years before the "practicum" became a college-wide institution. For

86. Cf. p. 218.
87. Obituary by Ellen A. Ganey, *Alumnae Journal*, May, 1935.

Sister Martha Julie Keehan, Economics, and Dr. Eva J. Ross, Sociology.

several years in the late 1950's and early 1960's senior economics majors joined foreign trade or economics majors from 27 area colleges participating in the World Trade Conference.[88]

Through judicious use of experts from government departments, business and labor Sister Martha Julie has ensured for economics students during her whole tenure as chair of economics the best in current economic theory and practice.[89] Students of the 1950's and 1960's will remember Dr. Henry Spiegel, Dr. Jeanne Pearlson, Mr. (later Dr.) Charles Wilber, Sister Olivia Kilbourn, Dr. Mary Jane Comerford Cronin, Dr. A. M. Piedra, and Dr. Charles Wilburn.

Dr. Cronin, known to students as Miss Mary Jane Comerford, Mrs. Cronin, Dr. Cronin, was one of Dr. Otenasek's majors who earned her M.A. in economics at Radcliffe College and doctorate at George Washington University. She joined the faculty full time from 1952 to 1954. From then she taught courses intermittently in the department until in 1966 she again returned to full time teaching for two years. Students of two decades appreciated her teaching as well as her interest in their advancement.

88. Cf. *Trinity Newsletter*, October, 1960.
89. A study of the catalogue for the 1970's will yield in the economics department a list of experts who have been called upon to share their specialties with economics students.

The economics department of the late 1970's, still under the aegis of Sister Martha Julie Keehan, continues to develop its policy of strong groundwork in fundamentals and emphasis on practical use of the facilities available in Washington.

Sociology

Sociology is one of the academic subjects that were open to the pioneer students of Trinity College. This first course, open to juniors and seniors, began in September 1903. During the first seventy years of the college two names stand out as great Trinity sociologists: Dr. William Kerby who directed the departments at both Trinity and Catholic University for more than thirty years, and Dr. Eva J. Ross who devoted twenty-nine years exclusively to Trinity College's department. Their great tradition has been worthily continued by Dr. Vincent dePaul Matthews whose teaching and influence make sociology of the seventies a vital force in tune with today.

In the Dean's Report[90] June 1904 we find that Dr. Kerby's weekly lectures in the "Elements of Sociology" awakened a lively interest in "that department of knowledge." The interest continued[91] in succeeding years until the dean reported in 1910: "The course in Sociology, open to the three upper classes, was chosen as an elective by about fifty students. The subject of Poverty and the methods of alleviating it was discussed during the first term . . . the members of the class made frequent visits to poor families in the city and in many cases gave material assistance." This interest led to practical application in the work of the Christ Child Society, the first student branch of which had been established at Trinity College.[92] The next year the Dean again has praise. "The excellent course," she wrote in 1911, "given by Rev. Dr. Kerby during the past years is bearing fruit in a most practical and praiseworthy manner. It has certainly developed the Social conscience of many of the Trinity students and awakened them to rise above the selfish spirit of the age." In 1920 the President's report mentions the "ever increasing interest in social problems and the demand for Social Workers." As a consequence, in addition to Dr. Kerby's courses, Dr. John O'Grady introduced a course in Applied Sociology (later called Social Work) and Miss Eleanor Downing took charge of Field Work. The President's 1921 and 1922 reports evaluate the social work: "Rev. Dr. O'Grady has conducted a course in social work, and for the first

90. Trinity College Archives.
91. The first student offering sociology as one of her major subjects graduated in 1908.
92. Cf. Chapter 6, Student Activities.

time, students have been engaged in case work in houses and hospitals under competent supervision."[93]

"In the sociology courses conducted by Dr. O'Grady, there has been a combination of scientific methods of conducting case work with the actual handling of such cases by the student. The lectures, given two hours weekly, have considered such vital subjects as 'The Family,' 'The Backward Child,' 'Delinquency' and 'Surveying the Institution.' When these problems had been carefully presented from a theoretical point of view, supplemented by reports as to the various methods used in solving them in various parts of the country, the interested members of the class, in order to get field work experience, were placed with different social agencies of the city, chiefly the Associated Charities. The cooperation of these agencies has been of great value in conducting the class. The nation-wide movement for the organization of Catholic charities and the steady demand for Catholic workers seem an assurance that our class in social service is a step in the right direction, taken at an opportune time."[94]

The "Dr. Kerby" mentioned in these excerpts was Iowa-born Rev. William J. Kerby, S.T.L. (Catholic University), Ph.D. (Louvain), (Docteur en Sciences, Politiques et Sociales), scholar and gentle but persistent crusader for social justice, for the dignity of each person, for lay participation in the work of the church. Though he was not one of the founders, he could easily be considered the male professor who has had the deepest most lasting influence on Trinity students during all the history of the college. Typical of the scholarly, dedicated professors of the young Catholic University who taught at both Trinity and the university, he gave of his best to both. He taught sociology at Catholic University from 1897 to 1934 and at Trinity College from 1903 to 1934. He was the principal founder in 1910 of the National Conference of Catholic Charities, editor of the *Ecclesiastical Review* from 1927 until his death, founder with Miss Agnes Regan in 1924 of the National Catholic School of Social Service which a quarter century later joined with the department of sociology and social work to form the Catholic University School of Social Service.[95] He was also chaplain for the students of Trinity College from 1914 until his death in 1936. There is a commemorative plaque in his honor in the foyer of the Main Building, a

93. An interesting sidelight on the attitude toward social sciences and social work of some members of the Advisory Board can be found in the minutes of that board for June 10, 1914.

94. This paragraph written in 1922 is from Sister Raphael (Pike)'s third President's Report.

95. *Trinity College Record*, Vol. 31, No. 1, Autumn, 1936, pp. 5–7. Cf. *Ecclesiastical Review*, Vol. XCV, No. 3, Sept. 1936, pp. 25–33; *Catholic University Bulletin*, Memorial Number, Sept. 1936, pp. 1–8, 11–12; *Catholic World*, October 1936, pp. 35–40.

large portrait photograph in the Marble Corridor, and Kerby Hall was named for him after a poll of the Alumnae Association. The Kerby Foundation was started in 1937 by friends and former students to keep alive the kind of work he did and spread knowledge of his ideals and principles.

In an appreciation written soon after Dr. Kerby's death, Rev. John J. Burke, C.S.P., a life-long friend, described his contribution to the Church, to people as individuals, to the Catholic University through teaching, writing, lecturing and fostering social service. In the following paragraphs, he shows Dr. Kerby's profound dedication to Trinity College.

> Through almost all these years at the Catholic University, Dr. Kerby gave himself, with a fidelity unequaled, to the future and the fortunes of Trinity College, one of the first higher colleges for the education of Catholic young women in the United States. We of the present who know its success and see it well established and flourishing, may imagine that neither special effort nor sacrifice accompanied its inauguration and its planning. But forty years ago, exceptional courage, high confidence, strong conviction in the cause of the higher education of women were not common. Dr. Kerby was faithful from the beginning even unto his death. He served Trinity College both as professor and as chaplain. In its chapel he preached every Sunday for many years. He advised with its officials. He was devoted to it as a father is devoted to his favorite child.
>
> We record that fidelity here because it reveals the man, the priest, Dr. Kerby. His courage, though he inwardly wrestled with the demon of pessimism and of doubt, was stable, unyielding. Trinity to him was not only a college: it was also a cause—the cause of the Catholic lay women of the future. To that cause he gave himself: and through his service and his sacrifice that cause has been forwarded in the United States.[96]

An indication of the students' long lasting positive reaction to his influence may be found not only in the popularity of his sociology classes and in alumnae achievement in social service but in appreciative letters written after his death and the fact that, by student request, he gave the Baccalaureate Sermon for the classes of 1904, 1910, 1914, 1920, the Cap and Gown Sunday Sermon for 1930, 1932, 1934, and the Commencement Address for 1934, spanning eight college generations.[97]

Throughout the 1920's up to 1934, Dr. Kerby, with Dr. John O'Grady in "Applied Sociology," continued teaching and chairing the sociology department. In 1934 after thirty years at Trinity College, succumbing to ill health, he retired from teaching, but continued until his

96. *Ecclesiastical Review,* Sept. 1936, p. 230. Cf. *Catholic University Bulletin,* Sept. 1936.
97. A list of his writings, articles, sermons, lectures, would be too long for this work. His books included *La Socialisme aux Etats, The Social Mission of Charity, The Young Priest and His Elders, Prophets of a Better Hope, The Impact of Years,* and *The Considerate Priest.*

death as the students' chaplain. The department was kept alive for the rest of the decade by Dr. O'Grady until his retirement and by Mr. (later Dr.) Percy Robert with Dr. Paul Hanley Furfey for social statistics.

In September 1940, Dr. Eva J. Ross joined the Trinity faculty. Born in Ireland of Scottish and English parents, she was educated in England and came to the United States in 1930. She became a U.S. citizen in 1950. With a B. Comm. from the University of London, an M.A. from St. Louis University, and a Ph.D. in sociology from Yale University, she had experience as an economist in London and Paris and as a college teacher in several Catholic colleges before coming to Trinity College. She taught both economics and sociology at first while she revised and modernized the content of the sociology major. "Sociology today," she wrote in 1964,[98] "is a much more complex subject than it was before World War II." Traditionally, prerequisites for a sociology major had included economics, biology, social statistics and introductory psychiatry. The first three were retained in the "new" major, but course work in sociology concentrated on its changed methodology and aim as a social science, de-emphasizing the social service area. She always professed a high regard for Dr. Kerby and his work, but believed that the field of study needed a different approach in the 1940's. In 1950, Dr. Ross re-introduced courses in social work with practical field work under Dr. Dorothy Abts Mohler (1950–1955) and Miss Genevieve O'Leary 1956–1964. This was not, however, as an essential part of the major, but as a closely related field much appreciated by the students.

A good rationale for Dr. Ross's attitude as a sociologist may be found in the 1964 article quoted above:

> Founded as a separate academic discipline one hundred and twenty-five years ago, sociology still seems to be misunderstood by the majority of nonprofessionals. In part the reason may be that people are frequently misnamed as sociologists when in reality they may be social workers, social philosophers, social planners, or simply interested in a general way in people and their social relations. Another reason for the widespread misunderstanding of sociology's aim and practice lies in the fact that the outlook and methods of sociologists have changed considerably over the years. Until the fairly recent past, the discipline was still discovering its own specialized meaning and its practical potentialities as a separate branch of science, so that the main body of facts and theories which have real pertinence today are of relatively recent origin. As with all the sciences, great strides have been made in its development since World War II. Earlier theories and the findings of scholars made even as recently as the nineteen-thirties chiefly have their places today only in the history of the subject, necessary to provide the scholar with a literate background of his field, with an explanation

98. "Sociology at Trinity," *Alumnae Journal*, Winter '64, p. 107. Cf. also "Sociology in its Historical Setting," *Alumnae Journal Supplement.*

> of the changes which have taken place within the discipline, and with valuable insights for the current formulation of scholarly hypotheses, approaches, and methods.[99]

She began her work at Trinity College in 1940 when the "great strides" were beginning and continued as a devoted, scholarly teacher, a writer active in professional societies, an ardent Catholic laywoman until her retirement and death in 1969.[100]

In her twenty-nine years as chair of the Sociology department, she was joined at various times by Miss Jean Hewitt, Dr. C. J. Nuesse, Rev. Daniel Lowery, Cecelia Fitzpatrick Maloney and Agnes Renehan Collins (both Sociology majors who had gone on to graduate work), Cletus Brady as well as the teachers of social statistics shared with other departments. Dr. Dorothy Abts Mohler, an eminent social worker, teacher at NCSSS, and at Catholic University after the amalgamation of NCSSS with the university, taught social work courses from 1950–1955. Miss Genevieve O'Leary continued these courses until 1964. In the late 1960's Dr. Ross, though not neglecting the theoretical, was emphasizing the service aspect of sociology, working in the sociology of religion and outlining for students the many career opportunities open to them.

Dr. Ross received an honorary D. Litt. from St. Bonaventure University (1956), a Fulbright Fellowship as professor at the University of Columbia at Bogota (1961), National Science Foundation and National Endowment for the Humanities Foundation research grants and participated in national and international professional meetings during her twenty-nine years as a Trinity professor. On the occasion of her receiving the *Pro Ecclesia et Pontifice Medal* after twenty-five years of service to the college, a colleague wrote:

> Scholar, author, lecturer, professor—Dr. Eva J. Ross, Chairman of the Department of Sociology at Trinity College, has responded fully to the need for highly competent lay Catholic leadership in the world today. Combining the best of Catholic and secular training, augmenting education with practical experience, enriching academic knowledge with considerable travel and extensive professional contacts, Dr. Ross has achieved distinction in her chosen professional field. She has tirelessly and generously shared her rich competence with her readers and audiences and with more than a generation of students at several Catholic colleges. By doing her chosen work well, by being both a Catholic leader and a leader in her profession, she has served *maxima cum laude.*[101]

99. *Alumnae Journal*, Winter, 1964, p. 107.
100. In addition to basic college and high school texts in economics and sociology, she published *A Survey of Sociology*, 1932; *Belgian Rural Cooperation*, 1940; and (with Rev. Ernest Kilzer, O.S.B.) *Western Social Thought*, and many periodical articles.
101. Excerpt from citation by Edna Fluegel, Ph.D., Professor of Political Science, May 30, 1965.

A plaque in her memory was placed in Room 230 by friends and former students, November 21, 1978.

Rev. Dr. Vincent dePaul Matthews joined the Trinity faculty in 1966 and succeeded Dr. Ross in 1969. He has effectively brought the department into the 1970's. The introductory statement in the 1975–76 catalogue (p. 85) gives an idea of the contemporary sociology in tune with today's problems. "The department's policy," it states, "is to emphasize a multi-disciplinary approach combined with practical work experience. Development along specific career lines is encouraged: to this end, in addition to the traditional sociology program, specializations are offered. . . ." Four such areas are listed and described: Community Mental Health, Criminal Justice, Court Management, and Urban Studies. An article in the *Alumnae Journal* in 1972 shows the very active participation of sociology students in practica and internships throughout the Washington area.[102]

Psychology

Psychology at Trinity College has had a distinguished history, though full major work was not offered until after 1950.

The psychology major of the 1950's, however, was not a beginning but the fuller development of a long tradition of sound, scientific psychology with its roots in the very source of modern psychology. The names of Edward A. Pace, who introduced psychology at Trinity in the first year, and of Thomas Verner Moore, who taught here until the middle 1940's, were internationally known names in their day and are permanently notable.

Wilhelm Wundt's laboratory in Leipzig might be called the birthplace of scientific psychology. "Wundt," as Boring says in his *History of Experimental Psychology*, "is the senior psychologist in the history of psychology. . . . When we call him the 'founder' of experimental psychology, we mean both that he promoted the idea of psychology as an independent science and that he is the senior among 'psychologists.'"[103]

Among the earliest of the young Americans who studied under Wundt in the laboratory in Leipzig and who came back to found psychological laboratories in their universities was our own Dr. Pace. Boring writes:

> America was close behind Germany in adopting the new psychology, and it also took its cue from Wundt. Stanley Hall visited Leipzig in the first year of Wundt's new laboratory, and founded in America, six years after Wundt began the *Philosophische Studien*, the *American Journal of Psychology*,

102. "Education in an Ivory Tower . . . or a College Without Walls," *Alumnae Journal of Trinity College*, Winter, 1972, pp. 7–11, pictures.
103. Edwin G. Boring, *History of Experimental Psychology* (New York: 1929), p. 310.

thus the second journal of experimental psychology in history. The proportion of Wundt's students from America was very large. Cattell was his first assistant. The following list, arranged chronologically . . . is, I think, almost complete for Wundt's American students before 1900: G. S. Hall (d. 1924, Clark), J. McK. Cattell (New York), H. K. Wolfe (d. 1918, Nebraska), E. A. Pace (Catholic University),[104] E. W. Scripture (Vienna), F. Angell (Stanford), E. B. Titchener (d. 1927, Cornell), L. Witmer (Pennsylvania), H. C. Warren (Princeton), H. Gale (Minnesota), G. T. W. Patrick (Iowa), G. M. Stratton (California), C. H. Judd (Chicago), G. A. Tawney (Cincinnati).[105]

The first published catalogue of the college, 1901–1902, lists a course in psychology described as follows:

An outline of the history of psychology, *illustrations of experimental methods*: practical aspects of the *science*: introduction to the philosophy of the mind. [Italics mine.]

Though the earliest catalogue did not list the faculty, we know that psychology courses were taught in the first decade by Dr. Pace[106] or by Dr. Shields who was a physiological psychologist.

The wording of the course in General Psychology remained the same until the catalogue for 1909–1910. Dr. Thomas Verner Moore came to teach introduction to philosophy at Trinity in 1910 to relieve Dr. Pace, who, however, continued to teach psychology courses and History of Education until 1919 and ethics here until 1924. The new wording is similar to what is found in the catalogue until 1958:

Psychology. The methods employed in psychological research are explained and illustrated. An historical outline of the important problems is given, and the connection is shown between the results of scientific investigation and the questions of the soul's nature, origin and destiny.

In 1915–1916 another course in Genetic Psychology was added, taught by Dr. Pace. There was also offered in the catalogue for 1908–1909 a separate course in Psychology of Education, not just part of the older course in Pedagogy. Psychology was separated from Philosophy in the catalogue listing in 1918–1919 when Dr. Moore came back to the subject after being listed under Biology from 1912. Two other courses, Experimental Psychology and Clinical Psychology, were added. Mental Hygiene was added in the 1930's.

Later in the decade and in part of the next the course offerings were reduced to general psychology, mental hygiene and educational psy-

104. Died, 1938.
105. Boring, Edwin G. *History of Experimental Psychology*, New York, 1929, p. 344.
106. The Class of 1911 wrote in Vol. I of the *Trinilogue:* "Our acquaintance with Dr. Pace dates from Sophomore days when in the vast precincts of O'Connor Hall, we followed him down the labyrynthian mazes of physical psychology to the staccato accompaniment of the stone-cutter's hammers in the new wing."

chology. Reawakened interest in the post-World War II period led to the healthy growth of the department and the establishment of a full major.

The 1915 President's Report mentions the visit of G. Stanley Hall of Clarke [sic] University who was in Washington for the twenty-fifth anniversary of the Catholic University.[107] At Trinity College he "expressed much surprise at the development of the College . . . and spoke of excellent graduate work of one of our recent graduates at Clarke University." The 1921 report announces that Dr. Moore "is back with us" after a period of service and study in Europe. "This year," it continues, "he has opened a new course in Experimental Educational Psychology, and his fortunate students have had the benefit of his experimental studies and experiences in conducting a seminar. This year they have dealt with child problems in social psychology. In connections with this, they may attend a course in clinic [sic] psychology at Providence Hospital."

Dr. Moore, who up to this time was a Paulist priest, was away again for the year 1923–1924 in Fort Augustus, Scotland, preparatory to founding, with other university professors, a priory of the English Benedictines in Brookland.[108] During this time two of his doctoral candidates, John Rauth and Thomas G. Foran, taught his psychology courses at Trinity College. As Dr. Rauth and Dr. Foran they collaborated with Dr. Moore (Dom Thomas Moore, O.S.B.) during the 1920's, Dr. Moore reserving for himself the general psychology in which he "tried out" the chapters of his *Dynamic Psychology* and *Congnitive Psychology*, the clinical psychology and a senior seminar. From 1928 to 1930 Dr. Foran taught educational measurement rather than psychology and after that date concentrated his efforts at Catholic University. Dr. Rauth was replaced by Rev. J. E. Haldi for one year (1928–1929) and returned to Trinity College as Dom J. Edward Rauth, O.S.B. to continue teaching general psychology until his sudden death in 1945. In 1930, Dr. Moore introduced mental hygiene as a course required for all seniors and continued to teach it until 1947.

The decade of the 1930's was a lean time for psychology at Trinity as for much of life. Only the essential required courses were offered until 1937 when Dr. Helena O'Neill re-introduced child psychology. She also established an excellent reading clinic, in which students could

107. An interesting sidelight on this is a 1970's letter from Addie Keenan Fitzgerald: "I attended the Mass at St. Patrick's Church on the 25th anniversary of the founding of the Catholic University, at which time for the first time all 3 American Cardinals attended, O'Connell of Boston, Farley of N.Y. and Cardinal Gibbons who later presented me with my B.A.

"I remember G. Stanley Hall, friend of Dr. Pace, entering the church. They had been classmates under Wilhelm Wundt in Leipzig."

108. St. Anselm's Priory, now Abbey, on South Dakota Avenue, N.E.

learn and practice remedial methods for the benefit of elementary school children from nearby parochial schools until Dr. O'Neill left to join the Navy in 1943.[109] These courses which serviced the Education Department were a presage of the interchange between the two departments that lasted through nearly twenty years until the establishment of full major work in both psychology and education.

Dr. Gertrude Reiman (T.C. 1926) taught child psychology at Trinity from 1943 to 1947 while continuing her work as psychologist in the Child Center at Catholic University. It was she who finished the year for the students of Dr. Rauth's general psychology course after his sudden death. In 1951, the course in mental hygiene which had been taught since 1947 by Dr. Dorothy Donley Dowd, M.D., a practicing psychiatrist, was transferred from psychology to the newly updated department of Physical Education and Health. It was still required of seniors but in 1953 Dr. Dowd became "consultant" in mental health. From 1954 to 1960 Dr. John R. Cavanaugh taught the senior mental hygiene, again under the aegis of psychology, until 1960.

Dr. James A. Vander Veldt, O.F.M., of the psychology department of Catholic University, taught general psychology at Trinity from 1947 to 1963 except for one year, 1958–1959, when the university questioned his dual role. From 1959 he was listed, with full permission of university authority, as lecturer at Trinity College and professor at Catholic University.

The names of three people have stood out in the nearly eighty years of psychology at Trinity College, those of Dr. Pace and Dr. Moore, whose influence has been traced, and Sister Margaret Marie Finnegan[110] who joined the department in 1958. Sister Margaret Marie [who later dropped the Marie] quickly rejuvenated the department, introduced updated courses, and established the psychology major. Known to students of the 1960's as "Sister Psych" she became the embodiment of the subject at Trinity and an advocate of its place in the liberal arts curriculum. Writing in 1959 she said:

> What, then, is the position of psychology in the liberal arts College? Fifty or sixty years ago, the teaching of scientific psychology was a new academic venture. In general, its educational value was mistrusted. Liberal studies might tolerate the physical sciences, but this new development appeared expensive, disorderly, undisciplined. Admittedly, however, rational psychology had investigated problems of human behavior, analyzing man's nature, his activities and his powers in the light of philosophical tenets. Consequently, it was possible for Ebbinghaus, speaking of scientific experi-

109. Cf. "Trinity in Uniform" in Chapter 8. Helena O'Neill graduated from Trinity in 1928. She later became Mrs. Emmet Scanlon.
110. A.B. Trinity College, M.A., Ph.D., Catholic University.

> mental psychology, to remark that it had "a long past, but a short history." And so, under the patronage of philosophy, scientific psychology was tolerated on the fringe of the academic world of that day.
>
> Today, happily, the aura of distrust is no more, and psychology enjoys a more or less peaceful coexistence with the other disciplines in the liberal arts college. Indeed, the situation today is such that it is possible for a psychologist to claim, somewhat aggressively: "Whether we like it or not, our society is tending more and more to think in terms of the concepts and methods spawned and nurtured by psychologists. And whether we like it or not, psychology and psychologists will continue to be a consequential factor in the making of social decisions and in the structuring of our culture."[111]
>
> In the curriculum which emphasizes the liberal arts, it is important to realize that the basic goal of the psychology course is intellectual, for psychology, no less than other fields, is charged with the responsibility for educating a cultivated and reflective elite which is manifestly able to achieve relatively high levels of intellectual maturity.[112]

With Dr. Vender Veldt until 1963 and with a series of competent psychologists[113] as lecturers (now called adjunct professors) in the various specialized fields, she continued to administer and develop the department until she was appointed academic dean of the college in 1970. During her deanship (1970–1974), she maintained her interest in psychology and taught at least one course a year. Dr. Fredda Steinman joined the department in 1967, chaired it from 1970 to 1976 and has contributed significantly to its work. Dr. Richard Sansbury has been a member of the department since 1974. Sister Margaret Finnegan, after a year of study both in England and the United States, returned full time to psychology and since 1977 has again chaired the department. An indication of the extent and value of the major in psychology can be gained by a look at the work of alumnae who were psychology majors, and from the catalogue statement of offerings. The 1977–1978 catalogue shows twenty-two courses from introductory to graduate level, under the direction of Sister Margaret Finnegan, Ph.D. (Chair), Dr. Steinman and Dr. Sansbury, prefaced by the statement:

> The psychology department offers two concentrations for majors.
>
> CONCENTRATION I. Designed primarily for students who wish to continue on to graduate training in psychology (e.g., clinical, counseling, learning, physiological, developmental, sensory). Required courses are Introductory (121), Statistics (222), Developmental (251) *or* Social (255), Physiological

111. Sanford, F. H. Notes on the future of psychology, *Amer. Psychologist*, 1951, 6, 75.
112. *Alumnae Journal* Supplement: Psychology, Autumn, 1959, p. 5.
113. They stayed one to three years. Their names can be found in the catalogues of the period.

(232), Sensation and Perception (380), Learning (381) and Experimental Seminar and Laboratory (385). Two other courses in psychology are to be elected.

CONCENTRATION II. Designed primarily for students who intend to work in psychology-related fields where a psychology background is helpful, but graduate training in psychology is not necessary (e.g., psychiatric social work, special education, vocational rehabilitation, social work, community mental health). Required courses are Introductory (121), Statistics (222), Mental Health (200) *or* Physiological (232), Developmental (251) *or* Social (255), Sensation and Perception (380) *or* Learning (381), Systems (356) and one laboratory in psychology (385 or 386). Two other courses in psychology are to be elected.

That statement is an outline of the full flowering in the last quarter of the century of the "experimental, scientific" psychology announced in 1900.

Education

The statement of the education department in the current catalogue (1977–78) begins with a sentence that echoes the basic principles underlying nearly eighty years of teacher training at Trinity College. "Students are expected to pursue teacher-training programs within the context of a well-balanced liberal arts education."

Though formal courses in "pedagogy," initiating the Education Department, began in 1903–1904 when the first class were seniors, "teacher education" may be said to date from 1900 when the "well-balanced liberal arts education" began. Dr. Thomas E. Shields,[114] a physiological psychologist and eminent educator, founder of the Education Department at the Catholic University, began a seventeen year record of service to Trinity College students with the 1903–1904 course in "Princi-

114. Thomas E. Shields (1862–1921) grew up on a farm in Minnesota and was educated for the priesthood in St. Francis Seminar, Milwaukee, Wis. and St. Thomas Seminary, St. Paul, Minn. He earned an M.A. at St. Mary's Seminary in Baltimore and the Ph.D. in Physiological Psychology at Johns Hopkins University, Baltimore. He taught psychology in the St. Paul seminary from 1895 and came to the Catholic University to teach psychology in 1902. His book, *The Making and Unmaking of a Dullard,* not only describes his own childhood and adolescent struggles to attain his potential intellectual development, but is an indication of the source of his sensitivity to the child's problems in learning. In 1907 he was promoted to the rank of professor of psychology and education. He wrote "Notes on Education" for the *Catholic University Bulletin* (1907–1910) and in 1911 established the *Catholic Educational Review,* founded the *Sisters' College,* and organized the Catholic University Press. The whole April, 1921, issue of the *Catholic Educational Review* is a memorial to him. A resolution of appreciation of his life and service from the Faculty and Students of Trinity College appears on p. 247 of that issue as well as one from the Rhode Island Chapter of Trinity College Alumnae on p. 249. The *Trinity College Record* also carried editorial appreciation and letters from alumnae across the country.

ples and Methods of Pedagogy." Dr. Shields, from the turn of the century until his death, had an influence on Catholic education similar to that of John Dewey of Columbia Teachers College on the public schools. Dr. Shahan in the early years taught "History of Ancient and Medieval Education," and Dr. Pace, "History of Modern Education." Even before this there is indication of an incipient practice teaching program in the Dean's Report of 1902–03. She wrote: "Among the Junior Class are seven who intend to teach, and to give them opportunity to practice the art, we began in March to allow them to teach classes in Languages; during the year they had been permitted to tutor (deficient or) conditioned students. . . . The students were willing to be practiced on and the regular teacher was present to approve or criticize her substitute. In this way we hope to send the future teachers out with some experience, as well as the theoretical knowledge . . . from courses in Pedagogy that will be among the electives offered to Seniors next year."

Three courses in the "History of Education" were first listed in the catalogue of 1902–1903 to be elected next year:

A. The development of educational theories in relation to the history of civilization. Greek and Roman education. The early Christian schools. The universities. The great leaders of educational movements.
B. Principles and Methods of Pedagogy—Theory and art of teaching. The problems of education.
C. A comparative study of the secondary schools of France, Germany, England and America.

This offering remained unchanged until 1908–1909 when a more complete course was presented and the department title became Education. The first mention of "the certificate" occurs in the Dean's Report of June 3, 1907. Writing of the twenty-two members of the class of 1907 who had done "excellent work" for four years, she continues: "A large proportion of these young ladies are desirous of obtaining teaching positions as teachers in High Schools. Seventeen have followed the course in Pedagogy and will receive the certificate." At that same June 3, 1907 meeting the Advisory Board decided, after lively discussion, that the college should shape the courses in "pedagogy" so as to meet certification requirements in various states. Though very good arguments for the usefulness of education courses were put forth, the consensus seemed to favor having the students major in a subject to teach and take education courses to learn how to teach them and for certification. The next year the college president announced that "courses in Pedagogy had been brought in line with the New York Board of Education requirements to make the students eligible for the New York State teaching certificate without further examination. The requirements for the Certificate of Education, which was awarded at Commencement in addition to the degree, appear in the catalogues from 1909 to 1928,[115] with very little change in wording to keep the vocabulary current. The original statement follows:

> A certificate will be given to students who have satisfactorily completed the work outlined in the several courses of this department together with Course D (Psychology) and Course E (Ethics) of the Department of Philosophy. In connection with Courses E and F of the Department of Education, opportunities for observation in the city schools are provided. Candidates for the Certificate of Education are required to do at least twenty hours of such observation work.

It should be remembered that, though it was still listed in the Philosophy Department, psychology was taught from the experimental point of view rather than the philosophical.

The "more complete course" introduced in 1908 consisted (in addition to ancient, medieval, and modern history of education and the science and art of study) of philosophy and psychology of education and of general and special methods. This remained the basic program for three decades, with the addition before 1920 of separate courses in "school administration and classroom management"; in "educational measurements and psychology of elementary school subjects" in the 1920's; in health education in the 1930's, and in "remedial reading" in 1941. A Teacher's Registry was maintained at Trinity College from 1911 to 1928, a forerunner of the placement office. In 1912 the Dean could report that sixty alumnae were teaching in high schools and academies in various parts of the country. Since the alumnae at that time numbered about 180, this represented one-third of the graduates. The Dean's Report of June 1920 states that twenty-seven of the class of 1919 were teaching, about 43% of the class.

Dr. Shields continued until his death in February 1921 teaching the four basic courses, alternating them two a year so that students could fit them into their junior and senior years. Dr. Pace continued the history of education courses until 1920 when he was succeeded by Dr. Patrick J. McCormick[116] who had been teaching "school management" at Trinity since 1915. Dr. Edward Jordan took up Dr. Shields' courses in February 1921 and continued to teach alternately psychology and philosophy of education at Trinity until 1934.

Names of teachers of education remembered from the 1920's and 1930's are (in addition to Dr. Jordan), Dr. Frank Cassidy, Dr. George

115. A manuscript copy is pasted into the Trinity College Library copy of the 1908–1909 catalogue.
116. Author of the text used in history of education courses for three decades, later Dean of the Sisters College, and Rector of the Catholic University.

Johnson, Sister Marie Louis Hummel,[117] and Dr. Felix M. Kirsch, with Dr. Thomas Foran for educational measurements (1927–1929) and Arthur Monahan for school administration (1930–1932). The President's Report, 1923, states: "Dr. Anna Nicholson conducted a large class in Methods of Teaching, while Dr. Edwin Barnes has given a course . . . in Public School Supervision of Music."

The 1940's brought a change. Sister Marie Raymond Lane came full time to the department, and Dr. Helena O'Neill established the Reading Clinic for elementary school children and taught remedial reading. The war struck. Dr. O'Neill joined the Navy, rising quickly to the rank of Commander, and Sister Marie Raymond left for work elsewhere. From 1943 Sister Columba Mullaly kept the department alive, teaching two courses a year in sequence until 1948. Dr. Joseph Gorman from Catholic University finished out the decade.

The 1950's was the time of change from emphasis on secondary to emphasis on elementary teaching. Miss Dolores Martin and Miss Carol Rayhill developed the plan, and the former, as Mrs. Dolores Martin Deegan, directed it from 1952 to 1954. This work was carried on through the 1950's to 1965 by Sister Margaret Loyola Carrigan and Sister Helen Lawrence Dawson, while Sister Ann Francis Hoey taught guidance and counseling and Principals of Secondary Education in those years with Sister Rita Buddeke for psychology and testing, and Sister Joseph Mary Donohue directing the Reading Clinic and teaching Special Education courses.[118]

The air was full, in the middle of the 1950's, of discussions of the needs of our schools, of the teacher shortage, of the enormous increase in the school age population. Whether Johnny could or couldn't read was a debatable question, but the fact that Johnny's younger brothers and sisters in ever-increasing numbers would be needing more and more teachers if *they* were to learn to read was an indisputable fact. Therefore, the offerings of the Education Department were enlarged in 1950 to include courses in elementary school teaching, in practice teaching, and in reading improvement.

Although a larger number of alumnae had, up to 1960, entered teaching than entered any other field, the training of teachers had never been the chief aim of a Trinity education. That aim has been and is the development of truly educated Catholic women able, in whatever sphere they find themselves, to take their full share in American life, spiritual, intellectual and civic. It still seemed to us more important to form educated young women who can teach, than to concentrate on

117. Cf. p. 93.
118. Cf. also "Trinity's Part in Helping the Exceptional Child," *Alumnae Journal*, Spring, 1955, pp. 5–8.

the techniques and methods of teaching to the detriment of the firm foundation of subject matter and intellectual maturity. For this reason, education was not even then made a major field of concentration at Trinity College.[119] This policy was not confined to Trinity but was in conformity with some of the best thinking in higher education. It was the theory behind the Yale Program of that time.

Arthur Bestor, author of *Educational Wastelands*, had in his 1955 book a powerful statement of this thinking that is so much in accord with the Trinity view that I cannot refrain from a long quotation from it here. He wrote:

> At the undergraduate level the education of the future teacher should be an education in the liberal arts and sciences. This ought to be self-evident. The ideal of liberal education is to produce men and women with disciplined minds, cultivated interests, and a wide range of fundamental knowledge. Who in our society needs these qualities more than the teacher? We increasingly recognize that the doctor, the lawyer, and the engineer, if they are to achieve true professional eminence, must receive balanced training in many intellectual disciplines not directly related to their professions. How much more does a teacher need such education! For him the fundamental intellectual disciplines are not supplements to, but the very essence of, his professional stock in trade. The teacher never knows when he may be called upon to give instruction in any or all of them. The students whose work he directs have a right to expect of him a genuine and sympathetic understanding of their various intellectual interests and ambitions. Whatever else a teacher may need, he must possess ready command of a variety of intellectual skills and a fund of accurate knowledge. Otherwise he can never make any significant or enduring impression upon the minds of his pupils, and his efforts as a teacher will be greeted by them with little real respect.
>
> The prospective teacher is entitled to a liberal education not so much for utilitarian as for broadly humane and civic reasons. Before he can be a teacher he must be a man and a citizen. He attends a college not primarily to acquire knowledge that he can pass on to others but to acquire intellectual discipline that he can use in the conduct of his own life. If his undergraduate program is directed by vocationally-minded advisers—by professors of pedagogy, for example—the liberal and liberating components of his education are almost certain to be neglected. The prospective teacher, when misguided in this fashion, approaches each course with the idea of carrying away from it only such bits of information as he can see the possibility of utilizing in some future job. Though on paper he may appear to be devoting a good deal of time to the liberal arts and sciences, in fact he is filling his head with communicable information rather than developing in himself the ability to think at an increasingly mature level.[120]

119. The one exception will be found in the carefully planned program for the education of the young Sisters of Notre Dame de Namur under the auspices of the college.
120. *The Restoration of Learning*, New York (Alfred A. Knopf), 1955, pp. 242, 243.

The whole area of teacher preparation and certification had changed very much since 1900. Most of those who graduated in the twenties or before received at Commencement, in addition to the degree, a Teacher's Certificate recognized by the United States Bureau of Education.[121] Sixteen credits in education and twenty hours of observation earned a credential that would be acceptable in any state. As a result many, the majority I think, went forth to teach their major subject—or perhaps something else, if it was needed—in high schools in all parts of the country. No one expected any to teach in elementary schools. In the thirties the situation changed very much. State Departments of Public Instruction, which had been developing and growing in importance, had evolved their own sets of requirements for teachers on the various levels. Fred O. Pinkham, Executive Secretary of the National Commission on Accrediting, writing in the May, 1954, *Association of American Colleges Bulletin* described the complex situation as follows:

> Fifty years ago, 3,000 local authorities were certifying teachers on the basis of local examination. Seldom were college credits required. Today certifying authority is almost universally centralized in state departments of education, and prescribed college credits have virtually replaced examination as the basis for certification of teachers.
>
> There is an amazing amount of diversity of teacher certification practices throughout the country. At present, there are approximately 1,000 separately named teacher certificates. One state issues 60 kinds of certificates, another issues only one kind of certificate. Requirements for "comparable" credentials vary from less than one year of college education to more than four years for elementary teachers and from less than three to five or more years' preparation for secondary teachers. State requirements in so-called professional courses vary from none to 60 units for the "same" certificate. (p. 234)

To make the complication of the problem even more evident one must consider the fact that Trinity College had alumnae in every state in the Union, that her student body in 1956 for example was from thirty-one states, three territories, and nine foreign countries. An additional factor to be considered was the fluctuating student attitude toward teaching. In the thirties and early forties few students took education courses or showed interest in teaching. A revived interest in the field placed greater emphasis on teaching in the elementary grades rather than in high school. All these elements had to enter into the policy and planning for teacher training at Trinity.

The Department continued to offer the essential courses which all states, in spite of the diversity, either required or accepted. Such were history of education, philosophy of education, educational psychology,

121. Cf. p. 106.

child and adolescent psychology, and principles and methods on both the secondary and elementary school levels. Other widely advocated courses such as testing, guidance, and special methods in particular subject matter were offered in alternate years as the demand arose. The administration and members of the education department kept up-to-date on various state requirements and had at hand for reference the Chicago University Press publication *Requirements for Certification*, compiled by Woellner and Woods. Students who wished to teach were encouraged to study the requirements of their state and to consult local authorities about opportunities. They were urged to plan summer session work in the home state to fulfill specific requirements. Arrangements for practice teaching were made with the public school authorities of the District of Columbia as well as with the parochial schools of the vicinity.

It was possible for a student to earn twenty-four credits in education courses. Much depended, of course, on the student herself, when she decided that she wanted to teach, what her other classes were, what were her ability and aptitude for teaching, how well she planned. That the plan worked is shown by the fact that all except one of the students who wanted to teach from the Class of 1955 were teaching in 1956. Enthusiastic reports from and about them seemed to indicate successful experience.

In the years since 1965 the Master of Arts in Teaching program,[122] undergraduate majors in elementary or secondary education, bilingual-multilingual programs, bilingual-bicultural programs, and special education courses have all developed under four Directors of the MAT who also acted as department chairmen: Dr. Roland Goddu, Dr. Edward Du Charme (Ducharme), Dr. Robert Grant, and Dr. James Van Dien. These have been assisted by Mrs. Hortense Fitzgerald, Sister Maureen Brogan, Sister Marita McGrath, Sister Jeanne McGlone. Dr. Phyllis Herson, Miss Nancy Grayson, Sister Frances Elizabeth McCarron, Sister Marie McMain, various adjunct specialists, and members of other departments.

An indication of the continuity as well as the extent of growth and development in teacher education appears in the current (1977–78) catalogue statement and the five pages of course offerings that follow it.

EDUCATION

Students are expected to pursue teacher-training programs within the context of a well-balanced liberal arts education. A minimum of 80 credits in academic content courses is normally required, including a distribution of courses in the General Program.

122. The MAT program will be treated in the section on graduate work.

Many state departments of education specify a particular distribution of academic courses as well as professional education courses for teacher certification. Students seeking to comply with state certification requirements should consult with their program coordinator early in the sophomore year.

Teacher-training at Trinity College emphasizes field-based instruction in a practicum setting. Many of the courses listed below require observation and practicum experience so that the student has exposure to the classroom and its demands prior to the student-teaching experience. Student-teaching is the culmination of the teacher-training program and is usually scheduled in the senior year. It requires full-day participation in the schools five days a week for an entire semester. Placements appropriate to the student's major area are made in the public and private schools of the District of Columbia and surrounding counties.

In reflection of the department's commitment to the demonstration of competence in the field, the comprehensive examination is in two parts. One half is behavioral, based on departmental observations of the student-teaching experience. The other half consists of a written examination of general pedagogical theory and the specific curriculum and methodology of the student's major area.

In addition to the courses listed below, qualified juniors and seniors may be permitted to take advanced courses offered in the Master of Arts in Teaching program.

Majors are offered in the following areas: elementary education (allowing for concentration in an academic subject or in bilingual/multicultural education); early childhood education; special education with an emphasis on teaching the mentally retarded. The department also offers a concentration in secondary education and participates in the music-education major.

So teacher training at Trinity College continues to fulfill its promise into a ninth decade.[123]

Sciences and Mathematics

The sciences, chemistry, physics and biology, as well as mathematics have had a position of prestige in the Trinity curriculum since the pioneer years. Mathematics was included in the first year, laboratories for chemistry, physics, and botany were equipped and ready for use in September 1902 and botany developed into biology by 1912. The Dean reported May 13, 1903: "The new laboratories were opened and twenty-five students elected Science: five chose Botany, ten chose Chemistry and ten Physics. Each course required five hours work weekly, divided between laboratory and lecture work."

The first botany laboratory was in what is now room 244. Chemistry and physics shared a larger laboratory at the end of the south wing on

123. "Teaching About Teaching," James Van Dien Jr. *Alumnae Journal*, Autumn, 1964, pp. 14–15.

second floor. The 1907 President's Report mentioned a steady development in the sciences and better equipped laboratories.[124] "The advantages afforded by the College laboratories," the report continued, "are supplemented by visits to the great scientific centres in Washington—the Bureau of Standards, the Agriculture Department, the Botanical Gardens, the Smithsonian and other institutions" where the students were "courteously received and accorded exceptional opportunities for deriving benefit." This use of Washington as a laboratory is echoed in each generation and culminates in the seventies in the internship program.

The 1901–1902 catalogue carries the statement:

> The college is not yet prepared to offer courses in Science which lead to a Bachelor's degree. Consequently, there are at present no "Science Groups."
>
> The instruction which is here outlined gives such an acquaintance with these sciences as is required in a liberal education.
>
> Every student is obliged, in the Junior Year, to follow one of these electives [Botany, Chemistry, Physics].

In addition, a course in the history of science was required of seniors. This became elective by 1905 and dropped out of the catalogue before the end of the first decade to be re-introduced in the chemistry department in 1945. The science requirement for every student moved from junior to sophomore to freshman year as the years passed, but it continued as a requirement through all curricular changes until the 1970's.

In 1907 the decision was made to allow candidates for the A.B. degree to choose a science as one of their "majors," and in 1909 the requirements for the Bachelor of Science degree were adopted. An excerpt from the President's Report, May 3, 1909, is a good summary of the policy from the beginning. Special attention should be given to the footnote about the B.S. degree granted in 1905. The report says:

> In the scope of the College as originally planned provision is made for a third baccalaureate degree—the B.S. Up to this time it has not been thought necessary or expedient to undertake a course of instruction leading to this degree, and students who desired to specialize in science were encouraged to pursue the A.B. course, with Physics, Chemistry, or Botany as one of their major subjects. From year to year, however, the work in the sciences has developed in scope and efficiency, notwithstanding the fact that these departments have been sadly hampered by lack of space. While the inadequacy of our laboratories still precludes the thought of advertising a special

124. It expresses gratitude to Bishop Garrigan of Sioux City, Iowa, a co-founder of the college and benefactor until his death in 1919; and to Bishop Harkins of Providence, R.I. Cf. President's Report, May 13, 1903, p. 2.

course in science, our facilities for such a course, if pursued by only a small number of students, are sufficient for thorough work.[125] These facts in connection with the consideration that provision ought to be made for those young women who are specially fitted for scientific studies and may wish to become teachers of science, urge us to take measures for granting the B.S. degree. A program, which is only provisional, has been drawn up by the Instructors of the Science Department, and is submitted for consideration. The requirements for the Bachelor's Degree in Science, like those for the degree in Arts and in Letters amount to sixty-six one hour courses,[126] and the entrance requirements are nearly the same as those which must be fulfilled by the aspirant to the A.B. degree. There is, however, one important point in which the proposed requirements differ from those of the two baccalaureate courses now established: Latin is eliminated both from the studies prescribed for admission and from those required in the College course. Other colleges of the first rank which offer the B.S. degree give prominence to modern languages in the requirements for this degree and omit the classical languages; but the question naturally arises whether in our College this total elimination of Latin from a baccalaureate course is not a departure from what may almost be regarded as a principle in real Catholic culture. [It was adopted, however.]

As early as 1908, the President's Report mentions the need of a science building, though more than thirty years would elapse before the opening of the new building in 1941.[127] Meanwhile botany moved in with zoology when the new laboratory was equipped on the north side of second floor South Hall.[128] Biology later grew to two large rooms (now 259 and 260) and shared with physics for many years a lecture room on the first floor. As soon as possible after the completion of North Hall, the physics laboratory and lecture room were equipped on first floor South Hall and the Chemistry department was able to occupy the whole east end of second floor South for its large laboratory, balance and supply rooms, at least one private laboratory, and a lecture room.

125. It will be remembered that in June 1905 the B.S. degree was conferred upon Mary Alice Gray, A.B. 1904, who did special work in Chemistry during a year of post-graduate study.
126. This means one hour for a *year*. It would equal a requirement of 132 semester hours.
127. Cf. Dedication Memorial Volume T.C.A. for pictures, press clippings and texts of speeches. Hugh Stott Taylor of Princeton was the principal speaker and representatives of many colleges and universities attended the convocation.
128. Cf. President's Report June 4, 1913, p. 2: "During the vacation a biological laboratory was fitted up and well equipped thanks to the kind generosity of our ever devoted friend good Bishop Garrigan, whose interest in the welfare of Trinity has never flagged from the moment of its foundation. The work in Biology has been under the able management of Reverend Dr. Moore, and great enthusiasm in the lectures and laboratory periods has been manifested by the students who eagerly followed the courses. It is hoped that the Science departments will expand as time goes on, and that from year to year we may be able to increase their equipment."

The science departments moved into the new Science Building in November 1941 to continue to provide for women the strong scientific foundation considered especially important during World War II and beyond. An idea of the quality of teaching in the next twenty years is shown by an excerpt from the President's Report 1959–1966.

> In 1965 a committee of outside examiners was invited to study Trinity's science curriculum and departments, and make any recommendations it considered necessary for improvement. The College was rightfully proud of the commendation it received from this committee for the quality and variety of courses offered, and for the dedication and competence of its science faculty. One recommendation made was the introduction of a required course for juniors and seniors not majoring in science, to be taught on a high level with a philosophical, theoretical, conceptual orientation. This was inaugurated in 1966 on an elective basis with presentations from the area. The visiting committee members were:
>
> Dr. Sterling B. Hendricks, Chairman
> Head Scientist, Mineral Nutrition Laboratory
> U.S. Department of Agriculture
>
> Dr. Jane M. Oppenheimer
> Professor of Biology, Bryn Mawr College
>
> Dr. George T. Reynolds
> Professor of Physics, Princeton University
>
> Dr. Frederick D. Rossini
> Dean of the College of Science, University of Notre Dame

The article, "Sciences at Trinity," by Sister Marie Therese Dimond, *Alumnae Journal*, Spring, 1967, also gives an overview of the departments in the late 1960's.

Biology

Sister Louise of St. Stanislaus[129] began teaching botany in the new laboratory September 1902 and continued even after the expansion of the department until 1917 when illness forced her retirement. The rather vague description in the original catalogue announcement became by 1902–1903, when botany was first taught, a sequence of four courses: General Botany, Systematic and Economic Botany, Cryptogramic Botany, and Plant Biology. The full catalogue statement for general botany indicates a scientific thoroughness that has consistently characterized the department since: "This course, introductory to all other courses in Botany, includes the outlines of the morphology and physiology of plants and of classification. An herbarium of the higher plants found in

129. Cf. p. 93.

the locality is required. Lectures, recitations, laboratory and field work." This departmental offering had grown to seven courses before 1912 when the first course in general biology was opened by Sister Raphael (Pike)[130] and Dr. Thomas V. Moore, C.S.P.[131] Sister Raphael, one of the original faculty and a qualified M.D. and A.B., up-dated her biological knowledge by studying biology with Dr. Parker at the Catholic University.[132]

Plans for including zoology in the curriculum, thus making possible a department of biology, were impeded in the early years of the century by the controversial "evolution question." Both Dr. Pace and Dr. Moore performed for the college the important task of demonstrating to the ecclesiastic authorities the need for scientific study of controversial topics by students in Catholic higher education. A *de facto* basis for a Trinity education from the earliest years, this principle, once it was explicitly established, made possible future development in other departments[133] as well as in biology.

The original full catalogue statement of general biology[134] laid the foundation and set a pattern for the steady progress of the department in the seven decades since then.

> GENERAL BIOLOGY
>
> This course is designed to acquaint the student with the fundamental principles of animal and plant life as a preparation for the further study of botany and zoology. It also furnishes an opportunity for gaining a practical knowledge of general biology.
>
> By the study of the amoeba and other protozoa, saccharomyces, protococcus and non-pathogenic bacteria, the student becomes familiarized with the unicellular organisms; by the study of hydra, obelia, mucor and spirogyra, with the multicellular.
>
> The earthworm, crayfish, perch, frog and rabbit are chosen as typical forms of animal life. The liverwort, moss, fern, pine and sunflower are studied to introduce the student to botany.
>
> The course is conducted by means of lectures, laboratory work and field excursions. Special attention is paid to the drawing of objects studied, to

130. Cf. pp. 89, 108–111.
131. Dr. Moore had a long and fruitful career at Trinity College as well as at the Catholic University. From 1908 to the mid-1940's, he taught successively philosophy, biology, psychology and mental hygiene. A Ph.D. from Catholic University, he studied medicine in Bonn, Germany, finishing the M.D. degree at Johns Hopkins because of World War I.
132. Sister Mary Isabelle (Mahoney) (of chemistry) and Sister Marie Louis (Hummel) also attended these courses.
133. Notably psychology, education, literary criticism, philosophy, theology and the social sciences.
134. 1913–1914, p. 98. The biology course had already been taught for a year before this statement appeared.

the killing, fixing and sectioning of specimens, the preparation of media, as well as the staining and mounting of slides and other methods of microscopic technique.

It is desirable that those who enter this course have an elementary knowledge of physics and chemistry.

Other courses will be added as need demands.

In 1916 Sister Julitta Larkin came to study with Sister Raphael and Sister Louise and to assist the latter in botany. She studied also with Dr. Ulrich of Johns Hopkins University who came on Saturdays for advanced biology courses for her and for Sister Berchmans Julia. The next year Sister Julitta replaced Sister Louise of St. Stanislaus who was ill and who died in 1918. When Sister Raphael was appointed president of the college, Sister Julitta took over the direction of the biology department. An excellent teacher as well as a meticulous scientist, she placed her stamp on the department which she guided with a firm hand for forty years. She earned her doctorate from the Catholic University, was listed in *American Men of Science* from the early 1930's, and kept up consistently with scholarly work in her field through professional societies and scientific publications. Dr. Edith Rich, '32, of St.

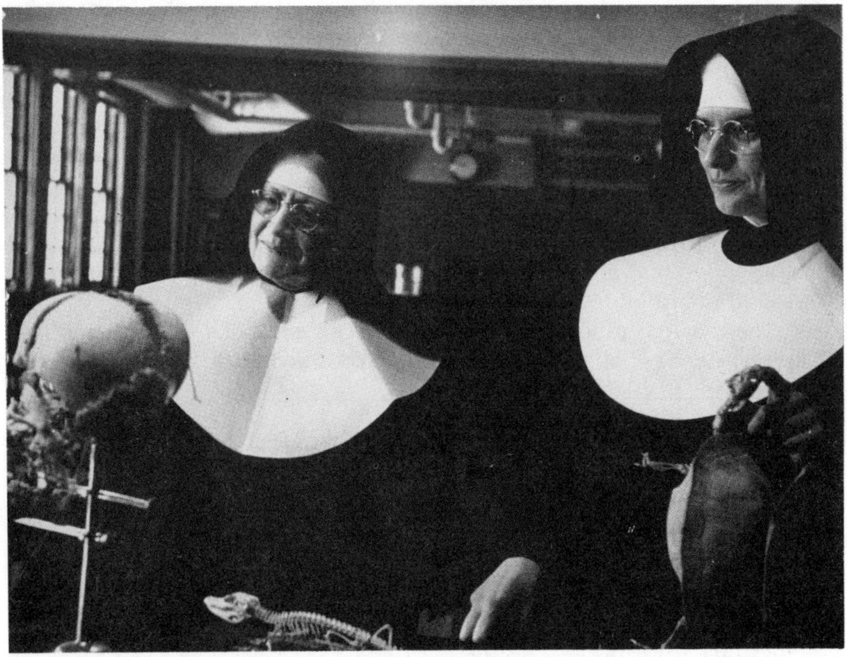

Sister Julitta Larkin with Sister Marie T. Dimond. (l.)

Louis, who had studied with her in the early 1930's and been a colleague in the department from 1937 to 1949 wrote after her death[135]:

> For many who asked her help she was an informed and prudent counselor.
>
> Trinitarians who studied biology under Sister Julitta remember the well-organized courses, the clear lectures and the quiz sessions enlivened by a ready wit. A perfectionist herself, she expected a high level of performance; and the students responded because they both feared and loved her. Those who are doctors, teachers, or scientists now, owe her much for starting them on their way. Many hundreds more, who may no longer remember the Mendelian ratio, cannot forget how to think honestly. All who knew her had to be influenced by the example of a completely dedicated and holy woman, calm and wise, with a sensitiveness and tenderness too seldom shown.

In 1918 the biology department offered (in addition to the introductory general biology described above) general botany and several advanced botany courses, animal histology and technique, comparative anatomy of vertebrates, embryology, physiology, and hygiene, microscopic drawing, as well as the philosophy of nature which was open to all students of science. By 1920 bacteriology, neurology and a senior seminar ("Biological topics of general interest to students in Biology, Philosophy, Psychology, and Education") had been added.[136] "Hygiene" had been dropped from the physiology course, and the elementary zoology and botany courses were consolidated into one introductory biology course.

With Pauline Wright, '21 (1922–1927), Sister Catherine Joan Skelly (1933–1946), Edith Rich (1937–1946) and Sister Marie Therese Dimond (1948–1958) and others[137] for shorter times during these years, Sister Julitta "built up the department not only with dedication, but with an unusual degree of foresight."[138] For two decades the offerings continued to follow the same pattern, but the faculty kept abreast of progress in biology and new scientific developments were consistently incorporated into existing courses. In 1967, Sister Marie Therese Dimond

135. *Obit. Alumnae Journal*, Spring, 1960, p. 136. Her life as a deeply committed Sister of Notre Dame, her community activities, her work in the Sunday School of Holy Rosary parish, her advice and practical help to Sisters teaching high school science, her unassuming, no-nonsense example of true goodness to all who knew her in community do not have a place in the academic history of the college, but all signify Sister Julitta to all who knew her or lived with her.

136. A forerunner of the contemporary bio-ethics in the association of other departments with biology.

137. Names appear in relevant catalogues.

138. Cf. Sister Marie Therese Dimond, "Sciences at Trinity," *Alumnae Journal*, Spring, 1967, pp. 161–163.

wrote: "Beginning as early as 1949–1950, the biology curriculum has undergone a radical although gradual reorganization in course division and sequence as well as in course content. . . . Women meet no (or at most very little) prejudice in a biological career, and opportunities are numberless."[139]

In 1958, Sister Marie Therese Dimond, who had been associated in the department with Sister Julitta for ten years, succeeded her. Since then, with Mrs. Barbara Hogan (1958–1972), Sister Elizabeth Henry Bellmer (1960–date), Dr. Gladys King (1961–1971) and others for shorter times[140] she has worked to maintain the high standards of the department as well as to keep it in accord with ever changing modern developments in the field. The current catalogue statement[141] reflects the continuity and change of the last twenty years.

> The principles and facts of biology often provide a basis for personal and societal choices in many aspects of life. For the non-science students the department accordingly offers a variety of courses, ranging from those designated as general program to electives such as human anatomy and physiology, human population problems, botany, and marine zoology. For biology majors the department offers a strong program leading to the B.A. or B.S. in biology. Certain courses in this program are also appropriate to majors in the other sciences. A secondary concentration in Bioethics is available to non-majors as well as to majors. (See below.) For the B.S. in Medical Technology, see section 11.
>
> The biology major follows a core curriculum of designated courses in biology, chemistry and physics; she then has considerable latitude for further choice of science, mathematics or psychology courses which will enable her to pursue her particular goal or chosen field of study. With the aid of a faculty adviser, she may thus prepare for laboratory or pharmaceutical work, scientific editing, teaching, professional school (e.g. medicine), or graduate study in biology or a related field (biochemistry, biophysics, animal behavior, neuropsychology, public health, bioethics).
>
> Washington metropolitan area facilities utilized include the Smithsonian Institution, the National Zoological Park, and the three largest libraries of their kind—the Library of Congress, the National Agricultural Library and the National Library of Medicine. The facilities of the Marine Science Consortium at Wallops Island, Virginia, are used for field studies.
>
> In fine, Trinity offers the biology student the advantages of a small-college environment with close faculty-student, student-student relationships, at the same time providing contact with leading exponents of biological thought.

One can note in this statement echoes of the original statements of 1902 and 1912 in the context of the world of the late 1970's.

139. *Ibid.*
140. Names in relevant catalogues.
141. 1979–1980, pp. 52–53.

Chemistry

"Chemical laboratory work" was introduced in September 1902. This statement in the President's Report marks the beginning of the Chemistry department. Sister Mary Isabelle (Mary Mahoney) had arrived at the college in April, 1902, to set up the laboratory, in preparation for teaching the course described in the 1901–1902 catalogue as

> Introduction to General Chemistry: The course is designed to meet the wants of students who take only one year of chemistry. The subject will be taught by lectures, recitations and laboratory work. A series of well-selected experiments illustrating the principles of chemistry will be required.
>
> *Five hours weekly*

By the next year a full chemistry offering appeared in the catalogue.[142] It is given here showing the revision of the introductory course.

> Course A—General Chemistry.—This course is designed to meet the wants of students who take only one year of chemistry. It includes a study of the principal elements and their compounds, and such an investigation of the fundamental laws governing chemical changes as is necessary for advanced work. Lectures. Recitations. Laboratory practice.
>
> *Five hours weekly.*
>
> Open to Freshmen, Sophomores, and Juniors.
>
> Course B—Qualitative Analysis.—A course consisting of lectures, recitations and laboratory work in the systematic methods of analysis. The elements are studied in their qualitative relations.
>
> *First semester, five hours weekly.*
>
> Open to students who have completed Course A.
>
> Course C—Quantitative Analysis.—A laboratory course embracing the most important and typical methods in gravimetric and volumetric analysis.
>
> *Second semester, five hours weekly.*
>
> Open to students who have completed Course B.
>
> Course D—Organic Chemistry.—A course consisting of lectures, recitations and laboratory work. A careful study is made of the principal classes of the compounds of carbon.
>
> *First semester, five hours weekly.*
>
> Open to students who have completed Course A.
>
> Course E—Organic Chemistry.
>
> *Second semester, five hours weekly.*
>
> A continuation of Course D.
>
> Course F—Advanced General Chemistry.—A course offering an opportunity for more extended study and investigation to those who have completed Courses B and C or D and E.

142. 1902–1903, p. 51.

This general pattern of courses continued until 1921 with the exception of the "Chemistry of cooking" which was tried in 1913 and 1914 as part of an abortive non-credit "Domestic Science" sequence which seemed to some of the faculty of that era to be "timely."

The President's Report of 1913 mentions the expansion of chemistry into the newly bought building on Lincoln Road.

> The building on Lincoln Avenue [Red Rose Inn, Graduate Hall, Old Cuvilly] has been entirely renovated and temporarily fitted up for scientific purposes. For some time the department of Chemistry has been handicapped in its laboratory room. Provision has been made in the 'Science Annex' as it is to be called, for development of the different courses, as well as for private laboratories [for research] for the Science Teachers.

Sister Mary Isabelle, a competent chemist and excellent teacher, directed the Chemistry Department until she was appointed Dean [of Students] in 1921. She was replaced by Sister Marie Mechtilde, M.A. (Helen Mahoney, '15), her own sister and former student, who taught Chemistry until her death in 1933. Meanwhile, Historical Chemistry was added in 1911, the Teaching of Chemistry and Food Chemistry in 1915, and Physical Chemistry in 1920. Biochemistry, which has since developed into a major sequence, came later—in 1934.

After the reorganization of 1932 when one major subject with one or more related minors became the center around which degree requirements were arranged, the chemistry major consisted of twenty-four semester hours in courses above the prerequisite basic inorganic chemistry. These were supported by mathematics through calculus, at least general physics, possible minors in biology or physics and by a knowledge of either French or German.

Sister St. John Nepomucene[143] (Elizabeth Finnessey '15) directed the Chemistry Department from 1933 until her retirement in 1965. She had taken a degree at M.I.T. and been a state factory inspector in Massachusetts before becoming a Sister of Notre Dame. She also did considerable graduate work in chemistry at the Catholic University of America. She was active in local and national groups of the American Chemical Society through the years and established a student chapter at Trinity College. In her later years she focused especially on the History of Science Section of the A.C.S. of which she was secretary-treasurer, writing papers in the field, both for publication and for presentation at meetings. She was in her later years elected a Fellow of the American Institute of Chemists.

143. Alumnae "Cum Laude," Sister St. John Nepomucene Fennessey, '15, *Alumnae Journal*, Spring, 1968, p. 134.

Sister St. John Nepomucene (Elizabeth Fennessey '15) with Elizabeth Healy Leffson '37.

Sister St. John in her long tenure was joined in the department by Adele Cavanaugh (1933–1937), Elizabeth Healy, later Leffson (1937–1944; 1959–date), Dr. Elizabeth Rona (an eminent atomic physicist, who left Trinity for Oak Ridge Laboratory, 1941–1947), Dr. James Hoare (1949–1954), Dr. Irena Roberts (1955–1965), Sister Frederika Jacob, Ph.D. (1959–1965), and others for shorter times.[144] Since 1965 Dr. Lilli Hornig (1965–1968), Dr. Alicia Kirkien-Konasiewicz, later Kirkien-Rzeszotarski, though still "Dr. K." (1966–date) have headed chemistry joined by various others for shorter times.[144]

The late 1950's brought the "advanced chemistry seminar" which gave an impetus to undergraduate research, and in 1961 a course in radio-chemistry appeared, sponsored by both chemistry and physics departments. By 1967 "Research Topics" constituted a separate course for qualified students while all majors participated in the "Department Seminar." The 1970–1971 catalogue records besides the basic pattern already in operation new courses: Chemistry and Photography, Chemistry of Life, Chemistry of Drugs, Chemistry and Environment, and Group Theory.[145]

The Department at the end of the 1970's has become "Chemistry-Biochemistry" which offers majors in chemistry or biochemistry and

144. Names in college catalogues in years of their teaching here.
145. Cf. "The Traveling Radioisotope Laboratory," by Sister St.John Nepomucene, *Alumnae Journal*, Summer, 1960, pp. 199–200.

"participates in the following interdepartmental majors and special programs: mathematics/chemistry, physics/chemistry, physical sciences, medical technology and the dual program in engineering."[146]

Physics

As in the other two sciences, physics courses began in September, 1902. The first vague announcement of 1901 developed in the catalogue of 1902–1903 into a series of five courses based on General Physics, a two semester course described as follows:

> *General Physics*—Lectures, readings, recitations and laboratory exercises in the fundamental principles of the science. Matter; motion; energy; properties of solids, liquids and gases; nature and effects of heat.
>
> *First semester, five hours weekly*
>
> Light, its transmission, reflection, refraction, absorption and dispersion; magnetism; electricity.
>
> *Second semester, five hours weekly*

For the first two years Sister Blandina, the mathematics teacher, taught physics.[147] Sister Antoinette Marie (Antoinette Pratt) succeeded her in September, 1904, and continued to teach physics until 1915 even while she studied history with Catholic University professors for the Ph.D. Sister Aloysius Marie (Mary Emma Metz) came to Trinity in 1914, replaced Sister Antoinette Marie in physics the following year, and continued to devote herself whole-heartedly to the physics department and to *her* students until her retirement in 1955. Writing after Sister Aloysius Marie's death in 1961, Eileen Collins Treacy wrote:

> One of the first nuns to teach physics at the college level, Sister was for many years chairman of our Physics Department; actually for a long time she was the only faculty member in the Department. Every student who took physics then knew her and loved her. She was an inspiration to all of us, but especially to me, for she was my teacher, my associate, and my dearly beloved friend. Even after her retirement, I called upon her many times for assistance. . . .
>
> Sister Aloysius Marie will be remembered by hundreds of Trinity alumnae as one of the outstanding personalities of their college years—a stimulating and thorough teacher, a religious of true humility and charity, but above all an understanding and devoted friend.[148]

146. Catalogue 1979–1980, p. 55.
147. Since Sister Antoinette Marie Pratt did not come to Trinity until September 6, 1904, she could not have been the original physics teacher.
148. *Alumnae Journal*, Autumn 1961, p. 16. Cf. *Record*, June, 1919, pp. 151–153. "The Underground and Subsea Wireless," by Irene Rieckleman '21, Visit of Chemistry and Physics majors to the laboratory of James Harris Rogers.

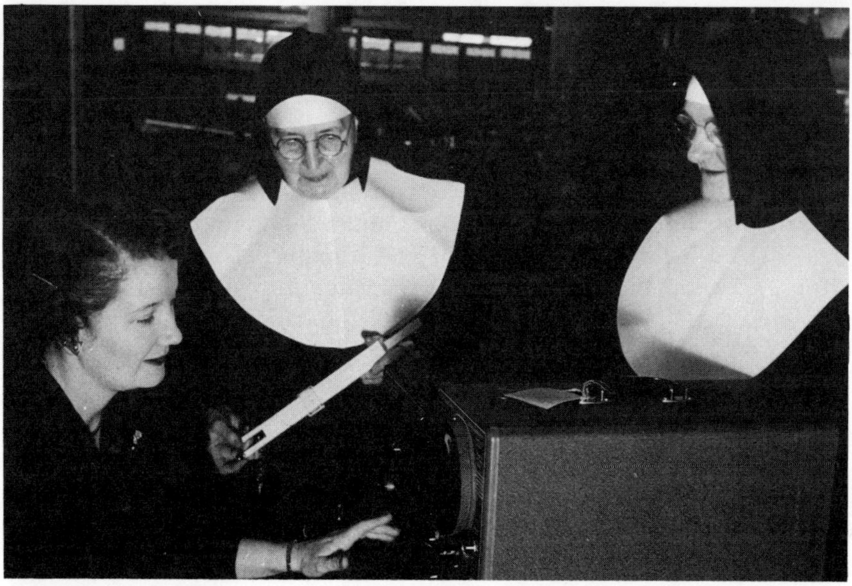

Sister Aloysius Marie (Metz) with Eileen Collins Treacy '36 and Sister Mary Robert Grandfield. (r.)

Her interest in the welfare of her students, both professional and personal, continued beyond their graduation until her death in 1961.

The years alone in the department mentioned above lasted from 1915 to 1938 when Eileen Collins, '36, M.A., joined the physics department and taught until her marriage in 1941. As Eileen Collins Treacy she has been back at Trinity since 1943. During the last thirty years in addition to Sister Aloysius Marie (until 1955) and Mrs. Treacy, members of the department were Sister Mary Robert Grandfield (1946–1969), Jane O'Boyle (1946–1949), Dr. James Hoare from chemistry (1949–1954), William Whalen (1957–1969), Sister Patricia Julie Sullivan, Ph.D. (1960–1965), Dr. Karen Weis Kershenstein (1968–1976) and others for shorter times.[149]

The original five-course program included: Advanced Physics (mechanics of solids, liquids, gases; magnetism; electricity, light, heat); Wave Motion and Sound; Ether-Waves; Electricity. Students were eligible for each of these only after successfully completing the ones before. Late in the first decade a course in "General Descriptive Physics" was added presumably for students who did not intend to carry the subject farther. By 1918 this had been dropped from the physics offerings and those taking only one course in physics were again required to take the

149. Names in relevant catalogues.

regular general physics course. A sort of individual student research course was introduced at the same time: "Selected Problems assigned for investigation, experimental work and discussion." When physical chemistry was first introduced in 1920, Sister Aloysius Marie taught the small select class for two years before the chemistry department reclaimed the course. From 1928–1932 introduction to "Quantum Theory and the Problem of Atomic Structure" and a separate course in "Radioactivity and X-Rays" were offered. The teaching of physics was listed from 1922 until the *1960's*. Like all such departmental courses, it was considered a "special methods" course in education, offered only when need arose. "An introduction to modern physics" was listed as early as 1934. This became by 1949 "Fundamentals of Modern Physics: Electron physics, Radio Activity, Nuclear physics." A separate course in the principles of radio communication was listed in 1942, though "conductivity of gases, x-rays, and radio-activity" dates from the late 1920's as mentioned above.

The department was alert to the developments in physics of the 1940's and "sputnik furor" of the 1950's. The offerings of the 1965–1966 catalogue reflect this. A research seminar in solid state physics had been introduced in 1957. This developed in 1959 into a course, "Introduction to Solid State Research." By 1965 the physics listing included, in addition to general physics which emphasized "basic principles and their relation to the space age," Mechanics and Wave Motion; Electrodynamics; Atomic and Nuclear Physics"; Introduction to Solid State; Advanced Laboratory Research; Theoretical Physics and Introduction to Quantum Mechanics.

Writing in 1967 Sister Marie Dimond could say of the physics department:

> Although the number of majors in Physics has never been large (the first three graduated in 1914), it has been steady, and, in addition, many of the mathematics majors have had physics as a related subject. Trinity is almost unique among Catholic women's liberal arts colleges in having a really good physics major program and was the first college to offer an undergraduate course in solid state physics. Last year a chapter of Sigma Pi Sigma, the national honor society for students of physics, was established on campus, the first such chapter to be established at a women's college. Opportunities for graduate training and for professional careers in physics are limited only by the students' ability and interest.[150]

The 1970's brought the addition of more of what might be called "applied or service" courses: physics of music, household physics, physics of photography, as well as inter-departmental majors:[151] physics/

150. "Sciences at Trinity," *Alumnae Journal*, Spring 1967, p. 161.
151. Reminiscent of the double majors of the early years of the college.

chemistry, mathematics/physics, physical sciences, and a dual degree program in engineering with the University of Maryland. Scientific developments and the prohibitive expense of increasingly sophisticated equipment lead to the 1977–1978 catalogue announcement ending the separate physics major. It states:

> The department offers a minor in physics and collaborates in the following interdepartmental majors and programs: physics/chemistry, mathematics/physics, physical sciences, dual degree program in engineering.
>
> Because the region of overlap between physics and chemistry is continually increasing, preparation for graduate or professional research in certain areas of science requires that a student interested in either field take advanced undergraduate courses in both. The interdepartmental physics/chemistry major is designed to make such study possible within a coherent structure.
>
> The mathematics/physics major aims to fulfill the needs of students who would normally concentrate in mathematics but prefer more of its applications to physics than a straight mathematics major would offer.
>
> The departments of chemistry, mathematics and physics together offer a major in physical sciences culminating in a B.S. degree to be pursued only under the dual degree program in engineering sponsored by Trinity and the University of Maryland College of Engineering.

The physics department reflects, perhaps, more than any other the explosive discoveries and changes the world has witnessed since 1902. Its faculty have labored mightily to help students keep abreast of developments.

Mathematics

As has been seen in the description of the early years,[152] mathematics dates from 1900 for those who had the preparation for college courses especially "for students intending to specialize in science" which was not yet offered. For the first three years courses in solid geometry and plane and spherical trigonometry were required of all freshmen. There were also non-credit courses in entrance mathematics for those who had to remove entrance conditions. After the publication in the catalogue for 1903–1904 of a more complete program of mathematics, there is no indication that mathematics was required of all students in the college. An entrance requirement of algebra through "quadratics and beyond" and of plane geometry persisted until the 1975 non-differentiated "sixteen units from the basic academic disciplines." Though no "group" is listed for mathematics in those early years, one of the thirteen students of the class of 1905 (the second class

152. Chapter 3, "Pioneer Years, 1900–1904," p. 104. Also Chapter 4, "Administration and Faculty," pp. 89, 91–92.

to graduate) received her B.A. in Latin and Mathematics, and one of the five of 1906 offered German and Mathematics. Combinations of mathematics with one of the sciences earned a Bachelor of Science rather than a Bachelor of Arts. During the first twenty-five years of college,[153] one or two students in each class except 1914 offered mathematics as one of their major subjects. Even in 1914 there were three combinations with science implying the necessary background in mathematics. In the 1920's the number increased. In the classes of 1923 and 1924 eight students offered mathematics as one major and in 1925 six in addition to popular combinations with science.

The 1902–1903 catalogue shows eight mathematics courses including "Theory of Equations and Determinants" for students who have taken differential and integral calculus, and the history of mathematics "for advanced students of mathematics." By 1906 the theory course was divided with separate treatment of equations and determinants, and a course in advanced algebra was added. In 1908, analytical mechanics (mathematical theory of mechanics) was added. Since 1911, a Teachers' Course has appeared in the catalogue for the benefit of prospective secondary school teachers. The original description was "critical review of algebra and geometry with a view to modern methods of teaching." For six decades this description remained, although presumably the "modern methods" did change, and the mid-sixties brought the addition of a course in contemporary mathematics for elementary school teachers. In the 1970's it is simply "teaching mathematics in secondary schools" and is joined in the Education Department by "Curriculum and Methods of Teaching Elementary Mathematics."

From 1913 to the early 1930's, graduate courses such as vector analysis, projective geometry, and the already mentioned mathematical theory of mechanics were offered. As a result of the curriculum reorganization of 1932, the single major with pre-requisites, major requirements, and recommended related minors was formulated.[154] A "reading course" for seniors (1946) became by 1951 the senior coordinating seminar. Statistical methods courses date from 1920 when mathematics for science majors became for several years differentiated into separate courses for physics and chemistry majors. Programming for electronic digital computers joined the course offerings in 1959, followed in the 1960's by data processing, symbolic logic, probability theory, complex function theory and topology. Interdepartmental majors in mathematics-chemistry, mathematics-economics, and mathematics-physics were introduced in 1970.

The departmental statement in the 1975–1976 catalogue gives a good description of the contemporary program:

153. *Degrees Conferred* 1904–1925. Trinity College Archives.
154. Full statement in 1934–1935 catalogue, pp. 39–42, 64–66.

The department offers a strong major program; interdepartmental majors in conjunction with the Chemistry, Economics and Physics departments; specialized courses needed by students majoring in biology, chemistry, economics, education, physics, psychology and sociology; and introductory courses in the cultural aspects of mathematical thought.

Students in the computer programming courses use Honeywell 1648 computers via four terminals at the college.

Well-qualified freshmen are granted advanced placement. These students usually finish their major courses by the end of their junior year and continue on to independent honors work at Trinity or take graduate courses at the various Consortium universities.

Students with a major in mathematics or one of the interdepartmental mathematics programs are prepared to continue their study in graduate and professional schools, to go on to systems analysis and programming or computer research, teaching, engineering, statistical or actuarial work and other professional positions.

The department's offerings also serve the following interdepartmental programs: Mathematics/Chemistry, Mathematics/Economics, Mathematics/Physics, Physical Sciences, Dual Degree Program in Engineering (see sections 4, 10)

Sister Blandina of the Sacred Heart (Abigal Shea) of the original faculty began teaching mathematics in 1900 and carried the first class through to graduation in 1904. She was joined in 1902 by Sister Marie Cecilia[155] (Josephine Mangold) who came to assist in the teaching of German while she studied mathematics with Sister Blandina. Sister Marie Cecilia succeeded her instructor in 1904 and continued directing the mathematics department for thirty years until her death in 1934. She was a gentle, quiet scholar, deeply interested not only in mathematics but in her individual students. During her long tenure on the Trinity faculty she continued friendly collaboration with her contemporaries[156] in the mathematics department at Catholic University, joining them in solving many an intricate mathematical problem to their mutual benefit. Sister Mary Kostka (Clara Kemper) joined the department in 1917 and continued to teach courses in both German and mathematics until she went to Japan to direct the work of the Sisters of Notre Dame in Okayama[157] where she worked until her death in 1961. She was replaced at Trinity College by Sister Mary Edwina who remained only a short time and by Sister Thomas Marie (Catherine Maloney), an

155. Cf. p. 91. Sister Marie Cecilia earned an M.S. from Trinity and an M.A. in Mathematics from Catholic University. Sister Blandina's obituary in the *Record* April 1914 tells of her later life.

156. The name of Dr. Landry is the only one that surfaces. More research should add others.

157. Sister Mary Kostka was one of the American Sisters interned during World War II, was re-patriated on the Gripsholm in 1944, but returned to Japan after the peace. She founded the Sheishin University College for Women in Okayama and other flourishing schools.

Emmanuel College alumna who replaced Sister Marie Cecilia after her death. From 1934 to 1938 Dr. Thomas Finan of Catholic University taught mathematics at Trinity and Sister Mary Robert Grandfield from 1934–1941. Sister Thomas Marie was an enthusiastic, competent mathematician, beloved by her students. She earned her M.A. from Catholic University and was nearing her doctorate in mathematics there when fatal disease struck and she died October 7, 1943. Her obituary[158] by Margaret Metzer, one of her majors who had graduated three months before, embodies the thoughts of all:

> A few weeks ago we gathered at Ilchester for the funeral of Sister Thomas Marie. On every face could be read the same thought, "I can't believe it." Her death came as such a shock to most of us. Former students had received letters a few short weeks before, present students had her in class a few days ago. And yet we gathered at Ilchester for her funeral. God in His kindness and mercy had seen fit to release her from this earthly exile. And who of us was more deserving to be released than she. We who have known and loved her cannot feel sad. You who knew her familiar smile as she walked the halls of Trinity may feel sad but we who have had her in class can only feel a great happiness that God has seen fit to reward her tireless efforts with us. How deserving those efforts were of reward only a roll call of her grateful students can tell.
>
> Her In Memoriam cannot be written with words in pen and ink. It cannot be written by any of us. She wrote it herself, wrote it indelibly in he hearts of her students and all who knew her. It is written in the countless marriage blessings all Sister's girls were sure to receive, written in the countless mementoes she made for every Class Day, Christmas and Easter. It is written in the minutes of the Math Club meetings that meant so much to her, written in the friendliness and warmth that fills the rooms on Second South. We learned our Calculus and Differential Equations there, learned to know our Mathematicians, but above all we learned to know Christ there.
>
> Yes, we gathered at Ilchester for Sister's funeral. It wasn't a sad day for us. We thought too much of Sister to be sad that she was finally with the God that she had loved and served so well in this life. Second South will not be the same, the Math Library will not be the same. Yet Sister with her bright smile, cryptography books, handfull of little white cards, her everlasting, "I mustn't be late for chapel" and her sunburned nose on May Day will watch over us always. Trinity has lost a teacher but gained a Patron. We gathered at Ilchester for her funeral but little do we know how great was the gathering that welcomed her to Heaven.

Young Dr. Mary Varnhorn who had joined the faculty in 1940, was now left suddenly alone in mathematics. Once again professors from Catholic University helped fill the sudden need. The *Alumnae Journal* quoted above has on page 14 the announcement: "Dr. Otto Ramler and

158. *Alumnae Journal*, Autumn, 1943, p. 7.

Dr. Mary Varnhorn with Dorothy Mortell Barrett '45. (l.)

Mr. Raymond Moller of the Catholic University are conducting the courses formerly taught by Sister Thomas Marie."

Dr. Varnhorn, a graduate of the College of Notre Dame of Maryland, earned her doctorate in mathematics at the Catholic University. She has taught at Trinity College from 1940 to 1978. During these years, commuting from Baltimore, she has devoted herself unstintingly to the mathematics department and to the individual needs of her students. In 1965, she was one of nine faculty members who received the *Pro Ecclesia et Pontifice Medal* for twenty-five years or more of service to higher education at Trinity College. Her citation at that time praised her commitment to the demanding work of the classroom and her devotion to leading each student through the advanced theory, the sophistical terminology to the mystery, the "angular essence," the "why" that underlies them. Trinity mathematics majors have gone on from the base of their thorough training to responsible positions in government, business, and education where their achievements have reflected favorably on the college.

From the 1940's to the mid-sixties Dr. Varnhorn was ably assisted in the department by a series of mathematicians, most of whom, like the adjunct professors of the present, stayed only a year or two as their expertise was needed. Of those who remained longer, three should be mentioned: Jane O'Boyle who soon turned to administration, holding several responsible positions, including Registrar and Associate Dean; Sister Catherine Marie Lee, who after four years also turned to administration, assisting Sister Mary Mercedes in the Registrar's Office, directing the food service and dining hall, and holding the office of Registrar for ten years, until her retirement in 1977; and Dorothy Mortell Barrett, one of Dr. Varnhorn's earliest majors, who has ably taught one or more courses in the department since 1954.

Dr. Marsha Sward joined the department in 1968. She has actively participated in the innovations of the last decade and has won the respect and affection of her students.

Philosophy

Philosophy is another of the departments that dates from 1900 and was established by one of the "greats" of the early years. Dr. Edward A. Pace.[159] The statement in the catalogue 1900–1901 sets the general pattern.

> The course in philosophy extends over four years. It leads the student gradually from a preliminary survey of the subject to the study of psychology, ethics and natural theology. Its purpose is to impart the training in method and the acquaintance with fundamental problems which are required for more advanced work. A clear understanding of principles as a necessary preparation for research in special lines, is aimed at throughout the course.
>
> Instruction is given by means of lectures, recitations, and practical exercises.[160]

Though psychology was listed until 1919 in the philosophy department, it has already been noted that it was taught as an experimental

159. A co-founder of the college. Cf. Chapter 1 and the section on the psychology department of this history.
160. p. 17.

social science even in those years. The "four year course" in philosophy required of all students, and established in the early years, remained standard for four decades. It consisted of logic, introduction to philosophy, history of philosophy, and ethics.[161] Courses in modern philosophy and aesthetics appear first in 1915–1916. Sister Fidelis (Dolle) joined Dr. Pace in 1901 and taught logic and the history of philosophy for most of the first decade, while Dr. Pace continued to teach various courses, especially the senior ethics until 1924.

That Dr. Pace, an eminent scholar, was to his Trinity College students a popular teacher can be seen from early *Trinologue* excerpts. Revering his national and international achievements, they nevertheless felt his personal interest in *them* enough to tease him.

The Class of 1913 wrote:

> "Cherish your illusions," advises a certain eminent optimist, and to aid us to preserve ours is no doubt the reason why our course in Ethics is held in trust until our Senior year. The various systems of education, Rousseau's and Pestalozzi's and hosts of others have been drawn for us by Dr. Pace, scorned or praised, according to their deserts, with his deft touch that is unrivalled. But in Ethics, the master course, the iconoclast of all our treasured theories, is where this renowned Doctor is most at home. . . .
>
> Not only in the moral order, however, does Dr. Pace shine, for he is equally eminent as psychologist, musician, and gold medal encyclopedist. Yet it is safe to predict that 1913 will remember him as the great scholar, who unhampered by notes and inspired by the druidical beauty of the Soldiers' Home Park, where his gaze often wanders, dispensed much wisdom on the ethics of the press, art, and the stage.[162]

Their predecessors of 1912 put it more succinctly:

Dr. Pace
We learned all about Pestalozzi
In our ethical tests guessedalozzi,
In his courses we dote
On each marginal note,
But we're glad we can now restalozzi.[163]

This attitude of affectionate admiration was characteristic of student reaction to him from the beginning to 1924.[164]

161. Dr. Pace's reputation as an interesting and lively teacher dates from the first academic year. The Annals of the college for Feb. 18, 1901 state: "Dr. Pace's lecture was particularly fine Subjectivism being the subject. Sparkles of dry wit accompanied all his expositions of theory and made the dry bones of logic most enjoyable to his auditors."
162. *Trinilogue*, 1913, p. 13.
163. *Trinilogue*, 1912, p. 14.
164. "Souvenir of an Uncle," by Marguerite Pace Corcoran, in *Alumnae Journal*, Summer, 1967, pp. 240–243.

In 1907, Dr. William Turner joined the department for history of philosophy using his own book as text. Two years later he took over the logic, developed *Lessons in Logic*,[165] and continued teaching until his appointment in 1919 as bishop of Buffalo, NY. Dr. Turner was also a popular professor, teased in the first volume of the *Trinilogue* (1911) for his lavish use of Greek terms and of the blackboard for "chirographical and etymological illustrations" in his explanations of the most complex syllogisms or the exigencies of the categorical imperative. The class of 1915, intrigued by the medieval Latin verse, "Barbara Celarent," used by Dr. Turner to try to help them memorize the various forms of syllogisms, set the whole thing to music and serenaded him with a harmonized choral ode. The President's Report for 1918–1919, announced that Dr. Turner had been named Bishop of Buffalo, a loss to the college where he had taught for twelve years and had "given valuable and generous service to Trinity and the Philosophy Department and endeared himself to Sisters and Students in countless ways."

Dr. Thomas Verner Moore, C.S.P.,[166] was teaching introduction to philosophy when he assisted in the establishment of the biology department and Dr. Charles Dubray, S.M. took over his philosophy course. Meanwhile, Sister Berchmans Julia (Julia Schumacher)[167] a young science teacher was doing graduate study in philosophy under Dr. Turner, earning her M.A. in 1913 with a dissertation: "Berkeley and the Existence of God."

In addition to the basic courses outlined above the department offered, from 1909 to 1915, a senior elective course of "Lectures and Seminars in Philosophy." A glance at the content of this course will indicate why it developed after 1916 into "Contemporary Philosophy." The catalogue description was

> 1. Lectures and discussions on topics such as the following: Agnosticism, Pantheism, Evolutionism, the Immortality of the Soul, Determinism, Pragmatism.
> 2. Critical study of philosophical essays selected from current numbers of leading reviews and magazines.

In the middle of the second decade Aesthetics was also added to the philosophy offerings. Both courses were taught by Dr. Charles A. Dubray, S.M. until 1923. Sister Berchmans Julia succeeded Dr. Turner in 1918, teaching logic, introduction to philosophy, history of philosophy and after 1923 aesthetics until 1932.[168] The catalogue of 1924 places the philosophy department for the first time in its alphabetical position

165. Catholic Education Press, 1911, 1929.
166. Cf. Psychology section.
167. Cf. Chapter 4, pp. 114–118.
168. The year she was appointed president of the college.

instead of following the religion-scripture-church history write-up and Dom Francis M. Walsh, O.S.B., began fourteen years of teaching senior ethics.

The decade of the 1930's continued the pattern set by Dr. Pace with Dr. John K. Ryan in introduction to philosophy (1932–1946), Dom Francis Walsh and later Dr. Edward Talbot, O.M.I. in ethics, Dr. Edward Roelker in logic. The entrance into the department in 1938 of Sister Ann Julia (Helen Kinnirey)[169] marked the beginning of a moving force which vivified and modernized the teaching of philosophy at Trinity College for more than thirty years, led to major work in 1956 and is still influential in the mid-1970's.

The basic pattern of courses required or offered during the forties was similar to that already described. The innovative element first became apparent through Sister Ann Julia's method of teaching the revised content of courses and the integration of logic with other subject matter fields. "Illustrations from the sciences" had long been listed in the logic course description, but the description of Philosophy 105 (1940–1947) shows a new approach.

> LOGIC, THEORETICAL AND APPLIED.
>
> The course gives an introduction to deductive and inductive logic. The union of the course with English 105 makes possible simultaneous training in the fundamental processes: reading, writing, and reasoning. The study of the scientific method is correlated with the freshman science courses.

With Dr. John K. Ryan, Dr. Talbot, and two other Oblates of Mary Immaculate, Dr. Raymond Hunt and Dr. Joseph Supple, who both taught religion as well as philosophy, Sister Ann Julia continued to concentrate on the freshmen until 1947 when she extended her innovative work to other courses. While Father John B. Mulgrew, O.P. taught ethics, she re-organized and taught the basic courses: logic and epistemology, general metaphysics, and an outline of the history of philosophy (the "philosophia perennis").

The elective courses were taught in a three-year sequence, thus allowing students to take all without the department having to offer all every year. Sister Ann Julia taught the aesthetics, which was required for art and music majors and popular with others. Dr. Ferrar Smith, O.P. (1952–1956) and Dr. Robert O'Donnell, C.S.P. (1959–1962) taught modern and contemporary philosophy. In the 1950's Sister Helen James John[170] (1954 to present) and Sister Sheila Doherty (1955–1963) joined the department. Requirements for a major in philosophy,

169. A.B. Trinity College, M.A. Columbia University, Ph.D. Catholic University. Post doctoral work at several universities.

170. A.B. Trinity College, M.A. Catholic University of America, Ph.D. University of Louvain, Belgium.

Sister Ann Julia Kinnirey, Ph.D. (r.) with Sister Helen J. John, Ph.D.

including reading list and coordinating seminar, were first stated in the catalogue of 1955–1956. In 1963 Sister Sheila left teaching to devote full time to her work as Director of Admissions. Sister Helen James John continued working with Sister Ann Julia (to 1975), with Dr. Max E. Guzikowski (1964 to the present) and Roland Cronkhite (1961–1971). She has contributed much to research and to the curricular changes of the 1970's.

From 1950 to 1964 ethics was not offered in the philosophy department while eight to ten hours of moral theology were required of all students. Ethics was re-instated as a senior philosophy course in 1964 with Dr. Guzikowski as teacher. The early 1960's brought the "Western Culture"[171] course (Philosophy-History 113), another example of integration of more than one subject matter field. It was described as a "sketch of the development of the basic concepts in Western thought in the context of the political and social history, closely correlated with English 107."

171. Taught by a team: Sister Ann Julia, Sister Helen James and Sister Joan of the History Department.

Dr. Max Guzikowski.

Changes in course names in the 1970's when logic became the "Art of Critical Thinking" and ethics "Why be Moral?" give an indication of departmental adaptation to changing times. "Man's Freedom," "Ethical Choice," "Existential Phenomenology" and "Bio-ethics" also show further contemporary orientation. Bio-ethics, which was pioneered in 1975 by Dr. Guzikowski and Sister Marie T. Dimond of the Biology Department, later grew through the collaboration of Sister Helen James John and Sr. Marie Dimond into a secondary concentration in bio-ethics offered currently in the biology department.[172]

The current statement introducing departmental offerings reflects the continuity underlying eighty years of development.

> Philosophy courses confront students with fundamental issues and options—in understanding reality, in making moral decisions, in sharing life with

172. Cf. "Background for Bioethics at Trinity," Summary Report of Helen J. John, S.N.D., assisted by Marie T. Dimond, S.N.D., August 1979.

> others. They also provide direction and practice in using intellectual analysis and clarifying experience through reflection. Thus, students are helped to deal with central questions in their own lives. Some courses utilize a variety of source materials, methods and perspectives to explore selected areas of special importance and relevance, either professional or personal, in depth. Others familiarize students with the Western philosophical tradition through direct study of great works of the past; trace relationships between philosophy and other aspects of man's culture and history; or introduce students to historical research and analysis in philosophy.[173]

Though all students are no longer required to take certain courses at the same time, Dr. Guzikowski and Sister Helen James John are actively "confronting students with fundamental issues" as the ninth decade approaches.

Religion-Theology

Religion courses have been part of the Trinity College curriculum since 1900. The 1900–1901 catalogue, which covered freshman courses only, states that the course will include doctrine, bible, and liturgy. In order to insure the students the full value of the degree as granted in other institutions of higher education (120 semester hours of academic work), the requirement for a Trinity degree was set at 132 semester hours. This allowed for eight hours of religion and four of scripture in addition to the customary one hundred and twenty. The subjects were always presented as college credit courses, not as "addenda."

The introductory statement in the first full four-year catalogue, 1901–1902, set the pattern and remained unchanged until 1937, though course descriptions and offerings changed as will be seen later.

> It is the aim of the College, as a distinctly Catholic institution, to offer to its students every opportunity to obtain a thorough knowledge of Catholic doctrine and practice. Hence the courses in religion form an organic part of the College curriculum. They are conducted with a view to solid religious formation; therefore, the work is so arranged that students who remain four years, the full time for degrees, will have studied a systematic exposition of fundamental truths.[174]

The courses aiming toward that "solid religious formation" had settled by 1902 into a pattern of four courses required of all students, one for each year of the students' college career. These courses, each one hour a week for a scholastic year, were listed in the catalogue until 1924 as:

173. Catalogue 1975–1976, p. 105.
174. p. 30.

1. *Apologetics* including revelation, tradition and scripture, Christianity and non-Christian religions, the Church and the churches;
2. *God and Man* including the unity and Trinity of God, creation, original sin, the incarnation, the redemption, the Mother of God;
3. *Sanctification* including grace, the sacraments, the sacramentals, the constitution and life of the Church, worship; and
4. *Religious Law and Sanction* including the precepts of God and the Church, virtues, sin, the counsels, the future life.[175]

In addition to these religious courses, freshmen and sophomores had one hour a week of Church History. The introductory rationale for church history in a woman's college, which appeared in the original catalogue 1900–1901 and which was retained without change (except in capitalization) until 1922 when church history was incorporated into the history department and listed as a history course, deserves to be quoted in full.

> The History of Religion of Jesus Christ is the story of the true emancipation and elevation of womankind. Hence, it is eminently proper that the History of the Catholic Church, the divinely appointed custodian and interpreter of the will and the spirit of Jesus Christ, should be thoroughly taught in any school of higher studies for Christian women.
>
> The aim of this teaching will be to draw out the critical sense; to enable the student to be self-helping that she may judge correctly what is false, misleading or imperfect in historical literature; to acquaint her with all that pertains to the nature, whereabouts, use and criticism of original authorities; to give her a full and accurate notion of the principal epochs, problems and institutions of Church History.
>
> As women have been incalculably ennobled by the spirit and institutions of Christianity, special attention will be paid to the office, condition and services of Christian woman as exemplified in the History of Catholicism.
>
> The discoveries of the last half century in the Roman Catacombs and in early Christian literature will be utilized as occasion arises.[176]

The First Twenty Years

For two years, 1900–1902, Dr. Philip Garrigan, Vice-Rector of The Catholic University of America, taught religion and acted as the students' chaplain. The religion course outlined in the catalogue was given

175. This course offering, preceded by the introductory statement given above appeared in the catalogues of the college from 1902–1903 to 1923–1924.
176. Catalogue 1900–1901, p. 18. Probably written by Dr. Thomas Shahan.

on Sunday morning.[177] When Dr. Garrigan was appointed first bishop of Sioux City, Iowa, the "scholarly series of Sunday morning lectures continued"[178] with Dr. John Creagh as the instructor as well as students' chaplain until 1907. The Very Reverend Dr. Charles Grannan gave, in 1902, "much valuable aid in the preparation of a systematic course in Biblical Studies" and continued to teach Trinity students using the latest findings of biblical scholarship until 1908 when he was replaced by Sister Marie Louis Hummell, an apt student of his courses. That year the "committee on studies" of the Advisory Board gave as its opinion that the Scripture course was "rather advanced for a College course" and should be modified. Though the course descriptions in the catalogue were not changed, the manner of teaching was, presumably, better adapted to undergraduate students. Dr. Thomas Shahan taught the church history until he was appointed Rector of the Catholic University in 1909. From 1910 to 1912, Sister Jeanne of the Nativity (Mary Murphy) filled in as church history professor until Dr. Nicholas Weber began his long tenure in that position, 1912–1947. During that time he was replaced at least twice: in 1914–1915 Sister Clare Lawler of the history department taught his courses while he was studying in Europe and in the 1940's Sister Carmelita Fennell taught church history while Dr. Weber was absent on necessary business for his religious order, the Marists.

In 1908 Dr. Charles Aiken[179] began a Trinity teaching career that lasted until 1923 and Dr. John Webster Melody became the students' chaplain to continue in that[180] office until 1914.

Though the early catalogues listed reference books such as Gueranger's *Liturgical Year,* Shand's *Christian Apology,* and Wilmer's *Handbook of Religion* for collateral reading, student memory seems to indicate that no *textbooks* were used for the courses. Some idea of the method of teaching during the first decade of the century may be gained from a letter of a pioneer student. Sister Wilfred (Elsie Parsons '04) answered in 1968 a query about textbooks in the early days of the college in a letter to Sister Helen Sheehan.

> Your idea of the early religion—and other theoretical—courses at Trinity is the right one. The Religion courses at Trinity—during the first four

177. One wonders how later students would have reacted to this scheduling. The pioneers seem to have taken it in stride.
178. President's Report, 1903.
179. It is possible that the Rev. Charles Aiken was still a candidate for the Ph.D. when he was first teaching at Trinity because there is extant the story that the Trinity students were privileged to attend the doctoral oral at Catholic University of their brilliant young religion teacher with a Harvard degree. The first catalogue list of faculty (1912) records him as Very Rev. Charles Aiken, S.T.D.
180. Students' religious activities will be treated in Chapter 6.

years—used no text-books. In fact I doubt that any such existed for college students at that time—unless perhaps the Jesuits ran some kind of outlines for the students in their classes. But Trinity was the first Catholic college for women in the U.S.—such used to be our boast—and both we and our professors were pioneers in the field. I think we might have been affronted by a text-book (except in language courses), the Professor was the fount of knowledge, he was supposed to be an authority in his field; he talked, we students listened carefully and took notes, and we were proud of our notes, we took them on small sheets of paper, and copied them into note-books after class. This gave us a good chance to fill in any gaps by consulting other members in the class. It also made us review and discuss the material among ourselves. Those were the days when students loved to talk about their courses, their professors. I think that some of our Professors were graduates of German Universities, where such customs prevailed. For our first two years we had Dr. Garrigan, Vice-Rector of the University, and after he became Bishop of Sioux City, we had Dr. Creagh who had just (I think) received his doctorate. He was a brilliant young man and an inspiring teacher. Our Religion classes used to be held on Sunday mornings at 10–11. I do not recall any special grumble at this. Mass was at 7. Our Religion courses must have included our Church History, given by Dr. Shahan, our philosophy by Dr. Pace and our Scripture—in Senior year—by Dr. Grannan. But all these courses were given in lecture form, innocent of any "discussion" from the students, although there were often lively enough ones out of class, when one could catch a Professor on the wing. For outside reading, there were references, especially in Church History, but the Trinity Library, in its first year, consisted of about 300 volumes in two small rooms on Third South. Definitely our courses consisted of what our Professors gave us, but what they gave us was probably vastly better than what books of the time would have given us. I do not believe this was the deprivation it would now be called, because I know that our minds were greatly stimulated to love learning, and that we received it as disciples—learners—not young people who imagined they already knew most of what they were being given. In fact I think the early student atmosphere of Trinity was very much what one reads of medieval universities: a sort of intellectual excitement.

Well, there it is; no text-books on religion, philosophy, Church history or Scripture (except the Bible, of course). Much later Dr. Cooper introduced his own text-book into his religion class, but I do not know if he was the first.[181]

A second 1968 letter from Anna P. Butler '08, who taught English in Cambridge, Massachusetts High School and was head of the English Department there for many years, gives another contemporary view of the early religion classes.

181. The "no textbook" statement in these subjects applies to the first decade only. Before Dr. Cooper's series of *Religion for College Students*, Dr. Turner had published his own texts *Lessons in Logic* and *History of Philosophy*, Dr. Weber his *Church History*.

> As for your request concerning textbooks used in religion classes, I am almost sure that we had none. We used large linen covered note books to take notes from the lectures and from such notes we studied to derive our knowledge of the subject. I remember we had both Dr. Creagh and Dr. Aiken for dogma and Dr. Grannan for Scripture courses. Very vividly I recall the type of examination we had one year. I think it was in Dr. Creagh's class. His question was as follows: Delilah did so and so and so and so. What do you think of Delilah? For two hours we were supposed to write our thoughts of Delilah. One rather modern student handed [in] her paper with the answer: "I think Delilah was one game sport." The proctor of the examination captured the student and made her come back to the classroom to write her supposed reactions to Delilah's conduct. . . . How things have changed! I suppose even the word "dogma" may be taboo today.

The first *Trinilogue*, 1911, gives in a serio-comic way the students' appreciation of Dr. Aiken and his classes, no longer on Sunday morning since about 1907, but part of the weekly schedule of classes. This "write-up" of the Very Reverend Charles F. Aiken, S.T.D., deserves quotation in full.

> Other courses may come and other courses may go, but Religion lectures go on throughout our College life. Here Caps and Gowns win no distinction; those who follow the Pedagogy courses, and those who are doing penance in the Science Laboratories, sit down in peace together. The 9.20 period on Monday is surely the triumph of Liberty, Equality, and Fraternity: the Declaration of Independence, storming the Bastille, and the Communist Manifesto, have not done so much to put mankind on an equal footing as the little announcement in the year book: "Religion is prescribed for all students." We obey a powerful race instinct when we express our pleasure that this equality is worked out under green banners, even if some of the learning inscribed on those emerald sheets, has filtered down to us by way of Puritan-originated-Harvard. With what breathless interest we have found certain resemblances between Sabellianism and the myths of the Egyptians, Hindus, and Laplanders! But seriously speaking, no matter what feature of our college curriculum we might cheerfully sacrifice, we would insist on clinging to that 9.20 period on Monday.

Who, besides Dr. Aiken, taught religion in the second decade is difficult to pinpoint, but student memory again gives, at least, Sister Odilia, whose doctorate on the German mystics as well as the government ban on the teaching of German during World War I plummeted her from her flourishing German Department into teaching freshman religion. She used *Manual of Christian Doctrine* by a Seminary Professor, "revised in accordance with the code of 1918," Philadelphia, 1919. This was from the Christian Brothers' religion course and was the 36th edition with a preface (presumably to the first edition) dated 1902. Sister

Odelia was determined to be on firm ground, while she continually petitioned the administration to be replaced "by a priest."

That petition was finally answered with the advent of the Rev. John M. Cooper, Ph.D., S.T.D.[182] in 1923 with his new series of textbooks for college classes, more appropriate for the post-war students of the 1920's and 1930's.

The Second Twenty Years

Dr. Cooper was the founder of the department of religious education at the Catholic University and an ardent anthropologist who later became full professor of that subject. The course descriptions in the catalogue for 1924–25, though headed by the time honored introductory statement, followed the content of Dr. Cooper's *Religion Outlines for Colleges*. This form for religion offerings with changes only in course numbers continued in the catalogues until 1937. Because of its historic value as an example of change of emphasis to suit the times, it is given here in full from the 1934–1935 catalogue (p. 77).

101. Motives of Catholic Life.
The dogmas of faith supply the dynamic for living the ideal of Catholic life. Study of Christ, our great Model, as exemplified in the Gospels.
Prescribed for Freshmen. *One semester, two hours weekly.*

126. Means of Catholic Life.
Prayer and the sacraments, the sources of grace and the aids to live the Catholic ideal of life.
Prescribed for Sophomores. *One semester, two hours weekly.*

151. Ideals of Catholic Life. Love of God and of neighbor as summing up the Catholic ideal of life. Human needs, charity, and the works of mercy. Human rights, justice, and the commandments.
Prescribed for Juniors. *One semester, two hours weekly.*

176. Life Problems.
A discussion of the bearing of Catholic truths and ideals upon the more important aspects of spiritual development, marriage and the home, life-tasks, and leisure-time activities.
Prescribed for Seniors. *One semester, two hours weekly.*

That Doctor Cooper was a revered and well-liked teacher is evidenced by student appraisal as well as teasing that appears in campus publications and by alumnae reminiscences. An example from the 1929 *Trinilogue* is typical.

182. Cf. Catholic University Rector's reports 1924–1926 and *Catholic University Bulletin*, April 1926, p. 24; January 1927, p. 2. Also *Trinity College Alumnae Journal*, Autumn, 1941. Obituary, *Alumnae Journal*, Summer, 1949, pp. 118–119.

> Easy-going—charitable—just. Broadminded—diplomatic—sincere. A renowned author—a well-liked—respected teacher. His experiences interesting—his anecdotes diverting. Pleasant—obliging—sympathetic—refined.
>
> We shall remember especially his attractive personality—his never-failing good humor—his love of life—his interest in his students—in his North American Indians—in all humanity.

He continued teaching at Trinity until 1941 when he resigned to give full time to anthropology.

Others who taught with Dr. Cooper in Trinity's religion department were Dom Benedict Brosnahan, O.S.B. (1926–1943), Dr. Maurice Sheehy (1930–1942, Dr. William Russell (1934–1943). The scripture courses also continued until the mid-1930's with Sister Marie Louis Hummel until 1927 and Dom Benedict until 1937. Scripture was again prescribed for freshmen in the transition program 1943 to 1948 when it was incorporated into the theology sequence. It reappeared as a major emphasis of the program of the 1960's. Liturgy as a separate course emerged in 1929 and continued to 1943. It was supplemented by liturgical singing.[183]

The first indications of change in the long established religion sequence of Dr. Cooper came with the advent on the faculty of Dr. William Russell, a student of Dr. Cooper and nephew of Dr. Kerby who had succeeded his uncle as students' chaplain. In 1937, Dr. William Russell wrote a new introduction to the departmental offerings showing the continuity of aim with a change in emphasis from a "solid religious formation" to supplying "motivation, incentive and guidance" toward love of God and neighbor.

> The courses in Religion form an organic part of the College curriculum. In fact they aim to unify and to integrate under one goal all the subjects which the student pursues. The motive dominating the entire four years is that which was laid down by Christ Himself, namely, the doing of those things which please God. The will of God is that the student should love God and love her neighbor. That is the essence of Catholic life. Emphasis, therefore, is placed on *giving* rather than on mere learning. The ideal contribution which Trinity students are asked to make to American life is a cultured and supernaturalized personality which flowers in love of God and neighbor.[184]

The basic text was Dr. Russell's own *Christ the Leader*, supplemented by some of the Cooper series.

183. Cf. Music Department section of this chapter.
184. 1937–1938 catalogue, p. 78. Unchanged until 1944. Dr. Russell also wrote a small booklet on the Trinity College religion program which was printed and circulated circa 1940, but the author has not been able to locate an extant copy. A 1937 letter to Charles M. O'Hara, S.J. from Sister Berchmans Julia, President, says that "Dr. Russell is experimenting now."

The Third Twenty Years

When Dr. Russell resigned in 1943, there began what now appears as a transition period lasting until 1948 with no introductory statement in the catalogue. For one year (1943–1944) Sister Ann Francis Hoey taught freshmen the *Life of Christ*, with Dom Benedict Brosnahan, Dr. Edward Dowd, and Dr. Gerald A. Ryan teaching the sophomores and juniors and Dr. Eugene M. Burke, C.S.P. pioneering his senior course: theology of the new testament. Others who taught in the department during those years were Dr. Joseph Supple, O.M.I., Dr. John F. Carvlin, C.S.P., Dr. Raymond Hunt, O.M.I., and Sister Carmelita Fennell.[185]

When Father Louis Ryan, O.P., began his "Introduction to Theology" for the freshmen in September 1947, the second step in transition from "Religion" to "Theology" was taken. The catalogue of 1948–1949 first used the departmental title *Theology*. Father Ryan was joined by two other Dominicans, Fathers Robert Conway and John B. Mulgrew. These three worked with Father Eugene Burke on a four-year theology course, based on the *Summa Theologica* of St. Thomas Aquinas supplemented by contemporary works in the Thomistic tradition. This course formed part of the core of the Trinity College curriculum for fifteen years (1948–1963).[186] The introductory statement (quoted here from the 1956–1957 catalogue, p. 74) gives the "theo-centric" rationale of the department during those years.

> The purpose of the department of Theology is the presentation of a thorough, organized knowledge of the Catholic religion. The general principle of organization is theocentric, that is, centered on God. God is the principal subject of Theology, first, as He is in Himself, then, as He is the origin of all things and their ultimate destiny. This destiny in God is achieved by man through the Way which is Christ. This theocentric principle of Christian theology determines the material organization of the courses.
>
> However this synthesis of knowledge is not achieved by reason alone nor by faith alone, but by a combination of faith and reason. Theology is faith seeking understanding through reason. Thus the documents of faith, the holy Scriptures, the authoritative definitions of the Church and the teachings of the Fathers and Doctors are studied as the positive sources of Theology. Nevertheless the work of reason is not neglected in the penetration and understanding of the significance of these sources. The framework of reference is determined according to the threefold function of Theology: first, to defend (apologetic), second, to explain (explication) and finally to

185. It should be noted that the Paulists, Oblates, and later the Dominicans, like the Sisters of Notre Dame, were seldom called "Doctor." They preferred the title "Father" or "Sister" even when the necessary initials followed their names.
186. Cf. "Theology at Trinity," Eugene M. Burke, C.S.P., S.T.D., *Alumnae Journal*, Spring, 1950, pp. 106–108.

> draw conclusions (scientific). Therefore, the curriculum follows the theocentric organization and the reasoning method of the *Summa Theologiae* of St. Thomas Aquinas.
>
> Nevertheless, while the department of Theology stresses these objective principles, it is by no means unmindful of the adaptations that must be made in the interests of the students, who are not preparing to be professional theologians, but Catholic laywomen pursuing liberal arts studies at the undergraduate level. The aim is an understanding of the Catholic religion by the student at the same intellectual and scholastic level as the other courses of the curriculum. For this reason, the special problems of contemporary life receive special emphasis.

Other Dominicans who helped develop the "theologians" of the fifties and early sixties were Fathers Urban Voll, Lewis A. Springman, Cornelius Thomas Kane, Thomas Heath, Justin Hennessey, Leo Duprey and others whose names may be found in the catalogues and in the memories of students of the time.

The Fourth Twenty Years

The year 1963–1964 was another transition year, transition to the "scriptural approach." Father Burke continued teaching the seniors with three Sisters of Notre Dame, Sister Anne (Mary Louise Norpel), Sister Mary Eileen Paul, and Sister Charles Mary (Sarah Fahy) for the other classes. Though no introductory statement appeared in the catalogue from 1964 to 1975, the course descriptions indicate an emphasis on "election, encounter and response." Electives, "Readings in Theology" and "Theology of Dialogue" were introduced. In 1967–1968 the introductory statement was incorporated in the general statement on curriculum.[187] That year, too, an enlarged theology program included not only Catholic doctrine with "post Vatican II" trends but courses in ecumenism and in modern Jewish thought. A major in theology was announced; Sister Mary Louise Norpel (Sr. Anne) returned after a leave of absence in which she completed the work for the Ph.D.; Mr. Edward Foye was chairman and Father Eugene Burke taught his last Trinity classes.

When the reorganized catalogue of 1975–1976 re-instated departmental introductory statements, that for theology again reflected contemporary thought. It continued essentially unchanged through the rest of the decade.[188]

> Because Trinity is a Catholic college, theology is essential to its identity and curriculum. The department's main purpose is to provide students with an

187. Catalogue 1967–1968, p. 11.
188. Quoted here from 1978–1979, pp. 106–107.

> intellectual appreciation of the Christian tradition and way of life. To achieve this end, courses have been constructed to introduce students to the various methodologies used in theological studies and to the major areas of the discipline: scriptural, historical, systematic. In addition to developing ability for critical thinking and effective expression within the theological discipline, the department is also concerned with making clear to students the interrelatedness of theology with the other liberal arts.
>
> Courses offered as part of the General Program are in the 100–200 level.
>
> Students who are interested in graduate work in religious studies are advised to take a minor concentration in theology with a major in a related field. e.g. history, literature, philosophy, psychology, sociology.

In the years since 1964 those who taught in the department, in addition to Sister Mary Louise Norpel (1963–1978)[189] were Edward J. Foye (1964–1968), Sister Kathleen Murray (1968–1971), Sister Joan Gormley (1971–), Emil Piscitelli (1967–1971), Rabbi Bernard Mehlman (1968–1975) and other lecturers (or adjuncts) whose names can be found in the relevant catalogues and in the memories of their students.

Discussion of the influence of the students' chaplains, what is now called "campus ministry," is deferred to Chapter 6, Student Activities.

Fine Arts: Music and Art

Though the teaching of music and art at Trinity College began in the pioneer years, it consisted chiefly of piano lessons for students who had achieved some degree of proficiency before entrance and of "studio art," both of which were offered in addition to the regular courses of study and carried no academic credit.[190] A course in the history of art carrying academic credit was introduced in February 1901 and appears in the catalogue of the next year (1901–1902). Courses in the theory of music (harmony, both elementary and advanced) first appeared in the 1923–1924 college catalogue, along with history of music and methods of teaching and supervising music in schools. Full major work in both art and music dates from 1940. The Glee Club, the Choir, and the small orchestra called the Euridyce Club were under the aegis of the music department from the early years. Of these, the Glee Club alone survives into the 1970's in the form of the Concert Choir.[191]

189. Cf. Pastoral Ministry graduate program which she initiated and directed (1973–1978).
190. In 1902–1903 Drawing or painting for special students in Art was $100.00, but for students in the regular college course the fee was $50. Twenty years later the fee was $75 for students in the regular college course. In 1902–1903 the extra fee for two piano lessons a week and use of an instrument for practice was $100.00 (equal to the full tuition charge). Twenty years later it was $150.00, though tuition had risen to $200.00.
191. Cf. Chapter 6, student activities, for clubs and recitals/concerts from 1900 to 1977.

Music Group. Commencement, 1904.

MUSIC

The first "regular music teacher," Sister Euphrasia of the Sacred Heart[192] (Anne Delany) taught at Trinity College from 1902 to 1905. Before that the annals are not clear on this subject. Sister Mary Hilda (E. McDonald) was the organist from November 1900 to July 1901, but whether she also "gave lessons" is not recorded. Early faculty members generously used their talents for the benefit of the students. Sister Ann Madeleine, the French teacher, taught singing and Sister Louise of St. Stanislaus, who came to Trinity in 1901 to teach botany, seems to also have filled in as organist during her first year. Sister Euphrasia was succeeded from 1905 to 1910 by Sister Helen Loyola (Loyola Teresa Leonard). After a hiatus, presumably filled as in 1901 by willing substitutes, Sister Josephine of the Angels (Mary Esther Smith) came in 1912 to rule vigorously in the music rooms at the end of South Hall and at the organ in chapel until 1924.

The President's Report, June 7, 1916, records a musical event, the forerunner of many summer workshops and summer sessions that span the years to the late 1970's. "Last summer," (1915) the report states, "a special Summer School session was held here for the Music Teachers of our various schools throughout the country. Lessons in the best methods of piano instruction were given by Mme. Von Unschuld, the celebrated Austrian pianist, and satisfactory work was accomplished by many of the Sisters in attendance." This is the first mention of Mme. Marie Von Unschuld "the celebrated pupil of Leschititsky" [sic] who is

192. Not to be confused with Sister Mary Euphrasia Taylor.

Orchestra, 1920's.

listed in the college catalogue from 1917 to 1921 as Supervisor of Music. She had established her own conservatory of music in Washington to which she devoted full time in the early 1920's. From 1925–1942, "Madame" appears again in the catalogue. Her last appearance was in the 1941–1942 list which, for the first time, ranked faculty. She was ranked as Professor of Music with a D. Mus. after her name.

The President's Report, June 6, 1917, announces a "Bulletin of Information" about the music department, giving requirements for a "Diploma with Teacher's Testimonial." This is the school music program that Mme Von Unschuld directed as "Supervisor of Music." It continued to offer opportunities to Trinity students through 1925 with courses by Helen Corbin Heinl 1922–1925, Mrs. George Cullen 1923–1924, and Dr. E. N. Barnes 1924–1925. School music and high school and normal school music were among the music offerings until the end of the decade.

After the first full entry for music in 1923–1924, consisting in the courses mentioned in the opening paragraph of this section and a page of regulations for "practical courses" especially in "pianoforte," there was little change in the offerings until the major requirements of 1941.

Recital Room, 1940's.

Sister Frances Immaculata with Howard Mitchell, Director, National Symphony Orchestra.

Concert Choir, 1970's.

One significant exception was liturgical music required of freshmen taught by Malton Boyce, B.Mus. (1930–1935), by Miss Helen Kuhn (1940–1943) and Sister Frances Immaculata (1936–1940; 1944–1963). After Vatican II this course was discontinued.

In 1941 the music department moved to the first floor of the newly renovated Cuvilly Hall, the old Red Rose Inn building and annex. The major courses included elementary harmony, advanced harmony and music literature, keyboard harmony, counterpoint, school music and "applied music": voice, violin, piano, and organ. A recital or joint recital was required as part of the comprehensive examination for majors. In 1951 Sister Frances Immaculata described the work of the music department in the *Alumnae Journal*.[193]

The continuity and progress of the next twenty-five years is succinctly expressed by the introduction to departmental offerings in the catalogue of 1977–1978 which include a practicum in choral administration, and internships at WGMS Radio Station and with the National Symphony Orchestra. School music is included under an interdepartmental major: Music/Education. The statement follows:

> The Music Department offers a Bachelor of Arts Degree in Applied Music and in Music Education. While most majors select piano or voice as a per-

193. Summer, 1951, pp. 144–146.

> forming area, one may also major in other instruments, such as flute, guitar, violin or organ.
>
> The aim of the music department is to train capable and qualified performers and teachers. The college attempts to achieve this end within the framework of a broad, liberal culture. It offers courses giving thorough understanding of theoretical subjects as well as practical applications through performing media.
>
> Career options in the field of music are many and varied. Opportunities are presented in performing, teaching, liturgical music, and in the public media of radio and television. Music therapy is a relatively new and quickly expanding field.
>
> The Music Department serves the entire student body through its performing organizations, such as the Concert Choir and Opera Practicum, and also through the service courses open to all students, such as Music Appreciation, Music History, and the practical skills courses in notation, harmony and ear training. Chamber music groups are arranged and offer performances on an informal basis.

Since Sister Josephine retired in 1924 the music department has been directed by Sister Marie Elinor (Mary Driscoll) 1924–1928, Sister Rose Marie (Marie Bourk) 1928–1934, Sister Frances Immaculata[194] (Gladys Harrington) 1934–1963, Sister Mary Clare (Mary Clare Mylett) 1964–1968, Peter McCarthy (1968–1972), and Dr. Sharon Schafer since 1972. Among other members of the department who will be remembered by alumnae are Dr. Jean Eichelberger Ivey, one of Trinity's first music majors and now a well known composer and Professor of Electronic Music at the Peabody Conservatory in Baltimore (1945–1953), Mrs. Lucille Tingle Masson (1943–1960), the Cordero sisters: Vivienne Cordero Conn (1943–1953) and Audrey Codero-Plitt (1943–1947), Miss Antoinette Melignani (1953–present), Sister Barbara Harkins (1956–1960).[195]

Art

The minutes of the Faculty Meeting (the Senate) February 25, 1901, state: "The course in Art [sic] to open on 26th inst. under Sr. Anne de Marie. All Teachers [are] invited to attend it." Thus began the history of art courses at Trinity. The catalogue for 1902–1903 first carries the art offering (p. 53). Four courses in the history of art were projected as well as "technical instruction in drawing and painting." Sister Florence Louise (Catherine Delaney) who had graduated from art school before becoming a Sister of Notre Dame, arrived at Trinity in February, 1902, to set up the art studio, teach history of art and act as Secretary of the College. For twenty-five years, until her retirement in 1927, she was

194. Obituary, *Alumnae Journal*, Autumn, 1973, p. 18.
195. Others for shorter periods. Their names may be found in relevant catalogues.

not only the artist *par excellence* and public relations director, but performed many of the duties that now fall to the admissions office and supervised the assignment of students' rooms. Her handsome, imposing presence, and exquisite courtesy impressed parents and eminent visitors alike.[196]

The President's Report, May 13, 1903, comments: "The course of Art lectures which has assumed systematic shape this year, is well calculated to exert a beneficent influence in our educational system. Provision has also been made for students who desire technical instruction in drawing and painting."

During the first commencement week, the O'Connor Art Collection and the building which houses[197] it were formally accepted and dedicated. Dr. Thomas Shahan gave the address at the dedication of the Gallery, May 31, 1904, "The Educational Value of the Fine Arts." During the next academic year (1904–1905) Dr. Shahan gave a course of lectures, "The History of Christian Art" in order to make use of the new gallery.

For more than twenty years, history of art classes were held in the O'Connor Art Gallery, though not exclusively there. The inner rooms of the gallery which had at first been projected as studios were never used as such. The drawing and painting studio was in a large room on second floor south (260). In the 1920's, when the main building was over-crowded, Sister Florence Louise moved the studio to her own office, which later became the Registrar's Office in the 1930's when "studio work" was not offered. As early as 1905–1906, the catalogue gives a good description of the method of class instruction in history of art. "Instruction," it states, "is given by means of lectures, illustrated by blackboard diagrams and representations, photographs, parallels of historic ornament, and lantern projections." In fact, the first slide projector on campus was for the art department.[198] The slides it projected were 4″ × 4″ hand-painted glass slides of which a collection still existed into the 1940's, though there was no extant projector to show them. The present excellent 2″ × 2″ slide collection and projector catalogued and housed in the library have an honorable history back to pioneer days.

The Dean's Report, June 1924, notes the formation of the Art Journal Club formed for the purpose of reviewing and discussing articles and

196. The students, however, as irreverent in the first quarter of the century as at any time, happily teased her. She was known in private to generations of Trinity students as "Floppy Lou," a most inappropriate nickname.

197. Trinity College Archives. Also Chapter VII of "Miles Poore O'Connor, California Philanthropist" 1823–1909 by Sister Helen Cecilia Miller, unpublished M.A. Dissertation, U. of San Francisco, 1957, and Chapter 7 of this history.

198. This excludes the stereopticon or "magic lantern" mentioned in annals of the first year, which was used as entertainment.

essays published in leading Art Journals. This club was so popular that the number of members had to be limited to fifty.[199] The Dean also announces in this report that twelve students are taking sculpture with Miss Clara Hill. She was "one of America's leading women sculptors—a pupil of Augustus St. Gaudens and for many years she conducted a studio in Florence, Italy." Miss Hill taught sculpture 1924–1927 in the small mezzanine room between first and second floor which is now used as a storeroom by the registrar's office. When she died in 1935 the Washington papers[200] called her a "famed Capital artist." "Studying first under the famous Augustus St. Gaudens, she later went to Julian Academy, where she worked under Puesch, and the Colarossi Academy, where she studied with Injabert in Paris. . . . She received the grand prize at the Seattle Exposition of 1909 and from time to time . . . other awards for her sculpture." She maintained studios in New York and Washington. Her grateful former students gave the ornamental fountain in the South Court (Seymour Court) at Trinity College in her memory.

From 1927 to 1941 studio art was not offered at Trinity, though the history of art has continued its unbroken record to the present. It was taught in the 1930's (1928–1940) by Mr. Albert Burnley Bibb,[201] 1940–1943 by Simonetta de Vries, and 1943–1978 by Ilona Deak-Ebner Ellinger with occasional assistance from others.

A full major in art, including both history of art and studio work, was established in 1940. Sister Jeanne Marie (Marie Michel) equipped the new studios in the renovated Cuvilly Hall and taught painting, design and modeling until 1945. Dr. de Vries and Sister Julia (Helen Stokes) of the Latin Department taught history of art, the latter specializing in classical sculpture and architecture. In 1943 Ilona Ellinger, M.F.A., replaced Miss De Vries, and in 1945 she took over the direction of the department teaching both history of art and studio art, though Sister Julia continued to teach the classical period until her retirement because of poor health in 1947.

Mrs. Ellinger during her first years at Trinity also continued her history of art studies at Johns Hopkins University where she received the Ph.D. degree in 1946. She taught studio work in the "Old Cuvilly" studios, in the artificially lighted rooms in the ground floor of South Hall in Main, and finally (from 1960) in the new Fine Arts Wing. In 1951 she wrote in the *Alumnae Journal*[202]

199. It must have been short-lived, however, because it is not mentioned later.
200. Cf. Obit., *Washington Post*, July 8, 1935.
201. Cf. C. U. Rector's Report 1926, p. 69, as well as *Trinilogues* of the period of his teaching here.
202. Summer, 1951, pp. 147–148.

> We are not, to be sure, able to produce finished artists—the five hours available weekly for art work naturally can not give the same results as does the full-time program of an art school, equipped with professional models and installed in roomy, north-windowed studios. Nevertheless, during a four-year curriculum the student is acquainted with portrait and figure drawing, with still life, landscape and portrait painting, and with the elements of design, lettering and composition. She uses charcoal, pastel, pen and ink, watercolor, tempera and oil paints as her medium. Special attention is given to the needs of a student who is planning to make a career of her art work. If she is to become a medical illustrator, she can spend more time on anatomical drawing; or if she is interested in construction and drafting she can get a special course in mechanical drawing from Sister Aloysius Marie.

The art major established in 1940 was weighted toward studio art with a history of art balance. After a few years only, the weight was shifted to history of art, though all majors were required to take "applied art." This plan persisted into the 1960's and the new building. With the arrival of Sister Anne Elizabeth Beringer (1966–1975) and Dr. Liliana Gramberg (1967–present),[203] the departmental offerings in studio art widened to include sculpture again as well as modern design, and printmaking, etching and other courses in current demand, such as photography and photojournalism.

In the mid-1970's the department was offering two majors: history of art and fine art. The current goals of art majors are best described in the introductory statement in the 1977–1978 catalogue.[204]

> The department offers majors in history of art and fine art as well as participating in the interdepartmental French/art history major. The history of art program provides a focus, through art, for the study of man's social and cultural development. Professionally, it may lead to curatorship of public or private galleries and museums; art criticism for newspapers or magazines; teaching and research after completion of a graduate degree (M.A., Ph.D.); participation in archaeological excavations or service as docent in galleries or community organizations.
>
> Within the fine art major, students take prescribed foundation courses, then develop their programs along traditional lines or with specialization in visual communication. The fine art program can serve as a foundation for subsequent study (B.F.A., M.F.A.) or, with appropriate education courses, for teaching at elementary or secondary level. A fine art major with speciali-

203. The names of other members of the department, who taught studio art for shorter periods, appear in the catalogues in the 1960's and 1970's.
204. Pp. 47–48. Cf. *Trinity News*, April, 1971. *N.B.* as this is going to press the faculty have introduced as *new* the Fine Arts major which had been approved ten years before!

zation in visual communication provides an introduction to the field for students seriously considering careers as graphic designers or photographers.

The list of courses which follows this description reflects not only some continuity with the past in the history of art courses and aesthetics, but contemporary focus as in "the American film," "United States Art," "Documentary Photography" and museum internships, and practica in visual communication.

Physical Education

In the last years of the nineteenth century when the higher education of women was still a controversial question, one strong contention was that the long hours of study would be detrimental to the health of the students. To combat this adverse criticism, the founders and faculty of Trinity College were concerned from the beginning about student physical fitness. The building (then only the South Hall wing) provided no place for exercises in common, but there was the great outdoors: the wooded campus, the surrounding area, the nearby "pretty little village" of Brookland and the wide expanse of North Capitol Street, newly cut through as far as Michigan Avenue. All students were encouraged to take daily walks and to engage in informal outdoor games. For indoors there were Indian Clubs! The dean wrote in 1902: "An effort was made to have regular hours for physical exercise, but that not being found practicable . . . Indian Clubs were given to each student and she was encouraged to use them privately.[205] Copies of the daily class schedules of students of the time show "walk" scheduled along with English and Latin and history. The health of the students appears as a vital concern in all the early dean's reports. An Athletic Association was formed by the students in 1902. The Dean reported in 1904: "The health of the students has been excellent throughout the year. Nearly all belong to the Athletic Association formed in the College. Daily exercise in the open air has been an invariable rule strictly enforced. A great need, however, has been felt during the Winter months for a gymnasium, as Tennis, Basket Ball and other outdoor sports are then suspended."

After the completion of O'Connor Hall (the central portion of the Main Building), the large room under the auditorium was used as a gymnasium. The Athletic Association not only promoted outdoor exercises, but arranged "competitive games of basket-ball and tennis during the spring months." Thus began the lively intra-mural competitions

205. Dean's report, May 14, 1902.

that flourished in the 1920's and 1930's and culminated in the intercollegiate sports competitions of the second half of the century.

The first mention of a teacher for physical exercise occurs in the President's Report of 1912. "Miss Elsie Kernan," she says, "conducted the classes in Elocution and Physical Culture, during the past year with gratifying results." There is oral evidence, from members of the Class of 1911, that Miss Kernan's teaching career at Trinity began in 1910, when they were seniors, but no documentary proof has been found. Her name appears first in the catalogue of 1912–1913, but when she retired in 1941, she had been at Trinity for 31 years.[206] The first eleven years she combined "gymnastics" with "elocution" and dramatics. In 1961, she was present to celebrate with her first students their Golden Jubilee of graduation.

From 1918 to 1921, Miss Camille Desio conducted "Physical Training" which must have been swimming using the newly opened pool, because Miss Kernan was still listed as teaching Elocution *and* Gymnastics. From 1921 Miss Kernan confined herself to Elocution and Dramatics and a series of competent young teachers[207] took over the swimming and "gymnastics," which became in 1924 "Physical Education" with a new format in the catalogue. A course in hygiene which had been in the catalogue as "required" for first-year students from 1901 to 1911 and elective until 1916, was re-introduced in 1922 and Girl Scout training courses were popular in the 1920's and 1930's. Field Hockey was introduced in the mid-1920's so that the first issue of the *Alumnae Journal* (December 1927) could report a lively intra-mural hockey tournament with 1930 leading.

The Dean's reports continued to show concern for the students' health. In 1918, Sr. Mary said: "The Swimming-Pool, Tennis Courts, and Basket-ball Campus have afforded pleasant recreation and exercise, and at the same time contributed to the good health of the students. The Swimming-Pool has been open all through the scholastic year, and has been well patronized by a large majority of enthusiastic swimmers." That swimming pool, built in 1916 at a cost of $25,000, was the result of the first "big" Alumnae drive for funds and was to be the first step toward a much needed gymnasium building. Described in the catalogues from 1917, it still serves as the one permanent physical education facility, though after sixty years it is tiredly struggling along as

206. An editorial in the April, 1935 *Trinity College Record* pays tribute to Miss Kernan's "remarkable gifts of ingenuity, discernment and discrimination, verve and vitality to engender a true appreciation of the art inherent in the drama." The Dramatic Society had honored her twenty-fifth year.

207. Their names are listed in the catalogue and a complete list of Physical Education teachers from 1911–1977 is in the Trinity College Archives.

the focus of efforts for a new modern gymnasium which should house its olympic sized successor.[208]

In 1926, the Dean reported that the college was handicapped by the "lack of equipment, especially our lack of place where indoor basket ball and tennis might be played in the winter season. However," she continued, "an effort has been made to arrange various seasonal sports and this has worked out fairly well. The students now have field hockey, tennis, basket ball, archery, swimming and such track exercises as are suitable for girls. They are also able to take lessons in horseback riding and to go out through the beautiful bridle parks of Washington attended by a riding master. One idea is to have as many lesser sports as possible so as to draw in a large number of students according to their respective abilities. From time to time the students ask to be allowed to engage in intercollegiate games, but for the present it seems best to confine ourselves to developing intra-mural athletics."

Miss Elaine Scanlon, director of Physical Education 1934–1942, enlivened and modernized the program in the 1930's, introducing modern dance as one of the activities. Her work was continued through the next decade by a series of excellent teachers[209] until the advent in 1949 of Miss Margaret Durbin, the beloved "Durb," who personified Trinity Physical Education for twenty-nine years.

In an article[210] on physical education as an integral part of the curriculum, Miss Durbin described the objectives and philosophy that governed her long administration of Trinity College Physical Education and bequeathed to the late 1970's a firmly based department. She wrote:

> There is only one true concept of physical education; it strives to develop the whole individual: *organically*; so that the human organism is able to sustain adaptive effort, which means that the body is trained to work and to recover quickly from fatigue, while carrying on routine and emergency activities of life—specifically, man performs tasks best when conserving and not wasting energy; *emotionally*, for an individual cannot follow his impulses as there are strict rules to obey, and he must also think of his fellow-players; *intellectually*, for he *must* think and plan, whether he plays in an individual, dual, or team sport, as well as render quick decisions and make judgments regarding his opponents; his capacity to anticipate accurately may decide his or his team's success or failure; *neuromuscularly*, for there must be coordination of mind and muscle, so that mind controls the action

208. The need for a gymnasium, first expressed in 1905, was listed among the needs of the college continuously from 1911. There is hope in the late 1970's that a gymnasium may be in sight at last.
209. Cf. footnote on preceding page.
210. *Alumnae Journal*, Winter, 1951, pp. 52–55.

Miss Margaret Durbin.

involved in a complicated situation without waste of energy or movement; just as the mind must work behind the wheel in the driving of a car, so too the mind has to work behind the ball for the best coordinated results.

Here at Trinity the fallacies stated earlier do not prevail; it is true the students must take physical education for two years to fulfil the requirement but they have a choice of physical education activities according to their interests, preferences and abilities, and these activities are taught in classes by trained leaders. But there are students, not having had physical education previously, who regard their course at Trinity from one of the fallacious viewpoints already mentioned, e.g., that a course in dancing will slim the hips or eliminate a bulge, as the case may be. However, it is not uncommon for that same student at the end of a course in physical education to realize that something more has been gained than what she had originally anticipated: she has learned a new skill—she has had a variety of new experiences—she has made new friends—she has now a new conception of body control and poise; all this, perhaps, without losing an ounce of weight and without regrets of any kind.

Physical education fosters development of the individual as a whole. Society demands that that individual be capable of working alone as well as part of a group. Here at Trinity we feel it essential that each student participate in a team sport in which she must make instantaneous choice in several courses of action, complicated because of restriction by rules and unexpected moves on the part of opponents. To hesitate, to make a mistake in judgment are errors that may lose the game. Repetition of such errors denotes inefficiency and will cause the player to lose prestige with her group. Team sports, therefore, improve cooperation, loyalty, sportsmanship, which are integral assets of a well-developed member of society.

Aside from team sports, every fall and spring a greater number of students sign up for the very popular game of tennis. Each girl is placed in a class with others of her playing ability and taught the techniques and theory of the sport for both singles and doubles play. We urge the girls to participate in the tennis tournaments sponsored by the Athletic Association in order to get experience which will enable them to move up to the last, and by far the most difficult, advanced classes. By the time a student reaches this level she has had much tennis instruction and is ready to be coached in the very fine points of tennis so that she will play a "winning game." It is from this last level that the varsity tennis team is chosen—a team with a record of which Trinity College can be proud for we are now holders of the very beautiful Wightman Intercollegiate Tennis Trophy.

Not only is a good physical education program concerned with the development of the whole individual, but also in preventive measures that will protect, safeguard and prolong the life of that individual. At Trinity a year ago we were shocked to learn about the large number of students who were non-swimmers, but who, nevertheless, took canoes down the Potomas River without supervision or safety measures of any kind. We have taken precaution in hand, and, commencing with the present Freshman class, every student must be able to swim in order to get her degree. Others will have to pass a swimming test before permission to take out canoes and boats will be granted them. Swimming classes are held all year long, but the winter term is by far the busiest. The American Red Cross has set up standards for swimming and we comply with these in every way. Non-swimmers are placed in Beginner classes; when they have completed all the skills in this level, they move on to the Intermediate, then to the Swimmer, and finally to the Advanced swimming classes. Every other year, we offer Senior Life Saving Courses to those who qualify to take them. We already have a large number of Life Savers at Trinity, and this year, many more students will take the courses. Several girls have requested an Instructors Course so that they can teach swimming during the summer, and we are, at present, trying to make the necessary arrangements with the Red Cross, to offer it. Last year, we started a Swimming Club, setting up very high standards for admittance to the group. The club met one night a week, and after working hard all year, presented on May Day a delightful water ballet with the story of Cinderella as its theme. It was very enthusiastically received by the spectators, and this year, because so many qualified for the group, we founded another club. There are not many schools that can claim two very active swimming clubs. Trinity can.

We also have intra-murals in hockey, basketball and softball, along with tournaments in tennis, ping-pong, badminton, and archery, all sponsored by our most active Athletic Association. The success of these tournaments is due primarily to the excellent leadership of our club president, Lola Blank,[211] and her co-workers. Not only the freshmen and sophomores participate in these activities but also the juniors and seniors, thereby proving that upperclassmen recognize their need for sports as a stimulating and necessary adjunct to study. Each year we plan our intra-mural sports and tournaments in such a manner as to satisfy the needs and wishes of the students, in addition to these, the Athletic Association sponsors varsity competition for the more advanced and skilled students in order that they may compete with outside colleges. Needless to say, such competition has definitely proved very successful in that Trinity is now well known in the District for its good sportsmanship and very fine team play; win or lose, the girls return refreshed in body and mind.

To open the season, the Athletic Association sponsors an all-out Athletic Week in October to acquaint the new students with their various activities. In May on Founders' Day their final activity of the year is a superb Field Day, starting early in the morning with games and contests; even the faculty participate in a softball game against a selected student team. This is followed by a May Festival at which the A.A. gives out the awards to those students earning the required number of points. Last year a new award, a white blazer, was given to two juniors who not only had earned over 2500 points, but also had other qualifications of outstanding leadership in the school and in physical education.

This year marks the initiation of the awarding of "tokens"—sterling silver charms to varsity team members and to winners of the various tournaments.

Best of all, our most recent addition this year has been a corps of ten cheer leaders who were selected from a large group of contestants for their performance. Captained by Betty Ann Scileppi, they have attended all our varsity games, encouraging a large cheering section which, I know, has

211. Daughter of Consuelo de Pasquale Blank '19, whose daughter, Lola Sullivan '77 was Athletic President the year Miss Durbin retired and an enthusiastic founding member of the latest activity, the Crew.

> thrilled our varsity players into playing far better games and enabling Trinity to be victorious in the Hockey Schedule. As basketball varsity play will begin soon, Betty Ann has made her plans so that our cheering section can give our very able and successful squad full cooperation, in the hope of enabling our team to end the season, as it has in the past, as District Champions.

In 1951 the department name was changed to Physical Education and Health with resident nurses and consulting physicians listed. During the next quarter century, Miss Durbin, with the help of assistants like Miss Barbara Elbery who stayed ten years, and of specialists in various activities, continued to develop and deepen the influence of exercise, athletics, and good health habits on successive generations of Trinity students. The affection and admiration of students and alumnae at her retirement dinner in 1977 were a fitting tribute to her outstanding work for the college.[212] She was active in many local and national physical education associations, served for a time as Chairman of the College Association of Coaches, was a member of the Executive Board of the D.C. Division of Girls' and Women's Sports, a life member of the National Association for Health, Physical Education and Recreation. Miss Judith Newton who succeeded her faces the future still bright with the hope of a gymnasium building at last. Meanwhile, she enthusiastically administers the Fitness Center in the former Notre Dame Auditorium as well as the varied activities of the department.

Capsule Description of Status and Accreditation

Trinity College was the first Catholic college for women founded specifically as an institution of higher education for a clientele of national scope, not evolving or developing out of a secondary school.[213] Founded at the end of the nineteenth century when women's colleges were comparatively new, the college established entrance requirements and curriculum of a high standard in order to insure the students an education of university level. Before the first degrees were conferred in 1904, the college was accreditated by the Regents of the State of New York. In 1907 and 1914, Trinity College was ranked among colleges of the first grade by the United States Commissioner of Education, a prestigious place at the time. The U.S. Bureau of Education no longer engages in accreditation nor, so far, does its successor the new Depart-

212. Cf. 1977 *Trinilogue* dedication to her and the *Trinity News* July, 1973, p. 4.
213. Several existing Catholic institutions in various parts of the United States in the late 1890's added post-graduate years to established academies to complete a college course and granted degrees under charters from their individual states before Trinity College. This explains the conflicting claims sometimes encountered.

ment of Education. In 1917, the American Association of Universities (AAU) established its list of approved colleges.[214] Trinity College was placed on that original list. In 1920, the college was included in the list, compiled by the American Council on Education, of colleges of high grade whose graduates were prepared to be accepted at European Universities. A member of the Association of Colleges and Secondary Schools of the Middle States since 1921, the college has been evaluated in 1950, 1961, 1968, 1979 and re-approved as "a good college with exciting intellectual activity and unusual morale." The Middle States Association is one of the five regional associations now responsible for accreditating in the United States. There has been a chapter of Phi Beta Kappa at Trinity College since 1971.

NOTE.—*The following letter*[215] *from the United States Commissioner of Education will answer the inquiries that have been made concerning the rank of Trinity College with the other leading institutions of the country:*

DEPARTMENT OF THE INTERIOR
BUREAU OF EDUCATION
WASHINGTON

March 30, 1914.

SISTER CATHERINE ALOYSIUS,
President of Trinity College,
Washington, D.C.

DEAR MADAM,

Doctor Samuel P. Capen, this Bureau's Specialist in Higher Education, has now completed his investigation of the standards of Trinity College and of the standing of students in this college who have entered other colleges and universities of a standard grade. It gives me pleasure to state on the basis of this examination and Dr. Capen's opinion that Trinity College should be ranked among the colleges of first grade.

Yours sincerely,

P. P. CLAXTON
Commissioner.

1914–1915 First appeared in front of catalogue—continued in each issue through 1929–1930.

214. The AAU discontinued its list in 1947.
215. President's Report to Advisory Board, May 1903. Advisory Board Dean's Report 1912 re: C.U. Affiliation and Letter of U.S. Commissioner of Education, March 1914.

1975 Commencement. l.-r. Sister Margaret Claydon, Hon. Pierce Flanigan, Sister Mary Ann Cook, Sister Ann Julia Kinnirey, Rev. Dr. Eugene M. Burke.

Graduate Programs 1904–1977

Before the first degrees were granted in 1904, the faculty were planning a graduate program. The Advisory Board at its meeting, June 1, 1904, appointed the Dean, Sister Mary (Henretty), Dr. Edward A. Pace, and Dr. Thomas J. Shahan as a committee "to study the matter of requirements" for the Master of Arts degree[216] and to report by November. That report appears in full as Appendix VI of this history. The President's Report for the academic year ending June 2, 1905, records the initiation of the program:

> The opening of the department of graduate work, and the conferring of the degree of Master of Arts mark the year under review as one of the large significance in the history of the College. The requirements and regulations for the degree were drawn up by the Committee appointed at the last meeting of the Advisory Board and, as stated in the report that has been presented this afternoon, were formally adopted by the College Faculty. I take

216. The form A.M. from the Latin was used at Trinity to designate the Master of Arts as was A.B. for the Bachelor of Arts for more than sixty years.

> pleasure in expressing my grateful appreciation of the services of the Very Rev. Dr. Shahan and the Very Rev. Dr. Pace who acted as members of that Committee. The Dean's Report, which includes some details as to the qualifications of our first graduate students and as to the nature and extent of the work undertaken and accomplished by them, will help to convey a more adequate idea of the scope, standards, and methods of the graduate department. As three of the four graduate students enrolled are members of Trinity's class of 1904, it is a satisfaction to note that the success with which they pursued studies of advanced grade reflects high credit upon the thoroughness of their undergraduate training. The degree of Master of Arts will be conferred upon two of these students and will stand in truth for advanced liberal culture, for ability to undertake scholarly research, and for tested efficiency in teaching. May Trinity's A.M. always have a content as noble, be as richly deserved and as gladly bestowed. The student to whom the degree of Bachelor of Science will be awarded deserves also high credit for excellent work of advanced grade. Her course was shaped toward the attainment of a second bachelor's degree in order that, by avoiding the necessity for writing the thesis required for all candidates for the A.M. degree, more time might be secured for actual laboratory practice. Our fourth graduate student, a Bachelor of Letters of Smith College, (Class of 1904), has been pursuing undergraduate courses leading to the A.B. degree, and has shown an earnest and intelligent appreciation of the advantages afforded by a Catholic college.[217]

The further details given by the Dean consisted in the complete report of requirements and the following paragraph:

> Three of the graduates who received the degree of Bachelor of Arts at Trinity College last June returned in September for post-graduate work. Two of them have fulfilled the requirements for the degree of Master of Arts drawn up by the Committee appointed by this Board at the last meeting. Miss Rudge, whose subjects are Latin and English, has presented a Thesis entitled "Vergil's Imitations and Imitators as Studied in His Eclogues." Miss McEnelly, whose subjects are Greek and German, has presented a Thesis on "The Name and Epithets of Odysseus." Miss Gray, wishing to specialize in Chemistry, has preferred to work for the degree of Bachelor of Science. Miss Casey, who received the degree of Bachelor of Letters at Smith College last June, has followed the Senior Year Course and will receive the degree of Bachelor of Arts.[218]

Trinity College continued to offer a master's program until 1930. Up to that time fifty master's degrees had been conferred at commencement.[219] Forty more were earned by Sisters of Notre Dame, who in

217. President's Report June 1, 1905.
218. Dean's Report, June 1, 1905. Cf. Appendix VI.
219. Cf. Printed booklet "Trinity College Degrees Conferred 1904–1925" and the catalogues 1926–1930.

those days did not appear at public functions, even commencement. The degrees were conferred privately, the records are in the Registrar's Office and copies of the dissertations (theses) are in the library.

Trinity College, though authorized from the beginning to do so, has never conferred the Ph.D. degree earned in course. In 1914 in answer to the application of a young woman, who had earned a master's degree at George Washington University, to do part of her work for a doctorate at Trinity the Advisory Board discussed the possibility of extending graduate work.[220] She wished to take major work in Gaelic under Dr. Dunn of the Catholic University and to take the two minor requirements at George Washington where she was an assistant librarian. The question for discussion was widened from the specific case by a second topic proposed by the Dean.

"From time to time our students have asked if it would be possible for them to obtain the degree of Doctor of Philosophy at Trinity. Knowing that women are debarred from the work of the Catholic University, does the Board think that provision should be made at Trinity?"[221]

The decision, which was ratified by the Board of Trustees at its Annual Meeting in October 1914, was against accepting the present applicant,[222] but for studying further the possibility of an arrangement with the Catholic University. ". . . it would be wise," the members thought, "to allow a year to consider the matter, and to confer with the Rector of the University and the Dean of the Sisters' College. A final settlement seem[ed] advisable, since the Sisters' College has been receiving applications which it cannot accept." That last clause meant that young Catholic laywomen were already seeking admission to the Catholic University through the Sisters' College which was for religious women only.

The rector of the university at that time was Dr. Thomas J. Shahan who had been a co-founder and on the faculty at Trinity 1900–1909 and who retained his deep interest in the college. The "arrangement" (which seems to have been oral since the author cannot find documents) provided for lay women in the doctoral program to study at Trinity under the direction of Catholic University professors. The degree would be conferred by the university. This agreement lasted through the 1920's until the Graduate School of Arts and Sciences was established at Catholic University and graduate lay women were

220. Advisory Board Minutes, June 10, 1914.

221. *Ibid.* It should be remembered that it was lay women who were "debarred." The first step toward education of women at the Catholic University had been made several years before when the Sisters' College was established. Cf. *The Catholic University of America 1903 to 1909*. C.U. Press, 1950, pp. 220–221. Also, Shields' *The Sisters' City* by Colman J. Barry, O.S.B.

222. The arguments pro and con were summarized in the minutes of June 10, 1914 quoted above.

admitted as students. The first four doctoral degrees granted to lay women were actually conferred at the Trinity College commencement. They were conferred in 1921, 1922, 1926, 1927 on Miriam Elizabeth Loughran[223] (T.C., A.B., 1917, M.A., 1918) in Economics, Psychology and Sociology whose dissertation was "The Historical Development of Child-Labor Legislation in the United States"; on Marie Cecelia McGrath[224] (U. Michigan 1918; A.M. U. of Pittsburgh 1920) in Psychology, Sociology and Ethics whose dissertation was "A Study of the Moral Development of Children"; on Miriam Frances Dunn (A.B. Smith College 1921, A.M. Trinity College 1922) in Psychology and Philosophy whose dissertation was "The Psychology of Reasoning"; and on Pauline Wright (Trinity College A.B. 1921, A.M. 1922) in Physiology, Psychology and History of Science whose dissertation in collaboration with others was "A Study of Anion and Cation Effects on Water Absorption by Brain Tissue."

In view of a widespread belief among those who do not know the history of the college that for the first twenty years the academic program was wholly literary, a look at the dissertation topics of those earning master's degrees in the "oughts" and "teens" might be enlightening. There were certainly topics drawn from English, classic and modern foreign literatures, but the following topics show wider interests: *The Labor Press* (1908), *Individualism in Education* (1912), *The Philosophy of Butler's Analogy* (1914), *A Comparative Study of the Economic and Social Factors in the Development of Colonial Massachusetts and Virginia* (1915), two different studies of *The Development of the Woman Suffrage Movement* (1916, 1920), *Concomitants of Amentia* (1918), *Some Anticipations of Modern Scientific Theories in Lucretius' De Rerum Natura* (1916), *Platonism in Berkeley* (1914), *The Functions of Mathematics in the Development of Insurance* (1920), *Dental Care of the Children of Washington* (1917).[225]

A second step toward co-education at the Catholic University of America affected the graduate program at Trinity College. In the late 1920's the university established its Graduate School of Arts and Sciences gathering into one separate school graduate students who had formerly studied in their separate departments. Lay women were to be admitted to the Graduate School. The first two lay women registered in the new Graduate School were Trinity College alumnae, Helen Kin-

223. Of Springfield, Massachusetts, later Mrs. Francis J. Rooney of Chicago who as Dr. Miriam Loughran Rooney was for many years an outstanding civic leader and worker for social justice. The Dean's Report, June 4, 1921, notes this first Ph.D. to a lay student of Trinity College and the public press publicized the "first lay woman to receive a Ph.D. from Catholic University."

224. Later Sister Marie McGrath, I.H.M., of the Marygrove College faculty.

225. Booklet: "Degrees Conferred, 1904–1925." Privately printed by Trinity College with an addendum with degrees to the Sisters. T.C. Archives.

nirey (A.B. Trinity College, A.M. Columbia University) and Mary Hannon (A.B., A.M. Trinity College). An agreement was worked out between Trinity College and the Catholic University whereby undergraduate women would be students of Trinity College and graduate women would be registered at the university. From 1930 to 1935 graduate lay women at Catholic University lived on the Trinity College campus in "Graduate Hall."[226] The arrangement about undergraduate and graduate women was published in the Trinity College catalogue from 1932 to 1941. It had been, however, a "gentleman's agreement" without written contract and by the decade of the 1940's was largely forgotten by the university where undergraduate women were gradually accepted, thus completing the third and final step toward a fully co-educational Pontifical University, a thing unthinkable in 1897. (*O Tempora, O Mores!*)

Trinity College re-entered the field of graduate work in the third quarter of the century with master's programs in specialized fields. The Master of Arts in Teaching,[227] the Master of Arts in Pastoral Ministry, and the Master of Business Administration. These programs became co-educational, while the undergraduate college is still a woman's college.

As mentioned in the section on the education department,[228] a Master of Arts in Teaching was developed at Trinity in the early 1960's. A summer program for Sisters of Notre Dame teaching in elementary schools was established[229] leading to a Master of Arts in Teaching. In 1966, Dr. Roland Goddu began the co-educational Master of Arts in Teaching Program focused on teaching in urban schools. It was one aspect of Trinity's continuing commitment to the community. A 1968 brochure stated: "Built on a base of strong content area resources, the Master of Arts in Teaching Program is assigned the delicate task of preparing career teachers, particularly for the inner-city. The program provides Trinity's reach to the people of the city and to difficult problems of our society." Though a few students from other cities have received pre-service training and degrees in the program, nearly all the hundreds of M.A.T. graduates of the past decade have been in-service teachers[230] in the schools of the District of Columbia and surrounding urban jurisdictions.

226. The old Red Rose Inn building which had been called Graduate Hall since 1919 (?) and was in 1940 renamed Cuvilly Hall when it housed the Music and Art Departments.
227. "Trinity: A Catalyst in an Urban Setting," Roland J. B. Goddu, *Alumnae Journal*, Summer, 1967.
228. p. 240. The four directors are listed there, as well as faculty.
229. Discontinued or combined with new M.A.T.
230. Cf. "Trinity's Unique Degree Program," *Washington Star*, July 18, 1971.

The statement from the 1977–1978 catalogue[231] serves as a summary of the ten-year development of the M.A.T. program as well as a factual description of its present status.

The Master of Arts in Teaching

In keeping with the traditions of Trinity College for quality education and community service, a co-educational Master of Arts in Teaching (MAT) Program was established in 1966. From its inception, the program has emphasized teacher-training for urban schools. Both pre-service training and advanced training for in-service teachers are offered. There are approximately 400 men and women enrolled, many of them in-service teachers from the schools of the District of Columbia and adjacent counties, who attend part-time. Courses are scheduled in the late afternoon and evening for the convenience of teachers and working students. Two six-week summer sessions are also given.

The MAT program is oriented toward the needs of practicing teachers and school personnel. Courses are designed to keep educators abreast of the latest developments and trends in curriculum, instructional methods, school organization, and utilization of personnel. Several programs are given on a cooperative basis with schools recognized for leadership in their respective fields. These afford the opportunity for on-site practicum instruction by faculty in daily contact with the real world of the schools. The program in School and Parent-Community Relations is offered in cooperation with The Home and School Institute, well known for its pioneering efforts, publications and parent-training sessions.

The program for experienced teachers requires 33 credits for the degree. Pre-service trainees pursue a program of 39 credits, including student-teaching and an accompanying seminar. All students take at least 18 credits in an area of concentration. In addition, each student completes a research-based field study together with a course in educational research and writing (total of six credits) in his or her major field. Students have the opportunity to acquire the equivalent of a minor in a second field by taking all 12 elective credits in one area. Concentrations currently offered include:

Art Education
Bilingual/Multicultural Education
Early Childhood Education:
  Curriculum and Instruction;
  Administration
Guidance and Counseling
Reading
School and Parent-Community
  Involvement
Special Education–Teaching
  the Mentally Retarded

Courses are offered to meet the certification requirements of the District of Columbia and other jurisdictions. Thus degree programs may be shaped to obtain either initial teaching certification or certification in another field, such as guidance and counseling or special education. An advanced certifi-

231. Pp. 116–117.

cate program (30 credits beyond the master's degree) is offered in educational administration and supervision.

In-service teachers interested only in a particular course or courses are welcome to register as non-degree students. Each summer the program offers for credit a number of workshop courses specially designed to meet the needs of the non-matriculating in-service teacher. The MAT program sponsors a Summer Middle School for grades five through nine, which provides additional opportunity for field-based teacher-training in the summertime.

In its brief existence, the MAT program has been the recipient of numerous grants and recognitions. In its initial years it obtained a grant from the Ford Foundation and participated in Teacher Corps and the Prospective Teacher Fellowship Program of the Educational Professional Development Act. In 1973, it received a certificate of excellence from the American Association of College for Teacher Education for its Bilingual/Multicultural Education Program. In 1974, it was the recipient of a D.C. Title I (HEA 1965) continuing education grant, administered through the Washington Consortium of Universities, for a program in parent development and community arts and crafts education. In 1976, the Office of Education awarded a National Teacher Corps Grant for an Arlington-Trinity Training Complex in bilingual-multicultural education.

The M.A.T. at Trinity is flourishing, heading into its second decade.

From 1973 to 1978 Trinity College offered Master of Arts in Pastoral Ministry. This was another way the college reached out to the needs of women. Sister Mary Louise Norpel, its initiator and director, was Chairman of the Theology Department under which the program operated. More detailed listing of requirements may be found in the catalogues for relevant years. The following excerpt from the catalogue for 1977–1978[232] gives a succinct description of the work in pastoral ministry.

Pastoral Ministry

In 1973, at a time when opportunities to prepare for a wide variety of ministries were not readily available to women in the Church, Trinity established a graduate program in pastoral ministry. Although the program was designed particularly to equip religious women for new forms of ministry, it was opened to both women and men, religious and lay. The college offered two options: a four-semester sequence leading to a Master of Arts in Pastoral Ministry, and a two-semester certificate program.[233] The first certificates were awarded in May, 1974; the first degrees, the following year.

Since the inception of this program, unique in 1973, changing attitudes toward the role of women in the Church have caused many seminaries and universities to open their full-time ministry training programs to religious and lay women. With a view to complementing, rather than duplicating, programs available elsewhere, Trinity is currently exploring programs more

232. P. 117.
233. *Ibid.*

> specifically oriented to the preparation of lay persons, especially women, for service in the Church. The original pastoral ministry program will be terminated with the graduating class of 1978.

The exploration mentioned above culminated in the Education for Parish Service for lay women in the Washington Archdiocese. Since this is not a graduate program and is in its initial stage at this writing, no further description will be given.

The third graduate program of the 1970's, the Master of Business Administration, was described fully in the 1977–1978 catalogue.[234]

> Trinity College initiated a Master of Business Administration program in January, 1977. The new MBA is offered in the spirit of Trinity's long-standing educational goals: to foster commitment, personal growth and service to society. The program is designed to enable individuals to integrate the analytical skills and theoretical knowledge of liberal arts disciplines with practical managerial and business abilities. It aims to facilitate both entrance into, and promotion within, a variety of careers in the private and public sectors.
>
> The objectives of Trinity's MBA program follow.
>
> To educate managers who can cope and set directions, who have a vision of management that is relevant to the 1970's: managing in a time of decreasing and conserving resources, budget constraints, little mobility, energy shortages; managing in a time of increased valuing of human resources; managing at a time when scientific-analytic management models are merging with human relations management; and managing with a diverse work force that challenges managers to look at value issues.
>
> To provide students with the following analytical skills and interpersonal competence skills: ability to describe oneself and to articulate one's values (self-awareness); awareness of oneself in a cultural context, including the impact of various cultural backgrounds and organizational values on women, white males and minorities; ability to analyze organizational and operational problems to determine effective solutions; ability to take fiscal, technological and human factors into account in decision making; multiple leadership styles: negotiation, collaboration, how to be directive, participative and consultative; ability to function as change agents, which implies being able to understand and facilitate a change process; ability to moderate, generate and ignore conflict; and comfort with collaboration and interdependence.
>
> **Course of Study and Degree Requirements**
>
> The minimum number of graduate credits required for the degree is 36 if the student elects to major in management. At present the M.B.A. program offers a major in management only. By 1979 Trinity hopes to offer an additional major in finance; the marketing concentration may be possible at some later date. The finance or marketing major will require 39 hours. In

234. pp. 117–118.

addition, there are 24 hours of prerequisites required at the undergraduate or graduate level.[235]

The M.B.A. is just beginning. Its progress must be left to a future historian.

Special Programs of the 1970's

In addition to the older undergraduate programs mentioned in the subject matter section of this chapter, such as Study Abroad, exchange of students with Catholic University in some departments, Work-Study Experience, and dual degrees in law and engineering,[236] the eighth decade inaugurated new ones. First among these was the Degree Completion Program[237] begun in the spring semester 1970 under the able director of Dr. Joan Kinnaird, Professor of History. It was designed to enable women whose college careers had been interrupted at an earlier date to resume their studies at Trinity College for a Bachelor of Arts degree.[238] Applicants' previous academic records were evaluated by a faculty committee to determine the transfer of credits from other liberal arts institutions. To qualify for a degree students had to fulfill Trinity degree requirements (e.g. course distribution, comprehensive examinations in the major field) and take at the college at least 32 of the 128 degree credits. Accepted candidates "moved directly into the undergraduate community." They attended classes with regular students, enjoyed the same privileges, and met the same standards. Degree completion students, however, enjoyed some flexibility in time and course load to enable them to meet family and/or career obligations. The college, through its Student Self-Help program, furnished a baby-sitting service on campus with fees arranged between the mother and student baby-sitter.

The concern of the college for the education of women extended beyond degree completion students to provide under the guidance of Mrs. Denise Loftus ('50) opportunity for adult women to begin or further their higher education in the Continuing Education program where an individual could take courses for credit or audit them, aim toward a degree or deepen her knowledge for enjoyment or career

235. Cf. 1977–1978 catalogue, pp. 118–120 for prerequisites and course requirements.
236. Cf. Catalogue 1977–1978, pp. 21–22.
237. Cf. Brochure 1970 in T.C. Archives; catalogues since 1971; "Belated Return to Academia or Who's Going to Babysit with the Children," by Georgia Knightly '72, *Alumnae Journal*, Spring, 1972, pp. 4–7.
238. This program like the graduate programs had precedent in the early years of the college. The Dean's Report, 1915, mentions an "older student," a Boston school teacher for twenty years who used her sabbatical leave to spend her senior year at Trinity and receive the A.B. in 1915.

advancement. One feature was STEP, *Saturday* Trinity Education Program, later *Sustained* Trinity Education when no longer confined to Saturdays. Lecture series and workshops for or about various careers for women[239] were a feature during the years of the seventies, following the seventy-year custom of the college to provide such services for students and alumnae.[240]

The Semester in Washington begun by the political science department in the late 1960's has become established in the 1970's. In 1974 it was described as follows:

> SEMESTER IN WASHINGTON. The College offers an opportunity for students enrolled at other colleges to spend a semester of study and field work in the nation's capital, and to do primary research in one of several vital systems of the American way of life. Students may elect up to eighteen credit hours and may select any combination of available offerings which meet their particular needs.
>
> The Semester in Washington, a co-educational program, presents the student with unique opportunities to witness at firsthand the operation of the national government; to engage in evaluative research in the evolution of government agencies and programs on the municipal level; to perform practica in economics at the Federal Reserve, Department of Agriculture, Federal Trade Commission, or Internal Revenue Bureau; or to take a private tutorial in History or American Studies using the Library of Congress as well as any of the several libraries or resource centers in Washington.[241]

A specialized degree in science, Medical Technology, also dates from this decade. It is described as the Medical Technology Fourth Year. "After three years of study at Trinity, and after passing the comprehensive requirement, students enrolled in this program will spend a fourth year (51 weeks) as part of an internship at either the Washington Hospital Center, or Fairfax Hospital, or the Oscar B. Hunter Laboratory School of Medical Technology. A comprehensive examination covering the topics studies during the internship will be administered at the place of training."[241]

The *Trinity Upward Bound Program* was founded in 1968 with the help of federal funds. It uses college and community resources to provide a preparation for college for inner-city young men and women. Academic classes and related activities are held daily in the summer and on Saturdays during the academic year. Trinity faculty members

239. For example, *Woman's Place Conference Series*, February-March 1975; *Wednesdays for Women*, October-December 1976; Mini-Courses Fall of 1974; *Try College for a Day* seminars, November 1975.
240. Dean's and President's reports and *Alumnae Journal passim*. Cf. Catalogue 1977–1978, pp. 24–25 for present information on education of adult women.
241. Catalogue 1974–1975, p. 23.

are among the TUB faculty and Trinity undergraduates have served as volunteer tutors in the program.[242]

Library

A brief history of the Trinity College Library is appropriate in this chapter on the academic program because from its beginning the library has been a valuable support to classroom work. The librarians have been, through the years, curriculum-oriented and the faculty library-oriented, so that book selection has kept progressively abreast of trends in the subjects taught in the college. Whether the library occupied two small rooms on third floor South Hall (1900–1903); a larger, well-lighted room (260) on second floor South Hall (1903–1905); two and then three spacious "apartments" in the O'Connor addition (234, 236, 238) over the front door on second floor (1905–1923); or nearly the whole of South Hall first and ground floors (1923–1963), it has been a focal point of study. The space and the collections with difficulty kept pace with the needs of the growing student body and the more varied curriculum. In 1941, when the Science Building opened, a science library was included. This was reincorporated into the main library in 1963 and the space used for additional laboratories. It was not until 1963 that at last the new library building became a reality.[243]

The history of the library has been written in many short articles by Sister Mary Patricia,[244] by Sister Helen Sheehan,[245] and the *History of the Library of Trinity College* by Sister Dorothy Beach.[246] The competence and dedication of these three women who have headed the library, have been a major factor in the continuity in policy as well as the growth and development of the collections and of technical services. As early as 1902 the President's Report mentions generous donations to the library "without which the work of the College would have been impossible." By 1903 the library "had quite outgrown the two little rooms originally assigned to it." The 7000 volumes ("nearly all reference works") were moved to a large room on second floor South Hall, and the cry for additional space began. This perennial plea of the librarian was destined to continue until the opening of the new building. Faint rumblings are again heard in the 1970's. During the early years the library was administered by members of the faculty. In 1902

242. Catalogue 1974–1975.
243. "The Big Move," *Alumnae Journal*, Spring 1963, pp. 177–180. Pictures.
244. Usually unpublished, but used by president and dean in annual reports; also in *Historical Sketch*.
245. N.B. *Alumnae Journal*, Spring, 1957. Cf. *Small College Library* by Sr. Helen, a volume which displays the wisdom gained in many years of guiding the T.C. library.
246. Unpublished Master's dissertation, Catholic University, 1951.

Library Reading Room, 1902.

Library Reading Room, 1923–1963.

One of Library Reading Rooms, 1963– .

Sister Mary Patricia (Butler)[247] arrived to teach English and take charge of the library. With her built-in book sense, she set herself to increasing the collection and to studying the then latest methods of classification. In 1905 there were over 13,000 volumes classified by the decimal system transferred during the Christmas vacation of 1905 "to apartments in the O'Connor Building which afford twice the amount of shelf room and ample space for large tables."[248] The President told the Advisory Board in 1906: "The College has engaged the services of Miss Jeannette Cooney of Washington, D.C. who received her diploma in Library Science at George Washington University" to catalogue and arrange books "according to the latest and most helpful methods." One can be sure that Sister Mary Patricia worked along with Miss Cooney and that when the job was finished there was little about the "latest and most helpful methods" that escaped her. She developed through her own in-service training into an excellent librarian whose work could be built on by the professionals who succeeded her. Both the President and the Dean mentioned the library in their reports for 1903–1904. Sister Mary (Dean) said that during the year "about five hundred valuable works on Philosophy, Literature and Science have been added to the library either by donation or by purchase. The magazine club of which all the

247. Cf. pp. 88ff.
248. President's Report May 31, 1906.

students are members has enabled us to secure some of the best periodicals in our own and in foreign languages."

Sister Georgiana (President) told the Advisory Board: "I have also the pleasure to announce the receipt of an important communication from Mrs. Alice M. Bannigan Sullivan, of Providence who offers to found a library that is to bear her name, and desires to begin at once with a collection of five hundred volumes to which additions will be made annually." The next year the Dean reported the first donation of books for the Alice Bannigan Sullivan Library of English Literature. "These seven hundred and fifty volumes," she said, "have been of invaluable assistance to all the departments of the College and especially to the students engaged in post-graduate work. Many other valuable books have been added to our collection, especially to the Latin and Greek libraries."

The description of the library in the midst of the first decade of the college is that written by Sister Mary Patricia as an appendix to the president's report and to Sister Fidelis' "History of the College," 1906.[249] It is given in full here to preserve it for future readers.

The College Library—1906

The general library occupies temporarily two large rooms in O'Connor Building. This collection and the various departmental libraries number together (April 1906) about 14000 carefully selected volumes. The library grows from year to year not only in the number of books but in the facilities afforded for methodical study and research. It is now being classified according to the decimal system, and catalogued according to the latest approved methods. In the reading-room the current numbers of the leading magazines and newspapers are kept for the use of students.

Several valuable collections of books have been presented to the College. The Father Mundy Library, numbering about a thousand volumes was acquired through the will of the Reverend John F. Mundy, scholar and priest of Cambridgeport, Mass. It consists chiefly of theological, philosophical, and historical works. Some notable volumes are the following: the complete works of St. John Chrysostom in Greek and French, the complete works of St. Gregory Nazianzen, St. Basil, St. Augustine, St. Thomas Aquinas, with valuable treatises by later theologians and philosophers. The Anna Hanson Dorsey Collection, the working library of that gentle pioneer in American Catholic literature, was presented by her daughter, Miss Ella Loraine Dorsey, of Washington, D.C. A small but interesting Celtic library was bequeathed by the late Humphrey Sullivan, of Hopkinton, Mass. One of the richest collections, and one destined to grow annually in extent and value, is The Alice Banigan Sullivan Library of English Literature. This

249. Typescript, T.C. Archives.

library was established in 1904 by Mrs. James Edmund Sullivan of Providence, R.I. More than seven hundred volumes were sent "as a beginning" and this number has since been increased to about twelve hundred.

Valuable accessions to the general library have been made through the Trinity Associate Boards of Columbus, Ohio, and Boston, Mass.; also through the Alumnae Association of Worcester, Mass. The generosity of other benefactors enriched the library with such gifts as the following:

A complete set of the Jesuit Relations and Allied Documents, Cleveland edition, 60 volumes.

The Official Records of the Union and Confederate Armies, War of the Rebellion, 126 volumes.

Library of the World's Best Literature, 31 volumes.

Hoefer's Biographie Generale, 46 volumes.

La Grande Encyclopedie, 31 volumes.

Century Dictionary, 10 volumes.

Totius Latinitatis Lexicon, Forcellini, 6 volumes.

Glossarium Mediae et Infimae Latinitatis, Cange, 6 volumes.

Thesaurus Linguae Graecae, Stepano, 9 volumes.

Bryan's Dictionary of Painters and Engravers, Revised and Illustrated, 5 volumes.

The Silva of North America, Henry Sprague Sargent, 18 volumes.

This description, and the following excerpt from the President's Report of 1911, give an idea of the widespread interest in the college and its library in the first decade of the century. At least a paragraph on the library has formed part of the "state of the college" report given at each commencement through the years into the 1970's.

At the opening of the scholastic year prospects for the library were rather gloomy. Our chief benefactress, Mrs. Sullivan of Providence, was no more, and in her the Library of English Literature she had so generously founded, lost its mainstay for the present and its hope for (the) future increase. Almighty God inspired other donors, however, and the librarian is able to report a most prosperous year. From the first of May, 1910, to the first of May, 1911, she recorded eleven hundred titles on her accession-book. Of these, 186, mainly on religion, came from a friend who desires no name to be mentioned. 175 came from Mrs. Edwin Barrett Hay, a member of the Ladies' Auxiliary Board, in memory of her husband. The books are in a handsome oaken case, also her gift, and for the present have been placed in the Social Hall. They will be known as the Edwin Barrett Hay Collection, having been thus marked on a handsome book plate. There are some valuable works on the History of Writing and Writing Materials, a subject in which Mr. Hay was greatly interested. These volumes are of special use and worth to the class in Latin Manuscripts.

> The Sisters of Notre Dame, Waltham, Mass., sent us 100 volumes, including a fine set, bound, of The American Catholic Quarterly Review, and a Hudson's Shakespeare; while our Sisters at North Capitol Street made us a Christmas gift of The Flatey Book, a fac-simile of the old manuscript, and fifteen volumes of Anglo-Saxon Classics and the Epics and Eddas of Northern Europe,—a numbered Memorial Edition.
>
> A visitor to the Commencement Exercises of 1910, the Rev. James E. Cassidy, Vicar General of Fall River, Mass., has sent us since then 16 volumes, mainly rare out-of-print books, including the four folio volumes of the only edition of Agassiz's Monumental "Contributions to the Natural History of North America."
>
> Through one of our Sisters, William T. Connelly, Esq., of Lowell, Mass., presented to the College Vols. 1 to 60 of The Catholic World, richly bound, being his own copy. Many of these volumes are now very rare.
>
> 105 volumes came from our students past and present, some spontaneous gifts, some in ready response to an appeal for certain needed works. Of these 105, thirty-five were from the Literary Society of the College; 25, including a set of Abbott's "Famous Characters of History," from Miss Edith McDonald, Class of 1911; 12 from Miss Katherine Walsh, Class of 1910, including an edition de Luxe of Lossing's History of the United States; and 12, a fine edition of Browning, from Miss Loretta Greene, once a member of the Class of 1908.

Alumnae of all decades, student clubs, and friends of the college continued this generous pattern of giving to supplement the small library budget. Though a complete list of these donors would be out of place here, three names, representing varying types of donor and gift, appear as examples. The Rev. John Butler of Cambridge, Mass., Sister Mary Patricia's brother, gave many rare books over the years, making possible Trinity's small, but valuable Rare Book Collection. Miss Marie Heide of New York repeatedly in the 1920's and 1930's, gave both money for the general collection and more than 100 books for the German Library. Dr. Arthur Deering of the English department donated his library of modern novels and plays.

Sister Mary Patricia continued to administer the library (full time after the first few years) until 1934. Her book-sense, not only in acquisition but in weeding out, produced an excellent basic collection of 39,320 volumes on which to build. She had assistants whose names did not appear in the catalogue and are therefore lost to history. She also inaugurated a system by which faculty members from departments such as English and history whose students were steady library users supervised the library in the evenings and on week-ends. This cooperative schedule made it possible to keep the library open until 9:30 p.m. with a minimal full-time staff. It continued until 1963 when the new building and a larger professional staff made a different arrangement possible. She also inaugurated in the early depression years the use of students on the "self-help program" to take charge of the reserved book desk.

Dorothy Petty, '30 (later Mrs. John B. Holden), who joined Sister Mary Patricia after graduation as assistant, is not listed in the catalogue. Nor was Miss Elizabeth Belle Tyler, an experienced professional librarian who came at the end of the 1920's to re-catalogue the whole collection using Library of Congress cards, though retaining the Dewey Decimal System. Sister Marian Timothy Walsh was the first assistant librarian to appear in the catalogue list (1931). She earned a library science degree at Catholic University and remained in the Trinity library until 1945. She returned as science librarian from 1962 until her death in 1973.

Trinity's second chief librarian, Sister Helen Sheehan, came in 1934 to replace the aging Sister Mary Patricia. She had, after receiving the A.B. from the college in 1924 and before becoming a Sister of Notre Dame, earned the Bachelor of Library Science degree at Simmons College in Boston and had several years' experience in libraries in her native Manchester, N.H. She brought to the position of Trinity College librarian youth, energy, organizing ability as well as professional training, experience, and an unlimited dedication to the ideal of a curriculum-oriented library at the service of students and faculty. With wisdom and delicacy of feeling she learned from and cared for her predecessor

Sister Helen Sheehan, Librarian, with Sister Dorothy Beach (l.) and Mary Klein (r.).

who continued to be listed in the catalogue as Consulting Librarian until 1939.

A comparison of enrollment and library statistics for the decade of the 1930's, the depression years, shows a steady, though slightly slower, growth in the library collection even in the years of lowest enrollment. In 1934 when Sister Helen arrived the enrollment had fallen to 282, the lowest since 1918 and lower than any later year to the present. The library of nearly 35,000 volumes in 1929 was not only being re-catalogued and weeded, but grew by about a thousand volumes a year to 40,367 in 1935. For the rest of the decade, Sister Helen continued the modernization of the technical services, developed a flourishing system of student library aides (helped at first by N.R.A. and later by the college financial aid program) and began the relentless quest for more space. That quest brought about the gradual occupation, in the next three decades, of the whole of the first and ground floors of South Hall until, as she said, her "grasping technique had been perfected, but there was nothing left to grasp" and a new building was imperative. Meanwhile, she led the library out of the depression decade and into "the war years" with a well-weeded, well-organized, basic collection of 46,000 volumes with, as one Catholic University professor remarked, "no trash." This had increased by the year of "the big move" (1963) to 80,000 volumes.

With an efficiently organized corps of student aides whom she ruled as a "benevolent tyrant" and, at least, two professional assistants, Sister Helen directed the library through thirty more years and three Middle States Association evaluations until her retirement in 1972. From the mid-1950's when the need for space had again become acute, she spent much time on the study of college library buildings. A first plan which never passed the preliminary stage was developed. It included a fine arts center to house the music and art departments. "All our present requirements and our probable future needs," she wrote, "were organized into a preliminary program which was given to our architects, and which they transferred to what looks, on paper, like the ideal library plan for Trinity."[250] The combination idea was, however, rejected. A fine arts wing was added to the Main Building and Sister Helen continued her research. The Development Office under Sister Martha Julie Keehan collected funds, the alumnae, polled by a questionnaire about building gymnasium, student center or a library, opted three to one for a new library.[251] Allard and Joutz, successors to Mur-

250. "The New Library and Fine Arts Center," by Sister Helen, S.N.D., Librarian, *Alumnae Journal*, Spring, 1957. The architects' renderings are in the Trinity College Archives. The architects were Murphy and Locraft of Washington.

251. Showing the importance of the library in the minds of sixty years of Trinity students.

phy and Locraft, planned a simple, functional building. Mr. Francis Friel of Philadelphia, an internationally known civil engineer member of the Trinity Lay Board of Trustees, obtained the services of his friend John McShain to build at cost and himself supervised construction every step of the way. Ground was broken October 28, 1961; the date stone laid on Cap and Gown Sunday, 1962; and the building formally dedicated May 31, 1963 with Dr. Louis B. Wright, Director of the Folger Shakespeare Library, as principal speaker. The continuity of the new building with the early days was symbolized, as Ellen Ganey wrote, ". . . on the morning of 'The Big Move' when teachers and students carried the now famous 80,000 volumes from the hallowed shelves of South Main to the new Library, there appeared at Notre Dame Chapel a slight young man asking to offer Mass in the customary fashion of Trinity priest-relatives. He was Father Richard Butler, grandnephew of Sister Mary Patricia, our first incomparable librarian."[252] Sister Helen enjoyed nine years in the building she worked hard to obtain. In 1979, through the efforts of the Board of Trustees, alumnae, many friends professional and personal, under the charming (clever), competent leadership of Sister Dorothy Beach, Sister Helen was honored at a ceremony celebrating her contributions to the Trinity College Library. The building was re-dedicated "The Sister Helen B. Sheehan Library" and a gift of money for books from the alumnae was presented by Mary Hampe Muir '47, one of her devoted former student aides.

Sister Dorothy Beach,[253] A.B., M.A., M.L.S., brought to the position of Librarian broad knowledge and twenty-two years valuable experience as chief assistant to the librarian and as well as reference librarian. At the beginning of her association with the Trinity library, she wrote its fifty-year history as her dissertation for the Master of Library Science degree.[254] During the years since then she has familiarized herself with all aspects of library administration including modern technical developments, and has judiciously selected competent professionals to assist in specialized fields which can no longer, in the late twentieth century, be a *detailed* part of the librarian's own work. Sister Dorothy became in 1972 the librarian of a collection of 127,921 volumes. In seven years this number had grown to 150,127. She has shown herself not only a proficient, competent, highly literate administrator, but an educator in the tradition of her predecessors deeply concerned with the role of the library in the educational program of the college.

252. *Alumnae Journal*, Spring, 1963, p. 177.
253. Formerly known as Sister Francis Mary.
254. "The History of the Library of Trinity College," unpublished dissertation, Catholic University of America, 1951.

Sister Helen Sheehan in the 1970's.

Sister Dorothy Beach, Trinity's third Librarian.

Among the professional assistants in the library in the years since 1940 are Elizabeth O'Connor, 1940–1946; Mary Catharine McCarthy, 1946–1948; Sister Dorothy Beach (formerly Sister Francis Mary), Assistant to the Librarian 1950–1972 when she succeeded Sister Helen as Librarian; Mary Klein, 1953–1965, reference librarian; Mary Feldman, 1964–1972, technical services; Sister Mary Elizabeth McNally, 1967–1977, order librarian; Clare Ruppert, 1968–1977, curriculum librarian for the M.A.T.; Vivian Templin, 1965–1980, readers services; Sister Doris Gruber, 1972 to present, periodicals librarian; Sister Therese Gaudreau, Acquisitions Librarian, 1975– ; Karen Leider, 1976 to present, cataloguer; Sister Therese J. Remy, 1979–1980, media specialist. The names of others who assisted in the library for short periods may be found in the catalogue for relevant years.

As the college approaches the end of its eighth decade it still has a curriculum oriented library organized to meet the standards of the late twentieth century with a capable librarian planning for future development as well as for present needs.

CHAPTER SIX

Student Life

THE PIONEER students of the Class of 1904 entered college as freshmen in the first week of November, 1900. The events of the first four years are described briefly in an earlier chapter.[1] The pattern of widespread geographic distribution appeared in that first student body. The twenty-two students came from twelve states (Connecticut, Iowa, Kansas, Massachusetts, Missouri, Montana, New York, Ohio, Pennsylvania, South Dakota, Utah, Wisconsin) with two from Washington, D.C. Two were older women registered as "hearers," who presaged in rudimentary form the continuing education of the 1970's. Student life on the Trinity campus as it has developed from the first impetus of the pioneer students (the classes of 1904, 1905, 1906, 1907) and deans (Sister Josephine Ignatius and Sister Mary), will be the subject of this chapter. Chapter 3 has given a vivid, at times first-hand, account of the years to 1904. This chapter will trace student life as it evolved, developed, changed, and reflected contemporary life during eight decades.

The members of that first class that gathered from such widely separated areas of the country were "liberated women" of their time by the very fact of qualifying for and entering college. They enthusiastically embraced their role of pioneers. They studied hard, began student clubs and other activities, set patterns and standards for classes that followed. They chose red for their class color and happily led the student body as "top class" while one more class was added each year until they had been the first sophomores, the first juniors, the first seniors, bequeathing their class color to the incoming class of 1908. On the afternoon of their degree day, June 4, 1904, they formed the Trinity College Alumnae Association whose line they led until their 65th reunion in 1969.[2]

1. Chapter 3, "Pioneer Years, 1900–1904," pp. 65–82.
2. As of this writing one of the original students, Marie Rotterman, is still living though she is very feeble and lives in a hospital in Dayton, Ohio. Another of those who registered in 1900, but did not remain to graduate, Jessie Johnston Fretz, is still a loyal Trinity supporter in Oregon. She is vigorously anticipating her 100th birthday. Both were present at Trinity for their 65th reunion.

To the Trinity women of the first decade of the century under the first two deans, Sister Josephine Ignatius (1900–1903) and Sister Mary (1903–1921) the college owes the firm foundations of the student life that has weathered the years. From that time date the Glee Club; Dramatics; the Athletic Association (1902); The Literary Society, Le Cercle Français 1906, a Current Events Club, the Christ Child Society, working for the poor; *The Trinity College Record* begun by the last of the pioneer classes (1907), published quarterly for sixty years (1907–1967) and revived in the late 1970's; the friendly helpfulness of sister classes; the class colors which have formed subtle ties between generations of alumnae; the long struggle for student self-government which was at last achieved by 1913, the tenth Trinity class; Founders' Day called May Day, with games, pageants, the Maypole, strawberry supper, and May Procession; the Baby Party; Halloween parties and "sings"; the Trinity Tea when the whole college was "at home" to friends; the Senior Serenade on the evening of the last examination; the interest in presidential elections and the opportunity for each student some time during her college career to attend an Inauguration, beginning with McKinley's second, March 4, 1901[3]; the development of the college spirit that has kept thousands of alumnae close to their Alma Mater through the fast changing twentieth century world.

The quality of student life in each era has been strongly influenced by the deans. Alumnae will identify with their own Dean of Students. As has been mentioned earlier the first two deans supervised both the academic program and the other activities of student life.[4] Sister Mary (Henretty), dean from 1903 to 1921, knew each student well and took individual interest in the studies, conduct, aspirations, life work, and families of all students who attended Trinity through its first two decades. She embodied the concept of "The Dean"—respected, loved, caricatured, sung to, remembered as "Sister Mary, Dean." No member of the twenty classes who knew her had any idea that she had a family name (Henretty). Because it was not customary at that time for sisters of Notre Dame to have pictures taken, the only extant pictures are "pirated" snapshots, taken by students or young alumnae[5] and treasured for years. One such, enlarged and framed, was given to the college by Margaret Salloway '09, dean of Boston Teachers' College, nearly fifty years after graduation.

After studying the entrance requirements, the extremely heavy academic schedule required of all students of those years, and the later

3. Cf. *Trinity Newsletter*, Jan. 1961, "Inauguration Tradition Dates from McKinley," and Dean's Notebook 1901.
4. Cf. pp. 96–101.
5. There must have been passport pictures for that trip to England and Belgium and perhaps others, but the author has not found them.

accomplishments of early alumnae, one might expect that the first decade's students would be a solemn lot. A description by one of them, Lillian Callahan 1908, gives a different picture.[6] "The contemporary college student," she wrote,

> is not a sharp-featured, spectacled, ink-spotted, quoter of Aeschylus or other interesting ancients, but rather she is a bright, lively young person, who flits about here, there, and everywhere, seemingly an almost positive contradiction of the well-known axiom that a body can not occupy more than one place at the same time. Her dress is made according to good taste and the latest fashion, and she is much more apt to be heard quoting the report of a recent foot-ball game than any more remote piece of intelligence.
>
> But she is clever, this college girl of to-day, if she be at all typical. Her accomplishments are as varied and useful as her character is many-sided. She can scribble off a class song at a moment's notice. She can direct the decoration of the "gym" for any occasion with such skill and good taste as to call forth the most admiring "Ohs" and "Ahs" from her co-workers on the committee. She can make the most delicious of rarebits, play basketball, or write a French play with almost the same satisfactory results. And it must not be supposed that her acquirements along more practical lines have hindered the intellectual development of the modern girl. On the contrary, every teacher will admit that the best-prepared student is the one who is quick and versatile, able to set about any sort of work with ease, and with the probability of successfully accomplishing it.

She is "mentally healthier, because she is more natural. She is keen, broad-minded, and splendid (sic!); wide awake, eager to learn, and quick to see, with manifold interests and varied enjoyments." Lest we turn away from a prejudiced account, the author continues.

> Of course she has her faults, the college girl of to-day, to make her more human. They are mostly the defects of her qualities. Sometimes her mind is too broad, and lacks real depth. Sometimes she has so many interests, that when she tries to do justice to them all, a scattering of energies and lack of concentration ensues. Sometimes, alas, what might have been wit or cleverness degenerates into mere flippancy, and this is above all to be deplored. Occasionally academic work suffers at the hands of a girl who craves a reputation for showier talents. But the well-balanced, responsible student has sense enough to realize that a just proportion should be observed always, and she acts accordingly.[7]

During that first decade of the century higher education for women was no longer a "curiosity," so that our Trinity author could state:

6. "The Evolution of the College Girl," *Trinity College Record*, June, 1908, pp. 3–6. Cf. Sister Wilfred's description of the pioneers of 1904, pp. 66–69. See also MS magazine *Woman*, March 25, 1902, article about student life by Marie Rottermann.
7. *Ibid* p. 4.

> Today[8] the college woman stands before the world as worthy to be honored. She has been tried, and has not been found wanting. Her day as an experiment has passed; she is tacitly recognized as a success. Now it is not alone a few daring ones who receive the benefits of a college education; it is becoming more and more the rule, rather than the exception for the high-school girl graduate of sufficient intelligence and means to take a course in a more advanced institution. Not only those who are preparing to teach or to do some sort of professional work, but any one who wishes to broaden her views, to develop her individuality and adaptability, will find opportunity in the modern college.

The advantage of the wide geographical distribution of students' origins characteristic of Trinity College is brought out well by this perceptive senior of 1908.

> And so it is that girls come together from all parts of the country—the staid, conservative Bostonian, and the breezy maiden from the far West, the easy-going Southern girl, and the vivacious Canadian. They live together, study together, play together, gossip together. For four years they form a little world all their own. They exchange views on every imaginable subject, from the deepest religions questions to the ideal husband, and the latest styles of hair-dressing. They experience, all of them, some disappointments and failures, as well as triumphs and pleasures. Their sympathies are widened; their views become broader. The Eastern girl discovers that Boston, even including its suburbs, does not encompass the universe, nor the more important part of it. The Western girl begins to have an increasing respect for conventionalities, and to realize that many things that may be done with impunity at home in the West, are not always strictly proper for a young lady in more conservative regions. The maiden from the sunny South adds enthusiasm to her many charms, and the Canadian becomes somewhat more subdued, without losing one bit of her vivacity or interest. And every girl after four years of life with a hundred or more others of various types and dispositions, after having passed through the vicissitudes of college experience, the dark side and the brighter side, must have developed to a greater or less extent unselfishness, consideration for others, and adaptability to circumstances.[9]

Another student of the period expresses the need of true "college spirit," "all that is best and highest in college life." This spirit, she wrote,[10] "is not only the outward manifestation of loyalty and enthusiasm, but it is the character-development of true and noble women." The author isolates five elements of this spirit which should permeate a healthy, active student life. She placed first "student-body government" under which students could develop their "sense of responsibil-

8. 1908.
9. "Evolution of the College Girl," *Record*, June 1908, p. 5.
10. "The Making of College Spirit," Beatrice Gavagan, 1908. *Trinity College Record*, June 1908, pp. 17–20.

ity" under a "code of honor" and "rule of conduct" directed toward the "general good" and be the "regulating medium between faculty and students."[11] The other elements of college spirit were:

2. a respect for authority which did not exclude *just* criticism (not "promiscuous criticism") but developed a "mutually accepted standard of justice";
3. interest in college activities ("Nothing is so detrimental to growth as indifference . . . better be among dissenters than remain absolutely uninterested");
4. college publications ("The *Record* has done more than anything to arouse and strengthen interest");
5. athletics, with its rivalry and competition, which "brings the whole college together for a common purpose." "Assemblies of this sort (the spring track meet) necessitate individual effacement and so create a spirit of democracy."

Finally, Miss Gavagan of 1908, in summing up, gives to the student of the eighth decade a demonstration not only of her own "sense of responsibility," but a hint of the difficulties of her contemporaries in laying the foundation which has undergirded student life since.

> College spirit is not only concerned with general activities, but also influences our daily life and mode of conduct. Our every action reflects for or against the college. We can not all win laurels or accomplish great feats, but we can do even more by showing individual good will. The true and loyal spirit of the whole student body can accomplish more than the great successes of a few. More necessary and more valuable than the amount of work that each one contributes is the added strength and support of cooperation. Dissension and discord impede progress, and this condition prevents our own development. In giving support and loyalty to our college we are aiding in the building of an institution which must necessarily become a part of ourselves. The greater and more perfect this institution grows, the more cause we have to be proud of our share in it. So the student body—composed of every student—must consider it a stringent duty to further the development of a strong and loyal spirit for the honor of the college.

It is not necessary to depend on later reminiscence or on conjecture in describing student life of even the very earliest years. There are contemporary student accounts extant in the two issues of the manuscript magazine, *The Woman*,[12] for March and May 1902, as well as in its successor, the already quoted *Trinity College Record* which published from

11. Full student participation in self-government did not materialize until several years later. Cf. section on S.G.
12. Its very title is significant. Cf. Dean's Report, June 1, 1904, p. 3.

its beginning in 1907 until the 1920's a section on College events called "The Chronicle" or "Under the Red Roof."

The Dean's Report of June 1, 1903 rather staidly summarizes the year's activities for the Advisory Board:

> The students have enjoyed during the past year a wholesome amount of social life. The Cecilian Society gave a Musicale on the feast of their Patroness. The Dramatic Society presented a very amusing play on Washington's Birthday, and the classes gave several afternoon "Teas" to which their friends were invited. Besides this, they enjoyed the privilege of attending a concert given by Madam Nordica, a Sacred Concert given by the Washington Choral Society, and a lecture by Hon. Bourke Corcoran.[13]

Student descriptions from the first decade are more detailed.

Generous quotations from Marie Rottermann's[14] lively descriptions in the March 25, 1902 issue of *The Woman* will show the seeds of continuity in student life in the context of turn of the century mores and style of writing. Her account is illustrated with snapshots. She wrote

> O those first days of strangeness and loneliness in the winter of nineteen-hundred! Their pleasures and pains only those can tell who will ever stand as Trinity's pioneers. Full well I remember those unfinished halls, those uneven floors, those paneless doors, those wood-shavings, that sawdust and over all the incessant noise of the inexorable hammer!

This gradually settled down, though the process was disconcerting at times as Marie recounts. Students and their furniture had to take refuge in corridors while floors were shellacked and polished. For example, "Confident that she may now rest secure (one) patient miss for the third time arranges her room in all neatness, when to her unbounded consternation, upon revisiting her apartment, she finds furniture dislodged and floors disordered, for the men have been putting up the molding!" By 1902, "all this has changed, and life at Trinity has assumed a more cheerful aspect."

> . . . One would not need to live long among the students to see that there is an amount of deep and earnest study. The class hours attest this. The lessons alotted (sic) for preparation are far from being short or easy, and any pretence even of knowing them, must be the result of real work. And then the girls must be given credit for an extension of general knowledge and culture, which may not indeed be the means of raising their class standing, but will surely make them the greater factors intellectually and socially in future life.

13. Dean's Report, June 1, 1903: Sister Mary Josephine's last.
14. One of the original students who entered Trinity in November, 1900. Cf. Sister Wilfred's (Elsie Parsons '04) ten year reminiscence, pp. 66–69.

> . . . the fact that in our days of books, books, books, the seeker for truth finds it just as easy to get knowledge first-hand without at the same time supplying the teacher with extra work . . . the student of Trinity has extraordinary advantages, for besides a very good collection of volumes within the walls of the college, she enjoys the benefit of the Congressional Library, one which might prove cause for envy to many not so fortunate. Nor is this mere theorizing, for the girls do avail themselves of these opportunities, and their class acquaintance with Cicero, Sophocles, Shakespeare, Goethe, Lamartine and the like is supplemented by work which will be of equal value to them when college days have come to an end.

After a section on Trinity as a Catholic college which will be quoted under "Campus Ministry," Marie comes to social life. Though this might be amusing or quaint to the student of the 1970's, it is typical college life of the era and shows that Trinity students were "with it" from the beginning.

They were also creatively active in providing entertainment for each other with parties, singing, dramatics, athletics among themselves when no visitors were present. The teas which are frequently mentioned in accounts of the first decade were accepted, popular social events of the time. Miss Rottermann continued:

> Of a want of social functions, I think no one will be found to complain, for (picture of a tea table with 4 hostesses and *young man*) the Sunday afternoon teas, and the Friday evening receptions must be ample field for each one to display her social tendencies, or her lack thereof.
>
> But there are other social affairs in the college, which though less formal, are for this very reason often more enjoyable. I refer to the gatherings around the proverbial chafing dish, the tea-kettle and the coffee pot. All hail! Where is the girl who has never indulged in such pastime. What can be merrier than a group of girls gathered around the table, where the pale alcohol flame gleams, while they eagerly watch the progress of the ingredients that are the beginning of the most delicious molasses candy? And then the lively pulling, each vying with her neighbor in giving forth in the shortest possible time that crisp substance of lightest hue. Or the stirring and beating of that most palatable concoction—fudge! Again a somewhat subdued company may be fortifying itself against the afternoon's drowsiness with a cup of first quality after dinner coffee.[15] Or a demure body sipping its tea in one or other of the rooms, while a subject of common interest is discussed. Then there is the jolly crowd regaling itself with cocoa in the intervals between a merry chorus, to the accompaniment of a piano or the tuneful mandolin. And at the conclusion of such scenes of merrymaking, not the least interesting, though not the pleasantest part of the entertainment, is that dainty domestic operation—dish-washing.

15. Dinner for many years was at noon.

Saturday mornings for more than fifty years were devoted by the students to thorough room cleaning and "the renovation of dilapidated wearing apparel." An excerpt from Marie's 1902 description of the pre-vacuum cleaner and pre- "who cares?" era is both amusing and indicative of the caliber of the pioneers.

> For a stranger visiting Trinity on a Saturday morning, what a scene would present itself. Arrayed in fitting apparel with a bounteous supply of apron, and a dusting-cap of any conceivable material those dignified damsels may be seen in postures and occupations the most varied. One is vigorously sweeping rugs, another directing the course her long brush broom shall take, while a third on her knees is scrupulously trying to extricate from intricate corners (sic) and crevices every particle of dust; while still another seems expending all her vengeance, and all her muscular energy, too, on the poor pillows that adorn her room. Then books are dislodged and subjected to the inevitable duster; every trinket and monstrosity is removed from its place, and made to undergo the same ordeal.

After the cleaning, the needle took over. Mending—"and if no other duty presses she may add a few stitches to a daintier piece of needlework, which she commenced in the hour when the Dean was gravely discussing social ethics." (snapshot of group with sewing)

During all this, "merry voices," "snatches of song," "startling announcements" sound lightheartedly through the corridors and Marie philosophizes that ". . . if a young cavalier in search of a charming, intellectual and thrifty mate could be the unseen witness of such scenes, he would make it a point to pay somewhat frequent visits to Trinity teas—and who can tell the rest? I dare not."

So much for "home-life." "Visits to the city, for a call, for shopping, for the theatre, a concert or a lecture are by no means infrequent. For all these Washington offers unusual advantages and the Trinity girl on principle seizes her opportunities." Most of these outings were daytime affairs. Thursday and Saturday matinees at the National Theatre or the Belasco of happy memory were traditionally patronized by Trinity students for many years until the advent of "late permissions."

When the student of 1902 "returns to the college after an afternoon of pleasure, she is overjoyed to find one, two or even three letters awaiting her. For though miles away, home and home friends are not forgotten, and long absence is but the prelude to a happy homecoming."

Predecessors of the radio, moving pictures, television, and blaring hi-fi's helped amuse the pioneer students, too. As early as 1901 another form of music besides piano, mandolin, and the ever present formal and informal song became popular at Trinity. Dr. Dumont, rector of the Theological College and later donor of several valuable art objects, gave to the college one of those new fangled talking machines called a phonograph or graphaphone and "sixty-four tunes." This "elegant" acquisition is mentioned frequently in the Dean's notebook and the convent annals as the center of entertainment for visitors as well as for student gatherings and the Sister's recreation.

On the visual side, a stereopticon or "magic lantern" helped to illustrate lectures on art, architecture and travel. A slide projector which showed 4″ × 4″ (sic) hand-tinted glass slides was acquired by the art department early in the decade for educational as well as recreational use.[16]

Lines of Continuity

Perhaps nothing could indicate the differences between the milieu of student life in the first and in the eighth decades of the century better than a comparison of the directions for reaching the college given in the catalogues of 1901–1902 and 1974–1975.

The college, says the first of these, "can be reached by the Brookland cars of the City and Suburban Electric Railway,[17] which pass the chief entrance to the grounds, or by the local trains of the Baltimore and Ohio Railroad which stop at University Station." There is no mention of horse drawn cabs from the station or of private carriages which also provided access to the college.

The announcement of 1974–1975 follows:

APPROACHES TO TRINITY COLLEGE

By Air:

National Airport—20 minutes by cab or limousine.
Dulles Airport—60 minutes by cab or limousine.

By Train:

Union Station—15 minutes by cab.

By Car:

From the North

The easiest approach to Trinity from the north is to take the Baltimore-Washington Parkway to the South Dakota Avenue turnoff and proceed to Monroe Street. Turn left at Monroe and continue straight to Michigan Avenue and then turn left again. Trinity will be just beyond the second traffic light on the left . . . or . . . Take the Baltimore-Washington Park-

16. For further glimpses of student life in the '00's see Kuntz, Frank, *Undergraduate Days* (1904–1908), Catholic U. Press, 1959 and a review of it by Marguerite Pace Corcoran '11 in *Alumnae Journal*, Winter '59, pp. 99–101.
17. The trolley line had been extended via North Capitol Street and Michigan Avenue to Brookland in January, 1900 a few months before the college opened.

way to New York Avenue and turn right onto North Capitol Street; proceed to Michigan Avenue and turn right. Trinity will be beyond the first light on the right.

From the South

Continue on Route 95 to the Potomac River. Take Alternate Route 1 to North Capitol Street and turn left onto North Capitol. Turn right onto Michigan Avenue. Trinity will be beyond the first traffic light on the right.

There is no mention of the Brookland bus, which replaced the trolleys in 1959 and still passes "the chief entrance to the college," possibly because the directions were chiefly for those coming from a distance and not just from "downtown." In the late 1970's the Brookland stop on the Metro subway[18] occupies the site of the "University Station," mentioned above.

The Brookland trolley car, memorialized in verse or essay by Trinity students through the years, with its successor, the bus, serves as a transition from the differences between early and contemporary student life and the lines of continuity that unite them.

There are many such lines of continuity linking the late twentieth century students with their predecessors of the early years. First, the Main Building itself, built in phases through the years 1899–1909, which has "seen it all" and remains the core of the developed campus, stands as a symbol of continuity. Less solid but a no less important link is student dependence on the telephone.[19] Other unbroken links can be found in a strong academic program demanding student effort[20]; an interest in woman's widening place in the world; guidance and counseling, not so called until c. 1940, which has reached individuals since the Dean's first visits to students' rooms for discussion of their studies in November, 1900; the search for and, in most cases, attainment of maturity[21]; the ten-years of work toward and the achievement of student self-government; the tendency to protest, dating also from 1900; interest in athletics; a singing spirit that has tended to permeate formal and informal student activities; and even the influence of color inherent in the chain of class colors which have fostered friendships and revealed common interests between alumnae even of different generations. "Oh, were you a blue class, too?" (Or a red or green or gold, of course.)

An overall view of the students and their Trinity life, divided into twenty-year periods, will be followed in this chapter by sections on

18. "Sic Transit, 25 Years on the Crosstown Bus," Jeanne Riordan Kelly '52; *Alumnae Journal*, Spring '78, p. 10; *Metro, Alumnae Journal*, Winter, '78, pp. 2–4.
19. Appendix VIII—Telephones, early numbers.
20. Cf. Chapter 5.
21. Cf. p. 157 ff.

Student Government; on Campus Ministry including the Sodality; on the ups and downs of the enduring clubs such as Glee Club-Choir, Dramatics, the Literary Society (Beta Sigma Phi), and *Le Cercle Français*; on Cap and Gown Sunday, on Class Days Trinity style, and on Commencements. Athletics will be mentioned incidentally because it has been included already with Physical Education.[22]

The First Twenty Years 1900–1921

Student activities of the first thirty years and beyond were centered chiefly on campus. There were, of course, trips to "the city" for shopping, visits and other social events, for sightseeing, or for study but all, except an occasional weekend with friends, were in the daytime. "Late" permissions, gradually getting later,[23] were a slow development at Trinity College. A present student might, as we have said, find the teas, the Friday evening parties, and even the athletics of the first decade quaint and amusing, but they were characteristic of college life of their time. They were accompanied by enduring protest against the prevailing "chaperone rule," by the pressure for more and more student self-government as well as by "pranks[24] and mid-night spreads" that lent zest to life and occasionally caused "unpleasant notoriety"!

The Dean's report, May 31, 1910, took the opportunity "to cast a brief glance backward to ascertain what has been accomplished in this interval. Sister Mary, too, was a woman of her time writing in flowing nineteenth century prose what might be more succinctly phrased seventy years later. She was, however, the wise and revered dean through the radically changing years from 1903 to 1921. After descriptions and statistics showing the ten-year progress, she reports on current student life. "On a few special occasions," she writes, "some of the students have been permitted to accept invitations to social functions in the city. It would not have been possible to grant this privilege had not Mrs. Carter and other members of the Ladies Auxiliary Board generously offered to chaperone the students and to afford hospitality in their homes over night."

As for student conduct she writes: "With the exception of the late infringement of College discipline by the Freshmen, there has really been a very satisfactory observance of regulations during the Scholastic

22. Chapter 5. Cf. "Women's Sports," a 78 year tradition. A.P.K. *Alumnae Journal*, Spring '78, pp. 2–4.
23. Cf. Student Government handbooks
24. For example, the hoisting of the green flag on the South Hall flagpole by freshmen in 1907 and the 1910 freshman frolic that got into the public press! Cf. Reminiscence of Bess McKeogh Manning '10 in T.C.A. and oral reports by Sister Julia (Helen Stokes '13): Dean's report May 31, 1910; newspaper clips in T.C.A.

Students with Bishop Garrigan, 1904.

year." One can observe the growth toward maturity of the class of 1910 by realizing who those seniors were of whom Sister Mary wrote. "In their first class meeting, the Seniors passed a unanimous resolution to co-operate with the Faculty and they have in great measure carried it into execution." They had been the childishly frolicsome freshmen who in 1907 hoisted the green banner of 1910 on the flagpole atop South Hall–and could not get it down! They graduated in the tenth year of Trinity and had the President of the United States at their Commencement.

The "late infringement"[25] mentioned in the 1910 report provides a transition from the first to the second decade of college life. The culprits were the class of 1913, introducing the burgeoning 'Teens, who were later as seniors, the first class to put into operation the long awaited Student Government. Of them Sister Mary wrote: "It is deeply to be regretted that the Freshmen should have planned and carried out a frolic which might have resulted seriously. All of us have felt keenly the exaggerated and in many points untrue report of the affair which has been circulated through the country by the newspapers. It is the first time since the foundation of the College, that the fair name of

25. The dean is reticent about the exact nature of "the infringement," but oral tradition says that they turned in a false fire alarm, and also raised a green flag over the Dome–*how* is not clear.

Students on South Hall steps, 1905.

Trinity College has been subjected to such unpleasant notoriety." (This was what hurt most! Apparently the 1907 affair had been kept largely *in camera.*) "The Freshmen," continued Sister Mary, "sincerely regret their conduct and are anxious to retrieve the good name of their College and their class." They did not, however, forget it. The present writer remembers hearing of it years later told enthusiastically by the president of that freshman class whose name, Helen Stokes of Scranton, Pa., was the only one to appear in the press. Having been the first vice-president of Student Government, she graduated with high honors as a Latin and Greek major, earned an M.A. from Trinity, and became a Sister of Notre Dame. As Sister Julia she earned further graduate degrees from Catholic University and Oxford in England and taught many years in the Latin Department of the College.[26]

The second decade brought the fulfillment of Student Government (1913); *The Trinilogue* (1911); room-mates (1912); World War I with

26. Cf. Chapter 5, p. 191. For a good student description of Trinity life in the mid-teens, cf. "Student Life at Trinity," Marion F. Walsh, reprints from *Notre Dame Quarterly* in T.C.A.

Student Group, 1913.

Basket Ball, c. 1912–13.

"war work"[27] and "war relief"; more intense agitation for Women's Suffrage and its attainment; the great Flu Epidemic; the Washington Trinity Dance sponsored by the Washington Alumnae Chapter first at Rauscher's and later at the Willard Hotel reached by chartered trolley car; greater participation in off-campus activities such as social work and Sunday school teaching; Teachers' Certificates from the U.S. Bureau of Education; the beginning of the Wekanduit Bureau as the active arm of the Foreign Mission Society, the emergence of the more formal pattern of Trinity's color-linked Class Days,[28] and of the Odd-Even rivalry of happy (?) memory; the acquisition of the Rose Estate and the use of the "Red Rose Inn" building successively as chemistry laboratories and "domestic science" laboratory, as an infirmary, as "Graduate Hall," with a new wing added for experimental psychology; and the opening of the swimming pool, called in the catalogue "the natatorium." The end of the decade brought the conferring of Trinity's first honorary degree on Elizabeth, Queen of the Belgians, who was visiting the United States with King Albert after World War I.[29]

Two topics important to the second decade which will not appear elsewhere are the patriotic involvement in "war work" during World War I, and the experience of the great Flue Epidemic as it affected Trinity students. They deserve more than a mere listing.

War Work

Excerpts from the Dean's Reports for 1918 and 1919 provide first-hand, concise reports. Sister Mary wrote, May 25, 1918:

> Never, perhaps in all history has there been a time in which there was such an earnest and imperative call on College Women for patriotic service as at the present day. With the deeper realization of her duties and responsibilities, there comes a stronger desire to respond to these appeals to the best of her ability. This has undoubtedly been the case at Trinity during the past scholastic year. While the College curriculum has in no way been curtailed, the students have found time for volunteer service. A Bureau of War Activities has been established here at the College and results show the sympathetic interest and cooperation that has been accorded to the organization. One branch of the work taken up with the keenest enthusiasm is the knitting for Army and Navy Chaplains. Many complete sets consisting

27. Dean's report 1918.
28. By the Gold Class of 1915. Cf. section in this chapter on "class days"; and *Alumnae Journal*.
29. T. C. Archives and *Trinity College Record*, Nov.-Dec. 1919, "Our Royal Guests," pp. 216–219 and frontispiece picture.

of sweaters, helmets, scarfs, socks, and mittens, have been furnished by the students.[30] An Auxiliary Branch of the Catholic War Relief Service and the Red Cross Society have also been established at Trinity, and a large supply of garments for the hospitals have been made by the students. The importance of the Bureau is not only evident in this practical line, but also in the financial aid given to deserving charities. By means of various entertainments for which a small fee has been charged, by contribution boxes placed in the registration office, quite a large amount of money has been collected and distributed to the Belgian Milk Fund, the Polish Relief Fund, the Nurses' Aid, the Foreign Missions, and the Knights of Columbus Fund.

Mr. D.J. Callahan gave a talk to the student body in the Auditorium on War Savings Stamps. This was immediately followed by a room to room canvas for the sale of war-stamps with the result that several hundred dollars were invested in them by the students. Miss Rankin,[31] Member of Congress, recently delivered an eloquent appeal here on the purchase of Liberty Bonds. Quite a number of the students have purchased Liberty Bonds on the installment plan. The Senior Class has also invested in one for the benefit of Trinity. Here in Washington and in all parts of the country the various Chapters of our Alumnae Association have also purchased Liberty Bonds, and are devoting themselves generously to war work in their respective localities.

Mrs. Norton from the Food Commission explained to the students Mr. Hoover's aims and methods for conservation of food. In compliance with the request of the Food Administration, a Course in Dietetics and Food Conservation has been given throughout this Semester to the Seniors and many other students. Three classes of twenty-five students each, have followed a course in Hygiene and Home-Nursing under an able instructor from the Red Cross Center. Their certificates for same have just arrived. Several of the Seniors have completed a business course in Stenography and Typewriting in the city so that they may be better fitted to fill the positions now open to women. A couple of our Seniors and a few of our Alumnae have decided to enter the Nurses' Training Camp at Vassar[32] during the summer, that they may fit themselves for hospital service. Several of the students are attending the clinic under Rev. Doctor Moore and doing work in the Juvenile Court to prepare for Social Service.

Quite a number of the students have taken Civil Service examinations and expect to work during the vacation in order to do their bit to help out the Government.

The senior class which Sister Mary lauds in her report was the famous Class of 1918 who had to reduce their commencement festivi-

30. One cannot avoid the memory of a World War I song: "It's not the socks of sister's/that raise the blooming blisters/It's the LAST, LONG MILE."
31. First woman in Congress. Mrs. Jeannette Rankin.
32. They were the precursors of the "Women in Uniform" cited in *Alumnae Journal* in the 1940's and later.

ties to a bare minimum because of the war and who were deprived of a Silver Jubilee celebration because of the restrictions of World War II. Their Golden Jubilee in 1968 was consequently a very special affair; but some were kept from coming to reunion by the riots of 1968.

The Great Flu Epidemic

In September, 1918, the dreaded Asian Flu struck Trinity. For eighteen years the Deans had been reporting on the excellent health of the students. A few cases of diphtheria at home in the early days caused a week's postponement of September registration. Slight ailments here and there, colds and "grippe" were mentioned, but nothing like this! Sister Mary wrote May 31, 1919 after nine months:

> Registration day last September brought with it such an overflow of students that our residence halls were taxed to their utmost capacity. Scarcely, however, had the rooms and schedules for more than three hundred young women been satisfactorily adjusted when the dreaded Influenza made its appearance at the College. Realizing the serious nature of the malady, Classes were suspended by the Doctor's orders, and four of our largest schoolrooms were converted into a hospital ward. Since it was impossible to secure nurses, the Sisters devoted themselves in an heroic manner, day and night, to the care of the dear patients. Thanks to the goodness of God and the untiring ministrations of the Sisters, though eighty of our large family were attacked by the disease, there was not one fatal case and all speedily recovered without sustaining any serious effects from the illness. Conditions were sufficiently normal to resume some of the classes on October twentieth. By November third, the quarantine was lifted and scholastic labors were resumed on scheduled time. Classes were held on Saturday till the Christmas holidays to make up the work lost during the period of the Influenza.

The whole "hospital" program at Trinity was organized by Sister Raphael (Pike), of the biology department, one of the original faculty and an M.D. herself. She acted under the authority of the college physician because she had not been in practice for some years, but her medical knowledge made possible the successful operation. Several Sisters of the Trinity community also went out into the neighborhood to take nursing care, food, and personal attention to the poor and neglected who were struck by the disease.

Those who experienced those weeks in the fall of 1918 have vivid memories of the time and each has stories to relate. This short summary serves as a reminder. Eye-witnesses or their descendants must fill in the details.

Rose Arbor, 1922. Notre Dame Chapel partly built.

The Twenties and Thirties 1921–1941 *"Post-War and Depression"*

The students of the period "between the wars" under the guidance of Sister Mary Isabelle Mahoney (1921–1924), Sister Wilfrid Parsons '04 (1924–1932), and Sister Angela Elizabeth Keenan (1932–1942) faced the rapidly changing mores of the post-war prosperity and the great Depression. The 1920's brought the shortskirted, bobbed-haired flappers who began the long struggle for the right to smoke on campus[33] and continued the agitation for late (and later) permissions for off-campus activities, as well as earnest work toward the strengthening of student government and of the honor system. Under a flippant exterior, the student of the Twenties strove to "get to the bottom of things." She widened her field of interest in politics, in parliamentary law, in social work and in girl scouting. While continuing the college traditions, she emphasized bridge games almost non-stop rather than taffy pulls, tea-dances downtown rather than teas, and made "blushing bunny", cinnamon toast or fudge in the kitchenettes rather than on the old-fashioned chafing dishes. Worldly wise as she supposed herself, she continued to enjoy the "goodies" from home that arrived in weekly laundry cases

33. Not achieved until 1950!

Daisy Chain, 1925. Notre Dame Chapel completed.

from home which had become popular before World War I[34] and continued in vogue well after World War II. The Wekanduits also sold sandwiches and French pastries for the missions, doing a roaring business.

Lights (except the minimum fire-lights) were turned off by a central switch on the "dormitory corridors" at ten o'clock sharp. The library closed and student proctors on the halls were off duty at nine-thirty when the lights all over the building gave a warning "blink." Student life was well adjusted to this regime. Studying was done early, except for crisis occasions when "sitting up under the fire-lights" became necessary. Baths were finished and flash lights and strictly-forbidden candles prepared for the late evening social life "after lights." There were two "night chaperones" who roamed the halls to be responsible for safety and to attempt to maintain quiet for those who really wanted to sleep. The Dean of Students made periodic appearances, too. The informal campus social life of the era flourished "after lights." Parties, games, profound discussions (literary, political, philosophical or on fashions, mores and men) made for lively evenings. One of the contemporary songs to the Dean refers to this "night life": "Girls and

34. Cf. "Corporal Mercy," verse by Frances D. Patterson '14, *in Trinity College Record*, Feb. 1913, p. 47.

lights together go out promptly at ten." No students were permitted to go down below the third floor after ten p.m. and no male visitors were entertained in student rooms, except an occasional parent visiting his daughter.

This was also the period of campus development when Notre Dame Chapel and Alumnae Hall were built, when landscaping of the grounds began in earnest.[35] The end of the decade brought the stock market crash of October 1929 and the gradually deepening depression.[36]

A preview of the worries which would be brought on by the changing times may be seen in the first post-war Dean's Report. Sister Mary wrote calmly enough:

> A new department was added this year to satisfy the demand for typewriting and stenography and it has been most popular among the students. While the lessons are given outside the regular College course, and do not count toward a degree, it is a great satisfaction to those who have completed the Course to feel that they possess a valuable asset in it which will be of service to them in later life.[37]

The stress being laid, however, on vocational training, the "almost necessity" of adding to the curriculum Domestic Science, Secretarial work, Interior Decoration and such like branches" brought a cry from the heart. "Verily," she wrote, "may we say that this vaunted age of progress aims to sweep away the old foundations of knowledge and replace them by a super-structure of an evanescent and commercial type."[37]

In the summer of 1921 Sister Mary left Trinity for what would be called today a sabbatical year. In 1922 she went to Emmanuel College in Boston where she was president until 1928.[38] After eighteen years of directing both studies and student life, she was replaced by two Deans, Sister Mary Isabelle, and Sister Berchmans Julia.[39] The work of the latter has been treated in the chapter on the academic program.[40] Sister Mary Isabelle, the competent and popular chemistry teacher came to the office from twenty years of rewarding work with students in her beloved laboratory and lecture room. Not only did she face the

35. By Mr. James Allan and the firm of Olmsted Bros. Cf. TCA.
36. Cf. Chapter 4, pp. 114–117 for the college during the depression and beyond.
37. Dean's Report, May 31, 1919. It should be noted that "Domestic Science" had a shortlived trial in the Teens and the others never materialized unless one considers them as aspects of the Master of Business Administration and the expanded art courses of the 1970's.
38. An idea of her influence on Trinity students may be found in the appreciative obituary by Marie Rottermann in *Alumnae Journal*, Nov. 1936; *Record*, Autumn, 1936.
39. Cf. Chapter 4, pp. 96–101.
40. Chapter 5, pp. 176–177.

difficult task of succeeding Sister Mary, but she faced courageously a student body of young women of the liberated post-war years. Neither she nor the students understood each other, yet Sister Mary Isabelle held her ideals high and worked through three years trying to solve the problems that faced her.[41]

At the end of her first annual report, which summarized the achievements of the year, she wrote

> One cannot fail to realize that the problems confronting the young people of the present day are more complicated than those of the past generation. The need of a thoroughly Catholic education is more imperative than ever before. Great are the responsibilities of the Catholic College to the Church and to society to send forth into the world women, not only well educated and carefully trained in the secular sciences, but women deeply inbued with those spiritual principles which alone can carry them safely through life.[42]

Three years later, in her annual report in which she listed the intellectual, athletic, and social activities of the students who were joyfully making use of enlarged spheres of interest, she still worried about the grave responsibility of the college. Her 1924 report clearly reflects her view of the situation. She wrote[43]:

> They face greater difficulties than the graduate of a decade ago[44]—the spirit of restlessness, of incessant craving for pleasure and novelty is to be found on all sides and the young woman of today needs depth of character, firmness of will, nobility of purpose to enable her to fulfill faithfully her duty and accomplish the special work God has entrusted to her as her particular mission in life. The Church needs the educated Catholic woman, Society needs the educated Catholic woman, and the duty of the Catholic College preparing young girls of the present day to meet the needs of the times and to qualify for the Lay Apostolate is indeed urgent and freighted with weighty responsibility.

Sister Mary Isabelle was fortunate to have during her years as dean the advice and counsel of a great woman whose depth of understanding and width of vision made possible the changes necessary for the time, Sister Raphael Pike, president of the College 1920–1929. Of her,

41. Cf. Administration of Sister Raphael as President. Chapter 4, pp. 108–109.
42. Dean's Report, June 7, 1922. Cf. Chapter 4, pp. 108–113 for a description of the college 1921–1932.
43. June 4, 1924, pp. 12, 13.
44. A decade before, Sister Mary had been reporting the changing problems from those of a decade before that. Deans have always had to cope with changing student bodies. The caliber of the alumnae indicates how well they succeeded even though they could not see it at the time.

Loretta Lawlor '15, first executive secretary of the Alumnae Association, wrote in 1930:

> In that difficult decade, just closing, many trying adjustments have been found necessary. . . . It is again characteristic (of Sister Raphael) that these adjustments were accomplished with dignity and with a real understanding of the changing currents of the life around her.[45]

In the summer of 1924 Sister Mary Isabelle was relieved of the "grave responsibility" which she had bravely faced for three years so that she could return to teaching chemistry—this time at Emmanuel College in Boston. She spent more than twenty-five years helping to develop competent woman chemists in the increasingly scientific age from the 1920's through World War II. In 1961, soon after her death, Ellen Devitt Kramer '21 wrote of her[46]:

> It is as a chemistry teacher that Sister Mary Isabelle is to be remembered and loved. Her scrupulous preciseness and scientific exactitude, combined with a natural reticence and a fine Puritan conscience, were, unhappily, no qualifications for the Dean's Office, which she herself realized more keenly than anyone else . . . [she] recruited us [as teachers] for the Sunday School classes she went out to teach each week. She enjoyed the Dramatic Club she counseled for some years. . . . was always close to her own family as well as interested in her science majors' ventures in the outside world. . . . Beneath a cool New England reserve, she hid a stout, warm heart.

When Sister Wilfred du Sacre Coeur (Elsie Parsons '04) became Dean the "flaming twenties" were in full swing and she was ready to cope with them. She was the first alumna to hold an administrative office in the college, one of those "liberated women" of the pioneer class, a Ph.D. in Classics who was avidly interested in constitutional history, in current politics, in social change—and in the students, their life and their problems. Like Sister Mary, she came to the office from the Latin Department and was replaced in her upperclass major courses by a Professor from another university, Dr. Roy J. Deferrari.[47] She continued to teach constitutional history which was required of all seniors. For five years until the great stock market crash of October 1929 and three years into the Depression she influenced student life by her penetrating insight into problems, her wisely humorous advice, her encouragement and her very firm prodding where need occurred.

45. *Alumnae Journal*, Vol. 3, No. 1, June 1930. The whole passage is worth re-reading.
46. *Alumnae Journal*, Winter '61, p. 74.
47. Cf. p. 191.

Sister Wilfred due Sacre Coeur (Elsie Parsons '04), Dean, 1920's.

The Thirties

For purposes of this history the decade of "the thirties" comprises the years 1929 to 1941, from the "Crash" to World War II. In campus terms it stretches from a newly completed *Alumnae Hall* to the opening of the *Science Building* a month before Pearl Harbor.[48] It was at first a period of declining enrollment, and of precarious finances, followed by gradual recovery toward the later 1930's. It was, however, a time of high student morale, serious attention to the academic side of life, generous work for the needy, practical, whole-hearted facing of financial difficulties caused by bank failures which wiped out student club and publication funds, and of the continuation of already established work for social and interracial justice and of service to others. A Debating Society, founded in 1927, flourished throughout the period, as did the Catholic Evidence Guild in the later years, after the spark set by Frank Sheed's lecture, "The Catholic Intellectual Revival."

Work for the service clubs such as Wekanduits, the Christ Child Society, and the Sodality was supplemented in the earlier 1930's by

48. Cf. Chapter 4, pp. 108–118.

extra fund raising and direct student help to those made destitute by the depression. They cooperated with the Washington Catholic Charities and with the pastor of St. Martin's parish. A manuscript memo[49] to the dean signed by Harriet Lyons is headed "Trinity College Charity Plan." It promised boxes of food for twelve poor families a week ($25 to $30 per family). Special boxes would be prepared at Christmas with toys and clothes added. The "adoption" of families for Christmas boxes did not stop with the Depression, but continued into the 1960's when each class was assigned a family from St. Martin's or St. Anthony's parish for whom they provided new outfits of clothes, appropriate toys and a full Christmas dinner with extra staples for afterwards.

At the bottom of the 1932–1933 plan, which included January to June weekly collections to be given to Catholic Charities, is a memo in Sister Angela Elizabeth's writing:

Amount of Money	
Nov. to Feb.	$330
Feb. to May	250
To Good Shepherd	50
	$630

That total of $630 is no mean sum from the small student body, who were also struggling to stay in college and to replace club and publication funds lost in the bank failures. A *Times* article March 1933 reports a "spirited student government meeting" at which it was stated that $2500 was needed to cover debts of the "societies." For this latter need a student Reconstruction Finance Commission was organized. The first of the events planned by that group was the famous "Old Home Weekend," March 31 to April 2, 1933, in which the entire student body participated on campus.[50] It was described in the *Trinity Times* of March 30, 1933, as "one of the most important features among the plans of the Reconstruction Finance Committee." It opened Friday evening with a variety show in O'Connor Auditorium, directed by Mary Louise Hickey '33, consisting of "from fifteen to twenty skits plus surprise treats." A full list of Miss Hickey's committee and of the cast of the

49. Dean's Scrapbook. The plan covered Oct. 1932 to May 1933. This same scrapbook contains letters of thanks from the Asst. Director of Catholic Charities, Rev. Lawrence J. Shehan (later Cardinal Archbishop of Baltimore) and from Miss Margaret Wallace in Dr. O'Grady's office (herself a Trinity alumna, 1925) who says they have started the same program at various other Catholic institutions using Trinity College as a model.
50. Humorous verses, "Saga of the Winter of 1932–1933," published in the 1933 *Trinilogue* is a good example of student spirit in the "dark days."

show appears in the *Times* article.[51] The show was preceded by a Waffle Supper in Alumnae Hall dining room. Saturday afternoon was filled by a bridge tournament in Social Hall, followed by a Water Carnival in the swimming pool. Saturday evening a "rousing debate" (subject not disclosed beforehand—and not known to the author now) gave scope for an "amusing and inspirational display of oratorical ability and ample opportunity for self-expression." The weekend closed Sunday afternoon at a tea in Social Hall. Tickets for the Old Home Weekend were $3.00 per person with the "added attraction" of a Theatre Permission for juniors and seniors and an extra ten o'clock permission for sophomores and freshmen. Members of the RFC in charge of ticket sales were Ruth Cox, Harriet Lyons, and Mary Andre. The proceeds of the weekend went far to replenish empty club coffers.

This type of on-campus-weekend to raise funds was so successful that another was held two years later, December 13–15, 1935. "The banks haven't failed," says the article in the Dean's Scrapbook, "but '36 wants to have the finest *Trinilogue* ever and to support a winning debating team." There was "a great list of events!" "Haven't you heard," it continued, "some stray information about Mary Kate Bland's operetta (modern version of Tannhauser—enormous cast!), Anarita Kelly's original show, Anne Moore's water carnival . . . ?"

The bankrupt 1933 *Trinilogue* was aided by the Boston, New York, and Rhode Island Chapters of the Trinity College Alumnae Association. The *Trinity Times* of May 2, 1933 expressed thanks for this aid to the *Trinilogue.* The clipping in the Dean's scrapbook reads:

> The splendid spirit of the Alumnae Association and the cooperation between graduates and undergraduates was evident recently in the financial assistance given by the Boston, Rhode Island and New York Chapters to the *Trinilogue.* In their respective meetings the chapters very generously voted in favor of complimentary advertisements for the yearbook.
>
> The Boston Chapter under the able leadership of a group of its younger members, conducted a dance of social, as well as financial, success, at the Salem Country Club on April 18. For the success of this function, the class of '33 is especially indebted to Catherine Crimmings, Dorothy Poor, Kathleen Grady, and Marie Mutrie, all of '32, Helen Rafter '31, Eleanor Hickey '29 and Mary Field '27.
>
> The Massachusetts Club with the able assistance of Mrs. Michael J. Lyons, held a bridge and tea on Easter Monday in the Philomatheia Club in Newton.

51. Dean's Scrapbook 1932–1933. There is also a song to the Old Home Weekend in the 1933 *Trinilogue* among the Senior Serenade songs. It was set to the popular tune, "Button Up Your Overcoats" and expresses good student spirit. The first four lines give the theme: Open up your pocketbooks/Now the week-end's here/What though banks are closed/They can't stop our cheer.

There was an appreciation of Alumnae help to 1933 published in the *Alumnae Journal*, May, 1933 by Aileen Crimmings, president of the class. She praises generosity as a virtue and adds the Philadelphia and Washington Chapters to those mentioned in the *Times* article, continuing

> This year, as never before have we witnessed here at Trinity some of the finest examples of generosity ever known to us in our lives—the generosity of our Alumnae to the Class of 1933. Not only did they aid us in our Commencement activities but they made possible the publication of our *Trinilogue* and *Record*. And so it is to the Alumnae of Boston, New York, Rhode Island, Philadelphia, and Washington that we wish to express our deep appreciation for the loyalty and interest which they have shown us and the work they have done for us. Their manifestation of cooperation has left a lasting impress on our minds and hearts, and we of the Class of '33 are anxious to join these various Chapters of Alumnae next year in the hope that we in the future may give them our undivided interest, and cooperate with them in their endeavors as they have done with us in ours this year.

During these years the Alumnae not only gave to the students examples of outstanding work in Catholic Action and Social Service, but more directly helped them by a Student Loan Fund, an Alumnae Scholarship Committee, and a Vocational Guidance Committee reported especially at the 1932 and following meetings of the Association.[52]

Freshman Week, testing and orientation were begun in the late 1920's by Sister Wilfred (Parsons) and became an important feature of the opening of college during the 1930's. The Student Government and Class Officers, and the Washington Club members cooperated with the dean in making freshmen feel at home. Printed programs for the week during succeeding years until the present are available in the Archives.[53] Sister Angela Elizabeth began the Saturday bus trips for freshmen to federal government and historical sites in Washington. Her scrapbooks preserve lists of freshman groupings and destinations for the years up to 1942.

The dwindling size of the student body did not affect its intellectual quality. When the American Council on Education developed its yearly Psychological Test for College Freshmen, Trinity College participated from 1927 to 1947 after which no new test was issued. An examination of the tables of percentile ranks of colleges shows the classes entering Trinity College in the 1930's were high on the list, ranking in the highest ten of 152 colleges all during the depression years. These students

52. Cf. also p. 115 and *Alumnae Journal* Nov. 1932, pp. 12–13 and June, 1933, pp. 72–73.
53. Dean's Scrapbooks and envelopes of programs of various eras. T.C.A.

Monsieur Beaucaire, *Notre Dame Auditorium.*

experienced the 1932 re-organization of the curriculum,[54] were (1935) the first students to face senior comprehensive examinations in their major subjects, and after graduation made full use of their preparation in responsible positions in government, business, education, social service as well as at home managing a family. (Cf. Chapter 8.) Their extra-curricular activities were developing into what was called a decade later "co-curricular" and were more intercollegiate. The students of Latin VI gave a performance of Plautus' *Menaechmae* on "May XIX, MCMXXXIII," though the Classical Society had died out. The annual French plays of Le Cercle Français continued through the decade with unabated zest. The Literary Society kept up its thirty-year tradition of sponsoring lectures by prominent contemporary authors and reviewing new books not only of fiction and poetry, but of political, economic and social interest.[55] These last were supplemented by articles and reviews in the *Record.*

English majors entered the A.A.U.W. Poetry Contest for Washington college students. February 6, 1933 Cathleen Chrystal won third prize and an honorable mention in this competition beginning a "tradition" of Trinity poetry winners in this and other contests, notably the *Atlantic Monthly* awards in later decades. Though the author makes no attempt at complete coverage she mentions here that Margaret Pal-

54. Curriculum re-organization, 1932. Cf. pp. 176–177 and *Alumnae Journal* articles cited there.

55. Minutes of Literary Society 1902–1966, Archives of Trinity College. Cf. section on this club later in the chapter.

lansch '40 won second prize in the A.A.U.W. contest in her senior year and later winners will appear in their own time.

Political activities, presaged in the earlier years of the college by interest in women's suffrage and by the mock-elections every four years, became more pronounced and spread to cooperation with other colleges in the critical 1930's. One reads in the Dean's Scrapbook of a Democratic rally staged by colleges, October 18, 1932 at the Central Democratic Committee. Ruth Cox, president of the Debating Society, spoke as the representative of Trinity College. She maintained that women would play an important part in the November elections. The "suffrage cause gave many thousands of American women their first practical understanding of the meaning of democracy," she said, while she defended the woman's viewpoint in politics. "What should political achievements be measured by, if not in terms of human well-being? What is government for except to promote the security, education and happiness of all the families of the country, and it is a woman's place to show that government is for that purpose. Woman must make the family the center of politics rather than the *political boss* or the *dollar bill.*" (Italics added)

Although most of the student body, except a few seniors, were under 21 and therefore not eligible to vote, there was a lively political rally in the South Court[56] on November 7, 1932, the night before elections. It was organized by the Debating Society. There were song-leaders, soapbox orators, hecklers for Republicans, Democrats, and Socialists, a roll call of states, and a torchlight parade was featured followed by a straw vote in O'Connor Auditorium.[57]

Interest in the various clubs which had been traditional at Trinity continued during the decade. A list of these with foundation dates appeared in the 1931 *Trinilogue* and is inserted here for the benefit of future readers.

Foundation Dates of Organizations and Publications
as listed in 1931 *Trinilogue*

Student Government	1912 (Class of 1913)
Our Lady's Sodality	1904
The Record	1907
The Trinity Times	1926
Literary Society	1901
Debating Society	1927

56. Now called Seymour Court.
57. That November 8, 1932 saw the election of FDR who appointed a Trinity alumna, Jane Hoey '14, to establish the Federal Bureau of Public Assistance which grew into the Department of Health, Education and Welfare. He had known her for her work on New York State Crime Commission while he was governor. Her biography appears in *Notable American Women* (Vol. IV) as founder of H.E.W. (q.v.) and she is mentioned many places in this history.

Dramatic Society	1901	
Glee Club	1901	
Eurydice	1902 (orchestra)	
Le Cercle Français	1907	
Deutscher Verein	1928	
Wekanduit Bureau	1917 (active arm of Foreign Mission Society)	
Christ Child Society	1909	
Chemical Society	1914	

State Clubs—Informal Clubs
Characteristic of '30's which did not survive into '40's.

New Jersey, Chicago (*sic*), Pennsylvania, Massachusetts, New York

Washington Club	1927	
Athletics	1903	Teams pictured: Basketball Hockey Swimming Riding Archery Track Tennis

Addenda from 1933—	International Relations Club	1931
	Press Club	1931
	El Circulo Espanol	1932

Not only national, but international affairs interested the Trinity students of the 1930's. The International Relations Club dates from 1931. In the spring of 1932 various embassies in Washington held Diplomatic Sunday Evening Salons. March 19, Dr. Eric Menke gave a lecture on the German Youth Movement at the German Embassy, which was attended by members of the International Relations Club and other seniors. There were other such Sundays at the Austrian, Spanish, and Danish embassies. The Deutscher Verein, Le Cercle Français, and El Circulo Español kept alive interest in life in the countries where those languages were spoken, while the relevant departments gave courses in their "civilization" or culture. Margaret Wohnlich '33 represented Trinity College at the Convention of International Relations Clubs at Bucknell University, in November, 1932.

Participation in the activities of the Catholic Conference on International Peace, of which Trinity had a college chapter, interested many undergraduates of the period. The Fourth Annual Students' Catholic Peace Federation, March, 1940 is reported with pictures and a *N.Y. Times* clipping in the Dean's Scrapbook.

Sister Angela Elizabeth Keenan, the dean of students 1932–1942, was a Phi Beta Kappa graduate of Smith College, a teacher in the Bos-

Sister Angela Elizabeth Keenan, Dean, 1930's.

ton Public High Schools before she entered the Sisters of Notre Dame de Namur. She earned her Ph.D. in classics at the Catholic University while teaching English at Trinity College. She exercised a strong influence on the students in the activities described in this chapter, strengthening morale in troubled times, enlarging their cultural appreciation, inspiring, prodding, advising, scolding as need arose. It was she who encouraged the students to support the struggling new National Symphony Orchestra under Hans Kindler. She organized and carried through the Tuesday Afternoon Lecture Series that brought to the campus distinguished authors, artists, and other professional men and women.[58] She worked with the Vocational Guidance Committee of the Alumnae to set up a Vocational Guidance Bureau for students and young alumnae[59] which developed into the Guidance and Counseling Service of the Dean's Office under Sister Ann Francis Hoey.

Sister Angela Elizabeth was also devoted to the spiritual welfare of the students, to greater integration of the day students into college life, as well as interested in works of service to others outside the college such as Sunday school teaching, and vacation schools of religion for

58. Changed in the 1940's to Thursday afternoon.
59. Cf. p. 115 and footnotes there.

children in North Carolina. A large album of pictures in the Trinity Archives memorializes the work of the "Pineers", Trinity students and young alumnae, chiefly from Washington, who ran religious vacation schools at Southern Pines, N.C., under her supervision in the late 1930's. She enthusiastically backed the students' work for the children of St. Vincent's and St. Joseph's Homes for Orphans, and the Christmas plays and parties for them sponsored by Student Government and the Dramatic Society. The play was always a Nativity play, sometimes from the medieval cycles and sometimes modern versions. She encouraged the cooperation of Trinity students with the work of Brother Maurus, O.S.B. of St. Anselm's Priory, for the children of the Brookland neighborhood.

At the outbreak of World War II, Sister Angela Elizabeth was not ready to face responsibility for a new and different generation of Trinity students and gladly returned to the classroom teaching English literature until 1947 when she was appointed dean of Emmanuel College in Boston. Her contribution to Trinity College will never be forgotten, especially by the students and faculty of the 1930's.[60]

One of the seldom mentioned, but great traumas of the 1930's was the necessary postponement of building the new science building and the consequent suspension of the college from the prestigious A.A.U. list.[61] With the help of Alumnae fund raising and of careful economy of the college, the administration managed to finish the Science Building just before Pearl Harbor, 1941. Both Sister Berchmanns Julia who had stayed on as vice-president under her successor to supervise the construction and Sister Angela Elizabeth could leave office with the satisfaction of knowing the place on A.A.U. list was restored.[62] The college faced a new threat—WAR. The generation of the forties were vitally affected by war, even more than that of the 'Teens.

The Third Twenty Years[63] *1941–1961*
The Forties

The students of the 1940's were again a wartime generation followed by participants (however unaware of it) in the usual post-war boom.

60. After her retirement from office at Emmanuel College, Sister Angela Elizabeth wrote and published, *Three Against the Wind*, the biographies of the two foundresses of the college, and one of the eminent members of the first faculty: Sister Julia McGroarty, Sister Mary Euphrasia Taylor, and Sister Raphael Pike.
61. Cf. pp. 117–118.
62. Ironically the year Sister Angela left Trinity, 1947, marked the discontinuing of the "list" by the Association of American Universities.
63. As background for this section, read pp. 118–134, the administrations of Sister Catherine Dorothea Fox and Sister Mary Patrick Feddon.

Entertaining Servicemen, U.S.O., W.W. II.

The decade at Trinity began in 1941 with the opening of the long-awaited Science Building[64] a month before Pearl Harbor and the transformation of Graduate Hall into a Fine Arts Center (old Cuvilly Hall) to accommodate the newly established majors in art and music.[65] It was a period of song, of on-campus activities and of active day student participation, of Trinity's first black students, of greatly strengthened student government, of "Joe's" at its heyday, of study "when necessary," but also of the Christian Culture Program that required hard study; a period of apparently carefree college life with a strong undercurrent of serious purpose. Brothers, fiancés, fathers, and most undergraduates from nearby universities were in the armed services. Blackouts, first aid lessons, defense activities, U.S.O. services, as well as news of alumnae in uniform brought the war very close.

The freshmen who entered Trinity in September 1941 became "the war class." Their reception into the Sodality and of the Trinity Medal on December 8 coincided with the Pearl Harbor attack that precipitated the United States into World War II. Their comprehensive examinations coincided with Victory in Europe Day (V-E). That night they all went to South Fourth to see the light on the Capitol dome, which had been dark since their freshman year. Their commencement was drasti-

64. *Alumnae Journal*, Autumn, '41, pp. 9–10. Dedication, June 1942, *Alumnae Journal*, Summer '42, p. 97.
65. *Alumnae Journal*, Spring, '42, pp. 77–81.

Commencement, 1944.

cally curtailed because of civilian travel limitations to facilitate troop movements across country from European battlefields to the Pacific. The class of 1944, the sophomores when the war began, lost many members in the summer of 1942 because of parental fear that Washington would be an early target for enemy bombing. They graduated only sixty-two seniors at a ceremony memorable not because of war, but because the eminent speaker, Dr. George Johnson, collapsed during the address and died fifteen minutes later on stage in Notre Dame auditorium.[66] The juniors that year, 1943, shared campus war activities for two years and graduated in time to get into varied defense jobs (in and out of uniform) in the wider field of service.

The fall of 1942 brought a new Dean of Students, Sister Ann Francis (Catherine Hoey '24), to the office near the "S.G. Door."[67] She devoted herself whole-heartedly to the students of the 1940's, 1950's until 1961, the longest tenure in that office of any dean. Even Sister Mary who symbolized "Dean" for the students of the first twenty years presided as dean for only eighteen years. Because of the larger classes of the postwar '40's which continued through two more decades, Sister Ann

66. *Alumnae Journal*, Summer '42, pp. 100–103. Editorial, obituary by Ellen A. Ganey.

67. The offices occupied in the late 1970's by the Academic Dean and her secretary at the south end of the Marble Corridor for more than fifty years (from 1921) housed the Dean of Students and the Student Government. All students left campus and returned through the adjacent door, called "S.G."

Francis is known to, and knows well, more than half the alumnae of the college.

Sister Ann Francis earned her Master's degree in English, and her doctorate in guidance and counseling at the Catholic University of America. Her dissertation was appropriately *Problems and Guidance Resources of Catholic College Women.* Of her work as dean, no better description can be found than that of Ellen Ganey in the citation for Sister Ann Francis when she received the Pro Ecclesia medal after twenty-five years at Trinity College.[68]

> A professional educator, she became fascinated with the great contributions . . . by modern psychology, weighing these in the light of her own good sense and experience. She has mingled with notable success the wisdom of the old with the advanced methods of the new, adapting whatever might be useful to each particular situation with extraordinary perception and judgment.
>
> Most of her work has been in counselling—actually she was an inborn counsellor before the word became fashionable. And so we find her for twenty-five years at Trinity, giving nineteen of those years to the office of the Dean of Students, from the troubled time of World War II almost to the turbulent years of the sixties with their emergence of "The New Breed." We may wonder just how new Sister Ann Francis considers this breed. Ever interested in a strong, "involved" student group, thirteen years ago she conceived and saw student-executed the ingenious idea of the Sophomore Workshop whereby second-year students evaluate their own education (the very privilege students are now clamoring for the world over). The establishment of this Workshop merited the 1957 Richard Wellington Award of the National Student Association. It was Sister Ann Francis who designed and initiated the Senior Guidance Committee, an effective means of implementing the traditionally sound influence of old Trinity students upon younger ones, a phase of college life important to preserve and nurture in our modern times of larger classes and multiple interests beyond the campus. Such measures as these illustrate Sister Ann Francis' foresight and executive skill. Her regard for the law, no student would question, but the fact that a rule was not made to be "hard and fast" was well understood, too. Her flexibility in such matters is best demonstrated by the phrase oft-quoted in many a Class Day play—"under the circumstances—yes!" . . .
>
> One who worked with her as a Student Government president defined her secret briefly and well: "The teachers and mothers among us recall Sister's wonderful gift of guiding by suggestion, or teaching by drawing out, of trusting in the maturity and integrity of the individual without a hint of doubt." Her girls found her quiet without being silent, serene but never aloof, friendly with no intimation of familiarity. She was given neither to

68. June 4, 1967 Program in T.C.A. Student appreciation of Sister Ann Francis is epitomized in the dedication of the 1960 *Trinilogue* to her; p. 10. Cf. also *Newsletter,* March, 1957; *Alumnae Journal,* Summer '61, p. 183, "To the Dean," by Sally Finnegan Harrs, '59.

> probing nor pushing, but by some inscrutable spiritual insight she seemed always sensible of the complexities of life, the sufferings of youth, the indefinable searching going on in each human soul. This was partly achieved through a keen memory of her own student days—with marked accent on the humorous aspects. This same sense of humor doubtless accounts in good measure for her excellent sense of proportion. It is due also, as the young alumna just quoted has indicated, to her willingness to induce others to greatness while leaving her own part unacknowledged. So, for virtually two decades, we see her as Dean, the able and wise support of strong presidents of the College, the patient and unfailing generator of a student organization showing steady development and robust vitality. The spotlight never seemed to fall on her; not that she avoided it—she simply directed it elsewhere. This adroit kind of persuasion to the good, this lifting up of others to full stature without even revealing the hands which do the elevating, is possible only in a person of true magnanimity, in a woman who understands fully what it means to love.

Sister Ann Francis went on from the dean's office to teaching in the education department, to being the Superior of the community of Sisters of Notre Dame living at Trinity, to Director of the Oxford group for two years. In the late 1970's she still lives at Trinity acting as liaison between the Alumnae Association and the college administration, joyfully greeted by returning alumnae of all ages.

An eyewitness account of Trinity girding for war supplements what has been written here about the early years of the 1940's.

> Trinity of 1942 faces Commencement and a chaotic world, one that changes hourly. In the very midst of the bewildering, crowded confusion of the wartime capital, it has maintained a great measure of steadiness and strength. In no way have these Trinitarians of today closed their eyes to all that lies before them. They are well aware of the challenge that confronts them. The battle of Pearl Harbor brought the war home to them that first week with the death of the brother of one of our Juniors—a gallant son of Georgetown who not many months before had come often to our S.G. door. Though they know it is their generation who will pay the terrible cost of this war, they are neither frightened nor despairing. They go about their work with new regard for its importance. They fill their Prom Weekend with every kind of laughter and loveliness that youth and courage can devise. They learn all the lessons the Red Cross can teach for first aid treatment in time of disaster. Yet they *lead* the conference for peace, the Peace of Christ, learned practically and thoroughly as to application according to the plan of Pius XII. Hourly—all day long—there is one of them at prayer in the chapel and the Mass on Friday of each week is offered for the fathers, brothers, friends in service of all Trinity. A startling number of the Seniors (underclassmen, too) are engaged to be married.[69]

69. *Alumnae Journal*, Spring, 1942, p. 83. Editorial by E.A.G. Cf. pp. 121–122.

The 1942 *Alumnae Journal* was devoted in large part to discussions of work for defense, on and off campus. Sister Catherine Dorothea wrote on "Trinity and Defense," telling of cooperation among twenty-five privately controlled liberal arts colleges for women as well as activities on campus.[70] The editorial gives a vivid picture of the momentous first blackout on campus.[71] The Autumn, 1942 *Journal* brought the first of a series of articles on "Trinity in Uniform," In this issue too, appears a report of the Representatives of National and Diocesan Leaders of the National Council of Catholic Women held at the National Catholic School for Social Service, January 25, 1942. Ellen A. Ganey '27 and Alice Corcoran '32 represented the Trinity Alumnae and were impressed by our alumnae among these Catholic leaders: Anne Hooley '15, director of the Women's division of N.C.C.S., Catherine Schaefer '27, research secretary of N.C.W.C.,[72] Lucy McAnany '33, Ruth Craven '28 of the Women's Council staff, later Executive Secretary, and Ellen Hughes Carlin '28 of the Cleveland Diocesan Council. Though not present here, Trinity alumnae have held leadership positions in many NCCW Councils, notably in Peoria, in Columbus, in several New York cities, as well as in Asheville, N.C., Philadelphia, Pittsburgh and Washington, D.C. Plans and early stages of work for service men, for their families, for the newly gathered "boom-town" war workers were outlined. Such work was being done and expanded by N.C.C.S., U.S.O. units. The Pope's Peace plan, and the problems of post-war recovery were on the program Catholic women, like all other women in America were mobilizing for both war and peace. Echoes of this could not escape the college campus.

The students not only entered eagerly into the defense and service activities already mentioned, but they did it very practically. A Commission for Defense was organized to co-ordinate student work, led by Barbara Archibald '43 for 1941–42, Gertrude Moore '43 for 1942–43, Margaret Claydon '45 for 1943–44 and by Molly Kramer '46 for 1944–45. They took over the waitress work in the dining hall, (All meals were still served in those days!) and used the money to buy U.S. Bonds for scholarships. These bonds matured long after their graduation, so that in the 1960's entering students received financial aid from the classes of 1944, 1945, 1946, 1947. They went to work on farms, in factories and offices during summers to ease the labor shortage. The Winter '43 *Alumnae Journal* has a cover picture: *Dance-Bound girls conserve gas and tires.* This was from the Washington *Times-Herald* newspaper for

70. Winter, 1942, pp. 47–49.
71. *Alumnae Journal*, Winter, 1942, pp. 49–51.
72. Catherine Schaefer was in the midst of a long career of service with the N.C.W.C. which culminated in her tenure as representative of the U.S. Catholic bishops at the United Nations. Cf. Chapter 8.

November 14, 1942, where it was captioned: "Mindful of the nation's need of avoiding unnecessary automotive travel, the girls of Trinity College last night elected to use streetcars in traveling to their dance."[73]

The 1944 *Trinilogue* has an illustrated section called "War Effort, in Which We Serve." Headed by the campaign of prayer for peace, as well as for relatives and friends in service, the war effort included typing classes, first aid courses, volunteer nurses aides in understaffed hospitals, blood donors, defense stamp sales, filling in for labor shortages in the dining-hall, nutrition courses, and Scout work with children. The Class history provides a contemporary student account of the impact of war.

> On December 8, 1942, [sic] we were jarred from our sophomore slump and gradually our perspective changed. Msgr. Ligutti's advice to "marry a farmer" didn't sound so strange in our ears, with trips to Bermuda and other sophomoric gossamer plans cancelled. We plunged into a world of tourniquets and slings, met in the corridors with blankets and radios for air-raid practices, and whiled away tedious blackout hours at movies in the auditorium. Some of us packed boxes at the Belgium Embassy, and all of us took on jobs for defense. Notices appeared on bulletin boards showing our ingenuity—"Check your weight—1 cent"—"Cement South American relations; learn the rhumba—5 cents." At our Victory Ball the Allied Nations were colorfully represented in the grand march.
>
> When exams rolled around we trekked in streams to the lighted nook in O'Connor and advised the freshmen of the futility of studying for the biology midyear. On the eve of our class day Suzanne Lebkicher and Mrs. Thuee made a midnight dash to "Woodie's" and saved the day with yards and yards of bunting for our "well," with its *patriotic motif.* The days grew warmer and we stepped forth in crisp pinafores and pastel chintz dresses. *Silver wings* and *gold bars* appeared on our sweaters. (Italics added)

Scattered through the rest of this lighthearted class history were allusions that showed that wartime still prevailed. References to "the *Record* Bond Rally, at which a galaxy of Trinity movie stars appeared, including Rita (Jean Conroy) Hayworth, who auctioned off her chic hat . . . our first trip to the Washington Press Club Dance in the street car . . . Georgetown's last Victory Ball. . . . We thought that rayon stockings were awful, but there was no heat in the buildings, or so it seemed, and we wore them and our fur coats to our 8:15 classes . . . and somehow we located dates and went to our very own Junior Prom and our last formal for the duration."

Like their predecessors of the 1930's, they had stayed "at home" for a closed weekend with varied attractions to raise money for the benefit of the Defense Fund. One new feature of that weekend was an enor-

73. Though the students seemed unaware of it their "war effort" was simply reviving the method of travel to dances required of students of an earlier era.

mously popular faculty show (without the Sisters, of course, in those days) which parodied the annual student Wekanduit Show and was entitled Wekanduit II, an eye-opener for the students on the extent of faculty awareness of their foibles and covert activities. It may have sparkled, but did not outshine the next year's Wekanduit Show, the Walsh-Alberti production, complete with roosters that crowed at dawn!

By 1944 the Commission for Defense had become the Victory Commission. A "Victory Report" in the *Alumnae Journal,* Winter '45,[74] quoted from the *Trinity Times,* is another student-eye picture of their war effort.

> "What is Trinity doing for the war effort?" is a question which has been asked of us many times. Here is our answer, in black and white, covering October and November.
>
> With classes alternating in sponsoring V-Day every Friday, the sale of stamps and bonds has met with great success.
>
> The juniors and sophomores went well over the 100 per cent mark, with top honors going to the sophomores. A special salute is due the freshmen who sold on their V-Day, November 10, five times as much as any other class. Their spirit has won our admiration, and we're predicting great things for them.
>
> For another job well done we express our thanks to the sophomores and freshmen for their service in the dining hall, and to those girls who helped in the cafeteria. This has netted a total of $532.
>
> * * *
>
> The weiner roast on November 8 was well-attended, and $57 was added to the Victory Fund. From the sale of coca cola in both the Main Building and Alumnae Hall, a profit of $35 was realized. With the Victory campaign only three months old, we have almost earned the $750 needed to buy our first $1,000 War Bond. Every Trinity girl should take pride in that achievement, and especially in the part which she contributed. October and November have given us something to live up to.
>
> The Catholic USO has asked for thousands of scrapbooks to be sent overseas. Trinity girls may now be seen poring over magazines, snipping out pictures, cartoons, quizzes, cross-word puzzles, short stories, and other bits of interest.
>
> Outside wartime activities include rolling bandages at St. Martin's from 10 to 10 on Wednesdays, and at the Benedictine Convent from 9 to 6. Work at hospitals is being done by Nurses' Aides and jangoes. Trinity's blood donors' honor roll is on the Defense Bulletin Board in S.G. Scrap paper is collected from the hall closets each week and a large pile has been stored in the basement.
>
> December 8 was proclaimed a national day of prayer for peace by the National Victory Commission. Observance of that feast at Trinity included Mass sung by the students, reception of freshmen into the Sodality.

74. P. 47. Cf. *Trinilogue* 1945, pp. 166–167 for another description and good pictures.

The book exhibit in the library solved Christmas gift problems for many. Through the courtesy of the Newman Book Store, 20 percent of the sale price of each book went to the Victory Fund. In this way approximately $65 was turned in.

Work for peace continued in the midst of war and the students persevered in their participation in national as well as in regional student associations. In December '41, Celeste Solari '42 and Doris Pettit '43 attended the Capital Peace Federation at Dumbarton College at which Celeste spoke on "The Economic Basis of a Just Peace." The

A Symbolic Class Day. "Well," 1945.

chairmanship of the newly established Commission on International Relations of the National Federation of Catholic College Students (NFCCS) was delegated to Trinity and Rita Schaefer '42 was unanimously named National Chairman. Jane Marilley '44 wrote a good description of NFCCS and Trinity's part in it in the *Record*, December, 1943 (pp. 107–109).

The strengthening of student government and the increased participation of students in intercollegiate organizations are described in the separate section on Student Government later in this chapter.

While the war was still raging on two fronts in 1943, the upward climb of student enrollment began. That September, 147 freshmen registered. The next year the freshman class was 173, while only 62 had graduated in June. September 1945 brought 154, though the "war class," "The Big Noise of '45," had graduated only 100 strong. The post war larger classes had arrived! This was the beginning of the predicted growth that culminated in 1965 with the registration of the largest class of 364, pictured on the cover of the *Alumnae Journal*,[75] crowding every space of Social Hall in Main.

The first of these "larger classes," 1947, gives a humorous student's-eye view of life in 1944–1945.[76] It is both typical of a student year of the time and specifically unique for this class.

> Sophomore year burst upon us, and ours was the feeling of 'ground accomplishment.' It was the general opinion that the average soph had only four 8:15's instead of five, not to mention later permissions. With a new sense of pride we took our freshmen out to breakfast and moved from the right side to the left in the back of O'Connor.
>
> This was the year Annapolis week ends were in vogue, and filled mail boxes were consolation for the lonely Saturday nights, (we must admit there was a minority that held out for the Army) while serious ponderings on the "isness" of chocolate cake and the pursuit of our newly acquired majors overtaxed the gray matter. The merits of 'half pearl' and 'whole' were seriously discussed as we ordered T.C. pins. Still strong were the 'gold' gym suits, but the Order of the Chic Black Stockings had been abolished. [A student landmark, indeed!]
>
> After the sorrows of mid-years, we recuperated our spirits for a frolicking semester week end, then more quietly entered Fr. Schoberg's retreat. Forty-five was the spring of the President's death and V-E Day. Serious sophomores hung their Well with golden emblems of Faith, Hope, and Charity. This, too, was the year of "Sophomore Misses," song hit from forty-seven's class day play, 'T.C. Canteen.'
>
> In May, after freshmen and juniors had departed, we dressed in long gowns and carried the daisy chain down the Marble Corridor for our now

75. Autumn, 1965.
76. *Trinilogue*, 1947, pp. 190–191.

senior sisters. Suitcases were packed, and of course we would write. But we'd be back. We had made a down payment on those rings, hadn't we?

A comparison of student activities of the forties with the 1931 list cited earlier[77] shows that the State Clubs and Debating Society had disappeared, the language clubs had anglicized their names, but were thriving, with Italian added. Eurydice had become the Music Club. Mathematics, art, and sociology had appeared, as well as the Chemical Society, a collegiate member of the American Chemical Society.[78] In 1946 the Interracial Club, affiliated with the Interracial Council of Washington, drew interest by "energetic discussions of the economic and social problems of the negro."[79] From this time a strong emphasis on social and interracial justice, and on international relations permeated student activities. In 1948 two black students, Barbara Black and Hariett Parker, from Notre Dame High School, Moylan, Pa registered as Trinity freshmen. Because Washington was still a segregated city they were advised by their families, pastors, and teachers in Pennsylvania to live with black families in the city for their own comfort. Though the number of black students increased slowly through the fifties it was the early sixties that brought significant increase in numbers, resident students, and an organized recruitment program especially in Washington.[80]

All during the war years the students showed a strong, sympathetic interest in the plight of the Sisters of Notre Dame in the battle areas, notably Belgium, Rome, and Japan. *The Record*, June '43, published excerpts from all three places. The *Alumnae Journal* published letters from Sister Julie Chisholm,[81] former English professor, who was in Namur, Belgium, throughout the war; from Elena Bisletti '41 in her native Rome[82]; from You Couroux-Mangin, former French exchange student, with the French army in North Africa; from Mabel Shannon '21 with the American Red Cross in refugee camps in North Africa; from Marilyn Maloney '42 a civilian Actress Technician in Germany in 1946; as well as from other Alumnae in uniform on all fronts.

77. Pp. 340–341.
78. Press or publicity student organizations have flourished or languished throughout the history of the college, depending much on faculty support and encouragement. At times during the eighty years informal groups such as the Trinititians, all redheads, and the granddaughters, whose mothers or grandmothers attended Trinity, have flourished for brief intervals. Their existence was chiefly ceremonial, marked by a picture in the *Trinilogue*.
79. The alumnae had been far ahead of undergraduate Trinity students in this area, having been active in promoting interracial justice as early as the 1920's, if not before.
80. Directed by Sister Sheila Doherty.
81. *Alumnae Journal*, November 1940, pp. 5–11. About bombing of Namur; Autumn '45, pp. 11–13, reaction to V.E. Day.
82. Winter '45. Cf. *Record* June '43, pp. 187–190, and pp. 214–217.

In 1946, when American colleges were "adopting" institutions in war torn areas, Trinity College adopted The Notre Dame Teacher Training College in Bastogne, Belgium, which had been in the midst of the Battle of the Bulge in December 1944 and had served as a hospital for American troops. The 101st Airbourne Division under Brigadier General Anthony McAuliffe ("Nuts") fought bravely to repulse "the bulge" and to weaken German forces in that area.[83] Students, their parents, alumnae and friends of Trinity College rallied to build up a fund that would enable the Sisters of Notre Dame to rebuild their teacher training college.

The class of 1946 history tells of senior year (1945–1946).

> In September we returned to T.C. joyful in the knowledge that ours was to be the first post World War II graduation. Missing several of our members (newspaper clippings of weddings told the tale), we moved across to the left hand front seats in Notre Dame and whispered plans for Cap and Gown Sunday. . . . The old peace-time social life got under way with more dances, and more civilians with shiny gold discharge buttons haunting the parlor.

The end of war brought a blossoming of the interest in international relations which had been growing for more than ten years. An article by Marie Therese Lynch '47 on the NFCCS and its International Relations Commission, of which she was chairman, appeared in the *Trinity Times*[84] and was reprinted in full in the *Alumnae Journal.*[85] She shows the early and vital interest in the new United Nations Organization. "The commission," she wrote, "at the beginning of the fall term, outlines a proposed plan for study and action which the colleges are asked to approve. If the majority approve the plan, the International Relations Clubs of the colleges devote at least part of their time to this national program. This year the national plan centers around the United Nations: its organization and function." That year they hosted on campus a model Security Council, held a United Nations Information Day, and sent Miss Lynch as a delegate to the Leadership Workshop at Notre Dame University.[85] The 1947 *Trinilogue*, an elegant production with illuminated quotations on the divider pages, commemorated the fiftieth year of the founding of the college, and was dedicated to the Foundress, Sister Superior Julia, S.N.D. (Susan McGroarty). An introduction: "High Souled Hopes" is a very good account of the years 1897 to 1900 before the college actually opened. It does not, however, include a class history, thus depriving us of the

83. Box: Bastogne, T.C.A., especially albums of pictures of before and after, and the booklet "A rendezvous with destiny."
84. November 14, 1946.
85. Autumn, 1946, pp. 18–19.

1947's own version of student life in their time, though Ila Ware '50 wrote a series of sketches in the *Record* (Feb. 1948)[86] that reflect some aspects of student out-of-class activities when she was a sophomore: awaiting the mail, trips to Joe's (discreetly incognito as "Jay's"), and chapel visits. These excerpts show by implication many day-to-day customs and activities that time has erased and can serve well as a mid-century contrast to those from the early years.[87] Like the earlier accounts they appear here at length.

". . . To Get a Letter"

Wedding bells, doorbells, New Year's bells, all arouse a certain amount of expectation, excitement, and turmoil, but in the intensity of their effects they cannot compare with the ten o'clock class 'bell at T---- College. Ten o'clock electrifies its hearers with the thought, "Mail call!" For sheer speed effected, it surpasses the eight o'clock dormitory bell that shocks you from the deep, deep languor of sleep; the assembly bell, nagging you as you struggle out of your gym suit three flights and five minutes above O'C---- Auditorium—yes, even the "ten-minute bell," warning of mealtime. Consider my own case this morning as typical. . . .

Almost before the bell has stopped vibrating, I jostle my way through the crowd bubbling out of English A, and head for the narrow back stairs. (Common opinion claims that using the broad front staircase takes too much time.) There is a fascinating possibility that Dad has come through with the check at last. Or perhaps Jack has written. If he can get a weekend to come down for the dance, he should have written by now. Let's see, I wrote last Friday . . . he got it Monday at the latest . . . today's Thursday—oh, it's just got to be there! By the time I've reached the steps, I have consoled myself with the theory that if by some freak of chance he *hasn't* written, at least I may get a letter from Marie. She always writes such interesting odds and ends. I wonder what she's been thinking about lately? Wait till I write her what happened yesterday—will she laugh!

As I reach the Marble Corridor and swing around the landing to start down the next flight, it has occurred to me that Mother hasn't written for over a week, now. Of course, she's busy, but I'd just love to get one of her lively notes. Over a week—you don't suppose there's anything wrong? My goodness, what's holding up the girls in front? Oh—oh, a bottle-neck at the foot of the steps, where the door opens up into the basement corridor—I just can't be late for Essay class again!

I stand in line, absently watching the expressions of the girls struggling upstairs. They were early, and already have their mail—lucky creatures. Jeanne comes up one step at a time, concentrating on a pink sheet, her lips moving slowly over each word. Behind her, Pat is eagerly trying to read two missives at the same time. And here's Anne with no letter, staring moodily at the stairs spiraling above her. What if I don't get one either!

86. Pp. 75–79.
87. Pp. 318–321.

Helen stumbles up, chuckling aloud at the deckled page bobbing in her hand, looking around for someone to share the joke. By the way, I haven't heard from Kitty for awhile—one of her epistles would be just the thing to brighten up Phys. Ed.—what a wit!

Ah, our line is moving now. As I duck under the low ceiling and push open the heavy door, another thought occurs to me. It's just possible that my brother might succumb to a sudden urge to write. Joining the current pulsating toward the P.O. door, I meditate on the idea. Of course, he's busy at college, and he's already written one letter, which fills his quota for the semester.

Tripping over a jumble of laundry cases, none of which is mine, I gather myself together, inhale to a full five-foot-five, and plunge desperately into the churning mob of the Post Office. A year's experience enables me to wriggle toward the package list with a minimum of sweater sleeves snagged in my spiral notebook. Bracing myself momentarily against the flood-tide of other determined students, I hopefully scan the list. No luck.

Now, it is comparatively simple to move with the tide and struggle within reach of Box 324. Peering over the shoulder of a wistful senior peeking timidly around the office-door to see if Sister has put *all* the mail out yet, I stretch one arm nearer to my box. Hurray, there's something in it! Daddy? Mother? Jack? Marie? Kitty? my brother? Eagerly I seize the precious thing and draw it out. Oh, no. No! NO! I stare down. Not a letter, but an emphatic, pencilled note: "Miss W-----, will you kindly call for your laundry *at once!*"

". . . Will Pass and Be Forgotten With the Rest"

We were just sitting there at Jay's, waiting for Marg to finish her cigarette and listening to Dina and Kathy argue about their theories on poetry. I started to twirl my empty coke bottle in aimless, lazy circles across the table, half-interested in the green reflection sparkling over the scarred wood, when one of those scars tripped my attention. It was a name, awkwardly dug into the pine: "Joan Murray, '40." Then I realized that the table was covered with names, hundreds of them, carved and charred in a fading crisscross: "Betsy, '45"; "N.M.H."; "Claire F"; "Pat"; "Mac." Fascinated with my discovery I lifted the salt-shaker from its accustomed place in the corner and found where a "Gretchen" had recorded her presence in square, deep-set characters—how long ago? Blurred into the wood itself, the older names seemed to share a secret immortality underneath layers of later imprints. A few more years of thick white dishes and heavy glasses rattling over the surface would obliterate the '40's as well, and then a new generation would add *their* quota. I wondered about those names. How many girls, five, nine, thirteen, even eighteen years ago, had sat in this same booth drinking a coke, smoking, arguing, reading, or thrashing out some campus problem. . . .

Jay's must have been much the same to them as it is to us. Of course, the fluorescent lights shadow the haze of smoke with a bluer tinge, and, on occasion, the plaster walls have renewed their beige-and-green decor, but the same dingy clock, surrounded, I suspect, by the same clutter of dangling cards displaying razor blades, sunglasses, and bottle openers, dominates the room from its corner, high above the front counter. And surely no one has replaced the framed menus which, on the back wall, announce their glad tidings in blue letters and celebrate them in red flourishes: "Hot dogs—15¢"; "Toasted pound cake with fudge sauce—20¢." Indeed, I doubt if returning students would consider a new semester as promising, if any other sign than that of the same grandeur—and antiquity—as the menus did not "Welcome T-----!" from the rear left wall. Glancing at the old wooden coat-rack by the door (how many styles of jackets and coats have been hung up there!) it occurred to me that the changelessness of Jay's is part of its charm; the shabbiness, part of its tradition. Not for this place the blaring modernity of a jukebox; even if there were room for one, Jay would never install it. Here, conversation still provides the only entertainment, and laughter the only amusement. As the flood of talk swirled about me, I realized that when they were here, "Joan," "H.W.N.," "Mary T," and all the others had talked about the same things: the lit test, the phone call, the Saturday campus, the chances of a 1.5. For a moment, I could even imagine that they were the ones crowded into the booths around us. Then, the fancy changed, and the girls were those coming *after* we had gone. I watched Jay behind the counter, ringing up someone's bill. He'd always be there, in his blue-striped shirt and voluminous white apron, cashing checks, taking orders, cancelling forgetful requests for hamburgers with "It's Friday, girls!"

Dina and Kathy declared a temporary truce, Marg ground out her cigarette, and suddenly we were leaving. "C'mon, we only have ten minutes to get back." We shrugged into our coats and straggled out, but just before we left, I looked back and smiled, knowing that one more name had been carved into the third booth against the wall. Then I shut the door behind me.[88]

". . . the Beauty of Thy House"

Benediction in the chapel becomes especially "other-world" when the sacristan floods only the sanctuary with light. Then, darkness swirls about the vast arches high above, where the dim-figured evangelists keep silent watch, and eddies down across the pews, to pile up as shadows in the corners and sift toward the marble line of tracery which is the sanctuary rail. There it dissolves in a cloud of soft light which flows about the golden monstrance shining on the long, gleaming altar, while, beyond the altar's soaring canopy, mosaics sparkle in golden echoes from the ceiling's dim greenness.

The silence, the stillness of the great empty chapel; the stillness, the raptness of the worshipper's mind, press toward the Radiance, as if wait-

88. The author was unaware that before she graduated Joe's would be a thing of the past. Sensing the approach of "smoking on campus" Joe made arrangements to retire to Florida when the Trinity smoker opened February 3, 1950.

> ing. At length, desire finds expression in a note of music which, almost imperceptible at first, softly penetrates the gloom of the nave and touches the monstrance with melody. Then, as if transported by the contact, the tone weaves itself into a pattern of harmony and envelops the whole chapel with the rich color of sound. Caught up in its sweeping tide, the mind is impelled across the shadow-pattern of the pews to the sanctuary, the light, and the Host.

Sister Catherine Dorothea, writing of the students of 1948, said: "They regard no field of human endeavor as unimportant or uninteresting. With equal zeal they turn from the study of St. Thomas to organize a scout troop at an orphanage, and from an afternoon at the Library of Congress to an evening at the Christ Child Settlement House."[89]

Mary Theresa Shea '51 presented a good overview of student clubs in the late 1940's in the *Alumnae Journal*, Autumn, 1950.[90]

"Life at Trinity College," she wrote, "is composed of religious, academic, and social activities which intermingle and suffuse one another, producing a unified atmosphere in which the student lives and grows into a cultured citizen. The student is not, however, merely a passive member of the college community, but, in fact an active contributor to the unity of school activities through her participation in each phase of college life." This was to be the first in a series of articles to keep the alumnae up-to-date on college life. Others on Student Government, Sodality, and national student organizations followed. These will be cited in later sections of this chapter. In true Thomistic fashion for 1951 were the Thomists *par excellence*, Miss Shea organized her discussion. "In general, . . . clubs meet once a month, dues are paid once a year and all clubs, with a few exceptions, are open to all students. In particular, clubs can be divided into co-curricular and extra-curricular."

Under co-curricular clubs were language clubs: French, German, Italian, and Spanish Clubs which presented Mardi Gras each year.[91] In the late 1940's, the Spanish Club had a special activity, the sponsorship of two Italian war orphans, paying their board in a convent in Italy with the proceeds from an annual tea dance in January. Literary, chemical, mathematics societies, as well as art, music, sociology and international relations were all co-curricular. The Athletic Association, the Christ Child Society, the Wekanduit Bureau ("Weekies"), Washington Club work with Br. Maurus for the underprivileged children he

89. *Alumnae Journal*, Autumn, '48, p. 14.
90. Pp. 8–10.
91. The Mardi Gras Carnival dates from the early 1930's and at times has been a very impressive pageant with floats and dances—all in the Alumnae Hall Cafeteria.

gathered at St. Anselm's, Choir and Glee Club, as well as student publications complete Miss Shea's list. For each club, of either category, she mentioned its chief activities and ended her article with the statement:

> When a student panel presented the material of these articles at a faculty meeting last spring, the only comment from the audience was "How do they do it all?" The question is a good one, but can be answered readily, if we return to the idea in our opening comments. Life at Trinity is carried on in a unified atmosphere. [The typical Trinity Thomist!]

A glance at Student Government Booklets of the period will show also that a rather strict regime governed the number of clubs in each category a single student could join. The choice was hers, but the number was regulated to avoid dissipation of effort. As in the past, all students were members of student government, of Sodality, and of the Athletic Association.

The decade of the forties ended and the fifties began with the celebration of the fiftieth academic year of the college, 1949–1950. This opened with a Jubilee Weekend November 3–6, 1949. It opened on Thursday, November 3 with a Mass of Thanksgiving for students and faculty with His Excellency, the Most Reverend Patrick Aloysius O'Boyle, Archbishop of Washington, as celebrant and the Reverend Edmond Benard, of the Theology School of Catholic University, as preacher. Saturday was a full day beginning with a 10:00 a.m. Solemn High Mass of Requiem for Deceased Founders, Faculty, Alumnae and Benefactors. The Rt. Rev. Patrick J. McCormick, Rector of the Catholic University was celebrant and the noted Father Ignatius Smith, O.P. preached. Present at this mass were two elderly Paulist Priests, Fathers Thomas S. O'Neill and Richard Cartwright who had been among the Paulist Seminarians who were the choir at the Dedication, November 22, 1900.

In the afternoon at an Academic Convocation, attended by representatives of more than a hundred institutions of higher education, the college conferred honorary degrees on three outstanding Catholic women: Mother Mary Joseph, O.P., foundress of the Maryknoll Sisters; Jane M. Hoey '14, Director of Public Assistance for the federal government and loyal alumna; and Professor Helen C. White, writer, scholar, and Professor of English in the University of Wisconsin. The academic procession of seniors, representatives of the alumnae, faculty, and guests was historic in a special Trinity way, because the Sisters of Notre Dame changed a fifty-year custom and marched in their proper places with the faculty for the first time instead of sitting secluded in the transept observing. As usual one turns to Ellen

Ganey's editorial in the *Alumnae Journal*[92] for an unsurpassable description quoted in full earlier in this history[93] in the administration of Sister Catherine Dorothea.

On Sunday the Solemn Pontifical Mass of Thanksgiving was celebrated by the Most Reverend Amleto G. Cicognani, Apostolic Delegate to the United States with the Right Reverend Edward B. Jordan, vice-rector of Catholic University and for years a Trinity professor, as Assistant Priest; Rev. Aloysius K. Ziegler as deacon, and Rev. John Carr, C.S.P. sub-deacon. The Paulist Students furnished the music as their predecessors had done at the dedication fifty years before.

Trinity's Choir showed the worth of its fifty-year experience by singing at both the Thursday and Saturday masses, and performing Montani's *Jubilate Deo* at the Convocation. The *Trinity College Record* under the editorship of Ila Ware published special jubilee issues that year with beautifully lettered and illuminated covers by Sheila Walsh '50 as did the *Trinity Times*. Both are featured in the 1950 *Trinilogue,* thus giving an idea of the students' appreciation of their fifty-year-old college.

The students of the late 1940's were like their predecessors, an intelligent group of young women making good use of the educational opportunities of the college, while enjoying an apparently carefree social life.

Sister Catherine Dorothea Fox, president of the college, using data provided by the Dean of Studies' Office as well as her own experience on the College Board, described the excellent achievement of Trinity students as shown by the Graduate Record General Education and Advanced Tests.[94] "It should be noted," she wrote, "that these examinations test knowledge gained not only through formal courses, but through all the various media of intelligent living." The results of tests taken in April, 1949, show the mean scores of Trinity sophomores and seniors to be consistently higher than those for comparable women, and even of men and women, except that the sophomores were slightly below in the field of physical science.

The year's celebration culminated at Alumnae Reunion in the midst of which the Class of 1950 graduated. The students' part in the celebration was a pageant, "Trinity Through the Years," written by Anne McMaster '50, and produced by the Dramatic Society. This intrigued

92. Winter '50, pp. 56–59. The program for the three days was elegantly printed, as was a booklet with all the speeches of the weekend, T.C.A.
93. P. 125.
94. "The Graduate Record Examination," Sister Catherine Dorothea, S.N.D. President. *Alumnae Journal*, Spring, 1950, pp. 109–111. This includes a description of Trinity's participation, 1945–1948, in the Inquiry into Post War Conditions in American Colleges.

Maypole in South Court. 1950's or 1960's.

the press and a full page feature with pictures appeared in the Washington papers.

The Fifties 1950–1961

The class of 1950, the seniors during the fiftieth academic year, are the link between the two parts of this section of the history. They spent most of their college years in the 1940's, but led the way into the new decade. Exuberantly Irish because their class color was green, they solemnly dedicated the statue of St. Patrick (bought with three years of class savings) on their Cap and Gown Sunday, September 1949.[95] No matter that the class roll showed names of English, German, Italian, Danish, French, Austrian, and Slavic origins as well as Irish, St. Patrick was the patron of the whole green class of 1950. Saying farewell to them in the 1950 *Trinilogue*, 1952 wrote: "Still we'll always think of you as our own jolly junior sisters, shouting 'Top o' the Mornin'' in our

95. Picture on cover *Alumnae Journal*, Autumn, 1949.

ears at 5:00 a.m., marching to 'It's a Great Day for the Irish' at your Junior Prom, and brightening up the Woolly West with a touch of green." The blues of 1953 wrote that they hoped that they could "keep the Trinity spirit . . . learned from the daughters of St. Patrick."

Perhaps the most momentous event, from the students' point-of-view, that marked the beginning of Trinity's second half-century was the opening, February 3, 1950, of the Students' Smoker. Since the early 1920's the petition for permission to smoke on campus had been regularly on the Student Government agenda. The same subject was hotly debated at alumnae annual meetings, generating resolutions formally presented to the college. Though Trinity had been an innovative leader in student activities as well as in academic excellence through the years, in this matter of smoking on campus she lagged far behind others. When the decision was announced telephone wires from students to alumnae, and alumnae to alumnae buzzed across the country from coast to coast. A blot on their Alma Mater's prestigious escutcheon had been at last removed!

The cafeteria in Alumnae Hall, the downstairs area now occupied by the faculty dining room and the Education for Parish Service Program, was designated for the Smoker. Student Government took charge and appointed a committee to supervise order and clean-up. Two new songs entered the Trinity repertoire, "Smoke Gets in Your Eyes" and "You're in My Dreams." Eight years later, before new Cuvilly Hall was opened, the class of 1958 described the activities in the smoker.

> In every season the smoker remains a center of student life. It is a world of tension surrounding piles of books at exam time or spontaneous laughter inspired by skits and impromptu entertainments. Here the plans for projects, class days, or special weekends are born. Discussions range from the morning's mail to the President's annual budget. Sunday brings an excuse for song fests, smoker-style.

The years have brought "smokers" to all buildings and smoking permitted in students' rooms in the fireproof buildings, though not in the Main Building—yet! The contemporary student would find it hard to realize the importance of that first Smoker or to accept the regulations that surrounded it. They might well, however, learn much from the clean-up program in force in the 50's.

In the decade of the fifties which was opened so auspiciously by the events described above, the long tradition of song continued. Music in both formal and informal events permeated student life. Joint glee club concerts with men's colleges, pioneered by Georgetown-Trinity in 1951, flourished. Student written and choreographed musical comedies on Class Days, revived in the 1940's after a period of published one-

West Point Cadets at Trinity. Eisenhower Inauguration.

act plays, reached a high degree of popularity.[96] A 1952 class day musical scored and directed by Dorothy Sennett and choreographed by Margaret Schnellbacher ("the DeMille touch in Wekie or Class Day shows")[97] was professional as well as popular. Later Kitty Solomita '57 was the indispensable accompanist. The more frivolous side of student life was reflected in the light humor of class day "spoofing" of faculty and administration and in the witty political and social satire of the Washington Club Show, a production rehearsed through the summer each year and performed early in the fall semester. One such musical stands out in memory, the 1958 Washington Club musical featuring Anne and Jeanne Dahlsteadt '59, identical twins, as rival candidates in an election campaign.

This was the era that witnessed the birth of the Trinity Belles, counterparts of the Georgetown Chimes, and of the first tea dance *on campus,* at which the students entertained the West Point Cadets who had marched in the Eisenhower inaugural parade. Roller skating (ice skating when possible), picnics and hiking, boating on the Potomac and yachting with paper yachts on the pond in the South Court—all found a following. Laundry cases from home still flourished until the advent

96. Cf. Section on Class Days later in this chapter.
97. 1952 *Trinilogue,* p. 120.

of the Gordon-Davis service. The telephone was still popular and busy, bringing an "invitation for Saturday night, a plea for six blind dates," a "long distance from home" or "just a quiet conversation." The parlors welcomed "a continuous stream of people" and "though not exactly our own living rooms" were nevertheless "beloved." "For often the room is filled with young men in tweeds or flannels—and lately in uniforms—waiting more or less patiently while upstairs we try to hurry."[98]

The Belles have had good times and bad in their thirty years of existence. Begun in 1950 by members of the class of 1952, The Belles were a student organized and directed double "barber shop quartette" which grew later to a triple quartet. The 1952 *Trinilogue,* page 189, pictures a group of the original Belles: Dorothy Sennet, chief organizer and pianist, Caroline Wagner, Mary Alice Patton, Regina Forsney, Eileen O'Connell, Frances Quinn, Joan Galloway, Mary Louise Cullen. Patricia O'Rourke, "Fifty-two's First Lady . . . a T.C. Belle whose disposition harmonizes as well as her voice" was not in this picture. For most of the decade they were considered not exactly *comme il faut* by the music department because their harmony and choice of songs did not conform to classical requirements. The twelve member group, however, was very popular, though in the unwilling position of "poor relation" to the time-tested Glee Club and Choir. They went confidently ahead and won places in intercollegiate competitions. They were in demand for student parties, and recorded their singing.[99] Gradually they took their place as a distinguished asset to college activities, invited by faculty, administration and alumnae as well as by students to perform at their functions.[100] The cover "blurb" on the 1962–1963 recording catches the confident spirit of the Belles:

> In 1950 Washington was introduced to the harmonies of the *Trinity Belles.* Now in their second decade of music-making, the Belles have expanded their audience from the intercollegiate to the "international set." By popular request they have entertained at political functions in the Nation's Capital as well as having renewed their welcomed acquaintance at college dances and other social scenes.
>
> Under the persuasive pitchpipe of Jo Ann Smith, the *Belles* can usually be found enlivening such familiar "haunts" as *Gusti's,* the *1789* and *Cuvilly Smoker.*

The 1950's were indeed a decade of music, all aspects of it "from Gregorian hymnody to barbershop harmony."[100]

98. 1953 *Trinilogue,* p. 182.
99. Copies of albums made by the Belles of *1962* and *1969* are extant in the T.C. Archives.
100. Cf. 1957 *Trinilogue,* pp. 68–69.

Cap and Gown Sunday Group, c. 1948.

In describing the fifties it seems necessary to give emphasis to the lighter, more frivolous and to the service sides of college life, because this was the era of the Trinity "theologians,"[101] of Woodrow Wilson, NDEA, and Fulbright Fellowships, of many national or university grant fellowships for graduate work in nearly all fields of the curriculum of "Honors" seminars or individual honors work, and even of foundation-funded undergraduate research which occupied summer vacations. Academic work was a serious matter in the Fifties. The concerns aroused by Sputnik and the curricular reorganization reflected in student attitudes.[102] The Student Education Committee also dates from this era. The Confraternity of Christian Doctrine, begun on campus in the 1930's blossomed into an even more effective, efficient work in the hands of zealous students of the 1950's. The 1952 *Trinilogue* describes the initiation of a Sodality Council to coordinate the activities of Sodality with those of Wekanduits, C.C.D., the Christ Child Society, and the Interracial Club.[103] The Sophomore Workshop in Liberal Arts Education, a student-initiated, senior-directed attempt to help off-set the dreaded "sophomore slump" was an achievement of the 1950's that

101. Cf. pp. 273–274. The class of 1951 was first class to have theology for four years and grew to consider themselves as "Thomists *par excellence.*"
102. Cf. Chapter 5, pp. 180 ff.
103. These activities as well as Student Government will be treated in more detail later in this chapter.

continued in the next decade and won from the National Student Association its prestigious Welling Award in 1957. The fifties also saw the *Trinity Times* rated All-American for superior work, for a stretch of years from 1952.

No description of the early fifties would be complete without reference to Ellen Ganey's "Passing of the Mid-night Bus",[104] a typical E.A.G. editorial, or Dorothy Sennett's "Permissions."[105] Both deserve re-reading to catch the flavor of an era. We shall include here an excerpt from the first and cite the second in the student government section. Thus wrote Ellen in 1982

> The first S.G. assembly of the year 1952–53 brought a storm of cheers and applause that re-echoed through the closed doors of O'Connor Auditorium down the far length of the Marble Corridor. Pausing in our work-a-day affairs, we thought—more permissions! Yes, there were more and later permissions—up to 12:30 for Seniors. But more than that, there was the announcement, called and repeated ecstatically in eager young voices throughout the Smoker immediately afterwards—no more buses for Trinity students returning from dances. Our readers know that we are forward-looking, that we have rejoiced in and approved, however tacitly, all the wonderful innovations, scholastic and social, of Trinity's last twenty years. We have endeavored to be—and felt at once humble and proud in being—of Trinity with every class— of every color; Red, Blue, Green, Gold—of every decade—the dear beginnings of the "oughts," the thrilling years of the first war, the turbulent twenties, the thoughtful thirties, the phenomenal forties, the . . . well, never mind! The buses are gone! Our armor is pierced—our brave front broken—for an era has passed and we can but look back—just this once—in unashamed and wistful longing.
>
> No Trinity bus. What is Washington coming to? The Trinity bus—butt of Georgetown and C.U. jokes for thirty years—summarily disposed of in an S.G. assembly of our brash young in this year of '52! This is truly the end of our half century. What are solemn convocations and grave sermons but the conventional trappings of a date? It is some seemingly inconsequential incident that really marks the end of one period and the beginning of another. The midnight bus is gone.
>
> Truly this is the end of Trinity's verdant youth—her days of fairy tale. Where else in the world could you find scores of lovely Cinderellas scampering en masse from a lighted ballroom to board their corporate carriage home? Where else could you find their gallant princes, in tails and toppers (or only borrowed tuxes) clustering round in gallant dejection, the price of supper still safely in their pockets against next week's laundry bills? And Mrs. Pattison—fairy godmother of how many years—futilely scanning street and doorway for the last laggard who finally approached, rosy and trium-

104. *Alumnae Journal*, Autumn '52, pp. 10–11.
105. *Alumnae Journal*, Winter '52, pp. 62–63, cited in Student Government Section.

> phant, the young scamp at her heels bearing his telltale accolade of lipstick on his manly chin—the while her tractable sisters sat in decorous and jealous silence awaiting her? Ah, innocence and youth—what is there left to fret against? No Trinity bus! How grown up we are! How mature, how good, how responsible!

Two mid-decade mini-descriptions of student life[106] will serve as both continuity and contrast to the 1902 descriptions earlier in this chapter.

> Potomac-ing all year round, literally and figuratively they seize the bright red ball of spirit from the past and carry it through their activities, their studies and their attitudes. Facing the reality of their new found field of research and the multitude of term papers, reports and monthlies . . . [they] have learned the advantages of scheduled play: it follows scheduled work! So look for them roller skating at the Tidal Basin, or picnicking in Rock Creek Park. See them at the University intramurals, where their enthusiasms lends [sic] to the cheering section. Hockey tunics and "tea" dresses—they'll mix and match them: there's always time for a change! Time for some golf: A walk to B'land! "See you in the Caf?" Annapolis calls, Georgetown visits and Quantico arrives! Carefree sparkle and cheerful gleams continue from tennis games and basketball intramurals to a Sophomore whirl at the Shoreham Ballroom. (*Trinilogue*, 1954, p. 147)

The 1956 version is more succinct.

> The scene viewed with stress on inscape—week and weekend . . . "Arooney it's Friday" . . . and colored Monday . . . "Take some shirts to B'land for me? or Never mind, I'll do them myself . . . an all-important letter that never came . . . small tragedies of Grecian proportions followed by a great joy—"You had a long-distance last night, will call tomorrow" . . . the postdinner questions: "Buy me a cup of coffee, pay you later" . . . "Is there an assembly today?" . . . "Have you done the reserve reading for the quizzle?" . . . from eleven o'clock sub-zero classroom to hasty lunch in tropical dining room . . . "What's on for the weekend?" . . . "Wouldn't be caught dead at that rat-race" . . . "I need a short freshman for a blind date, are you game?" This 1956's casually evolved vernacular. (*Trinilogue*, 1956, p. 156)

The end of the decade found Trinity students, wearing Shetland sweater sets and knee socks, still trekking to B'land, "The Traditional Goal of Athletic Ambulators," and dreaming of a new dormitory building replacing the "Old Quads."[107]

106. From *Trinilogue*, 1954, p. 147 and 1956, p. 156.
107. *Trinilogue*, 1957, pp. 80, 83, 88. New Cuvilly Hall.

The Fourth Twenty Years[108] *1961–1977*
The Sixties

In spite of glowing *Times* and *Trinilogue* accounts of athletic prowess and social success, Sister Ann Francis could still write in 1961 of the new decade Trinity students as academically oriented.[109]

> The 1961 Trinity student, she wrote, is a complex, many-sided person of varying moods, ideas, and opinions. She is, of course, young, with all the maddening inconsistencies of that period—notably, procrastination—from the arrival at Mass two minutes after it has started to the paper finished a minute ahead of the class at which it is due. She is, however, working towards the maturity that only experience and age can give. She takes the business of getting an education seriously, for the most part. The revised four-course curriculum is Trinity's attempt to assure its students "that you go to college to learn." It is hoped, too, that their classes give them the sense of achievement which comes from intellectual effort. Whether it is, that more is demanded of the present-day student academically by way of independent work in seminars, on honors programs even for a selected group of freshmen, or whether it is part of the current educational zeitgeist, the current Trinity student generally puts her scholastic commitments first.

Sister Ann Francis continued with more about the use of Washington as a laboratory for course work, and about Student Government and the Honor System as maturing influences. These will be incorporated into later sections of this chapter.

The sixties were the era of the new library (1963); of the first Parents' Weekend, February, 1960; of undergraduate Honors Convocations twice yearly beginning in October 1959; of our first African students; of the *Look* article and the *Mademoiselle* "Cookie Cutter" article, January, 1963; of the advent of the Early Admissions Program, 1961; of two new dormitory buildings (Cuvilly late '50's and Kerby, 1965); of the Music and Art wing, 1960; of the "new liturgy" 1963–the present; of continuing interest in politics, national and local, manifested by the very active bi-partisan Political Club as well as campus chapters of Young Republicans and Young Democrats; of student publications in science and philosophy: *Scope* and *Thought and Belief*; of the March on Washington and Martin Luther King's speech "I Have a Dream," 1963; of the assassination of a President, 1963, and of his brother, Robert, and of Dr. King in 1968, with ensuing riots; of the reorganization of Student Government to form the Student Association, and, through the early years of the decade, the continued flourishing of the social event of the year, the

108. As background for this section re-read Sister Margaret Claydon's administration, 1959–1975, pp. 134–149; and Sister Rose Ann Fleming, 1975– .
109. *Alumnae Journal*, Spring, 1961, Section 2: "The College Student."

Angelica and Perpetua, First African Students.

"S.G. Tea," Trinity's "At Home" to her friends on the Monday before Thanksgiving each year. The decade ended in student unrest reflecting the spirit of other campuses and of the country.[110] The *Trinilogue*, 1963, though very "modern" in its layout, in its use of lower case in captions shunning capitals whenever possible, shows a student life still interested in traditional activities. May Day (Founder's Day) the day after senior comprehensives in May; "*The* Tea" on the Monday before Thanksgiving when the student body was at home to friends from four to six; The Court Sing on Cap and Gown Sunday; Student Government: "A gift from the past, the promise for the future . . . fostering personal integrity, directing the day-to-day . . .[111] government whose

110. A good picture of the early 1960's college girl is found in *The American College Girl*, by K.C. Cirtaulus (N.Y. Citadel Press), 1962. The author's list of permissions to quote provides a brief selective bibliography of contemporary books on the subject.
111. P. 66.

ideals proclaim the heart of living Trinity . . . "[112]; the Christmas Party for orphans and for the whole college; senior guidance and sophomore workshop, as well as, all the Clubs and Societies mentioned in earlier decades, the "new liturgical movement" and the "new library."

The Deans of Students who worked with the students to deal with the problems as well as the pleasant times of the sixties were Sister Mary Joan Kentz, a member of the class of 1940 and president of student government that year, 1961–1963; Sister Janice Marie Moran, who had been Assistant Dean of Students with both Sister Ann Francis and Sister Mary Joan and to whom the 1963 *Trinilogue* was dedicated, 1963–1965; and Sister Francis (Ann Gormly '45) who returned to her family name while in office and who faced with the students the turbulence and reorganization of the end of the decade, 1965–1971. At the beginning of her term as Dean of Students, Sister Janice Marie Moran characterized the student government as the exercise of "initiative under counsel." She praised the "enduring student-faculty relationship of shared responsibility which the oldest alumna vividly remembers and the newest student quickly recognizes as the Trinity way of life."[113] In this she described the college spirit of the mid-1960's, 1962–1966.

These years saw the construction and dedication of the library building, a practical demonstration of the academic emphasis on campus, as well as a flowering of student social awareness and personal involvement in community needs, in continuity with their predecessors. Both during the year and in vacations students continued to demonstrate that liberal education "liberates the mind from the limited goals of mere utility or personal convenience." They traveled in summer—young alumnae for all year—to volunteer services as teachers in North Carolina, Colorado, and Texas. They tutored homeless children from D.C. Junior Village. They answered "an urgent appeal . . . from Annandale, Virginia, for volunteers to tutor Negro children who had transferred to newly integrated schools." (Virginia schools were a decade behind D.C. in school integration.) "Each Saturday morning they conducted classes in arithmetic, reading, and other elementary school subjects, under the auspices of the Christian Family Movement."[114] Cuvilly Lounge on Wednesday evenings found Sodality members teaching English on a one-to-one basis to Spanish-speaking children newly arrived from Mexico and Venezuela, while on Wednesday afternoon thirteen other student volunteers supervised study periods in nearby public schools: Noyes, Brookland, and Shaw.

112. P. 235.
113. *Newsletter*, November, 1963. Cf. *Newsletter*, July, 1962.
114. *Newsletter*, July, 1963.

Hockey still flourished.

The Wekanduit Society raised transportation money for Mary Anne Tietjens and Michaela Carberry, newly graduated, to mission schools in British Honduras for a year's teaching, and for Gail Moreschi for summer volunteer work in a settlement house in El Paso, Texas. Three others of 1963 worked for a year in the Extension Volunteer Program, while undergraduates staffed vacation schools in North Carolina and Washington, D.C.[115]

The mid-sixties were also the era of continued activity in undergraduate research and of the search for academic excellence, of widening interests in international as well as in national affairs, of courses in East Asian and Russian civilization, of larger groups of foreign students (now called "international students"), of study of the "critical" languages: Chinese, Portuguese, Russian, as well as the traditional foreign languages. A chapter of the American Academy of Poets was

115. *Ibid.* Cf. "All College Apostolate in Community Service," *Newsletter*, February, 1964, pp. 1, 5.

established on campus and Trinity poets continued to win local or national awards.[116] The first chapter of Sigma Pi Sigma, the physics honor society, to be granted to a woman's college was installed at Trinity, March 19, 1966.[117]

The Sophomore Year in England ("the Oxford Program") dates from 1965.[118] The research of Dr. Irena Roberts into the need for education of the mature woman[119] in the early 1960's led to a new diversification of the student body in the Degree Completion and other Continuing Education Programs which developed from it in the next decade.[120] These and the graduate programs (M.A.T., Pastoral Ministry, and M.B.A.) brought to the undergraduates the maturing influence of older women as well as a few men on campus with them. Sister Ann Francis Hoey was interviewed on the Patti Cavan T.V. Show on "Educating the Mature Woman".[121] Carol Widmann '60 and Rosemary Durkin '60 appeared on the Hazel Markel Show with Dr. Irena Roberts, who was doing the research mentioned above, and Mrs. Chester Bowles.

From 1967 to the end of the decade a change of student attitudes toward government, toward college, toward life became noticeable at Trinity as on other college and university campuses. The search for "meaning" was begun by a new generation. In her report for 1967–1968, Sister Ann Gormly wrote of the Student Association: "The continual dialogue and excellent communication with faculty has made the officers seem part of the 'establishment' in the minds of the students with a consequent loss of prestige. The consensual approach tends to dilute the sense of power, something very desired and perhaps needed by young people still unsure of their own worth. Change has come too quietly to be appreciated. Student disinterest was demonstrated at the installation of new officers. Only a handful of personal friends came for the ceremony."

It was in this report also that Sister Ann first mentioned having the student religious activities under someone, other than the Dean of Students,[122] who could give more attention to it. She mentioned a change in more traditional events. "The old Thanksgiving tea was to have been a Christmas Open House as last year. It finally was changed to a spring picnic on the hockey field and was a great success." "There is increas-

116. *Newsletter*, May, 1964, p. 4. List of charter members, both students and alumnae, mostly of '50's and '60's, but including Helen Linehan Porter '07.
117. *Newsletter*, May '66, p. 4.
118. *Newsletter*, November 1965, February and July, 1966, August 1967. Cf. *Alumnae Journal*, Winter 1966, pp. 104–107.
119. *Newsletter*, July 1964; *Trinity News*, December 1969, pp. 3, 5.
120. For M.A.T., *Newsletter*, May 1966, pp. 1 and 4.
121. *Newsletter*, October '61; cf. April, 1961.
122. This was effected later by Dean Winifred Coleman. Cf. Section on Campus Ministry.

ing pressure," she wrote, "against class days and little interest in the activities surrounding graduation itself. The honors convocation was very poorly attended, indicating student lack of interest in such events."

Sister Ann reviewed residence life at Trinity and the changes taking place here and on other campuses. She mentions "the move from the house-mother approach to a more counseling-oriented or more academically-oriented approach in the college world in general." It should be remembered that counseling, both personal and academic had been traditionally functions of the deans, who *were*, from the 1940's to the 1960's, professionally trained and who supervised those of staff or faculty who shared these activities. The campus spirit at the end of the decade is succinctly stated by Sister Ann when she writes of "the speed of change on our own campus that has made obsolete some of the notions I had in this area two years ago."

Transition to the Seventies

Meanwhile students were still interested in the quality of education, in wider political and social movements. They sponsored all-college forums on "Higher Education and Catholic Colleges,"[123] "Urbanization,"[124] and on the Trinity curriculum. They participated with the president and deans in the Cultural Series sponsored by Cabinet members at the State Department and other departmental reception rooms.[125] They benefited from the experience of President Barnaby Keeney of Yale, who spoke at their Leadership Conference in the spring of 1965.[126] In 1969, the largest class graduated (274 + 7 M.A.T.s), addressed by one of their own members, Diana Sixsmith,[127] and the decade ended with unrest caused by tragic incidents on the Kent State and Jackson State campuses as well as by the assassinations already mentioned.

"The year 1969–1970 was unique," wrote the Dean of Students in her report. "It will always be hard to understand how a year that began with so much promise under capable student leaders, and that reached a climax in February with the acceptance of Task Force proposals bringing desired academic change, and the Rathskeller in which to share a renewed sense of community, could by mid-March become a house divided against itself."[128] But it did! "Moratorium,[129] boycott, Cambodia: those concerns generated the interest of about seventy-five percent

123. *Trinity News*, June '69, pp. 2, 5, also p. 1.
124. *Trinity News*, February '69, p. 2.
125. *Ibid.*
126. *Ibid.* June '68.
127. *Trinity News*, June '69, pp. 2, 5, also p. 1.
128. Dean of Students' Report, 1969–1970, p. 1. (Sister Ann Gormly).
129. Cf. *Trinity News*, December 1969.

of the students. The more traditionally collegiate kind of activities stimulated little enthusiasm."[130]

With the growing number of black students on campus Sister Ann wrote in that same report: "Aware of my own inadequacies in the area of work with black students, I made an effort this (last) summer through reading and attendance at a black college to come to a better understanding of their way of thinking and their problems. Faithful participation in the trying meetings of the Black Experience Committee, which spent a good part of the year preparing a report on this topic, was the principal way available to me during the year to show special concern for the black students."[131]

That, after twenty years of integration on the Trinity campus, black students were very much a part of student life, however, is shown by the election of Jeannette Jackson president of the senior class of 1970 which office would be hers for as long as she chose to exercise it as an alumna. The speaker at the Cap and Gown Sunday breakfast was Mrs. Elizabeth Duncan Koontz, Director of the Women's Bureau of the Department of Labor. "Mrs. Koontz, the first Negro to head the Women's Bureau and the first of her race to be president of NEA, is also a U.S. Delegate to the United States Commission on the Status of Women."[132] Black faculty members were appearing also. Sylvia Washington '58, a Woodrow Wilson and Fulbright Fellow was teaching in the French Department from 1961 to 1967 and returned as Madame Bâ from 1969–1974 when she returned to Senegal with her diplomat husband and to the faculty of the University of Senegal. Mrs. Hortense Fitzgerald in the M.A.T. program, and Dr. James R. Haynes in Economics, and Mr. Joseph Clare, Director of the Upward Bound Program were here in the late 1960's. Since that time the presence of black faculty members has become so accepted as to be seldom emphasized.

In the spring of 1970, many of the students, misunderstanding the faculty tenure regulations, rose in defense of some of their popular young teachers whose contracts were not renewed. Under the capable direction of the top officers of the Student Association, Barbara Shambo and Helen Gallagher, and encouraged by the teachers affected, they boycotted classes for nearly a week.[133] A special meeting of the Board of Trustees was called to consider a position paper signed by 470 students[134] and to listen to student presentations. Mr. Hugh P. McFadden, Chairman of the Board, stayed on campus for several days,

130. Dean of Students' Report, 1969–1970, p. 1. (Sister Ann Gormly).
131. Dean of Students' Report, 1969–1970, p. 14.
132. *Trinity News*, August, 1969, p. 1. Cf. p. 353 for first black students, September 1948.
133. *Trinity News*, April, 1970, p. 2. Cf. Dean of Students' report cited earlier.
134. Board of Trustees papers. T.C.A. The undergraduate enrollment 1969–1970 was 787. The 470 who signed the position paper were a little less than 60% of all.

"after the college was again in running order" to discuss the matter with students. The Trustees issued the following statement:

> The action of the administration in giving terminal contracts and notices was discussed at length. Faculty and student representatives participated in the discussion. Members of the Board explained that the notices were given to implement a policy decision previously made by the Board, which is aimed at bringing the budget into balance and eliminating present and projected operating deficits.

Since the proper procedures had been followed, "the Board unanimously agreed that the request to reconsider must be declined." The Board took steps, however, to encourage student opinion and find more effective methods of making it known. A "Policy on Disruptive Demonstrations" was approved by the faculty and by the faculty-student Senate and issued from the President's Office, November 6, 1970.

That last year of the decade ended with student rallies, as well as special masses for the victims of unrest at Kent State and Jackson State colleges. Though the "disturbances" of the spring semester had caused faculty and administration to worry about what might happen at the commencement ceremonies, there was little difference from those of any other year.[135] A few black gowned seniors wore symbolic white armbands for peace and to memorialize their fallen comrades, but all 197 approached the dais with dignity to receive their degrees from Sister Margaret Claydon, President. At that commencement 14 men and women received the Master of Arts in Teaching. Honorary doctorates were conferred on the new presidents of area universities: Dr. James Cheek, Howard; Rev. Robert J. Henle, S.J., Georgetown; Dr. Clarence Walton, Catholic University. The Class of 1970's crusaders for peace were urged by the speaker Senator George McGovern of South Dakota to get back to "a reasonable application to the principles of the Declaration of Independence and the Constitution."

"Let us," he said, "rededicate our nation to peace and the healing of our nation. Let us reaffirm the inalienable rights of every human to 'life, liberty, and the pursuit of happiness.' That is the cry that gave us birth, and that is the way to greatness for America." These are things that the Class of 1970 had been trying to do in its own way. Rev. Dr. Vincent Mathews of the Sociology department who gave the Invocation,[136] showed that he understood both the aspirations and the troubles of the generation. His invocation impressed both students and guests at the ceremony and is reprinted here in full.

135. *Trinity News*, July, 1970, pp. 1, 4, 5. Minutes of the Board of Trustees.
136. *Trinity News*, July, 1970, p. 4.

A Prayer for 1970

Invocation at Commencement, May 31st
by Reverend Vincent Mathews
Associate Professor of Sociology

Oh God, let this generation always ask: what is truth?

Let them always be discontented with injustice and burn with impatience.

Let them be creators of a new world rather than builders of walls against change.

Let them be despised agitators fighting against public opinion rather than bandwagon reformers waiting for opinion to change, flitting like butterflies after the safe and popular.

May neither the years nor the heavy responsibilities of life tarnish their ideals.

Whatever the cost, let them honestly face problems rather than avoid them, and fight the easy compromises that sell principles for pottage.

But above all, let them never build their happiness or security on the blood, sweat, or servitude of black, brown, red, yellow or white brothers.

Give them courage to be losers, for one cannot win much without risking much

And let them learn from your Son that jail, death on a cross, or a mocking world does not mean failure.

That in pursuing ideals to the very end, they are truly following Him.

Amen.

Along with other worthwhile activities[137] in senior year, the class of 1970 initiated and carried through a project which had lasting influence on student life: the metamorphosis of the snack bar in Cuvilly Hall into the campus rathskeller, the Red Rose Inn, where beer and light wine could be served. This proposal had been voluntarily submitted to the Board of Trustees, though such action was not necessary, because the students wanted their approval.[138] The choice of the name Red Rose Inn reflects the history of Cuvilly Hall which stands on the site of Rose Estate which was bought by the college in 1913,[139] where in the early years of the college a noisy and somewhat disreputable roadhouse operated under the name of the Red Rose Inn. For a fuller history of the use of the property by the college and reminiscences of those who knew both old and new Cuvilly Hall, see Chapter 7.

137. Cf. Dean's Reports cited above.
138. Minutes of the Board of Trustees, October 25, 1969.
139. Cf. *Trinity News*, July, 1970; *Washington Star* interview with Sister Teresa, I.J., circa September 1957 in T.C.A.: President's reports.

Dean Winifred Coleman.

At the end of the 1970-71 year Sister Ann Gormly left Trinity College for a sabbatical year and administrative work for the Sisters of Notre Dame at Ilchester, Maryland. She was honored by the student body at a dinner April 29, 1971 at which they not only toasted her for her five years' service as Dean of Students, but presented her with a check from the four classes to enable her to travel on her sabbatical year in Brazil.[140]

Miss Winifred Coleman,[141] who had been Catholic Woman of the Year in 1963, succeeded Sister Ann Gormly, to become the "Dean of the Seventies." She came to Trinity from fourteen years of service as the popular Dean of Students at Casanovia College in New York. The first laywoman to hold the office of dean at Trinity, she brought with

140. *Trinity News*, June, 1971, p. 2.
141. *Ibid.* pp. 1-2. Dean Coleman served Trinity 1972-1981.

her a record of successful academic and professional activities, including graduation from Le Moyne College in Syracuse, a Master's Degree in guidance and student personnel from Marquette University, membership in at least five national organizations, and listing in Who's Who of American Education, of American Women, in the East, as well as listing in International Biography. She was active in the American Personnel and Guidance Association, the Central New York Council of Girl Scouts, the National Association of Women Deans and Counselors, the International Federation of Catholic Alumnae. All of which helped to prepare her to face the changing students of the seventies with sensitivity, objectivity and aplomb, to which she added her own brand of humor to help her through many a difficult situation.

The Seventies

The new scholastic year 1970–1971, the transition to the Seventies, found the students in good order, the "new curriculum"[142] in full swing. Cap and Gown Sunday mass was celebrated outside, with the altar on the portico of Notre Dame Chapel and the president, Sister Margaret Claydon, could write in December[143]:

> Students are actively engaged in the work of their courses but they are also involved in those extra-curricular offerings which make college more meaningful and sometimes even fun! Father Schrider and the Campus Ministry have been seeking ways to make the faith more truly a part of the lives of this generation.
>
> Almost all of the Trinity Students spend part of their day in work experience, either in fulfillment of personal goals as volunteers, or for financial aid, or as part of their practical courses for academic credit in which students have an opportunity to test theory in "real-life" situations. These positions bring them into the city where they become more aware of the advantages of going to college in the nation's capital. Many courses this semester will increase this activity even more in the future as our Washington Semester program combines the offerings of Political Science, Sociology, and other departments into a cohesive unit for a work study experience. . . .
>
> The Service Council has undertaken several projects this year and on a regular basis Trinity students visit St. Ann's Infant Home and the Washington Hospital Center. Many, too, tutor children from Junior Village, and work with handicapped children.

These students were in continuity with the four pioneers who went with two Sisters of Notre Dame, November, 1900, to begin the Sunday School in St. Anthony's parish in Brookland, and all those of the

142. Cf. Chapter 5.
143. *Trinity News*, December, 1970.

decades between with their Girl Scout troops, social work, and care for poor families at Christmas and Easter.

"The students of the seventies," the president continued, "have expressed an increased interest in developing their creative talents and we note that many more are registering in art and music. Sculpture, painting, design as well as voice, instrument and musical theory registrations are rising."

The seventies saw the maturing of programs begun in the previous decade and the consequent change in the composition of the student body mentioned earlier. Students became accustomed to older women on campus. Many teachers from the Washington schools in the MAT classes, the Religious in the Pastoral Ministry Program and the married women in Degree Completion and Continuing Education programs mixed freely with the traditional undergraduate women, benefiting all groups. The cosmopolitan, geographically and racially integrated character of the student body gained an element of integration of age groups. Young children of married students were cared for in a student operated nursery and baby-sitting service. Young families appeared at Commencement for mother's graduation.[144] The college became more accustomed to Trinity's own undergraduate women returning to classes to finish their degree course after marriage. More undergraduate students found off-campus jobs.

Practica in their major subjects, internships in government, business, communications and art history came into their own in the seventies. They helped many students to appreciate the realities of life after college and to develop a mature, practical program, arranging on- and off-campus time efficiently. This had been traditionally the experience of practice teachers, social workers, as well as volunteers in group work with children, but practica, internships, and paid jobs widened the opportunities as the new decade progressed. This is well described in the articles "A College Without Walls," and Patricia McGuire's "Working Students" in the *Alumnae Journal*.[145] Though a computer center had been installed on campus in 1966 under the aegis of the Mathematics department, and administrative offices initiated some computer use, computer technology grew rapidly, interesting and affecting the lives of both faculty and students through the seventies and beyond.

A swing toward student interest in "traditional" activities showed itself. College-wide organizations like student government, athletics,

144. For an example see Georgia Knightley's article in the *Alumnae Journal*, Spring, 1972, pp. 7–11; "Pastoral Ministry," by Sister Mary Louise Norpel, *Alumnae Journal*, Spring, '74, pp. 6–7.

145. "College Without Walls," *Alumnae Journal*, Winter, '72, pp. 7–11; "Working Students," Patricia McGuire, '74, *Alumnae Journal*, Winter, '74, pp. 10–11; *Newsletter*, March, '74, pp. 1-3.

campus ministry as well as many of the clubs of long standing such as dramatics and glee club evoked student participation with a strong "seventies emphasis." The choir became the liturgical singing group. The glee club became the concert choir. Athletics became much more inter-collegiate and added the crew to other teams. Dramatics added miming to its repertoire and returned to O'Connor Auditorium for plays after sixty years in Notre Dame Auditorium, which in turn was fully occupied by the Fitness Center.[146]

That the sophisticated students of the seventies with their greater freedoms in life and in study retained much of the Trinity spirit in common with their predecessors is shown by these excerpts from Deby Hyde's talk to her classmates at their senior luncheon.[147]

> We've all been through a lot together, and that is an understatement.
>
> That first day—remember September 1973?—we passed each other in the halls of Main: confused, bewildered, excited, scared. An ID? A senior sister? A roommate? Washington, D.C.!? *What an I doing here?* It seems so long ago—but you do remember, don't you?
>
> The next four years saw us through course selections, passing statistics, changing courses, going off to our first internship, and, of course, how many all nighters were there?, and what about those comps! . . .
>
> We have danced the night away; we have cried for days; we have felt as though we spent our lifetime plowing through *Middlemarch*!
>
> At one time or another we have all hated each other. We have all loved each other. But above all else, we've made it! Yes, Trinity's Class of 1977 has pulled through. We knew that we could do it, we had our doubts at times, *but we did it*!
>
> *And we did it together!*
>
> Throughout our years here some of us have been recognized for our participation in class and school functions. Today, Mary has expressed special thanks to certain people. . . .
>
> Each and every member of the Class of 1977 deserves a very sincere "thank you". At one time or another each one of you has provided an understanding ear, an encouraging smile, a friendly hello. Each one of you has done something to make Trinity a better place for someone. Each one of you has given a little of yourself to someone here and, as a result, you have made the Class of 1977 what it is today.
>
> Going back again to that autumn day in September 1973, didn't we think we were off to a new adventure, a new wider world? Funny, don't you feel some of the same feelings now—scared, excited, nervous, daring? Who would have ever thought, back in 1973, that 1977 would come so quickly and some of us would be holding back the tears. We are truly off now to a

146. See sections of most of these activities later in the chapter. For athletics see pp. 284–290 of Chapter 5. For crew see *Trinity News*, September, 1976, p. 4. Pictures and news.

147. *Newsletter*, Spring, 1977, p. 4.

wider world, "the wide wide world". But we will always be the Blue Class of 1977, a bond not just in words, but one of friendship.

Looking back over this survey of eight decades of student life at Trinity College, one can still observe the strong thread of continuity binding the pioneers to late twentieth century women, but not as stereotypes. Trinity women have always been individuals characteristic of their own times. A study of the alumnae makes that clear. (Chapter 8) The rest of this chapter on student life will trace the development of the more enduring activities that have weathered the years, with mention of a few which influenced students for many years but no longer exist on campus. Student participation in the government of their campus life has held such an important place from 1900 that it will be treated first. The others will follow, not necessarily in the order of importance.

Student Government

The pioneer Trinity students were very conscious of their status as women of a university grade college. They shied away from anything that might make them seem like boarding school girls. They expected to work hard but not *too* hard. Within a month of the opening of the college the Dean "notified the faculty" of the first student protest against the extremely heavy daily schedule. "Some of the students," she said according to the minutes,[148] "were fretful under so many hours of labor. They counted to her 28 hours; she showed them it was $21\frac{1}{2}$ hours which divided by 5 days gave 4+ each day." They were probably including singing at 5:30 each week day except Thursday and the organized "Social Hour" after dinner which was unpopular. That Social Hour had been adopted November 4 before any student had arrived and was "superintended" by a different teacher each evening. It was the subject of their next protest and abolished before Christmas of that first year,[149] and student-faculty discussions got under way for the establishment of a Student Advisory Council. This first hesitant step toward student participation in government was definitely in place by the second academic year. That it had already started in the second semester of 1900–1901 is implied in the minutes of the College Advisory Board, May 9, 1901.

The chair, Dr. Phillip Garigan, "advised liberal government" for the students. There was a discussion of "the present strict order" which seemed unfair to the students by transferring holidays to Saturday. "Accidental holidays," the Board thought, "do not belong to the fac-

148. *Senate Meetings*, Vol. I, p. 7. (Earliest faculty minutes.) T.C.A.
149. *Senate Meetings*, Vol. I, p. 3, p. 10.

ulty, but to the girls." "There should be representation of the students' views, of their wishes. . . . In other colleges the form of government adopted by the students gave them the right to protest." The Dean replied that there was the same right at Trinity . . . not yet organized as a government."[150] The chair advised a "House Committee of the Students." The students, he thought "might enjoy all the liberty consistent with good order and the best college discipline." This became the students' Advisory Council (or Board) with representatives of each class, who met with the Dean. The first recorded meeting (extant) was dated simply October 1901.[151] It began "as soon as the Class officers were elected, the Societies organized and officers elected." "The Dean called together a Students Advisory Board consisting of The Dean, Miss Redfern, the Presidents and Vice-Presidents of the classes and the Presidents of the Musical, Dramatic and Literary Societies." The chief business of that meeting dealt with social events: The Sunday Afternoon Teas and the Friday Evening Receptions were discussed in some detail and an individual tax of $1.00 levied for "a Tea Fund." Miss Redfern (the chaperone) was asked "to receive this money and to buy all that was necessary, kettle, cloth and flowers, etc.—as well as eatables and to take charge to give out the latter." Contemporary snapshots of one of these teas appeared in The Woman, the manuscript student magazine of spring, 1902.[152]

As early as January 12, 1902 the students questioned: "Should officers be nominated from the resident body only?" This was discussed but no action taken "for fear of breaking up class spirit." The "general sentiment" of the students was satisfaction with the way college life was progressing, except for "being obliged to rise on Saturday morning as usual in time for breakfast. A late sleep was asked for and the privilege of staying in one's room on Saturday morning if one so desired." A compromise easing the situation slightly, was reached.

"The Sunday Teas were discussed and the Dean told the Board that the Sunday afternoons had been spoken of as a "Courting School"; this was thought to be so absurd and uncalled for that it was resolved *to pass it by unnoticed.* (italics added)."

Through the next two years the students' board met monthly and discussed many matters momentous or trifling, but important to the students: noise that would disturb others, visiting each other's rooms, whistling, an "address of appreciation" for the President, Sister Lidwin, who left Trinity in 1902; conduct in the dining room, proctors and their duties, class attendance, new regulations in regard to use of the

150. Advisory Board minutes, May 9, 1901 (1st meeting). T.C.A.
151. The formal Minute Book of the Students' Advisory Council begins in October, 1901. T.C.A.
152. Original in T.C.A.

telephone, mail distribution, registration when leaving campus, hot water, hot meals, elections, "how to reach the girl who laughs at everything, as reg. of college, etc. and who never looks at anything seriously." Reading the minutes for the first three years from the perspective of nearly eighty years, one senses that Sister Josephine Ignatius, the Dean, considered the students' board as a help for her in disciplinary matters. She seems to have presided at the meetings, dictated the chief points of the agenda, and channeled faculty complaints. The elected students emerge as polite, but self-reliant individuals, articulate in presenting the students' point of view and "sticking to their guns." They were in no sense, however, the self-governing body which they were seeking.[153] An entry in the Dean's Notebook[154] shows that she could discern possibilities. "The Students," she wrote, "elected a Committee to investigate the disturbance in the College halls on Saturday evening after 10 p.m. . . . It was the first case of Students Self-Governing Board or Association and seemed to impress the school. . . . " The Dean had set members of the student board to work looking into student government organizations at other colleges and formulating a plan for Trinity College.[155] This resulted in a formal presentation of a "Proposed Agreement between the Faculty and Students at Trinity College concerning Student Government." The letter of presentation and the appeal to the President and Faculty, given in full below, were signed by representatives of the three classes then in college: 1904, 1905, 1906. A form of agreement, a proposed constitution and by-laws accompanied the letter.[156]

Trinity, May 10, 1903.

The Dean of the Faculty,
Trinity College.

Dear Sister Josephine:-

In accordance with your request, we have gone over carefully the Self-Government Association Constitutions of Bryn Mawr, Wellesley and Vassar, and drawn up tentatively what we believe would be a practicable form on which to organize a Students' Association here.

The time has been so short that we have not been able to consider the question as thoroughly as we should like, nor have we been able to bring it before the classes for general discussion; but we have tried to express our interpretation of the public opinion in the College, and think the attached sheets will serve as a working basis for the organization of the Association,

153. Cf. President's Report, June 1, 1905. Paragraph about Students' Advisory Board, p. 8, T.C.A.
154. March 26, 1903. T.C.A.
155. Implied by the letter to the Dean which is given here in full.
156. Originals in T.C.A., Box: Student Government.

to be ratified, of course, Article by Article, by the whole student body after the Association is formed.

We ourselves are heartily in favor of the fullest possible measure of Self-Government, and believe it would be of great and permanent benefit to both the Students and the College. The life-long interest that graduates of other Women's Colleges show in their Alma Mater, in contrast to the indifference of most of the graduates of Boarding-Schools, is, we believe, entirely due to the fact that during their College course they have been directly concerned with the successful government of the institution, and thus feel themselves a part of it, so that their strong College spirit lasts even after leaving; while the Boarding-School girls, being subject to rules which they had no voice in making, feel no personal responsibility or interest in their observance, and leave the School only glad to be freed from its restraints.

We have prepared the data in the form of an Agreement between the Students and Faculty, a Constitution, and a set of By-Laws; and, in addition, attach a petition for an extension of our opportunities for social life, which, if granted, we believe will do much to promote good feeling among the students and do away with the spirit of discontent and complaining which prevail under the present restrictions.

Respectfully yours,

/s/ Florence E. McMahon '04
/s/ Marguerite M. Brosseau '05
/s/ Katharine O'Neill '06

TO THE PRESIDENT AND FACULTY OF TRINITY COLLEGE:

We, the undersigned, in the name of the students of Trinity College believing from our knowledge of the conditions at other Women's Colleges, that a measure of social life is not incompatible with a high degree of scholarship, but rather necessary to that symmetrical development of character which is the end of true education, do hereby petition the President and Faculty to withdraw the stringent prohibition thus far in force in regard to our going out and entertaining in the evening.

We believe that girls who are old enough to come to College have sufficient self-reliance to be trusted with, and profit by, a certain amount of intercourse with people of the world, and that greater freedom in this respect would further develop that self-reliance, and lead to the individual judgment and intelligent insight into character and life which are looked for in an educated woman.

It has been said by many great educators, among them Cardinal Newman, that much is to be learned from people as well as from books, and the cosmopolitan society of Washington offers exceptional advantages in this respect.

Therefore, we earnestly recommend this matter to the serious consideration of the President and Faculty, and on the part of the students, pledge ourselves to observe the following regulations, to be inserted in the By-Laws of the Students' Association, in case it is acted on favorably:-

1. The hour of closing the College shall be 10 P.M.
2. All evening callers shall leave the College not later than 9:45.
3. Students who are to be out with friends after 6:30 P.M. shall notify the Dean personally, and shall return not later than 10 P.M.
4. Special permission shall be obtained, and an approved chaperon provided, for the theatre, dances and all public entertainments.

/s/ Florence E. McMahon '04
/s/ Marguerite M. Brosseau '05
/s/ Katharine O'Neill '06

Signed: May 12, 1903.

The text of the proposed constitution and by-laws appear as Appendix X of this history. The carefully worded, practical document was submitted to the Committee on Discipline of the College Advisory Board which rejected it in spite of the fact that Dr. Garrigan had recommended in the 1901 meeting some form of student self-government.[157] The Board of Trustees ratified the decision and the students continued through ten more years before the Student Government Association came into being. Meanwhile, the Students' Board, with a new Dean, Sister Mary, strove to serve the student body. Minutes of their meetings until 1910 are extant. A notation by Sister Mary, Dean, July 1911 about the change in the make-up of this Board ends the book. The next two years were transition years culminating in September, 1912 in the first tentative steps of student government with the class of 1913's officers acting also as student government officers.

In The Dean's Report, May 30, 1912, Sister Mary wrote:

> In my estimation, the principal problem with us in regard to increased numbers is the matter of discipline. (current enrollment 162 students) In most of the large *non* Catholic Colleges, the solution of this problem is found in the system of student government. The opinion of this Advisory Board was averse to the establishment of such a system at Trinity College, when the subject was discussed at the meeting, held in May, 1903.
>
> From my experience in the matter, I would be a strong advocate of granting a modified form of self-government at Trinity. Though there has been apparently no serious infringement of discipline during the past scholastic year, yet it is much to be desired that there should be more hearty co-operation on the part of every individual student in observing regulations that are in the best interests of all. Trinity students should agree to keep reasonable regulations from a sense of duty rather than fear of penalty. Such a system also tends to develop the student's sense of responsibility and give her a maturity of judgment which many of our catholic young girls lack.

157. Advisory Board Minutes, T.C.A.

The Advisory Board decided that "A Modified Self-Government by The Student Body should be given a trial." The board of Trustees ratified this decision and the class of 1913 returned in September 1912 to find the "dream" had become a *fait accompli.* Their senior officers, Blanche Driscoll, President, Helen Stokes, Vice President, became concomitantly the officers of Student Government. In her next report, June 4, 1913, the Dean wrote: "A Constitution was drawn up and a Board elected by the students with two faculty members to regulate the affairs of the Association. In some respects the results have been satisfactory, though there is still room for improvement. . . . " By June 10, 1914, she is still a bit hesitant about the success of the new student government, but she says: "There is every evidence that better results will be obtained when the booklet containing the Constitution and Rules and of the Association is printed and available for distribution to each student. This we hope will be done by September."

Meanwhile Jane Hoey and her fellow officers were working hard to establish the new government on a firm basis. The "Chronicle" section of the *Trinity College Record,* December, 1913[158] carried the following item.

> September 26—Miss Hoey, the President of the Student Government Body at Trinity, summoned a mass meeting in O'Connor Hall to present her plan of procedure for the coming year. From that night we all felt that the honor system depends upon the students themselves. The new system is still progressing; but, like all great enterprises, it must necessarily travel a rough road, with many impediments, and its brave captain must expect many disappointments. However, the Class of 1914 is determined to establish a firm footing for the honor system before its exit into the wide world. All hail to its success!

The success of the project, thought barely satisfactory by the Dean, resulted in a lasting effect on later classes by the formulation of the first Student Government Booklet, mentioned above. This included the agreement between faculty and students and a Constitution for the association. It is interesting to note how much of the material in the 1903 proposed agreement, though worded differently, appears in this first printed version. The agreement is given in full here, with a few annotations of slight changes made in later years. It remained unchanged in fundamentals in each biennial revision and publication until 1965. Its final paragraph was still in the Student Association agreement in the 1978 revision of the *Handbook.*[159]

158. p. 308.
159. The change from Student Government Booklet (or Handbook) to Student Association Handbook took place in 1966–67. A chart of the new organization is on pp. 8–9 in that first publication. (Copies in Dean of Students' Office and in T.C.A.)

AGREEMENT[160]

Between the Administrative Board
and the Student Government
Association of Trinity
College

Whereas the Administrative Board of Trinity College believes that the institution of a partial ("partial" omitted 1925) Student Government would, by fostering a spirit of loyalty among the students and by aiding the growth of character, make for the best interests of the College, and whereas, the students of Trinity College, recognizing this fact, desire to assume the responsibility for the conduct of the students in the college life.

The Administrative Board of Trinity College hereby authorizes and charges the Student Government Association to exercise the powers hereinafter committed to it with the utmost care for order, for liberty, and for the maintenance of the best conditions of college life.

Whereas, neither the Faculty nor Students desire that this government be absolute, it is expressly provided that in every case where a question of suspension or expulsion shall arise, the ultimate responsibility and decision shall rest with the Faculty. The Association may, however, place before the Faculty the data concerning any such case and draw their attention to the apparent need of such a penalty.

It shall be within the power of the Administrative Board to withdraw the responsibilities and powers granted in this document, or of the Student Government Association to relinquish the same, ten days notice being given in either case. The Student Government Association expects that from time to time as the occasion shall arise the Administrative Board will entrust to it more power in such measure as shall be deemed advisable. (This sentence was deleted by the early 1930's.)

The Administrative Board of the College is pledged to support the Student Government Association to the full extent of its power by enforcing all decisions made in accordance with this agreement. The members of the Association on their side are pledged to co-operate with the authorities of the College to maintain the standards set for Trinity in scholarship and personal conduct.

The Administrative Board of Trinity College then delegates to the Student Government Association power and responsibility concerning the following matters:

1. The care of registration of students for such absences as are hereinafter stated.

2. The entire management of the fire-drill.

3. The maintenance of order and decorum in the halls, private rooms, dining room, and library. (Dining Hall and Library were transferred to sections of by-laws by 1940's.)

160. Original Student Government Booklet, 1914, preserved in Dean of Student's Office, Trinity College, pp. 1–5.

4. The general supervision of the student societies in such a way as shall be hereinafter stated.

5. The enforcement of parliamentary law at the business meetings of all classes and societies.

6. The prescribing and administration of penalities for breaches of all rules of the Student Government Association provided such breaches are not so serious as to imply suspension or expulsion from the College.

7. The preservation of all records of actions taken by the Student Government Association.

8. The control of registrations before and after regular vacations. (Deleted by 1934.)

9. The jurisdiction in matters affecting the spirit of harmony and loyalty which should exist among the members of the Association.

The Faculty reserves for itself the regulation of all affairs that are strictly academic.

This agreement is intended to define in so far as is possible the province and powers of the Student Government Association, but it must not be understood to be complete in every detail. When a question arises, therefore, as to whether a subject not mentioned here lies within the jurisdiction of the Association, it shall be referred to a Joint Council between Faculty and students. This Council shall consist of all the members of the Executive Board and in addition to this, a number of Faculty representatives, equal to the number of student representatives on the Board. These Faculty representatives are to be specially appointed in each case by the President of the College, who shall act as chairman of the Council either in person or by proxy.[161]

This agreement shall require, to be valid, the signatures of the President of the College, of the Dean, and of the President and Vice-President of the Student Government Association.

Sister Catherine Aloysius,
President of Trinity College

Sister Mary,
Dean of Trinity College

Marie Ryan,
President of Student
Government Association

Anne Sarachon Hooley,
Vice-President of Student
Government Association

Italics were used in the sections dealing with suspension and expulsion from 1917.

161. Wording for this section was soon (1917) changed to "it shall be referred to the Administrative Board of the College through the Executive Board of the Association."

The following article by the 1914–1915 President of Student Government, Marie Ryan '15, is printed in full here because it gives a thoughtful student evaluation of the early experiences of student government at Trinity and seems to express the standards and spirit which continued in student struggles to achieve a viable self-government.

STUDENT GOVERNMENT[162]

"The old order changeth, yielding place to new."

When it became 1913's good fortune to return to Trinity to reign as the high and mighty dignitaries of this institution, a delightful surprise was awaiting not only the Seniors, but even the unsophisticated lower classmen. To the astonishment of every Trinitarian, by a free act of the Faculty, Student Government was thenceforth to be the law and order of Trinity. As a natural consequence of this form of government, a radical change was brought about in many phases of college life, for transference of power always introduces a new state of affairs. It is Macaulay, I believe, who declared that "a growing and struggling power always gives annoyance, and is more unmanageable than an established power." Realizing this fact the students of Trinity must feel deeply their debt of gratitude to 1913 and 1914, for the masterful way in which an experimental Student Government was brought into the fields of success. To a certain extent, however, Student Government at Trinity, thought now in its third year, is still something of an experiment, at least in so far as we have not yet reached the heights of perfection. Each succeeding year will add the wisdom of experience, and we hope that in the near future a system will be evolved that will solve all our present problems, and make the path of the future Trinitarian as free from difficulty as any path can be when it leads undeviatingly upwards.[163]

Student Government at Trinity, however, is in no sense to be considered entirely absolute and completely free from faculty supervision. Supreme and unlimited power in the hands of the students is not to be desired, for the recipients of self-government must be prepared gradually for the tasks encountered in holding the reins of authority. Neither should Student Government be interpreted as a severance of the bond between Faculty and students. On the contrary, Student Government draws the Faculty and the students into closer union and more intimate communication. One of the very principles of Student Government is greater co-operation between Faculty and students, and more thorough understanding by the Faculty of student problems. To return the compliment, as it were, the students try in every way to prove worthy of the trust and confidence placed in them by striving to attain the high ideals for which Trinity stands.

In some ways this system may be considered as in keeping with present-day tendencies, with democratic ideals, and with republicanism, since in all purely human governments the question of absolute authority and of

162. *The Trinity College Record*, December, 1914, pp. 221–224.
163. Miss Ryan's youthful optimism did not foresee the student struggles of the late twentieth century when Trinity students are still trying to "make it work."

monarchical ideas is now relegated to dreamers, who, if not yet quite forgotten, dwell in a world of yesterdays. Today in the politics of every country throughout the world the desire is to govern by the consent of the governed. The person charged with holding the reins of power must not be an august being, the embodiment of the phrase, "L'état, c'est moi," but must be an ordinary mortal of the "unaristocratic" class. In many respects, therefore, Student Government may be considered as a movement with twentieth-century ideals. Student Government, however, does not reject authority; it simply substitutes for coercion the voluntary choice of what is right and good, leaving to the students themselves the power to punish the minor deviations from the straight and narrow path of duty. The system not only supposes, but strengthens a high public spirit among the students; it appeals not merely to their honor and self-respect as women, but to the fundamental principles which must, to a Catholic, be the motive and sanction of action, now and in the years to come. Student Government means the recognition by the student body of the right line of conduct in any given circumstances, their free decision to follow that line, their condemnation of what is petty or deceitful, foolish or wrong. The very atmosphere and spirit at Trinity are so truly democratic, in the best sense of the word, that within our college walls there may be said to exist a veritable republic with the Faculty exercising a kind of hegemony of the untyrannical type. Student Government so places power in the hands of the students that at Trinity we have a government of the students, for the students, and by the students.

Last spring after countless meetings and endless detail work on committees of various kinds, a formal agreement was at length drawn up between the Administrative Board of the College and the Student Government Association. This precious document states clearly and definitely the province and powers of Student Government. Under its jurisdiction fall such important matters as the care of registration, the entire management of fire-drills, and the maintenance of order and decorum not only within the college precincts, but also in the city of Washington and in the beloved town of Brookland. The daily routine of Student Government work includes numerous other points of less importance, such as the inner workings of the House and Social Committees, the enforcement of rules, and the bestowal of the much-dreaded campuses on forgetful members of our association.

It is almost needless to mention our knowledge of our weaknesses and limitations in Student Government, but strong and hopeful in our faith we find a motto in the words of the Bishop of Peoria when he exclaims, "Failures for those conscious of inner power are like trumpet calls to rally to renewed attacks," and again when he declares that "Consciousness of defect is the evolutionary principle which urges us towards completeness." Ever hopeful for assured success in our Student Government, we know that our system of law and order must progress and move steadily forward till in the end perfection in the fullest measure will be the crowning glory of Student Government. Years may pass before the pinnacle of success is attained, but time is merely a minor consideration when there exist confidence in results and loyalty to the standards cherished by every Trinitarian. Of first rank among these standards is that of the ideal Catholic woman. In whatever paths of labor her life work may lead her, in whatever fields of action circumstances may place her, the Trinitarian will be better prepared for every duty, and will more easily meet the demands made upon her, after having lived four years under Student Government. This force and factor in college life not only trains and molds character, but it directly fits the student for the responsibilities of later years.

Such are our hopes for Student Government. With these sentiments, we feel secure that no blame can lawfully be laid at our door for "hitching our wagon to a star." Realizing that the earnest support of every student of Trinity is at our command, that the glorious spirit of harmony permeates every phase of our college life, we plead for enthusiastic co-operation and for continued interest in Student Government. It is our hope that true college spirit may flourish and thrive, and call forth from every Trinitarian the most beautiful fruits of the virtue of loyalty. Confident of the ultimate success of Student Government we say with Tennyson:—

"That which we are, we are;
One equal temper of heroic hearts,
Made weak by time and fate, but strong in will
To strive, to seek, to find, and not to yield."

Marie Ryan, '15.
President of Student Government

The constitution and by-laws printed in 1914 have been the subject of student discussion ever since. Yearly petitions for changes in details, especially in by-laws have been a continual fact of Trinity life. The biennial revisions of the handbook, prefaced by the signed agreement, reflect changes in accord with changing times. A complete analysis and comparative study would be a worthy research project. Its scope is too great for this history. Highlights, or perhaps milestones of these changes, will serve to bring student self-government at Trinity up to the verge of the ninth decade.

One can perceive a development in student participation in government, especially in the late 1920's in cooperation with Sister Wilfred Parsons, and the 1940's and 1950's with Sister Ann Francis Hoey. Annual or at least biennial petitions for changes in the by-laws have centered chiefly in a few areas: the plea: (1) for later permissions for off-campus activity ranging from the early 8:00 or 9:00 p.m. "late" permissions to mid-night, to 2:00 a.m. to overnight with proper safeguards in the 1970's; (2) for male visitors, from Sunday afternoon in the parlors to the "free" visiting of the late 1970's. The 1976–77 amendment to By-law Five allows male guests in Cuvilly and Kerby lounges only, with strict regulations. Each student is responsible for the behav-

Student Government Assembly, 1950's.

ior of her guests[164]; (It should be remembered that most resident students of the mid-seventies lived in those two halls. The move back to Main and Alumnae had not yet begun.); (3) for more week-ends for resident students (now a moot question); (4) for greater involvement of non-resident students in government from the first steps of the Washington Club to the birth of the Association of Commuting Students. The Washington Club had been organized in 1927. By the 1940's day students were participating enthusiastically in college activities. The Washington Club president was a member of the Student Government Board on a par with presidents of the residence halls. Day students have held major class offices. For example: Patricia O'Rourke was senior president of 1952, Marcella Jordan, freshman president of 1956, and Jeannette Jackson senior president of 1970. This involvement depends on the attitude of the non-resident students themselves as well as on the whole student body. (5) For smoking on campus, culminating in the establishment of "The Smoker," in 1950. The latest Handbook (By-law 7) reads: "Students may smoke on campus only in residence areas and public lounges. Smoking in residence halls may be

164. A very good history of "By-law Five" and of the Student Affairs Committee, written by Sister Mary Frances McCarthy for the Board of Trustees is extant in the T.C.A.

restricted by the residents;" (6) for fewer restrictions on the use of alcoholic beverages. Early booklets do not mention alcoholic beverages. An abuse would have been a serious offense against the decorum expected of all students and subject to the judgment of the Administrative Board. Up to, at least, 1969 no student was permitted to keep or consume alcoholic beverages on campus, though by that time, within the laws of the District of Columbia, and with the approval of the Administrative Board, such beverages could be served at student-sponsored functions. The latest Handbook available at the time of writing states:

> Consumption of alcoholic beverages on campus is permitted in residence halls, *subject to restrictions* imposed by the residents of a given hall; it is prohibited on the grounds and in all instructional and administrative areas of the college (including Social Hall during business hours).

The problem of drugs on campus characteristic of the sixties and seventies involved violation of District and federal law and called forth a statement of college policy, quoted here from the 1975–1976 Student Handbook.

> By-law 8. Drugs
>
> Violations of the District and federal laws concerning illegal sale, use or possession of drugs on campus are subject to judicial action.
>
> N.B. This by-law should be read in conjunction with the following policy statement:
>
> Because the illegal sale, use or possession of drugs may be prosecuted as a crime, the college would be doing a disservice to its students to fail to take any steps to discourage violations of the law. The reason for establishing a drug by-law is to protect the welfare of the community. Since the college is genuinely concerned with the welfare of the individual student, every instance of violations of by-law 8 will be handled on an individual basis. Action, subsequent to a violation may include personal counseling, and medical aid, and/or campuses, suspensions, and expulsions, according to the usual procedure of the Judiciary. The confidentiality of all judicial matters will be guaranteed to the extent permitted by law to all individuals involved.

Student attitude toward their government in the mid-1940's is distilled into these excerpts from the *Trinilogues* of 1945 (p. 30) and of 1946 (p. 37). Accompanied by pictures of the receiving line at the Trinity Tea, and of officers at work in the old Student Government Office, 1945 wrote

> Student Government is above all a matter of individual honor in which Trinity has a deep and healthy pride. The fulfillment of the trust placed in

> every student shouts to a cynical world that ideals are practical after all. And then there is the lighter side of this very serious business of personal integrity—our gracious Gloria presiding at assemblies, suppressed fire drill giggles, the formal beauty of the S.G. tea. Student Government plays an important part in the accomplishment of Trinity's aim—to develop well-rounded Christian women, true and gay, honorable, with minds and hearts lifted to God.

The 1946 version complements that of their predecessors:

> '46 is proud of Student Government. Signing that extra late minute, groaning over a Saturday campus but wandering down to S.G. from eleven to seven—these little things make real the honor system at Trinity, emphasize the important thing—personal integrity.
>
> S.G.-sponsored, too, was the party atmosphere of the formal tea, fire-drill attacks of giggles, closing the little blue books with a pledge-flourish, and eight's during the week.
>
> So for the last time, '46 gathers in the marble-corridor singing, "Here's to you, S.G."

The celebration of the golden jubilee of full-fledged Student Government was celebrated by the whole college community in 1964. Programs of this event are extant in the Trinity College Archives.[165] An article, "S.G. After Fifty Years, Old Fashioned, New Fangled," by Catherine Kaufmann, '65, the incoming president of the Association, appeared in the *Alumnae Journal*.[166]

The active participation of Trinity College students in the National Federation of Catholic College Students (NFCCS) and the more wide-spread National Student Association (NSA) was most effective from the 1930's to the end of the 1960's when student unrest tended to blur organizational affiliations. From 1942, Trinity College held the Commission on International Relations of NFCCS with Rita Schaefer '42 its first national chairman.[167] In 1954 NFCCS established CURA (College and University Relief Association) to provide scholarships for students from the southern and southwestern sections of the country. The CURA activities at Trinity were described by Wilda Marrafino '57 in the *Alumnae Journal*,[168] "Student Government—CURA." Unique among campus CURA programs, the student helped earn money for the scholarships by benefits, entertainments and other projects, not just leaving it to the Administration to donate them as at other colleges.

165. Student Government Box, Closet 3, T.C.A.
166. Summer, 1964, pp. 250–251. Pictures.
167. Cf. pp. 351–352, 394 and for Sophomore Workshop, p. 363.
168. Winter, 1955, pp. 81–82.

The detailed listing of permissions,[169] "privileges," punishments, registration of absences from campus have all but disappeared from the student handbook to be replaced by clarifications of By-laws 5, 6, 7, 8. Saturday campuses, dress inspection before formal dances, the feverish counting of "late minutes" are unknown to the Trinity student at the beginning of the ninth decade, though she still considers Trinity a strict college.

The Honor System that has animated Student Government for more than seventy years[169] has been a subject of development, of discussion, of examination and of concern to generations of Trinity students. The fact that it has been debated and accepted by students of various eras is an indication of its vitality on campus even through the "turbulent years." It was implied in the student constitution from the beginning and cherished by students of the teens and '20's. "The Honor System" as a separate statement appeared first in the Student Government Handbook in 1929. This was essentially unchanged in each revision until the reorganization of 1967. Since then statements have been re-worded, but the students who will graduate in the ninth decade are still deeply concerned about applying its principles and convincing their more reluctant companions of its value.

In 1961, Sister Ann Francis Hoey wrote with nineteen years of experience as Dean of Students:

> Admittedly, the most potent non-academic factor in the life and development of the Trinity student is the honor system. The honor system booklet, compiled and written by a member of the class of 1960, is as important to each student as the more detailed Student Government handbook. For nearly every Trinity student, honor gains strength in the process of daily college living. It is as our representative in the pages of this supplement truly states "part of the tradition." The Trinity student is still a respecter of tradition. She holds on to most of the old ones while willing to call something done once a "new tradition."
>
> This then is the thumb-nail sketch of the girl who is today in the process of becoming the Trinity woman of tomorrow. It may help you to identify the statements of the Trinity representative at the conference described in this supplement and to recognize where the student developed under the aegis of the All-holy Trinity must necessarily be expected to differ from the picture of the typical student portrayed in the following pages.[170]

The expanded statement, "The Honor System at Trinity College" in the 1980 Student Association Handbook[171] embodies all that has gone

169. Cf. Excerpt from "Chronicle" section of the *Record*, p. 386; and "Permissions," Dorothy Sennett, '52, S.G. President, *Alumnae Journal*, Winter, 1952.
170. *Alumnae Journal*, Spring 1961, Section 2.
171. *American Alumni Council Supplement*, "The College Student," pp. 4–5.

before and demonstrates that this distinctive element of Trinity has weathered the rebellions and protests of the last fifteen years and is still a part of college daily living, debated, re-worded, but still there.

A person choosing to attend Trinity College becomes a member of a community. As such, the person participates in both the academic and the social life of the college. A significant part of this life is the honor system, established in 1913. Meant to bring about "the formation of persons prepared and willing to make decisions, and to serve in effecting them," the honor system rests on three principles: the integrity of the individual; a mutual agreement of trust among all members of the community, including students, faculty and administration; and a sense of responsibility for living out this trust by respecting one another's rights and upholding regulations established for the good order of the community.

What does the honor system mean in the concrete? To a large extent, student life is self-governed. Various organizations, notably the Student Senate and the residence councils, develop most of the regulations governing student life. To ensure that these regulations reflect real needs, all of them must be approved by student vote. The Senate may initiate review of any change of college policy. Such changes are then subject to review and approval by the Committee on Student Affairs and/or the Trustees Committee on Student Interests. A student chairs the Judiciary, a faculty-student organ administering the honor system.

In the social sphere, individuals enjoy a high degree of privacy, commensurate with their responsibility. There are, for example, no residence directors living on each dormitory floor. Students are expected to follow hall regulations, voted yearly by each dormitory, without such supervision.

In the academic sphere, too, students enjoy a number of privileges. Library procedures are simplified, and resources made more accessible by a shelf reserve system, resting on the assumption that students will remember classmates' needs; books in particular demand are so designated and left on the open shelves, with the understanding that they are not to be removed from the library.

Perhaps the most tangible privilege granted because of the honor system is that all testing is unproctored. In addition, semester examinations are self-scheduled.[172] Because of this second privilege, students can schedule their examinations at the times most convenient for them during the examination period. In addition to agreeing not to cheat, students commit themselves to maintaining the integrity of examinations by not discussing their content until the examination period is over.

The honor agreement which students sign affirms their intention of living according to the principles of the honor system in both the academic and social aspects of their lives at Trinity. The agreement reads as follows:

> I realize the responsibility involved in membership in the Trinity College community. I agree to abide by the rules and regulations of this

172. This was voted on by the faculty each semester and was revoked after a few years' trial. Student examinations are again scheduled, but not proctored.

> community. I also affirm my intention to live according to the standards of honor, to which lying, stealing and cheating are opposed. I will help others to maintain this responsibility in all matters which I judge essential to the common good of the community.
>
> Under this agreement, individuals declare themselves responsible for striving to conduct their lives in accordance with the honor system's principles and the community's regulations. They also agree to support others in the same effort. They participate, then, as individuals and as members of a community.

In addition to statements in handbook and catalogue the students have from time to time issued small separate booklets on the Honor System. Two extant in the Archives are by Jacqueline Shea, Student Government President, 1960 and by Bridget Globenski, Chair of the Judiciary, marked in pencil 1977.

For about ten years, from the autumn of 1953 to the mid-1960's the student government conducted Sophomore Workshops on college life and the meaning of a liberal arts education to help counteract what was popularly called "the Sophomore Slump." Annette Pieslak, President of Student Government, and the senior class of 1954 organized the first of these for their sophomore sisters of 1956. For more than twenty years from the mid-1940's the Student Government administered in cooperation with the Dean of Students the Senior Guidance Committee for the orientation and guidance of the freshmen. Each senior guide advised no more than five freshmen. In addition to the more informal, chiefly social help of her "Junior Sister" (whose existence dates from the earliest years), and her "Sophomore Sister," the freshman was integrated into Trinity College life. In the reorganization of Student Government Senior Guides gradually metamorphosed into Peer Counselors, under the Dean of Students and the Counseling Center.

Academic counseling remains with the Academic Dean and Faculty, and religious counseling with the Chaplains and Campus Ministry.

Chaplains—Campus Ministry

Trinity College has from the beginning been a Catholic college for women, not just a college for Catholic women. In the very first published catalogue (1900–1901), this statement appeared: "Trinity College has for its purpose the higher education of women under the auspices of the Catholic Church. As a first step toward the attainment of this end, its courses of study are planned according to the best standards of our American educational system." The college aimed at scholastic excellence in a Catholic atmosphere. This atmosphere has been achieved in varying degrees of success in a changing world, as well as through exterior changes in Catholic practices. A few of the contributors to that atmosphere have existed since the beginning. The fact that mass has been celebrated, at least once but usually twice daily, in chapels on campus since October, 1900, should rank first among these. Second, religion-theology, scripture, church history have been an integral part of the curriculum continuing as a leaven even in the years of upheaval in the late 1960's and in the 1970's. A re-reading of the section "Religion-Theology" in Chapter 5 would complement what is presented here as part of student life.[173] Third, a convent of Sisters of Notre Dame de Namur has existed on campus since October 1900 and by its presence has been an outward symbol of Catholicity as well as a "powerhouse of prayer" for the welfare of the college and home for many of its faculty.

The chaplains for the students, who were revered and who strongly influenced student life during the early decades were all part-time at Trinity. They all held full-time often important jobs elsewhere, but were so interested in the welfare of the Trinity College students that they have left an indelible impression. In fact, the first *full-time* campus minister was appointed in 1975.

Dr. Philip Garrigan, vice rector of The Catholic University and one of Trinity's founders, acted as the students' chaplain from 1900 to 1902 when he was appointed Bishop of Sioux City, Iowa.[174] A contemporary expression of the students' opinion of him is found in the second issue of the manuscript magazine, *The Woman*, (Trinity Sunday, 1902): "So much has already been said, and so much is felt in every heart that it seems almost superfluous to revert to the painful subject of Right Reverend Bishop Garrigan's departure, yet our paper would be incomplete without some mention of it. Words cannot accurately convey any idea of the deep and heartfelt regret that this leave-taking occasions *to every student of Trinity* [italics added], since all have been made partakers in the benefits of his untiring zeal in our behalf. Time nor labor did our devoted chaplain spare that our welfare and comfort might be furthered. Personal inconvenience was disregarded where the happiness of his children might lose thereby. In short, nothing that might in any way secure more fully our well-being was left undone. Ever priestly, ever friendly, untiringly he labored for us; untold acts of thoughtfulness, of deep interest, and of true devotion are the records of his fatherly career among us." Prayers and best wishes followed him to his new field of labor as the students joined in "a unanimous and hearty God Speed."

Dr. John Creagh succeeded Dr. Garrigan, acting as chaplain and teaching the course in religion from 1902 to 1907, "the scholarly series

173. Cf. "Religion-Theology" section, pp. 266–275.
174. Cf. Chapters 1, 2, and 3 *passim*.

of Sunday morning lectures."[175] Dr. Creagh was described much later by a student of '04 as "a brilliant young man and an inspiring teacher." Early in the decade the religion course was changed to another day to be part of the regular schedule. From 1907 to 1914 it was taught by the chaplain, Dr. John Melody and other religion courses had been added. A member of the class of 1908, Anna P. Butler described her religion classes in a letter quoted in Chapter 5. She wrote, "I remember we had Dr. Creagh and Dr. Aikin for dogma and Dr. Grannan for Scripture courses."[176]

A student's eye-view of the Catholic atmosphere, written in 1902,[177] gives a good idea of its earliest existence. Due notice must be taken of the currently popular somewhat pompous prose, and of contemporary church terminology.

> . . . but she (Trinity) is distinctively a Catholic institution, and hence the religious element is easily discernible throughout her dealings. The student begins her day by attendance at Mass and this with devout demeanor and the frequenting of the Sacraments shows that she is Catholic not only in name but in practice.
>
> Nor is there an absence of religious instruction. Every Monday morning there is an exposition of the Sacred Scriptures; the prayer at the opening of class[178] is prefaced by a reading from the lives of the Saints, from Holy Writ, or some part of the Church's liturgy. Once a week the dogma of Catholicism is expounded in detail, and here the student may arm herself with the arguments with which to overcome future attacks on the religion she professes.[179] An annual retreat and frequent sermons are justly calculated to help us in our strivings for perfection and an increased use of the missal [quite *avant garde* in 1902] and the reading of the Bible show that a wholesome interest in the ritual has been aroused. The bi-weekly Benediction of the Blessed Sacrament may not go unmentioned for it is a ceremony every truly Catholic girl must love and feel regret when compelled to forego it. [Post Vatican II students might not even know of this devotion and still be staunch Catholics.]
>
> Although there are no common night prayers, the tabernacular God is not forgotten and visitors many does He receive . . . to find renewed courage for the morrow's duties.

Though the students' day began with Mass, as mentioned above, attendance was voluntary, except on Sunday. The first students soon

175. Cf. pp. 267–268.
176. Cf. *ibid.*
177. *The Woman*, Ms Magazine, March 25, 1902, pp. 58–60.
178. The traditional "Trinity Prayer" composed by Dr. Pace and indulgenced by Rome was regularly said before each class by students and professor alike until the last fifteen or twenty years, but the readings described here did not survive the first year or two.
179. Typical of the attitude of the Church at the turn of the century.

realized the value of daily attendance at mass, and established a custom which they passed on to entering freshmen through the years. The habit acquired at Trinity of celebrating with the priest at weekday mass became so much a part of the lives of many that parish priests from Maine to Florida to Ohio to Iowa to California could identify Trinity alumnae by their presence each morning. After the first decade there developed patterns of attendance when weekday congregations ebbed and flowed. By the 1920's, large attendance could be expected in October and May in honor of Our Lady, in November to pray for the "Holy Souls," at a period of preparation before Christmas, at examination times twice a year, in Lent, and, if one stayed at college, during Holy Week and Easter. Up-to-date liturgical observance became the hallmark of religious life at the college.

The earliest students were encouraged to use the missal to participate with the priest instead of burying themselves in the long entrenched private prayerbooks or saying the rosary, beloved at other times but not during mass. The Latin responses, usually recited in parish churches by an altar boy, were made by students. For many years senior Latin major claimed this privilege, each "taking a week" in rotation being "the server," although from the front bench—no woman could have been allowed in the sanctuary. They were forerunners of the student "ministers of the Eucharist" as were the Sodality members who helped the Sister Sacristan through the years.

Pope Pius X's proclamation of frequent, even daily communion, for the laity (December 30, 1905) was immediately heeded by the students. They petitioned[180] to have their mass time changed to seven o'clock (a.m.) so that it would be before breakfast and they could receive communion while observing the ritual fast from midnight. That remained the hour for the students' daily mass for more than fifty years—and it was *daily* including Saturday. The disappearance of a Saturday students' mass was a late loss brought about by many changes in life style, as well as in liturgical patterns. It will be remembered that until the 1920's there were few day students ("day-hops", commuting students) and they were envied by the residents because of their greater freedom of action. The college liturgical schedule was made with the residents in mind. It was assumed that day students participated in their own parishes. In the mid-1940's when the number of "Washington Club" members had grown to nearly one fifth of the total student body, they began petitioning for a "more reasonable time" for daily mass so that they could attend on campus. Monsignor Aloysius Ziegler, students' confessor (1941 to late 1960's)[181] offered to celebrate his daily mass in Notre Dame Chapel at eight o'clock. Gradually the eight

180. By Rosaline Brownell, 1911, Cf. *Class History, Trinilogue,* 1911, p. 72.
181. Cf. "Appreciation" in *Alumnae Journal,* Summer, 1967, p. 231.

o'clock students' mass became the norm and Sunday mass moved later and later into the morning. When the new Cuvilly Hall was opened in 1959 Dr. Ziegler, while continuing the 8:00 a.m. mass in Notre Dame Chapel, celebrated mass there at least once a week until illness brought his devoted Trinity apostolate to a close. The liturgical renewal of the 1950's and the radical changes of Post Vatican II days have evolved a varied schedule of student masses at noon, night, and Sunday morning in various chapels on campus: Notre Dame for great events and for Sunday mornings (in good weather!), the Sisters' chapel in Main, Cuvilly, and Kerby chapels. As early as 1963, Reverend Doctor Gerard Sloyan, Chairman of the Religious Education Department at C.U. and President of the Liturgical Conference, celebrated mass with homily at noon each week day, and was available in the early afternoon for consultation.[182] He was called Religious Counsellor rather than chaplain.

An annual students' spiritual retreat was an integral part of the Trinity program from the second year.[183] For more than sixty years the midyear examinations were scheduled to end on a Tuesday. The rest of that week beginning Tuesday evening and ending at Mass on Saturday morning all Catholic students were "in retreat." No resident student left campus. Day students, who were involved in their parish activities made the retreat if they wished. Many did. They gathered in chapel at least three times a day for spiritual conferences by the "retreat master or director," who was carefully chosen each year from among the eminent preachers of their time who exhibited an understanding of, and the ability to "reach," college age students. Most of these priests through their talks and the sacraments, helped students to understand themselves better and to grow in appreciation of their religion. Individual Alumnae may remember to their sorrow the few who were ineffective, but even they must admit that not all four of their college years produced such a "dud." An atmosphere of quiet prevailed for the three days. Students observed complete silence in corridors and public rooms. Though the comparative silence in the students' rooms depended entirely on individual attitude, it allowed students to reflect, read—or play bridge or do their laundry—as their inclination directed. A festive mass on Saturday morning, followed by celebration at breakfast officially showed that the college was "out of retreat." An immediate exodus "to town" for shopping, matinees, movies, lunch or "tea" followed.

One such "end of retreat" is especially memorable, that of 1922. It was the day of the snowstorm that caused the collapse of the Knickerbocker Motion Picture Theatre at 18th Street and Columbia Road. The

182. *Trinity Newsletter*, November, 1963; *Trinilogue*, 1965, p. 43.
183. First Annual Retreat for the students, Feb. 3–6, 1902. Rev. James E. O'Neill, D.D. from St. Mary's Seminary, Baltimore. Cf. Dean's Notebook.

Trinity celebrators were caught downtown by the unexpected severity of the storm as they emerged from stores, theatres or "tearooms." The streetcars (predecessors of buses) moved slowly or stopped completely. Frantic calls to the Dean's Office made her aware that most of the stranded Trinitarians plodding their weary way on foot would certainly not be back for the eight o'clock deadline. They straggled in weary and hungry. Only next morning did they hear of the Knickerbocker Disaster which occurred in the evening. Hearty souls trudged through piled snow to cross town "to see what they could," praying for the victims, and thanking God that they had been "downtown," not "uptown" at 18th and Columbia Road during the great storm of 1922.

As times have changed, the scheduling, format, and character of student retreats have differed. The first change was having a separate retreat for freshmen with its own director, concomitant with the upperclass retreat. In the 1970's smaller volunteer groups gather at various retreat centers off-campus for week-end retreats with a director of their choice with whom they plan the exercises. Several such retreats occur each year, meeting the spiritual needs of the post-Vatican II student.

When Notre Dame Chapel opened in 1924 it became the center for up-to-date liturgical celebrations in accord with its *avant-garde* design[184] for American churches. Only the "new" gothic-type vestments were worn. In the late 1950's when liturgical reform was progressing toward the official changes soon to come in the Vatican II decisions, Father Sloyan introduced on summer Saturdays mass in English facing the people and "new" hymn books such as the *People's Hymnal* for congregational singing. These ceremonies were in Notre Dame Chapel because the Catholic University authorities had not yet reached that stage of renewal. Each Saturday there would be a congregation of several hundred, most of them religious from the Catholic University and Trinity summer sessions. Many took these latest liturgical developments back home to their various dioceses—to the concern of some bishops who continued to be worried at least until after the promulgation of the Constitution on the Liturgy.

Liturgical singing, too, has through the Music department and the choir kept pace with twentieth century changes. Late 19th century church music had become more and more operatic, distracting by its elaborate form from the eucharistic celebration itself. By the end of the century a strong movement toward simplification emerged. The use of plain chant, and simpler forms of polyphonic music was already evident by the turn of the century. Even before Pius X's *Motu Proprio for the Reform of Church Music,* November 22, 1903, at the solemn high mass for the dedication of the college the music was Dumont's Sixth

184. Pendant crucifix, free-standing altar, freedom from "furbelows".

Tone Gregorian Mass.[185] The *Liber Usualis* of plain chant published by the monks of Solesmes was provided for both students and Sisters. The students' choir, which co-existed with the Glee Club and dates from the pioneer years, sang high masses for feasts and other college religious functions for more than half a century into the era when congregational singing became popular. They practiced at least an hour a week, in addition to Glee Club practice, under the direction of the Music Department chairman, assisted in the 1930's by Malcolm Boyce, and in the 1940's by Miss Helen Kuhn. One hour a week of liturgical singing was required of all freshmen to supplement the course in liturgy from 1929 to 1943.

In line with these earlier developments new books of sacred songs for congregational singing began to appear. An excellent example of these, the English edition of *Biblical Hymns and Psalms,* by Father Lucien Deiss, was prepared for publication[186] by a group, chaired by Brother Aelred, F.S.C. and inspired by the enthusiasm of Miss Christiane Brusselmans, in the Music rooms of Trinity College. Copies for all students, as well as for the Sisters were bought and used as part of the liturgical renewal on campus in the 1960's. Other newer hymn books have been used in the intervening years, but even in the late 1970's Deiss I, as it has been called, has continued to hold its place with them and with Deiss' *Biblical Hymns and Psalms II.*

Dr. John Melody for twelve years and Dr. William Kerby for nineteen years influenced the students from 1907 to 1935. Both men were revered for their scholarship, admired as deeply religious priests, listened to as good preachers and loved as friends and counsellors whose sound advice affected the lives of many, long after Degree Day. Dr. William Russell, nephew of Dr. Kerby and disciple of Dr. Cooper,[187] founder of the Religious Education Department at C.U.A., brought changes to the teaching of religion[188] at Trinity, while he continued his uncle's work as chaplain until 1943. He prepared and the college printed a small booklet on religion at Trinity College, but no copy seems extant on campus at this time.

During all the years until the 1960's the pattern of mass attendance, described above, continued. The religious activities, like other student activities, were co-ordinated by the Dean of Students. A series of monthly devotions developed gradually and was printed in a small booklet, *Traditional Devotions,* by Sister Ann Francis Hoey. Notable

185. Sung by a choir of Paulist Seminarians. Cf. p. 74 which quotes from *The Historical Sketch of Trinity College*, pp. 33–34. November 22, 1900.
186. World Library of Sacred Music, Inc., Cincinnati, Ohio, 1965. A list of collaborators appears on p. 4 of the first edition.
187. Cf. pp. 271–292.
188. Cf. p. 272.

among these are two that were popular with the students of the time: Triduum for Parents (three days preceding the Thanksgiving holidays) and the Novena in honor of Feast of the Immaculate Conception culminating in the celebration of the feast, December 8, and the reception of the freshmen into the Sodality of the Blessed Virgin Mary. A third, the Church Unity Octave (Jan. 18–25) presaged the interest in ecumenism of post-Vatican II.

For two years (1943–1945) a panel of priests from the Trinity faculty celebrated the daily mass in Notre Dame Chapel, while the Paulists officiated at Sunday mass and delivered the weekly sermon. In 1946 the Paulists Fathers, who had celebrated mass for the Sisters of Notre Dame since 1916 and still do, became the students' chaplains. The Paulists by their very mission to the church in the United States, are usually in the vanguard of contemporary liturgical, ecumenical, and spiritual movements as well as Newman Club work on secular campuses. For more than fifteen years Trinity students were beneficiaries of this influence, moving forward with the times. Other Paulist involvement at Trinity College is recorded elsewhere in this history.[189]

The November, 1963, *Newsletter*[190] announces:

> The Rev. Gerard Sloyan, Chairman of the Religious Education, celebrates a noon Mass and is available for consultation afterward in the early afternoon. Father Sloyan is President of the Liturgical Conference and is the author of many widely-read works on biblical cathechesis.

He was called Religious Counsellor rather than chaplain. Father Sloyan began the daily short homily and though he is mentioned above in the description of the changing pattern of mass times, his contribution to campus ministry is repeated here for continuity.

In the period of the late 1960's various priests from the Catholic University faculty and surrounding religious houses (Dominicans, Franciscans, Oblates, Atonement, and possibly others) celebrated the noon mass with homily. The Dean's Report, 1969, states:

> At the present time religious affairs on campus refers primarily to liturgical services. A team of excellent priests took care of the three Sunday masses at 12:30 a.m., 10:30 a.m. and 4:30 p.m. Three sub-groups of the Religious Activity Board, each having a real sense of identity and loyalty to "their mass", met during the week and prepared the Sunday liturgy. We owe a great deal to the Paulist seminarians for their help with the 12:30 and 10:30 and to Father Geaney for his help in the preparation of the 4:30 Sun-

189. Cf. section on Paulist Fathers and Trinity College in Chapter 5 and Chapter 7 for Paulist teachers in the academic program.
190. p. 3. N.B. Father Sloyan was following the precedent of the founder of his department and of Father Russell mentioned earlier.

> day Mass. Mass was said for the convenience of faculty and students at 12:05 Monday through Friday in the Main Building Chapel.
>
> Confessions were heard weekly by Father Geaney and periodically by Father Etten. Father Etten found that the students who came were not concerned with confession. They wanted a complete course in post-Vatican II religion. He felt there was something we badly needed to do, but pressure from his studies did not leave him time to investigate the matter further.

From 1970 to 1972 Reverend James Schrider, S.J., is listed as chaplain. Then began the Campus Ministers.

Campus Ministry

The *Trinity News*, Fall, 1972, announces the new chaplain who will direct the campus ministry.

> Father John George Lynch, C.S.P.,[191] brings an interesting background to Trinity. A native of Minnesota, he was ordained a Paulist Father in 1962, in New York City. He received his B.A. and M.A. from St. Paul's College, Washington, D.C., a Masters in Theology from St. Michael's College of the University of Toronto, an S.T.D. from the Institut Catholique de Paris, and did further work at the University of Strasbourg and L'Ecole des hautes etudes de la Sorbonne. In addition to his work at Trinity, Father Lynch is teaching at St. Paul's College. He has had varied experience as a chaplain at Holy Cross Hospital, a chaplain in a Georgia mental hospital, and as Newman Club Chaplain at the University of West Virginia.
>
> To aid in the Campus Ministry work, Father Lynch has appointed two associate chaplains: Mr. James Traynor, a Paulist seminarian, and Mr. John Wojcik, a Carmelite seminarian.

In an open letter to parents, Winter, 1973, Father John George Lynch wrote: "Campus Ministry at Trinity College is still new and beginning. As chaplain, I have found Trinity both challenging and exciting. There are many moods on our campus. The spirit of those who feel at home mixes with the spirit of the angry and deceived. Like any family, there are those who are lost and drifting, those enthusiastic and alive. All these moods are expressions of life and are hopeful signs to me. . . . Campus Ministry calls to life worship and prayer in the Trinity community especially in the celebration of mass. It is my hope, also, to help bring together the many facets of campus life."

Father John George Lynch wrote an article on the Sacrament of Penance in the issue of the *Alumnae Journal*[192] which focused on "the idea

191. It is important to mention the middle name since there is a Rev. John Edward Lynch, C.S.P., at St. Paul's who is a professor at Catholic University. Cf. also "New Directions," *Newsletter*, Winter, 1972, p. 1.
192. *Alumnae Journal*, Autumn, 1973, pp. 5–7. Cf. also the editor's note for that issue signed A.P.K. (Annette Pieslak Kane '54) on the inside front cover.

of liturgy as summit and source of our lives as Christians" and "Campus Ministry at Trinity, A New Look" in the Spring, 1974 issue of the same journal.[193] Father Lynch distinguished between the office of chaplain and the direction of the campus ministry. He considered himself chaplain *and* director of the ministry program. He wrote: "Ministry in all its forms means sharing moments of consequence—those times, important times, when ties are quickly established." In 1973, Father Lynch ordained the first lay ministers of the eucharist on campus. They were Sisters of Notre Dame. Cf. *Trinity News*, December, 1973. In 1975 Father Lynch left for other fields of apostolic work and Sister Eileen Holohan, S.N.D., who stayed with the Trinity ministry less than a year, came. She was the first *full time* campus minister, assisted by various priests for mass.

From 1976 to 1980 Reverend Patrick Powers, O.S.A., was the energetic, devoted director of campus ministry. He took seriously his position of chaplain, considering it to include that of confessor and of director of all campus ministry. From the beginning he made accessibility a top priority. "I am available," he said in an interview soon after his appointment, "for suggestions and open to people in regards (sic) to the direction they want Campus Ministry to take." He "wished to break down barriers that might exist between himself and students and to be accepted as a person, not as a judge."[194] He worked in close cooperation with St. Martin's Parish on North Capitol Street. In a leaflet "Campus Ministry 1978–1979" Father Powers outlined the scope of his work. "The aim of Campus Ministry is to bring the Gospel message to everyone connected with Trinity College." The leaflet lists not only the liturgy schedule, but six types of student volunteer work outside the college, prayer meetings, and the staff: himself, an assistant Brother Gerry Shaw, O.S.A. and four students, one from each class. The Campus Ministry also handled: Convert Classes, Pre-Marital Investigations, arrangements for weddings at Trinity, Confirmation Instruction, Sacrament of Penance—anytime, Liturgical workshops especially for lectors and extraordinary ministers. Though office hours were 10:00 a.m. to 5:00 p.m., many an evening saw lights on and Father Powers at work.[195] Father Powers ordained students as ministers of the Eucharist.

For the last two years of his work at Trinity, Father Powers taught at least one course in the Theology department. He regretfully left Trinity in 1980 for a larger apostolate as Catholic chaplain in a state university in Florida.

193. *Alumnae Journal*, Spring, 1974, p. 5.
194. Cf. *Alumnae Journal*, Autumn, 1976, p. 12.
195. In the evenings he was usually "assisted" by Angel, his beautiful, elderly, blond collie dog. Angel loved the social life, but was never allowed on campus during working hours.

As this is being written Miss Lorraine Carey is Campus Minister, assisted by Father David Buescher and Father Richard Sparks, C.S.P., is Campus Minister.

Chaplains—For Students

1900–1902	Dr. Philip Garrigan, Vice Rector of Catholic University
1902–1907	Dr. John T. Creagh, Professor at Catholic University
1907–1916	Dr. John Melody, Professor at Catholic University. Cf. *Trinilogue*, 1911–1915
1916–1935	Dr. William Kerby, Professor of Sociology at Catholic University and at Trinity; Founder of Catholic Charities; of the National Catholic School of Social Service (NCSSS) which is now incorporated into the C.U. School of Social Service; Co-Founder and long editor of the *Ecclesiastical Review*: cf. pp. 224–226 and footnotes appended there.
1935–1943	Dr. William Russell, Professor in Religious Education Department, Catholic University; author of *Christ the Leader*: nephew of Dr. Kerby.
1943–1945	A panel of priests on the Trinity faculty celebrated daily mass in Notre Dame Chapel and the Paulists officiated at Sunday mass and delivered the weekly sermon.
1946–1961	Paulist Fathers, students' chaplains. (They had celebrated mass for the Sisters of Notre Dame since 1916 and still do to date.)
1963–	Rev. Gerard Sloyan (S.T.D., Ph.D.); Began noon mass and daily homily; cf. *Newsletter*, Nov. '63 and *Trinilogue*, 1965.
–1970	Various priests from C.U. and surrounding religious houses (Dominicans, Franciscans, Oblates, Atonement, and diocesan).
1970–1972	Rev. James Schrider, S.J.

Campus Ministers

1972–1975	Rev. John George Lynch, C.S.P., Professor at St. Paul's College; cf. *Trinity News*, Fall 1972, Winter 1975, *Alumnae Journal*, Fall 1973; Spring 1974, assisted by Mr. James Traynor, a Paulist seminarian, and Mr. John Wojcik, a Carmelite seminarian; First Eucharistic

	Ministers, S.N.D.s, Sept. 1973; cf. *Trinity News*, Dec. 1973.
1975–1976	(less than a year) Sister Eileen Hollahan, S.N.D., first full time; assisted for mass by various priests as above.
1976–1980	Rev. (later Dr.) Patrick Powers, O.S.A.; cf. *Alumnae Journal*, Autumn 1976, p. 12.
1980–	Miss Lorraine Carey, M. Div., assisted by Father David Buescher and Fr. Richard Sparks, C.S.P.

Confessors—Spiritual Directors

1900–1902	Dr. Philip Garrigan; cf. chaplain, religion teacher
1902–1907	Dr. John T. Creagh; cf. chaplain, religion teacher
1907–1910	
1910–1916	Dr. John F. Fenlon, S.S.; cf. *Trinilogue*, 1911–1916
1916–1918	Dr. William Turner; cf. p. 262.
1918–1921	Dr. Patrick J. McCormick, Professor of Education, Trinity College and C.U. Dean, Sister's College.
1921–1923	
1923–1941	Dr. John M. Cooper; cf. p. 271.
1941-late 1960s	Dr. Aloysius K. Ziegler; cf. *Alumnae Journal*, Summer 1967, p. 23, and *Trinilogues* 1940's and 1950's.

Penance and reconciliation have been administered under the campus ministry with no one "confessor" appointed.

Until the ferment of change in the sixties, each Trinity student, in addition to the Student Government Association, belonged to and paid dues to the Athletic Association, the Sodality of the Blessed Virgin Mary, and the Foreign Mission Society. As early as 1903 the Dean's Report mentions athletics as an already established organization. Since there were no "gymnastics" and no gymnasium, it states, an Athletic Association had been formed. Two tennis courts and a basketball court had been provided and a daily walk encouraged, which was "generally practiced."[196] The Athletic Association has been incorporated into the section on Physical Education in Chapter 5. This should be re-read in conjunction with this description.[197] Its progress can be traced through the *Trinilogues* since 1911. Teams listed in the 1931 volume (cf. p. 406 of the typescript) were basketball, hockey, swimming, riding, archery,

196. Dean's Notebook, October 23, 1901. "Lawn Tennis court fixed today. D.G."; copies of students' schedules of classes for the early years reveal "walk" entered like any class. Also, "a daily walk before breakfast was suggested to Michigan Avenue and back." Faculty Minutes, January 12, 1901.

197. Pp. 284–290.

track, and tennis—all intramural. Intercollegiate competitions and the crew were later developments.

An "Overview of Clubs" at Trinity at the beginning of the 1950's by Mary Theresa Shea '51 is cited earlier in this chapter.[198] The Sodality, the Foreign Mission Society of which the Wekanduit Bureau was the active arm, the Christ Child Society, and later the Confraternity of Christian Doctrine (C.C.D.) were the closest related to Campus Ministry.

The Sodality of the Immaculate Conception of Blessed Virgin Mary, a worldwide association established by the Jesuits in the seventeenth century was formally inaugurated at Trinity College "on the eve of the Feast of the Immaculate Conception, 1904, on the occasion of the *Golden Jubilee* of the Proclamation of the Dogma of the Immaculate Conception of the Mother of God."[199] Sister Mary was at her most eloquent in describing the scene.[200]

> At 5 P.M. His Excellency the Apostolic Delegate Falconio came to Trinity accompanied by Rev. Father Stickney. The ceremony was most impressive. The Reverend Delegate robed in Golden cope, preceded by the master of ceremonies, Rev. Fr. Morgan, two acolytes and Rev. Dr. Creagh, and accompanied by Deacon, Rev. Dr. Melody, and sub-deacon, Rev. Fr. Stickney, in gold dalmatics, entered the sanctuary which was aglow with lights and adorned with choicest white flowers, especially our Lady's altar. After the *Veni Creator* was sung, Rev. Dr. Creagh delivered a magnificent eulogy on our Mother Immaculate. The Rev. Delegate then blessed the Medals and himself enrolled all the Students to the number of seventy six in the Sodality. He gave a brief address then proceeded to bless the new crown with which Rev. Dr. Creagh crowned the statue of our Blessed Mother. Solemn Benediction followed and the singing of the *Te Deum* closed the impressive ceremony.[201] After supper the young ladies were presented to His Eminence (sic) and after spending a pleasant half hour with them, [he] granted them a holiday and left for home.

The Trinity College Sodality was placed under the patronage of St. Paula, a fourth century educated lady, a pupil of St. Jerome, the great scripture scholar. December 8, Feast of the Immaculate Conception, according to a statement inserted in the Sodality Roll Book about 1914 became "the Special Feast of the Sodality. On this day each year, the

198. P. 358.
199. *Ms* statement inserted in original roll book of the Sodality. T.C.A. Note that this is one society *not* started by the class of 1904. They had graduated.
200. Dean's Notebook. December 7, 1904. Cf. Faculty Minutes, Jan. 12, 1901. Dr. Garrigan thought sodality "not necessary at least at this time."
201. Note that this took place in the chapel which until 1909 was in the present room 250. Pictures of the chapel and of the shrine described are extant in T.C.A. From 1909 to 1923 the chapel was in the large southwest room now occupied by Admissions and from 1924 to the present Notre Dame Chapel has been in use.

members of the Sodality have a High Mass celebrated in the Trinity College Chapel for all the members ever enrolled, living and dead. On this occasion the Sodality also furnishes the flowers for the altar. On the evening of the same day there is a sermon in the Chapel and all new Catholic students are enrolled in the Sodality. The ceremony is closed with Benediction." That the order of exercises for this enrollment remained essentially the same for more than fifty years is evidenced by typed copies of the "Order of Exercises" and Act of Consecration dating from various periods from 1904 to the mid-1950's.[202] The students' chaplains Dr. Creagh, Dr. Melody, Dr. Kerby, Dr. Russell[203] acted as directors until 1941. Dr. Aloysius K. Ziegler, the students' confessor, for the next twenty years was also Sodality director during those years.

A typical Sodality reception began with the singing of the *Veni Creator,* followed by a sermon, or "instruction," admission of candidates which consisted of the reading by the President of the Sodality of the complete list of new members, the blessing and conferring of medals, the Act of Consecration by all present, and a hymn. This was followed by Benediction. The Seniors entertained the new members at a party in the parlors or Social Hall to complete the day.

Until 1933 the new sodalists received a blue-ribboned medal which was the property of the sodality and returned afterwards to be distributed and worn at meetings. Each December 8 saw white-clad, white-veiled freshmen led into the chapel of that era by Cap and Gowned seniors to be received into the sodality at a solemn Benediction of the Blessed Sacrament. On December 8, 1933 Sister Angela Elizabeth Keenan, Dean of Students, introduced the "Trinity Medal," which was received and kept by each freshman, at the Sodality Reception. Later, Sister Janice Marie Moran, Assistant Dean of Students and moderator of the Sodality, restored the original selective idea of membership in that society and the sodality reception ceremony was confined to those who wished to join and were accepted. The whole freshman class, however, still received the Trinity Medal as a token of acceptance into the college community. In this way not only Catholic students but all who wished to do so have been involved in the reception ceremony.

The Trinity Medal

The medal is symbolic of Trinity and of Mary, the Mother of God, Notre Dame. The face of the medal reproduces the original high-relief statue of Mary which is on the pediment over the front portico of the chapel, a seated Madonna holding the Child Jesus. The inscription

202. T.C.A. Box: "Student Activities" and Sodality Scrapbook, T.C.A.
203. Cf. section on Chaplains—Campus Ministers, pp. 397–409.

brings out clearly the intimate connection of Our Lady and the Holy Trinity:

> "Hail, beloved Mother, storehouse of the Wisdom of God, radiant resting place of the Trinity."

The reverse side shows a time-honored symbol of the Trinity. Within the circle of eternity are trefoils and triangles. In the center trefoil is the word DEUS; on three other trefoils around the circle are the three words PATER, FILIUS, SPIRITUS. Each of the trefoils is connected with the center by a bar bearing the word EST and with each of the others around the circle by the words NON EST. Thus the intricate doctrine of the Triune God is symbolized graphically.

Wekanduits

Until the turn of the century when Trinity was founded, the Catholic church in the United States was still considered a "mission" church, receiving help from Europe through the Propagation of the Faith. Mission efforts of the Church in this country were for the neglected parts of the U.S. itself. The first twenty years of the new century witnessed a growing interest among American Catholics in missionary work in other lands, chiefly the far east. This interest on campus culminated in the establishment in 1917 of the Trinity Foreign Mission Society, open to all students, with the smaller Wekanduit Bureau as its active arm. By 1919, Trinity had joined the National Catholic Students Mission Crusade, the first women's college to do so.

A student description of the beginnings, attributed to Dorothea Naumann '20, heads the Wekanduit Scrapbook.[204] An outline for a talk "Pioneer Days of the Wekanduit Bureau," given at Trinity c. 1920 by Eleanor Downing '18 and a copy of a paper prepared for the New York School of Social Work in 1920 by the same alumna provide information on student aims and attitudes on the subject of foreign missions. The first of these sources begins

> In the spring of 1917 a group of girls here at Trinity, impressed with the critical condition of the foreign mission field, organized a foreign mission society. They were imbued with the idea that this society should become a permanent institution in the college and, in order to bring this about, they decided that personal service should be the means adopted for raising funds. Personal service was made to include a range of activities from typing and sewing to shoe polishing. The students who performed these ser-

204. T.C.A. Closet 3. Dorothea Naumann later joined the Maryknoll Sisters and was a founding member of that missionary congregation's cloistered contemplative group. Miss Naumann was featured in *The Shield*, Nov. 1936 on the occasion of her perpetual vows as a cloistered Maryknoll Sister (Sister Christopher, M.M.).

> vices for [other] students called themselves the Wekanduit Bureau and constituted the active branch of the Foreign Mission Society. The entire student body were invited to identify themselves with the work for the missions by joining the Society, with membership dues at one dollar a year. It has become traditional to give sixty cents out of every dollar received as membership dues to the Propogation [sic] of the Faith. . . . In January 1919, the Trinity Foreign Mission Society joined the Catholic Students Mission Crusade,[205] which had received the approbation of Cardinal Farley and Cardinal Gibbons and had as its Honorary President Bishop Shahan of the Catholic University. Our purpose in joining was to identify ourselves with a National Movement. As the first women's college to join, we pledged ourselves to conduct a campaign for the purpose of enlisting other women's colleges in the Crusade. We urged that they adopt the Wekanduit method of raising funds. . . . We made no attempt to affiliate the newly organized Bureaus with our own. We explicitly stated that we would not exercise any control over their funds.[206]

The organizing members of the Wekanduit Bureau in 1917 were one junior, two sophomores, and six freshmen: Eleanor Dowing '18, Alexandrine Acerboni '19, Constance Curtis '19, Dorothea Naumann '20, Louise Keyes '20, Catherine Manion '20, Catherine McCarthy '20, Hester Curtis '20, Alice Mulligan '20.[207] Their ideas of personal service to raise money for the missions and personal communication between the donors and recipients permeated the activities of the Wekanduits during their sixty years of effectiveness at Trinity College.

The words of one of the founding members make the first of these clear in the description quoted above. The second shows in the same document:

> When the Bureau was first organized the girls had a specific missioner in mind, whose mission they wanted to help. There was always the personal equation existing between the missioner and the Bureau which has stimulated interest and kept it at a high pitch. Through correspondence the girls are kept in touch with the missioner and they have the satisfaction of knowing how his work is progressing and what his needs are.

The annual report for 1918–1919[208] gives an idea of the widespread interests of the early Wekanduits. It is therefore inserted here in its entirety.

205. Though the writer does not mention it, two Trinity students, Dorothea Naumann and Alexandrine Acerboni "petitioned the Crusade to admit women."
206. *Wekanduit Scrapbook.* T.C.A. Closet 3.
207. Names gathered from early Wekanduit documents, and articles in *The Shield*, *The Field Afar*, and several articles in *The Trinity Times*, notably one by Elaine Werebold '38. These are in the *Wekanduit Scrapbook* without dates.
208. *Wekanduit Scrapbook.* T.C.A. Closet 3.

ANNUAL REPORT 1918–1919

Trinity Foreign Mission Society

The Trinity Foreign Mission Society has realized	$1042.50
The WEKANDUIT BUREAU, the active part of the Society earned	758.00
Membership dues from students and founders	284.50
Total	$1042.50

The funds have been disposed of as follows:

To the Trinity Wekanduit Burse at Maryknoll	$200.00
To the Propagation of the Faith	115.00
For the support of one of the pioneer American missioners in China	100.00
For the adoption of a Korean orphan	100.00
To Fr. Gavin Duffy for schools in India	70.00
For the education of a native catechist in China	60.00
To Mother Mary Paul in British South Africa	50.00
To Rt. Rev. Bishop Crimont for his mission in Alaska	30.00
For the founding of a school in the Philippines	30.00
For the erection of a hospital in India	25.00
To the Dominican Mission in China	25.00
To the Carmelite Mission in India	10.00
Total	$815.00
Balance	$227.50

The WEKANDUIT BUREAU has conducted an extension campaign for the purpose of establishing similar organizations in all the Catholic women's colleges. Up to date Wekanduit Bureaus have been established in:

St. Catherine's College,
St. Paul, Minn.

St. Mary's College,
Monroe, Mich.

St. Mary's College reports that its Bureau has already earned $200.00.

Wekanduits, through the years, considered at their monthly meetings appeals from missionaries, allotted funds to those they chose, and kept up correspondence with them. They contributed to burses for the education of missionaries, and in the spirit of personal communication cooperated with the Maryknoll Sisters and with the Medical Mission Sisters from the pioneer days of both congregations. They sent help to Notre Dame de Namur missions in Japan, China, and Africa.

The original services offered by the Wekanduits were multiplied through the years to include running the student telephone switch board under contract with the college, the selling of homemade sandwiches and French pastry and later, candy and cookies in dormatory corridors in the evenings, breakfast-in-bed on Saturday, the pressing of gowns before Cap and Gown and Baccalaureate Sundays, the sponsoring of lectures, card parties, running a campus agency for a professional dry cleaning company, the providing on commission of birthday cakes from a local bakery, and finally and most notoriously the annual Wekanduit Show. This last musical or variety show, a friendly "take off" of life on campus (faculty and students) was zealously rehearsed in secret and invariably a great success—for the missions and socially.

Two faculty moderators of the Wekanduits, Sister Mary Kostka Kemper in the 1920's and Sister Fredericka Jacob '52 in the 1960's became missionaries themselves in Japan and Africa respectively, thus carrying out the "personal approach." Through thirty years from the early 1930's, Sister Margaret Mary (Fox) was moderator, encouraging, organizing, and sometimes browbeating Wekanduits to greater efforts for the missions.

As late as 1968 appeals were still coming in to Wekanduits from India, Alaska, the Philippines.[209] By the 1940's the "We-kan-do-its" had become on campus simply "Wekies." Periodically, articles in the *Times* or speeches at student gatherings outlined the history of the group and explained its name to later generations.

After the Japanese-Chinese War, the Chinese revolution and other "upsets" in Asia, when American missionary efforts became practically impossible in that part of the world, Wekanduits turned to helping the Latin American church and to Africa. The campus unrest of the late sixties, and a changing concept of "mission" finally ended the half-century of Wekanduit endeavor. Outlets for student zeal in the late '70's and beyond are provided by the activities of Campus Ministry.

The Christ Child Society

Another activity requiring personal service for others that flourished through many years from 1909 until the late 1960's was the Trinity College branch of the Christ Child Society.

The Christ Child Society had been founded in the late 1880's by Miss Mary Merrick, before Catholic Charities were organized and when the St. Vincent de Paul Society was the only Catholic relief agency operating in the city. "In her girlhood a physical handicap destined (Miss Merrick) to a life of invalidism but her valiant spirit overcame all handicaps and following the light of the Star of Bethlehem, she led count-

209. Wekanduits Scrapbook. T.C.A.

less souls into the field of social service where in the child of poverty, they found Christ Himself, the Babe of Bethlehem."[210] Clothing destitute children, especially making layettes for infants, visiting the poor in their homes, boarding children in need of fresh air in Brookland farm houses were early activities. These led to the Fresh Air Farm, the Christ Child Camp, a headquarters building first at 1101 H Street, N.W., then at 2550 K Street, N.W., called Christ Child House, and centers in various parts of the city, a Settlement House at 324 Indiana Avenue, N.W., Clinics, a Convalescent Home, and a new Settlement House on Capitol Hill. The Christ Child movement has continued to serve the poor long after the death of its foundress. Through the years Trinity alumnae have served on its boards, and labored in its many good works, continuing devoted service begun as students.

An article about the Christ Child Society[211] which shows also its many Trinity connections was written in 1963 by Dorothy Callahan Callahan '17, then president of the Society. "To the Trinity alumnae, the Christ Child Society is a familiar recollection. It may be the dolls dressed for Christmas, Easter baskets for convalescent children at the Christ Child Home, infant night gowns and kimonos served for layettes, Christ Child Tag Day at the College, or volunteering at the Christ Child Settlement House." She continued[212]:

> No one knows how many Trinity women have been a part of it. They are credited with helping establish branches in other cities. Josephine Farrell Bonner '19, and Julia O'Neill Collins '27 have been especially active in Pasadena, California; Frances Kushing Butler '51, in Detroit and Clare Corcoran Reynolds, '27, "Dickie" Thomas Hauser '21 and her daughter Mary, '59, in Chicago. Several have usually been on the Board in Washington.
>
> We are delighted to have a large number now in the Junior Guild. At a National Convention I met Ruth Harahan Mouquin '18 and Susannah Harahan Markey '18 from their active New Jersey Chapter (their late sister, Catherine '21, an able social worker, was also on our Board). Also Bess Fitzgerald '19 from Massachusetts and "Puddy" Griblen Crowley '36, who was President of the South Bend Branch last year. Perhaps this story will uncover more.
>
> The College, itself, has always been most sympathetic and cooperative to the Christ Child Society. Sister Marie Louis and then Sister Aloysius

210. *The Early Years of the Christ Child Society*, (1887–1937), by Mildred C. Merrick, p. 53. Privately printed, Washington, D.C., 1960, p. 1, T.C.A. Cf. "A Story of the Christ Child Society," Dorothy Callaghan Callaghan '17, *Alumnae Journal*, Summer 1963, pp. 312–318.
211. "A Story of the Christ Child Society," Dorothy Callahan Callahan '17. *Alumnae Journal*, Summer, 1963, pp. 312–318.
212. *Ibid.* pp. 312-313. Cf. also "Christ Child Society," *Trinity College Record*, April, 1910, pp. 87–90.

Marie[213] were our loyal friends for many years. They instilled into their Christ Child students an appreciation and understanding of the work, as their successor, Sister Catherine Marie does now.

Record books, minute books, clippings and correspondence covering the years from 1910 to the early 1960's preserved in the Trinity College Archives provide evidence of student activity in the Christ Child Society. As late as the 1964 *Trinilogue*[214] the Christ Child Society is listed as part of the Religious Activities Council. Words from that entry provide a fitting end for this description, and an indication of lively Christ Child work in the mid-1960's.[215]

> Volunteer service at St. Vincent's Orphanage and Christ Child Settlement House . . . tutoring and being tutored by the younger set . . . Oh that new math! . . . arts and crafts instruction . . . supervised play . . . a trip downtown at Christmas to see Santa Claus . . . sightseeing excursions on week-ends.

Confraternity of Christian Doctrine (CCD)

Though Trinity students had been teaching in various parish Sunday schools, with the Sisters of Notre Dame from the College, since that first group who opened St. Anthony's Sunday School in November, 1900, that apostolate had almost died out by the 1930's. Parish schools had been opened in six of the parishes and the work of the Confraternity of Christian Doctrine was beginning to grow in our area. The S.N.D.s continued directing the Sunday School at Holy Rosary Church at 3rd and F Street, N.W. until the 1950's, but Trinity students seldom accompanied them.

In 1937, the apostolic energy of an earnest group of students was reenkindled by participation in a successful Vacation School in Southern Pines, North Carolina. Out of this grew the Trinity branch of the Confraternity of Christian Doctrine, a diocesan based movement under the general direction of the NCWC.[216] The CCD had been instituted by Pope Pius in 1905, to be in every diocese in the world. Yet in 1950 much work remained.

A brief typewritten history[217] of the beginning of CCD at Trinity College is filed with the CCD records in the Archives. The section quoted here is the best description the author could find.

213. These were faculty moderators of the Trinity Christ Child Branch. Sister Aloysius Marie, of the physics department, devoted herself to encouraging the work for at least thirty-five years.

214. P. 38.

215. P. 39.

216. National Catholic Welfare Conference. Now developed into the NCCB, the National Conference of Catholic Bishops.

217. No date; anon. Probably 1942 according to internal evidence.

A brief history of the development of the Confraternity work will account for the present scope of activities among the students of Trinity College. Five years ago, twelve Trinity College students and two pupils of Trinity College Preparatory school at Ilchester, Maryland, engaged themselves to act as teachers, helpers, and fishers, for a religious vacation school planned for the children of Southern Pines, N.C., and of the surrounding countryside. Their work began during the Lenten retreat for the students of the college. The intervals between retreat exercises were utilized for the preparation of visual aids and project work for the coming session of the religious vacation school. This foretaste of the work aroused enthusiastic interest in the members of the group. Aside from this acquaintance with the teaching materials used in the vacation schools and a few preparatory meetings to discuss their plans, no other preparation for the actual work of teaching was given until the group assembled at the Academy of Notre Dame, Southern Pines, N.C., the scene of the religious vacation school. Here they were initiated into the work of fishers and helpers in earnest as they travelled throughout the surrounding country contacting Catholic families and obtaining pupils for the school whom they agreed to transport themselves if the ordinary school bus route was too inconvenient. Each student was assigned to work with a Sister. The partnership idea worked effectively as the trained catechist was able to supervise the activities of the student teachers and, at the same time, the student was free to use her initiative and resourcefulness in dealing with the problems that arose. The first group met the challenge admirably and the very tangible results went a long way toward developing permanent interest in catechetical work among the students. Convinced of its worthwhileness, the group were eager to enlist themselves in the work for the next season.

This first experience of engaging the students in religious vacation school work led to the following conclusions: (1) association with the Sisters was one of the best means of guiding the activities of the young teachers; (2) the definite objective of preparing for the work of teaching religion acted as a spur to study the literature connected with the Confraternity of Christian Doctrine movement; the more cognizant the student was with the principles underlying the various activities, the deeper the interest and the more desirable the outcomes of the student's work; finally, (3) the assumption of responsibilities for certain phases of the work of the school, picture study, project work, recreation, pageant, made for greater interest and, at the same time, greater joy in the work.

The third and fourth years in the development of the Confraternity work found the students studying discussion group methods under the direction of their Chaplain, the Reverend William H. Russell, of the Department of Religious Instruction at the Catholic University and of Religion at Trinity College. Their attendance at these discussion meetings gave them an insight into the technique of handling this important phase of Confraternity work.

With no diminution of interest in the work already launched, the Confraternity of Christian Study Group during the past year added a very important feature to their activities. The number of incoming students who

> needed additional instruction in order to follow the course in Religion offered material for the work of the Confraternity members. Under the direction of Reverend William H. Russell, several of the very able students were interested in caring for the needs of these students and became deeply interested in this phase of religious instruction. These teacher students met with the Dean, Sister Angela Elizabeth, to discuss the problems they met with in their work of instruction and to obtain direction in solving them. During the second semester, they were given a faculty sponsor to act in the same capacity to their group as the respective sponsors act for the various other extra-curricular activities.

From material deposited with the T.C. Archives it is possible to follow the activities of CCD at the College from 1937 to 1967 when they seem to have been swallowed up as were many others in the widespread campus unrest. The faculty moderators from the anonymous 1942 appointee through Sister Marie Therese Dimond in the late 1940's, Sister Ann Julia Kinnirey in the 1950's to Sister Elizabeth Henry Bellmer in the 1960's encouraged, helped organize, cooperated with the Archdiocesan CCD, notably Father Joseph Gedra, and gave the instruction necessary for the students to earn CCD teaching certificates. Numbers of students holding such certificates varied from 21 to 48, but an average of, at least, 35 was maintained through the 1950's and 1960's.

The Trinity College membership was certified first by Reverend Cornelius Collins, Director, National Center, Confraternity of Christian Doctrine, N.C.W.C., 1312 Massachusetts Avenue, Washington, D.C., authorized by the Archbishop of Baltimore (.n.d.). January 11, 1949, a new certificate (in Latin) was issued to Trinity College by Archbishop Patrick A. O'Boyle.

Student speeches or printed articles describe the work at different periods. On April 3, 1949, Vivienne Lambert '49 gave a talk "We Have a Confraternity and We Value It," at an area Regional CCD Meeting at Dumbarton College. May 8, 1950, Father Gedra held a Confraternity Day for college students of the Archdiocese with mass at the National Shrine on C.U.'s campus and all other activities at Trinity. April 28, 1951, the First Archdiocesan Cathechetical Congress[218] organized by Father Joseph E. Gedra was held in Notre Dame Chapel at Trinity. Cecelia Fitzpatrick '52 spoke on "Problems Faced by Teachers," and Rosemary Albus '53 on "The Apostolate of Good Will."

Cecilia Fitzpatrick '52 distinguished herself in her college years (and even after graduation) by her efficient management of the logistics of assigning teachers, and providing for transportation to and from assign-

218. Note that the Washington Archdiocese only started to operate separate from Baltimore in 1947.

ments.[219] The classes were held for the children of various parishes on Saturday mornings. Usually classes were conducted in six or seven parishes a year, by arrangement with pastors and local CCD workers.

The 1963–1964 report of activities which may be taken as an example of the continuing work names co-chairmen Mary Ann Brady and Mary Frances King, with a council of "heads of each activity," Chairman of Teachers, Claire Crabtree, had three to five students in seven "local areas": St. Camillus, St. Joseph, St. Peters, Junior Village, St. Vincents, St. Andrew, Our Lady of Sorrows. The training course enrolled 31. Ten discussion groups centered on Trese's *Guide to Christian Living* and the liturgical movement in the church, timely in the year of Vatican II. Pat Hishike and Seton Cuneen were enlisting and preparing students to participate in summer vacation schools. Groups were cooperating with Wekanduits and the Foreign Students Council making visual aids for use of teachers in Brazil and Africa.

Meanwhile, vacation schools had been held at various times. A letter from Sister Angela Elizabeth Keenan describes programs in Hyattsville and Ardmore in 1940. A letter from Sister Peter Claver Fahy '23, SMBT, praises the work of Trinity students in Gadston, Alabama in 1964. A *Trinity Times*, Vol. 35, No. 1, (1961), article by Nancy Leyendecker gives details of vacation schools on The Mass in North Carolina at Shelby, Leaksville, Hendersonville, Southern Pines, Warrenton, summer of 1961. A successful vacation school was conducted in Clifton Forge, Virginia in 1964.

Trinity students are listed in the 1966 and 1967 programs of graduations of CCD aspirants in the Archdioces of Washington. Nothing later appears in the records, but many students trained in the Trinity CCD program went back to their home dioceses and continued their volunteer work. Many a child in a distant part of the country has benefited through the years from their efforts, a leavening effect unknown to others.

Class Days—Trinity Style

Those unfamiliar with Trinity student life need a distinction here between one of the days of the traditional Commencement Week and the carefree song-filled, color-tied celebrations during the scholastic year when each class enjoys a day that remains a focal point for alumnae in their memories of college years. The development of the full-fledged Class Day of the middle sixty years of the century (1920's to

219. No college bus was available in the '50's nor were resident students allowed cars on campus. The Washington CCDers did yeoman work in those days in addition to teaching.

1980's) was gradual. Though the Gold Class of 1915 claimed the honor of instituting the custom, red classes since the first, 1904, had fastened on Valentine's Day for celebration, as the green classes from 1906 claimed St. Patrick's Day. The class of 1915 chose May 4 in the midst of spring for their special day, followed by their sisters the blues of 1917 who chose Columbus Day, later changed to Armistice Day.

The program for the day consisted at first of decorations in the dining hall and songs at meals. From this developed the full Class Day Program representing the team work of most of the members of the class preparing through many weeks, or even months. The day began with mass, attended by the whole college, followed by the gathering at the decorated Well for the march of the celebrating class to the decorated dining hall, singing their "marching song." Several of these "marching songs" became traditional, such as "Here's to the Class that Claims our Praise" dating from the 'teens, or 24's memorable "Red Roof," or "All Hail to Our Class '25" sung to the rhythm of "The Stars and Stripes Forever."

Appropriate words were written to the melodies of popular songs and sung before and after classes, at meals, at the Well. By 1921 the elaborate decoration of the Well (second to fourth floors!) and the wearing of "costumes" by the celebrating class evoked student concern. A movement to simplify Class Days was strong enough to limit the Well decoration to second floor and reduce costumes to sweaters and skirts with a touch of the proper color. Gifts to members of the celebrating class, songs to various classes were part of the dinner program and remained. The original skits at the evening party grew into original plays or musicals in the auditorium, dwindled to published one-act plays by Dramatic Society members, and returned again to originality in the mid-1940's with original musicals replete with local innuendo.[220]

Class Days have changed drastically as life in these United States has changed. The students of the late 1970's still celebrate—not at the traditional times, but on more pragmatically chosen dates. The "childishness" of earlier years may be gone, but the teamwork, the carefree sociability, the deep friendships, the organization and decision making, as well as the cleanup operations of those days were not wasted.

Nothing could catch the spirit or the changing character of Trinity Class Days better than an article by Ellen A. Ganey, "An Achronism? Enigma? Paradox?"[221] It is reprinted here, lest we forget.

> Our young photographer had followed the sophomores from Notre Dame Auditorium to the Smoker where he strolled casually about in the

220. Cf. pp. 362–363.
221. *Alumnae Journal*, Winter 1958, pp. 75–80. Includes three pages of pictures.

crowd, his camera slung over his shoulder in much the way a minstrel of old carried his lyre. He warily skirted relaxed groups at tables, squatted, jumped, stood on tiptoe, and generally engaged in the spirited athletic endeavor peculiar to all good photographers. Then he strolled and skirted some more, sampling the coke and cookies and shaking his head the while in fascinated amazement as he murmured, "I can't believe it! I just can's believe it!" We, trailing him with our own coke and cookies and watching too for the next good spot for a squat, jump, or stand-on-tiptoe, inquired, "Can't believe *what*?" "Why, that . . . they're the way they *are*!" this obscure remark gave us a slight pause. It all seemed familiar and usual enough . . . after all, this was Class Day! . . . "Oh, you mean all this unsophisticated stuff?! . . . "Yes, I guess so . . . it's just so *different*." . . . "I suppose it is . . . Look! how about that?" . . . He was off about his business and we filed away his comments for later consideration.

The milieu of Trinity was certainly not alien to him—nor the feel of things behind the milieu. His own mother had played *her* "unsophisticated" part on other Red Class Days. And yet—he had been so astonished.

Class Day on other campuses refers ordinarily to one of the festivities of Senior Week at graduation, as, of course, it does also at Trinity. But Class Day to a Trinity girl means something quite different in its first connotation. It means the eleventh of November or the fourteenth of February or the seventeenth of March or the fourth of May, and it is suffused—not with a rosyglow—but with blue or red or green or gold, as the case may be.

The pace of life at Trinity has changed as it has everywhere else. Trinity has grown and matured; the late teenagers blossoming into their twenties who grace her campus today are not the same as those of other generations. Of course, they are still young, still occasionally foolhardy after the fashion of the young; they are still extraordinarily single-minded about unimportant things—like proms and week ends, still surprisingly shortsighted when they should be taking the long view—like not-much-income-while-he-is-in-law-school-but-we-know-we-can-manage-it. But they are far freer than we ever were, far more responsible, and—let us be honest—getting through college is a more serious business and a greater accomplishment (though paradoxically a more common one) than it was in "our day," even though that day may have been but five years back. Today's Trinity lady respects and upholds most of the old traditions—a few, we suspect, she clings to with a kind of tolerant charity because she senses we would be hurt if she did not. She adds quite regularly new customs of her own; she discards unceremoniously trifling habits she considers in the way. In a word, she is quite judicious and fair about the whole matter of traditions.

There is not very much time for play these days. Club activities are sober and time-consuming, and, as increasingly later permissions keep step with the times, life beyond the campus takes on a very natural and salutary attraction. What place, then, has Class Day in the life of today's Trinity student? A most important one!

Of all the year's activities, Class Day requires the most time and effort on the part of the greatest number, with little to show in results but fun and good fellowship. The day's programs with their attendant backgrounds are becoming steadily more elaborate. The Well, of course, goes up the night before—or should we say the *decorations* in the Well. Either way, it is hard to explain to the uninitiated. We overheard a remark made one day in the parlor—"The Well? . . . Well, the Well is . . . er . . . the Well . . . I thought you said you'd dated Trinity before!" The Well decorations consist still of a large *pièce de résistance* suspended, literally in thin air, by what seems to be the most fragile of cords fastened to the four pillars. The surrounding balustrades (this is on the second floor, remember) are covered with scenes relating to that piece of signal importance (often electrified to light and move these days) which floats in midair. The Art Gallery side carries an inscription interpreting the whole, linking its significance to the class itself.

Additional décor consists in placards affixed to classroom doors, illustrating the theme of the day and proclaiming in time-honored witticisms some pertinent impertinence. The foyer of Alumnae Hall, too, is decorated; while the class color predominates, strict adherence to one color no longer prevails, and there are usually some touches of the colors of the three other classes, signifying thus graciously their part in the general Trinity scheme. This applies to *all* classes, not just the sister class, for the old odd-even rivalry is long since dead.

A headress of an appropriate sort is worn in lieu of the old costumes (space hat with a map of the world on it made a cap for this year's sophomore). Seniors wear academic dress out of courtesy to the class celebrating, and from each mortar board swings a tassel of the proper color. All members of the class—and indeed everybody in the school including feminine members of the lay faculty wear garments of the color of Class Day. A great variety of hues is displayed, as you might imagine; for instance, on February 14, deep crimson to pale coral!

Menus are chosen by the class celebrating, and no matter how extraordinary the combinations may be, the culinary department respectfully adheres to them.

Class Day is vocalized by unceasing song. The Green Classes still persist in the unholy practice of opening their day at a very early hour by singing "Top o' the morning to you" throughout the corridors and flinging open the doors of non-green sleepers. Everyone sings at assembly (where special permissions are traditionally given by the Dean), sings at classes, sings in the dining room, (where all the tables have been decorated—very cleverly too—the tables of the celebrating class by members of the sister class). The traditional knock song is part of the repertoire at dinner, and classes still sing back and forth to one another as they have these many years. Singing persists throughout the play, culminating with a grand finale when the whole class is crowded on the stage. At the end of the play the class president publicly thanks each committee chairman and presents her—on the stage (though she may not be immediately recognizable due to the part she has played) with a gift from the class in token of appreciation. Thereupon the Vice President makes a speech of appreciation to the President and presents *her* with a gift, and everyone sings some more.

Immediately thereafter all repair to the Smoker where a skit is put on by the sister class and attended by the officers of administration of the College as well as by the whole school. More singing ensues, though everyone is hoarse by this time.

This, in general outline, is today's Trinity Class Day. We have not even mentioned the several delicate touches—like a small floral tribute for every faculty member who shares the same class color (the color handed down every four years since 1904 and '05 and '06 and '07), as well as a great basket of flowers for the Dean. Then there are presents from "my Junior" and "my Senior" and "my Freshman," not to speak of other friends—all festively wrapped like birthday presents. A great number of congratulatory messages—many of them telegrams—are read before the play by the Class President—messages from mothers and fathers and friends and absentee members, messages from Trinity's own V.I.P.'s and likewise from potentates at home and abroad whose offices have been solicited for these very letters! messages from the colleges of boy friends, from "the Blue (or Red or Green or Gold) Sisters," and from "Lady Bedcheck."

The play is invariably an original production with an enormous cast, exceedingly funny, though usually filled with cryptic remarks utterly meaningless to all but the students themselves and perhaps the hapless professor who recognizes his own phrases adroitly wedged into the most seemingly irrelevant dialogue. These innuendoes are delivered with poker-faced sobriety and greeted with hilarious enthusiasm by the audience. It would seem, then, that a Class Day play though admittedly clever, would have scant appeal for any but the immediate family. On the contrary! Class Day plays draw alumnae-mothers of students (sometimes from considerable distances), boy friends, small brothers and sisters, the College President and the Chaplain, professors of theology and psychiatry, of sociology and political science, chairmen of the departments of art and speech and physical education, members of the class who have left to be married or transferred to other colleges or just left to take a job at the Pentagon, and again—all the Red—or Green—or Blue—or Gold—Sisters in the house. Why? It defies any rational explanation.

Class Day is one long, full day of ludicrous nonsense and childlike exuberance, or rapier-like satire and undisguised sentiment. It is an anachronism if *Alice in Wonderland* and *Gulliver's Travels* and *A Midsummer Night's Dream* are anachronisms. It is an enigma in somewhat the same way that a Christmas tree and a wedding cake and a champagne toast to the newly christened are enigmas. In short, it is a paradox—in appearing to be irrelevant and inconsistent it is actually relevant to and consistent with the very essence of Trinity. For knowledge is not the only handmaid of Faith: so too are laughter (cf. G.K.C., "In Defense of Nonsense") and firm friendship (cf. St. John, First Epistle, Chapter 3).

Happy Class Day!

Cap and Gown Sunday

The question of academic dress as a "uniform" for students at Trinity College became one of the items discussed at the first meeting of the

Advisory Board, May 9, 1901.[222] It was introduced by the president of the college. Saying that this was one of the "very important factors sometimes in the esprit (sic) of the College," Dr. Garrigan, chair of the meeting, invited discussion. Though Sister Lidwin "was for Cap and Gown," the dean "Sister Josephine said she was in doubt—Vassar after a lengthy discussion had decided against Cap and Gown; Smith and Bryn Mawr were divided, the former still discussing it and the latter had adopted it. Some thought it lent a masculine tone and manner." In the lively discussion that followed varied opinions emerged. "Miss Dorsey stated that the Mother Provincial had said last year, when the question was submitted, that she thought she would reserve it for Senior year, as a mark of merit for those girls who having worked through the full course had conquered its difficulties and won their degree." The result of the discussion was a "mandate" to the president to form a "Committee on Uniforms," with herself as chairman. The committee thus formed consisted of Sister Lidwin (president), Sister Josephine (dean), Miss Olive Risley-Seward, Mrs. Thomas Carter, and Miss Ella Lorraine Dorsey.

No official report of this committee was given at the 1902 meeting, but "Miss Risley-Seward said she would like to see the Trinity students designated by some distinctive gowns rather than that of the ordinary college student." The Committee on Uniforms was replaced by a "Committee on Cap and Gown" to report at the next meeting. Though no separate report appears in the minutes of the 1903 meeting, the decision to reserve the Cap and Gown for senior year had been taken. A paragraph of the Dean's Report at that meeting announces the decision. "The Committee appointed to look into the question of adopting the Cap and Gown report a favorable answer. The students were consulted and replied though their representatives, that they desire the cap and gown of the regulation form and color, but for the Senior class alone. So caps and gowns will be worn by Trinity's students of the Senior class in the fall of 1903."

The first Cap and Gown Sunday was October 4, 1903. The entry in the Dean's Notebook for that day will be given in full since it describes the beginning of an unbroken tradition linking the first students with those of today.

> "October—1903. 4th, Mass of the Holy Ghost by Rev. Dr. Creagh.[223] The Students sang the Mass very well and the celebrant preached a beautiful sermon on Christian education. This day will be memorable as the occasion on which *Caps* and *Gowns* were first worn at Trinity by the Seniors. Having put on their scholastic costume, the young ladies marched in line to the

222. T.C.A. *Advisory Board Minutes,* Book I.
223. The students' chaplain.

Chapel[224] and occupied the first two benches. The day was a gala one in honor of the event, a fine dinner being given to all and the tables were beautifully decorated with wild flowers. Souvenir verses were presented to each Senior which they appreciated very much.[225]

Oct. 5th.

On this day and for the rest of the week, the Seniors wore their caps and gowns to all *lectures* and *recitations.*"

This first Cap and Gown Sunday had two elements: the line of march to chapel and the college-wide celebration in honor of the seniors. The festivities at dinner, which was at noon in those days, point to the fact that the Mass was after breakfast. The *Motu Proprio* in favor of frequent, even daily, communion had not yet been promulgated. When it was, Trinity students immediately petitioned for early Mass so that they could receive communion,[226] without breaking the required fast from the previous midnight.

The 1907 account reflects this in the change to festivity at breakfast.

A more perfect day could not have been desired than October sixth, nineteen hundred and seven, when the Seniors donned their caps and gowns for the first time. It was indeed a very imposing sight as the fourteen Seniors marched into chapel to the impressive strains of the organ. When mass had been celebrated, all assembled in the dining hall for breakfast, where the Seniors' tables had been tastefully decorated with their class colors, red and white, by the Sophomores. After the underclasses had taken their places, the wide doors were thrown open and the Seniors entered with slow and stately march to the loud applause of all. During breakfast cameras were much in evidence and the memory of Cap-and-gown Sunday was fixed indelibly.[227]

"Cap and Gown Sunday, September 28, 1913 marked the opening of the scholastic year," wrote Sister Mary in her report for 1913–1914. The student account of the day shows the beginning of the emphasis on song which developed into the "Court Sing" and more recently the "Well Sing."

September 28—Nature put on her sunniest smile when 1914 donned their caps and gowns for the first time, and it was universally admitted that the Senior march to chapel was a most impressive sight. According to a tradition almost as old as the college, the Mass was read by the Right Reverend Monsignor T.J. Shahan, Rector of the Catholic University, who gave us the honor of a splendid sermon, urging the Seniors to live up to the dignity of which cap and gown are symbols, and make the Trinity sands of time

224. The present room 250.
225. Cf. Dean's Report, June 1, 1904, p. 2.
226. The origin of the 7:00 a.m. students' Mass which lasted for sixty years.
227. *Trinity College Record*, Dec., 1907.

> famous with the footprints of 1914. The Sophomores, as usual, showed their loyalty in their zealous preparations to receive the Seniors as they marched into the dining-room, for the tables were decorated as only 1916 could have done it. Everything was delightful. The greatest surprise of all was given in the marvelous wealth of song lore which 1914 rendered. The truth of the matter is, they had been saving the richness of their voices for three long years, and, with a generous chorus, they made the rafters of dear Trinity ring on this famous day. After breakfast, the unique feature of the day was realized in a grand march of the Seniors and Sophomores, who paired off in true sisterly spirit. Then the camera fiends had their sway, and the result is we have many pictorial reminders of our groups around the grounds. The rustic bridge played a prominent part in the scenic backgrounds. It was certainly the best day ever![228]

The marching song of 1914 became a traditional senior song surviving to even today, though rhythms change with fashions and class numerals are adapted. Marian Welch '14 wrote[229] of the freshmen who with the other students were waiting in the Dining Hall:

> They strain to catch the words, and rising with the others, as the Senior President brings her line into the dining hall, the thrill of college spirit springs up, never to die.
>
> So here's to the class that claims our praise,
> Here's to our friendships strong;
> Here's to our merry college days
> Of laughter and of song.
> Here's to our College, best on earth,
> Here's to 1914,
> Here's to her rare and sterling worth,
> Here's to our white and green!

From 1909 to 1924 the "Senior Line" marched proudly the full length of the Marble Corridor from the chapel at the south end to the dining hall at the north.[230] The first Cap and Gown Mass in Notre Dame Chapel was September 24, 1924. After the opening in 1929 of the dining rooms in Alumnae Hall the Seniors marched around the Main Building while the other students hurried via the northern short cuts to be in place to receive them when they arrived.

All these years until the mid-1930's the celebration of Cap and Gown Sunday was an entirely "in house" festivity. Students and faculty only,

228. *Trinity College Record*, Dec., 1913. Student history was a bit vague. The "tradition almost as old as the college" of having Monsignor (later Bishop Shahan) preside and preach was a seldom broken tradition of the 'Teens and early 1920's, but it did not go back into the first decade. Dr. Shahan was a revered teacher until 1909 when he was appointed Rector of C.U.
229. "Student Life at Trinity," *Notre Dame Quarterly*, circa 1915.
230. There were no fire doors to impede their progress. *They* date from the early 1970's.

joining to honor the seniors at Mass, breakfast and the "Sing" in the South Court (now called Seymour Court). Sister Angela Elizabeth, Dean of Students, and the Student Government officers thought that parents and friends would like to share in the celebration and sent invitations to Mass, brunch and the sing. A President's reception for seniors, guests and faculty on the preceding Saturday evening was inaugurated by Sister Margaret Claydon in the 1960's.

The time of the Mass has changed with the scheduled time of the regular students' Sunday Mass from 7:30 a.m. to 7:00 a.m. back to 7:30 to 8:00 to 10:30 to the current 11:00 a.m. The seniors no longer march to the dining room, but meet their guests on the chapel lawn and accompany them to reserved tables in Alumnae Hall. The other classes participate in the "Sing" after brunch, but have been crowded out of places in chapel and dining room by increasing numbers of guests as well as larger numbers of seniors.

The custom in the early years of senior visits in the evening to freshmen has also died out. The freshmen provided refreshments and eagerly waited for their impressively cap and gowned guests. The traditional sunny weather did not always materialize. The song fest was driven inside by rain a few times, causing the decision in the late 1970's to have the sing around the Well rather than outside. The custom of

Cap and Gown Sunday, 1977.

seniors wearing their caps and gowns for the first and last weeks of the academic year, to Sunday Mass, and to any all-college ceremony remained in the student Tradition Book until 1974, but has now fallen into disuse. Cap and Gown Sunday, however, still remains, as the ninth decade approaches, a highlight of the college year.

One feature of the program of this day that has endured through the years is the presentation of the "Book of Traditions" and the class banner in the appropriate color to the incoming freshman class by the junior class president. These had been entrusted to her by the graduates of the previous June for the class would inherit their color. Thus has the unbroken color chain endured. The traditional "Odd Born in Us" song was lustily chanted by odd numbered classes to counter the "Even Clap" through three decades. These were replaced by the 1940's by the less boisterious and more sentimental "Remembering" sung by red and green classes ("evens") and "Friendships of Gold and Blue" sung by the "odds."

The Trinity Tea

Teas, popular social functions of the period, are mentioned by Deans and students alike from 1900. The regular Sunday afternoon teas given by the students for their friends,[231] teas to which the students were invited by members of the Ladies Board and other friends in the city flourished. The description of one of the latter appeared in *The Record*[232]:

> Mrs. Thomas Carter gave a Tea in honor of the Senior Class Tuesday, April thirtieth. The decorations were gold and white, the class colors, while the class flower, the marguerite in evidence everywhere, made 1907 appreciate more the thoughtfulness of Mrs. Carter, who omitted no detail toward making the affair the success which it proved. Among the guests were many people prominent in diplomatic circles of the city. Georgetown and The Catholic University were well represented, both students and professors of the latter being present.

The Trinity Tea when the whole student body was "at home" to guests dates also from the earliest years. *The Record*[233] announced the hope that it "will continue one of Trinity's established traditions." That hope was fulfilled until the turbulent years of the 1960's. The 1907 item follows:

> On Tuesday, November twenty-sixth, the students gave their Thanksgiving Tea. The hall was effectively decorated in pink and smilax. The col-

231. Cf. p. 319 for description and snapshots from 1902.
232. June, 1907, p. 83.
233. December, 1907, p. 78; June, 1922, pp. 141–142.

> lege pennants and banners were gracefully arranged and gave that little touch to the scene which made it a college function. The large attendance was encouraging and it is to be hoped that the Tea will continue one of Trinity's established traditions.

Since the number of guests in 1906 had been estimated as over three hundred, the "large attendance" in 1907 must have reached at least that number. Gradually *the Tea* became settled on the Monday before Thanksgiving. An especially graphic account by Dorothy Flynn '22 appears in the June 1925 *Record.* Printed "At Home" invitations were sent by students and faculty, and numbers grew with the years. By the 1940's, parlors, the Marble Corridor and Social Hall were decorated by florists, and catered refreshments were served in Social Hall to as many as 1500–2000 guests. A fountain in "The Well", and the receiving line of Student Government and Class officers greeted guests in one of the parlors. This pattern continued under the direction of the Vice-President of Student Government, the students' official social chairman, until The Tea like other activities succumbed to change.

Clubs

A list of "societies" (clubs) in the *Record*, February, 1913 (p. 67), the 1931 *Trinilogue* tabulation of existing "organizations" with foundation dates,[234] and Mary Theresa Shea's ('51) article "Students Clubs" in the *Alumnae Journal*, November, 1950, all provide evidence of the durability of student organized activities. Two of the most durable, founded in 1901 deserve more than passing notice here: Dramatics and The Literary Society.

Dramatics

The Dramatic Society,[235] founded at the beginning of the second academic year of the college, must have included practically the whole student body. As the college grew in numbers of students the society established requirements for admission by audition, and the limitation of numbers to twelve members from each class: freshman to senior. All

234. Cf. p. 340.
235. The records of membership, dues, productions from the beginning were still extant as late as 1950, but the author knows nothing of them since. The evolution from "Shakespeare Dramatic Society" to "Drama Club" is indicated informally in the text. Many programs, printed and mimeographed from all eras exist in the Archives, but not the society's records. *Trinilogues* 1911 to date provide sources of information about Dramatics. Re-read pp. 210–211 of chapter 5 for some background for this section, the connection with speech classes.

members paid dues which, with admission fees to plays, helped pay the cost of production and royalties. In the late 1940's "dramatics" began to accept, in addition to full members who were "actors", associate members whose desire was for backstage work on costumes, sets, production in general. The distinction between types of membership soon died out, so that in the eighth decade, "the Drama Club" focuses on producing plays using the varied talents of all who want to join them.

The first major production of the "Shakespeare Dramatic Society" was a dramatization of Tennyson's "The Princess" on April 23, 1902, produced and coached by Sister Florence Louise (Delany) who had just jointed the faculty two months before. The day was significant because April 23 is not only Shakespeare's birthday, but the feast of St. George the time honored patron of England. The Dean's notebook, under April 23, 1902, throws light on customs of the time. "A holiday in honor St. George. Students ate in Sisters' Refectory as the stage occupied $\frac{1}{4}$ of St. Helena's Hall.[236] At 7:30 the Shakespeare Dramatic Association presented the Princess of Tennyson in a creditable manner. Followed by chocolate and cake at 9 p.m. At 9:30 all were in their rooms. Day scholars spent the night here."

A four page formal printed program with a crest (T.C. "Unitas in Trinitate"), a title page, "arguments," list of acts and songs, and the cast of characters still exists to memorialize the event.[237]

In addition to the frequent informal skits by any and all, a pattern emerged of four plays a year, one by the "dramatics" members from each class. These were open, for an entrance fee, to the whole college, but not to "outsiders." For many years a passion play was produced in Lent for Washington audiences, especially from nearby parishes. The major productions (presaged by "The Princess" mentioned above) were Greek classical dramas, or Shakespeare, Sheridan, or Goldsmith given during commencement week. Not only were they of high cultural tone, but they solved the problem of costumes for male characters.

As in Shakespeare's time, boys played the female roles, so at Trinity College male parts were played by Trinity women—*but* trousers were unacceptable for costumes. Until the end of the 1920's, the heroes or villains of modern plays produced at Trinity were authentically made up and costumed to the waist, but gym bloomers completed the attire! Pictures of well produced modern plays in the teens and twenties will show male characters strategically standing behind tables or leaning

236. The large multipurpose room at the southwest corner of the first floor, used until 1909 as both dining room and reception room, with curtain dividers so that it could be used as two rooms or one as required.
237. Copy in Dean's Notebook.

gracefully over the backs of armchairs, lower half hidden. Miss Kernan with the support of Sister Marie Mechtilde Mahoney finally succeeded in getting rid of this taboo before 1930, but it took until 1957 for men to penetrate Trinity College produced plays. That year the cast of "Blythe Spirit" included one Georgetown student and one from Loyola in Baltimore. The dam was broken and present day students have never even heard of or could they believe that such a ban ever existed.

From 1904, the first commencement, until 1922 the senior play at commencement was produced outdoors: on the "roof of the boiler room"[238] with the audience facing it, seated about where the pond is; in the south court with the audience on the surrounding "veranda;" or on "the Aventine," the hill where the library building now stands. The stage in O'Connor Auditorium was the usual place for other plays (as well as for "rained in" commencement plays and May Day Pageants). Cycloramic curtains, scenery flats, footlights and a dimmer were acquired over the years, though all sets were room-height in the lofty stage alcove and Pope Leo XIII (now on the center stairs) overlooked all productions. 1922's "Twelfth Night" was "rained in" at the last minute making the need of an indoor stage even more evident.

The 1923 Commencement Play, "The Taming of the Shrew," inaugurated the much larger stage in Notre Dame auditorium. For the year 1923–24, that auditorium was used as the students' chapel while the chapel upstairs was being finished. Baccalaureate Mass, 1924, marked the opening of the Notre Dame Chapel. From 1924 for fifty years the stage in Notre Dame, with footlights, overheads, electrically operated curtain, dimmer, and specially built sets for each play was the place for all plays: commencement, Class Day musicals,[239] dramatic society productions. Productions with experimental return to cycloramic curtains, with bare stage, with "levels," and "divided stage" effects drew audiences to Notre Dame Auditorium. The first play "in the round," Williams' "Glass Menagerie," was on the floor of the auditorium, surrounded by the audience.

The gradual encroachment of physical education and physical fitness activities on the facilities of Notre Dame auditorium, plus the ever present student desire for change sent the "Drama Society" back to O'Connor auditorium which had long since been converted into a lecture or recital hall. All the trappings of dramatic productions had been removed, a speaker's podium and amplifying system installed, and direct access to the music department arranged. There the "Drama Club" of the late seventies and beyond is producing excellent plays (from Greek Drama to farce) using original stage sets, and increased

238. Which is, since 1960, the foundation of the art and music wing.
239. See pp. 361, 419 ff.

ingenuity in rigging lights and making costumes, carrying on Trinity's interests in the drama in ways that suit their own generation.

The Literary Society (Beta Sigma Phi)

"The Literary Society of Trinity College was established in the year 1901, under the name of Saint Teresa's Literary Society, having as object the development in its members of an ardent interest in literature. It had a membership of twenty-three students." This statement entitled "History of the Beta Sigma Phi Society" by Margaret McDevitt '04 appears on the first page of the bound volume of "Minutes of the Literary Society 1905–1920." Perhaps the most effective of what were called later "co-curricular" clubs, the Literary Society endured until the late 1960's. Five bound volumes of minutes and membership lists from 1904 to 1966 are extant in the Archives. Immediately following Margaret McDevitt's statement in the 1905–1920 volume the constitution of the society appears in full. It was to be known as Beta Sigma Phi[240] (Books and good-Fellowship). The aim was to develop in its members "an ardent interest in literature and an ability to read magazines with a view to derive from them the greatest possible benefit." New members had to be proposed by sponsoring members and voted on by the group. They had to be interested students of English. A slightly revised constitution is appended to the Minutes of May 30, 1908, giving the name in Greek and introducing a pin inscribed BSϕ. After the advent of the *Trinity College Record* in 1907, publication of at least one piece of writing in the *Record* became a requirement for admission. Changes in twentieth century interests are reflected in the subjects discussed at meetings. Authors for discussion and guest speakers in the first decade were contemporary and predominantly, but not always, American. They included James Whitcomb Riley, Winston Churchill, Rudyard Kipling, Mark Twain, R.L. Stevenson, Eugene Field, Thomas Nelson Page, Maurice Francis Egan, Edmund Stedman, and some women: Mary E. Wilkins Freeman, Celia Thaxter, Agnes Repplier, Myra Kelly, Mrs. Humphrey Ward.

In January, 1908, a formal "public" meeting was held for the whole college and guests on John Greenleaf Whittier. The printed program lists speeches, readings from Whittier's works, a vocal solo, and a piano solo. This practice of a public meeting in January or February, with a guest speaker became a specialty of the society through most of its history. The 1909 speaker was the Director of the "International

240. Sometime between the original St. Teresa's Literary Society and 1905, it had been known as Upsilon Tau. Perhaps some members still wanted that because the membership voted October 17, 1906, that the name should be definately changed to Beta Sigma Phi.

Bureau of American Republics;" his topic: "Why the young ladies of Trinity College should be interested in Uncle Sam's Prestige Abroad." The present Trinity College student's interest in international and inter-American affairs has a long tradition!

Several times in the first years the Minutes mention concentration on contemporary novels and poetry. Other genres were not excluded and Shakespeare "cropped up" periodically. By the 1920's Kathleen Norris, Edith Wharton, Mary Roberts Rinehart, Willa Cather, Susan Glaspell, Virginia Woolf, and Dorothy Canfield were added to the "women writers" of special interest. In the 1930's, Edna St. Vincent Millay and Sheila Kaye-Smith were studied and evaluated. Meanwhile, males were not neglected. A lecturer on Shakespeare rubbed shoulders with the popular humorist, Stephen Leacock. Fitzgerald's *This Side of Paradise* evoked "interesting discussion," Sinclair Lewis' *Main Street* and *Babbitt* represented best sellers, while Joseph Lincoln's "local color" and Joseph Conrad's sea stories came under review.

The Society for the year 1922–1923, took as a body, a correspondence course given by Columbia University "in the Study of Current Literature" and started a circulating library to give members access to the books studied. The names of Sinclair Lewis, Dorothy Canfield, Joseph Hergesheimer, Hugh Walpole, Mary Roberts Rinehart appear among the authors discussed. One meeting was devoted to some "modern novels . . . that express the Catholic spirit." Several meetings the next year were devoted to compiling, at the request of *America,* a list of the ten best Catholic books "of the last hundred years. After narrowing suggestions down to forty, discussing, voting, defending favorites, the list of ten was sent to *America.*[241] The author has not examined its final fate, or how it compared with lists sent by other Catholic colleges.

The Society continued on an even keel into the 1930's, new names of authors appearing and a few old ones still holding interest for a new generation. More poetry, drama, and biography returned to the program: Edwin Arlington Robinson, Edna St. Vincent Millay, T.S. Eliot, Eugene O'Neill, Thornton Wilder, John Drinkwater, Douglas S. Freeman's *Robert E. Lee.* A study of the Minutes from 1935–1940 shows the discussion and criticism of twenty-six novels, five plays, two volumes of poetry, and several biographies or non-fiction. Nineteen of the authors were women, twenty-one men.[242]

The continued enthusiasm that characterized the Literary Society's activities owes much to its Honorary Presidents (faculty moderators)

241. Literary Society Minutes 1920–1934, p. 63. T.C.S.
242. A complete list of authors and works can be found in Literary Society Minutes 1934–1950. T.C.A.

with whom the other officers worked closely. They are listed here lest their names be forgotten.

Sister Julie de la Ste. Famille (Chisholm)	1901–1922
Sister Julia of the Trinity (McDonald)	1922–1929
Sister Julie again for a year	1929–1930
Sister Mary Mercedes	1930–1934
Sister Helen Sheehan	1934–1946
Mr. William Force Stead	1946–1958
Sister Dorothy Beach	1958–1966

Literary's years from 1946–1958 belonged to Mr. Stead,[243] a member of the English faculty (1941–1958). Excerpts from the obituary by Anne McMaster Reardon '50, a former student and colleague in the English department shows better than the author could why Trinity students revered him.

> Our image of him was based partly on the externals of British tweeds, a scholarly bearing, a self-deprecating wit, and the kind of unfailing courtesy which Shaw defines as "having the same manners for all human souls." It was enhanced by an other-world aura derived from the few facts we knew of his history: a native of Washington who had finished his education at Oxford; an Anglican clergy man who baptized his friend T.S. Eliot; a published poet who became the friend of Yeats, Robert Graves, and the Sitwells.
>
> What lay behind the image and made him the man we were honored to know, was something we never analyzed. Even now it seems difficult to connect him with strife or indecision or sorrow, yet some of these must have been present in his conversion to Catholicism, in the life-long invalidism of one son, in the giving of his other son to the Benedictines, in his return to America after twenty-five years abroad.
>
> Searching as students do for the perfect symbol, we decided that what he represented was the period he taught—nineteenth-century England. We were crediting his courtesy to a bygone age; his kindness to what he thought of as a simple, less stressful way of life. Now having lived and learned and understood a little more, we know the nineteenth century can no more claim him than our own can. No matter how frenetic the age he lived in, he would achieve serenity; no matter what pessimism or uncertainty or discouragement he absorbed from the atmosphere, he would remain innocent. We could not have met another like him in the nineteenth century any more than we could meet him in the twentieth or twenty-first, or, I suppose, ever again.

Beta Sigma Phi discussed and reviewed through two world wars and the great depression until the student unrest and riots of the late 1960's ending as one of the casualties of that unhappy time.

243. Cf. *Alumnae Journal*, Winter 1965, pp. 59–66. "Mr. Stead Presents an Old Friend"; Spring, 1967, p. 190 (obit.).

Crew, a new sport.

Other Activities

The activities of the various music groups, which have been popular from the opening days have been incorporated into the text of chapters 3, 5, and 6 and will not be described separately here. They have strongly influenced many Trinity students of each generation. They are the Glee Club (1901) which became the Concert Choir in 1970's, the choir (1900) (recently the liturgical singing group); Eurydice (1902) an orchestra; The Cecilian Society, a combination of glee club and orchestra which performed on state occasions and was later called the Music Club; the Trinity Belles, at first frowned on and later promoted by the Music department.[244] Along the way there was a Mandolin Club and other groups of which we found no written record.

Athletics, an enduring activity, is incorporated into the section on physical education and throughout this chapter. The language clubs, too, appear with the relevant sections in Chapter 6.

Of the foreign language clubs, *Le Cercle Français,* founded in 1907, proved the most durable. The Classical Society (*Noctes Atticae*) produced Latin plays and flourished in the first three decades, but had disappeared by 1931. *El Circulo Español* appears in the 1919 *Trinilogue,* but not in 1931. It was later revived as the Spanish Club in the 1940's, languished in the 1960's, and has again come to life in the late 1970's. A

244. Cf. pp. 363–364.

Deutscher Verein,[245] founded in 1928 after the revival of the German department in the post World War I years, continued as the German Club until it too succumbed to changing times.

The Record's first issue[246] stated: "The Cercle Français, which was instituted at the opening of this scholastic year, has for its purpose 'the promotion of interest in the French language by the study of its literature.'" The program for its March meeting included two songs, a recitation in French and a farce (cast listed on p. 78). This farce marks the beginning of the presentation of French plays and playlets which endured through at least fifty years. "The presentation of *Les Précieuses Ridicules* did exceeding credit to the participants as linguistic scholars and dramatic artists. It was another evidence of the versatile character of The Trinity stage."[247] A more ephemeral but popular comedy "Hâtez-vous Lentement" amused audiences periodically as it was revived for each generation of students. As the eighth decade ends, the French Club still flourishes with members earnestly improving their conversational skills, enjoying current French "movies" in the city, interested in the activities of the Washington Alliance Français.

This survey of student life at Trinity College will end with a glance at the celebration of Founders' Day (May Day) and appropriately the crowning events of a students' college career Commencement Week.

Founders' Day

The celebration of Founders' Day,[248] a carefree, all-college day in May, dates from the first academic year of Trinity College, 1900–1901. May 1, 1901, the students, freed from class for the day, joyously entered into their first May Day, mixing traditional devotions to Our Lady, vigorous outdoor games and athletic contests, and a sedate Maypole Dance. Since other colleges had Founders' Days, May Day was dedicated to the courageous founders of Trinity, now immortalized in marble in the foyer of Main, but at that time known personally by all twenty-two pioneer students. The threads of continuity linking the first May Day-Founders' Day with those of eighty years later are the Maypole dance and athletic events. Trinity students have wound and unwound the maypole in the stylish long skirts of the "oughts" and "teens," in the shorter afternoon dresses of later decades, again in long

245. Evidence of well produced German plays, as well as programs of recitations or essays appears in the *Record* in the decade of the teens, but no reference to a club. They seem to have been presentations of the department.
246. April, 1907, p. 83. Cf. also December 1907, p. 78.
247. *Record*, June, 1913. Under date of April 11 in the "Chronicle".
248. Cf. "Founders' Day," by Ellen S. Ganey and profusely illustrated with Vincent Shields' picture, *Alumnae Journal*, Spring, 1962, pp. 144–149.

formal gowns in the forties and fifties (all these usually in white or pastel shades), in the slacks and shorts of later informal garb, but they have always included this essentially medieval form of May Day celebration in their Founders' Day activities.

For sixty years at least, the day began with the whole college at Mass, and ended with the May Procession led by the seniors in Cap and Gown followed by the rest of the student body in white or light colored dresses, all sunburned and glowingly transformed from the rough and tumble athletes of the day, by the SND's, and by other faculty members.

Older alumnae remember nostalgically the old May hymns sung at Mass and in the procession, especially the "Trinity May Hymn"[249]:

> Trinity hails thee from campus and woodland
> All its spring beauty greets you today.
> Joyfully hailing you
> Gladly proclaiming you
> Queen of our College
> Dear Queen of the May.

Two cherished May Day activities of the earlier years are completely unknown in the eighth decade: May baskets on the seniors' doors, and the strawberry supper provided by the Sodality and served on the South Veranda by Sisters of Notre Dame wearing to protect their habits the "blue aprons" which were seen by the students at no other time of the year. The May baskets were first given by the Class of 1908 to the seniors of 1905. A 1907 description of this custom is from the *Record*[250]:

> Loyally following the pretty tradition established by their sister class, the Freshmen, by a tremendous effort, rose at sunrise on May Day, and filled baskets with May flowers to hang on each Senior's door. The yellow heart's-ease and violets intended to carry out the color scheme of 1907; and tied with yellow ribbon to the handles of the baskets were short verses which told as well as could be told in rhyme by any one who has not had the benefit of the Junior poetry course, of the enduring pride and love felt by 1910 for the "grand old Seniors."

In 1907, the *Trinity College Record*[251] notes that "for the first in the history of the College" [seven years!] it rained. There was no procession, and the Maypole and supper had to be indoors. The rain must

249. Words by Denise Roach '22 set to an English S.N.D. hymn. The words are the refrain quoted from memory by the author.
250. June, 1907, pp. 83–84.
251. June, 1907, pp. 83–84. Compare this with the 1962 article cited above. Cf. also a description of the "bright and clear" Founders' Day in the June, 1917 *Record*, p. 211, the cover picture of the pageant, 1947, *Alumnae Journal*, Spring, 1947.

have begun late in the day, however, because "the most interesting event of the day was the baseball game," for

> You may talk of the mirth of a dance,
> Or the joy of an afternoon tea
> But, oh, what compares with the trance
> That a game of baseball brings to me!

The game between upperclassmen and freshmen was rained out in the fifth inning with a score of 14-8 in favor of the upperclassmen. The tennis tournament was postponed.

The 1914 "bright and clear" Founders' Day followed much the same pattern as the earlier ones. By mid-century Founders' Day had become "a sports day in May . . . on which all classes are suspended and games are the order of the day" and cook-outs had replaced strawberry suppers. Sports had become extramural and in the eighth decade crew and long distance running vie with tennis, basketball, hockey and the, now traditional, faculty-student soft-ball game. Even the date is seldom in May since the changes in the academic calendar. Nevertheless Founders' Day still flourishes, linking contemporary students with the pioneers.

Commencements

The culminating point, the attainment of the proximate goal of every college student's life is the conferring of the degree which she has earned. The story of commencements, then, provides the ending to this chapter on student life at Trinity College. In 1902 and 1903 there were at Trinity formal closing exercises attended by faculty and friends.[252] The prototype Commencement Week of 1904 set the pattern for forty years until the exigencies of World War II caused the shortening of festivities from a week to a weekend. The shorter format has been followed since then, though the importance of the chief event, the conferring of degrees, has always held pride of place.

At the turn of the century there was an established custom at colleges and universities to spend a week in celebration by and for the graduating seniors. The Commencement Week of 1904, Trinity's first was not unlike that at women's colleges of the day. Copies of the invitations, program for the week, and programs for each event are preserved in the Archives of the College, as well as those of all years since then. The four and a half by three and a half inch printed program for Commencement Week, 1904, appears below.

252. The large scrapbook of commencements in the T.C.A. has copies of the programs for these events as well as of the solemn ceremony establishing the Sodality on the fiftieth anniversary of the dogma of the Immaculate Conception.

SUNDAY, MAY 29,

10 A.M.

Solemn Pontifical High Mass.
Celebrant,
The Right Reverend Philip J. Garrigan, D.D.,
Bishop of Sioux City, Iowa.
Assistant Priest,
Very Reverend Charles P. Grannan, D.D.
Deacons of Honor,
Very Reverend Thomas J. Shahan, D.D.
Very Reverend Edward A. Pace, D.D.
Deacons of the Mass,
Reverend John D. Maguire, Ph.D.
Reverend John W. Melody, D.D.
Master of Ceremonies,
Reverend George A. Dougherty.

Baccalaureate Sermon
Reverend William J. Kerby, Ph.D.

MONDAY, MAY 30,

5 P.M.

Presentation of the "Antigone" of Sophocles.
The Dramatic Society.

TUESDAY, MAY 31,

3 P.M.

The Opening of the O'Connor Art Gallery.

The Very Reverend Thomas J. Shahan, D.D., will speak on behalf of the donors, Judge and Mrs. M.P. O'Connor of California, and will deliver an address on "The Educational Value of the Fine Arts."

Concert by the Musical Society.

WEDNESDAY, JUNE 1,

10 A.M.

Class Day Exercises.

2 P.M.

Meeting of the Advisory Board.

THURSDAY, JUNE 2,

10 A.M.

Conferring of Degrees.
His Eminence James Cardinal Gibbons.

Address. "The College Woman."
Charles P. Neill, Ph.D.

3 P.M.

Organization of Trinity College Alumnae Association.

A separate program for the Conferring of Degrees dates from the earliest classes, listing the names of all candidates as well as the order of exercises. The 5 × 8 inch leaflet was enlarged in the early 1960's (1962) to 8 × 11 inches, but otherwise follows the same basic pattern.

This first Commencement Week is notable not only for its status as leader, as pattern, but because of the dedication of O'Connor Art Gallery, and the inauguration of O'Connor Auditorium. It is described at some length in an article in The Guidon, July, 1904.[253] Programs for all commencements since then are preserved in the Trinity Archives.[254] Descriptions of a few, only, will be presented here to note special features and to show the principle of continuity and change that runs through this whole history of Trinity College.

253. "Commencement Week at Trinity College," *The Guidon*, an illustrated monthly Catholic Magazine, Manchester, N.H. July, 1904, pp. 3–9. (8 pictures) T.C.A.
254. A list of speakers forms Appendix XI of this volume.

An article on "Student Life at Trinity," by Marian Welch '14 in the Notre Dame Quarterly[255] re-creates for us from the student's point of view the Commencement Week of 1914.

> To the world in general, the proceedings of commencement appear to last from Sunday until Thursday noon, and so the calendars say, but those acquainted with the internal workings that are necessary to turn out completely finished young ladies, are accustomed to weeks and weeks of endless preparation. Quiet is needed for a final essay perhaps. Fancy the distracted state of one's mind when intermittant strains from a glee club rehearsal and a mandolin practice come impartially up the well. Dire, indeed, is the effect on the final essay of such a combined scraping and carolling with, every now and again, the hammer of the stage builder. But what matters a Saturday sacrificed, or a nerve shattered, when Baccalaureate Sunday marks a perfect beginning to a perfect end. This year even the usually fickle weather smiled with unasked-for ardor, it is true—but still a smile is a smile, in every clime, and as such is always appreciated. Right Reverend Bishop Allen of Mobile was the celebrant of the Pontifical High Mass, and our professor of Sociology, Rev. Dr. Kerby, delivered the Baccalaureate sermon. His subject was "Prayer," and it would be impossible to describe the effect that his words had upon us. Every one was moved and thrilled but hardly more than we expected, because experience had been an efficient teacher and we knew our confidence could not be misplaced.
>
> Monday offered the play as its special attraction, "A Midsummer's Night Dream" it was, and with its pastoral setting in the court, was certainly a treat. To the audience on the surrounding porch, the forest that so suddenly had grown and thrived before the eyes of the girls, looked staunch and sturdy, indeed, and when the groups of rainbow fairies danced from out its shade, the scene was rightly named a dream. Talent displayed itself, of course, from Hermia and Helena, looking truly beautiful in spite of the obvious fact that love was eating out their inmost hearts, down to Peter Quince and Nick Bottom, who made our gray walls ring with laughter at the antics of his ass-ears. Puck wove his thread of mirth through it all, and looked like the green and gold sprite he was, as he danced and vanished, and danced again among the trees. If a pale, yellow moon had only lent its glamour to the presentation, I am sure the delighted spectators would have really believed themselves in the kingdom of the shining Oberon and his beauteous Queen Titania. As it was, the things of an everyday world were forgotten for a space, and the onlookers enjoyed a truly beautiful Midsummer's Day Dream.
>
> On Tuesday, the Cecilian Society gave the final concert, and, on Wednesday, came the great Class Day. One is not surprised to know that Class Day is the long anticipated goal, the pride and joy of every college girl, when one witnesses the beauty and solemnity of it all. Fancy forty-one girls in shimmering white, each with a long-stemmed American Beauty rose in

255. Reprints in T.C.A., closet 4.

her right hand, answering the summons of a compelling march, and stepping slowly down Assembly Hall toward the flower-dressed stage. Fancy them, too, arranged in a great semi-circle on that stage, singing with the depth of feeling only parting ones can express, the words of their class song. As the chorus says so truly, it was and will be *ad infinitum.*

To thee, Alma Mater, we consecrate ever
The thoughts of our hearts and our hands endeavor,
As a bond which even the years cannot sever,
    Through our length of days,
    As a pledge of praise,
Unto thee forever,
    Listen to us as we tell
    Trinity, to thee, farewell.

Only that "farewell" is tempered by the hope, the certainty, that some day the magnet will draw us surely back.

The real purpose of four college years, however, no matter how frequently it is lost to sight,—comes as the fitting culminating achievement of Commencement. Right Reverend Bishop Garrigan of Sioux City conferred the degrees on 1914, and his presence was particularly significant in that 1914 was the tenth anniversary of Trinity's first graduating class, and, to the pioneer girls, Bishop Garrigan has always been a cherished friend. The hoods of purple and gold with the white band indicative of the degree took away that sombre air that clings so persistently to a cap and gown, and after the stirring words of Bishop Garrigan and Hon. Mr. Haaran of New York, who delivered the address, the knowledge that one's tassel reposed on the other side of one's cap, caused a glow to warm forty-one hearts. The realization that all was over, the surety that days like Trinity days would never come again, the bidding good-bye to friends whom circumstances were to carry to all parts of the country, made an ache that time can only help to alleviate. But the song we used to sing so often, tells us a consoling truth that is not hard to remember:—

There may be a change in the weather,
    There may be a change in the sea,
There may be a change altogether,
    But T.C. will never change for me.

Graduates of the late twentieth century would not be so detailed nor so fulsome in expression, but the essence remains.

Individual classes remember their own commencements as different for various reasons. The Vice President of the United States, Honorable James S. Sherman, gave the address for 1909. The class of 1910 had the President of the United States, The Honorable William Howard Taft, for their commencement speaker, his presence preceded by Secret Service inspection and the provision of a sufficiently sturdy armchair. Both 1918 and 1945 found their activities severely curtailed because of

World Wars I and II respectively. The dedication of Notre Dame Chapel in which they participated shortly before commencement gave 1924 the opportunity of being the first to have their Baccalaureate Mass in that beautiful new building. Though 1934 was "a depression class,"[256] no indication of the effects of that dark period marred their solemn, happy, final ceremonies with the Rector of The Catholic University as celebrant of their Baccalaureate Mass and Archbishop Michael J. Curley of Baltimore, Chairman of the Board of Trustees, presiding at the conferring of degrees. Perhaps the most memorable of all Trinity College commencements was that of 1944. Their commencement speaker, the Rt. Rev. Msgr. George Johnson, Ph.D., a former faculty member, head of the department of education of The Catholic University, founder of its Campus School, executive director of both the National Catholic Education Association and the education department of the National Catholic Welfare Conference,[257] collapsed toward the end of his address and died fifteen minutes later on Notre Dame stage. The degrees had been conferred. At the request of Archbishop Curely the graduates filed out of the auditorium followed by the whole audience. Silently they proceeded upstairs to the Chapel where they prayed for their dying friend. The "Unfinished Address" was printed and widely circulated by Sister Catherine Dorothea, president of the College. A copy is preserved in the Trinity College Archives. The classes of 1925, 1950, and 1975 graduated in the midst of celebrations of the 25th, 50th, and 75th Jubilees of the College feeling somewhat overshadowed by the larger events.

A study of the list of commencement speakers[258] reveals that both houses of Congress, the Supreme Court, the Cabinet and other Federal Agencies, as well as state and city officials have addressed Trinity graduates, and after 1935 outstanding alumnae of the College appear with satisfying regularity. In 1906 Senator Thomas H. Carter of Montana, in 1917 and 1925 Senator David I. Walsh of Massachusetts, in 1918 Representative George F. Shaunessey of Rhode Island, in 1928 Representative Charles A. Mooney of Ohio, in 1958 Senator John F. Kennedy of Massachusetts, in 1962 Senator Thomas Dodd of Connecticut, in 1965 Senator Eugene McCarthy of Minnesota, in 1970 Senator George J. McGovern of South Dakota, in 1971 Representative John Brademas of Indiana, all brought the United States Congress to Trinity's Commencement. Justice William J. Brennan, Jr. addressed the class of 1960.

The complete list (Appendix XI) shows cabinet members, Federal government agency heads, prominent lay men and women in educa-

256. Cf. pp. 335–338.
257. Now called the U.S. Conference of Catholic Bishops.
258. Appendix XI.

tion, science, social work, journalism, local or state government from all sections of the country. They indicate the national character of the student body through the first eighty years.

These final ceremonies of a Trinity student's college life, held in O'Connor Auditorium, Notre Dame Auditorium, on the Hockey Field, or the Library steps, and once in the National Shrine of the Immaculate Conception have crowned the student life of thousands and appropriately conclude this chapter.

PART III

Non-Academic Influences

CHAPTER SEVEN

Granite, Sandstone, Boards and People

The non-academic influences.

WHETHER OR NOT one accepts Mark Hopkins' assertion that a college's needs are a student and a teacher seated on a log, it is necessary in our time to have a rather extended log: buildings, campus, helpers of all kinds to provide the working environment for faculty and students. This chapter will attempt to describe the special ambience, the "Divine Milieu"[1] that has been an essential element in a Trinity College education during more than eighty years. It has been there, permeating work of classroom, lecture hall, laboratory, library,[2] contributing to the hallmark of excellence, taken for granted by students, remembered by alumnae, the "something different" that cannot be found in the catalogue. It has been provided, too, by a succession of good friends who have made possible the work of the college by generous material help and practical advice through the years. The oldest of the associations of such friends is the Ladies Auxiliary Board of Regents, 1898–1978, and the Advisory Board of prominent Catholic Laymen and women and eminent educators, 1901–1926. Worthy successors to these were the Father's Club, the Lay Board of Trustees later called the President's Council, and the Friends of Trinity.

Sisters of Notre Dame de Namur

It is impossible to overestimate the influence of the Sisters of Notre Dame de Namur, or of the educational ideals of St. Julie Billiart in the foundation and growth of the college and in the solidity of its changing educational program through the years.[3] The influence has also been exercised effectively by the many Sisters of Notre Dame who have worked at the College though not on the faculty or administration. Their contribution is a valuable part of the history of Trinity College. As part of the celebration of the seventy-fifth anniversary of the col-

1. Cf. Teihard de Chardin, S.J.
2. Detailed in chapters 4 and 5.
3. Cf. Chapters 1, 2, and 5.

lege, a celebration which lasted from November 1972 to December 1975, at a Mass of Thanksgiving for the Sisters of Notre Dame,[4] Sister Columba Mullaly, S.N.D., Ph.D., gave the sermon, excerpts from which are appropriate here.

> "How good is the God of Israel to those who are right of heart."
>
> This verse from the psalms, inscribed above the statue of St. Julie Billiart in the right transept, reminding us of her own frequent exclamation: "How Good is the Good God," sets the keynote of our thanksgiving today. It echoes in the gospel we have just heard and in our songs of praise to God. We thank God for Trinity's seventy-five years as a woman's college in Washington, as a Catholic college, but especially today for the service of the Sisters of Notre Dame de Namur to that college, through all these years of change, and of development in the role of women in higher education, in civic, social and economic life, in the church. Our hearts glorify the Lord for the achievement of the past as we face steadfastly toward the future with hope and confidence that the Most Holy Trinity will be with this college which bears His name.

After a resume of the foundation and the growth of the College with expressions of gratitude to the many who had contributed to that development, who have already been honored, the speaker continued:

> This thanksgiving celebration focuses on the service of the Sisters of Notre Dame at Trinity College, a seventy-five year service without which there could be no college today. Since October 25, 1900, when the Sisters moved into a not-quite-finished South Hall, there has been a Notre Dame Community at Trinity, contributing, in addition to teaching and administration, essential services that often go unsung, and a certain indefinable something that has made a Trinity education unique above and beyond the scholastic attainment. Among these unnamed I choose a quartet to symbolize the contributions of all.
>
> Sister Mary Stephanie,[5] Matron of the College, housekeeper *par excellence*, was known to all students who lived "under the Red Roof" until her death in 1947. With a corps of helpers, she preceded both Sisters and students to "get the place ready" for occupancy. She organized cleaning and maintenance, forthrightly supervised the students' care of their own rooms, acted as a practical, no-nonsense guide, counselor and friend, inspiring a healthy respect as well as deep affection in Trinity women for nearly five decades.
>
> Sister Mary St. Roque,[6] gentle, dignified, a person of deep faith and sparkling Irish humor, was sacristan for nearly fifty years. She began her service in 1903 when the chapel was still in what is now Room 250; moved to the large room at the south end of the Marble Corridor in 1909 and from

4. November 16, 1975, Notre Dame Chapel.
5. *Obit. Alumnae Journal*, Spring, 1947, pp. 106–107, E.A.G.
6. *Obit. Alumnae Journal*, Autumn, '58, p. 5. E.A.G.

1924 joyfully cared for this beautiful Chapel to Notre Dame during its first quarter century.

Sister Cecilia Josephine,[7] from 1913–1929 was supervisor and director of the students' dining hall while it was in the present Social Hall. When Alumnae Hall opened she became its housekeeper and the ardent champion of the students who lived there. Though she ruled them with a firm hand, residents of Alumnae Hall could do no wrong in Sister Cecilia's eyes. "Her building" came from her twenty-four years of care as perfectly in order as at its first opening.

And, last, Sister Teresa of the Infant Jesus,[8] the keeper of the gate, who came to Trinity in 1901 and was portress at Trinity from January 1902 to her death in 1959. Today, we might call her receptionist, but that would not have suited "Sister Blue Glasses" at all. With unruffled aplomb she was impartial hostess to the important guests of the college and to the quite as important (but no so notable) guests of the students; to statesmen and cardinals, to bishops by the dozens and college boys by the hundreds, to parents of students; to Eamonn de Valera and Sinclair Lewis, to Elizabeth Queen of the Belgians, and to the President of the United States. She was an unofficial public relations person for the college for nearly sixty years.

We raise our voices in thanksgiving to God for the fruitful years since 1900, remembering the favorite quotation of the foundress of the college, Sister Julia McGroarty: *Non Nobis, Domine*, not to us, O Lord, but to Thy name give glory. It is fitting that we end with the same wish for the college in the years ahead that Dr. Conaty expressed in 1900; *Vivat, floreat, crescat*. May Trinity College live on, grow and flourish into the 21st century and beyond. The Good God *is* very Good!

In addition to that "quartet," five more should be included here. Sister Marie Liguori Wall, little known to the students, labored for their welfare on the grounds or in the basement, from 1903 until her death in 1950. She had charge of the bedding for resident students, remaking or repairing mattresses with her own mattress machine during the hot summer months, stitching hundreds of mattress pads, supervising the cleaning and maintenance of the ground floor, and personally locking all doors[9] before the advent of night watchmen or security guards on campus.

Sister Marie Edward Tivnan was the cheerful, witty college printer and telephone operator, 1913–1950. She printed all official notices of the College as well as mid-year and final examinations until the predominance of "objective type" or other specially constructed tests and of multiple copiers. She personally delivered telephone messages to

7. *Obit. Alumnae Journal*, Summer, '53, p. 199. E.A.G.
8. *Obit. Alumnae Journal*, Summer '59, p. 202 by E.A.G. Cf. *Newsletter*, March 1957. Another Sister Teresa of the *Sacred Heart* was portress before "Sister Blue Glasses," cf. *Annals III*, Feb. 17, 1902.
9. Except those subject to Sister Teresa's authority.

administration or faculty members before the advent of the switch board or the first private branch exchange (PBX) both of which she operated in her later years.[10]

Sister Edward Marie Connolly, assistant to Sister Mary Stephanie 1921–1947 and later post-mistress *par excellence* who organized a devoted student volunteer corps of sorters whose efficiency out-classed paid workers before or since, was affectionately known in private as "big Eddie." She ruled with an iron hand and a soft heart.

Contributing to the preservation of the Main Building and exercising a significant influence on the students of their time were two successors of Sister Mary Stephanie: Sister Mary Martha McGrath and Sister Lidwin Marie Genau, who moved from "upstairs" to continue her service as receptionist at the Main Desk. Tangible expression of student appreciation appears in the dedication of the 1958 *Trinilogue* to Sister Mary Martha and of the 1967 *Trinilogue* to Sister Lidwin Marie.

These, with the Sisters of faculty and administration, are symbols of the many Sisters of Notre Dame who have lived and worked at Trinity College through eighty years.

Boards and the People Who Served on Them

Except for the Board of Trustees, the governing board of the College which dates from August, 1897, the Ladies' Auxiliary Board of Regents holds pride of place among those associations dedicated to helping Trinity College. For eighty years, 1898 to 1978, the "Ladies' Board" served the College well. Its founding and early work are described in Chapter 2. In addition to the minutes, at least three short histories are extant in the T.C. Archives: one anonymous, dated January 1911, a second by Miss Nelly Feely, 1934, and a third by Sister Catherine Marie Lee, 1960's.

"The Board is organized as the Auxiliary Board of Regents of Trinity College and consists of ladies who have associated themselves together for the purpose of assisting and equipping[11] Trinity College." So stated the original constitutions. The scope of the association and the states for which the original "regents" assumed responsibility appear earlier in this history.[12] Associate Boards were organized in New York City, Brooklyn, Albany and other up-state cities, Boston, Worcester, New Haven, Pawtucket, Cincinnati, Cleveland, Columbus, St. Louis and other parts of Missouri, Montana, Virginia, Newark, N.J., Pitts-

10. The students' switchboard was separate, operated by the Wekanduit Society until the PBX.
11. This word was dropped in 1936 and the name became the Trinity College Auxiliary Board.
12. P. 43 ff.

burgh, and Spokane. Some of these were short-lived, but all contributed publicity as well as material gifts of books, scholarships or furnishings for the new College. The St. Louis Board was the first to complete a scholarship. The Cleveland Board furnished O'Connor Auditorium,[13] which has been renovated and refurnished at least three times since the pioneer gift. A "Montana Room," used by Montana scholarship students until the mid-1920's, was furnished by the Montana Associate Board under Mrs. Thomas Carter; and Mrs. Peter Larson, Honorary Regent of that Board, gave the crystal chandelier which still graces the foyer of the Main Building. The Associate Boards gradually became inactive, having fulfilled their purpose, while their work in various sections of the country was continued by Alumnae Chapters. The 1901 catalogue lists five associate boards with their presidents, the 1911 lists twenty-one, the 1925 lists nineteen, but by 1954 there were no board members outside the Washington Metropolitan Area. By direct contribution, by lectures, concerts, balls, card parties and other activities (there is a program for a "Ladies Minstrel Show" given by an Associate Board, but without identity of place or date), the Auxiliary Board has through the years contributed to Trinity College.

Miss Seward, Mrs. Carter and especially Miss Dorsey traveled extensively in 1899 and early 1900 in the interests of the College. The ladies of the board were hostesses at the elegant reception for dignitaries at the Dedication of the College, November 22, 1900, described in a three-column spread in the *Washington Post* of the next day. Since that time, successive members of the Board have worked not only for the scholarships, books and furniture mentioned before, but in 1922 to 1924 for $3500 to pay for the Marble Communion Rail in Notre Dame Chapel; the next year, for a full set of gold vestments as a jubilee gift; 1927–31 for a Student Loan Fund of $4865 which was used in the depression years, but which grew to $6406 and was transferred to make the Anna Hanson Dorsey scholarship available yearly instead of every four years.

There is continuity between the board of 1898 and that of the 1970's in many ways. Many members are alumnae of the College or have daughters who are alumnae or students of today. There is continuity in the presence of the Sisters of Notre Dame—no longer needing to be represented because the habit inhibits, yet still imbued with the spirit of St. Julie and devoted to the apostolate of Trinity College. One special continuity I cannot fail to choose from many. Staunchly assisting Sister Mary Euphrasia in the early work for Trinity was a young member of the North Capitol Street community, Sister Gertrude of the Blessed Sacrament (Margaret Dempsey). She was one of the original

13. Cf. Bronze plaque in the Marble Corridor.

incorporators of the College and the only one of the founders who came to Trinity permanently. For thirty-five years she was treasurer of the Ladies Board. Five of her nieces and at least three grand-nieces have graduated from the College: Three of those nieces, Mrs. Charles Fahy (Mary Agnes Lane), Misses Regina and Alma Neligan, brought that continuity to 1973 as honored members of the Trinity College Auxiliary Board in its seventy-fifth year.

The activities of the "Ladies' Board" continued until 1978, rounding out eighty years of service to the College. That year it disbanded in favor of a new group of both men and women called the "Friends of Trinity."

The Advisory Board of educators and prominent lay Catholic men and women was organized by the Board of Trustees of the College during the first academic year and held its first meeting at the end of that year, May 9, 1901. In Book I of minutes of the Advisory Board[14] pasted opposite the May 9, 1901 minutes is a statement which makes clear the function of this board: "The government of the College is vested in a Board of Trustees of which His Eminence Cardinal Gibbons is President. The Members are elected from the Community.[15] The Trustees are assisted by the Advisory Board which holds its first meeting today—and The Ladies Auxiliary Board of Regents."

At that first meeting with Dr. Philip Garrigan, Vice-Rector of The Catholic University in the Chair the ground work was laid for the board's support and advice to the trustees of the young college. Ten members (a quorum) were present. Those unable to attend sent messages indicating lively interest in the work.

Those present were

Very Rev. Dr. Garrigan in the Chair
Mother Provincial Julia
Sister Lidwine, President
Sister Josephine, Dean
Mr. A. A. Wilson
Gen. Vincent, U.S.A. (ret.)
Mrs. Carter, Pres. Auxiliary Board
Miss Risley-Seward, Hon. President Aux. Board
Miss Charlotte Lincoln
Miss Ella Loraine Dorsey

14. Not only the manuscript minutes of the Advisory Board for more than twenty-five years, but professionally typed copies with supplementary material are preserved in a large scrapbook. (T.C.A.)
15. In turn of the century language "community" here means the Sisters of Notre Dame de Namur, especially those living at Trinity College.

Sister Mary Euphrasia, Treasurer of Trinity and Manager of the Auxiliary and its Associate Boards, was present by special invitation of the Mother Provincial.

Letters of regret were received from Mrs. Ward of New York and Miss Carey of Cambridge, Mass., who were prevented by illness from being present; from Mr. Walter George Smith of Philadelphia, and Mr. Charles J. Bonaparte of Baltimore, the former detained by an engagement to lecture before the University of Pennsylvania, the latter by an engagement of long standing; a telegram from Judge Daily of New York, who was detained by a case in Court; a letter from Monsignor Conaty, detained by a Committee meeting of Trustees; and a letter from Miss Lindsay of St. Louis. A telegram from Mrs. Ward was presented by Miss Risley-Seward empowering her to vote for Mrs. Ward during the meeting.

Excerpts from the minutes are enlightening for late twentieth century readers, especially Dr. Garrigan's remarks as well as his conduct of the meeting which set the pattern for future meetings.

> The Chair's address was full of pith and inspiration, its dominant notes being the need for Trinity College, its great importance as a factor in the educational system of our country, the great benefit it will be to the Catholic women of America, and through them to society generally; he dwelt with force upon the fact that Trinity has not time to grow as the other Colleges have done through 25 years of experiment, but must enter into full-fledged competition with them from the very start. This competition is a valuable one, for it is not merely a competition of endowment and numbers, but a determination to work out and adopt the soundest and best methods, basing them on the highest standard.
>
> He further stated that Trinity deserves and ought to have the best support the Advisory Board can give it, and spoke of the honor the Faculty have done the members in associating them with this great work.
>
> "We shall pass away but Trinity will stand and the work we put into it will live. The dignity of helping to found this College, destined for such a noble use is ours, the honor of helping to evolve its educational system is ours, and we may feel sure, if we put our best efforts of mind and soul into this work to which we are specially invited, that a portion of the reward will be ours."
>
> He reminded the Board that it was created by the Trustees for the purpose of advising in all matters of discipline and curriculum, and urged full and free discussion of every point of interest and information.

The members were fully informed by the President and the Dean on the state of the College and the progress to date, and by a report from the Ladies' Auxiliary Board. A committee on "the order of business" (agenda) was elected to start work immediately. The Chairman stated that the usual way of transacting business by any deliberative or advisory body is to appoint committees—standing committees that shall prepare the material to be presented to the Board for action. That he would like suggestions from the Board as to what committees should be created. That today was an abnormal meeting, we had no order of business, no rule of procedure. Since the two important subjects on which the Board would advise the College were "studies" and "discipline," the Board established two standing committees to study these two areas. After work by the committees, the whole Board would discuss proposals to be submitted to the Board of Trustees.

After a recess for "an exquisite lunch" provided by the College, the Committee on the Order of Business reported a form of agenda that was accepted. This format for meetings remained in force throughout the Advisory Board's existence. Its simple practicality fitted the needs of this Board and could be a model for successors. It follows here:

> On reassembling the first business was the Report from the Committee on the Order of Business, Gen. Vincent, Chairman
>
> 1- Call to order,
> 2- Prayer,
> 3- Minutes,
> 4- Report of President of Advisory Board
> 5- " " " " College,
> 6- " " Dean of College
> 7- " " Standing Committees,
> 8- Unfinished business,
> 9- New business.
>
> Accepted and the typewriting of a certain number for use suggested.

In accord with the Chair's advice, "full and free discussion" characterized not only this first meeting but those to follow. The possibility of student self government[16] was brought up as well as general regulations of discipline, the curriculum, and the degree to be granted. Discussion of questions of changes in the by-laws, method of compiling agenda and above all the definite determination of the membership of the standing committees resulted in the appointment of a corresponding as well as a recording secretary, a request that the Dean provide ahead of time a list of important items for discussion at meetings, and the final list of members of the two standing committees including those who had not been able to attend the first meeting. Because the committee membership included prominent Catholic lay people from various parts of the country, the final lists appear here in full.

16. Cf. pp. 381 and Minutes of Advisory Board.

Committee on Discipline

Dr. Garrigan,
Sister Lidwine,
Miss Risley-Seward,
Mr. Bonaparte,
Mrs. Ward,
Miss Lincoln.

Committee on Studies

Monsignor Conaty,
Sister Josephine,
Miss Carey,
Mr. Smith,
Judge Daily,
Mrs. Carter,
Miss Lindsay,
Miss Dorsey.

Decisions of the Board of Trustees of the College were influenced often during the first quarter century by the advice or proposals of the Advisory Board. This fact appears in the chapters on the academic program and on student life in this history. This very helpful board became inactive after 1926, and was disbanded in 1935.[17] Meanwhile, the Ladies' Auxiliary Board and the National Alumnae Association and its growing number of chapters continued to stand firmly behind the administration. The Fathers Club,[18] the Lay Board of Trustees[19] (called after 1971 the President's Council) begun in 1956 were valued successors of the Advisory Board. The re-organization of the Board of Trustees (the governing board of the College) to include lay members brought the College administration into position to face the late twentieth century.[20] The names of chairmen of the re-organized Board of Trustees are listed in Appendix XII.

The Hon. Charles Fahy, Justice of the United States Appellate Court, an erudite lawyer of national reputation, presided at the organi-

17. Board of Trustees Minutes October 25, 1935.
18. A six member Washington Advisory Council established by the Board of Trustees, January 22, 1954, met during that year and suggested a Fathers Club as its successor. The Fathers Club was established in 1955.
19. Under Sister Mary Patrick Furden and Mr. James Nagle, first Director of Development, the Lay Board of Trustees was launched in 1956 with letters of invitation from Archbishop Patrick A. O'Boyle.
20. Cf. "The Trinity Board of Trustees," Sr. Margaret Claydon, S.N.D., President, *Alumnae Journal*, Winter, 1969, pp. 60–61; and p. 144 of this history.

zation of the Fathers Club, May 21, 1955. Characteristically, he introduced himself, presenting his credentials as of close association with Trinity College. His two sisters, he said, were Trinity alumnae, as were his wife, Mary Agnes Lane '19, their three daughters Anne, Sarah and Agnes, his wife's sisters and at least two cousins.[21] Though Judge Fahy passed over his legal credentials, his legal mind and language are apparent in the constitutions of the new group.

The statement and list of officers in the 1958–1959 catalogue[22] describe clearly the scope of the Fathers Club.

> The Fathers Club of Trinity College was organized on May 21, 1955. Its purpose as set forth in the second article of the Constitution, is "to afford to the fathers of the students and graduates and to others as authorized, the opportunity to acquire directly a more intimate understanding and personal acquaintance with the physical, intellectual, social, civic, moral and spiritual program administered by Trinity College in the education of their daughters"—and secondly, "to provide the Sister Administrators of the college with experienced masculine counsel and advice on current major problems and technical and financial planning, to the end that Trinity College shall continue to meet the needs of our young women of the future for a Christian education in the liberal arts."

Executive Officers for the Year 1958–59

President, William L. O'Donovan, Rye, New York
Vice-President, J. Eugene McMahon, Buffalo, New York
Secretary, Thomas R. Padgett, Washington, D.C.
Treasurer, Leon E. Dahlstedt, Washington, D.C.
Ass't Sec.-Ass't Treas., Sister Alice Clement
Consultant to the President of Trinity College, The Hon. Charles Fahy, Washington, D.C.

Board of Directors

Chairman, Sister Mary Patrick, President, Trinity College
John M. Bailey, Hartford, Connecticut
Eugene V. Colligan, Plandome, New York
Patrick F. Crowley, Wilmette, Illinois
E. Flynn Ford, St. Louis, Missouri
Louis Glunz, Chicago, Illinois
James F. Knipe, Cleveland Heights, Ohio
Arthur J. McGinnis, Allenhurst, New Jersey
John J. Power, Jr., Youngstown, Ohio
John A. Volpe, Winchester, Massachusetts

The Fathers Club continued activities until the mid-1960's providing valuable services to the whole college community. Its two chief lasting

21. Cf. p. 451 ff.
22. P. 84. Cf. later catalogues to 1963.

accomplishments were Parents' Week-end[23] which had been preceded by Father-Daughter Days, and the suggestion of and strong support of the Lay Board of Trustees.

THE LAY BOARD OF TRUSTEES-PRESIDENT'S COUNCIL

The Lay Board of Trustees[24] came into existence in the same year that the Development Office became a separate entity in the college administration, both under the aegis of Sister Mary Patrick Furden. The twenty-seven original members, who elected officers and adopted a constitution at their first meeting on December 6, 1956, were from twelve widely separated states and the District of Columbia.[25] The officers chosen at that meeting were Frank J. Keeler, Chairman; John J. Power, Vice-Chairman; Edward J. Duffy, Treasurer. According to Article IV, Section 1 of the constitution, Mr. James Nagle, Director of Development, became Secretary, and Sister Alice Clement (now Sister Monica Davis) became Assistant Treasurer.

An article[26] by Jane E. Marilly '44, one of the charter members, is a good description of the Board's first two years.

> Two years ago His Excellency, the Most Reverend Patrick O'Boyle, Archbishop of Washington, appointed for Trinity College a Board of Lay Trustees. His action was prompted by the Catholic hierarchy's deep concern in the continuing obligation to provide for our nation and the world women of high moral principles, sound in values, and sensitive to opportunities for service. This particular group was chosen because of their personal interest in Trinity and conviction of the value of independent liberal arts education.
>
> The Board was inaugurated to take on a vital role in the immediate and long-range development of the College. It is made up of twenty-seven voting members—outstanding representatives of industry, business, and the professions, and experienced in financial matters—and ten *ex officio* members. Seven of the charter members are alumnae, and voting members. Almost all the male members have Trinity connections, being fathers or husbands or both of Trinity alumnae.
>
> The very capable and devoted Chairman of the Board, just elected for a third year, is Mr. Frank J. Keeler, Vice President of the Chase Manhattan Bank. He heads up an Executive Committee which is concerned with the affairs of the Board in the interval between the semi-annual meetings at the

23. First Parents Week-end February 12–14, 1960. *Newsletter,* Jan. 1960. *Alumnae Journal,* Winter, 1960, pp. 89–93, pictures.
24. Not to be confused with the governing board, the reorganized Board of Trustees, which has a majority of lay men and women as members. Cf. *Newsletter,* March, 1957, and November, 1956; *Alumnae Journal,* Autumn '58, pp. 17–20, and three document boxes in T.C.A.
25. Appendix XIV gives the complete list of charter members.
26. *Alumnae Journal,* Autumn, 1958, pp. 17–20.

College. The other officers are Mr. Hugh P. McFadden of Hellertown, Pa., Vice Chairman; Mr. John O'Neil of Washington, D.C., Treasurer; Director of Development Florence T. Judge, '23, Washington, D.C., Secretary; and Sister Alice Clement, '34, Assistant Secretary-Treasurer. Besides the Executive Committee, there are four standing committees within the Board concerned with special phases of Trinity's development program.

After a complete listing of members of the standing committees and of the *ex officio* members, Miss Marilley continued and the *Journal* editor added a note:

The charter members of the Board will serve through the end of this fiscal year; then a third of these members will be elected for a term of one year, a third for two years, and a third for three years. Thereafter, appointments to the Board will be made through the Nominating Committee consisting of the President of the College and two members of the Board who are to be appointed by the chairman.

The Board has four major objectives, as set down in its Constitution:

1. To confer with the President and Administration of the College on general procedures and policies which concern the overall current and future development of Trinity.
2. To concern itself with the broad public relations program of the College.
3. To assist in furthering the identity of Trinity as an outstanding liberal arts college for women in the nation.
4. To perfect itself as a truly functioning lay board in all matters referred to it or which may originate and which affect the well-being of the College.

It is hoped that the Sisters of Notre Dame de Namur devoted, inspiring, and dedicated to their mission of teaching and counseling, will find in this new lay association the effective backdrop against which can be projected a thrilling concept of a greater Trinity.

* * * * * * * * * * * * * * * *

NOTE: One of the most generous and intensely interested members of the Lay Board is not mentioned in this account. Mr. William J. Nixon, husband of Leonie Crowe, '19, of New Rochelle, N.Y., died only a few days after the Board met at the College in October. Mr. Nixon was present at this meeting, as he had been at all previous ones, for even his illness could not diminish the deep concern and ardent enthusiasm he felt for the welfare of the College. As a member of the Fiscal Policies Committee, he made a valuable contribution to the initial work of the Board. Himself a staunch alumnus of Bowdoin, he had a sincere and chivalric devotion to his wife's alma mater that was as delightful as it was beneficial—The Editor.

Mr. Frank J. Keeler, the enthusiastic charter chairman of the Lay Board, guided the organization through its first three years. He presented to the president of the College a handsome gavel which is still used at formal meetings and keeps alive the memory of his services to Trinity College.

In late 1959, Mr. Keeler resigned leaving a record of devoted service to Trinity College as the charter chairman of the Lay Board. Hugh P. McFadden of Hellertown, Pa.[27] succeeded him. Mr. McFadden, a prominent lawyer, a Knight of St. Gregory, was an ardent champion of Trinity as the husband of one alumna, Dorothy Kinney '29, and the father of another, Nancy '57. He drew on his legal experience, as well as his experience as a trustee of Lehigh University in his service to Trinity College. Working closely with Sister Margaret Claydon, he was deeply interested in the quality of the academic program, the welfare of the faculty, and the upgrading of faculty salaries. After his term as chairman he continued as a member of the Lay Board, "had a considerable share in the re-drafting of the by-laws" of the re-constituted Board of Trustees of the College, and was elected its first Chairman January 4, 1969. His calm, firm and capable handling of student protest in the boycott of classes in 1970 brought about an amicable settlement of that crisis. In his retirement he retains his lively interest in the college.

In October, 1961, the following officers were elected by the Lay Board: Charles A. Eisenhardt, Jr.,[28] a prominent Cincinnati businessman, chairman; Francis S. Friel[29] of Bryn Mawr, Pa., a civil engineer, vice-chairman; and Edward Duffy, Essex Falls, N.J., a member of the New York Stock Exchange, treasurer. Mr. Duffy had been treasurer since 1956 and was repeatedly re-elected until 1966. They were re-elected for another year in October 1962. All three of these men "gave invaluable guidance during one of the most significant periods of the College's development."

Eugene McGovern, Treasurer of the Conduit and Foundation Corporation of N.Y., and a director in several other New York corporations, succeeded to the chairmanship in October 1963.[30] Thomas E. Moran, New Canaan, Conn.,[31] president of Moran Towing and Transportation Company, N.Y., followed as chairman of the Lay Board, assisted by vice-chairman James L. McMahon, Short Hills, N.J. and New York City; and treasurer John O'Neill of Akron, Ohio and Washington, D.C. In 1968 Vincent de Paul Goubeau[32] of Philadelphia, Pa. and Salem, Mass., was elected chairman. He initiated, supervised, and carried through the transformation of the Lay Board of Trustees into

27. *Newsletter*, Jan. 1961, p. 2; *Alumnae Journal*, Winter, '69, pp. 60–61.
28. *Newsletter*, July, 1961, p. 2 *vita*, Jan. '62, p. 3; Jan. '63, p. 3.
29. *Newsletter*, January, 1962, p. 2; Oct. '62, p. 1 (datestone of library).
30. *Newsletter*, Nov. '63, p. 2 (vita); cf. "Tribute," *Newsletter*, Nov. '67, p. 1.
31. *Newsletter*, Nov. '66, p. 2; cf. Nov. '67, p. 1.
32. *Trinity News*, Feb. '68, p. 2.

Vincent Goubeau, President of the President's Council receives an award. Mary Field Goubeau '27, foreground.

the President's Council and served as its first chairman and representative to the Board of Trustees. The Lay Board of Trustees 1956–1971 and the President's Council since then have advised and supported the president of the College during the years of growth, the acquisition of land and the erection of three buildings (Library, Cuvilly and Kerby), the establishment of the Trinity Award, as well as in countless other matters of scholarship or discipline. These organizations have worked closely with, and at times supervised the Development Office of the College.[33] For that reason the history of development at Trinity College is placed here.

Development Office

Though a formal Development Office with a full-time Director of Development dates only from 1956,[34] the fund-raising and public relations activities implied by those titles have been carried on since 1897, effectively supporting the work of founders, of administration and of faculty. Sister Mary Euphrasia's[35] lists of possible donors, personal visits to important Washington residents, lobbying of Congress, man-

33. For more details about the Lay Board/President's Council cf. T.C.A. three document boxes.
34. *Newsletter*, November, 1956, p. 3; Cf. *Newsletters* and *Trinity News*.
35. Cf. Chapter 2.

agement of a nationwide publicity program, as well as the establishment of the Ladies' Auxiliary Board (q.v.) indicate a comprehensive plan that sounds very "modern"—and that brought on her severe criticism from her Sisters because she infringed the strict rules of conduct in force at the turn of the century for Sisters of Notre Dame.

The College administration in collaboration with the Ladies' Board, and other friends, and especially with the growing Alumnae Association quietly continued development programs through the first two decades of the century culminating in the erection of award-winning Notre Dame Chapel.[36] Sister Raphael, President of the College (1920–1929), brought into focus the resources of the College for fund-raising, by organizing a Trinity College Building and Endowment Fund and engaging the services of the John Price Jones Company, professional fund-raisers. An Alumnae Office rent-free at the College, with Loretta Lawler '15 as full-time fund-raiser begun in 1923 was the nucleus of the present Alumnae Office. That students, as well as alumnae were interested appears in an article from the *Record*[37]:

ACTIVITIES PRELIMINARY TO THE TRINITY CAMPAIGN

To everyone who is interested in the progress of Catholic education in general and Trinity in particular this is a most important year, for it marks the opening of the campaign for the Endowment Fund. For the excellence of Trinity's training, from a religious as well as a scholastic standpoint, makes its extension eminently desirable.

A convention of the delegates from all the organizations connected with Trinity met at the College on October 28 to make preliminary plans for the campaign, of which the intensive work is to be done next March. Plans were submitted and discussed by the various delegates, and much of the final detail work was done. A most encouraging letter of approbation and support was received by the convention from the Most Reverend Archbishop Curley. The meeting was a very successful one and contributed materially toward further unity in an already compact and efficiently functioning organization.

The Advisory Board was represented by Monsignor Doherty, and there were also delegates from the Ladies' Auxiliary Board, the Student Government Association, and the College Building Fund. The following officers of the Alumnae Association: The Misses Miriam Greene, '16, President of the Alumnae Society; Loretta Galligan, '10, Secretary; Martha Logan, '09, Treasurer; Nellie O'Mahoney, '04, Boston; Bertha Strootman, '10, Buffalo; Anna Boyle, '12, Cleveland; Jennie Hoey, '14, New York City; Loretta Lawler, '15, Pittsburgh; Mary Leonard, '23, Cincinnati; Miriam Loughran, '17, Washington, D.C.; Alice Leonard, '18, Scranton, Wilkes-Barre;

36. For sources of money for chapel see Board of Trustees Minutes, October 26, 1921 and T.C.A. "gifts."
37. June, 1922, pp. 226–227.

> Elizabeth Jones, '19, Philadelphia; Mary Duncan, '20, Waterbury; Helen Somers, '22, Worcester; Sarah O'Neil, '23, Chicago; Mrs. Fitzgerald (Mary MacMahon, '11), Conn. Valley; Mrs. Aubrey Fennell (Catherine Moorman, '16), Cincinnati; and Mrs. George Gibbs (Gladys Flynn, '21), Minneapolis.
>
> Many of the Chapters have already decided upon various activities which are to take place before the actual opening of the campaign. For example, the New York Chapter has arranged for a theater party during the Thanksgiving holidays, the proceeds of which are to be devoted to this purpose; it also intends to open a gift shop.
>
> We in the College have also tried to do our best toward the good cause, and although it is, of necessity, very little in comparison with these larger efforts, still, to be platitudinous, "Every little bit helps." Hugh Walpole says that one's own experiences cannot be platitudinous, because of the very personality with which one has invested them, despite the fact that such expressions often appear so. Perhaps on the strength of that the quotation will be forgiven. Most of our efforts have been in the direction of parties and entertainments of various sorts. The epidemic of bridge, which has swept over so many schools during the last few months, has really justified its existence at Trinity. Aside from providing endless diversion and intellectual development, it has formed the basis for the Pascal Party which was given recently, and for the O'Connor Bridge. The Dramatic Society's contribution to the fund consisted in a very entertaining and well-acted play, "The Turtle Dove." Not to be outdone, the Titian Society provided a riotous minstrel, and the Literary Society is to show "A Connecticut Yankee," or some other equally interesting moving picture in the near future.
>
> Undoubtedly there will be numerous other parties and devices for swelling the fund before the academic year is at an end.

In June 1923 Sister Raphael described in some detail for the Advisory Board this first "Fund Drive." "The long contemplated effort of our Alumnae to raise a million dollar Building and Endowment Fund has begun," she wrote. "Such a figure as this would have frightened us a few years ago. Now we have learned to think in millions, because life, even for intellectual needs, makes greater demands on material things, and since these things have proved themselves indispensable, they necessarily claim our attention. Times may again be as they were before the war, but hardly in this generation, and Trinity cannot wait so long."[38] Then follows a campaign report for 1921–1923.

An account of all money collected for the College 1897–1901 shows a total of $288,037.74 (note the .74!).[39] The O'Connor gifts for building, in 1904 and 1905, the center wing of the Main Building amounted to about $145,000.00 plus the art collection. In the years to 1921 the Sisters had amassed $214,328.41 toward the $500,000.00 needed for building

38. Advisory Board minutes June 2, 1923. T.C.A. especially pp. 7–9 of President's report.
39. T.C.A. Drawer II. Sister Mary Euphrasia folder.

Notre Dame Chapel.[40] Now, as Sister Raphael stated, the sights were higher. Remembering the immense cost-of-living increase in the years from 1900 to 1980,[41] one can more easily realize the comparative value of the contributions to the college in the first half of the century.

The 1923 John Price Jones campaign backed loyally by the alumnae realized a large enough part of the $647,000[42] needed for the new dormitory-dining hall to have the name Alumnae Hall given to the building. As with the Main Building and the Chapel, the rest of the cost was paid by loans from Washington banks, paid back gradually and in full before a new project began. Alumnae Association presidents worked with College presidents during the depressed 1930's when the great need was a science building.[43] The Jubilee Fund for the Science Building, started by Catherine Cummings '32, as alumnae president, aided substantially the completion in 1941 of that much needed addition to the Trinity College complex. The annual Alumnae Fund grew steadily during the 1940's.

From the opening of the Alumnae Office in 1923 until 1956 when the Development Office as a separate entity was established a steady effort to raise funds for the College as well as to assist in other ways was evident. Several names recur frequently in descriptions of development efforts during these years: Loretta Lawler '15, Catherine Crimmings '32, Edith Callaghan '31, Mary Agatha Kelly '24, Marcella Seymour '24 and Antonia McGinnis Thayer '25, as well as all the alumnae presidents of those years and Ellen A. Ganey, the eminent alumnae executive secretary who engineered in the 1930's the change-over from "annual dues" to the Alumnae Fund which was well established to form a basis for the Trinity Fund of the later decades.

The chief aim of the forties, in addition to the routine annual aim for the needs of the College, was for a $50,000 Jubilee Gift in 1950. This gift, duly achieved, was used to restore the O'Connor Art Gallery. Sights were then set on better music and art facilities, a library building, a gymnasium, and further dormitory space. All these became the work of Development Directors as well as presidents of the College and the Alumnae Association from 1956 to the present. Mr. James Nagle, mentioned above, established the office in 1956. He continued as Director until late 1957, and was succeeded by Florence Judge '23,[44] former Commander in the Waves, former Alumnae Association president and active business women, until July, 1959. Sister Martha Julie

40. Board of Trustees minutes Oct. 26, 1921; and folder in T.C.A. Drawer VI.
41. Cf. Statistical Abstracts of the United States.
42. Board of Trustees minutes, October 26, 1927.
43. Cf. Administration of Sr. Berchmans Julia pp. 114–118.
44. *Newsletter*, July '58.

TABLE VIII. *Fund Growth, Grand Totals—5 Year History*

	1960	1961	1962	1963	1964
Alumnae	$113,299.26	$154,338.44	$110,435.56	$131,152.79	$174,411.40
Parents	19,061.57	19,476.49	39,484.01	43,267.25	48,849.51
Students	6,183.52	7,912.00	4,100.00	4,481.56	5,436.24
Friends	4,405.87	6,326.00	9,308.44	38,022.75	49,030.26
Business, Foundations and Matching Grants	24,270.36	7,630.79	31,541.51	46,113.49	39,444.55
TOTALS	$167,220.58	$195,783.72	$194,869.52	$263,037.84	$317,172.96
Alumnae Percent Participation	49.2%	57.0%	61.0%	54.8%	55.5%

Keehan,[45] as Vice-President for Development (1959–1963) managed the fund drive for the library building. The alumnae, surveyed, had chosen between the library and a gymnasium as the first building to be built. Sister Martha was followed as Development Director 1963–1965, by Sister Ann Paul Schumann T.C. '45,[46] and (1965–1975) by Roger Schifferli[47] who managed the New Resources and Concerned Action programs of the late '60's and the 1970's. Mr. Schifferli was the director of longest tenure (1965–1975) and did excellent work in building up the fund.

Throughout the 1950's the total of gifts and grants grew but not steadily as is shown by articles *passim* in the *Newsletter*. The 1957–58 total[48] is reported as $407,971; the next year it was $205,097; and in 1959–60, $331,290. This last must be calculated in a different manner, because Table VIII given above quoted from the 1964 Fund Report shows a lower amount for 1960. Continuing the history of the Fund, from data found in annual fund reports, the 1964–65 total was $301,234.28 (New Resources Booklet). By 1970 it had increased to $1,074,956.[49] The establishment in 1964 of a Development Council with Raymond A. DuFour[50] as first chairman to give "Lay Leadership for Ten-year Plan," and of a National Fund Committee in 1966 with Elizabeth Sullivan Ritter and Oscar Hunter as co-chairman and successors announced annually in the *Newsletter*, significantly aided the development work for New Resources and Concerned Action Programs through the decade and into the 1970's. The 1970–71 New

45. *Newsletter*, October '59; *Alumnae Journal*, Spring '60, pp. 138–139.
46. *Ibid.* Nov. '63.
47. *Ibid.* Feb. '65; Nov. '65 *et al.*
48. *Ibid.* Dec. '58.
49. *Newsletter*, Dec. 1970.
50. *Newsletter*, Nov. 1964.

Resources total was $810,444.[51] The 1973 total was announced[52] as $829,000 plus $263,000 in Government Grants. The goal[53] for the next two years was $1,500,000 over the period, the LXXV Fund to celebrate the seventy-fifth anniversary of the opening of Trinity College to students ($750,000 each year).

Having achieved the seventy-fifth anniversary goals Mr. Schifferli resigned to go to Loyola College in Baltimore. Mr. Edward Peabody administered the Development Office from 1976–1978. As this chapter is being finished Mrs. Roseanne Casey (1952) has become the Director of College Relations, organizing in addition to the fund, publicity for the notable visit of Pope John Paul II to Trinity College.[54]

Trinity College and The Catholic University

The early chapters of this history show that the college has enjoyed close and cordial relations with the Catholic University of America from the beginning. An article "Solemn Opening of Trinity College[55] which appeared in the Catholic University Bulletin described the dedication mass, November 22, 1900 and quoted from Msgr. Conaty's sermon. Msgr. Denis O'Connell, Rector of Catholic University told the Advisory Board in 1905 and 1907 that Trinity College was "an extraordinary success." In preparation for the celebration of the 1939 Golden Jubilee of the Catholic University, Dr. William Russell prepared an account[56] of the close relations between the two institutions which merits liberal quotation here, even at the risk of some repetition. He wrote:

> The history of the Catholic University and that of Trinity College are entwined. The story of the origin and of the beginnings of Trinity cannot be separated from the chronicles of the University because of the participation of the University professors in the inception of the school around the bend. In 1914 Bishop Shahan said: "Trinity College is rightly known as the eldest daughter of the Catholic University." (*Trinity College Record*, Vol. VIII, p. 114.) The vision behind each institution was pioneer in outlook and national in scope. Dr. Garrigan's view in 1914 was: "I rank the establishment of Trinity and of the Catholic University as the two most important events in the history of the Catholic Church in our country." (*Trinity College Record*, Vol. VIII, p. 112.) Both schools were conceived by people of noble and broad aims; both had to contend with misunderstanding and opposition. Since the golden jubilee of the University finds removed from this

51. *Newsletter*, Dec. 1971, p. 4.
52. *Ibid.* Nov. 1973.
53. *Newsletter*, Dec. 1974.
54. Cf. *Alumnae Journal* and *Trinity News.*
55. Reprint in T.C.A. C.U. folder, Drawer III.
56. June 6, 1938. Copies are in the T.C.A. Possibly published in the *C. U. Bulletin.*

earth the builders who laid firm the foundations of Trinity it is fitting that there be recorded in the annals of the University its share in the origin and development of the "eldest daughter." . . .

Then follows a succinct history of the events recounted in Chapter 2 of this volume (q.v.). Dr. Russell, having conferred with his uncle Dr. William Kerby and with Sisters of Notre Dame who knew the origins, writes graphically of the early difficulties. He continued:

We are so accustomed to Catholic colleges for women today that we find it difficult to reconstruct the educational horizons of only forty years ago. Female academies dotted the land at that time; and there were perhaps ten colleges for non-Catholic women. But in Catholic circles the academy was considered "higher education" for women. So unthought of were Catholic colleges for women that Trinity was first called "post-graduate" by some people. The honor for the first charter for a Catholic women's college goes to the School Sisters of Notre Dame of Baltimore, who, already possessing an academy in that city, obtained from the legislature of Maryland a charter for a college in April, 1896. However, there does not seem to have been given to the plan any publicity. What is unique and original about the plan for Trinity is that its founders visioned it as a national institution which would have its faculty strengthened by the addition of professors from the University. . . .

There was much difficulty in securing a suitable site. At that time the present Michigan Avenue extending up to the University from North Capitol Street was not even a path. However, twenty acres of the present site were finally purchased early in June.[57] The only approach was from the rear of what is now Trinity. The name "Trinity" was given by Sister Julia.

On June 15 news of the purchase and of the plans leaked out. Overnight Trinity became a topic of country-wide discussion. Its proximity to the University naturally brought the latter institution into the picture. Attitudes already formed toward the University undoubtedly did much to influence in some quarters the views that were soon spread in regard to the college for women. The newspapers found that the discussions were "news" and played up some of the personalities involved. The clear statement of Cardinal Gibbons in his letter of approval: "working in union with, though entirely independent of the Catholic University," did not allay the suspicions that were aroused. Trinity was reported as being a "wing" of the University; coeducation was intended. It was suggested that teaching at Trinity might be good sport for the professors since they had so few to instruct at their own school. Jokes were spread concerning the possibility of female philosophers. Reports of this nature were also sent to Rome. Thus a delay ensued until difficulties could be cleared up in the eternal city. Meanwhile Congress had granted a charter to Trinity on August 20, 1897. On October 2 of the same year Cardinal Rampolla wrote Sister Julia that Rome had no opposition to the plan.

57. For $80,000.00 Financial Report 1898–1901, T.C.A.

It had been the intention of the Sisters from the first to proceed slowly, but the unfavorable publicity necessitated further delay. Financial difficulties loomed large. Congress had to appropriate the money to open up Michigan Avenue, which road eventually gave a new access to the University as well as to the college. Public opinion had to be re-educated and in this matter the University officials did heroic service. The clear-headed but dogged determination of Sister Mary Euphrasia was an example to everyone. Particularly do Bishops Conaty and Garrigan deserve high praise for their unflinching and courageous espousal of the cause. They never wavered in their allegiance to Trinity. Bishop Shahan soon entered the lists and with pen and voice became a formidable champion of the college. It is also a co-incidence that he who is in reality the founder of the Catholic University should also have added the final argument which strengthened support for Trinity. Bishop Spalding was to give two lectures for the University in Washington in January of 1899. The Sisters asked if he might be induced to give a third in the interests of the college. Graciously Doctors Conaty and Garrigan decided that one of the two should be set aside for the Sisters. Thus originated the famous Spalding lecture on "Women and Higher Education," which was spread broadcast throughout the land and which helped to make enthusiasm for Trinity universal. . . .

Dr. Russell gives here an appreciative account of the services of Dr. William Kerby to the College which repeats what is expressed in an earlier chapter.[58] He ends his account with reference to the Catholic University professors who "walked through the mud to dispense lore at Trinity." "For the sake of accurate record," he wrote, "a list of the men from the University who taught at Trinity is here appended." The complete list appears as Table IX to provide a permanent record of the University's cooperation with Trinity extending well beyond the "Jubilee Year." The ending dates were brought up to date in the 1940's by Sister Catherine Dorothea Fox, President of Trinity College.

Chapter 4 mentions the admission of lay women to the Catholic University as students in the newly organized Graduate School of Arts and Sciences.[59] The 1932–33 Trinity catalogue describes an agreement with the University providing that Trinity would refer all graduate women to Catholic University and stop its own graduate program. Reciprocally the University would send undergraduate applicants to Trinity College. Unfortunately, that had been a "gentleman's agreement" with, as had been customary for forty years, no written documents. After the Jubilee Celebration of 1939, and the advent of World War II the University turned interestedly toward undergraduate women, losing sight of the "agreement." Perhaps the late administrators did not even know of it. Young women were admitted to the schools of

58. Chapter 4.
59. Cf. p. 113 and catalogue 1932–1933.

TABLE IX. *Catholic University Professors Who Have Taught at Trinity*

Starting Date	Professor	Subject Taught	Ending Date
1900 Oct.	Dr. Garrigan	Chaplain to students	Dec. 1901
Nov.		Religion	Dec. 1901
Nov.	Dr. Kerby	Chaplain to Sisters	Sept. 1916
Nov.	Dr. Pace	Philosophy	June 1924
		Psychology	
Nov.	Dr. Shahan	Church History	1909
1901 Dec.	Dr. John J. Creagh	Chaplain to students	Nov. 1907
		Religion	1907
Sept.	Dr. Charles B. Grannan	Scripture	1909
1902 Sept.	Dr. Kerby	Sociology	June 1932
1903 April	Dr. M. F. Egan	English	1907
1904 Feb.	Dr. Shields	Education	Feb. 1921
1905 Sept.	Dr. Kerby	Economics	June 1914
1906			
1907 Nov.	Dr. Melody	Chaplain to students	June 1916 (?)
1908	Dr. Charles Aiken	Religion	1924
	Dr. William Turner	Logic 1909	1911
		History of Philosophy	1919
1909	Dr. T. V. Moore	Philosophy	1911
1910			
1912	Dr. T. V. Moore	Biology	
		Psychology 1918	1947
1911	Dr. Dubray	Philosophy	1923
1912	Dr. Weber	History	
1915	Dr. McCormick	Education	1924
1916	Dr. John A. Ryan	Economics	
		Political Science 1920	1945
1918	Dr. Leo McVay	Education	1919
1920	Dr. Filippo Bernardini	Italian	1932
	Dr. Delauney	French	1922
	Dr. John O'Grady	Applied Sociology	1940
1921	Dr. Edward B. Jordan	Education	1937
1922	Dr. Joseph Dunn	Gaelic	1932
		Irish History	
	Dr. Crocianus Capellino	Italian	1924
1923	Dr. Thomas G. Foran	Psychology	1930
	Dr. John M. Cooper	Religion	1941
	Dr. Patrick Browne	History	1930
	Dr. Donald A. MacLean	Political Science	1939
		International Relations	
	Dr. George W. Johnson	Education	1927

(continued)

TABLE IX. *(continued)*

Starting Date	Professor	Subject Taught	Ending Date
1924	Dr. John E. Rauth	Psychology	1944
	Dr. Frank Cassidy	History of Education	1940
	Dr. Francis A. Walsh	Ethics	1938
	Dr. Roy J. Deferrari	Latin	1931
1926	Dom Benedict Brosnahan	Religion	1944
1927	Dr. Felix M. Kirsch	Education	1940
1929	Dr. William M. Deviny	Economics	1940
1930	Dr. Maurice S. Sheehy	Religion	1941
	Dr. Joseph P. Christopher	Italian	1937
1932	Dr. John K. Ryan	Philosophy	1945
	Dr. Edward G. Roelker	Logic	1938
1933	Dr. William H. Russell	Religion	1943
	Dr. Paul Furfey	Social Statistics	1937
1934	Dr. Edward J. Finan	Mathematics	1938
	Dr. Percy A. Robert	Sociology	1943

Airview of Campus, 1960. Still "a third of a mile from the University."

drama, music, nursing and finally to the Arts and Sciences. In the mid-1940's the University catalogue carried the statement that both men and women might apply as undergraduates to all schools of the University—except theology. That came much later. The University is *still* a pontifical university, but it now admits women.

Though the free exchange of professors was no longer in operation after 1941, Catholic University faculty members have continued to teach at Trinity College as "lecturers" or "adjuncts" and the coalition of Colleges and Universities has made possible an exchange of students, both graduate and undergraduate. Chapter 5, of this volume, "The Academic Program," makes this clear.

Cordial relations between administrators continued and Rectors and Trinity College Presidents conferred often together, but the close connection was broken. Trinity has become indeed "a separate institution, half a mile from the gates of the University." Catholic University's first lay president and Trinity's president Sister Margaret Claydon were appointed, in the 1970's, as the two non-clerical members of the American Delegation to the Second International Congress of Delegates from Catholic Universities sponsored by the Sacred Congregation for Catholic Education where they gained the approval for American "free standing colleges" to be recognized as of university grade.

As this volume goes to press, it seems significant of ties with the beginnings when a son of a Trinity College alumna, Rev. William James Byron, S.J. is president of the Catholic University of America. He is the son of Mary I. Langton Byron, T.C. 1918, carrying on good close relations between the two institutions.

Trinity College and the Paulists

The Paulist House of Studies at the Catholic University of America opened in 1889, the year the University itself opened. Paulists were, therefore, on campus eight years later when Trinity College came into being "down the road." Individual Paulists were interested in and helpful to the new college from its beginning. Paulist seminarians, directed by Mr. Finn, one of their number, sang at the laying of the cornerstone of the Main Building, December 8, 1899, and at the mass of dedication, November 22, 1900. Later, as Father William Finn, C.S.P. their director formed the nationally renowned Paulist Choristers. Among the seminarians in 1900 were Richard Cartwright and Thomas S. O'Neill who, as old and prominent priests, were present at the anniversary mass in Notre Dame Chapel, November, 1949, opening the Fiftieth Academic Year of Trinity College.

At the Solemn Dedication, November 22, 1900, Father John J. Burke, C.S.P. (later editor of the *Catholic World*, and even later, circa

1919–1936, General Secretary of the National Catholic Welfare Conference) was master of ceremonies at the Solemn High Mass. According to the Dean's Notebook[60] he added to his liturgical duties the role of general helper in the conversion of the large reception room[61] into a chapel, staying until late the evening before to tack down the carpet on the predilla and doing other heavy work for the Sisters.

Both the Dean's Notebook[62] and the President's Report[63] describe the Requiem Mass for Sister Julia McGroarty, Foundress of the College, which was celebrated in the College Chapel, December 12, 1901, the "month's mind" of her death. The celebrant was Bishop Conaty. Father Walter Elliott, C.S.P.,[64] Superior of the Paulist House of Studies at Catholic University, delivered a "touching eulogy" on the text: "I have found Him Whom my soul loveth." "The music of the Mass was beautifully rendered by a choir of Fathers and Scholastics, also from Paulist College."

Throughout its history Trinity College has had a close relationship with the Paulist Fathers. The annals described lectures, retreats, concerts, and general helpfulness at Commencements and other special events. Since 1914 they have been chaplains for the Sisters of Notre Dame who live at the College, and from 1945–1950 were also chaplains for the students.[65] From 1972 to 1975 Reverend John George Lynch, then a Paulist, was students' chaplain and head of campus ministry.

The list of Paulist members of the Trinity faculty spans many years. Dr. Thomas Verner Moore, C.S.P., taught psychology at Trinity from 1909 to 1922 when he became a Benedictine and continued his scholarly and teaching career as a Monk of St. Anselm's both at Trinity and at Catholic University for more than twenty more years.[66]

Father John Carvlin, C.S.P. was the very popular teacher of sophomore religion in the 1940's. Father Eugene Burke (who like the Sisters never used the title "doctor" though entitled to it) influenced hundreds of Trinity women through his senior religion-theology courses and personal interest in their problems for more than twenty-five years, from 1944 to the end of the 1960's.[67] In 1948 Father Bourne, C.S.P. taught Church History for a year, before entering the Trappists in Conyers, Georgia. Dr. Robert O'Donnell, C.S.P. taught philosophy 1958–1961. Father George Fitzgerald taught in the Pastoral Ministry Programs in

60. T.C.A.
61. Southwest corner of Main Building.
62. December 12, 1901.
63. May 14, 1902.
64. Rector of the Apostolic Mission House, founder of *The Missionary* magazine, early companion and biographer of Fr. Hecker. When he died the June 1928 issue of *The Missionary* was a memorial to him. T.C.A.
65. Cf. Campus Ministry section.
66. Cf. Section on psychology.
67. Cf. Section on Religion-Theology.

the 1970's. The ministry of Father John George Lynch is described in the section on Campus Ministry.

A sampling of Paulist references from the archives indicates a continuing collaboration: "Rev. William J. Finn, C.S.P. of Chicago . . . came to this city with his band of choristers. A part of the proceeds of his concert was devoted to *The Anna Hanson Dorsey Scholarship*." (President's Report, 1909.) "April 8, 1921, Feast of Blessed Mere Julie. Solemn Mass sung at six a.m. Several students present with Srs. . . . after Benediction Rev. Father Lyons, C.S.P. delivered an inspiring instruction on our Blessed Foundress and her work."

An autographed letter dated June 14, 1924 from the Standard Hotel, Dublin, signed J. Elliot Ross, C.S.P. reports to Sr. Raphael, the president of Trinity, on his visits to the Notre Dame Training Colleges in Liverpool and Glasgow. The informal tone of the letter, its cordial "regards to all" and a specific message to Sister Teresa exemplify the interest of the Paulists in Trinity College and their friendship for the S.N.D.s there.

The president's report May 29, 1920 mentions using the "brick house facing Lincoln Road" (old Cuvilly) for students, with a small chapel to accommodate the overflow from the main chapel. Father Hopper, C.S.P. was the devoted chaplain for this.

It is both impossible and inappropriate to try to mention here all the Paulists who have contributed to the life of the College. From the "early great ones" of the turn of the century: Father Walter Elliott, Father Thomas Burke, the eminent preacher, and Father Joseph McSorley, there is a steady stream of names that live in the Trinity memory, in addition to those already mentioned. Lewis O'Hern, rector of the Apostolic Mission House and editor of the *Missionary*: John Harney, at one time Superior General of the Paulists; Joseph Malloy, John McGinn; C. Edward Lufrio; John Carr; John Paul; James McVann; Alvin R. Bergraff; Theodore C. Petersen; Benjamin Hunt, philosopher and Dean of St. Paul's College; Sean Foley; John Gaeney; as well as our *present Paulist friends* represent the priests and students of St. Paul's College who are all part of the history of Trinity College.

A glance through the description of the faculty and administration through the years will show that several other religious orders were sincerely concerned in the development of the College, notably the Benedictines, and Dominicans. They were members of the faculty and valued advisors to the early administration. Names appear in Chapter 4.

Auxiliaries

Trinity College has benefited during its whole history from the loyal, devoted industry of its non-academic helpers, many of whom served for twenty-five years or more. It is not possible to record a complete roll, but notable characters will be mentioned as their memory survives. One thinks of the engineers, of Sister Teresa's "assistants" at the front door, of the carpenters, painters, cooks and of the nightwatchmen and receptionists. For some, only the first name is now remembered and for others only the surname. This section, then becomes a reminiscence rather than a history since the author has no access to the original personnel records. It will, however, be of interest to alumnae of the various eras of their service.

The first of Sister Teresa's assistants at the front door appears to have been Alec, the ever polite, ever solicitous announcer of visitors or special delivery letters, written about with regret for his loss in the *Record*, February, 1914.[68] He was succeeded by Wesley Day,[69] the best known of front door factotums, who served with Sister Teresa from 1912 to 1937, immortalized in the traditional song, "Yes, Miss, Yes, Miss." He died in 1941 mourned by generations of Trinity College students. His successor, Ralph, a much younger man brought a vigorous energy to the work expected by the veteran Sister Teresa through the 1940's. Ethel Peary, until she transferred to the library, and Irene Hobson who still works as infirmary maid for the Sisters filled out the years of Sister Teresa's encumbency, cheerfully following rapid-fire orders issued from the "parlor dining room" at the north end of the Marble Corridor.

While we are at the Main front door it is appropriate to mention some of the night receptionists, those valued aides to the Dean of Students from the 1940's to the 1960's: Mr. Donegan, Mr. Scanlon, and especially Mr. Patrick Hassett,[70] as well as Mr. Lowe[71] in Alumnae Hall in the 1930's and 1940's.

There were the expert full-time carpenters Mr. Lonigan, Mr. Ellis, Mr. Groomes whose work spanned about three quarters of Trinity's history.

The *Alumnae Journal*, Autumn, 1962,[72] has a picture feature, "Some Other Jubilarians" presenting ten auxiliaries who had served the college for a quarter-century or more. Leading the list is that patriarch "Mr. Albert" Jones who worked at miscellaneous jobs chiefly in the basement corridor from 1906 for more than fifty years. In 1962, Albert was still a weekly visitor to the campus.

Lawrence Stewart,[73] in 1962 Superintendent of Building and Grounds, served the college from the 1930's to the late 1970's as gen-

68. P. 41.
69. Song: *Trinilogue*, 1936; *Alumnae Journal*, March, 1938; *Trinity Times*, December 10, 1937; *Alumnae Journal*, Autumn 1941.
70. *Newsletter*, June, 1971.
71. *Alumnae Journal*, Winter '48, p. 60.
72. Pp. 22–24.
73. Cf. *Trinity Times*, Feb. 4, 1976, pp. 1, 8.

eral helper, chauffeur, carpenter and expert upholsterer before becoming superintendent. He served five presidents and was "Sister Alice Clement's right-hand man" in the 1960's.

Others deserving recognition are Tommy Dee, painter; Billie Bonner, groundsman; Parker Price (Slim), chef; Larry Silvestro, engineer who carried on the work of the legendary early engineer, Mr. Brosnan; Dorothy Gaskins, assistant in the science laboratories; Ethel Peary in the library; and Paul Proctor.

The Proctor family like Albert Jones have served the college through most of its history. Beginning with Miss Annie in the early years Proctors have been "Trinity people." Amy Proctor was infirmary maid in the students' infirmary for twenty-five years from the late 1920's. Edward helped Sister Cecilia Josephine in Alumnae Hall and Paul[74] worked for many years with Sister Mary Stephanie and her successor. Paul progressed to Superintendent of Grounds in the 1970's and brought the Proctor presence to the 1980's, rounding out fifty years of service.

The names of five more loyal maids who worked for twenty-five years or more should not go unmentioned: Hattie Keyes, Alberta Lewis, Nicie Brown, Sally Mitchell, and Annie Banks who preceded them all by many years. These represent the small army of helpers that have enabled Trinity College to operate smoothly through more than eighty years.

The Campus

The original twenty-four acres of wooded, deeply ravined land bought from the Glenwood Cemetery Company has become a landscaped site for seven large buildings. Architects made clever use of the uneven character of the land to design buildings like the Main Building and Alumnae Hall which have varied numbers of floors to use the ravines to advantage. Cuvilly Hall, which is five stories high conformed to the two-story code of Fourth Street because it was in a low part of the campus and the roof rose just two stories above the Fourth Street level. By the time Kerby Hall was built there was no mention of restrictions. It rises its full height matching St. Paul's College across Fourth Street.

Though not the geographical center, the Main Building is the focal point around which the campus has developed. This first building, which took ten years to complete, was called "Trinity Hall" by the founders, but the name did not survive. The chronological evolution of the buildings may be seen in Table X.

74. Cf. *Trinity Times*, Feb. 25, 1976, p. 2.

TABLE X. *Chronology of the Buildings*

	Cornerstone	Ready for Occupancy
1. Main Building (originally to be called Trinity Hall, but really constituting the whole college for twenty-five years)	1899–1909	
South Hall	1899	1900
O'Connor Hall	1903	1904
North Hall	——	1909
2. Old Cuvilly Hall (also called Graduate Hall), bought 1913, enlarged 1920, renovated for art and music 1941, torn down 1957 to make room for new building.		
3. Swimming Pool (part of projected gymnasium, still needed)		1915
4. Notre Dame Chapel	1921	1924
5. Alumnae Hall	1927	1929
6. Science Building	1940	1941
7. Cuvilly Hall	1957	1958
8. Art and Music Addition to O'Connor Hall		1960
9. Library: Ground-Breaking, October 28, 1961		
Date-Stone, September 23, 1962	1962	1963
10. Ground was broken for a new residence hall on September 20, 1964—Kerby Hall	1965	1965

The inscriptions on the buildings facing the entrance gates express the essential spirit of the college:

MAIN ENTRANCE

Collegium deo uni trinoque sacrum. A college dedicated to the Trinity.

PEDIMENT OF NOTRE DAME CHAPEL

Ave Mater Alma Sapientiae Dei Receptaculum Praeclarum Trinitatis Triclinium

Hail Loving Mother, Glorious Vessel of the Wisdom of God, Dwelling Place of the Trinity.

LIBRARY

Scientia ancilla fidei. Knowledge the handmand of faith.

The grounds were landscaped about 1929 by Olmstead Brothers, Landscape Architects of Brookline, Massachusetts. At that time the college employed Mr. James Allan, a fifth generation landscape gardener to supervise the grounds. Mr. Allan's contributions to the campus for a quarter of a century were invaluable.

The original building of Trinity College, the Main Building, is a good example of turn-of-the-century institutional architecture. Solidly built of Port Deposit granite with red tiled roof and Mt. Airy granite finish,

Main Building, 1900–1904. South Hall only.

Main Building, 1904–1905 (no front entrance).

South View, c. 1905 showing boundary with Glenwood.

Main Building, 1905–1909.

it is one of very few buildings of its kind in the District of Columbia still in use for its original purpose, in this case, the higher education of women. Its red dome has been a landmark in Northeast Washington, on Michigan Avenue a block east of North Capitol Street, for eight decades. It symbolizes Trinity College to 8000 alumnae distributed in all fifty states and many foreign countries.

Built when the whole section, including the pretty little villages of Eckington and Brookland, formed part of the almost rural "outer suburbs" of the city, this building antedates all the existing buildings of the Catholic University of America and its surrounding houses of study except Caldwell and McMahon Halls. It forms now a nucleus, the core of continuity of the Trinity College Campus, linked architecturally to the white limestone Notre Dame Chapel and Alumnae Hall by the red tiled roof. They in turn continue to be linked to newer buildings by white stone construction.

The Main Building was planned in the last years of the nineteenth century and construction began in the spring of 1899. The first section, South Hall, was completed in the autumn of 1900. The central section with art gallery, auditorium, and students' rooms, was completed in 1904. The front entrance foyer, four parlors with classrooms and students' rooms above were added in 1905, and in 1909 the North Hall wing completed the E-shaped building with a 350 foot frontage on the newly extended Michigan Avenue opposite the eastern boundary of the Old Soldiers' Home park.

The architects, Edwin F. Durang and Son of Philadelphia, wrote in their descriptive booklet[75]: "It was decided in the first general plans to follow the prevailing type of architecture of the city. In consequence, a building classic in feeling was designed." Elsewhere in the same brochure the caption under a picture of the completed building mentions the "classic tone of the general design." The "tone" or "feeling" may be classic, but not the Greek-temple classic one associates with the term. The building is rather eclectic in a way that was typical of massive turn-of-the-century institutional architecture. The straight lines of the exterior, the Ionic pillars of the entrance porch, the roof-level pediments at the front of the three main wings are classic elements. The dome, however, and the treatment of some of the windows show renaissance influence.

The interior woodwork is red oak. The parquet flooring in four large rooms (two at each end of the building) is a feature of lasting value. Classic elements are more evident in the interior structural simplicity as well as in the decoration. The atrium-like light well at the center front of the building, rising four floors from the foyer to the dome with wide

75. Issued in 1909. T.C.A.

Main Building complete, 1909.

Air View, c. 1920.

stairways at two sides, is both classic in conception and a good example of late nineteenth century American style.

Plaster-covered iron columns support the ceilings in the two large rooms in South Hall (now 1970's, Admissions, Development and Alumnae offices, and Room 250) and at each floor level at the central light

Campus, 1929–1941. No Franklin Street.

Campus, 1941–1956. Franklin Street cut through. Lincoln Road closed.

well. Similar wood-enclosed columns in modified ionic style support the large stairways. The later construction methods of North Hall have dispensed with supporting pillars in the large rooms. The columns, as well as pilasters along the main marble-floored corridor, are Corinthian or composite in style. Heavily paneled and molded ceilings character-

Campus, 1977.

ize the four large rooms mentioned above as well as the central auditorium and the parlors near the main door.[76]

The buildings on campus are linked to the Main by architectural ties: Notre Dame Chapel and Alumnae Hall by their red tiled roofs; the other four by white stone construction, linking them to the limestone of the red-roofed buildings. The two courtyards formed by the wings of the Main Building became quadrangles by the placing of Alumnae Hall, but the names South Court and North Court remained until the 1970's when the South Court was named Seymour Court in honor of Marcella McHale Seymour '24, a great friend and longtime benefactor of the College. The North Court, long reserved for the Sisters has become a thoroughfare from the dining halls to the Main Building elevator.

Notre Dame Chapel[77]

The prize winning Notre Dame Chapel was the second building constructed by the College. Begun in 1920 it was dedicated in time for the Baccalaureate Mass of the class of 1924. It stands to the north of the Main Building, facing the Library. The inscription on the pediment symbolizes its position in the College.

76. A description of the use of various rooms in the Main Building by Sister Julitta Larkin, is in the Contents List of the Trinity College Archives.
77. Cf. p. 108; T.C.A. for *Record* and *Trinity Times* articles; Mary Godfrey's description in the *Trinilogue* of 1936 with pictures.

Notre Dame Chapel, 1924.

The pediment inscription of Notre Dame Chapel at once expresses its consecration to Our Lady and the quickening vision of the College of which the chapel is the heart and center. The whole architectural design and decoration of the chapel gives expression to the same theme. Completed in 1924, the structure won for its designers, Maginnis and Walsh of Boston, the 1925 Gold Medal for ecclesiastical architecture.

The style of the chapel is a simplified modern rendering of the Byzantine, executed in Kentucky limestone, with a red tile roof which links its design to that of the Main Building and Alumnae Hall. The only exterior decorations, apart from the strong, graceful structural lines, are the sculptured relief of Our Lady, seated with the Child in her arms, in the pediment over the main entrance, and the small bas-reliefs symbolizing her litany titles, Tower of David, Ark of the Covenant, carved under the eaves at the corners of the transepts.

Inside, the general simplicity of design carries attention forward to the sanctuary. The mosaic above the main altar depicts the Coronation of the Virgin in a setting inspired by Dante's description of the Earthly Paradise; it was designed by Bancel LaFarge and executed at the Ravenna mosaic factory in Munich.

On the baldachino, Our Lady is shown in white relief against a gold background, crowned and holding the Child, surrounded by a scrolled design of grapes and peacocks. The small arched windows of the sanctuary repeat a single Marian design, the potted lily, in tones of blue, green, and violet which grow deeper from the side windows to those in the center behind the altar.

The windows of the nave depict, in the central medallions, scenes from the life of the Blessed Virgin, her espousal with Joseph, the birth of Our Lord, the Crucifixion, and the Assumption. The upper and lower medallions symbolize her titles: Tower of Ivory, Fountain Sealed, Garden Enclosed, Ark of the Covenant, Seat of Wisdom, Vessel of Honor, Mirror of Justice, Mystical Rose, Morning Star, House of Gold, Gate of Heaven. The twined monograms, crowns, white roses, and fleurs de lis are Marian symbols integrated into the design of each of the nave windows. These symbols are used, with the monogram of Our Lord as well as that of Our Lady, in the rose windows of the transepts. The windows of the Chapel, with their unified themes, are particularly fine examples of contemporary stained glass; they were designed and executed by Connick of Boston.

The Marian theme of the decorations is carried out from the relief of the Annunciation above the entrance, through the small medallions of the lily and the monogram, A M R, on the columns at the back. These small motifs are repeated frequently, most notably in the borders of the windows, of the nave, and in the rose windows and those of the sanctuary. St. Teresa of Avila and St. Catherine of Alexandria, patrons of woman students, are represented by heroic statues in niches at the back of the chapel.

The dome, which rises to a height of sixty-seven feet, is supported by pendentives bearing reliefs of the four evangelists, each with his apocalyptic symbol. The inscription around the dome is the first six verses of the Magnificat; above the inscription are twelve arched windows of angels, with four archangels at the cardinal points. At the East stands Michael with sword and scales, signifying his rank as Captain of the Hosts of Heaven in service for victory and justice; near him are angels of wisdom and praise, bearing scrolls. At the West is Raphael with fish, signifying his service as guardian of Tobias; near him, angels of praise with musical instruments. The North is commanded by Gabriel, a lily symbolizing his service as messenger at the Annunciation; nearby, three angels with censers, symbols of prayer. At the South, Uriel stands with the sun, sign of eternal wisdom. Angels near him hold censers as symbols of prayer and thanksgiving for wisdom.

The transept altars honor the Sacred Heart of Jesus and Saint Julie Billiart, foundress of the Sisters of Notre Dame de Namur, who conduct Trinity College. The inscription of the Sacred Heart altar is from St. John's Gospel: AS THE FATHER HAS LOVED ME AND I HAVE LOVED YOU, ABIDE IN MY LOVE. That above the altar of Saint Julie is taken from the Psalms: HOW GOOD IS THE GOD OF ISRAEL TO

THOSE WHO ARE RIGHT OF HEART, and echoes the foundress' favorite aspiration: HOW GOOD IS THE GOOD GOD.

The mosaic above the main altar bears this inscription from Isaias:

> THOU SHALT BE A CROWN OF GLORY IN THE HAND OF THE LORD AND A ROYAL DIADEM IN THE HAND OF THY GOD . . . FOR THE LORD HATH BEEN WELL PLEASED WITH THEE. AND THE BRIDEGROOM SHALL REJOICE IN THE BRIDE.

The central scene is flanked by the forbidden Tree of Knowledge of Good and Evil, and by the Tree of Life. In the center, Christ sits in majesty, holding the book, symbol of the Word; Our Lady, crowned, is at His right hand. From the two central trees hangs the medallion with ornamental rose, symbol of the Blessed Virgin. Falling flowers thrown by angels and flowers on the ground signify the bounty of the Lord.

The chapel retains its beauty and its place in the group of buildings facing Michigan Avenue.

Other Buildings

Alumnae Hall and the Science Building the third and fourth buildings were, like the chapel, designed by Maginnis and Walsh of Boston.

Mosaic and Baldachino, Notre Dame Chapel.

Alumnae Hall, 1929 and Science Building, 1941 (l.).

Alumnae Hall[78] housed two large student dining rooms and serving rooms, a cafeteria downstairs (now the faculty dining room), kitchens, laundry, storerooms, and on the second and third floors students' suites of rooms. It has been in continuous use since 1929, though dining rooms have evolved into cafeterias and other rooms changed uses from time to time. It is a classically simple limestone building with a deeply recessed entrance. Over its front door is a carved stone medallion of the old form of the College seal.

The Science Building,[79] one of the best of its kind at the time, was dedicated with an academic convocation at Commencement 1942. It was finished just in time to escape the priority restrictions of World War II, it was occupied by Biology, Chemistry and Physics departments a month before Pearl Harbor. Designed and built following suggestions from the science faculty, it is still a functional building. Through the years, alterations have been made to include solid state and atomic physics, photography, psychology, and even computer science.

As has been seen earlier, a small tavern on Lincoln Road called the Red Rose Inn[80] was bought by the College in 1913. It was first used as a Science Annex, as an infirmary, as a dormitory annex, and as a house for graduate students. In 1941 it was remodeled for the Art and Music

78. Cf. Development Section.
79. Cf. T.C.A. for details.
80. "Red Rose Inn," Sister Angela Elizabeth, *Alumnae Journal*, Spring 1942, p. 77.

Cuvilly Hall, 1958.

Library, 1963.

Kerby Hall, 1965.

departments and called Cuvilly Hall in honor of the birthplace of Saint Julie, foundress of the Sisters of Notre Dame de Namur. By the 1950's the overcrowding in the Main Building made more dormitory space essential. Old Cuvilly by then was crumbling from termites. It was razed and a five-story white stone and glass dormitory, designed by Gaudreau and Gaudreau of Baltimore was built. It was dedicated and ready for occupancy in 1958. This new Cuvilly Hall[81] built with a long-range Government College Housing loan was the fifth building completed in the campus plan. It had, besides student rooms, a snack bar called appropriately the Red Rose Inn, a large first floor lounge, a chapel, an infirmary, and small lounges on other floors. It replaced Main as the center of student activities for two decades.

The evolution of the sixth building, the library, has been treated at some length in Chapter 5.[82] The building, completing the "front campus," was designed by Allard and Joutz, following suggestions from Sister Helen Sheehan.

Kerby Hall[83] named by Alumnae vote for Dr. William J. Kerby, popular sociology professor and chaplain, was the seventh building.

81. Cf. T.C.A. for details.
82. End of Chapter 5.
83. *Newsletter*, November '64 and November '65; *Alumnae Journal*, Summer '65.

Built, like Cuvilly Hall with the help of a government loan, it is a white stone and glass dormitory on the hill near the Fourth Street side of the campus. Designed by Allard and Joutz of Washington, D.C. and executed by Victor Beauchamp Construction Company, it can house two hundred students. Besides students' rooms, it has a large artfully designed lounge on the ground floor and a chapel, a lounge, and a sun-deck on the fifth floor. The completed part of the building was intended to be the central section of a curved structure. Changes in trends in students enrollment and in college architecture make it doubtful whether the two other wings will ever be built.

The advantages of the location of the campus in Washington, D.C., the Nation's Capital, have been mentioned frequently throughout this text and will not be treated again here. Suffice it to say that a beautiful campus in downtown Washington, four years of living in the capital, the opportunities for learning from the libraries, art galleries, and government departments, as well as internships in all of these form a special dimension of a Trinity College education.

PART IV

By Their Fruits . . .

CHAPTER EIGHT

Alumnae—The Product

THE ALUMNAE of Trinity College, that body of women who earned degrees, or a significant number of credits toward degrees, from the college, is too large a subject for a mere closing chapter of this history. The Alumnae Association should have a full length history published. This chapter is a brief overview, a kind of reminiscence of alumnae through the years. It is not possible to cite all individual achievements. Examples of loyalty, of achievement, of work for the college will be mentioned as representative of all. The *Trinity College Record* until 1930 and *The Alumnae Journal* since 1927 both offer sources for this chapter and for the suggested history as do the results of questionnaires sent periodically from the early 1920's to date to all alumnae.

The graduates of the first class, 1904, organized the Alumnae Association on the afternoon of their Degree Day, June 4, 1904. The first three local chapters (Boston, Worcester, New York) were organized in 1909. The Association was incorporated as an entity separate from the college in 1911.[1] The Association, in 1917, joined the Association of Collegiate Alumnae, later known as the American Association of University Women. It became a member, in 1919, of the Association of College Alumnae Secretaries, later formed with the men's organization into the American Alumni Council. At the first national convention of the National Council of Catholic Women in 1921 the Association was represented. The first Alumnae Council, consisting of national officers and representatives of both chapters and classes, was held in Washington, D.C., November, 1936 and has met every two years since then except during World War II. The Alumnae Fund, replacing annual dues, was established in 1942. It formed the strong base on which the Trinity Fund was built and is still a major part of that fund.

The Alumnae Office began in the 1920's when Loretta Lawler '15 was appointed by the College in 1922 as executive secretary of the Building and Endowment Fund, with an office provided on campus. Mary Gwinn '23 succeeded her in 1925, Esther Monahan in 1928. In 1930 Ellen A. Ganey '27 was appointed executive secretary of the Alumnae

1. Golden Jubilee Booklet, 1954, bound with *Alumnae Journal*. "Highlights in Alumnae Association History," TCA. This was used as source for this capsule history to 1954.

Ellen A. Ganey with Ann Whilfield. (l.)

Association, beginning an eminent forty year career in that office. She was given an assistant, Madeline Dowling, in 1951, and was succeeded in 1970 by Ann Whitfield '62, and by Anna Marie Condon McGovern '50 in 1972. Sr. Ann Francis Hoey '24 administered the office for an interim year 1971–72.

In 1904 there had been sixteen members of the Association. In 1954 there were 3,500 in 48 states and all over the world. The three chapters of 1909 had become 30 chapters in eighteen states and the District of Columbia. In 1975 there were 42 chapters, with thirteen regional directors available for consultation and information[2] and more than 7,000 members in the Association.

Two chapters that date from 1914, the Minnesota and the Washington, D.C. chapters are selected here to represent the chapters all over the country whose members have loyally supported the college, reporting yearly to the Association.[3] The Minnesota Chapter has remained small, while Washington has grown to the Metropolitan Area Chapter, been divided into five area chapters and come back together again.

Anne V. Culligan '14 and Blanche McCarthy Michael ex '14 wrote the history of the Minnesota Chapter in 1960[4] in an article which an editor's note calls a "fascinating account of one of Trinity's oldest and most

2. "Alumnae and the College and Vice Versa," Jacqueline Shea Fish '55, *Alumnae Journal*, Winter, 1976, pp. 6–9.
3. Yearly reports published in the *Alumnae Journal*.
4. *Alumnae Journal*, Winter, 1960, pp. 86–88.

Anne Marie Condon McGovern

far-flung chapters" that "demonstrates that loyalty has not to do with size or distance." The Minnesota Chapter grew out of the St. Paul Chapter which was organized in the summer of 1914 by seven Trinitarians from the Twin Cities and three from outside the immediate area. An old receipt book shows the first receipt dated August 17, 1914. Because of the small number of members, Trinity joined for good works with the Barat Club, but by 1920 they became more active as a Trinity group, electing officers in August, 1920, with Anne Culligan as president, and deciding in October to hold quarterly meetings with elections in June and to have a yearly luncheon for the students at home from Trinity.

Fund raising consisted chiefly in giving dances at Christmas when the students were home for the holidays (1920–1925) or in the spring at clubs or hotels in St. Paul or Minneapolis. "The last large fund raising party was held at the home of Mildred Flynn (now Mrs. Frank Kertson) in Minneapolis in 1931." The dances were rewarding socially and financially. The chapter, though small, was able to send from $100 to $300 a year to the Building Fund, and even one year $500.

From 1934 the chapter has held monthly meetings at which they did work for local charitable organizations and planned other ways of raising funds to add to the sum of the annual chapter donation which was sent to Trinity each year. The members cooperated with activities initiated either at the college or by other chapters and continued to recruit for students to go to Trinity. They "also established a tradition of attending Mass as a group once during the year." For several years before the 1960 article the Reverend George Garrelts celebrated Mass at the Newman Club on the University campus where he was chaplain.

They welcomed National Alumnae Association members and officers. From them they learned of the need of funds for the Science Building and gave a "Heat Table" in the Physics Laboratory. In October, 1959, the chapter sponsored the first regional meeting of alumnae in the area, inviting alumnae from Iowa, Montana, North and South Dakota, and Superior, Wisconsin, as well as representatives of the Milwaukee, Indiana, and Chicago Chapters. They estimated that, at that time, there were 70 Trinitarians in the region. The regional meeting, though attended by only twenty-nine alumnae was considered a success.

The history ends with a summary: "This, therefore, is the story of the development of the original St. Paul chapter of seven members. In 45 years we have branched out into the Minnesota Chapter with a present membership of 40 members, 29 of whom are living in the Twin Cities. The members outside the Twin Cities are not active members and do not pay dues. . . . The future may bring more Trinity daughters to the Twin Cities and there may be granddaughters going to Trinity from the area. Regardless from whence they come we will always be happy to welcome the Trinity alumnae into the Minnesota Chapter." This is a sentiment echoed by other small chapters of which this is a sample.

Washington Metropolitan Area—A Large Chapter

The second chapter that dates from 1914, the Washington Chapter, has been chosen as a companion sample because it did not remain small, but grew, after a slow start, into one of the largest chapters in the association. As has been shown earlier in this history, there were few Washingtonians in the student body in the early years. Alumnae from elsewhere married or worked in Washington and remained in the area. The increases in numbers of day students began in the mid-

1920's. Maude Gaynor, one of the original 1914 members wrote a brief summary of the chapter up to 1920,[5] which follows:

> The enrollment for the first twenty years of the Washington Chapter was only 25. It was fortunate that the Chapter's first president, Mrs. Jane McDonald Grogan, and its vice president, Mrs. May Sheridan Fahnestock, were such socially-minded ladies. They gave many tea dances in their own homes during their term in office. Both had sons at Georgetown College, so securing escorts for the girls was no problem.
>
> Another friend, who helped the Chapter sprout its wings, was a very gracious lady, Mrs. Thomas Carter, wife of the senator from Montana. Mrs. Carter was president of Ladies Aux. Board of the college and she too being socially minded, often had open house for her Board members on a Sunday afternoon. To these informal affairs the Chapter and the seniors were most welcome. Mrs. Carter also had sons so there were plenty of boys to meet and to date for future events.
>
> We held six regular meetings each year, the first and last being conducted at the college. The fund raising project centered around the gymnasium fund. By the early 1920's the Chapter had sponsored six very successful dances, and had accrued over the years the sum of $5000.00.
>
> Our first dance was held on Feb. 5th, 1915 at Rauschers on Connecticut Ave. opposite the Mayflower of to-day. Rauschers is just a memory, but in the 20's it was patronized by the ultra fashionable. There were two large ballrooms typically French in character, the appointments were those of the Louis XIV period.
>
> Because Rauschers had such a genteel atmosphere and the fact that no liquor was sold on the premises, the Faculty insisted that we have the first dance there.
>
> But the young blades of that day had to have a drink regardless of wishes of the Faculty, so at intermission they stepped over to the Grafton Hotel, filled their flasks and returned. The lads and lassies of that generation all carried flasks.
>
> In these early years the Chapter was incorporated. The young lawyer who drew up the papers for this document was Charles Fahy, now Judge Fahy, the husband and father of four alumnae.
>
> The high light of the '20's was the visit of the Queen of the Belgians to Trinity. The Chapter did their share in contributing $100.00 to the Queen's purse for her private charities.
>
> In May 1920 we joined the American Association of University Women and donated $150.00 to furnish a room in Trinity's name at the club house. In May of the same year the class of '20 entertained at the Club, Gertrude Lane O'Donnell acting as hostess, presented the seniors.

The location of the chapter in Washington at the seat of federal government and near the college itself has contributed to its development.

5. T.C.A.

The experience of its members over the years has been much like that of alumnae in other large chapters. On May 25, 1960 a meeting at the college featured the History of the Chapter written by Joan Bussler '57 and presented by Mary Coleman O'Donoghue '28. Maude Gaynor '12, Isabelle Cain Donohue '19, Mercedes Phelan Hayden '20, Florence Judge '23, and Florence O'Donoghue '30, were, as past presidents called on to describe their eras, but their enthusiastically received speeches are not available for quotation here. The "history" is, and follows, with gaps because of the missing speeches.

1914–1922

1492, 1776, and 1914 are founding dates of note. Lest anyone be unaware of the significance of the latter date, it should be noted here that on November 30th of that year, the Washington and Baltimore members of the Trinity Alumnae met at the college for the purpose of organizing the Washington Chapter of the Alumnae. After a charmingly appointed dinner given by Sister Superior in honor of the newly organized chapter, the first officers were elected, of whom Mrs. Lawrence Grogan, Class of '05 and Mrs. Bruce Fahnestock, Class of '04, served as President and Vice-President.

During its first year in existence, the young Washington Chapter established many precedents in its social and fund raising functions. Often, in fact, the two were closely related. Simply social were the "two delightful dances given by Mrs. Grogan at her home, where Georgetown University was largely represented," and the "no less enjoyable dance at which Mrs. Fahnestock was hostess, entertaining, in addition to the chapter members, many young men from the Catholic University." A brilliant social and financial success was the first annual dance of the Washington Chapter, held at Rauscher's, at which $350 was realized for the Gymnasium Fund.

The next few years found the young Alumnae chapter experimenting with the fund-raising potential of bridge (its potential was immediately proven), approving the decor of the New Willard hotel ballroom at the annual winter dance of 1919, expanding its membership ranks by welcoming many of the Trinity girls who came to the city to "do their bit" for the government, joining the Association of College Alumnae, and contributing annually to that fund which would insure the sound body for the sound mind of the Trinity girls—the Gymnasium Fund.

Here to tell us about the early years of the Chapter, about the Queen whom they entertained and the Regal Rauscher's where they danced, is Miss Maude Gaynor, who was President of the Chapter in 1921–22, and a member of it from its beginning.

* * * * * * * * * * * * *

1923–1927

The decade of the Twenties found the Chapter garnering more support for the Building Fund through its various socially successful financial affairs at places—some still about town, such as the Columbia Country Club and

Iron Gate Inn, some no longer on the local scene, Le Paradis, St. Mark's Cafe, the Wardman Park. Bridge, which came into its own as a social and financial whiz of an affair, was joined by an Annual Rummage Sale as a boon to the Building Fund. The Chapter continued to enjoy active participation in the Association of Collegiate Alumnae. Chapter meetings themselves were enlivened by book reviews, dramatic monologues, and musical programs featuring native chapter talent. Isabelle Cain Donohue, Chapter President in 1923, will tell us in both prose and doggerel, about the changes in the Chapter during the mid-twenties.

* * * * * * * * * * * * *

1928–1929

The twilight of the Twenties found a chapter member, Sister Julia of the Trinity, becoming Superior of the college, the introduction of a floor show and a big band at the annual dance, and the temporary replacement of the chapter president by a Trinity husband. Mrs. Mercedes Hayden, the replaced president of 1929, is here to tell us about the turning years of the Twenties.

* * * * * * * * * * * * *

1930–1939

New deals were not restricted to the national scene during the Thirties. In addition to the familiar deals at the ever-popular bridge meetings, new deals by the Washington Chapter included a one day retreat at the college for chapter members, a fashion show by Jelleff's, with chapter members as models, a Christmas party where children of the Alumnae and Santa Claus shared top billing, an annual Requiem Mass for deceased relatives of Chapter members, Study Clubs and Current Events Clubs. The popularity of many of these ventures has caused them to become favorite traditions of the Chapter years. Well-known speakers who graced the lecterns around which the Chapter gathered included Gilbert K. Chesterton, Dr. Fulton Sheen, Msgr. John A. Ryan and Msgr. William J. Kerby. Proceeds from lectures and benefits were shared by the Building and Endowment Fund, a Student Aid Fund, a Scholarship Fund, and the Notre Dame Project at Southern Pines, which was adopted as a Catholic Action project. Miss Florence Judge, the Chapter's own FDR and president of the Chapter in 1930–1932, is here to tell about that part of the Chapter's history which she helped to make.

* * * * * * * * * * * * *

1940–1949

The war effort of the first half of the Forties was reflected in the activities of the Washington Chapter. In one year, 3,636 volunteer hours were spent by members in such activities as canteen service, teaching of finger printing, O.P.A. rationing work, and housing inspection. The Day of Recollection and the Christmas Baby Party survived the lean war years when, according to a Journal report of 1952, "Miss Mary Virginia Burke performed almost superhuman feats in cornering sufficient ice cream to satisfy young appetites." Proficiency at stamp selling was gained by the many chapter members who helped man the Tuberculosis seal booth at the Mayflower and Statler Hotels. By late 1943, wartime conditions had made it inadvisable to attempt a prom, so funds were raised by means of bond raffles and card parties. In addition to the war effort, the Chapter actively supported a committee for Good Friday Observance of the Three Hours Agony.

The early post war years found the Chapter's social calendar returning to normal, while its Catholic Action activities increased manifold. The Baby Party was designed to help the needy children of the world, and later to assist the Little Sisters of the Poor. Financial aid was sent to Brittainy. European families were "adopted" by Chapter members, and cared for long distance. Members ran the local U.S.O. club for a weekend and provided food for the servicemen. Organization of a "14-20 Club" at the Christ Child Settlement House, cooperation with the Dominican Fathers' School of Theology for Laymen in sponsoring six lectures at Trinity on Contemporary Philosophy, work in the Community Chest Drive—these and many similar civic and social activities occupied the members. A tea for prospective students was first held by the Chapter in 1948. A lecture by Clare Booth Luce, with introduction by Msgr. Fulton J. Sheen was a highlight on the 1949 season and a fitting farewell to the eventful Forties, about which Miss Florence O'Donoghue, Chapter President 1942–1944, will now tell us more.

* * * * * * * * * * * *

1950–1960

Since the Fifties have more of the familiarity of current events than the nostalgia of history, it will suffice to say that the Chapter's social, intellectual and spiritual activities continued to increase, as did its membership. So large has it become in fact, that the Washington Chapter has nurtured several offspring chapters in nearby Virginia and Maryland

As the Washington Chapter brings to a close its forty-sixth year and reviews its past, it can note with pride its growth, its activities, its accomplishments, and above all, that spirit of its members which, like the Olympic torch, has been passed on from its founding until today.

Though Washington was chosen as the sample of a large chapter others should be mentioned especially the prestigious Boston Chapter which deserves a history of its own, and the New York Chapter which had some of the same experiences as Washington, dividing in several chapters. New York State like Massachusetts, Pennsylvania, and California, has several chapters, large and small which continue to spread the name and spirit of Trinity College.

The late 1940's was a time of emphasis on chapter activity. The *Alumnae Journal* published articles by Ellen A. Ganey '29, "Chapter and Alumnae Records"[6]; by Jane Marilley '44, "The Washington Chapter's

6. Winter '47, pp. 67–71.

Social Action Program"[7]; by Edith Callaghan '31, "So You Are Running a Chapter"[8]; by Frances Smith Adams '28, "Developing the Small Chapter."[9] Regional meetings began in 1948 with the first such meetings in Baltimore, New Jersey, and Chicago. Mary Field '27, national chairman for regional meetings, reported at the 1949 annual meeting on the plans for several more such gatherings planned for the summer and fall. As this activity has progressed the association has planned regional meetings in various parts of the country in the alternate years between Alumnae Council meetings which now meet regularly in Washington. Yearly informal meetings in Florida in the winter and on Cape Cod in the summer have become popular. The latter, "Campus on the Cape," at the home of Margaret Sheehan Blodgett '19 is famous in Trinity circles. The Pittsburgh Chapter was honored by the Distinguished Service Award of the Alumnae Association in 1972.[10]

The constitution of the association has been amended as needed and has been completely rewritten several times, notably in the 1940's under the able direction of Louise McCarthy '23, one of Trinity's eminent lawyers; in 1960 for the addition of Regional Directors to the Board; and most recently in the 1970's.

Though not chosen as a "sample" chapter for this capsule history, the Boston Chapter should not go unmentioned. It was one of the first three organized in 1909 and has during its long history represented the college with *eclat* in its area. The members have participated actively in recruiting students, following up their progress, as well as raising funds for the college. Each year, in company with the Philadelphia Chapter and others, the Boston Chapter donates scholarships to be awarded to students in financial need from their area. A poignant little story of the late 1940's indicates the far-reaching influence of the Boston Chapter. A senior with several alumnae in her family was weary from studying for her comprehensive examinations and began to worry about passing. She went in to talk to the Dean about her problem. "Sister," she said, "if I don't pass, I think I could take it, but *what would I say to the Boston Chapter?*"

As the college enters its ninth decade the nearly 8000 alumnae in all parts of the United States and many parts of the world are steadily acting as yeast to spread the Trinity spirit in their own environments. A fitting end to this capsule history would be to re-read the brief reminiscence of Ellen Ganey in the *Alumnae Journal*, Autumn '72.

7. *Ibid.*, pp. 71–72.
8. Winter '48, pp. 61–63.
9. Spring '49, pp. 87–88; "Chapter Activity Planning," by Ann McMaster Reardon, Summer '72, pp. 12–13.
10. *Alumnae Journal*, Autumn '72, pp. 20–22.

The roll of those who have led the Alumnae Association provides an opportunity to mention twenty-nine eminent alumnae whose devotion to Trinity College spans the Years.

PRESIDENT OF THE ALUMNAE ASSOCIATION

*Florence Rudge McGahan '04
*Eleanor Griffin Cloonan '04
*Alice M. Ryan '07
*Mary Murray McArdle '08
*Margaret Cummings '07
*Mabel Higgins Mattingly '07
*Jane M. Hoey '14
*Miriam A. Greene '16
*Margaret C. Norman '13
*Dr. Mary D. Walsh '15
Carolyn Kerwin Keating '15
*Helen C. Ormond '23
*Marie R. Madden '08
*Florence T. Judge '23
*Mary Hannan Mahoney '27
*Catherine C. Crimmings '32
Alba I. Zizzamia '31
Mary Agatha Kelly '24
Marcella MacHale Seymour '24
Regis L. Boyle '33
*Catherine Sullivan Shay '22
Margaret Gilmer Keller '33
*Helen Barrett Glennon '31
Mary Jane Ryan Malone '56
Jacquelyn Shea Fish '55
Jean Perry Connell '54
Anne Wolf Breidenstein '43
Marian E. Glennon '58
Patricia A. McGuire '74

*Deceased

A quick glance will give an idea of how the "yeast" mentioned above works and introduce a more extended listing of occupations.

A Trinity alumna, Jane Hoey '14, founded, under President Franklin D. Roosevelt, the U.S. Bureau of Public Assistance which developed into the Department of Health, Education and Welfare. A Trinity alumna, Marita Houlihan '37, directed for many years the Foreign Student Exchange Program of the State Department. A Trinity alumna, Patricia Caron Crowley '36, founded with her husband Patrick, the Catholic Family Live Movement. Two alumnae, Mary Catherine

Sister Ann Francis Hoey with Sister Margaret Finnegan, Dean (l.), Mary Jane Malone and Dr. Joan Gillespie, Trinity's first dentist.

Schaefer '27 and Alba Zizzamia '31, represented the Catholic Bishops for many years as director and assistant director of their office at the United Nations. A Trinity alumna, Sylvia Poor '42, discovered and isolated the sickle-cell anemia virus. A Trinity alumna, Patricia Sullivan Lindh '50, has been Assistant to the President of the United States for Women's Affairs and later an assistant Secretary of State. At least two Trinity alumnae, Anne Hooley '15 and Mary Hannon Mahoney '27, have been national presidents of the National Council of Catholic Women, while several were sought out by bishops to start that lay organization in their dioceses: notably in Columbus, Ohio; Peoria, Illinois; Asheville, North Carolina, and Washington, D.C. A Trinity alumna, Barbara Bailey Kennelly '58, is a member of the U.S. House of Representatives. A Trinity alumna, Cathleen Black '66, is publisher of *U.S.A. Today* and chairman of Gannet, Inc.

A Trinity alumna, Hester B. Curtiss, M.D., M.P.H. '20, has been an influential member of the Public Health Departments of New York,

Sheridan-Fahnestock Wedding Party with Drs. Pace, Shields, and Shahan.

Connecticut, Georgia, and Director of Public Health in New Mexico where she "virtually laid the foundations for that state's program."[11] She was Regional Medical Director, U.S. Children's Bureau, New York, with a ten-state area of jurisdiction. A Trinity alumna, Anne Barrett May '62, is director of HOPE: the Southwest Institute for Head Injuries, Phoenix, Arizona. A Trinity alumna, Dr. Andrea Kielich '71, has been president of the Oregon Chapter of the American Medical Women's Association.[12] A Trinity alumna, Dr. Constance Urciola Battle '63, is Medical Director and Chief Executive Officer of the Hospital for Sick Children, Washington, D.C. and is currently National President of the American Association of Women Physicians.[13]

11. Newspaper clipping, n.d. T.C.A. Cf. 1965 article quoted in section on Medical Profession.
12. *Alumnae Journal*, Summer, 1982, p. 11.
13. *Alumnae Journal*, Autumn, 1981, p. 7; Spring '86, pp. 8–9.

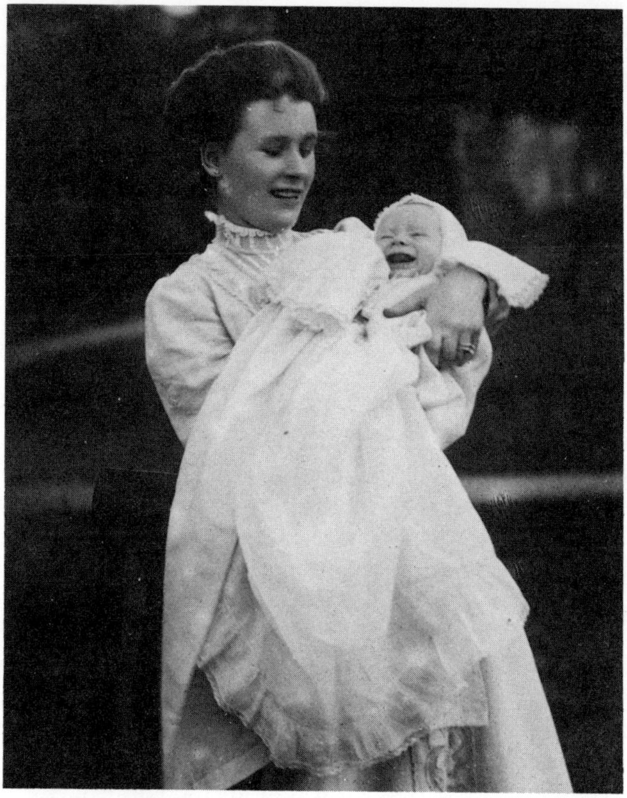

"The Trinity Baby," 1904's class baby, Sybil Fahnestock.

Occupations

The class of 1904 led the way in varied experience as in all other ways. In 1900 when they entered college there was a strong public opinion that higher education would prevent women from marrying. Yet the first Trinity alumna was married the day after the first commencement. May Sheridan married Bruce Fahnestock in Holy Trinity Church, Georgetown, with her classmates and their professors present.[14] Mrs. Fahnestock lived in Georgetown and years later, after the death of her husband, sailed the Pacific with her two sons, Bruce and Sheridan, and published a book *I Ran Away to Sea at Fifty*.

Eight of the sixteen members of 1904 married and one, Elinor Griffin Cloonan, was the mother of the first "Trinity granddaughter," Gertrude Cloonan '33. Members of the class taught in high schools in

14. Snapshots of that wedding are in the Trinity College Archives.

Ohio, New York and Massachusetts and Helen O'Mahoney managed the family coal business in Lawrence, Massachusetts. One, Elsie Parsons, entered the Sisters of Notre Dame de Namur and as Sister Wilfred du Sacré Coeur, taught Latin and Constitutional History at Trinity. She was Dean from 1924 to 1932. Another, Anna Coleman, after teaching history for twenty-five years in Pelham, N.Y. public schools, also entered Notre Dame and taught history at Trinity. Margaret McDevitt worked with Dr. Pace on the Catholic Encyclopedia before her marriage. Several went on to graduate work. Four earned the M.A. degree and Sister Wilfrid earned a Ph.D. from Catholic University.

By the end of the first decade of the century the long line of doctors, lawyers, social workers, volunteers, and teachers at all levels had begun. Women in politics, C.P.A.'s, judges, and alumnae in uniform for our country came slightly later.

The concern about the detriment of higher education to marriage and family life was long reflected in the yearly publication in the *Alumnae Journal* of the 1930's to 1950's of comparative research bureau statistics on the ten and twenty-five year graduates, showing that Trinity alumnae ranked above average for women's colleges in percentages of marriages and of number of children per marriage. Because of this concern and because the largest occupation of Trinity alumnae through the years has been that of mother and home manager, families are placed first among occupations. After World War II Trinity women tended more and more to combine their home activities with jobs outside the home in accord with the trend throughout the country.

Families

The emphasis on Trinity families falls into several categories: sisters, generations, lateral connections making "clans," and large families. Frequently there is overlapping.

In the first decade of the century the Dean's Reports mention younger sisters coming to Trinity because their sisters were happy Trinity students. Through the years three, four and five sisters of the same family have been Trinity students. Elinor Griffin Cloonan '04 was the first to have a daughter, Gertrude Cloonan '33, graduate from Trinity College as the first "Trinity granddaughter." In 1941 there were thirty-two "granddaughters" on campus. The numbers have fluctuated, regularly reported in the *Alumnae Journal*, but there has been a group each year to the present. Helen Linehan Porter of 1907 and Mildred Connelly Moran 1908 might be considered pioneers of the tradition of sending four daughters to Trinity. The *Porters*[15] *of Massachusetts* were

15. Pictured with their mother at commencement 1948, *Alumnae Journal*, Summer, '48, p. 149.

Mary Porter Herring '37, Eleanor Porter Curry '39, Margaret Porter Kuhn '41, and Alice Porter McNamara '48. The *Morans of Findlay, Ohio* were Anne Moran Maher '36, Elizabeth Moran Drake '38, Jean Moran Elsea, and Margaret Moran Drake '44. Elizabeth Kennedy Kelly 1907, whose sister Clara Lynch was in 1910, was the pioneer of Trinity "dynasties." Her daughters, the Kellys of Larchmont, New York were Margaret Kelly Kelly '37, Elizabeth Kelly Coakley '39, Catherine Kelly Lynch '40. Margaret's daughter, Susan Kelly '65, was Trinity's first great-granddaughter. Though she was at Trinity only one year, her picture at the Groundbreaking Ceremony for the library appeared on the cover of the *Alumnae Journal*, Autumn, 1961. Another of Margaret's daughters, Mary, graduated in 1976.

Katherine Walsh '09 and her sister Gertrude '12 of Davenport, Iowa, led the *Walshes of Iowa*. Their nieces were Kathleen Walsh Lindy '34, Rosemary Walsh Quail '38, Eleanor Walsh Meyer '44, and Sheila Walsh Murdoch '50. Two of Sheila's daughters, Sheila Murdock Phelin '78, and Sara, who stayed two years, made a third generation at Trinity.

Later, alumnae who had four Trinity daughters were Marie Kramer O'Neil '15, who will be mentioned later as part of a Trinity Clan; Francis Oddi McGowan '23, Katherine McGargee Curtin '23, and Mary Louise Dillmeier Connolly '44. The *Akron, Ohio, O'Neils* were Mary K. '41, Patience '46, Alice '49, and Margaret O'Neil Freer '52. The *McGowans of Asheville, North Carolina*, were Mary Frances Sappenfield '58, Jo-Ann Grimes '60, K. Patricia Stahl '61, and Margaret Rudd '63. The *Connollys*[16] *of Williamsburg, Virginia*, and Garden City, New York, were Kathleen '73, Megan '77, Melissa '81, and Cynthia '85. The *Curtins of Scranton, Pennsylvania*, were Frances O'Brien '48, Katharine Quinn '51, Mary Smith '54, and Leila Cuddy '55.

Other families of four sisters included the *Leonards of Wilkes-Barre, Pennsylvania*: Elizabeth McCole '15, Alice '18, Josephine '22, and Eleanor Brennan '25. The *Grogans of Washington, D.C.* were Anne Miskowsky '47, Mary Stohlman '50, Helen Orem '51, and Kathleen Neill '57. The *Gaffneys of Philadelphia* were Anne Horstmann '32, Mary '36, Catherine (Kate) Horstmann '38, and Elizabeth (Lisette) '44. The *Doody's of Washington, D.C.* were Ellen Hartke '27, Mary Stack '28, Sheila Sancorecy '32, and Elizabeth Schaefer '35, several of whom had Trinity daughters.

The *Moynahans of Springfield, Massachusetts* were Eleanor Bagley '58, Irene Splaine '61, Rosemary Kristofak '64, and Martha McMahon '67. The *DuBruls of Cincinnati, Ohio*, were Anna '21 (Mother M. of St. Kevin, S.A.), Marjorie Shields '35, Louise (Sr. M. Marcella, S.C.M.M.) and Denise '39. Marjorie had two T.C. daughters. The *Schaefers of Cape*

16. Picture of mother and four daughters, *Alumnae Journal*, Summer, '85, p. 9.

Charles, Virginia, were M. Catherine (Tish) '27, Mary '35, Agnes Shay '38, Rita '42. With the Doodys and Stocks they are part of a "Trinity clan." The *Feddis's of Cumberland, Maryland,* were Mary '78, Nessa '80, Noreen '83 and Oona '85.

There have been at least six Trinity families with five sisters: the Harahans of Richmond, Virginia, and Long Island, New York; the McCarthys of Ridley Park, Pennsylvania; the Skahans of Boston, Massachusetts; the Farrells of Pittsfield, Massachusetts; the Glennons of Rye, New York; and the O'Donoghues of Washington, D.C. The *Harahans* were Ruth Mouquin '18, Susannah Markey '18, Catharine Harahan '21, Virginia (Sister Catherine Virginia, S.N.D.) '30, and Theodore (Sister William Susannah, S.N.D.) '34. Both Ruth and Susannah had Trinity daughters. The *McCarthys* were Mary Tisdale '16, Catherine (Sr. M. of St. Victoria, R.G.S.) '20, Louise '23, Elinor Voelker '26, and Margaret McCallen '27 whose daughter Elinor Gossman '57 graduated from Trinity as did two daughters of the sixth sister, Florence, who did not come to Trinity: Florence Sullivan Christ '53 and Maureen Sullivan '54.

The *Skahans*[17] were Mary '21, Ruth McGeary '21, Eleanor Hickey '22, Frances Ford '23, and Sarah Deignan '23. Frances' daughter was Gloria Ford Murphy '54. Ruth had a step-daughter attend Trinity for a year. Eleanor's three daughters were all Trinity graduates: Mary Ellen Sullivan '49, Ruth E. Ziehm '55, Eleanor Head '59. Two of her granddaughters were Catherine Ziehm '79 and Eleanor Sullivan '80.[18]

The *O'Donoghues* of Washington, D.C. were Catherine '23, Mary '26, Helen '27 (Sister Helen Patricia, S.N.D.), Margaret '31 (Sister Alice Bernardine, S.N.D.), Bernardine Ebel '32.

The *Glennons* of Rye, New York, are a widespread loyal Trinity family. Helen Barrett Glennon '31 had at least one sister Marion Bertrand '33, five daughters and two nieces are alumnae. Her daughters, the *Glennons* of Rye, New York, were Marion '58, Helen Malloy '59, Anne McIntosh '61, Patricia Whamond '62, Frances Dunlop '71. Two nieces were Mary Domerecki '63, Anne J. Glennon '64. Helen herself was president of the Alumnae Association and her daughter Marion holds that position as this history goes to press. Helen's son Charles is a member of the Board of Trustees of the College and Nancy's daughter, Suzanne McIntosh is a freshman of the class of 1989.

Examples of *three generations* of Trinity alumnae include also the following: Josephine Heyl Loeffter '08, aunt of Ruth Hopkins Kilroy '30, mother of Virginia Kilroy '58.[19] Margaret Broughan McNamara '14, Anne McNamara Griffith '48, Anne Griffith '84 whose paternal grand-

17. Pictured together at Trinity's Golden Jubilee, *Alumnae Journal*, Winter '51, p. 76.
18. Eleanor Hickey pictured with 50 grandchildren, *Alumnae Journal*, Spring, 1972, p. 39.
19. Picture, *Alumnae Journal*, Summer '58, p. 178.

mother was also an alumna, Anna Clemons '15; Mary Geier Connolly '17, Anne Connolly Pacious '47, Mary A. Pacious '75; Consuela de Pasquale Blank '19, Lola Blank Sullivan '51 and Lola Sullivan Reynolds '77. Beatrice Randall Hoynes '24, Margaret Hoynes Knoblauch '48, and Mary Kay Knoblauch '71.[20] Marcella McHale Seymour '24[21] had two Trinity daughters, and two granddaughters: Isabel Fitzer '53, Marcella Lilly '55, Isabel (Mimi) Fitzer '84, Marcella (Muffet) Lilly '81. Another "dynasty" included Helen Holland Byrne '25, followed by Sheila Byrne Betts '50, Anne Betts '86. Helen had two T.C. sisters: Agnes Holland Cosgrove '17 whose daughter was Helen Mae Cosgrove Carignan '43, and Mae Holland '23.

Another type of Trinity family has been featured in the *Alumnae Journal*, the large family. The largest recorded such family is that of Rosemary Alexander '45 and John Walton. They had sixteen children including several sets of twins. Rosemary, herself the daughter of Catherine de Barbour Alexander '19 of Altoona, Pennsylvania, earned a Master's degree in mathematics and taught mathematics before her marriage. After the youngest was old enough to go to school, she too returned to the classroom teaching in the local elementary school.

Others cited in the *Journal* include Lola Saddlemire Quilty '44[22] with thirteen and two who boasted families of twelve children: Margaret Fitzgerald '23 and Judge John P. Cooney, Jr. of Providence, Rhode Island[23]; Margaret Ganey '35 and Dr. Paul O'Donnell of Washington, D.C. Marjorie DuBrul '35 and Richard Shields[24] of Cincinnati, Ohio pictured with their eleven. Margaret Haran '31 and Francis X. McElroy also had eleven. (*Alumnae Journal*, Spring '56). Catherine Newman '35 and Kenneth Krugh of Pittsburgh, Pennsylvania; Ruth Gilmartin '35 and James H. Lynch of Southampton, New York; Virginia Ryan '35 and John M. Wigglesworth of Chevy Chase, Maryland all had nine. Elizabeth McHugh '42 and Charles Donovan of West Newton, Mass., had twelve with at least one Trinity daughter (Cover Spring '67). Barbara Grauman '42 and Daniel J. O'Connell and Agnes Fennell '42 and James Healy each had nine.

Clans

Intermarriage between alumnae relatives has resulted in a number of what can be called Trinity Clans. Three of these are selected as

20. Picture, *Alumnae Journal*, Winter '72, p. 25.
21. Seymour Picture, Cover, *Alumnae Journal*, Summer '81.
22. Picture, *Alumnae Journal*, Spring '69, Cover and p. 169.
23. Cover picture, *Alumnae Journal*, Spring '48.
24. *Alumnae Journal*, Spring '60 and pp. 151–152 for the Shields, Lynchs, Krughs and Wigglesworths.

examples here. The O'Donnell-Lane-Neligan-Fahy-Ganey group stems chiefly from the lateral connections of Sister Gertrude of the Blessed Sacrament (Margaret Dempsey) a member of the original incorporating group, 1897–1900, who came to Trinity in September 1901. She was re-elected to the Board of Trustees to fill the vacancy of Sister Euphrasia, February 17, 1902 and was Treasurer of the College as well as board member, 1903–1935.[25] Her sister Mrs. Patrick Neligan delivered the announcement of the incorporation of the college to the newspapers for Sister Gertrude. Mrs. Neligan had two Trinity daughters: Regina '24 and Alma '25. Mrs. Thomas J. Lane, the third Dempsey sister had three Trinity daughters: Gertrude (Mrs. William F. O'Donnell) '15, Margaret '16, and Mary Agnes (Mrs. Charles Fahy) '19. Gertrude's one daughter attended Trinity in the 1940's, and one of her seven sons, Dr. Paul J. O'Donnell married Margaret Ganey '35, Ellen A. Ganey's sister. The Paul O'Donnells had twelve children,[26] three of whom graduated from Trinity: Eileen Jaczens '65, Mary Anne '75, and Claire '80.

Mary Agnes and Judge Charles Fahy's three daughters were Trinity graduates: Anne Sheehan '52, Sara, S.N.D. '53, and Agnes Johnson '57. Anne's twin, Charles, Jr., became a Benedictine monk of St. Anselm's Abbey and was ordained to the priesthood in Notre Dame Chapel at Trinity. Two of Judge Fahy's sisters were Trinity alumnae: Hannah '23 (St. Peter Claver, MSBT), and Agnes '25. The Judge himself was one of the founders and first president of the Fathers' Club of Trinity which developed into the Lay Board—President's Council.

The Devitt-Kramer-O'Neill-Mahoney-Metzger-O'Donnell clan joins alumnae from Ohio, New York, and various cities in the U.S. and Canada where the O'Donnells have lived, and seemed to reach a high point at the baptism in Notre Dame Chapel[27] of Siobhan O'Neil who had two great-grandmothers, two grandmothers, her mother and numerous aunts and cousins Trinity alumnae. Ellen Devitt '21 and Mary Devitt '25 were from Cleveland, Ohio. Ellen, president of 1921, married Dr. James G. Kramer of Akron, the brother of Marie Kramer '15. Their daughter, Molly Kramer Zeigler was the president of 1946. Marie Kramer married Augustine F. O'Neill. Their four daughters graduated from Trinity[28] and their son James, an Annapolis graduate, married Mary Helen Mahoney, president of 1945 and daughter of Marie O'Malley Mahoney '17 of Gloversville, New York,[29] whose second daughter Sally was in 1948. Marie Kramer's sister Magdalene '20

25. A biography of Sr. Gertrude by her niece, Mrs. Charles Fahy is in the T.C.A. as are the Minutes of the Board of Trustees. Vol. I covers her years as treasurer.
26. Cover, *Alumnae Journal*, Spring, 1960. Picture.
27. *Alumnae Journal*, Summer '78.
28. Cf. p. 505.
29. Cover, *Alumnae Journal*, Spring '45.

taught speech at Teachers College, Columbia, and was for years the Head of the Speech Department there. John Mahoney, Mary Helen's brother, married Patricia Corcoran '45. Mary Helen and Jim O'Neill's daughter Patricia was in 1981 and their son Michael who "worked on the Hill" in Washington married Margaret ("P.J.") O'Donnell, daughter of Margaret Metzger O'Donnell '43. They were the parents of Siobahan whose baptism began this saga. A cousin, John O'Neill of Akron and Washington, D.C., served the college devotedly on the Lay Board and the Board of Trustees.

A third example of a Trinity clan is the Powers-Heinze-Globensky-O'Neal group, led by the Powers sisters of Tulsa, Oklahoma, who fanned out taking their Trinity connections to Illinois, Michigan, New York, Maryland, Washington, D.C., Texas, and Italy. Maurice Powers Hanney's daughters were Patricia Washka '55, and Eileen Romero '59. Eileen Powers Heinze '23 also had two Trinity daughters: Eileen Globensky '51 and Mary Anne Romero, '52. Brigid Globensky '77 and Nora Globensky '86 are Eileen's daughters. Their brother, George Heinze, married Mary Ellen O'Neal '56 whose sister Kate O'Neal '68 married Charles V. Glennon of Larchmont, New York. George and Mary Ellen have three Trinity daughters: Mary Kayne '80, Catherine Anne '81, and Megan '82. George himself was a member of the Trinity College Board of Trustees.

One special family, unique as far as we know, is that of Florence Mattimore '25 and Martin R. P. McGuire of the Greek and Latin Department of Catholic University and long Dean of its Graduate School. They adopted six children over a period of eight years and brought them up as a happy, loving united family,[30] with Trinity daughters: Agnes McGuire Clarigio '60 and Helen McGuire Griffin '62.

There are dozens of others Trinity families throughout the country, and hundreds of Trinity alumnae married or single who cannot be mentioned here lest this history grow beyond control. Many of these are named in other parts of the book and all are part of Trinity's living history. Refer back to the dedication of this book and the beginning of this chapter to realize the appreciation the college has for all.[31]

Educators at All Levels

Teachers, educators at all levels from pre-kindergarten to graduate school, administrators from elementary school principals to college presidents form the second most numerous group of alumnae through

30. "Our Adopted Family," Florence Mattimore McGuide '25, *Alumnae Journal*, Spring, 1948, pp. 101–103.
31. The author does not dare attempt a selection of a few and cannot without a scientific survey refer to all! Look in the *Alumnae Directory*.

the years. At the solemn dedication of the College in 1900, a visiting bishop is reported to have said that the college would prove its success, if one graduate became a public high school teacher in a large city. He seems to have been referring specifically to Boston.

According to that prediction the college "made it" beyond all hopes. Six members of the first class, 37% of the class, went into high school classrooms in Ohio, New York, Massachusetts, Missouri, and elsewhere. Before 1910, the college could allude with pride to Marie Rotterman '04 teaching German and French in Dayton, Ohio; Anna Coleman '04 teaching history in Pelham, New York, High School; Alice Gray A.B. '04, B.S. '05 teaching science in St. Louis and later in Mobile, Alabama; Mary McKenna '07 beginning her long career as high school mathematics teacher in New York City; Marie Madden '08 doing the same in history; Anna Butler '08 in Cambridge, Massachusetts beginning a long popular career in English which led to her appointment to the English Department chairmanship at Cambridge High and Latin School; Elizabeth Loughran '08 heading toward the chair of the Department of Foreign Languages at Roxbury Memorial High School; and Margaret Salloway '09 beginning her forty years at Boston Teachers' College, many of them as Dean—not only teaching in Boston, but *teaching teachers* for Boston.

The proportion of alumnae in teaching established by the first class has held quite steady through the years. An analysis of an Alumnae Association survey in 1972 indicates that 34%, of those answering the questionnaire, were teaching. This is broken down to show that 13% of that group were teaching in college, 48% in high school, 27% in grade and pre-school, 5% were principals, and 7% were in special education to the handicapped, *et cetera*.

Without that complete up-to-date, scientific survey mentioned above, it is impossible to list all alumnae who have made education their life work, or even part of it. I shall follow the method used for families and mention a few in each era of Trinity history, letting them represent the many who have "lived Trinity" in this way, but must remain anonymous here.

The numbers of Trinity alumnae teaching in Catholic schools, academies, and colleges are considerably increased by the Sisters of Notre Dame who earned Trinity degrees either before or after entering the congregation, as well as by those in other Orders, who have distinguished themselves on the faculties of schools and colleges. Many of these Sisters are mentioned in various places in this history. Like their lay colleagues and even in this post-Vatican II era the main body of these Trinity educators must also remain anonymous in the interests of finishing the history.

We have seen the vindication of the 1900 prediction through the first decade. The Teens soon joined the growing numbers. From 1911, we cite Kathleen Greeley in Holyoke and Zita Simms in Attleboro, Massachusetts; Amy Broughan, public school principal in Chicago, Illinois; and Agnes Finnegan in New Britain, Connecticut. From 1912 came Anna Boyle in Sharon, Pennsylvania; Caroline Kempel in Akron, Ohio, Alma Madden in Brooklyn, New York, and Maude Gagnor,[32] a founder of the Washington Alumnae Chapter, who taught nearly forty years in the District of Columbia schools, part of them as principal, and who, retired and crippled through a freak car accident, continued service to others in volunteer parish work and never gave up her advocacy of Interracial Justice.

A "sprinkling" from the many in the Teens will show not only continuity but geographical spread. Frances Cashman '13[33] was academic teacher in Essex County Agricultural School, Massachusetts; Helen Cronin '13 at Manchester, New Hampshire High School; Alice Donovan '13 Head of the English Department, English High School, Lynn, Massachusetts; Alice E. Sullivan, Science and Latin in Lowell High School, Massachusetts. The Class of 1914 added not only Genevieve Caulfield teacher of the blind in Japan, Viet Nam, and Thailand, but Marguerite Duffy teaching Latin at Port Washington High School, New York; Margaret Gallagher in Philadelphia, Pennsylvania; Mary McSweeney Burke, English in Glens Falls, New York. Margaret McArdle '15 was head of the English Department in the Weehawken, New Jersey High School and Anne Sarahon Hooley '15 established and directed business schools in Kansas City, Missouri and in Latin America. Margaret McWeeney '15 taught in Providence, Rhode Island. The Bouillins '16, Ann E. and M. Louise were teachers of physical education in Clarksville, Tennessee. While Anna Brodbine '16 combined teaching in Boston with establishing her Travel Agency. Mary Rose Murphy '16 taught English at Hutchinson High School, Buffalo, New York, and Kathleen Smith '16 was a teacher in Riverdale, Maryland. Mary Judge '17 taught in Fall River, Massachusetts, and Eleanor McCormick '17 taught music in Pittsfield, Massachusetts, while Kathleen MacHale '17 taught mathematics at Southwestern High School, Detroit, Michigan. Also of 1917, Agnes Neary was a high school teacher in Johnstown, Pennsylvania, and Pearl Standt in Canton, Ohio. From 1918, Angela Burke in Springfield, Massachusetts; Kathleen Eagan Morris in New York City; and Eleanor Downing first at Trinity and later at St. John's University, New York, continued the tradition. From 1919 came not only Bernadette

32. *Alumnae Journal*, Winter, 1964, pp. 96–98.
33. Recipient of Julie Billiart Medal 1962, and mother of Trinity daughters.

Dore,[34] lifelong teacher and elementary school principal in the Washington, D.C. schools, but Mary Figueira (Sr. Ambrose, S.P.) in Evanston, Illinois; Elizabeth Fitzgerald in Peabody, Massachusetts; Regina O'Donnell, Dean of Discipline, Central High School, Providence, Rhode Island; Margaret Himstedt Letzig, District Manager, Educational Publications, Little Rock, Arkansas; Helen Shanahan, South High School, Lima, Ohio; and Mary M. Sullivan, teaching English in Jamaica Plain High School, Massachusetts.

The Twenties with much larger classes brought a corresponding increase in the number of alumnae in the teaching profession and a consequent problem of choosing a "sprinkling" to represent them. This problem becomes more acute as the decades pass. Beginning with the Class of 1920, we mention Jean Marshall in the high school in Fall River, Massachusetts; Inez O'Donnell in Pittsburgh, Pennsylvania; Magdalene Kramer from Akron, Ohio, teacher in and Head of the Speech Department, Teacher's College, Columbia University; and Louise Keyes, R.S.C.J., who distinguished herself in Sacred Heart Colleges in several parts of the United States and abroad.[35] From 1921 Katharine Brady taught history in Portsmouth (New Hampshire) Senior High School; Mary Rose Brennan, English in Walton High School, New York City; Eleanor Dean Campbell in Somerville, Massachusetts; Caroline Cassidy, French in Gloversville (New York) High School, and Margaret Crotty was a legend in Brighton, Massachusetts. Joining them from 1922 were Lillian Manganaro, Mathematics and Italian in Waterbury, Connecticut; Catherine Mullen, English, in Bangor, Maine; Carol O'Brien in Milwaukee, Wisconsin; Helen Dalton, Latin, in Warren, Massachusetts; and Alice Padgett, sociology at the Catholic University of America. Florence Enright '23 was high school principal in White Sulphur Springs, Montana; Catherine Haage Kacmarynski '23 taught for years at Hunter College, New York City and established the graduate and other significant programs at the College of New Rochelle, while Marian Schwartz '23 taught in high schools in Maryland. A few from 1924 will demonstrate the continuity of Trinity educators. While Priscilla Fogarty was teaching English in Springfield, Illinois, Helen McMahon was teaching history in Rosemont College, Pennsylvania; Helen Keller was a bacteriologist at the University of Cincinnati, Ohio; and Madeleine Guilfoyle Maldonado was teaching in Bogota, Colombia.

The Class of 1925 added among others, Rose O'Donnell, Wilkes-Barre, Pennsylvania, Helen Reagan starting her forty-year career as teacher and principal at Swansea High School (Massachusetts), Anne Hackett in Providence Central High (Rhode Island); Mildred Judge,

34. Julie Billiart Medal, 1967. *Alumnae Journal*, Summer, 1967, p. 220.
35. *Alumnae Journal*, Autumn 1982 and other earlier issues.

Special Education Supervisor for Indiana and Armstrong Counties, Pennsylvania; Julia Diggins, mathematics teacher, Washington, D.C.; Antonio McInnis combining family business management with teaching in Roanoke (Virginia) Community College; Frances Moore McGee in Lowell, Massachusetts; and Aileen Mize, directing Speech and Drama at the College of Notre Dame of Maryland.

Teresa Boylan '26 became a legend in Classics at Springfield High, Massachusetts, while elsewhere in Massachusetts others '26ers taught: Loretta Creed in Boston, Alice Barry in Jamaica Plain, Anne Marshall in Fall River, Margaret Kielty directing Adult Education in Fitchburg. Mary Hughes '26 taught in Parkersburg, West Virginia; Dorothy Strootmen in Buffalo, New York, and Florence Rormay in New Britain, Connecticut. Joining the ranks from 1927 were among others Eileen Dwyer, Arlington, Massachusetts; Mary Eagan, Providence Rhode Island; Margaret Finke, Dayton, Ohio; Regina Flannery Hertsfeld, heading Anthropology at Catholic University; Agnes Leahy, English at Buckley High, Hartford, Connecticut; Eleanor O'Kane teaching languages at Hollins College and later becoming a Sister of the Holy Cross on the faculty and dean at St. Mary's College, South Bend, Indiana; and Vera Whitty, Latin in Washington, D.C. From 1928, Olive Heneberger taught English at Brooklyn College, New York; Ethel S. Johnson, Mathematics at Canandaigua Academy (New York); Isabel Hesse in high school in Pittsfield and Helena Sullivan in Fall River, Massachusetts; and Catherine Weber in Ashland, Pennsylvania; while Anne McLoughlin established a school for medical secretaries in Washington, D.C., as well as holding administrative positions at Georgetown Visitation Academy and later at Georgetown University where she was University Registrar and Director of Records for years. Ending the decade, 1929 had Elizabeth Collins (Sr. Edwarda, I.H.M.) in Scranton, Pennsylvania, Miriam Leahy Nichols, teacher in and owner of a nursery school in Richmond, Virginia; Hilda Moorman, teaching English in Withrow High, Cincinnati, Ohio. There were also three in Connecticut, Catherine and Mary A. Flynn in Meridan, and Eileen King in New Britain.

From the turn of the decade, 1930, the distribution continues with Margaret Kinnirey teaching modern languages (later Guidance and Counseling) in Portland and Middletown, Connecticut; Helen Desnoes in Dallas, Texas; Bridgie Doughterty in Nesquehoning High School (Pennsylvania); Margaret McConnell Moe in Auburn, New York; Helen Marrocco in Paterson, New Jersey; Genevieve Steffan in Buffalo and Margaret O'Malley Davin in Kenmore, New York; and Mary Christine Swint in Weston High School (West Virginia). Keeping in mind the 1972 survey showing 34% of alumnae who answered in the field of education, and the necessity of brevity here, we shall go quickly through the remaining decades mentioning even fewer names.

The first forty years of the alumnae, however, produced several eminent Trinity S.N.D. faculty members who are mentioned earlier in this history,[36] but deserve listing: Sister Wilfrid du Sacre Coeur (Elsie Parsons '04), Sister Julia of the Trinity (Edith McDonald '11), Sister Julia (Helen Stokes '13), Sister Marie Virginia (Gertrude Smith '14), Sister Marie Mechilde (Helen Mahoney '15), Sister St. John Neponucene (Elizabeth Fennessey '15), Sister Therese of the Blessed Sacrament (Katherine Sullivan '17), Sister Helen (Helen Sheehan '24), Sister Ann Frances Hoey (Catherine Hoey '24), Sister Ann Julia (Helen Kinnirey '25), Sister Columba (Catherine Mullaly '25), Sister Alice Bernadine (Margaret O'Donoghue '31), Sister Catherine Marie (Katherine Lee '34), Sister Alice Clement, later called Monica (Monica Davis '34), Sister Mary Frances (Arline McCarthy '37), Sister Joan of the Blessed Sacrament (Mary Kate Bland '38), Sister Margaret Therese (Frances Evans '38), Sister Marie Therese (Marie T. Dimond '38).

For the reasons mentioned before, the remaining decades will be "spot checked" only. An increasing number of alumnae from these later decades are in supervisory positions, or in teaching or research in colleges and universities. Dr. Regis Boyle '33 is nationally known for work in promoting excellence in high school and college journalism. She has taught in the Washington, D.C. high schools and at the University of Maryland, received many awards, and is listed in at least four *Who's Who* volumes. Also from 1933 Margaret Gilmer Keller has distinguished herself in university teaching at Rutgers University in New Jersey. She has been honored repeatedly by the university, and most recently[37] was named Professor of the Year by the students.

Elizabeth M. Schneider has been teaching English at Western College in Ohio. Mary Louise Tindell Tietjens '37, after teaching English at Trinity, continued interest in education in New Jersey and currently is Director and teacher in the CCD program in the Newark Archdiocese.[38] Sister Rita Buddeke '37, taught high school mathematics and biology, taught in and chaired the Department of Education at Trinity, taught in graduate education at the Catholic University, wrote at least four textbooks before being appointed Vice President for Academic Affairs at Strayer's College. She was honored for achieving accreditation for Strayer's as a four year business college, and Middle States accreditation. She has been a consultant to the D.C. Mayor and to the archdioceses of Washington and of Richmond, Virginia. Sister Marie Therese Dimond '38 of the Trinity biology department has become an internationally known authority on turtles.

36. Chapters 4 and 5.
37. *Alumnae Journal*, Summer, 1982, p. 11.
38. *Alumnae Journal*, Summer, 1982, p. 11.

From the 1940's a token few must represent all. Joan Grace '42 taught at Seton Hall College; Rita Lynn '43 was teacher of Social Work at the Catholic University; Virginia McNamara '43, taught mathematics in Rochester, New Hampshire; Claire Horrigan '44 taught at Dumbarton College, D.C.; Cornelia Sullivan '44 taught high school in Hartford, Connecticut and Patricia Reynolds '44 in Lowell Massachusetts; Dorothy Mortell Barrett '45 taught mathematics at Catholic University and for years at Trinity. Moira Sullivan '46 has headed the biology department in Newton (Massachusetts) High School, Mary Cawley '48 has taught mathematics and been a guidance counselor at East Providence High (Rhode Island). Ellen Wagner Healy '49 is on the Indianapolis Archdiocesan Board of Education[39] and Margaret Thorne '49 has been Director of Testing Program for the College Entrance Examination Board.

Mona Bruno Shevlin '50 founded, in cooperation with Sister Ann Francis Hoey '24, the Vocational Counseling Bureau at Trinity and has taught Guidance and Counseling at the Catholic University while directing her own center in northern Virginia. She was appointed to the U.S. Commission for Counseling of Women and the D.C. Commission on the Status of Woman, and elected Conference Director for the Middle Atlantic Region of Counseling Center Directors. Jeanne Shook Prial '53 has been Principal of the Center School for Children with learning disabilities which is financed by the Boards of Education of nineteen districts from five New Jersey counties.

Norma Matarese Kacen '56 has been Executive Director of the Houston Teachers Association. She has spoken many times and published as well on the subject of improving education. Sylvia Washington Bâ, '58,[40] professor-scholar received both a Woodrow Wilson and a Fulbright Fellowship, studied at The University of Bordeaux and at Fordham using for her doctoral dissertation topic "The Concept of Negritude in the Poetry of Leopold S. Senghor." Besides being published by Princeton University Press, this book attracted the attention of the poet, himself then President of Senegal, who invited Sylvia to teach in the university there. As Madame Bâ, the wife of a young Senegalese diplomat, she taught French at Trinity captivating her students by her excellent teaching and her Paris fashions. Back in Senegal she is still on the university faculty.

From the sixties, several Trinitarians have combined medicine with education. Dr. Tatiana A. Assaykeen '61 is Assistant Professor of Surgery (Urology) and Pharmacology at Stanford University School of Medicine. She has a Ph.D. from the University of Virginia and has

39. *Ibid.*
40. Cf. *Alumnae Journal*, Autumn '81, p. 6.

written extensively in her fields. Marilyn Demorest Wang '65, Ph.D. Johns Hopkins, is a Research Associate in Audiology, University of Pittsburg School of Medicine. She, too, has published articles in her field. Jennifer Hart Lavail '65, University of Wisconsin, Ph.D. (Anatomy) has been a research fellow at Harvard Medical Department of Neuropathology and has written articles and abstracts. Sister Emily Mullin '69, a graduate nurse and master in tropical disease, teaches in a teacher-training and technical school in Zaire, Africa.

Not all teachers of this decade are in medical schools as a few examples will show. Joan Formato Ferrante '63 teaches in Montgomery County, Maryland, and keeps in close touch with the college as an officer in the Alumnae Association. Kathleen Mullin Mullinex '65 is Vice Provost of Columbia University,[41] Ann Marie di Stephano '69 is Assistant Professor of Education and Women's Studies at Washington University, St. Louis.[42]

As has been said before the problem of choosing a "sprinkling" of educators to represent the whole body has become more acute as the years have passed. For that reason not even a token will be chosen from the seventies. This section will end with the mention of Trinity alumnae who have been college presidents and a listing of representation from the related field of librarianship.

Two Sisters of Notre Dame de Namur who were Trinity alumnae have been presidents of Trinity College: Sister Julia of the Trinity (Edith McDonald '11) 1929–1932; and Sister Margaret Claydon '45, 1969–1975.[43] Sister Mary Frances, S.N.D. (Arline F. McCarthy '37) was president of Emmanuel College, Boston, Massachusetts. Sister Honora, S.S.J.[44] (Rose Callahan '23) was president of Regis College, Weston, Massachusetts. Sister Mariana Brady, S.P. '48, was president of Immaculata College, Washington, D.C. Carolyn Manuszak '54 is president of Villa Julie College, Stevenson, Maryland. Louise Keyes, R.S.C.J. '20, has held high academic offices in Sacred Heart College in St. Louis, Missouri; Newton, Massachusetts; Manhattanville, New York, and in India.[45]

Librarians

Since the library is an essential basis for a sound education on all levels and many Trinity alumnae have distinguished themselves in librarianship, a list of alumnae librarians spanning the years through the 1940's and showing territorial spread supplements the list of teach-

41. *Alumnae Journal,* Autumn, 1982, p. 7.
42. *Alumnae Journal,* Spring 1982, p. 6.
43. *Alumnae Journal,* Autumn, 1959, pp. 4–5; 6–7.
44. *Alumnae Journal,* Autumn, 1941, p. 7.
45. *Alumnae Journal,* Spring 1951, pp. 110–112; Autumn 1951, pp. 12–14.

ers. Again it is indicative rather than complete. The list: Lucile May '13, head librarian Superior, Wisconsin Public Library; Frances McManus '15, Philadelphia, Pennsylvania; Eileen McDonald '20, Waterbury, Connecticut; Marthe Augier '23, Supervisor Public Libraries, Department of the Seine, Paris, France; Sister Helen Sheehan '24, second librarian of Trinity College; Margery Grant '24, Villanova College, Pennsylvania; Teresa Callaghan '27, Chestnut Hill, Massachusetts; Kathleen Dooley '30, Lisbon, Ohio; Nancy Mango '31, Music Librarian, Pan American Union, D.C.; Elizabeth O'Connor, R.S.C.J. '39, Trinity College and Albany, New York and Manhattanville College; Margaret Donahue '42, Reference Librarian, Catholic University; Sister Dorothy Beach '43, third librarian, Trinity College; Mary Catherine McCarthy '44,[45] Syracuse, New York; Elizabeth Fitzgerald, secretary to Chief of Manuscripts, Library of Congress, D.C.; Sally Mahoney '48.

Marchand Hall Finnegan '53 describes in the Winter '68 *Alumnae Journal* the position of University Archivist. She is Archivist of the State University of New York and currently President of the Society of American Archivists.[46]

It is hard to gauge and almost impossible to overestimate the leavening effect of Trinity educators through more than eighty years. This effect continues in the present through the work of the education department and the various programs of continuing education.

Medical and Legal Professions

Alumnae in the medical and legal professions also date from the first decade of the college.

In 1965 Sister St. John Nepomucene (Elizabeth Fennessey '15) wrote for the *Alumnae Journal*[47] an article that makes an appropriate opening for this section. It will be liberally quoted here. She wrote:

> Last week an evening paper announced that the Soviets were training more physicians than we. Trinity need feel no compunction in this area. Since Honoria Shine, '09, received her M.D. from Woman's Medical College of Pennsylvania in 1913, there has been first a trickle—growing now to a full stream of women doctors who give Trinity as the source of their pre-medical education. To date there have been fifty-seven. Their medical schools range from Harvard to the University of Southern California, with one degree from the University of Rome (Concetta Mango Lettieri, '31), and among their postgraduate accomplishments we find a "Zeugnis" certificate from the University of Vienna (Elizabeth Herbert McDevitt, '22).
>
> The fields of specialization, while not all-embracing, are almost as varied as the medical schools. Cecilia Douglas Powers, '42, practicing with her

46. The author understands the difference between archivists and librarians, but this placement seemed logical.
47. Winter 1965, pp. 76–77.

husband, is our only doctor of veterinary medicine (University of Pennsylvania), although one of the class of '65 plans that as her future work. Pediatricians are in abundance, as are doctors of internal medicine and general practitioners. There are several psychiatrists, a neurologist, a radiologist, an anesthetist, a pathologist. We can claim even some surgeons, though surgery is a specialty thought to require physical strength of a kind not always attributed to women. An expert diagnostician was lost when Mary D. Walsh, '15, died last year. Of the total number of "our doctors" only two others, Katherine Degnan Miller, '10, and Germaine Güntzer, '23, have died to date.[48] General practice claims most of these physicians, although industry, school systems, hospitals, and governmental agencies all use their skills.

The recipient of most honors is our only doctor in Maryknoll, Sister Gilmary, O.P. (Eileen Simmons, '44) who received a presidential citation from the government of Korea for her work on a Tuberculosis Health Program for the Korean people. She was also cited for this achievement in the State Senate of Pennsylvania. Sister Gilmary had a feature role in "M.D. International," the nationwide NBC television show portraying the work of American doctors abroad. In 1963, Sister received the citation of the Commonwealth Committee of Woman's Medical College and was on the Duke University Symposium, Cross-currents in Contemporary Life.[49] Two of our doctors not only won the coveted T pin but were Student Government presidents at Trinity, Judith McMahon Musladin, '49, and Yvonne Thel Driscoll, '58, the latter carrying on her tradition by being class president at Woman's Medical. Three have received their M.D.'s *cum laude* from there, Sister Gilmary, Alice Teahan, '36, and Moyra Siu Moy, '49, who also won the Mosby prize for medicine. Georgetown has granted M.D.'s *magna cum laude* to Mary Gertrude Beck Maloney, '48, and to Sister M. Frederic (Eilene Niedfelt), '45, of the Society of Catholic Medical Missionaries, who also won two gold medals—one for the highest average for four years, the other as the highest in bacteriology. Sister also received honorable mention in at least six courses. This could not have been totally unexpected as Sister had been graduated from Trinity *magna cum laude*.

Others, too, showed promise in their undergraduate years, brought to happy fulfillment at the universities—like Veronica Zavatone, '59, who, having received the Mary Murray McArdle award here, was president of the senior class at Woman's Medical and elected to Alpha Omega Alpha, the honorary medical society. Student Government Vice President, wearer of the T pin and named to the collegiate *Who's Who*, Kay Leland, '60, was President of the Student Council at Woman's Medical in '63–'64 and received with her degree the Dr. Emily Macon Award for the outstanding student in pediatrics. Marie Lalor, '60, who was class secretary at Tufts Medical, '61 to '64, was the first woman from Woonsocket, R.I., to receive a medical degree since 1886! Patricia Bryan Wilber, '48, after receiving her

48. Since that date, Dr. Elizabeth Babbitt '57, Dr. Lucy Sikorsky '20 (*obit. Alumnae Journal*, Autumn, 1972); Dr. Monica Millitzer Reed, '32 (*obit. Alumnae Journal*, Autumn, 1967) have died.
49. Sister Gilmary's later honors will be cited in the list that follows.

> M.D. from Harvard was on a U.S. Public Health Research Fellowship at Tufts, 1953–54.
>
> Many are the publications of our doctors, Dorothy Donley Dowd, '26, psychiatrist, having the largest number, more than twenty-five. One of our most active alumnae, Hester Curtis, '20, with an M.D. from Yale and a Master in Public Health from Harvard, has worked a maternal and child welfare in New York, Connecticut, New Mexico, and West Virginia. As regional medical director of the U.S. Children's Bureau, first in Kansas City, Missouri, and then in New York, she covered nineteen states. Presently in Washington, Hester is now Medical Officer, Division of International Cooperation of the Children's Bureau of the Department of Health, Education, and Welfare.
>
> But the nineteen states covered by Hester Curtis seem but "local" in comparison with the extensive territory in which we find our Sisters of the Catholic Medical Mission Society. At the time in their Holy Family Hospital in Mandar, India, Sister Ignatius Marie (Ellen Desmond, '18) was the superior of this jungle hospital, Sister M. Barbara Taggart, '39, was assigned as surgeon (839 operations in one year) and for a few months Sister Marcella (Louise Du Brul, '37) was there. The map will show the present location of most of the thirteen Sisters who received at Trinity the pre-medical training which enables them to add to the C.C.M.M., the M.D.

The first Trinity physician was Dr. Honoria Shine '09,[50] a member of the sixth class to receive Trinity degrees. She specialized in pediatrics and public health and was a prominent citizen of Holyoke, Massachusetts. Her Clinic and Day Nursery earned the praise and respect of her city through nearly half a century. She received an honorary D.Sc. from Trinity at Commencement in 1959.[51]

Many of the line of Trinity physicians that followed Dr. Shine have been mentioned in Sister St. John's article and elsewhere in this history. A list of examples indicates to some extent variety of activity, continuity and geographical spread. Kathleen Degnan Miller '10, practiced in Greenwich, Connecticut; Mary D. Walsh '15, in New York City; Josephine Wimsatt Lohr '16, in Evanston, Illinois; Lucy Sikorsky '20, in Massachusetts and Albuquerque, New Mexico[52]; Paz Pamintuan von Heiland '21 was Professor of Bacteriology in Centro Escolar University, the Philippines; Dorothy Donley Dowd '26 practiced psychiatry in Washington, D.C.; Evelyn Merrick '28[53] was head of the Department of Rheumatology at Orange Memorial Hospital, New Jersey. While Margaret Bevine '31 was a pathologist at Bellevue Hospital, New York City, Concetta Mango Lettieri '31 practiced in Bergen, New Jersey and Juliana Swiney '31 was an eminent pediatrician in Bayonne, New Jer-

50. *Obit. Alumnae Journal*, Spring 1969, p. 139.
51. *Alumnae Journal*, Summer, 1959, cover and p. 196.
52. *Obit. Alumnae Journal*, Autumn, 1972, p. 24.
53. *Obit. Alumnae Journal*, Winter, 1968, p. 80.

sey; Monica Millitzer Reed '32[54] was a neurologist in Long Beach, California. Florence Leuthardt '42 was technician in the New York Public Health Services while Cecilia Douglas Powers '42 practiced Veterinary Medicine in Dover, Massachusetts; Elizabeth Babbitt Cordasco '57, of Flagstaff, Arizona earned her M.D. from Georgetown and practiced in her home state. Catherine Herlihy Beyer '58 is a pediatrician in rural Fayetteville, North Carolina.[55] M. Joan Gillespie '64 is a dentist in the Washington Area. Louise Donohoe Resor '70 is a neurologist practicing first in New York City and later in Connecticut. Mary Mauriello Kelly '70 practices in Seattle, Washington.

Mention of a few in the allied medical profession of nursing will indicate that Trinity women have not neglected this area of service. Anna E. Ryle '30 was Director of Nursing, Grasslands Hospital, Grasslands, New York. Mary Cuneen Gilhofer '31 was Nursing Instructor, St. Mary's School of Nursing, Louisville, Kentucky. Mary Mahoney Fergus earned her R.N. at Johns Hopkins University Hospital and practiced successfully in the east before moving to California. Katrina Quinn Weschler '44 of Erie earned a Master's degree in Nursing Administration at Yale and served efficiently in that field. Two later examples round out this sketchy list. Mary Teresa Curry '72 earned a B.S. in Nursing at Cornell and Patricia McFadden Schwartz '55 graduated with highest academic honors from Touro Infirmary School of Nursing, New Orleans, Louisiana.[56]

Lawyers and Judges

Trinity's lawyers began with Bertha Strootman Rodet '10, though Irene O'Crowley '07, who earned a Ph.D. at New York University did become an LLB and passed the New Jersey Bar in 1920. Miss O'Crowley, an early "libber" retained her maiden name after marriage and practiced law for many years in New Jersey.

A scattering of names of Trinity lawyers shows that Trinity women have "taken to the law" consistently through the years, often combining legal work with various other pursuits. Louise Welch O'Connor '17 was a lawyer in Beverly, Massachusetts. Margaret Sheehan Blodgett '19 uses her law in conjunction with her insurance business in Manchester, New Hampshire. She is also a licensed pilot[57] and the recipient of an Alumnae Achievement Award as well as sponsor of Campus-on-the-Cape. Charlotte Hogan Vogel '21 was a prominent lawyer in Columbus, Ohio. She was the first woman admitted to the

54. *Obit. Alumnae Journal,* Autumn, 1967, p. 28.
55. Picture. *Alumnae Journal,* Spring, 1973, p. 19.
56. *Alumnae Journal,* Summer '75, p. 11.
57. *Alumnae Journal,* Autumn '74, p. 5.

Order of the Coif at Ohio State University. Louise F. McCarthy '23[58] was a successful Philadelphia lawyer when she joined the Navy in World War II and was appointed instructor in the Wave Training Center at Smith College. She "worked up a course in Naval Law and taught it." She was later promoted and as Lt. Commander worked in the Navy Judge Advocate General's Office in Washington. After the war she became a partner in the law firm of Hugh P. McFaddan in Allantown, Pennsylvania. Agnes Sullivan O'Brien '24 of Kentucky and New York began as a social worker, branching out into ardent work for interracial justice, studied law and was a practicing attorney in New York City. Mildred Gott Bryan '28 was a lawyer in the D.C.-Maryland area. Helene Maxwell Dardis '31 was a lawyer in Massachusetts and in Arizona. Mary Shanafeldt Stanton '40 was a lawyer in Washington, D.C. Joan Conroy Geiler '44 was an Associate in a New York City law firm. Antonia Mangano '48[57] is deputy commissioner at the New York State Supreme Court. She works in family law. Helen O'Connor '50 was one of the first women to receive the LLB degree from Harvard Law School.[58]

Agnes Gilligan Nolan '52[59] is not only a partner in her own New York City law firm, but is an executive in her own real estate business.

The number of lawyers has increased rapidly in the last two decades so that the names cited here are indeed tokens only to indicate the continuity. One recent issue of the *Alumnae Journal* listed seven new law degreees which an examination of class letters and "Alumnae Notes" of other issues would show to be typical. Rosemary Mayers Collyer '68,[60] a Denver lawyer specializing in labor law, is one of a five-member Federal Mine Safety Commission appointed by President Reagan. Patricia Meyer Bromberg '69 practices in Morristown, New Jersey and Nancy Principe Scull '70 in San Diego, California. Trinity lawyers are active in legal aid, in family courts, in all areas of the profession. It is not possible to mention all here, though Trinity is proud of their record. Margaret McMorrow Love '73[61] is an Oklahoma City lawyer who has won at least one case before the U.S. Supreme Court. Patricia McGuire '74 is assistant dean of the Georgetown Law Center in Washington, D.C.

At least six Trinity alumnae are judges in various parts of the country. Charlotte Murphy '45 was the first woman in 112 years to be appointed to the bench of the U.S. Court of Claims in Washington, D.C. Mary Ann Killeen Ast '48 is Chief Justice of the Family Court in Erie County, New York. Patricia Herron '49 is a judge in the Superior Court of California in San Francisco. She also owns a California vine-

58. *Ibid.*, Autumn '53, p. 7.
59. *Alumnae Journal*, Summer '73, p. 18.
60. *Alumnae Journal*, Autumn '81, p. 15.
61. *Alumnae Journal*, Summer '85, p. 15.

yard. Barbara Coppeto '55 is a Judge of the Superior Court of Connecticut, who came to the bench from the law firm of Yudkin, Coppeto and Young.[62] Jane Drew Waller '68 is a judge in the Chicago, Illinois, area and Regina McGranery '67 is a judge in Washington, D.C.

Business and Industry

In no field have Trinity women demonstrated better the value of a strong liberal arts education as a basis for varied activities than in business. From Nelly O'Mahoney '04, Treasurer of the O'Mahoney Coal Company in Lawrence, Massachusetts to the young alumnae in the highly technical environment of the eighties Trinity women have penetrated and succeeded in a more and more complicated business world. From produce to publishing, from retailing to restaurants Trinity women have made their way. Again a spot check through the decades must suffice. No complete coverage is possible here.

Anne Hooley '15 ran schools for secretaries in St. Louis, Kansas City, and Mexico City. Anna Brodbine '16 left teaching to open her own travel agency in Boston, Massachusetts, which she efficiently directed for half a century. Florence Gaffney Doherty '17 was a bank bookkeeper in Detroit, Michigan. From 1918 were Margaret Dougherty O'Brien, insurance broker, New York City; Frances Dillon, owner, dry cleaning plant, Lowell, Massachusetts; Helen Flynn Stetson, Business Manager, Dry Cleaners and Furriers, Sarasota, Florida; Mary McCabe Lynch, Purchasing Clerk, Naval Shipyard, San Francisco, California. Margaret Sheehan '19 is lawyer and insurance underwriter, Manchester, New Hampshire; while Alma Shannon '19 was supervisor, Carnegie Teachers' Cooperative Investment Office, Yonkers, New York; Mary Gaffney Cornwell '20 was a statistician with Armour Company, Chicago, Illinois. Marie O'Reilly Nash '22 was a bookkeeper and secretary in University Heights, Ohio. Leonora Aprea '23 was Secretary of Lumberman's Mutual Casualty Company, Macon, Georgia, while Ruth Horan Davis '23 was an interior decorator in Wellesley Hills, Massachusetts, and Mary Leonard '23 ran the family produce business in Cincinnati, Ohio, at the same time being active in volunteer work for the handicapped.[63] Mary Devitt Plunkett '25 managed a hotel in downtown Cleveland. Margaret Donnelly Martineau '25 owned and operated a bookstore and was an officer, as was her sister, Mary Donnelly Leonard '25, in the family furniture business in Grand Rapids, Michigan. Antonia McGinnis Thayer '25, widow with one son, ran the family stone quarry in Eagle Rock, Virginia, and taught in the local community college. Genevieve Beauton Tierney '25 operated the family

62. *Alumnae Journal,* Autumn '81, p. 15.
63. *Alumnae Journal,* Spring 1955, p. 130.

Laundry and Dry Cleaning Company in New Haven, Connecticut. Orilia Hollis '26 was a secretary, Conde Nast Publications, New York, while Imogen Felin Haenn '26, as a widow, continued to run the family lumber business in Philadelphia, Pennsylvania. Florence O'Brien Patterson '26 was the first woman vice president of Erwin, Wasey Advertising Company and later Vice President of American Home Products, Inc., both in New York City. Josephine Farrell Miner '29 was the proprietor of Harvey Lake Inn, Northwood Center, New Hampshire, while Mary Ahern '29 was accountant and assistant-treasurer, National Lumber Manufacturers Association, Washington, D.C. Mildred Wolberg '30 was an insurance underwriter, Maplewood, New Jersey; Florence O'Donoghue '30 was an investment counselor in Washington, D.C.; Helen Barrett Glennon '31 was an executive in a travel agency, White Plains, New York. Regina Bartenback '31 was an executive in the Hamilton Paper Company, Evanston, Illinois, while classmate Edith Callaghan '31[64] was Retail Manager of Systems and Methods Department, Bamberger and Company, Newark, New Jersey; and Theodosia Grey Wood '31 owned a packaging company in Northwood, New York; and M. Elizabeth Brown '31 was Assistant to the Editor, McClure Newspaper Syndicate, New York City. Catherine Crimmings '32 was president and treasurer of J. J. Crimmings Company of Boston and later vice-president and treasurer of Russell Armstrong-Attenbury Company, Portland, Maine.[65] Marjorie DuBrul Shiels '35 was President and General Manager, Charles F. Shiels Lumber Company,[66] Cincinnati, Ohio. Jeanne Adele Hafner '42, Chicago businesswoman, was President of Chicago Bank Women.[67] Mary Virginia Long '42, manager of headquarters personnel, Union Camp Corporation, received a Tribute to Women in Industry (ITWIN) Award in Ridgewood, New Jersey. Mary Ellen White '43 owns her own talent agency in New York and Los Angeles. Jane Marilley '44[68] founded with Mary Hayden '26 Courtesy Associates in Washington, D.C., developed it to national and international prominence and directed the enterprise until her death in 1976. Agnes Gilligan Nolan '52, an attorney, owns her own very successful real estate company, Whitebread Nolan, Madison Avenue, New York City. Joan Payden '53[69] is a certified public accountant with her own investment company in San Francisco. Carol P. Neves '54 is a vice president of Merrill, Lynch, Pierce, Fenner and Smith, New York City.[70] Betty Duff Murphy '57 is a real estate broker in Middleboro,

64. Cf. "Value of an A. B. Degree," *Alumnae Journal*, Autumn '56, pp. 5–8.
65. *Newsletter*, February 1968, f. 4.
66. *Alumnae Journal*, Summer '74, p. 11.
67. *Alumnae Journal*, Spring '67, p. 201.
68. *Alumnae Journal*, Winter '52, pp. 60–61.
69. *Alumnae Journal*, Winter '67, p. 10.
70. *Alumnae Journal*, Winter '82, p. 8.

Massachusetts. Mary Ann Violet Schoeb '60[71] is an investment adviser in Washington, D.C. Patricia Boyle '60 was the first woman in the Chase Manhattan Trainee Program from which she joined the bank staff. Consuella Donahue '61 was Marketing Manager, Data Processing Division, I.B.M. Mary Curtin Smith '54 entered the same corporation soon after graduation from Trinity and became an IBM advisory systems engineer in the Syracuse, New York area.[72] Marion Glennon '58 is in the same corporation as a telecommunications specialist. Carolyn Raemondi Wall '64 was publisher of *Adweek* and President of Advertising Women of New York[73] and later publisher of *New York Magazine*. Diana Loftus Snowden '68 was recently appointed Commissioner on the Alaska Public Utilities Commission. She has been Vice President for Industrial Relations of Alascom, the largest private company in Alaska. In addition, she was for six years chair of the Alaska State Commission on Human Rights.[74] Meanwhile Cathleen Black O'Callaghan '66 has been rising in the publishing field.[75] From advertising sales for *Holiday* and other magazines, advertising manager and associate publisher of *Ms.*, she became in 1979 publisher of *New York Magazine*. In 1983 she was appointed publisher of *U.S.A. Today* and in 1985, Executive Vice President for Marketing of Gannet, Inc. She is the recipient of an Alumnae Achievement Award.

Maureen Dwyer '69 is senior vice president Erie Indemnity Company, managing company of the Erie Insurance Group. She is a chartered Property Casualty Underwriter. Margaret Hoffmann O'Brien '69[76] founded two restaurants: The Man in the Green Hat on Capitol Hill and Colonel Brooks in Brookland, D.C. Patricia Teufel '72 is an associate actuary for Aetna Insurance, Hartford, Connecticut.[77] Lisa Switzer '74,[78] CBS anchor in Portland, Maine and co-host, New Hampshire Public Television weekly public affairs program, was formerly a reporter for Concord Station WKXL. She is not the first Trinity woman in TV, but is cited here as a contemporary in the line that goes back to the early days of the industry.

Social Work, Girl Scouts, Volunteers

The emphasis on service to others has appeared in the activities of alumnae from the beginning, reflecting a spirit developed at Trinity

71. *Ibid.*, p. 7.
72. *Syracuse Post Standard*, Pictorial, November 26, 1961.
73. *Alumnae Journal*, Spring '82, p. 6.
74. *Alumnae Journal*, Winter '82, p. 8.
75. *Alumnae Journal*, Spring '73.
76. *Alumnae Journal*, Autumn '81, p. 8.
77. *Alumnae Journal*, Winter '82, p. 8.
78. *Ibid.*

College. Family life, education, the medical and legal fields are all service activities. Professional social work fostered by Dr. Kerby and his successors[79] in the sociology department holds an honored place among alumnae service occupations. An article in the Trinity College Record as early as 1910[80] calls M. Christine Ryan '12 a "pioneer in Trinity's Social Service Work." Mary Maxwell '11 was Director of the Department of Social Work, University Hospital, Iowa City, Iowa. Lucille Quinlan '12 was Supervisor of in-service training, Minnesota State Department of Social Work. Margaret Norman '13 was Director of Public Assistance, New York State Department of Social Welfare. Anne Culligan '14 was a supervisor of social workers in Minneapolis, Minnesota. Anna May McCaffrey Langley '14 was a social welfare caseworker in Amsterdam, New York.

Jane Hoey '14[81] was the most eminent and most widely known Trinity alumnae in social work. Born in Nebraska, she grew up and spent most of her life in New York City. She earned her Master's degree from Columbia University School of Social Work, which awarded her the first Lasker Award in 1955. She moved from one responsible position to another in city, state, and finally federal social agencies. Franklin D. Roosevelt, who had known her on the New York State Crime Commission called her to Washington as founder and Director of Public Assistance which developed into the Department of Health, Education and Welfare and as a member of the Social Security Board. She received many professional and academic awards but valued especially the Trinity honorary doctorate and being president of the Alumnae Association.

Dorothy Gallagher '15[82] was a volunteer in the clinic and social center in Kansas City, Missouri. She taught sociology at St. Teresa's College, Winona, Minnesota. She was a post-World War II social worker in France and did "a stint of teaching in the Mariana Islands." She received the Julie Billiart Medal from Trinity.

Catharine Harahan Norton '21 was an eminent social worker in Richmond, Virginia, and Washington, D.C. Alice Padgett '22 taught sociology at the Catholic University. Mabel Shannon '21 wrote for the *Alumnae Journal*[83] a description of meeting T.C. Medical Missionaries in India when she was attending the International Conference of Social

79. It is true that Dr. Eva J. Ross insisted on the distinction between sociology and social work, but she always had a course in social work available in the department.
80. Vol. 4, p. 151.
81. *Alumnae Journal,* February '36, p. 23; June '36, pp. 50–52; June '37, p. 83; Winter '50, p. 59; Summer '50, p. 167; June '41, p. 84; Autumn '55, p. 4; Autumn '66, p. 54; Autumn '68, pp. 31–32 (*obit.*); Winter '70, p. 73 (appreciation and portrait). Cf. also Box in T.C.A. Included in *Noted American Women,* 4th edition. Biography by Blanche Cole.
82. *Alumnae Journal,* Spring '72, p. 10.
83. *Alumnae Journal,* Winter '54, pp. 62–65.

Work in Madras. Marita Reddington '24 was supervisor of the Children's Bureau of the Catholic Charities, Washington, D.C. Florence Osbourne '25 was Supervisor, Child Placement Department, Catholic Charities, St. Paul, Minnesota. Margaret Wallace '25 was a social worker who held supervisory positions in Catholic Charities and other agencies in both Washington, D.C. and Baltimore, Maryland. This thin selection of social workers must end with two from 1930: Mary A. Dowling Day, Catholic Charities, Cleveland Heights, Ohio and Agnes Jerome, social worker in Fencastle, Virginia, letting Katherine Loftus Boucher '55[84] show that the line continues. It is interesting to note that 7% of those answering the 1972 questionnarie, cited earlier, were in professional social work.

Volunteers, Girl Scouting, Other Group Work

Related in many ways to social work is that of volunteers in civic, religious, and social service. Trinity alumnae through the years while listing their main occupation as family, business, or education, have devoted a part of their time to volunteer service. As in other parts of this chapter the mention of a few must represent the many.

The Alumnae Council of 1954 focussed on the topic of volunteer[85] work. Three articles by alumnae in 1955 put into perspective aspects of this alumnae activity: "The Volunteer in Civic Life," Catherine Cray Eichenlaub '21[86]; "Volunteer Work in Education," Mary Leonard '23[87]; "Volunteer Work Among the Aged," Eleanor Skahan Hickey '22.[88]

Mary Murray McArdle '08 was on the Board of the Troy (New York) Council of Social Agencies, and the Board of Directors of the Troy Community Chest[89] and Helen Coffey Sulzmann '33 was treasurer of the Troy Council of Social Agencies. Harvey Smith Kinsella was active in the Cana Conference Movement.[90] Elizabeth Sullivan Retter '20, active in New York City, is best known for the establishment and direction for many years of Casita Maria, a settlement house in the Puerto Rican area of the city.[91] Julia Thomas Conley '22 was active in Michigan for more than fifty years.[92] Hazel Ryan DeSmet '24 headed the March of Dimes campaign in the Chicago area, capping a long career of civic volunteer work. Marcella McHale Seymour '24 of Scranton,

84. *Alumnae Journal*, Autumn '74, p. 7.
85. *Alumnae Journal*, Autumn '54, pp. 15–19.
86. *Alumnae Journal*, Winter '55, pp. 77–80.
87. *Alumnae Journal*, Spring '55, pp. 130 ff.
88. *Ibid.*, pp. 17–19.
89. *Alumnae Journal*, Summer '42, p. 109.
90. *Alumnae Journal*, Autumn '45, pp. 8–9.
91. *Alumnae Directory*, 1950 and *Alumnae Journal*.
92. *Alumnae Journal*, Spring '82, p. 7.

Pennsylvania[93] was a social worker in Detroit who after her marriage made a career in social and civic volunteer work in the Detroit area, as well as life-long work for and devotion to Trinity College. Agnes Sullivan O'Brien '24 of Kentucky, a social worker-lawyer in New York City, was a charter member of the Catholic Interracial Council and an ardent crusader for interracial justice.[94] Isabelle Unrah '26 was Director of the Child Day Care Center in Mobile, Alabama, and worked for the Community Chest of that city. Patricia Caron Crowley '36 with her husband Patrick initiated and directed the Catholic Family Life Movement and was on the Papal Commission on Population and Fertility.[95] Margaret Owen Finucane '36 was on the Board of the Mercer County, Pennsylvania United Way for twenty years and was Board President of the area Mental Health/Mental Retardation organization.[96]

One should not omit the later "different" types of volunteer work such as Eurate Kasickas' '64 year of teaching in Kenya before starting her journalistic career, or that of Rosemond Kilmer '69 teaching with the Peace Corps in West Africa, or Anne Byrne '70 who worked as a Vista Volunteer in a deprived community in Florida. In the years since Vatican II the number of alumnae in parish work, in CCD, planning liturgies, or serving on parish councils has grown significantly.

Young alumnae of the early 1920's not only became interested in Girl Scout work but urged the students of that era to join in the work. An extra-curricular non-credit course for Catholic Girl Scout Leaders was established in 1921–1922. The Dean's Report, 1923, stated that the students had "shown considerable interest in the work and have profited by the opportunity of gaining experience in organization and leadership by taking charge of Scout Troups (sic) at St. Martin's School in the city and at Benedictine School in Brookland." That report also indicates that Mabel Shannon '21 was "in charge of the Girl Scouts." The interest in Scout leadership lasted into the 1930's but seems to have died out by 1940. Among alumnae in many parts of the Scout leadership on a high level has continued to the present. A list of a few such leaders follows. Like all such lists in this section it is indicative rather than complete.

Elizabeth Sullivan Ritter '20. National Board member for many years.

Mabel Shannon '21. Many years on the National Staff. Also National Board Member.

93. *Alumnae Journal, passim.*
94. *Alumnae Journal,* Autumn '44, pp. 7–11.
95. *Alumnae Journal,* Autumn '65 and other articles.
96. *Alumnae Journal,* Spring '82, p. 7.

Dorothy Flynn '22. Awarded Golden Eaglet Scout Award, 1922.

Mary Agatha Kelly '24. Westchester County Director, Archdiocese of New York director for Catholic Girl Scouting. Various executive positions in scouting in other geographical areas.

Dorothea Sullivan '26. Insular Director for Puerto Rico for two years in the 1930's, then in the National Office as organizer and field worker; in National Office, Personnel Division as advisor on Professional Work. After she left scouting for teaching on the university level she was on the National Board.

Mary Herrick Powers '29. Has also been on the National Board.

Elizabeth Ethol '40. Is a professional Scout worker. In 1962 she was Executive Director of the Sioux Trails Girl Scout Council. That year she was one of twelve women sent abroad to study and arrange for the international scouting exchange program. She is now in Florida and until recently actively involved in scout work.

As I have said, this is not a complete list. There are Trinity women in many areas of the United States in leadership positions in scouting.

Dorothea Sullivan '26, after her years in Scout work was appointed to the faculty of the National Catholic School of Social Service of the Catholic University of America where she introduced courses in Group Work and wrote at least three books on the subject. She was active as a lecturer and consultant to governmental and voluntary agencies, both in the United States and in numerous foreign countries. During leaves of absence from the University, she served as an adviser on youth services in occupied Japan (1948–49), in the United Nations Technical Assistance Administration in Italy (1956), in the U.S. Department of State's specialist program in Venezuela (1960), and as consultant to the Cuban Children's Program of the Archdiocese of Miami (1962–69).[97]

Writing, Music, Art

The line of published writers, among alumnae, dating from the first class, indicates the facility for self-expression which has been part of Trinity education into the ninth decade. From 1904, in addition to Sister Wilfred's (Elsie Parsons) voluminous periodical writing and her scholarly translations of the Latin Fathers of the Church, May Sheridan Fahnastock wrote the autobiographic *I Ran Away to Sea at Fifty* and Jessie Johnson Fretz published a novel at ninety! Helen Linehan Porter '07 published her poetry, Marie R. Madden '08 wrote many periodical articles and published at least two scholarly historical works. Claire Wallis

97. *Obit.* November, 1978. Edmund D. Pellegrino, President of C.U.A.

Callahan '11[98] was a journalist on a Philadelphia paper soon after graduation. In the 1930's she was Assistant Fiction Editor on the *Ladies Home Journal* and in the 1950's she was a columnist on the *Philadelphia Inquirer* and published books on antiques. Mary R. Walsh '12 of Auburndale, Massachusetts, was an author and literary agent. Frances Taylor Patterson '14 of Brooklyn, New York[99] and Carolyn Kerwin Keating '15[100] were the popular Trinity authors of the late 'teens and twenties. Frances wrote stories for young people. She was for years on the English faculty of Columbia University and gave the 1939 Commencement Address at Trinity. Her best known works are *White Wampum,* the biography of Kateri Tekakwitha, *The Long Shadow, the Story of St. John de Brebeuf, S. J.*

A list of alumnae writers who have published works in various specific fields will show continuity through the years. Margaret McBride '20 (M. Mary Genevieve, O.S.U.) wrote the *History of the Ursulines in Montana.* Mary Tinley Daly '24 was a journalist whose syndicated column, "At Our House," was read nationwide. Mary McEnery Stuhldreher '26 in *Many a Saturday Afternoon* described her travels with her football-coach-husband, Harry Stuhldreher, one of the famous "Four Horsemen of Notre Dame." Alba Zizzamia '31 translated Italian scholarly and literary works and Arline McCarthy '37 (Sister Mary Frances, S.N.D.) translated German theological and other scholarly works. Patricia McGerr '37 wrote popular mystery stories and at least one novel, *Marth, Martha,* the manuscript of which she gave to the Trinity College Library. Sr. Helen J. John '51 has contributed to anthologies and to periodicals in the field of philosophy, Frances Wimsatt Zureifel '52 used her two subjects of biology and art in her *Handbook of Biological Illustration* and other works. Virginia Pleus Bergen '58 is the author of *Psycho-Decorating, What Homes Reveal About People.* Anne Byrne McGivern '70 and co-authors have brought out a second edition of *Language Stories: Teaching Language to Developmentally Disabled Children.*

A selective list of alumnae writers and their experience, compiled by public relations in the 1960's carries on the line. Marilyn Moehlenbrock Angers '45, Associate Editor, *Coronet*; Editor, *American Beauty Magazine*; Catherine Dwyer Brady '59, Editorial Assistant, Sheed and Ward; Constance Burke '63 TV Continuity Writer WTIC, Hartford, Connecticut; Mary Dowling Daley '45, radio copywriter, freelance writer; Diane Divorky '61, Education Editor, *Boston Herald* (she is also a published poet); Patricia Fitzpatrick '56, Assistant Editor, *House and Garden, Glam-*

98. *Alumnae Journal,* Spring '71, p. 10.
99. *Alumnae Journal,* November '34, pp. 7–9; June '39, pp. 50–54; Winter '57, pp. 78–80, etc.
100. *Alumnae Journal,* Summer '75, p. 13.

our; Elizabeth McCoy Finn '61 Associate Editor, Haire Publications; Anne McNamara Griffith '48, editor of several magazines; Eileen Hanney '59, writer, *Glamour* magazine; Elizabeth Schmick Howard '61, freelance writer. Catherine Harrington Jensen '51, newspaper reporter and editor; Carolyn Conway Kermond, children's stories; Elizabeth Kraemer '58, *Time-Life International*, Germany; Margaret Acer Mumford '50, Society Editor, *Miami News*; Mary Juliet O'Donovan '61, Special Editorial Department, *Look*; Eleanor Montville Schaefer '49, promotion staff, *Life*, Assistant Promotion Manager, *Sports Illustrated*, Promotion Director, *Glamour*; Mary Patricia Simmons '43, Women's Editor, Washington *Evening Star.* Anne Marie Woodward '46 has wirtten on Housing for the Elderly.

Two members of the class of 1950, close friends at Trinity, have both become successful writers: Mary Ellen Lee Ballou[101] and Alice Mulcahy Fleming.[102] They have also been distinguished in local and national alumnae affairs. Marianne Novy '65 has published a scholarly work, *Loves' Argument: Gender Relations in Shakespeare.* Mary Frances Somers Heldhues '58 has written at least two books and several articles on the Chinese in Southeast Asia.[103]

Colette Hoppmann Dowling '58[104] published articles in national periodicals, film strip commentaries for the New York State Department of Education, and was a writer for the Bicentennial Commission before her best-seller *The Cinderella Complex* in 1981. Caryl Rivers Lupo '59[105] is a journalist, writer, and Boston University Associate Professor who has published several books including *Growing Up Catholic in the Fifties, Virgins,* and *For Better or for Worse.* Eurate Kazikas '64,[106] Associated Press Reporter in New York and Washington, freelance photographer in Vietnam and at Mt. Everest, a volunteer missionary in Kenya, winner of New York Business Women's Front Page Award might be called Trinity's journalist *par excellence.* Jeanne McManus '69 is Assistant Editor of the *Washington Post Magazine.*[107]

The New York Alumnae Chapter has formed a communications network[108] for alumnae in the area who are in publishing, advertising,

101. *Alumnae Journal*, Spring '64, pp. 176–177; Autumn '64, p. 28; Summer '73, p. 17; Winter '76, p. 10 and others.
102. *Alumnae Journal*, Autumn '64, pp. 8–10; Autumn '65, p. 26; Spring '72, p. 9f. (List of books); Fall '72, p. 23; Winter '73, p. 6–7; Winter '74, pp. 8–9, 12; Winter '76, p. 16; Autumn '82, p. 7; Winter '83, p. 9. *Readers Digest*, October 1982.
103. *Alumnae Journal*, Autumn '75, p. 12.
104. *Alumnae Journal*, Autumn '74, p. 7; Summer '81, p. 13, etc.
105. *Alumnae Journal*, Summer '72, p. 6; Summer '73, *Focus On*; Autumn '74, p. 4. Cf. "Grave New World," *Saturday Review*, April 8, 1972.
106. *Alumnae Journal*, Winter '74; Summer '76; et al. *Washington Post Magazine*, October 8, 1978.
107. *Alumnae Journal*, Spring '82, p. 6.
108. *Alumnae Journal*, Winter '82, p. 14.

broadcast or print, public relations or freelance writing. This seems to indicate a group of Trinity writers in the area. As this history goes to press we learn of the latest Trinity novel, *Maud Gone,* by Kathleen Rockwell '67.

For every Trinity author mentioned here there are others "out there" plying their art. The author feels not only guilt, but helplessness in the face of the exigencies of the history as a whole.

Music and Art

Music, both vocal and instrumental, has always held an honored place in Trinity life (cf. sections on the Music Department and on Student Life earlier in this history). Many alumnae have carried over the love of music into their later lives, but few have become professionals. Examples of those few will be mentioned here. Gertrude Borzi '30 was an opera and concert singer. Margaret Dooley's '24 beautiful contralto voice was heard in the New York opera and concert as well as on radio in the late 1920's and the 1930's.

Jean Eichelberger Ivey '44,[109] musician, composer, professor, concert pianist, and pioneer in electronic music, is the most widely acclaimed Trinity musician. Dorothy Sennett Werner '52 is also a concert pianist of note who has combined her art with a business career, managing a family, a horse farm, and a restaurant.

Art and Relatd Fields

Though art has been a major since 1940, the professional artists who have emerged in recent decades majored in various fields relating to their art as talent dictated. Some accomplishments of a few of them indicate their activity.

Ruth Garvey '55[110] was an artist at the coronation of Elizabeth II in England. Tessa Merdler Mahalek '62 and Ann Wigglesworth Barbiere '62 exhibited their paintings in the Trinity Art Gallery. Anne Burgess Askley '64[111] and Susan Davis '69[111] have both exhibited and have both painted covers for *The New Yorker.* Susan's work appears frequently in the *Washington Post Magazine.*

Elizabeth Ruzzin Lurie '62[111] is an artist in porcelain. Mal Stella '71[112] created the Crucifix in Assumption Church, Andover, Massachusetts.

109. *Baltimore Sun,* November 25, 1973. *Alumnae Journal,* Autumn '74, p. 4; Autumn '69; Spring '75, p. 9; Autumn '75, p. 12; Summer '76, p. 10. 60th Birthday Symposium and Concert at Trinity College, October 27 and 30, 1983.
110. *Alumnae Journal,* Spring '53, p. 104.
111. *Alumnae Journal,* Summer '82, p. 11.
112. *Alumnae Journal,* Spring '75, p. 24.

Gallery or museum curators of which there are several and actresses could be included here with art in a wide sense. Aileen Mize '25 had a brief career on the New York stage before a long career as Professor of Drama and Director of the College Theater at College of Notre Dame of Maryland, Baltimore. Virginia Burns Kelly '57 was an award winning student at the American Academy of Dramatic Art and a New York actress.[113]

An interesting development has appeared as older alumnae become artists in later life. Hester B. Curtis '20 held an exhibit of water colors at the 1981 Regional Alumnae Meeting. Julia Diggins Madden '25 after a career as mathematics teacher and author, studied painting at Catholic University. She has exhibited her paintings at Trinity. Florence Judge '23,[114] mathematician, Navy Lieutenant-Commander, teacher of mathematics for aeronautics, national officer in the Alumnae Association and briefly Director of Development learned weaving and established St. Jude's Weavers in Georgetown, D.C.

Politics and Government

Politics and government at all levels: local, state, national and international have interested students throughout Trinity College's history.[115] Before the end of the first month of classes in 1900 the students had visited Congress. Agitation for women's suffrage[116] mingled with their campaigning and mock presidential elections. Alumnae have held appointed government positions since the early decades of the century, but active participation in politics and elective office is a characteristic of later decades especially since World War II. From conversation or correspondence with alumnae as well as from informal reports in "Class Notes" the writer concludes that contemporary alumnae are active in local government in many parts of the country, but she cannot document that information. A few examples must serve. Mary Louise Gent Glosser '43 was Vice Mayor of Highland Beach, Florida. Joan Sperling '72 was Village Manager of "Martins Additions," Chevy Chase, Maryland.[117] Esther Herlihy Techlenbury '49 has been active in city government in Charleston, South Carolina, a long time member of the city council, and an officer of the South Carolina[118] Council of Democratic Women. Nora O'Neil Lambourne '36 is a member of the city council of Alexandria, Virginia[119] and wrote for the

113. *Alumnae Journal*, Spring '59, p. 159 *et al.*
114. *Alumnae Journal*, Winter '64, p. 132 (*obit.*); Spring '53, pp. 96–97.
115. Cf. Chapter. Student Activities.
116. Cf. for example: "Thoughts on Woman Suffrage," Kathleen MacHale '17. *Trinity College Record*, Feb. 1917, pp. 97–100.
117. *Alumnae Journal*, Spring '82, p. 11.
118. *Alumnae Journal*, Winter '82, p. 8.
119. *Alumnae Journal*, Spring '73, p. 17; Winter '76, p. 3.

Alumnae Journal of the "splendid confusion of local government." Patricia Queenan Sheehan '55 was mayor of New Brunswick, New Jersey and Commissioner, Community Affairs for the state of New Jersey.[120]

Names of a few government workers to represent the many help make my point. Mary B. Galvin '11 was Associate Chief, Internal Revenue Office, Providence, Rhode Island. Cecelia Kays '12 was a United States Foreign Service clerk, Laguna Beach, Florida. Mary Langton Byron '18 was an auditor, Veterans Administration, Philadelphia, Pennsylvania. Kathleen Harlow '25 worked for nearly forty years with the National Institutes of Health starting in the days when it was still the U.S. Public Health Service. Elizabeth Murphy '27 was Senior Microbiologist, Connecticut State Health Department and Marie K. Murphy '28, a biologist with the United States Public Health Service. Margaret Lawlor '35 worked with the United States Civil Service Commission. Marita Houlihan '37 was Program Officer, Exchange of Persons Division, U.S. Department of State in charge of exchange students and Fulbright Scholars.[121] Virginia Armstrong '50 was New York Regional Director, U.S. Civil Service Commission.[122] Patricia Sullivan Lindh '50,[123] after effective activity in Republican Party politics in Louisiana, was President Ford's Special Assistant for Women and later Deputy Assistant Secretary of State for Educational and Cultural Affairs. Nancy Lammerding '54[124] was social secretary to Mrs. Ford after having been in the Protocol Office, State Department, and the White House Press Office. Isabel Drane Wolf '55[125] was Director of the Office of Consumer Advice, U.S. Department of Agriculture.

Representing the workers "on the Hill," where Trinity has been in force in recent decades, we name Faye Padgett '61[126] Research Assistant to Representative Frank Thompson, Jr., Kathleen Hagan '69, Project Assistant to Senator Edward Brooke, Francie Glennon '71,[126] Staff Member for Congressman Peter Peyser.

Of Trinity alumnae in the League of Women Voters, we mention only Joan Humphreys Czarnechi '53, President of the D.C. League of Women Voters 1973–75[127] and Maureen Armstrong Allegaert '54, Vice President of the Scarsdale, New York, League of Women Voters.

120. *Alumnae Journal*, Spring '67, p. 60; Spring '68, p. 124 (Profile); pp. 126–127; Summer '71, p. 19; Autumn '81, p. 15.
121. *Alumnae Journal*, Autumn '64, p. 24.
122. *Alumnae Journal*, Spring '75, p. 9.
123. *Alumnae Journal*, Summer '74, p. 11; Summer '75, p. 11; Autumn '75, p. 12; Spring '76, pp. 9, 12–13; Winter '76.
124. *Alumnae Journal*, Autumn '74, p. 16.
125. *Alumnae Journal*, Spring '82, p. 7.
126. *Alumnae Journal*, Autumn '68, pp. 9–12.
127. *Alumnae Journal*, Winter '76, p. 6.

Enduring Symbol of Continuity: the Red Roof.

Barbara Bailey Kennelly '58,[128] Trinity's first Congresswoman began her career, soon after graduation in her home state of Connecticut. She was councilwoman on the Hartford City Council, Secretary of State for Connecticut, and Representative for the First District in the U.S. Congress. She gave the nominating speech for Geraldine Ferraro at the Democratic National Convention in 1984.

Fully aware of the sophisticated overtones attached by scholars to the term renaissance, we dare to sum up this section of the history

128. *Alumnae Journal*, Spring '76, p. 2; Winter '82, cover and pp. 204, p. 14; Winter '84, p. 17.

Enduring Symbol of Continuity: the Marble Corridor.

with the description of Trinity College alumnae used by Patricia McGuire '74:

> We are artists and lawyers, authors and mothers. We manage millions of dollars of other people's money, and we keep track of the Girl Scout Cookie receipts. We are doctors, nurses, and magic healers of kids of all ages. We run marathons and computers. We stump for our candidates; we are candidates! We are poets in the rhythm of life. We are Renaissance Women. We are Trinity Alumnae.

The author concludes this final chapter by applying to all the alumnae her often repeated words addressed to senior classes. "Such as you are, you are the best we have"—and Trinity College is proud of you!

Bibliography

Advisory Board Minutes and Proceedings, 1901–1926
Large scrapbook volume with typed and mimeographed material. In Trinity College Archives.

Alumnae Journal of Trinity College, 1927–1977. Vols. I-L.

Annals, Trinity College Community of Sisters of Notre Dame. Cf. *Journal.*

Annals of Notre Dame, Mt. Pleasant, Liverpool, England, 1893–1927.

Auxiliary Board of Regents of Trinity College. ("Ladies' Board"). Minutes 1898–1978. Volume 1898–1903 is in two versions: the original and what seems to be a "fair copy."

American Colleges and Universities. American Council on Education, Washington, D.C., 10th edition, 1968.

Archives of Trinity College, Washington, D.C.

Baltimore Archdiocesan Archives. Cardinal Gibbons papers, 1897.

Beach, Sister Francis Mary, S.N.D. *A History of the Trinity College Library,* unpublished M.A. dissertation, Catholic University of America, 1951.

Bernard, Jessie. *Academic Women,* Pennsylvania State University Press, 1964.

Board of Trustees of Trinity College Minutes 1897 to present.

Bowler, Sister Mary Mariella, O.S.F. *A History of Catholic Colleges for Women in the United States of America,* Washington, D.C., Catholic University Press, 1933.

Butler, Sister Mary Patricia. *An Historical Sketch of Trinity College,* 1897–1925. Privately printed.

Butler, Sister Mary Patricia (Sr. M. P.). "Trinity College," *Catholic Historical Review,* N.S., Vol. 5 (January, 1926), pp. 660–674.

Brownlee, Sister M. Francesca. *Endowment and Catholic Women's Colleges,* Catholic University Press, 1932.

Catholic University Bulletin. Catholic University Press.

Catholic World, The, especially Vols. LXIV–LXIX, 1896–1899.

Chafe, William H. *The American Woman.* Her Changing Social, Economic and Political Roles, 1920–1970, New York (Oxford University Press), 1972.

Clapp, Margaret. "Realistic Education for Women," *Journal of AAUW,* Summer, 1950.

Clebsch, William A. *From Sacred to Profane.* The Role of Religion in American History, New York (Oxford University Press), 1972.

Cole, Arthur C. *A Hundred Years of Mount Holyoke College,* The Evolution of an Educational Ideal, New Haven (Yale University Press), 1946.

Conaty, Thomas J. "The Work of Catholic Women in Education." Lecture, Boston, April 30, 1899. Copy in Trinity College Archives.

Conaty, Thomas J. Sermon at dedication of Trinity College, Washington, D.C. *U.S. Commissioner of Education's Report for 1899–1900.* Washington, D.C. Government Printing Office, 1901 (Whole no. 276), pp. 1395–1402.

Conaty, Thomas James. Cf. Hogan, Peter Edward, "Rectorship of Thomas J. Conaty."

Dean's Notebooks of activities of Trinity College.
Begins October 10, 1900. T.C.A.

DeVane, William Clyde. *Higher Education in Twentieth Century America,* Cambridge, Mass. (Harvard University Press), 1965.

Dewey, David Rich, Ph.D. *National Problems, 1885–1897,* Vol. 24 of *The American Nation, a History,* New York and London, 1907.

Dictionary of American Biography.

Doyle, Sister Margaret Marie. *The Curriculum of the Catholic Woman's College,* Notre Dame University, 1932.

Dressel, Paul L. *The Undergraduate Curriculum in Higher Education.* Center for Applied Research in Education, Inc., Washington, D.C., 1963.

Educational Ideals of Blessed Julie Billiart, by a member of her congregation. Translation from the French. London (Longmans Green and Co.), 1922.

Ellis, John Treacy. *The Formative Years of the Catholic University of America.* Washington (Catholic University Press), 1946.

Ellis, John Treacy. *The Life of James Cardinal Gibbons,* Archbishop of Baltimore, 1834–1921, Milwaukee (Bruce Publishing Co.), 1952, 2 vols.

Ellis, John Treacy. "A Guide to the Baltimore Cathedral Archives." *Catholic Historical Review,* Vol. XXXII, No. 3 (Oct. 1946), pp. 341-360.

Faculty Meetings 1914–1933. 2 bound notebooks labeled "Teachers' Meetings." T.C.A.

Foundation of Trinity College by Sister Mary Euphrasia Taylor. Three handwritten notebooks. T.C.A.

Fuess, Claude M. *The College Board, Its First Fifty Years,* New York (Columbia University Press), 1950.

Green, Constance McLaughlin. *Washington Capitol City, 1879–1950.* Princeton University Press, 1963.

Greene, Theodore P., ed. *American Imperialism in 1898,* Problems in American Civilization, Boston (D. C. Heath and Company), 1955.

Handlin, Oscar. "Immigration in American Life" in *Immigration in American History,* Henry Steele Commager, ed., University of Minnesota Press, 1961.

Harpers New Monthly Magazine, especially 1896–1897.

Hassinger, Robert, ed. *The Shape of Catholic Higher Education,* foreword by David Riesman, University of Chicago Press, 1967.

Hogan, Peter E., S.S.J. *The Catholic University of America 1896–1903.* The Rectorship of Thomas J. Conaty. Washington, D.C. (Catholic University Press), 1949.

Hug, Elsie A. *Seventy-five Years of Education: The Role of the School of Education, New York University, 1890–1965.* New York University Press, 1965.

Journal (*Annals*) of the Community of Sisters of Notre Dame at Trinity College, November 1900–December 1902. T.C.A. (Named *Annals* in references to distinguish from Sr. M. Euphrasia's Journal.)

Journal of Sr. Mary Euphrasia. Two small manuscript notebooks with jotted items to be "written up in *Foundations.*" T.C.A.

Julia, Sister (McGroarty), February 13, 1829–November 12, 1901. *Dictionary of American Biography*, Vol. X, pp. 244–245.

Julia, Sister (Susan McGroarty) by Sister Helen Louise, Benziger Brothers, 1928.

Latané, John Holladay, Ph.D. *America as a World Power, 1897–1907.* Vol. 25 of *American Nation: A History*, New York and London, 1907.

Lee, James Michael, ed. *Catholic Education in the Western World*, Notre Dame University Press, 1967.

Lewis, Nancy. "College Women and Their Proper Spheres," *American Association of University Women Journal*, May, 1954.

McAvoy, Thomas, C.S.C. *The Great Crisis in American Catholic History, 1895–1900*, Chicago (Regnery), 1957.

McNamee, Mary Dominica, S.N.D.deN. *Light in the Valley.* Berkeley, California, 1967.

Meng, John J., "Cahenslyism: The Second Chapter, 1891–1910." *Catholic Historical Review*, October, 1946, pp. 302–340.

Miller, Sister Helen Cecilia, S.N.D. *Myles Poore O'Connor*: Pioneer California Philanthropist, 1823–1909. Unpublished University of San Francisco Thesis, 1957. Copy in Trinity College Library.

Mitchell, Broadus. *Depression Decade, 1929–1941.* Vol. IX of *The Economic History of the United States*, New York, Toronto (Rinehart & Co.), 1947.

Morgan, H. Wayne. *William McKinley and His America.* Syracuse University Press, 1963.

New York Times. January to March, 1897. March to September, 1898.

Newcomer, Mabel. *A Century of Higher Education for American Women.* New York (Harper & Bros.), 1959.

O'Neill, Sister Mary Bernice, C.S.J., Ph.D. *An Evaluation of the Curricula of a Selected Group of Catholic Women's Colleges.* St. Louis University, 1937.

———————————— later edition. Maryhurst Press, St. Louis, Mo., 1942.

Power, Edward J. *A History of Catholic Higher Education in the United States.* Milwaukee (Bruce Publishing Company), 1958.

Reapers in the Fields of Notre Dame. Notre Dame Press, Cincinnati, Ohio. 1896–1898. In Trinity College Community Library.

Record of Teachers' Meetings at Trinity College. Washington, D.C., October 27, 1900–June 25, 1911. Ms. notebook. T.C.A.

Renewal of Catholic Higher Education, The by Charles E. Ford and Edgar L. Roy, Jr. Washington, D.C. (N.C.E.A.), 1968.

Rhodes, James Ford. *The McKinley and Roosevelt Administrations, 1897–1909.* New York, 1922. (Chap. II, pp. 21–22, "Secretary Sherman")

Rudolph, Frederick. *The American College and University.* New York (Alfred A. Knopf), 1962.

Sanford, Nevitt, ed. *The American College.* New York (Wiley & Sons), 1962.

Schlesinger, Arthur Meier. *The Rise of the City, 1878–1898.* Vol. I of *A History of American Life.* New York, 1933.

Shahan, Thomas J. "The Educational Value of the Fine Arts" in *The House of God and Other Addresses and Studies.* New York (Cathedral Library Association), 1905.

Shields, Thomas Edward. *The Education of Our Girls.* Benziger Bros., 1907, Chapter XI, "The Woman's College of the Future," pp. 251–275.

Spalding, John Lancaster, D.D. *Woman and Higher Education.* Privately printed pamphlet. Lecture January 16, 1899 at Columbian University, Washington, D.C. Copy in T.C.A. Later included in *Opportunity and Other Addresses,* 1900.

Statistical Abstract of the United States. 91st Annual Edition, U.S. Dept. of Commerce. Government Printing Office, 1970. Also other editions, i.e. 1923, 1936, 1973.

Sullivan, Mark. *Our Times,* The United States, 1900–1925. Vol. I "The Turn of the Century." New York (Scribner), 1928.

Trinilogue, The. 1911 to date. Yearbook published each year since 1911 by the senior class of Trinity College.

Trinity College: History of Foundation and Development. Typescript, pp. 13. April, 1906. T.C.A.

Trinity College Catalogue, 1899–1982.

Trinity College Journal, 1897–1900. Two small notebooks by Sister Mary Euphrasia and kept separate from accounts of North Capitol Street Community.

Trinity College Newsletter, 1956–1975.

Trinity College Record, The. 1907–1967. Quarterly magazine of students, published under the auspices of the English Department.

Tuchman, Barbara W. *The Proud Tower.* London (Hamish Hamilton), 1966.

Williams, Robert L. *The Administration of Academic Affairs in Higher Education.* Ann Arbor (Univ. of Michigan Press), 1965.

Woody, Thomas. *History of Women's Education in the United States.* New York (Science Press), 1929.

APPENDIX I

Mrs. Talty's Account of the Purchase of Land and Other Memorabilia

ONE MORNING in May or June 189- a group of Alumnae of the Sisters of Notre Dame were talking outside St. Aloysius' Church. Hearing that there was a new Superior at the Convent they hastened to welcome her. It was Sister Mary Euphrasia, the guiding star of the then not bought Trinity College. In telling her of our beautiful city reference was made to the city limits. After some little time, Sister Mary Euphrasia sent for the writer and questioned her about the city suburbs etc. She had in mind opening an academy such as Notre Dame always has in every big city.

The school at Kay St., while interchanging teachers with their most exclusive academies would always be known as a parochial school. The education given there followed the same scholarly schedule of Notre Dame's best academies but the *name* was lacking.

A very warm and continuing friendship was formed between Sister and Mr. and Mrs. Talty. Mrs. Talty suggested that Dr. Garrigan, then Rector [sic] of the Catholic University, be consulted, so a meeting was arranged. It was the birth of Trinity College—for Dr. Garrigan told Sister Mary Euphrasia that he had been obliged to refuse twenty women who had applied for admission to Catholic University. Finally after many "diplomatic conversations" Trinity was evolved. Sister Mary Euphrasia had a giant's task to convince[1] her order that higher education was demanded by young women who would get it elsewhere, if the Church, through her teaching orders, did not supply it. Many anxious hours were shared by us. The need was all so new and yet so terribly real. Finally consent was secured. Dr. Garrigan and others did all in their power to aid the project.

1. Letters of Sr. Julia and the *Foundations* by Sr. M. Euphrasia herself do not substantiate the idea that it was hard to convince "the order." Sr. Columba. Practical details: money, etc. caused the hesitations.

Mr. Talty, a business man of experience, was enlisted in the plans. He advised the Sisters to keep their plan secret, till a plot of ground was secured. We drove all over Washington and into every estate near the Catholic University. It was finally purchased by elimination. (We made the investigation presumably for ourselves.)

1. The Robinson estate now the Vineyard was too costly—$250,000. It was a site that Sister Superior Julia wanted but it was beyond their purse.

2. The Kate Chase Sprague estate—now St. Vincent's Home and School.[2] Mr. Geo. N. Beall and the writer called on the owner who interviewed us in the yard. He was almost surly. He said he would consult his real estate man. "Who is it?" "Redford Walker." "Oh! That is all right as he is a friend of my husband's." Mr. Beall had $500.00 to deposit. But Sister Julia and the other Superior had set their heart on this site. (Look at it now, shut in by freight sidings, an eye sore.) (Mr. Talty and Sister Mary Euphrasia wanted the Michigan Avenue property.) Before the negotiations for the Kate Chase Sprague site were even begun, the owner died and intestate. His grand daughter, being only 16, the estate was thrown into the orphans' court.

3. Glenwood Cemetery Property. (Now Trinity.) Sister Superior Julia positively refused to look at it. Sister Mary Euphrasia had sprinkled it with holy water one day while Mr. Geo. Beall and I walked around the place. There is a ravine on it and she would have none of it. One day Sister Mary Euphrasia tried to get her to look at it and we planned a little trick. Sister Mary Euphrasia told me to drive up there and get out and let down the bars and drive them in. She thought that if they saw this property they would realize its value and nearness to the Catholic University.

We arrived—I obediently tried to carry out our plan, but those who know Sister Julia know that she could not be fooled. She *demanded* to know *what* I was doing. I tried to beg her to go in. "No, I'll not buy a piece of ground with a ravine on it." It seems that when the Summit in Cincinnati was bought there was a slope which when they started to build necessitated a sub-basement and cost three thousand dollars to fill in. So she would not be caught again. (When Trinity was finished—on the map—, I roguishly asked her one day "What about the ravine?" "Oh! It's St. Julia's glen. It's ours—that makes a difference.")

Mr. Talty carried on all the negotiations as if he was buying for himself through Mr. Anton Heitmuller, a Director of the Cemetery Board. They finally agreed to sell twenty acres. We tried to get the Sisters to buy more land but they were afraid. The venture was assuming large financial burdens. They afterwards paid as much for seven acres as they did for the twenty.

2. *Note* by Sr. Columba: *Fd. S.E.* mention also a No. 4 the Stewart estate.

Mr. Talty was in a unique position to aid the Sisters. He was a contractor and builder and known and respected by all the District Bldg. He had a way of getting what he wanted. He had his men and bosses dig the foundation. Sister Mary paid them off weekly. He helped in every way and tried to reduce the expense and never took a cent commission, although he put his best men and bosses there and let his own work rest. Besides he maneuvered and planned till he got sewers, gas, and electricity on the premises. These were all ready when they were needed. One of his reasons for advocating this site, in preference to the Kate Chase Sprague was that through his friend, W. Kelly Schoepf, Manager of the Washington Railway, he knew that they planned to carry the Brookland traffic through Bloomingdale by way of Michigan Avenue. So even the car line was ready when Trinity opened her doors. Michigan Avenue was formerly just a rough country road encircling the Soldiers' Home on the South.

The property was returned to the Sisters of Notre Dame on June 10, 1897, Feast of St. Margaret. On this day we deeded the property to the Sisters. Sister Mary Euphrasia remembered that date till her dying day. She used to send a remembrance of her gratitude while she remained Superior at Kay Street. The first was a slender little bud vase, sterling silver and engraved "St. Margaret's Day, June 10, 1897." Mr. Talty did not like anyone to repay a kindness (and he had been more than kind) so he had me tell Sister not to do that again. Next year she had Sister Rosalie make us a dish of gelatin; John the Janitor, brought it out very pompously. When the Superiors went to Namur in 1901 she asked Maurice to let me go. I fancied she thought I might be of some help if Trinity was discussed but the Mother General did not allude to it in my presence but she gave me a bottle of Evans Pale Ale as I did not look very strong. As Roberta Potts and I had not had a chance to drink it we put it in our suit case. We were afraid when the gendarme searched our baggage at the frontier. Sister Georgiana, Sister Agnes of the Cross and Sister Joseph completed the party.

After the property was acquired the Sisters at Kay Street were sent out there often by Mr. Talty in those big herdics. He also sent ice cream and cake. Helen Talty and I had our lunch, fixed by Sister Rosalie, the cook, in a little basket, with two cups tied on to the handle. Their meal, even in the woods, was sacrosanct. These outings took place often. When the first sod was turned by Dr. Garrigan, Sister Mary Euphrasia invited Mr. Talty and me and the architects. A few colored laborers graced the scene. The Sisters did not want it in the newspapers but one of the Catholic University professors mentioned it to a newspaper woman. The breaking of ground for a Catholic Women's college was *news* and although I almost got down on my knees to the editor, in it went.

While the Sisters were busy with the cleaning etc., of the College, I brought them their dinner in a big basket from Kay Street. One day I got out of the surrey and helped the Sisters in with the basket. When I came back my mare, Fanny, had died. It was a hot day and I had driven her hard so as not to be late. Maurice was so good; all he said was "Don't worry. She'd have died some time."

As soon as possible Sister Mary Euphrasia started a group of ladies as a Board. They wanted to run the Institute as well as the College so a more elastic Auxiliary was formed which continues today to do great work for Trinity.

Sister Mary Euphrasia was not appointed Superior of the new College. If it was a cross to her, she never criticised the new order of things. She was a real religious. We were very intimate friends. Her loyalty was a fruit of her love of her vocation. On the day of dedication she was on the sidelines, looking on, and so were we—Mr. Talty and I. I can't remember ever getting an invitation to the ceremony, but Sister Mary Euphrasia sent us word to come. Sister Mary Euphrasia was sent West but she never forgot her advisors and helpers; June 10 was always a rallying point in our lives. Mr. Talty died June 10, 1903.[3] I received a long letter from her from California on that memorable day.

Under new management new friends helped to form the destiny of Trinity. I was never asked to join the Board. One day while paying a little visit to Trinity I was asked why I did not come to the meetings so (Innocence Abroad!) I determined I'd put my pride in my pocket and go. So I went—I was a surprise member; my name had not been presented. I was really *persona non grata*. Well, they managed it well and put me through, but it was really funny. My skin is thick so I continued to attend until other imperative duties prevented me.

Our Alumnae planned a big affair to spread the glad tidings of Trinity. We had Alumnae in every parish. We had a big meeting. I had a paper on Notre Dame and Trinity. We planned to have a branch in each parish and to keep alive the interest in Trinity. We were told that the Rector of Gonzaga (Fr. Gillespie) did not want us to form a center as we (St. Aloysius) had too many pressing needs. Sister Mary Euphrasia did not want to fight it. So that organization meeting failed of its purpose. She told me that as I was the leader in it, it would be better if I did not become a member of the original Board. There was no opposition to Trinity but a fear by the Reverend Rector that we would divert the funds away from St. Aloysius.

3. When Mr. Talty planned and worked with Sister Mary to save and get the excavations and foundation in as cheap and good as possible, I advised Maurice to do the work and charge as he would any other work and when finished to present a check of $5000.00 to Trinity as a donation but he did not like his light to shine before men and chose to render his services in a hidden manner. Maurice is one of the Founders of Trinity College but unknown.

Washington, D.C., April 18, 1898

Dear Madam:

You have been suggested as one who would naturally be interested in a project for the higher education of women. The Sisters of Notre Dame, in their zeal for Christian truth and the good of modern society, have undertaken to establish a college for women, the standard of which shall be in no way below that of Smith, Vassar, Wellesley, or Bryn Mawr. They have bought a beautiful site for the buildings in an exceptionally desirable locality of the National Capital, which is fast becoming the educational as it is the political centre of the nation, and where proximity to great libraries, universities and the scientific departments of the government lend peculiar advantages. We, the undersigned, feel that we owe it to our sex as well as to religion, to give our active co-operation in the work of erecting and equipping the first hall or building of a group to be known to future generations as Trinity College. The Sisters have proved themselves eminently fitted for educational work by their past success, but are debarred by their habit from going about in public to solicit patronage and assistance, and we women in the National Capital concerned, as many of us are, in the interests of far-away States and sections, have formed a plan of work in which we hope to enlist your practical interest, and we feel sure that much can be accomplished by good organization and Christian unity.

We enclose your copy of a pamphlet stating the plan and purpose of the College, and also a copy of Articles IV and V of our Constitution.

Should you be willing to join us in this work, which will be a monument for all time for those who take part in its inception, we shall be heartily glad to welcome you as one of us and communicate with you more in detail.

OLIVE RISLEY SEWARD, President

Marie Patterson, Vice President
Sara Carr Upton, Recording Sec'y

REGENTS

Mrs. R. P. Bland, Missouri
Mrs. Thom. H. Carter, Montanta
Mrs. Thos. H. Carter, Utah
Miss Daingerfield, Virginia
Mrs. Maurice Francis Egan, Pa.
Miss Ella Lorraine Dorsey, Md.
Miss Emily Mason, Virginia
Miss Marie Patterson, Missouri
Miss Roach, North Dakota
Mrs. Geo. Crogan Reid, D.C.
Mrs. W. C. Robinson, Connecticut
Miss Mollie Eliot Seawell, Va.
Miss Olive Risley Seward, N.Y.
Miss Sara Carr Upton, Maine
Mrs. Zebulon B. Vance
Miss Elizabeth Sherman, Ohio
Miss Charlotte Lincoln (pro-tem.), Ohio

Note: Pamphlets and other printed matter concerning the College, may be had on application to Sister Mary Euphrasia, Convent of Notre Dame, North Capitol and K Streets, Washington, D.C.

APPENDIX II

The Catholic World

(Volume 65) September 1897, pp. 861–2

As reports regarding the establishment in Washington of a Catholic college for women have been prematurely circulated, it was deemed advisable by those immediately concerned to publish an authoritative statement. Since the establishment of the Catholic University of America at Washington, inquiries have been made as to what the Catholic Church is prepared to do for the higher education of women. It has been decided to establish in Washington a women's college of the same grade as Vassar, thus giving young women an opportunity for the highest collegiate instruction. The institution is to be known as Trinity College, and will be under the direction and control of the Sisters of Notre Dame, whose mother-house is in Namur, Belgium. This congregation of religious women is devoted exclusively to teaching; their colleges in Belgium, England, Scotland, and their academies and parish schools in the United States, have won for them high distinction in educational work. Trinity College will offer to its students all the advantages of the best American colleges, and will have, in addition, those benefits that come from education given under the direction of experienced religious teachers.

The Sisters of Notre Dame have purchased twenty acres of land near the gateway of the Catholic University, at the junction of Michigan and Lincoln Avenues, and plans will be at once prepared for a suitable college building. The establishment of this college in the City of Washington offers opportunities to the students which can be found in no other city of our country; the libraries and museums, as well as many of the educational institutes and the scientific collections, offer advantages that cannot be equalled elsewhere in America, while its close proximity to the Catholic University will give to the students the rare privilege of following regularly the public lecture courses, or private courses by specialists having the endorsement of the university.

It will offer three courses of study, each extending through four years—the classical course, leading to the degree of bachelor of arts; the scientific course, leading to the degree of bachelor of science, and the course of letters, leading to the degree of bachelor of letters, and the course, leading to the degree of Ph.D.

This college idea has been under consideration for some time, and has met with the cordial approbation of his Eminence the Cardinal-Archbishop of Baltimore and the chancellor of the university, who welcomes its establishment in his diocese and near the university as a providential step in the higher education of Catholic women. It is to be a post-graduate school, and no preparatory department is to be connected with it. It is intended to supplement the good work of the academies and high-schools throughout our land, and the candidates for admission must have certificates of graduation from such school, or pass an examination before entering equivalent to such graduation.

Right Rev. Monsignor Conaty, Rector of the Catholic University, when questioned about this matter, stated that everything that could be done consistent with the interests of the university would be freely rendered for the encouragement of those who have so generously undertaken this great enterprise. He expressed himself as confident of the ability of the Sisters of Notre Dame to establish a first-class college, as he has had experience with them as teachers during the whole period of his ministry, and could certify to the thoroughness of their instruction and to the evident determination of being satisfied with nothing less than the best in all the departments of education which came within their scope. He feels confident that great success awaits the enterprise of the sisters, and is pleased to see their college seeking the friendship of the university, for in so doing they desire to be in close touch with the bishops of the church, under whose direction the university is placed. At least one answer is given to our Catholic women with regard to higher education; for the university frequently receives letters from all parts of the United States making inquiries concerning it.

For further particulars application should be made to Sister Julia of Notre Dame, K and North Capitol Streets, Washington, D.C.

APPENDIX III

Sister Mary Euphrasia Account June 1897–January 1901 (Handwritten)

STATEMENT

Sister Mary Euphrasia, Treasurer,

In Account with Trinity College, from June-1897-to-January-1901.

From June-1897-to-January-1899.		
Received by Gifts to Sister Superior Julia.	5,300	
" " Other Donations.	27,684.71	
" from Miss Eliz. Hill for Statue of B.V.	100	
" by Loan on House of Washington.	10,000	43,084.71
From January-1899-to-January-1900.		
Received from Sisters of Notre Dame.	10,989.94	
" " Miss Annie Leary.	15,000	
" " Various Persons.	225.12	
" by sale of Bishop Spalding's Lecture.	239.50	
" Interests on Deposits.	467.53	
" by Loan from Wash. Loan & Trust Co.	50,000	76,922.09
From January-1900-to-January-1901.		
Received from Convents of Notre Dame.	12,033.87	
" by Money of the Institute.	3,665.19	
" " Founders Fees.	1,750	
" from Associate Boards.	6,707	
" " Various Objects.	305.12	
" by Loans.	141,400	165,861.18

Sister Superior Julia's Private Account.
From February-1900-to-January-1901.

Received by Money of the Institute.	4,833.50	
" from Sisters and Friends.	2,160.82	6,994.32
Total Amount Received		292,862.30

STATEMENT

Expenditures.—From June-1897-to-January-1899.		
Paid for Michigan Avenue Property.	25,000	
" " Interest on Loan.	1,250	
" " Printing.	285.05	
" " Surveyors.	122	
" " Engraving on Certificates.	184	
" " Journeys.	20	
" " Postage.	38	
" " Stationery.	6.60	
" " News Directory.	5	
" " Furniture.	21	
" " Lawyers Fees.	52.25	
Check returned to Sister Superior Julia.	150	27,133.90

Expenditures.—From January-1899-to-January-1900.		
Paid for Michigan Avenue Property.	55,000	
" " Interest on Loan.	923.33	
" " Commission on Loan.	500	
" " Refunding of Loan to National Safe Deposit and Trust Company of D.C.	10,000	
Paid for Stone for the Building.	18,000	
" " Plans of Buildings.	1,200	
" " Certificates of Title.	130.10	
" " Journeys.	386.71	
" " Lawyers Fees.	152.00	
" " Postage, $30.30—Internal Revenue, 123.01	153.31	
Paid for Engraved Cut of Building.	20.20	
" " Advertizing in "Bulletin."	50.00	
" " Printing, $42.50—Stationery, 5.13	47.63	
" " Masses, $6.00—Telegrams, 6.65	12.65	
" " Sewing Machine.	35.00	86,610.93
Amount Forwarded.		113,744.83

STATEMENT

Expenditures. From January-1900-to-January-1901		
Amount brought forward.	113,744.83	
Expenses for the Building.	165,514.53	
" " the "Day of Dedication."	957.70	
" " Various Objects.	969.92	281,186.98

Sister Superior Julia's Private Account.		
Expenditures, From February-1900-to-January-1901.		
Paid for Furniture and Bedding.	3,295.21	
" " Steam.	1,000	
" " Draft sent to Sisters when in England.	100	
" " Books.	248.88	
" " Sheeting.	234.14	
" " Feathers.	106.75	
" " China—Table Ware.	132.24	
" " China—Students Chamber Sets.	102.50	
" " Shades.	210	
" " Mattresses.	84.95	
" " Ticking.	63.70	
" " Clothing.	54.31	
" " Brokerage, Freight & Custom House Duties.	517.81	
Gave Sister Lidwine for Trinity.	200	
Paid for Utensils.	93.86	
" " Journeys.	119.94	
" " Printing.	135.90	
" " Flag Pole.	50	
" " Candlesticks $36.00 Stationery $22.67	58.67	
" " Postage $4.00 Aurist $19.00	23.00	
" " Groceries $2.00 Washing $2.00	4.00	
" " Fruit.	14.90	
Total amount expended from June-1897–		288,037.74

APPENDIX IV

Miss Dorsey's Expense Account (Recapitulation)

(Handwritten)

Trinity College,
Washington, D.C.

By balance of Harp recital money	185.00
By return on mileage books	20.00
	205.00

In Treasury of
Aux. Board Fund

Recapitulation

Made good by Order: for salary forfeited by "excess leave"

30 days	100.00	Endowments	
5½ days	18.26	promised on	
	$118.26	said journey	
Expenses	231.73		
	349.99	$167,000.00	
		25,000	excess K of C

Rec'd. from Sr. Euphrasia, Tres. for	
Western journey June 15 to Aug. 1	$150.00
Aug. 13th–16th for *Plattsburgh & ret.*	33.17
For *Chicago* Oct. 11–16	36.56
and return	219.73
To excess of expenditure	
on Western journey	12.00
	231.73
	205.00
	26.73

Furnished by Mrs. Thos. H. Carter Prest. of Board, passes on North Pacific vc, from Chicago to Butte and return to St. Paul.

E.L.D. By checks 40: 14.25: 20.00 = 74.25

Yellowstone 6½ days		
Coupon-book for journey thro	22.00	
Extra day and a half	5.00	
Camp	2.00	
1st day	4.00 (?)	33.00
(Mrgt)		
Candy, Book - 75: Baths 1.00. Fees	3.30	
Flowers (Cleveland)	3.43	6.73
Stamps 45: Boys game 75:	1.20	
	1.30	
Boys papers 87: Med. 1.25 + 5:	.87	3.37
Papers 10: Tels. & Nashota 1.63	1.73	
Plates & pens 35: Ch. 75: Tickets 50:	1.60	
Toys 55: books 3.55: Postage 84	4.94	8.27
(Ellen)		
Hdkchfs. 50: Candy 80: Special 10	1.40	
Photos 1.00: Book 1.00: Boys 62	2.62	4.02
(Child)		
Candy 10: Change on hand		9.25
		63.64
		159.13
		222.77
		162.08
		63.64
		225.72

		Baggage	Meals	Attendance	Cars
21,000 mile ticket	60.00	W. 50	1.25	25	5
By rebate	10.00	20	65	25	30
	50.00	15	05	25	10
Sleeper to Cinn.	3.00	10	10	25	5
" " Chic.	2.00	25	25	1.50	10
Ticket Butte " Annabar*	5.15	20	10	20	15
Sleeper " "	2.00	25	5.00	25	10
" " St. Paul	13.00	25	50	25	10

Ticket & " " Chicago	14.25	Cl.	50	10	25	25
Boat & Trunk " Milwaukee	1.50		10	55	20	5
Boat train & Chair to Detroit	7.75	Ch.	50	2.35	10	50
	.25		10	80	25	10
Bay City & return	5.75		10	10	10	1.85
Chair both ways	.50		10	10	25	
Transfer to boat	.25		10	75	25	
Ticket & anteroom to Cleveland	3.75		25	1.00	25	
Sleeper to Washington	4.00		15	1.00	75	
	113.15		25	1.00	50	
*By rebate Annabar	.25		20	40	25	
	112.90	Ch.	50	1.00	25	
			10	75	25	
			10	10	15	
			10	10	25	
			10	95	25	
			10	50	25	
			10	65	50	
			50	15	25	
			15	1.00	25	
			15	75	25	
			6.15	25	25	
	Storage		65	22.25	25	
			6.80		25	
					25	
					50	
Insurance 3.70					10.50	
Laundry 1.59					22.25	
Telephones .30					6.80	
Telegrams .69					112.90	
6.28					1.85	
Cabs 1.50					7.78	
7.78					162.08	

Items of Report turned in to Sister Euphrasia, Treasurer, Trinity College by E. L. Dorsey.

Mem: Attention is directed to the fact that a slight mistake was made in favor of the College owing to the omission of (item) 65 cts. for trunk storage (item) 40 cts. one meal: (item) 20 cts. attendance:

APPENDIX V

Mimeographed, Handwritten Sheet

A SUMMARY of Questions most frequently asked, and the Answers authoritatively returned by the Superior of the Order through the Auxiliary Board at the Meeting of Nov. 28, 1899 at Washington, D.C.

---

1. *Is attendance at Chapel or Mass compulsory?*
   No. As at Oxford and elsewhere the day will always begin in the Chapel: but non-Catholics will be provided with other duties during the Mass itself.
2. *Will Sisters from Europe be brought here to teach in the College?*
   Only those who have been selected for their special talents, and who have been rigidly trained in American educational methods.
3. *Will lay teachers be admitted?*
   Yes.
4. *Will non-resident students be admitted?*
   Yes.
5. *Will the College open next Fall?*
   Yes.
6. *Will philosophical works other than those written by priests be used?*
   Yes, if the Philosophy be sound.
7. *Will the College be broad in its scope?*
   Yes.
8. *Will there be, when the College is organized a Board that will correspond to the Board of Directors of the Catholic University—a Board of the laity—an Advisory Council?*
   Yes.

Every question laid before the Sisters is discussed with great care, which accounts for the slow formulation of the three several questions that most vitally interest the public—discipline, curriculum, finance.

APPENDIX VI

The Fifth Annual Meeting of the Advisory Board of Trinity College

June 1, 1905.

REPORT OF THE COMMITTEE ON REQUIREMENTS FOR THE DEGREE OF THE MASTER OF ARTS

TO THE MEMBERS OF THE ADVISORY BOARD:

The Committee appointed by this Board on June 2, 1904, to consider the question of requirements for the degree of Master of Arts held a meeting at the opening of the present academic year and, as the result of its investigations, submitted to the President and Faculty of the College the following recommendations in regard to the degree of Master of Arts.

I. AS TO THE QUALIFICATIONS OF CANDIDATES

Candidates should be Bachelors of Arts of Trinity College, or of some other college, and should give satisfactory evidence of ability to carry on the work for the Master's degree.

II. AS TO THE PERIOD OF PREPARATION FOR THE DEGREE

Candidates should spend one year in residence at the College. Work for the degree "in absentia" should not be permitted.

III. AS TO THE NATURE AND AMOUNT OF WORK

The usual requirement should be one major and one minor subject. The candidate should be allowed to elect the latter from undergraduate courses, but in the former she should be required to elect work of advanced grade. A candidate may, however, at the discretion of the Faculty, be permitted to do all of her work in one subject, especially if her work for the A.B. degree has been highly satisfactory.

IV. As to the Means of Testing the Work

Every candidate for the A.M. degree should be required to present a thesis and should pass an examination on such thesis. This examination may be either oral or written, as the instructor in the student's major subject deems most advisable. It would be well for the candidate to present also some of the papers prepared during the year.

V. As to the Thesis

1. It should deal with the subject in which the candidate is doing her major work. The special subject of the thesis should be decided upon in the Senior Year when the candidate elects her major for graduate work. This will give her an opportunity to do preparatory reading during the summer vacation.

2. The length of the thesis will depend largely upon the nature of the subject chosen. A thesis written by a candidate whose major subject is mathematics or a natural science would be briefer than a thesis on a purely literary subject.

3. The thesis should be written in good English. It should show sufficient grasp of the subject undertaken and an appreciation of its relation to other subjects which it touches. It should evidence a thorough acquaintance with the sources from which it is drawn. As far as opportunity allows of a bibliography on the subject, this should be required as an appendix to the thesis.

4. The copy of the thesis submitted for examination ought to be typewritten. If, however, on examination the thesis proves to be very excellent and the student desires to print it in pamphlet form, or publish it in some good magazine, she should certainly be permitted to do so.

5. As a rule, the thesis should be presented a month before the candidate's final examination, i.e. if the examination be held about the middle of May, the completed thesis should be presented about the middle of April.

6. The merits of the thesis should be passed upon by a committee of three. This committee should be composed of, the instructor in the major subject, the instructor in the minor subject (or if the student's work consists of only a major subject, another member of the College Faculty) and in addition to these, one other competent person, preferably some one outside of the College.

These recommendations having been, as before stated, presented to the President and Faculty of the College, were by them formally adopted without modification.

Respectfully submitted by

THE COMMITTEE

APPENDIX VII

Career Highlights

Rt. Rev. Edward A. Pace

1891 Became Professor of Psychology until 1894 at C.U.A.
1892 Charter member of American Psychological Association.
1893 Welcomed to Washington the first Apostolic Delegate his former teacher and friend in Rome, Archbishop Francesco Satolli, who had recommended Edward Pace for the Professorship at C.U.
1894 Became Professor of Philosophy until 1935.
1895 Became Dean of the School of Philosophy until 1899. Delivered discourse at dedication of McMahon Hall. Helped establish the Catholic University Bulletin.
1896 Lectured at Catholic Summer School despite questions raised about his Liberalism and Orthodoxy.
1897 Co-founder of Trinity College for Catholic Women.
1898 Delivered address "The College Training of the Clergy" at his Alma Mater on the 50th anniversary of St. Charles College.
1899 Co-founder and first Director at the Institute of Pedagogy later to become the Department of Education.
1901 Editor of "Psychological Studies for the Catholic University of America."
1904 Co-founder and editor of "The Catholic Encyclopedia."
1906 Second term of Dean of School of Philosophy until 1914. Delivered sermon on 100th anniversary of Baltimore Cathedral.
1911 Co-founder and first Editor of "The Catholic Educational Review."
1912 Director of studies at Catholic University.
1914 Co-founder of Catholic Sisters College to train Teachers. Honored with Papal medal, "Pro Ecclesia et Pontifice."
1916 Helped inaugurate Sisters College in California. Helped in the Modern Translation of the Roman Missal entitled: "Mass Every Day of the Year."
1917 General Secretary at Catholic University until 1924.

1919 Prepared draft for Pastoral letter of American Bishops. Helped establish the National Catholic Welfare Council.

1920 Honored on July 15 by Pope Benedict XV as Protonotary Apostolic with title of Rt. Rev. Monsignor.

1922 Preached sermon on May 3rd at Consecration of Bishop Patrick Barry as fifth Bishop of St. Augustine. Elected member of Executive Board of the American Council on Education.

1923 Preached Sermon in commemoration of the deceased Alumni at the celebration of the Diamond Jubilee of St. Charles College.

1924 Vice President of the American Council on Education. Appointed Vice-Rector of Catholic University.

1926 President of the American Council on Education. Co-founder and first Editor of "The New Scholasticism." First editor of "Studies in Philosophy and Psychiatry." Co-founder of the American Catholic Philosophical Association. Lectured at School of Social Service in Washington. Co-founder of Catholic Sisters College in Washington.

1927 Elected President of American Catholic Philosophical Association.

1929 Scholarship Burse founded at Sisters College in the name of Monsignor Edward A. Pace, by the International Federation of Catholic Alumnae recognition of his services as moderator of the Federation. Appointed by President Hoover to be a member of the National Advisory Committee to discuss relations between the Federal Government and Education.

1931 American Catholic Philosophical Association honored Monsignor Pace by making their entire convention a tribute to him and his work in Catholic Philosophy. A volume of essays on philosophical, psychological and education subjects written in his honor were presented at a testimonial dinner on the occasion of his seventieth birthday.

1932 While convalescing from an operation he composed his well known "Prayer for the Catholic University" which was later used on October 12, 1938 by Cardinal Dougherty as the invocation opening the University's Golden Jubilee Year.

1933 On June 14 he presented President Franklin D. Roosevelt for the Honorary Degree of Doctor of Laws and composed the Citation which was broadcast nationwide on the Radio.

1934 Third term as Dean of the School of Philosophy. Leg amputated in January.

1935 Observed 50th anniversary as Priest on May 30. Received permission from Rome to say Mass sitting down. Congratulated by Pope Pius XI on Jubilee. The Baltimore Catholic

Review congratulated him with bold type headline: MONSIGNOR PACE YOU HAVE SERVED NOBLY Commemorative Issue of Catholic University Bulletin dedicated to him on his anniversary. Honored as Vice-Rector Emeritus of University. Honored as Professor of Philosophy Emeritus. Received Honorary Doctor of Laws Degree from Catholic University, bestowed by Archbishop Michael Curley as a rarity on one not a head of state. In conferring the degree Archbishop Curley said, "Although as Chancellor of the University I have bestowed degrees upon the heads of nations and distinguished prelates, no other occasion has brought me more personal pleasure than the present office of conferring this degree which honors a truly great educator and an outstanding prelate, my friend, Doctor Pace." Honored by Georgetown University on Founders day, by presentation of Cardinal Mazzela Award for achievement in the field of Philosophy.

1938 Passed away on April 26 at Providence Hospital in Washington. Memorial Issue of Catholic University Bulletin dedicated to Monsignor Pace included Eulogy by his close friend, Father Ignatius Smith, O.P. and a final tribute by Monsignor Maurice Sheehy. Picture and Obituary carried in many secular newspapers including the New York Times; and in many Catholic Weeklies including the Baltimore Catholic Review. Apostolic Delegate Archbishop (later Cardinal) Cicognani, and Archbishop Michael Curley among prelates at his funeral in the National Shrine of the Immaculate Conception. Gravesite prayers read by the bishop of his own Diocese, Bishop Patrick Barry of St. Augustine.

1941 Dedication of Starke church on October 13, the Feast of St. Edward by Bishop Joseph P. Hurley, Bishop of St. Augustine; dedication sermon by Monsignor Patrick McCormick Vice-Rector of Catholic University was a tribute to Monsignor Edward Pace, a native son of Starke.

1961 Commemoration of the 100th anniversary of the birth of Edward Pace in Starke observed by Catholic Philosophers in McMahon Hall at the Catholic University of America.

1963 Dedication by his Grace, the Most Reverend Joseph P. Hurley, Archbishop of St. Augustine of a Memorial Plaque in St. Edward's church to perpetuate for posterity the humility as well as scholarship of Monsignor Edward Aloysius Pace of Starke, Florida, on April 26, the twenty fifth anniversary of his death.

APPENDIX VIII

Requirements for Degrees

Catalogue, 1922–23

Bachelor of Arts (A.B.)

First Year	Units	Second Year	Units	Third Year	Units	Fourth Year	Units
English	(3)	English	(2)	English	(2)	Philosophy	(3)
Latin	(4)	2 Majors	(6)	2 Majors	(6)	History	(1)
Philosophy	(2)	Science	(4)	Philosophy	(2)	Amer. History	(2)
Scripture	(1)	Philosophy	(2)	History	(1)	Religion	(1)
Religion	(1)	Scripture	(1)	Religion	(1)	Electives	(8)
Electives	(6)	Religion	(1)	Electives	(4)		
		Electives	(2)				

Bachelor of Letters (B. Litt.)

First Year	Units	Second Year	Units	Third Year	Units	Fourth Year	Units
English	(3)	English	(4)	English	(4)	English	(4)
Mod. Languages	(6)	Mod. Languages	(6)	Mod. Languages	(3)	Mod. Languages	(3)
Philosophy	(2)	Philosophy	(2)	Philosophy	(2)	History	(1)
Scripture	(1)	Scripture	(1)	History	(1)	Philosophy	(3)
Religion	(1)	Religion	(1)	Religion	(1)	Religion	(1)
Electives	(4)	Electives	(4)	Amer. History	(2)	Electives	(3)
				Electives	(3)		

Bachelor of Science (B.S.)

First Year	Units	Second Year	Units	Third Year	Units	Fourth Year	Units
English	(3)	English	(2)	English	(1)	Majors	(5)
Mod. Languages	(3)	Mod. Languages	(3)	Majors	(6)	Philosophy	(2)
				History	(1)	History	(1)

Mathematics	(3)	Majors	(7 or 8)	Religion	(1)	Religion	(1)
Science	(4)	Philosophy	(1)	Second Science	(4)	Electives	(6)
Scripture	(1)	Religion	(1)	Electives	(4)		
Religion	(1)	Electives	(3)				
Electives	(2)						

*Two years of college work in French and German or Spanish or Italian are required.

Catalogue, 1932–33

Bachelor of Arts (A.B.)

First Year	Sem. Hrs.	Second Year	Sem. Hrs.	Third Year	Sem. Hrs.	Fourth Year	Sem. Hrs.
Religion	2	Religion	2	Religion	2	Religion	2
Scripture	2	Scripture	2	Church History	2	Church History	2
Logic	3	Philosophy	4	Psychology	4	Ethics	4
Argumentation	3	Major	10–8	Major	10–8	Major	10–8
Foreign Language	6	Related Subjects	6–8	Related Subjects	6–8	Related Subjects	6–8
Electives	6	Electives	4	Electives	8	Electives	8
English	4	English	6				
Science	8		–		–		–
	34		34		32		32

Pre-Medical Course (A.B.)

First Year	Sem. Hrs.	Second Year	Sem. Hrs.	Third Year	Sem. Hrs.	Fourth Year	Sem. Hrs.
Religion	2	Religion	2	Religion	2	Religion	2
Scripture	2	Scripture	2	Church History	2	Church History	2
Logic	3	Philosophy	4	Psychology	4	Ethics	4
Chemistry	8	Chemistry	8	Chemistry	8	Chemistry	4
Greek	6	Biology	8	Biology	8	Biology	8
Mathematics	6	Mathematics	6	Physics	8	Physics	8
*French or German	(6)	French or German	(6)	French or German	(6)	French or German	(6)
English	4	English	6			Electives	2
	–		–		–		
	31		36		32		(6) + 30

*A reading knowledge of French and German is required. In order to acquire this the student may take these languages in any year in which it is convenient.

APPENDIX IX

Early Telephone Numbers

(Referred to in Chapter 6)

1901	The catalogue lists as "pressing needs of the college" a telephone and a fire alarm.
1902–1903	Main 2057
1903–1904	North 754 (new exchange)
1905–1906	North 754
1906–1907	North 2970 (until PBX remained same for fifty years though others added)
Students'	North 3102
1910–1911	North 2970
Students'	North 2367

APPENDIX X

Student Proposals, 1903

PROPOSED AGREEMENT
Between the
FACULTY AND STUDENTS OF TRINITY COLLEGE
Concerning
STUDENT GOVERNMENT

WHEREAS THE students of Trinity College desire to assume individual and community responsibility for the conduct of the students in their college life, and whereas it is believed that such responsibility if given to the students will make for growth in character and power, and will promote loyalty to the best interests of the College,

The President and Faculty of Trinity College, with the approval of the Trustees, do hereby authorize the organization of the Students' Association of Trinity College, charging this Association to exercise the powers that may be committed to it with a careful regard both for liberty and order and for the maintenance of the best conditions for scholarly work.

I. To this Association the President and Faculty entrust the management of all matters concerning the conduct of students in their college life that are not strictly academic or that are not hereinafter withdrawn from the jurisdiction of the Association.

II. The authorities of the College reserve for themselves the right to regulate:

a. All chapel attendance.
b. All formal entertainments and athletic events at the College, and the invitations to such entertainments.
c. All matters pertaining to the use of college property and equipment.
d. All societies, organizations and publications.

III. The reservation of powers enumerated in Section II is to be understood as follows:

The Students' Association may legislate in regard to these matters, but all such legislation must be subject to the approval of those authorities to whom these matters have been committed by the Trustees.

IV. The enumeration of powers reserved to the authorities is intended to define, as far as practicable, the province of the Students' Association, but it is not to be understood as complete and all-inclusive. If question arises as to whether any subject is within the jurisdiction of the Association, it shall be referred for decision to a joint committee of seven, made up of a standing committee of three from the Faculty, a standing committee of three from the Students' Association, and the Dean of the College, chairman ex-officio.

V. The authorities of the College stand pledged to support the Association to the full extent of their power. The members of the Association, on their side, promise to co-operate with the President and Faculty in maintaining a high standard of scholarship and life.

VI. It shall be within the power of the authorities of the College to withdraw the powers granted in this document, or of the Students' Association to formally relinquish the same, thirty days' notice being given in either case.

Amendments to this Agreement proposed either by the Faculty or by the Students' Association shall be considered by the Joint Committee referred to in Section IV, and the agreement reached by the conferring committees shall be ratified by a two-thirds vote of the Faculty in the case of an amendment proposed by the Students' Association, or by a two-thirds vote of the Students' Association in the case of an amendment proposed by the Faculty.

VII. The Constitution of the Students' Association of Trinity College, appended to this document, shall be subject to amendment only on the acceptance of proposed amendments by the Faculty of the College.

There shall also be appended to this agreement a copy of the original By-Laws of the Student's Association as a memorandum of the initial status of the arrangement between the Faculty and the Association.

VIII. The Faculty may, on the unanimous recommendation of the Joint Committee (provided for in Section IV), place any of the By-Laws of the Association under the same provision as the Constitution so far as amendment is concerned.

IX. This Agreement shall require to be valid the signatures of the President and Dean of the College, representing the Faculty, the President and Secretary of the Association, representing the Association, and the President of the Board of Trustees, representing the Trustees.

____

____

____

____

____

PROPOSED CONSTITUTION of the STUDENTS' ASSOCIATION OF TRINITY COLLEGE

ARTICLE I

The name of this Association shall be the Students' Association of Trinity College.

ARTICLE II

The purpose of this Association shall be to control the management of all matters concerning the conduct of students in their college life that are not strictly academic, or that are not reserved to the jurisdiction of the Faculty by the terms of the Agreement.

ARTICLE III

All resident undergraduate students of Trinity College are ipso facto members of this Association.

ARTICLE IV

Section 1. The Executive Power of the Association shall be vested in a President, a Vice-President, a Secretary, a Treasurer, and an Executive

Board composed of the President, Vice-President and five other members.

Section 2.

a. The President and Vice-President shall be members of the Senior Class; the Secretary and Treasurer shall be members of the Junior Class; and the five members of the Executive Board shall be two Juniors, two Sophomores and one Freshman.

b. The officers and the Executive Board, with the exception of the Freshman member, shall be elected annually by May 15, and shall enter upon their duties at the beginning of the following College year. The Freshman member of the Executive Board shall be elected by October 15.

c. The term of all offices shall be one College year.

Section 3.

a. The duties of the President shall be to call together and preside over all meetings of the Association, and to act as Chairman of the Executive Board though with all the powers of a full voting member.

b. The duties of the Vice-President shall be to assume the duties of the President in the absence, or at the request, of the President, and to act as Secretary of the Executive Board.

c. The duties of the Secretary shall be to keep the minutes of the Association and a list of its members; to post notices of meetings; and to attend to the correspondence of the Association.

d. The duties of the Treasurer shall be to collect and care for the money of the Association, and to expend the same in accordance with the will of the Association under the direction of the President.

e. The duties of the Executive Board shall be to enforce the rules of the Association; to consider and pass upon all infraction of such rules; to impose penalties to the limit of recommending expulsion. It may, at its discretion, summon before it any member or members of the Association; its actions being subject to revision or repeal by the Association sitting as a judicial body, providing appeal from its actions is made to the Association within three days after notification of its actions has been made; all appeals to be made in writing to the Secretary of the Association.

ARTICLE V

The Legislative Power of the Association shall be exercised by the whole Association, one-third of whose members shall constitute a quorum.

ARTICLE VI

Section I. The Judicial Power of the Association shall be vested in:

1. The Association sitting as a judicial body. This body shall constitute the highest court, wherein the rule of a majority consisting of two-thirds of the members of the Association shall prevail.

2. The Executive Board constituting the lower court, before which all matters must first be brought, and from which alone an appeal may be made to the whole Association sitting as a judicial body.

Section II. In extraordinary cases the Association sitting as a judicial body, at the request of the Executive Board, and upon an affirmative vote of two-thirds of the members of the Association, may delegate its supreme jurisdiction to a special court consisting of the Executive Board and two members of the Association, the election of said two members to follow immediately.

ARTICLE VII

The Standing Committee of the Student's Association to form with the Standing Committee of the Faculty the Joint Committee referred to in Section IV of the "Agreement" shall consist of the President and two members from the Junior or Senior Class elected by the Association.

ARTICLE VIII

Section 1. There shall be an Annual Meeting of the Association held not later than May 15 for the purpose of electing officers for the ensuing year and receiving the report of the retiring Treasurer.

Section 2. A meeting of the Association may be called at any time by the President on her own motion, and must be called by her on the written request of five members.

ARTICLE IX

When the Association is sitting as a judicial body, and at the annual meeting for elections, a quorum shall consist of two-thirds of the members of the Association. In all other cases one-third of the members shall constitute a quorum, with all legislative, executive and judicial powers not prohibited in this Constitution, and may confer authority upon the Officers or upon the Executive Board, or upon any Committee.

ARTICLE X

Should a vacancy occur in any office of the Association or in the Executive Board, it shall be filled by special election as soon as possible.

PROPOSED BY-LAWS
of the
STUDENTS' ASSOCIATION OF TRINITY COLLEGE

I.

All members of the Association shall observe and co-operate in enforcing, the system of Self-Government embodied in the following rules.

II.

Provisions for Quiet in the Buildings

1. There shall be no disturbing noise in the College halls during hours of recitation.

2. There shall be general quiet throughout the buildings from 8 P.M. to 10 P.M. from Sunday to Thursday, inclusive. On Friday and Saturday evenings there shall be general quiet from 9 P.M. to 10 P.M., except in case of College entertainments holding after 9 P.M., in which case there shall be quiet 30 minutes after the close of said entertainments.

3. Students shall retire at 10 P.M. every evening, and there shall be absolute silence from 10 P.M. to 6:15 A.M.

4. There shall be perfect silence in the Library at all times.

5. Musical instruments shall not be used for any other purpose than practicing during the hours of recitation.

III.

Provisions for Order in the Dining Room

1. There shall be no unnecessary noise in the Dining Room.

2. Students are expected to be present for Grace before meals, and to remain until the hostess of their table says Grace after meals.

IV.

Provisions for Leaving the College

1. On leaving College the students shall register their name, destination and time of return. All registration must be canceled on return.

2. Students shall not register for return later than 6:30 P.M.

3. If for any reason a student is more than an hour delayed after 6:30 P.M. she shall send a telegram or telephone message to the Dean.

4. Students who will be out later than 6:30 P.M. must have special permission from the Dean.

5. Students may not go out Sunday afternoons without permission from the Dean.

V.

Provisions for Chaperonage

1. Students shall be accompanied by a chaperon approved by the College on a first visit to a Dentist, Doctor or Oculist, but in the case of prolonged treatment under an approved physician they may be accompanied by another student.

2. Students must be accompanied by a chaperon or another student for Singing Lessons and Music Lessons given in men's studios.

3. Without an approved chaperon no student shall attend games or entertainments at Men's Colleges.

4. Students may not take gentlemen through the Dormitories of the College without a chaperon.

VI. *ORDER*

All questions of Order shall be decided by Robert's Rules of Order except where they may conflict with the Constitution and By-Laws of the Association.

VII.

An annual tax of $.25 shall be levied on every member of the Association, and shall be collected by the Treasurer by October 15.

VIII.

Except in cases of special emergency, notice of any proposed meeting shall be posted on the Bulletin Board in each Hall at least 36 hours before the time appointed for the meeting.

IX. *ELECTIONS*

Section 1. Officers and Standing Committee. Nominations shall be made by acclamation at a meeting of the Association held at least one week before the Election; such nominations to be reduced to two by ballot; the two candidates thus chosen to be voted for by ballot, a plurality of votes decidng the election.

Section 2. Executive Board. The members of the Executive Board shall be nominated and elected in the same manner as the officers of the Association, except that it shall be at meetings of the Classes which they respectively represent instead of at a meeting of the Association.

X.

No student shall hold two Major offices, or more than two minor offices at the same time; but one Major and one Minor office may be held at the same time. The Major Offices are the President and Vice-President of the Association, the Presidents of all Classes and College organizations, including the College Glee Club. Minor Offices are all other offices of the Association, the Classes or other organizations.

XI. *REPRESENTATIVE BOARD*

1. This Board shall consist of representatives from each district in the College (the present building being divided into four districts known as St. Gertrude's, St. Teresa's, St. Agnes' and St. Julia's Halls), whose duties shall be to look after and report upon all matters of order and the observance of all rules in their districts and to confer with the President in reference thereto.

2. The representatives shall be chosen by the residents of the districts, and shall serve for one semester.

APPENDIX XI

Commencements, 1904–1976

	Commencement Speaker	Baccalaureate Sermon
1904	Very Rev. Edward A. Pace "The College Woman" Address for Opening of Art Gallery: Very Rev. Thomas J. Shahan "The Educational Value of the Fine Arts"	Rev. William Kerby Bishop Philip J. Garrigan, Celebrant
1905	Mr. Charles J. Bonaparte of Baltimore "Woman as a College Graduate" (Secretary of Navy designate "leading lawyer and reformer") (Cardinal Gibbons advises girls against suffrage)	Rev. John J. Creagh, D. D. "Wisdom in Education" Wisdom VII, 7–24 Apostolic Delegate Falconio, Celebrant "His Excellency Most Reverend Diomede Falconio, D.C. Apostolic Delegate"
1906	Hon. Thomas H. Carter, U.S. Senator from Montana Apostolic Delegate Falconio presiding	Very Rev. Edward A. Pace, D.D. Rt. Rev. Denis O'Connell, Rector, C.U., Celebrant
1907	Walter George Smith "Woman's Responsibility in Modern Life" (Apos. Del. Falconio confers degrees)	Rev. John D. Maguire, D.D. Rt. Rev. Alfred A. Curtis, D.D., Celebrant
1908	Hon. Victor J. Dowling of New York Cardinal Gibbons confers degrees	Apostolic Delegate Falconio Solemn Benediction Rev. John Melody, D.D. Sermon
1909	Hon. James S. Sherman Vice President of the U.S. Bishop Garrigan confers degrees	Rev. William Turner, D.D. (I Peter, III, 14) Bishop Garrigan, Celebrant
1910	His Excellency William Howard Taft President of the United States Apos. Del. Falconio presiding	Dr. William Kerby "Conversation," *Record*, Vol IV, No. 3 Apos. Del. Falconio, Celebrant
1911	Hon. Michael F. Girten of Chicago Cardinal Gibbons, presiding	Very Rev. Edward A. Pace, Ph.D. Apos. Del. Falconio, Celebrant
1912	Hon. Joseph P. Daly of New York City Cardinal Gibbons presiding	Rev. Thomas Shields, Ph.D. Bishop Louis S. Walsh, Celebrant Portland, Maine

1913	Conde B. Pallen, Ph.D. Bishop Garrigan presiding	Rev. William Turner, Ph.D. Most Rev. John Bonzano, Celebrant
1914	John H. Haaren, LL.D. Bishop Garrigan presiding	Rev. William Kerby, Ph.D. Bishop Edward T. Allen of Mobile, Celebrant
1915	Hon. Michael J. Ryan of Philadelphia Cardinal Gibbons presiding	Very Rev. Charles F. Aiken, D.D. Bishop Shahan, Celebrant
1916	Hon. Thomas W. Churchill of New York Apos. Del. Bonzano presiding	Rev. John W. Melody, S.T.D. Bishop Shahan, Celebrant
1917	Hon. David I. Walsh of Boston (Senator from Massachusetts) Apos. Del. Bonzano presiding	Very Rev. Edward A. Pace, Ph.D. Bishop Shahan, Celebrant
1918	Hon. George F. O'Shaunessey (Member of Congress from Rhode Island) Cardinal Gibbons presiding	? Apos. Del. Bonzano, Celebrant
1919	John A. Lapp, Ph.D. NCWC–Social Action Cardinal Gibbons presiding	Very Rev. Edward A. Pace, S.T.D., Ph.D. Bishop Shahan, Celebrant
1920	Hon. Francis P. Garvan Apos. Del. Bonzano presiding	Rev. William J. Kerby, S.T.L., Ph.D. Bishop Shahan, Celebrant
1921	Hon. Timothy S. Hogan, L.L.D. (Judge, Ohio) Apos. Del. Bonzano presiding	Rt. Rev. Msgr. Edward A. Pace, S.T.D., Ph.D. Bishop Daniel Feehan, Fall River, Mass., Celebrant
1922	Hon. Maurice Francis Egan Emeritus Professor of C.U. Minister to Denmark 1907–1918 One of C.U's first Lay Professors Friend of Trinity College from 1897 Archbishop Curley presiding	Rev. Thomas V. Moore, Ph.D. Bishop Shahan, Celebrant
1923	Hon. Wendell P. Stafford Assoc. Justice of Supreme Court of D.C. Archbishop Curley presiding Note: May 9, 1923 reception for New Delegate Pietro F. Biondi	Rev. John A. Ryan, S.T.D.
1924	Hon. Joseph Scott, California Archbishop Curley presiding Note: May 13, 1924 Dedication of Notre Dame Chapel	Rev. John M. Cooper, S.T.D., Ph.D. Bishop Shahan, Celebrant
1925	Hon. David I. Walsh, L.L.D. Senator, Massachusetts Archbishop Curley presiding Note: Jubilee Celebration, 1900–1925: Alumnae Reunion	Rev. George Johnson, Ph.D. Bishop Shahan, Celebrant

1926	Michael Williams Editor of *Commonwealth* Archbishop Curley presiding	Rev. Thomas V. Moore, O.S.B., Ph.D. Apos. Del. Fumisoni Biondi, Celebrant
1927	Hon. Thomas F. Woodlock Interstate Commerce Commission Archbishop Curley presiding	Dom. J. Albert Haldi, Ph.D.
1928	Hon. Charles A. Mooney Congressman from Ohio Archbishop Curley presiding	Very Rev. John A. Ryan, D.D., LL.D. "Ancient Ideals and Modern Life" Proverbs XXXI, 10
1929	Hon. Alfred J. Talley, M.A., LLD New York City Archbishop Curley presiding	Rev. Thomas V. Moore, O.S.B. Bishop John M. McNamara, Celebrant
1930	Edward A. Fitzpatrick, Ph.D. Dean, Graduate School of Marquette U. Archbishop Curley presiding	Rev. Edward B. Jordan, S.T.D. Bishop John J. Swint, Wheeling, W.Va., Celebrant
1931	Joseph J. Reilly, Ph.D. Archbishop Curley presiding	Dom. Francis Augustine Walsh, Ph.D. Apos. Del. Fumasoni Biondi, Celebrant
1932	Professor Hugh Stott Taylor Princeton University Archbishop Curley presiding	Very Rev. Nicholas A. Weber, S.M., S.T.D. Rt. Rev. James Hugh Ryan, S.T.D., Rector of C.U., Celebrant
1933	Dr. Charles G. Fenwick Bryn Mawr College—Historian Archbishop Curley presiding	Rev. Maurice Sheehy, Ph.D. Bishop McNamara, Celebrant
1934	Rt. Rev. William J. Kerby, Ph.D. Archbishop Curley presiding	Dom. Thomas V. Moore, Ph.D., M.P. "Our Spiritual and Moral Obligations" Bishop James Hugh Ryan Rector of C.U., Celebrant
1935	Anne Sarachon Hooley '15, A.M., LLB President of N.C.C.W. Archbishop Curley presiding (Note: First Alumna to give commencement address)	Rev. Edward B. Jordan, S.T.D. Jer. 11, 13 Bishop James H. Ryan, Celebrant Rector of C.U.
1936	Jane M. Hoey, A.M., Hon. LLD (1914) Dir. of Fed. Grants to States under Social Security Act. Bishop Peter Ireton of Richmond presiding	Rev. William H. Russell, Ph.D. Bishop McNamara, Celebrant
1937	Joseph J. Reilly, Hunter College Archbishop Curley presiding	Bishop Charles LeBlond of St. Joseph Rev. Maurice S. Sheehy, Ph.D.
1938	Ross J. S. Hoffman, Ph.D., Litt. D. New York University Archbishop Curley presiding	Rev. Felix M. Kirsch, O.M., Ph.D. Rt. Rev. Patrick J. McCormick, Vice-Rector, C.U., Celebrant

1939	Frances Taylor Patterson, T.C. 1914 Columbia University Most Rev. John M. McNamara, D.D. Aux. Bishop of Baltimore	Rev. John K. Ryan, Ph.D. Rt. Rev. Patrick J. McCormick, Celebrant
1940	Jerome G. Kerwin, Ph.D. University of Chicago Archbishop Curley presiding	Rev. Edward Talbot, OMI, Ph.D. Bishop Charles H. LeBlond of St. Joseph
1941	Hon. John A. Matthews, A.M., LLB, K.M. Judge of Court of Chancery of New Jersey Archbishop Curley presiding	Rt. Rev. John A. Ryan, D.P. Most Rev. Joseph M. Corrigan, D.P. Rector of C.U.
1942	Francis M. Crowley, Ph.D., Litt.D. Dean of School of Education, Fordham U. Archbishop Curley presiding	Rev. Edward Talbot, O.M.I., Ph.D. Rt. Rev. Patrick McCormick, Celebrant
1943	The Very Rev. Martin J. O'Malley, C.M., S.T.D., Rector of Kenrick Seminary, St. Louis Bishop McNamara presiding	Rev. Joseph Supple, O.M.I., Ph.D. Rt. Rev. Patrick J. McCormick, Celebrant
1944	Rt. Rev. Msgr. George Johnson, Ph.D. "The Unfinished Address" . . . died before finishing the address. Archbishop Curley presiding	Bishop John M. McNamara Aux. Bishop of Baltimore Bishop Patrick J. McCormick, Celebrant
1945	Leo J. Crowley, K.S.G. Foreign Economic Administrator Bishop McNamara presiding	Bishop Mathew Brady, D.D. of Manchester Bishop McCormick, Celebrant

Announcement instead of invitation to most people because of war regulations on travel.

1946	Francis M. Crowley, Ph.D., Litt.D. Dean, School of Education, Fordham U. Bishop McNamara presiding	Bishop Michael J. Ready, of Columbus, Ohio (formerly of N.C.W.C.) Bishop McCormick, Celebrant
1947	Robert H. Mahoney, Ph.D. Director of Secondary Education Hartford, Ct. (Husband of Mary Hannan '27) Bishop McNamara presiding	Very Rev. Ignatius Smith, O.P., Ph.D. Dean, School of Philosophy, C.U. Bishop McCormick, Celebrant
1948	Hugh Stott Taylor, Sc.D. Dean of Graduate School, Princeton U. Most Rev. Patrick O'Boyle, D.D. Archbishop of Washington presiding	Rev. Eugene M. Burke, C.S.P., S.T.D. Bishop McCormick, Celebrant
1949	Rt. Rev. Frederick G. Hochwalt, Ph.D. Secretary Gen., N.C.E.A. Archbishop O'Boyle presiding	Bishop John J. Wright, D.D. Auxiliary Bishop of Boston Bishop McCormick, Celebrant

1950	Rev. Eugene M. Burke, C.S.P., S.T.D. School of Theology, C.U. and Trinity C. Archbishop O'Boyle presiding Pageant: Through the years—1900–1950	Rt. Rev. Edward B. Jordan, Ph.D. Vice Rector, C.U. Rt. Rev. Robert B. Mulcahey, D.D. Rector, St. Luke's Church, N.Y.C.
1951	Rev. William E. McManus Assistant Director of Department of Education, National Catholic Welfare Conference	Rev. Louis A. Ryan, D.P. Theology Department, Trinity C.
1952	Magdalene Kramer, Ph.D. '20 Chairman, Dept. of Teaching, Speech and Drama, Teachers College, Columbia	Rev. Gerard F. Yates, S.J. Dean of Graduate School, Georgetown University
1953	Rev. John B. Sheerin, C.SP. Editor of *The Catholic World*	Rev. John P. Mulgrew, O.P.
1954	Rev. Theodore M. Hesburgh President, Notre Dame	Rev. Eugene M. Burke C.U. School of Theology and Trinity
1955	Alba Zizzamia '31 U.N. Observer for National Catholic Welfare Conference	Rev. Ferrer Smith, O.P. Dept. of Philosophy, Trinity
1956	Vincent E. Smith, Ph.D. Professor of Philosophy, Notre Dame	Rev. Joseph A. Sellinger, S.J. Associate Dean, Georgetown University
1957	Harold F. Collins, LL.D.	Rev. Philip M. Hannan Auxiliary Bishop of Washington
1958	Hon. John F. Kennedy U.S. Senator from Massachusetts	
1959	Rt. Rev. John Tracy Ellis Professor of History, Catholic University	
1960	William J. Brennan, Jr. Assoc. Justice of the Supreme Court	Rev. Edmond D. Benard Dean, School of Sacred Theology, C.U.
1961	John J. Meng, Ph.D. President, Hunter College	Rev. Frederick A. McGuire Exec. Secretary, Mission Secretariat, D.C.
1962	Senator Thomas Dodd Democrat—Connecticut	Rev. Eugene M. Burke Theology Department, Trinity College
1963	Robert F. Kennedy Attorney General, USA	Rev. Daniel L. Lowery
1964	Stephen G. Kuttner, J.U.D., S.J.C., J.C.D., LL.D., Professor of the History of Canon Law, C.U. Most Rev. Philip M. Hannan, D.D. presiding	Very Rev. E. B. Bunn, S.J.

1965	The Hon. Eugene J. McCarthy U.S. Senator, Minnesota Archbishop O'Boyle presiding	Rev. Gerard S. Sloyan Head, Religious Ed. Department, C.U.
1966	Donald F. Hornig, Ph.D. Special Assistant to the President for Science and Technology	Rev. Eugene M. Burke, C.S.P., S.T.D. Associate Profesor of Theology, Trinity Rev. Gerard S. Sloyan
1967	Richard H. Sullivan, A.M., LL.D., D.Hu.L. President, Assoc. of American Colleges Archbishop O'Boyle presiding	Rev. Thomas M. McLernon Rev. John Joseph McGarraghy Very Rev. Msgr. James C. Donohue, Ph.D. Director, Department of Education U.S. Catholic Conference
1968	The Hon. Ralph A. Dungan Chancellor of Higher Education, N.J.	Rev. John P. Whalen Acting Rector, C.U.
1969	Diane M. Sixsmith, '69	Rev. William P. Morgan Rev. David J. Joyce Rev. Robert I. Gannon, S.J. President Emeritus, Fordham U.
1970	The Hon. George J. McGovern U.S. Senator, South Dakota	Rev. Robert O'Donnell, C.S.P. President, St. Paul's College
1971	Hon. John Brademas, D.Phil. (Oxon) U.S. Representative from Indiana	Rev. Gilbert Hartke, O.P.M.A. Chair, Speech and Drama, C.U.A.
1972	Miss Jurate Kazickas, '64 Reporter, Associated Press	Most Rev. John J. Dougherty, S.T.D., S.S.D. Aux. Bishop of Newark, N.J.
1973	Lilli S. Hornig, Ph.D. Exec. Dir. Higher Education Resource Services Former Trinity College Chemistry Professor	
1974	M. Elizabeth Tidball, Ph.D. Professor of Physiology George Washington University Medical Center	
1975	Sister Margaret Claydon, S.N.D., Ph.D., L.H.D. President of Trinity College	
1976	Patricia Queenan Sheehan, '55 Commissioner for Community Affairs State of New Jersey	

Note: Clippings, copies of the addresses and notes and statistics on person giving opening remarks and report of the year included in the Scrapbook.

APPENDIX XII

Presidents of the Ladies' Auxiliary Board

Miss Olive Risley Seward	1899–1902
Mrs. Thomas H. Carter	(interim)
Mrs. Maurice Francis Egan	1902–1905
Miss Ella Loraine Dorsey	1905–1907
Mrs. Thomas H. Carter	1907–1932 (25 years)
Dr. Mary O'Malley	1932–1933
Mrs. John J. Noonan	1933–1936
Mrs. Peter John McGovern	1936–1939
*Mrs. Aubrey B. Fennell	1939–1942
Mrs. James E. Colliflower	1942–1945
*Mrs. S. Dolan Donahoe	1945–1948
Mrs. James F. Hartnett	1948–1951
Mrs. Charles J. Cassidy	1951–1953
Mrs. Paul Rodler	1953–1956
Mrs. John F. Victory	1956–1957
*Mrs. Charles Fahy	1957–1959
*Mrs. Edward A. Tamm	1959–1962
Mrs. Augustus Giegangack	1962–1963
Mrs. John R. Kennedy	1963–1964
Mrs. William B. Grogan	1964–1966
Mrs. Edward C. Moynihan	1966–
Mrs. Ralph P. Dunn	Sept. 1967–1969
Mrs. John J. O'Neill	1969–1971
Mrs. Ernest M. Fornili	1972–1974
*Dr. Dorothea Sullivan	became ill 1974
*Mrs. Edwin McManus	1975–1977
Mrs. John B. Daly	1978

N.B. 1942–43 catalogue Auxiliary Board moved from front to p. 89 in back.

*Trinity College Alumnae.

APPENDIX XIII

Chairmen – Re-Constituted Board of Trustees

Hugh P. McFadden (Jim)	January 1969–1971 Cf. *Newsletter*, February 1969
Paul Aiken	1971 to death May 25, 1974
Pierce Flanigan	1974–July 30, 1976 Cf. *Trinity News*, November 1974
Thomas E. Moran	1976–1978
George Sweeney	Jan. 1979–May 1980
Ignatius Horstmann	1980–

APPENDIX XIV

Trinity College Board of Lay Trustees

Charter Members

Mr. James H. Black, Chicago, Illinois
Dr. Regis L. Boyle, Washington, D.C.
Mr. Phil Braniff, Tulsa, Oklahoma
Mrs. Henry B. Coakley, Larchmont, New York
Mr. Harold F. Collins, Altadena, California
Mr. John D. Denney, Philadelphia, Pennsylvania
Mr. Edward J. Duffy, Essex Falls, New Jersey
Mr. Charles A. Eisenhardt, Jr., Cincinnati, Ohio
Mr. William F. Flaherty, Great Barrington, Massachusetts
Mr. Fred W. Herlihy, Orangeburg, South Carolina
Miss Jane Hoey, New York, New York
Mrs. Alphonse C. Kallan, Newton Centre, Massachusetts
Mr. Frank J. Keeler, Valhalla, New York
Mrs. Robert H. Mahoney, Hartford, Connecticut
Miss Jane Marilley, Washington, D.C.
Mr. William J. Nixon, New Rochelle, New York
Mr. Hugh P. McFadden, Hellertown, Pennsylvania
Mr. Martin F. O'Donoghue, Washington, D.C.
Mr. William L. O'Donovan, Rye, New York
Mr. John O'Neil, Washington, D.C.
Mr. John J. Power, Youngstown, Ohio
Mr. Arthur L. Quinn, Washington, D.C.
Mr. Andrew Saul, Washington, D.C.
Mr. Thomas G. Sennett, Royal Oak, Michigan
Mrs. Bartholomew Seymour, Grosse Point, Michigan
Mr. Francis J. Souhan, Seneca Falls, New York
Mr. Bernard J. Voll, South Bend, Indiana

Ex Officio Members

His Excellency, The Most Reverend Patrick A. O'Boyle, Washington, D.C.

The Rev. Eugene M. Burke, C.S.P., Washington, D.C.
Dr. Philip Caulfield, Washington, D.C.
Mr. William L. Galvin, Baltimore, Maryland
Miss Ellen Ganey, Washington, D.C.
Mr. Jasper Moore, Chevy Chase, Maryland
Sister Columba, S.N.D., Washington, D.C.
Sister Elizabeth Carmelita, S.N.D., Ilchester, Maryland
Sister Mary Patrick, S.N.D., Washington, D.C.
Mr. James E. Markham, Washington, D.C.

The Trinity Prayer

May the power of the Father
govern and protect us;
May the wisdom of the Son
teach and enlighten us;
May the love of the Holy Spirit
renew and quicken us;
May the blessing of the all Holy Trinity
Father, Son and Holy Spirit
Be with us now and forever. Amen.